Lecture Notes in Computer Science 13359

Advanced Research in Computing and Software Science
Subline of Lecture Notes in Computer Science

More information about this series at https://link.springer.com/bookseries/558

Ulrich Berger · Johanna N. Y. Franklin ·
Florin Manea · Arno Pauly (Eds.)

Revolutions and Revelations in Computability

18th Conference on Computability in Europe, CiE 2022
Swansea, UK, July 11–15, 2022
Proceedings

Springer

Editors
Ulrich Berger (iD)
Department of Computer Science
Swansea University
Swansea, UK

Johanna N. Y. Franklin (iD)
Department of Mathematics
Hofstra University
Hempstead, NY, USA

Florin Manea (iD)
Georg-August University Göttingen
Göttingen, Germany

Arno Pauly (iD)
Department of Computer Science
Swansea University
Swansea, UK

ISSN 0302-9743 ISSN 1611-3349 (electronic)
Lecture Notes in Computer Science
ISBN 978-3-031-08739-4 ISBN 978-3-031-08740-0 (eBook)
https://doi.org/10.1007/978-3-031-08740-0

This Springer imprint is published by the registered company Springer Nature Switzerland AG
The registered company address is: Gewerbestrasse 11, 6330 Cham, Switzerland

Preface

Computability in Europe (CiE) is an annual conference organized under the auspices of the Association Computability in Europe (ACiE), a European association of researchers from a broad variety of backgrounds who are connected to one another through their work in computability. The conference series has built up a strong tradition of developing an interdisciplinary scientific program that brings together researchers in all aspects of computability, foundations of mathematics, and computer science as well as the interplay of these theoretical areas with practical issues in computer science and with other disciplines such as biology, mathematics, philosophy, and physics. Its purpose is not only to allow researchers to report on their own ongoing work but also to broaden their own perspectives by engaging with the work of others from different backgrounds.

The motto of CiE 2022 was "Revolutions and Revelations in Computability". This alludes to the revolutionary developments we have seen in computability theory, starting with Turing's and Gödel's discoveries of the uncomputable and the unprovable and continuing to the present day with the advent of new computational paradigms such as quantum computing and bio-computing, which have dramatically changed our view of computability and revealed new insights into the multifarious nature of computation. The motto also hints at the historic role of the host city, Swansea, in the Industrial Revolution, as the world center of copper smelting in the 18th and 19th centuries.

CiE 2022 was the 18th conference in the series, and this was the second time it has been held in Swansea. Previous meetings have taken place in Amsterdam (2005), Swansea (2006), Siena (2007), Athens (2008), Heidelberg (2009), Ponta Delgada (2010), Sofia (2011), Cambridge (2012), Milan (2013), Budapest (2014), Bucharest (2015), Paris (2016), Turku (2017), Kiel (2018), Durham (2019), and, virtually, in Salerno (2020) and Ghent (2021). After two online CiE conferences, we were very happy to be able to hold CiE 2022 as a largely in-person meeting with some online elements.

The conference series has become a major event and is the largest international conference that brings together researchers focusing on computability-related issues. The CiE conference series is coordinated by the ACiE Conference Series Steering Committee consisting of Alessandra Carbone (Paris), Liesbeth De Mol (Lille), Gianluca Della Vedova (Executive Officer, Milan), Nataša Jonoska (Tampa), Benedikt Löwe (Amsterdam), Florin Manea (Chair, Göttingen), Klaus Meer (Cottbus), Russell Miller (New York), Mariya Soskova (Madison), and ex-officio members Elvira Mayordomo (President of the Association, Zaragoza) and Marcella Anselmo (Treasurer, Salerno).

Conference Structure and Program

The conference program was centered around tutorials, invited lectures, and a set of special sessions ranging over a variety of topics as well as contributed papers and informal presentations. The Program Committee of CiE 2022 consisting of 32 members, selected the invited and tutorial speakers and the special session organizers and coordinated the reviewing process and the selection of submitted contributions. The Program Committee selected 19 of the 34 non-invited submitted papers for publication in this volume. Each paper received at least three reviews by the Program Committee and their subreviewers. In addition to the contributed papers, the volume contains seven invited papers and 23 abstracts.

Invited Tutorials

- Dora Giammarresi (Università di Roma, Italy), *Two-Dimensional Languages and Models*
- Noam Greenberg (Victoria University of Wellington, New Zealand), *Recent Interactions Between Computability and Set Theory*

Invited Lectures

- Erika Ábrahám (RWTH Aachen University, Germany), *SMT Solving: Historical Review and New Developments*
- Thierry Coquand (University of Gothenburg, Sweden), *Sheaf Cohomology in Univalent Foundation*
- Liesbeth De Mol (Université de Lille, France), *Towards a Diversified Understanding of Computability, or Why We Should Care More about Our Histories*
- Damir Dzhafarov (University of Connecticut, USA), *Reverse Mathematics 2021*
- Harvey M. Friedman (The Ohio State University, USA), *String Replacement Systems*
- Svetlana Selivanova (KAIST, South Korea), *Computational Complexity of Classical Solutions of Partial Differential Equations*

Special Sessions

At the intersection of computability and other areas of mathematics. Organizers: Denis Hirschfeldt (University of Chicago) and Karen Lange (Wellesley College)

- Meng-Che Ho (California State University, Northridge), *A Computable Functor from Torsion-Free Abelian Groups to Fields*
- Bjørn Kjos-Hanssen (University of Hawai`i at Mānoa), *An Incompressibility Theorem for Automatic Complexity*
- Elvira Mayordomo (Universidad de Zaragoza), *Algorithmic Dimensions, the Point-to-Set Principles, and the Complexity of Oracles*
- Alexandra Shlapentokh (East Carolina University), *A Connection Between Inverse Galois Problem of a Field and Its First-Order Theory*

Computability theory of blockchain technology. Organizers: Arnold Beckmann (Swansea University) and Anton Setzer (Swansea University)

- Eli Ben-Sasson (StarkWare), *Ultra Scaling Blockchains with ZK-STARKs*
- Maurice Herlihy (Brown University), *Blockchains and Related Technologies: Which Ideas Are Likely to Endure?*
- Philip Wadler (University of Edinburgh), *Smarter Contracts: Applications of Haskell and Agda at IOG*

Computing Language: Love Letters, Large Models and NLP. Organizers: Liesbeth De Mol (Université de Lille) and Giuseppe Primiero (University of Milan) for the Council of the HaPoC Commission

- Troy Astarte (Swansea University), *'My avid fellow feeling' and 'Fleas': Playing with Words on the Computer*
- Juan-Luis Gastaldi (ETH Zürich), *Mathematics as Natural Language: Principles, Consequences and Challenges of the Application of NLP Models to the Treatment of Mathematical Knowledge*
- Maël Pégny (Universität Tübingen), *Are Large Language Models Models (of Language)?*
- Jacopo Tagliabue (Coveo Labs), *Are We There Yet? Meaning in the Age of Large Language Models*

Computing with bio-molecules. Organizers: Jérôme Durand-Lose (Université d'Orléans) and Claudio Zandron (University of Milano-Bicocca)

- Giuditta Franco (University of Verona), *DNA Library Evidence Strings*
- Maria Dolores Jiménez-López (University of Tarragona), *Processing Natural Language with Biomolecules: Where Linguistics, Biology and Computation Meet*
- Nicolas Schabanel (CNRS - LIP, École Normale Supérieure de Lyon), *Turedo a New Computational Model for Molecular Nanobots?*
- Petr Sosík (Silesian University in Opava), *Computability and Complexity in Morphogenetic Systems*

Constructive and reverse mathematics. Organizers: Samuele Maschio (Università di Padova) and Takako Nemoto (Hiroshima Institute of Technology)

- Makoto Fujiwara (Tokyo University of Science), *An Extension of the Equivalence Between Brouwer's Fan Theorem and Weak König's Lemma with a Uniqueness Hypothesis*
- Takayuki Kihara (Nagoya University), *Computability Theory and Reverse Mathematics via Lawvere-Tierney Topologies*
- Robert Lubarsky (Florida Atlantic University), *On the Necessity of Some Topological Spaces*
- Huishan Wu (BLCU Beijing), *Reverse Mathematics and Semisimple Rings*

Reachability problems. Organizers: Paul Bell (Liverpool John Moores University) and Igor Potapov (University of Liverpool)

- Kitty Meeks (University of Glasgow), *Reducing Reachability in Temporal Graphs: Towards a More Realistic Model of Real-World Spreading Processes*
- Olivier Bournez (École Polytechnique), *Programming with Ordinary Differential Equations: Some First Steps Towards a Programming Language*
- Véronique Bruyère (Université de Mons), *A Game-Theoretic Approach for the Automated Synthesis of Complex Systems*
- James Worrell (University of Oxford), *The Skolem Landscape*

Women in Computability Workshop

ACiE and this conference have had a strong tradition of encouraging women to participate in computability-related research since CiE 2007. In 2016, a Special Interest Group for Women in Computability was established, and in 2021, Mariya Soskova set up an online mentorship program associated with this group to connect junior researchers in computability theory with women mentors not just at the conference but throughout the year. These initiatives are anchored in the annual Women in Computability workshop, held this year with the following speakers:

- Troy Astarte (Swansea University, Wales)
- Dora Giammarresi (Università di Roma, Italy)
- Svetlana Selivanova (KAIST, South Korea)

Organization and Acknowledgements

The CiE 2022 conference was organized by the Theory Group of the Department of Computer Science at Swansea University.

We are happy to acknowledge and thank the following for their financial support: Association Computability in Europe, the Institute of Coding in Wales, the London Mathematical Society, and technocamps.

We are also happy to announce that CiE 2022 was held in cooperation with the Association for Women in Mathematics for the first time in the history of this conference series and supports its Welcoming Environment Statement.

The high quality of the conference was achieved through the careful work of the Program Committee, the Special Session organizers, and all of the referees, and we are very grateful for their help in creating an exciting program for CiE 2022.

May 2022

Ulrich Berger
Johanna N. Y. Franklin
Florin Manea
Arno Pauly

Organization

Program Committee

Marcella Anselmo   University of Salerno, Italy
Verónica Becher   University of Buenos Aires, Argentina
Ulrich Berger (Co-chair)   Swansea University, UK
Katie Brodhead   Florida State University, USA
Laura Crosilla   University of Oslo, Norway
Joel Day   Loughborough University, UK
Gianluca Della Vedova   University of Milan, Italy
Leah Epstein   University of Haifa, Israel
Maribel Fernández   King's College London, UK
Ekaterina Fokina   TU Wien, Austria
Johanna Franklin (Co-chair)   Hofstra University, USA
Lorenzo Galeotti   Amsterdam University College, The Netherlands
Sandra Kiefer   RWTH Aachen University, Germany
Susana Ladra   University of Coruna, Spain
Maria Emilia Maietti   University of Padua, Italy
Florin Manea   University of Göttingen, Germany
Klaus Meer   Brandenburg University of Technology
    Cottbus-Senftenberg, Germany
Dale Miller   LIX, École Polytechnique, France
Russell Miller   Queens College, CUNY, USA
Arno Pauly (Co-chair)   Swansea University, UK
Nadia Pisanti   University of Pisa, Italy
Solon Pissis   CWI Amsterdam, The Netherlands
Giuseppe Primiero   University of Milan, Italy
Ramyaa Ramyaa   New Mexico Tech, USA
Monika Seisenberger   Swansea University, UK
Anton Setzer   Swansea University, UK
Alexandra Shlapentokh   East Carolina University, USA
Reed Solomon   University of Connecticut, USA
Mariya Soskova   University of Wisconsin-Madison, USA
Peter Van Emde Boas   University of Amsterdam, The Netherlands
Andreas Weiermann   Ghent University, Belgium
Andreas Wichert   University of Lisbon, Portugal

Organizing Committee

Troy Astarte   Swansea University, UK
Arnold Beckmann   Swansea University, UK
Ulrich Berger   Swansea University, UK

Tonicha Crook	Swansea University, UK
Faron Moller	Swansea University, UK
Bertie Mueller	Swansea University, UK
Arno Pauly	Swansea University, UK
Olga Petrovska	Swansea University, UK
Markus Roggenbach	Swansea University, UK
Monika Seisenberger	Swansea University, UK
Anton Setzer	Swansea University, UK
John Tucker	Swansea University, UK

Additional Reviewers

Eric Allender
Uri Andrews
Stefano Berardi
Olivier Bournez
Vasco Brattka
Gabriele Buriola
Wesley Calvert
Douglas Cenzer
Francesco Ciraulo
Pieter Collins
Chris Conidis
Thierry Coquand
Walter Dean
Matthew de Brecht
Nuiok Dicaire
Jacques Duparc
Arnaud Durand
Guido Fiorino
Emanuele Frittaion
Samuel Frontull
Ziyuan Gao
Guido Gherardi
Daniel Graça
Ferruccio Guidi
Valentina Harizanov
Stefan Hoffmann
Mathieu Hoyrup
Hajime Ishihara
Takayuki Kihara
Bjørn Kjos-Hanssen

Manfred Kufleitner
Oliver Kullmann
Karen Lange
Steffen Lempp
Robert Lubarsky
Elvira Mayordomo
Tim McNicholl
Alexander Melnikov
Kenshi Miyabe
Larry Moss
Carl Mummert
Matthias Naaf
Takako Nemoto
Reino Niskanen
Hugo Nobrega
Dag Normann
Victor Ocasio González
Mizuhito Ogawa
Sebastian Ordyniak
Benedikt Pago
Fedor Pakhomov
Robert Passmann
Guillermo Perez
Iosif Petrakis
Christopher Porter
Pavel Pudlák
Michael Rathjen
Jan Rooduijn
Dino Rossegger
Luca San Mauro

Invited Tutorials

Two-Dimensional Languages and Models

Dora Giammarresi ⓘ

Dipartimento di Matematica, Università Roma "Tor Vergata", via della Ricerca
Scientifica, 00133 Rome, Italy
giammarr@mat.uniroma2.it
https://www.mat.uniroma2.it/~giammarr/

A picture, defined as a rectangular array of symbols chosen from a given alphabet, is
the two-dimensional counterpart of a string. Researchers were inspired by the attempt
to reproduce Chomsky's hierarchy for picture languages. In the past and more so in
recent years, the classical methods used to define string languages have been essayed
for picture languages, thus obtaining various formal models and picture language
families.

The tutorial presents the state of the art of formal definitions for picture languages.
The formal models considered are: 2D regular expressions, tiling systems, automata
and grammars of different types. Each picture language family will be presented by
means of typical examples that illustrate its expressiveness. Moreover each 2D formal
model will be compared with the corresponding string model to point out similarities
and differences. The two-dimensional perspective will show up with its intrinsic
richness whose we will analyze drawbacks and benefits.

Reference

1. Reghizzi, S.C., Giammarresi, D., Lonati, V.: Two-dimensional models. In: J.-É., Pin (ed.)
   Handbook of Automata Theory, vol. 1, pp. 303–333, EMS Publishing House, Berlin (2021)

MIUR Excellence Department Project awarded to the Department of Mathematics, University
of Rome Tor Vergata, CUP E83C18000100006 and OBPOBS Project funded by Tor Vergata
University, CUP E83C22001660005.

Recent Interactions Between Computability and Set Theory

Noam Greenberg

School of Mathematics and Statistics, Victoria University of Wellington,
Wellington, New Zealand

Since very early days, there has been a certain overlap between computability theory and set theory: one can view both fields as inhabiting two parts of a spectrum that starts with regular languages and polynomial-time computation, continues with partial computable functions and Turing reducibility, and then the hyperarithmetic realm, effective descriptive set theory, fine structure of the constructible hierarchy, and inner models for large cardinals. Thus the same diagonal argument was used by Cantor for the unctounability of the reals, by Gödel for the incompleteness theorem, and by Turing for the undecidability of the halting problem.

I plan to survey three areas which have seen recent activity.

1. **Higher randomness**. Both Martin-Löf and Sacks suggested strenghtening the notions of effective randomness to obtain nice closure properties. They considered randomness with respect to effectively Borel (hyperarithmetic) sets, and effectively co-analytic (Π_1^1) sets. This subject was later picked up and developed by Hjorth and Nies, and then Chong and Yu. In parallel, Hamkins, Welch and others have considered infinite-time Turing machines and related notions of higher randomness. At the extreme end we find randomness over Gödel's L studied originally by Solovay. I will discuss relativising randomness in the higher setting, and what this tells us about the different equivalent definitions of ML-randomness.

2. **Uncountable structures**. Computable algebra and computable model theory investigate the interplay between information and structure: what information can be stored in a structure or in its isomorphism type. By the nature of computability, this study is restricted to countable or separable structures. *Admissible computability* is a generalisation of computability to domains beyond the natural numbers, and can be used to study the effective properties of uncountable, well-ordered structures. I will in particular examine the case of free and almost-free abelian groups, related to Shelah's work on the subject.

3. **Effective Borel sets**. Shoenfield's limit lemma says that membership in a Δ_2^0 set can be understood as an approximation process, involving finitely many mind-changes. To understand membership in more complicated Borel sets, the extra ingredient needed is the Turing jump. Montalbán's "true stages" machinery allows us to dynamically approximate membership in Borel sets. It was one of the ingredients in Day and Marks's recent resolution of the decomposability problem. I will discuss other applications to descriptive set theory.

Invited Lectures

SMT Solving: Historical Review and New Developments

Erika Ábrahám

RWTH Aachen
abraham@informatik.rwth-aachen.de

Satisfiability modulo theories (SMT solving) is a relatively recent research thread in computer science, with the aim to provide algorithms and tools for checking the satisfiability of (usually quantifier-free) first-order logic formulas over different theories. Starting with relatively easy theories like equalities and uninterpreted functions, state-of-the-art SMT solvers nowadays provide support for numerous theories, including (quantifier-free) real arithmetic. For real arithmetic, some exciting recent developments combine traditional SMT solving ideas with a kind of counterexample-guided abstraction refinement using methods from computer algebra.

In this talk we give a historical review of SMT solving with a focus on arithmetic theories, describe our own solver SMT-RAT and discuss some of these fascinating new research directions.

Sheaf Cohomology in Univalent Foundation

Thierry Coquand ⓘ

Computer Science Department, University of Gothenburg
coquand@chalmers.se
http://www.cse.chalmers.se/~coquand

Abstract. In the introduction of his book on Higher Topos Theory, Jacob Lurie motivates this theory by the fact that it allows an elegant and general treatment of sheaf cohomology. It was realised early on that these ideas could be expressed in the setting of univalent foundations/homotopy type theory. I will try to explain in my presentation recent insights which show that this can be done in a maybe suprisingly direct way. Furthermore, all this can be formulated in a constructive meta theory, avoiding the non effective notion of injective resolutions.

Keywords: Univalent Foundation · Homotopy Type Theory · Constructive Mathematics

Towards a Diversified Understanding of Computability or Why We Should Care More About Our Histories

Liesbeth De Mol

CNRS, UMR 8163 Savoirs, Textes, Langage, Université de Lille
liesbeth.de-mol@univ-lille.fr

Abstract. In this talk I will argue that we should care more for and be more careful with the history of computability making a plea for a more diverse and informed understanding. The starting point will be the much celebrated Turing machine model. Why is it that within the computability community, this model is often considered as thé model? In the first part of this talk I review some of those reasons, showing how and why they are in need of a revision based, mostly, on historical arguments. On that basis I argue that, while surely, the Turing machine model is a basic one, part of its supposed superiority over other models is based on socio-historical forces. In part II then, I consider a number of historical, philosophical and technical arguments to support and elaborate the idea of a more diversified understanding of the history of computability. Central to those arguments will be the differentiation between, on the one hand, the logical equivalence between the different models with respect to the computable functions, and, on the other hand, some basic intensional differences between those very same models. To keep the argument clear, the main focus will be on the different models provided by Emil Leon Post but I will also include references to the work by Alonzo Church, Stephen C. Kleene and Haskell B. Curry.

Supported by the PROGRAMme project, ANR-17-CE38-0003-01.

Reverse Mathematics 2021

Damir Dzhafarov

Department of Mathematics, University of Connecticut
damir.dzhafarov@uconn.edu

Reverse mathematics is a foundational program in logic aimed at measuring the complexity of mathematical proofs and constructions according to the strength of the axioms needed to carry them out. Founded by Friedman in the 1970s, and principally developed by him and Simpson throughout the 1980s, it has become an incredibly active and far reaching area. Part of its appeal comes from its close, nearly inseparable connection to computability theory. The initial focus of the subject was a classificatory one, of categorizing different parts of mathematics into one of a handful of benchmark subsystems of second order arithmetic. Over time, interest has shifted to examples that defy this classification, giving rise to a zoo of mathematical principles with a rich and intricate web of strengths and interconnections. More recently, the subject has expanded to include notions and techniques from computable analysis, giving an even finer gauge with which to calibrate mathematical complexity, and offering new insights along the way. The talk will survey a bit of the history of the subject, some of the recent and ongoing developments, and offer a view of where it may be headed next.

Abstracts of Invited Talks

A Computable Functor from Torsion-Free Abelian Groups to Fields

Meng-Che "Turbo" Ho[1] ⓘ, Julia Knight[2], and Russell Miller[3]

[1] California State University, Northridge, Northridge, CA 91330,
USA
[2] University of Notre Dame, Notre Dame, IN 46556, USA
[3] City University of New York, New York, NY 10017, USA

In descriptive set theory, complexities of classes of countable structures are studied. A classical example is the isomorphism problem $\cong_r$ on the class of torsion-free abelian groups of rank r. Baer [1] gave a simple invariant for $\cong_1$, i.e., when two torsion-free abelian groups of rank 1 are isomorphic. However, Hjorth [3] showed that $\cong_1 <_B \cong_2$ and Thomas [6] generalized this to show that $\cong_n <_B \cong_{n+1}$. Recently, Paolini and Shelah [5] showed that the class of torsion-free abelian group with domain ω is Borel complete.

We compare the class of torsion-free abelian groups and the class of fields using the notion of computable functors defined by Miller, Poonen, Schoutens, and Shlapentokh [4], and the notion of effective interpretability. Harrison-Trainor, Melnikov, Miller, and Montalban [2] showed that the presence of a uniform effective interpretation between two classes implies the presence of a computable functor between them and vice versa. Writing $\mathfrak{TFAb}_r$ to be the class of torsion-free abelian groups of rank r and $\mathfrak{TD}_r$ to be the class of fields of transcendence degree r with characteristic 0, we show the following:

Theorem 1 (Ho, Knight, and Miller)

1. *There is a Turing-computable reduction from $\mathfrak{TFAb}_r$ to $\mathfrak{TD}_r$ that is uniform in r. That is, there is a Turing functional (uniform in r) $\Phi_r : \mathfrak{TFAb}_r \to \mathfrak{TD}_r$ such that for every $G, H \in \mathfrak{TFAb}_r$, $G \cong H$ if and only if $\Phi_r(G) \cong \Phi_r(H)$.*
2. *There is a uniform effective interpretation of $\Phi_r(G)$ in G. Thus, Φ_r can be completed to a computable functor in the sense of [4].*

References

1. Baer, R.: Abelian groups without elements of finite order. Duke Math. J. **3**(1), 68–122 (1937)
2. Harrison-Trainor, M., Melnikov, A., Miller, R., Montalbán, A.: Computable functors and effective interpretability. J. Symb. Log. **82**(1), 77–97 (2017)
3. Hjorth, G.: Around nonclassifiability for countable torsion free abelian groups. In: Eklof, P.C., Göbel, R. (eds.) Abelian Groups and Modules, pp. 269–292. Trends in Mathematics, Birkhäuser (1999)
4. Miller, R., Poonen, B., Schoutens, H., Shlapentokh, A.: A computable functor from graphs to fields. J. Symb. Log. **83**(1), 326–348 (2018)
5. Paolini, G., Shelah, S.: Torsion-free abelian groups are borel complete (2021). https://arxiv.org/abs/2102.12371
6. Thomas, S.: The classification problem for torsion-free abelian groups of finite rank. J. Amer. Math. Soc. **16**(1), 233–258 (2003)

An Incompressibility Theorem for Automatic Complexity

Bjørn Kjos-Hanssen

University of Hawai'i at Mānoa
bjoernkh@hawaii.edu
https://math.hawaii.edu/wordpress/bjoern/

Abstract. Shallit and Wang showed that the automatic complexity $A(x)$ satisfies $A(x) \geq n/13$ for almost all $x \in \{0,1\}^n$.

They also stated that Holger Petersen had informed them that the constant 13 can be reduced to 7.

Here we show that it can be reduced to $2 + \varepsilon$ for any $\varepsilon > 0$.

The result also applies to nondeterministic automatic complexity $A_N(x)$. In that setting the result is tight inasmuch as $A_N(x) \leq n/2 + 1$ for all x.

Algorithmic Dimensions, The Point-To-Set Principles, and the Complexity of Oracles

Elvira Mayordomo

Departamento de Informática e Ingeniería de Sistemas, Instituto de Investigación en Ingeniería de Aragón, Universidad de Zaragoza, Spain

Effective and resource-bounded dimensions were defined by Lutz in [5] and [4] and have proven to be useful and meaningful for quantitative analysis in the contexts of algorithmic randomness, computational complexity and fractal geometry (see the surveys [1, 2, 6, 12] and all the references in them).

The point-to-set principle of J. Lutz and N. Lutz [8] fully characterizes Hausdorff and packing dimensions in terms of effective dimensions in the Euclidean space, enabling effective dimensions to be used to answer open questions about fractal geometry, with already an interesting list of geometric measure theory results (see [3, 11] and more recent results in [7, 13–15]). This characterization has been recently extended to separable spaces [10] and to resource-bounded dimensions [9].

In this talk I will review the point-to-set principles focusing on the importance of the oracle that achieves the characterization of classical dimension in terms of an algorithmic dimension. For instance Stull [15] has been able to improve the Marstrand projection theorem by analyzing the optimality of the oracles in the point-to-set principles. I will discuss some open problems on the complexity of the oracles involved in the point-to-set principles for both the effective and resource-bounded cases.

Bibliography

1. Downey, R.G., Hirschfeldt, D.R.: Algorithmic Randomness and Complexity. Springer, New York (2010). https://doi.org/10.1007/978-0-387-68441-3
2. Hitchcock, J.M., Lutz, J.H., Mayordomo, E.: The fractal geometry of complexity classes. SIGACT News Complex. Theor. Col. **36**, 24–38 (2005)
3. Lutz, J.H., Lutz, N.: Who asked us? how the theory of computing answers questions about analysis. In: Du, D.Z., Wang, J. (eds.) Complexity and Approximation. LNCS, vol. 12000. Springer, Cham (2020). https://doi.org/10.1007/978-3-030-41672-0_4
4. Lutz, J.H.: Dimension in complexity classes. SIAM J. Comput. **32**(5), 1236–1259 (2003)

Research supported in part by Spanish Ministry of Science and Innovation grant PID2019-104358RB-I00 and by the Science dept. of Aragon Government: Group Reference T64_20R (COSMOS research group).

5. Lutz, J.H.: The dimensions of individual strings and sequences. Inf. Comput. **187** (1), 49–79 (2003)
6. Lutz, J.H.: Effective fractal dimensions. Math. Logic Q. **51**(1), 62–72 (2005)
7. Lutz, J.H.: The point-to-set principle, the continuum hypothesis, and the dimensions of hamel bases. Computability (2022). To appear
8. Lutz, J.H., Lutz, N.: Algorithmic information, plane Kakeya sets, and conditional dimension. ACM Trans. Comput. Theor. **10** (2018). Article 7
9. Lutz, J.H., Lutz, N., Mayordomo, E.: Dimension and the structure of complexity classes. Technical report (2021). https://arxiv.org/2109.05956
10. Lutz, J.H., Lutz, N., Mayordomo, E.: Extending the reach of the point-toset principle. In: Berenbrink, P., Monmege, B. (eds.) 39th International Symposium on Theoretical Aspects of Computer Science (STACS 2022), vol. 219 of Leibniz International Proceedings in Informatics (LIPIcs), pp. 48:1–48:14. Schloss Dagstuhl Leibniz-Zentrum für Informatik (2022)
11. Lutz, J.H., Mayordomo, E.: Algorithmic fractal dimensions in geometric measure theory. In: Brattka, V., Hertling, P. (eds.) Handbook of Computability and Complexity in Analysis. Theory and Applications of Computability. Springer, Cham (2021). https://doi.org/10.1007/978-3-030-59234-9_8
12. Mayordomo, E.: Effective fractal dimension in algorithmic information theory. In: Cooper, S.B., Löwe, B., Sorbi, A. (eds.) New Computational Paradigms. Springer, New York (2008). https://doi.org/10.1007/978-0-387-68546-5_12
13. Slaman, T.: Personal communication (2021)
14. Stull, D.: The dimension spectrum conjecture for planar lines. Technical report (2021). https://arxiv.org/arXiv:2102.00134
15. Stull, D.: Optimal oracles for point-to-set principles. In: Berenbrink, P., Monmege, B., (eds.), 39th International Symposium on Theoretical Aspects of Computer Science (STACS 2022) of Leibniz International Proceedings in Informatics (LIPIcs), vol. 219, pp. 57:1–57:17. Schloss Dagstuhl Leibniz-Zentrum für Informatik (2022)

A Connection Between Inverse Galois Problem of a Field and Its First-Order Theory

Alexandra Shlapentokh

Department of Mathematics, East Carolina University, Greenville, NC 27858
shlapentokha@ecu.edu
myweb.ecu.edu/shlapentokha

Given a countable field F and a finite group G the Inverse Galois Problem for F and G is the problem of determining whether the field F has a finite Galois extension L such that $Gal(L/F) \cong G$. We show that the Turing degree of this problem is less or equal to the Turing degree of the first-order theory of the field.

Ultra Scaling Blockchains with ZK-STARKs

Eli Ben-Sasson

StarkWare Industries Ltd.
eli@starkware.co
https://www.starkware.co/

Abstract. Scalable and Transparent ARguments of Knowledge (STARKs) are practically efficient cryptographic proofs that use minimal cryptographic assumptions and are capable of improving the scalability and privacy of blockchains. By now, there have been weeks during which STARK-based systems settled 33% more transactions than Ethereum, while using only 1% of Ethereum's computational resources.

This talk explains why STARKs and blockchains blend nicely together like wine and cheese, and will describe the "theory-to-practice" journey of STARK technology from the early days of PCP theory to blockchain rollups, layer 2/3 systems, and beyond.

Blockchains and Related Technologies: Which Ideas Are Likely to Endure?

Maurice Herlihy

Brown University
herlihy@cs.brown.edu
https://cs.brown.edu/mph/

Abstract. Blockchains and distributed ledgers have become the focus of much recent attention. Like many innovations, this field emerged from outside mainstream computer science, although almost all the component ideas were already well-known. As a new area driven mostly by technological and financial innovations, it can be difficult to distinguish accomplishment from aspiration, and especially difficult to tell which ideas are of transient versus lasting interest.

This talk surveys the theory and practice of blockchain-based distributed systems from the point of view of classical distributed computing, along with opinions about promising future research directions for our community.

Smarter Contracts: Applications of Haskell and Agda at IOG

Philip Wadler[1,2]

[1] School of Informatics, University of Edinburgh
wadler@inf.ed.ac.uk
https://homepages.inf.ed.ac.uk/wadler/
[2] IOG
https://iohk.io/en/team/philip-wadler

Abstract. Cardano is a proof-of-stake blockchain platform developed by IOG. Its smart contract language, Plutus, is based on Haskell, and supports both on-chain and off-chain components with a single sourcce language; and much of the software of Cardano is implemented in Haskell. On-chain components of smart contracts are compiled to Plutus Core, which is a variant of System F and has been formally specified in Agda. Property-based testing is used to compare the production implementation of Plutus Core with an evaluator derived from the proof of soundness of System F written in Agda. Astonishingly, IOG is one of the few firms to insist its products be based on peer-reviewed research.

Keywords: Smart contracts · blockchain · Haskell · Agda

References

1. Manuel M.T., et al.: The Extended UTXO Model. Financial Cryptography Workshops, pp. 525–539 (2020)
2. Manuel M.T., et al.: Native Custom Tokens in the Extended UTXO Model. ISoLA (3), 89–111 (2020)
3. Chapman, J., Kireev, R., Nester, C., Wadler, P.: System F in agda, for fun and profit. MPC, 255–297 (2019)
4. Peyton Jones, M., Gkoumas, V., Kireev, R., MacKenzie, K., Nester, C., Wadler, P.: Unraveling recursion: compiling an IR with recursion to system F. MPC, 414–443 (2019)

'My Avid Fellow Feeling' and 'Fleas'

Playing with Words on the Computer

Troy Kaighin Astarte

Swansea University

An early non-numerical application of computers was processing human language, such as in the field of machine translation; natural language processing remains a significant field today. But almost as soon as they were employed for serious language applications, computers were applied to playful or artistic endeavours as well. This talk explores two historical examples: one fairly well-studied, the other a new archival discovery. One is Strachey's 1952 program for randomly generating love letters, and the other a poetry programming competition held at Newcastle University in 1968.

In the early 1950s Christopher Strachey, a schoolmaster at Harrow, visited Manchester University to write some programs for its Ferranti Mark 1. This included a program randomly generate (rather mawkish) love letters. The letters were based on a template with blanks of particular types (adjectives, nouns, adverbs), and a pool of words which were inserted into the appropriate spaces at random. This program, which Strachey may have written with help from both Turing and his literary sister Barbara, represents a very early example of digital combinatory literature.

The University of Newcastle upon Tyne's Computing Laboratory underwent a period of change in the late 1960s: expanding teaching, experiments in new networked computing, and growing breadth of research. Such research topics included automatic typesetting, medical literature information retrieval, and bibliographic data processing—manipulating language. In this context the lab director, Prof. Ewan Page, announced a competition for the production of limericks or poems, written *as programs*, such that their output was also poetic. The competition saw entries by a number of PhD students and the ingenuity on display was high. Programs humorously explored existing algorithms, reflected on life as a PhD student, or referenced classic works of literature.

Various analyses of Strachey's work discuss its position as an early form of digital art, as a parody of attitudes towards love written by a gay man, and as a technical exploration. In my talk, I extend these analyses and consider how they apply to the Newcastle poetry competition. I argue that both examples show the crucial role of play in the practice of programming, and discuss how considering humans and machines together provides a better perspective on the perennial questions of the form "Will a computer ever write a symphony as good as Beethoven?"

Mathematics as Natural Language: Principles, Consequences and Challenges of the Application of NLP Models to the Treatment of Mathematical Knowledge

Juan Luis Gastaldi ⓘ

ETH Zürich, Zürich ZH 8092, Switzerland
juan.luis.gastaldi@gess.ethz.ch

Recent years have seen a remarkable development of deep neural network (DNN) techniques for data analysis, along with their increasing application in scientific research across different disciplines. The field of mathematics has not been exempted from this general trend. Indeed, various works have suggested the relevance of possible applications of DNNs to the treatment of mathematical knowledge at multiple levels [1, 2, 4–9, 12, 14–16]. Significantly, the vast majority of those results resort to neural models specifically developed for the processing of natural language (NLP), from word embeddings [10, 11, 13] to seq2seq [17] and Transformers [3, 18].

This circumstance is remarkable for several reasons. Starting with the fact that, while the computational treatment of natural language traditionally implied an effort toward the latter's mathematization, it is now the mathematical knowledge that needs to be conceived as a kind of natural language, thus suggesting novel and non-trivial articulations between both. Furthermore, these contemporary neural approaches entail a renewed interest in textual aspects of mathematics and their representational capabilities. More precisely, since mathematical texts (statements, expressions, symbols) are all DNNs can rely on to perform tasks involving mathematical knowledge, the success of these methods would imply a new fundamental role of mathematical texts, going far beyond the usual understanding of mathematical writing as a simple notation for a pre-existing mathematical content, or a more or less arbitrary syntax for an independently determined semantics. Finally, even more than any other field of application, these attempts in mathematics raise critical epistemological questions since the formal (i.e., non-empirical) nature generally attributed to mathematical knowledge contrasts with the radically empirical position assumed by connectionist approaches guiding the application of DNNs and characterizing the practice of natural language.

After reviewing the most relevant literature in the field, this paper assesses the philosophical stakes of recent attempts to apply NLP models to mathematical knowledge. It concludes by indicating the conceptual and technical challenges and orientations to be drawn from such applications for a linguistically-driven philosophy of mathematics.

This project has received funding from the *European Union's Horizon 2020 research and innovation programme* under grant agreement No 839730.

References

1. Alemi, A.A., Chollet, F., Een, N., Irving, G., Szegedy, C., Urban, J.: Deepmath- deep sequence models for premise selection. In: Proceedings of the 30th International Conference on Neural Information Processing Systems, NIPS 2016, pp. 2243–2251. Curran Associates Inc., Red Hook, New York (2016)
2. Bansal, K., Loos, S.M., Rabe, M.N., Szegedy, C., Wilcox, S.: Holist: an environment for machine learning of higher-order theorem proving (extended version) (2019). http://arxiv.org/abs/1904.03241
3. Brown, T.B., et al.: Language models are few-shot learners (2020)
4. Charton, F.: Linear algebra with transformers (2021). https://arxiv.org/abs/2112.01898
5. Charton, F., Hayat, A., Lample, G.: Learning advanced mathematical computations from examples. In: International Conference on Learning Representations (2021). https://openreview.net/forum?id=-gfhS00XfKj
6. Davies, A., et al.: Advancing mathematics by guiding human intuition with AI. Nature **600** (7887), 70–74 (2021). https://doi.org/10.1038/s41586-021-04086-x, https://doi.org/10.1038/s41586-021-04086-x
7. Kaliszyk, C., Chollet, F., Szegedy, C.: Holstep: A machine learning dataset for higher-order logic theorem proving (2017). http://arxiv.org/abs/1703.00426
8. Lample, G., Charton, F.: Deep learning for symbolic mathematics (2019)
9. Loos, S.M., Irving, G., Szegedy, C., Kaliszyk, C.: Deep network guided proof search (2017). http://arxiv.org/abs/1701.06972
10. Mikolov, T., Chen, K., Corrado, G., Dean, J.: Efficient estimation of word representations in vector space (2013). http://arxiv.org/abs/1301.3781
11. Mikolov, T., Yih, W.t., Zweig, G.: Linguistic regularities in continuous space word representations. In: Proceedings of the 2013 Conference of the North American Chapter of the ACL: Human Language Technologies. pp. 746–751. ACL (2013)
12. Peng, S., Yuan, K., Gao, L., Tang, Z.: Mathbert: a pre-trained model for mathematical formula understanding (2021). https://arxiv.org/abs/2105.00377
13. Pennington, J., Socher, R., Manning, C.D.: Glove: Global vectors for word representation. In: EMNLP. vol. 14, pp. 1532–1543 (2014)
14. Polu, S., Han, J.M., Zheng, K., Baksys, M., Babuschkin, I., Sutskever, I.: Formal mathematics statement curriculum learning (2022). https://arxiv.org/abs/2202.01344
15. Polu, S., Sutskever, I.: Generative language modeling for automated theorem proving (2020). https://arxiv.org/abs/2009.03393
16. Saxton, D., Grefenstette, E., Hill, F., Kohli, P.: Analysing mathematical reasoning abilities of neural models (2019)
17. Sutskever, I., Vinyals, O., Le, Q.V.: Sequence to sequence learning with neural networks. In: Proceedings of the 27th International Conference on Neural Information Processing Systems, NIPS 2014, vol. 2, pp. 3104–3112. MIT Press, Cambridge (2014)
18. Vaswani, A., et al.: Attention is all you need (2017)

Are Large Language Models Models (of Language)?

Maël Pégny

Universität Tübingen
maelpegny@gmail.com

Abstract. Large Language Models (LLMs) are extremely large deep neural networks trained on humongous amount of data. Primarily trained for part-of-speech prediction, i.e. roughly the task of predicting what comes next in a text, they have been able to display not only state-of-the art performances for this task, but also have shown a great versatility to be fine-tuned for many other NLP tasks. Recently, they have even shown a surprising ability to be used as a basis to build efficient models for non-NLP tasks on multi-modal data. LLMs are thus slowly emerging as some of the most crucial models in all of AI. In this presentation, I will try to articulate the epistemological consequences of this evolution. First, I will first examine the respective consequences of two different paths towards task-agnosticity in NLP and beyond (in-context learning and transfer learning), and then see whether they can be seen as a true road towards, if not the great General AI, at least a more general AI. Finally, I will try to articulate how this question of task-agnosticity relates to the nature of the knowledge produced by large opaque models.

Are We There Yet? Meaning in the Age of Large Language Models

Jacopo Tagliabue

Coveo Labs, New York NY, USA
jtagliabue@coveo.com

1 Long Abstract

There is no time like the present. With the advent of the "golden age of Natural Language Processing" [1] (NLP), a contagious enthusiasm on the capabilities of large language models (LLMs) started spreading from research institutions into the general public [2]. While critics, mostly from academia, have repeatedly argued that LLMs show limited "understanding" [3, 4], the pace of development of increasingly larger models doesn't seem to slow down [5]: are we there yet?

In *this* talk, we briefly review the two dominant traditions on *meaning* of the last century:

- the "symbolic" tradition, where *meaning* is mostly about deductive composition of atomic components which are *given*; for example, see the model-theoretic semantics in [8];
- the "neural" tradition, where *meaning* is mostly about statistical association of atomic components which are *learned*; for example, see the distributional semantics in [9].

While a satisfactory unification of the two approaches is ultimately desirable [7], we argue that the duality of meaning – which sometimes behaves like a function, sometimes like a vector – is here to stay, at least for the time being. Contrary to the symbolic camp, we stress the importance of a theory of lexical acquisition and analogical reasoning; contrary to the neural camp, we stress the importance of *true* zero-shot generalization and a more rounded (and less naive) view of what counts as "grasping the meaning" of something [6].

In particular, the two camps seem to fundamentally disagree not (only) on what counts as a good explanation, but what is there to explain in the first place. In this perspective, we discuss the famous architecture behind recent LLMs – i.e. the transformer [10] –, which has been successfully adapted to many sequential problems that have nothing to do with the original NLP problem [11]: whether language is simply yet another sequence prediction problem is a contentious issue with deep ramifications into linguistics and cognitive sciences.

Finally, we conclude showing recent progress made in *grounded* language models – including our own research –, and sketch a roadmap for investigating meaning in more ecological settings.

References

1. A golden age for natural language. https://www.forbes.com/sites/louisaxu/2021/12/01/a-golden-age-for-natural-language/. Accessed 21 Jan 2022
2. A robot wrote this entire article. Are you scared yet, human. https://www.theguardian.com/commentisfree/2020/sep/08/robot-wrote-this-article-gpt-3. Accessed 31 Jan 2022
3. Bender, E.M., Koller, A.: Climbing towards NLU: on meaning, form, and understanding in the age of data. In: Proceedings of the 58th Annual Meeting of the Association for Computational Linguistics, Online (2020)
4. GPT-3, Bloviator: OpenAI's language generator has no idea what it's talking about. https://www.technologyreview.com/2020/08/22/1007539/gpt3-openai-language-generator-artificial-intelligence-ai-opinion/. Accessed 23 Jan 2022
5. Using deepspeed and megatron to train megatron-turing nlg 530b, the world's largest and most powerful generative language model. https://www.microsoft.com/en-us/research/blog/using-deepspeed-and-megatron-to-train-megatron-turing-nlg-530b-the-worlds-largest-and-most-powerful-generative-language-model/. Accessed 29 Jan 2022
6. Lake, B.M., Murphy, G.L.: Word meaning in minds and machines. Psychological review (2021)
7. Baroni, M., Bernardi R., Zamparelli R.: Frege in space: a program of compositional distributional semantics. linguistic issues in language technology (2014)
8. Montague, R.: The proper treatment of quantification in ordinary english. In: Proceedings of the 1970 Stanford Workshop on Grammar and Semantics, Dordrecht (1973)
9. Mikolov, T., Kai C., Gregory S.C., Dean J.: Efficient Estimation of Word Representations in Vector Space. ICLR (2013)
10. Vaswani, A., et al.: Attention is All you Need. ArXiv (2017)
11. Janner, M., Li, Q., Levine, S.: Reinforcement learning as one big sequence modeling problem. ArXiv (2021)

DNA Library Evidence Strings

Giuditta Franco

Department of Computer Science, University of Verona, Italy
giuditta.franco@univr.it

Generation of a combinatorial library of n-long binary strings, especially by starting from few sequences and by applying yet efficient basic DNA operations, has a biological, technological, and algorithmic relevance. Namely, some DNA based research, including tools and technologies from life science, aim at improving the cost, speed and efficiency of technologies for writing and combining DNA or other information-storing bio-polymers. DNA-based digital data storage provides a valid alternative to current technologies: it is promising in terms of information density (orders of magnitude higher than traditional memories) and of stability (millennia versus years). From a computational perspective, the design of efficient molecular algorithms is a challenge for the development of new biotechnologies generating DNA libraries.

In the context of design and development of string algorithms for computational biotechnology, this talk revolves around a simple DNA library generation algorithm, which starts from four specific DNA strings and efficiently produces a library of 2^n different strings in linear time. It consists in an iterative application of specific null context splicing rules, which recombine a couple of strings (in which one given substring occurs) by producing a new couple of chimerical strings, and may be implemented in laboratory by an XPCR procedure (a variant of the well known PCR). Of course such an algorithm is correct (and complete) iff it produces the whole library of DNA strings. Correctness is proved from a theoretical viewpoint while the experimental feasibility needs to be demonstrated independently. In an experimental context, the algorithm outcome is proved by the existence, in the final pool, of two specific patterns called library *evidence strings*, which are specific cyclic strings with a motif four characters long. If they (both) are present in the pool after the execution of the algorithm, we are guaranteed that each single instruction (an XPCR based string recombination) had produced the expected result, then the whole library has been generated (with no experimental drawbacks).

The algorithm with the experimental work validating all the procedures are presented in the talk, as well as the concept of evidence strings, with their combinatorial properties. This is a nice showcase where a string combinatorial property allows us to assess the experimental success of a DNA algorithm.

Keywords: Computational biotechnology · DNA library · Molecular computing · Periodic strings · XPCR

Turedo a New Computational Model
for Molecular Nanobots?

Daria Pchelina[1], Nicolas Schabanel[2], Shinnosuke Seki[3],
and Guillaume Theyssier[4]

[1] LIPN, Université Paris 13
daria.pchelina@normalesup.org
[2] CNRS - École Normale Supérieure de Lyon
nicolas.schabanel@ens-lyon.fr
http://perso.ens-lyon.fr/nicolas.schabanel/
[3] The University of Electro-Communications
shinsek@gmail.com
[4] Institut de Mathématiques de Marseille (CNRS - Université Aix-Marseille)
guillaume.theyssier@cnrs.fr

Abstract. Different models have been proposed to understand natural phenomena at the molecular scale from a computational point of view. Oritatami
systems are a model of molecular co-transcriptional folding: the transcript (the
"molecule") folds as it is synthesized according to a local energy optimisation
process, in a similar way to how actual biomolecules such as RNA fold into
complex shapes and functions. We introduce a new model, called turedo, which
is a self-avoiding Turing machine on the plane that evolves by marking visited
positions and that can only move to unmarked positions. Any oritatami can be
seen as a particular turedo. We show that any turedo with lookup radius 1 can
conversely be simulated by an oritatami, using a universal bead type set. Our
notion of simulation is strong enough to preserve the geometrical and dynamical
features of these models up to a constant spatio-temporal rescaling (as in
intrinsic simulation). As a consequence, turedo can be used as a readable oritatami "higher-level" programming language to build readily oritatami "smart
robots", using our explicit simulation result as a compiler. Furthermore, as our
gadgets are simple enough, this might open the way to a readable oritatami
programming, and these ingredients could be regarded as a promising direction
to implement computation in co-transcribed RNA nanostructures in wetlab.

As an application of our simulation result, we prove three new complexity
results on the (infinite) limit configurations of oritatami systems (and radius-1
turedos), assembled from a finite seed configuration. First, we show that such
limit configurations can embed any recursively enumerable set, and are thus
exactly as complex as aTAM limit configurations. Second, we characterize the
possible densities of occupied positions in such limit configurations: they are
exactly the Π_2-computable numbers between 0 and 1. We also show that all
such limit densities can be produced by one single oritatami system, just by
changing the finite seed configuration. Third, we exhibit a universal turedo (and
consequently a universal oritatami system) that is able to build any finite shape

up to some upscaling from an asymptotically minimum size seed, and show conversely that uncomputably large upscaling is needed in general in this regards.

None of these results is implied by previous constructions of oritatami embedding tag systems or 1D cellular automata, which produce only computable limit configurations with constrained density.

Note that, reframing our results, we prove that doodling without lifting the pen nor intersecting lines and using only a 1-local view to decide for the drawing directions produce drawings as complex and as dense as can be.

Keywords: Molecular self-assembly · Co-transcriptional folding · Intrinsic simulation · Arithmetical hierarchy of real numbers · 2D Turing machines · Computability

Computability and Complexity
in Morphogenetic Systems

Petr Sosík ⓘ

Institute of Computer Science, Faculty of Philosophy and Science,
Silesian University in Opava, Czech Republic
petr.sosik@fpf.slu.cz

Keywords: Morphogenetic system · Membrane computing · Self-assembly ·
Turing universality · **P** versus **NP** · **PSPACE**

Extended Abstract

Morphogenesis, literally meaning *generation of the form*, lies at the core of many processes of both organic and inorganic nature, described in biology or geology. Morphogenesis inspires many ideas of human creation, e.g., in architecture, design and art. Basic principles of morphogenesis, in a nutshell, are controlled growth and self-assembly. Both these topics are often understood as (semi)-algorithmic processes, for a mutual benefit of biology, chemistry and computer science.

To capture algorithmic aspects of morphogenesis, we have created a formal model of morphogenetic growth called the *morphogenetic (M) system* [5]. The model unfolds in a 3D (or generally, dD) continuous space in discrete time steps. Spatial structure of the model is determined by the underlying so-called polytopic tile system in $\mathbb{R}^d$. It is based on a generalization of Wang tiles to arbitrary d'-dimensional polytopes of specified sizes and shapes, $1 \leq d' \leq d - 1$. Unlike Wang tiling or algorithmic tile assembly (aTAM) [1], the tiles (polytopes) are not present in an arbitrary many copies, but they are created by reactions of simpler shapeless atomic objects. These objects can mutually react and pass through a specific *protion channels* in tiles. Their "metabolism" is controlled by a set of evolutionary rules inspired by membrane systems with proteins on membranes [2]. Every object, either a tile or a floating object, has at each moment its specific position and orientation in $\mathbb{R}^d$, possibly changing as the system evolves. The combination of self-assembly and evolutionary rules provides the M system with feedback loops and hence with the ability of a surprisingly complex behaviour. We refer the reader to [5] for a formal description and detailed examples of M systems formation.

In previous publications we have used M systems as models of bacterial growth, self-healing properties and resistance to damages caused by, e.g., antibiotics [3]. Computer simulations with our freely available software package Cytos

Supported by the Silesian University in Opava under the Student Funding Scheme, project SGS/8/2022.

(https://github.com/mmaverikk/Cytos) were in a very good agreement with biological experiments. Here we focus on computational aspects of morphogenetic systems. After reviewing previous results related to their computational universality (in the Turing sense), we present two new results on minimal universal M systems.

Theorem 1. *There exists a universal M system in 2D with three tiles, 26 floating objects, one protion and 26 rules.*

We further extend the result to the case of self-healing M system which can recover from injuries to their structure.

Theorem 2. *There exists an M system in 2D with 8 tiles, 28 floating objects, 4 protions and 100 rules, that simulates a universal Turing machine M on any given input in linear time, and it is self-healing of degree 1, provided that injuries at each step only affect tiles and objects belonging to a single tape cell.*

Then we focus on computational complexity of M systems and we demonstrate how they can characterize the **P** versus **NP** borderline. M systems under standard definition can solve NP-complete problems in randomized polynomial time. We introduce *M systems with mass*, where mutual pushing of objects are at each step limited by a certain certain distance, due to their nonzero mass.

Theorem 3. *M systems with mass can solve in polynomial time exactly the class of problems* **P**.

Finally, we also discuss a possible relation of M systems to the class **PSPACE** and we conjecture that, even under the standard definition, they most likely cannot solve **PSPACE**-complete problems in a polynomial time. For a more detailed description of the results presented here we refer the reader to [4].

References

1. Krasnogor, N., Gustafson, S., Pelta, D., Verdegay, J.: Systems self-assembly: multidisciplinary snapshots. studies in multidisciplinarity, Elsevier Science (2011)
2. Paun, A., Popa, B.: P systems with proteins on membranes. Fundamenta Informaticae. **72**(4), 467–483 (2006)
3. Smolka, V., Drastík, J., Bradík, J., Garzon, M., Sosík, P.: Morphogenetic systems: models and experiments. Biosystems **198**, Art. No. 104270 (2020). https://doi.org/10.1016/j.biosystems.2020.104270
4. Sosík, P.: Morphogenetic computing: computability and complexity results. Submitted (2022)
5. Sosík, P., Smolka, V., Drastík, J., Moore, T., Garzon, M.: Morphogenetic and homeostatic self-assembled systems. In: Patitz, M., Stannett, M. (eds.) Unconventional Computation and Natural Computation. UCNC 2017. LNCS, vol. 10240. Springer, Cham (2017). https://doi.org/10.1007/978-3-319-58187-3_11

Computability Theory and Reverse Mathematics via Lawvere-Tierney topologies

Takayuki Kihara

Department of Mathematical Informatics, Graduate School of Informatics,
Nagoya University, Japan
kihara@i.nagoya-u.ac.jp

We present a new perspective of oracle: We consider an oracle to be an "*operation on truth-values*" that may cause a transformation of one world into another: A mathematical statement φ may be false in computable mathematics, but φ can be true in computable mathematics relative to an oracle α. This means that the oracle α caused a change in the truth value of the statement φ, and also caused a change from the computable world to the α-relative computable world. One might say that this is based on the idea that there is a correspondence between "*computations using oracles*" and "*proofs using transcendental axioms*". Such an idea is used as a very standard technique in, for example, classical reverse mathematics. Our approach is similar, but with a newer perspective that deals more directly with operations on truth-values. More explicitly, it is formulated using topos-theoretic notions such as Lawvere-Tierney topology, which is a kind of generalization of Grothendieck topology to an arbitrary topos.

In this talk, we will connect the structure of the Lawvere-Tierney topologies on a certain relative realizability topos (e.g., the effective topos; the Kleene-Vesley topos) with a certain degree structure in computability theory, based on previous work by Lee and van Oosten. For this purpose, we introduce a new computability-theoretic reducibility notion, which is a common extension of the notions of Turing reducibility and generalized Weihrauch reducibility. This notion can be thought of as a fusion of the notions of generalized Weihrauch reducibility and Bauer's extended Weihrauch reducibility. We introduce a realizability predicate relative to a "extended generalized Weihrauch degree", which is identical to the realizability relative to the corresponding Lawvere-Tierney topology, and then show some separation results on constructive reverse mathematics.

References

1. Takayuki K.: Degrees of incomputability, realizability and constructive reverse mathematics. arXiv:2002.10712 (2020)

The author's research was partially supported by JSPS KAKENHI Grant Numbers 19K03602 and 21H03392.

2. Takayuki K.: Lawvere-Tierney topologies for computability theorists. arXiv:2106.03061 (2021)
3. Takayuki K.: Rethinking the notion of oracle: A link between synthetic descriptive set theory and effective topos theory. arXiv:2202.00188 (2022)

Reverse Mathematics and Semisimple Rings

Hishan Wu

School of Information Science, Beijing Language and Culture University,
15 Xueyuan Road, Haidian District, Beijing 100083
huishanwu@blcu.edu.cn

We study rings and modules from the standpoint of reverse mathematics. In this talk, we mainly focus on semisimple rings and semisimple modules. Semisimple modules are often defined as modules that can be written as direct sums of simple submodules. In 2013, Yamazaki initiated the study of semisimple modules as well as other kinds of modules like projective modules and injective modules in reverse mathematics; he showed that the statement "every submodule of a semisimple module is a direct summand" is equivalent to ACA_0 over RCA_0. Semisimple modules have various equivalent definitions in classical algebra. We first discuss equivalent characterizations of semisimple modules in reverse mathematics. By choosing a different characterization for semisimple modules, We first discuss equivalent characterizations of semisimple modules in reverse mathematics. By choosing a different characterization for semisimple modules, we define a left R-module M over a ring R to be semisimple if every submodule of it is a direct summand. We view a ring R as left semisimple if the left regular module $_R R$ is semisimple. Based on such definitions of semisimple modules and semisimple rings, we study characterizations of left semisimple rings in terms of projective modules and injective modules in reverse mathematics. For instance, we show that ACA_0 is equivalent to the statement "any left module over a left semisimple ring is projective" over RCA_0 and that ACA_0 proves the statement "if every cyclic left R-module is injective, then R is a left semisimple ring". For more details of the work, refer to a recent paper in Archive for Mathematical Logic https://doi.org/10.1007/s00153-021-00812-4.

The Skolem Landscape

James Worrell ⓘ

Department of Computer Science, University of Oxford, UK
jbw@cs.ox.ac.uk

Abstract. We overview the Skolem and Positivity Problems for C-finite and P-finite recurrence sequences. We describe the history of these problems, their relevance to computer science, and the state of the art as regards decidability.

Keywords: Recurrence sequences · Skolem-Mahler-Lech theorem · Skolem problem · Positivity problem

1 A Landscape of Decision Problems

This talk aims to paint a landscape of decision problems for recurrence sequences. We consider sequences that satisfy linear recurrences with constant coefficients (the so-called C-finite sequences) and, more generally, we consider those that satisfy recurrences with polynomial coefficients (the so-called P-finite sequences). For example, the Fibonacci sequence is C-finite, while the sequence of harmonic numbers is P-finite. Many authors use the term holonomic in place of P-finite.

The two main decision problems that we investigate are the ***Skolem Problem*** (does the sequence have a zero term?) and the ***Positivity Problem*** (are all terms of the sequence positive?). From a computer science perspective, we consider these as canonical reachability problems for linear systems.

Decidability of the Skolem and Positivity Problems are open, both for C-finite sequences and for P-finite sequences. In the talk we will survey the history of the two problems, starting with the celebrated Skolem-Mahler-Lech theorem which characterises the structure of the set of zeros of a C-finite sequence. We will mention also subsequent variations and generalisations of this theorem to P-finite sequences, both in finite and zero characteristic. For further motivation, we will describe some of the many different guises in which the Skolem and Positivity Problems appear in automata theory, logic and model checking, analysis of algorithms, combinatorics, and related areas.

In the second half of the talk, we will describe partial decidability results for variations of the problems, including recent developments (of ourselves and others). We will, in particular, mention a recent proof that the Skolem Problem for simple C-finite sequences is decidable subject to two well known number-theoretic conjectures: the p-adic Schanuel Conjecture and the exponential local-global principle. In general, we will attempt to give a flavour of some of the relevant mathematics, which ranges from classical results in Diophantine geometry, such as the Subspace theorem, to more speculative number-theoretic conjectures, such as the periods conjecture of Kontsevich and Zagier.

In summary, the talk aims to give an idea of a landscape of decision problems for recurrence sequences, to explain why the problems are important, what is currently known in terms of partial decidability results, and why decidability of the central problems in this landscape remain open.

Contents

Calculating the Mind Change Complexity of Learning Algebraic Structures

Nikolay Bazhenov[1], Vittorio Cipriani[2]([✉]), and Luca San Mauro[3]

[1] Sobolev Institute of Mathematics, Novosibirsk, Russia
bazhenov@math.nsc.ru
[2] Università degli Studi di Udine, Udine, Italy
vittorio.cipriani@uniud.it
[3] Sapienza Università di Roma, Roma, Italy
luca.sanmauro@uniroma1.it

Abstract. This paper studies algorithmic learning theory applied to algebraic structures. In previous papers, we have defined our framework, where a learner, given a family of structures, receives larger and larger pieces of an arbitrary copy of a structure in the family and, at each stage, is required to output a conjecture about the isomorphism type of such a structure. The learning is successful if there is a learner that eventually stabilizes to a correct conjecture. Here, we analyze the number of mind changes that are needed to learn a given family $\mathfrak{K}$. We give a descriptive set-theoretic interpretation of such mind change complexity. We also study how bounding the Turing degree of learners affects the mind change complexity of a given family of algebraic structures.

Keywords: Inductive inference · Computable structures · Algorithmic learning theory · Mind change complexity

1 Introduction

Learning theory is one of the mathematical approaches that study the adaptation of a rational agent to an environment. In this paper, we deal with a particular style of learning called *learning in the limit* or *inductive inference*. Introduced by Gold [11] and Putnam [16] in the 1960s, this paradigm was meant to infer objects that were either formal languages or computable functions. Generally, such a paradigm is constituted by a *learner* that analyzes a growing amount of data about some *environment* and, in the limit, is able to get a systematic

Bazhenov was supported by the Ministry of Education and Science of the Republic of Kazakhstan, grant AP08856493 "Positive graphs and computable reducibility on them as mathematical model of databases". Cipriani's research was partially supported by the Italian PRIN 2017 Grant "Mathematical Logic: models, sets, computability". We also thank the anonymous referees for their careful reading of the paper and the valuable suggestions.

knowledge of it. In recent times, learning of mathematical structures, first considered by Glymour [10], received interest, with special attention paid to families of computable structures, like vector spaces, rings, trees, and matroids [9,12,15,17].

At each stage, the learner outputs a conjecture about the isomorphism type of the presented structure. That is, the learner either produces a new hypothesis or stays with its previous conjecture. The information provided to the learner may also be empty, and on the other side, the learner can output the symbol "?" whenever the information received so far is considered insufficient. The learning is successful if, in the limit, the learner eventually guesses the correct isomorphism type of presented structure. This paradigm is analogous to what, in classical algorithmic learning theory, is called **InfEx**-learnability: namely, **Inf** (for *informant*) stresses that the information provided to the learner contains both positive and negative information about the object to be learned; **Ex** (for *explanatory*) stresses that the learner needs to stabilize the correct hypothesis *in the limit*.

In [5], the authors obtained a complete model-theoretic characterization of which families of algebraic structures are learnable, using tools coming from infinitary logic. This allowed to witness the non-learnability of (apparently) simple families such as $\{\omega, \zeta\}$, where ω is the order type of natural numbers and ζ of integers. In [6], the authors built a family composed of two structures which is learnable, even if no Turing machine learns it. More recently, in [3] we presented a new hierarchy to classify the complexity of learning problems for algebraic structures via descriptive set-theoretic tools coming from the study of reductions between equivalence relations.

As the title suggests, the main theme of this paper will be the study of the number of mind changes made by a learner while learning a given family. This was already done for formal languages (e.g., in [1,8]), where the authors study which families are learnable when the number of mind changes allowed is bounded by some ordinal α. In this paper, we put the same constraint to the problem of learning algebraic structures. After some preliminaries (Sect. 2), we attack this problem in two different ways. In Sect. 3 we study particular types of families that we call *limit-free*, considering the partial order (poset) given by some suitable embedding relation on the family $\mathfrak{K}$, and we show that the mind change complexity of $\mathfrak{K}$ is affected by the height of such a poset. Our results characterize only families that are learnable with n many mind changes, where n is a finite ordinal. Secondly, in Sect. 4, following [3] and exploiting ideas from [14], we characterize certain types of families that are learnable with α many mind changes, with α a countable ordinal, in topological and descriptive set-theoretic terms. The last part of this paper is meant to study how the complexity of a learner, defined in terms of Turing reducibility, affects the number of mind changes required to learn a given family. This leaves further directions open, starting from the definition, suggested here, of the n-learning spectrum of a family of structures.

2 Preliminaries

2.1 Our Paradigm

We assume that the reader is familiar with basic notions and terminology from computable structure theory, as in [2].

Definition 1 ([3], Definition 2.2). *Let $\mathfrak{K}$ be a family of computable L-structures.*

- *The* learning domain *(LD) is the collection of all copies of the structures from $\mathfrak{K}$. That is,*

$$\mathrm{LD}(\mathfrak{K}) := \bigcup_{\mathcal{A} \in \mathfrak{K}} \{\mathcal{S} : \mathcal{S} \cong \mathcal{A}\}.$$

  As we identify each countable structure with an element of Cantor space (written as $2^{\mathbb{N}}$), we obtain that $\mathrm{LD}(\mathfrak{K}) \subseteq 2^{\mathbb{N}}$.
- *The* hypothesis space *(HS) contains, for each $\mathcal{A} \in \mathfrak{K}$, a formal symbol $\ulcorner \mathcal{A} \urcorner$ and a question mark symbol. That is,*

$$\mathrm{HS}(\mathfrak{K}) := \{\ulcorner \mathcal{A} \urcorner : \mathcal{A} \in \mathfrak{K}\} \cup \{?\}.$$

- *A learner $\mathbf{M}$ sees, by stages, all positive and negative data about any given structure in the learning domain and is required to output conjectures. This is formalized by saying that $\mathbf{M}$ is a function*

$$\textit{from } 2^{<\mathbb{N}} \textit{ to } \mathrm{HS}(\mathfrak{K}).$$

- *The learning is* successful *if, for each structure $\mathcal{S} \in \mathrm{LD}(\mathfrak{K})$, the learner eventually stabilizes to a correct conjecture about its isomorphism type. That is,*

$$\lim_{n \to \infty} \mathbf{M}(\mathcal{S} \restriction_n) = \ulcorner \mathcal{A} \urcorner \textit{ if and only if } \mathcal{S} \textit{ is a copy of } \mathcal{A}.$$

We say that $\mathfrak{K}$ is learnable, *if some learner $\mathbf{M}$ successfully learns $\mathfrak{K}$.*

Since our paradigm is defined on countable families of computable structures, we will omit the words "countable" and "computable". Notice that what here we call *learnable* is what in classical algorithmic learning theory is called **InfEx**-learnable. We also highlight that, since we defined a learner as a function, we can consider learners of different complexity: for example, a computable learner is simply a computable function from $2^{<\mathbb{N}}$ to $\mathrm{HS}(\mathfrak{K})$.

We now proceed in refining our paradigm in order to characterize n-learnability, that is, learnability where we allow only n many mind changes. Let ϵ denote the empty string and given $\sigma \in 2^{<\mathbb{N}}$ we indicate by σ^- the finite sequence σ without the last digit. We say that $\mathbf{M}$ *changes its mind at* σ if $\mathbf{M}(\sigma) \neq \mathbf{M}(\sigma^-)$ and $\mathbf{M}(\sigma^-) \neq ?$.

Definition 2. *Let $\mathbf{M}$ be a learner, $\mathfrak{K}$ be a countable family of computable structure, and let $c : 2^{<\mathbb{N}} \to$ Ordinals.*

- c *is a* mind change counter for $\mathbf{M}$ and $\mathfrak{K}$ *if*
  - $c(\sigma) \leqslant c(\sigma^-)$ *for all* $\sigma \neq \epsilon$, *and*
  - $c(\sigma) < c(\sigma^-)$ *if and only if* $\mathbf{M}$ *changes its mind at some* $\sigma \in 2^{<\mathbb{N}}$;
- $\mathfrak{K}$ *is* α-learnable *if and only if there is a learner* $\mathbf{M}$ *that learns* $\mathfrak{K}$ *and there is a mind change counter* c *for* $\mathbf{M}$ *and* $\mathfrak{K}$ *such that* $c(\epsilon) = \alpha$;
- $\mathfrak{K}$ *is* properly α-learnable *if* $\mathfrak{K}$ *is* α-learnable but not β-learnable for all $\beta < \alpha$.

Notice that, in the first point of the definition, one could define a counter c with the property that, for $\sigma \in 2^{<\mathbb{N}}$, $c(\sigma) < c(\sigma^-)$ even if $\mathbf{M}$ does not change its mind at σ. In this case, $\mathbf{M}$ would have different counters that are in a certain sense not "optimal" with respect to $\mathbf{M}$'s mind changes. Our choice allows us to associate a single counter c to a learner $\mathbf{M}$, so that, given $\mathbf{M}$ and once we have set $c(\epsilon)$, we can easily reconstruct c at any stage: this makes our proofs smoother.

2.2 Topology

In this paper, our paradigm and the equivalence relations involved, are defined on Cantor space. Such a space can be represented as the collection of reals, equipped with the product topology of the discrete topology on $\{0,1\}$. Given $\sigma \in 2^{<\mathbb{N}}$, let $[\sigma] = \{\alpha \in 2^{\mathbb{N}} : \sigma \subset \alpha\}$ be a *cylinder*. These cylinders form a basis of Cantor space. Given two finite strings $\sigma, \tau \in 2^{<\mathbb{N}}$, we write $\sigma \sqsubseteq \tau$ to denote that σ is an initial segment of τ ($\sigma \sqsubset \tau$ in case σ is a proper initial segment of τ). For any topological space, we say that a point x is *isolated* if there is an open set O such that $O = \{x\}$. If x is not isolated, then x is a *limit point*. We shall now define the Cantor–Bendixson derivative of X (see [13] for more on this topic). Given any topological space X, let $X' = \{x \in X : x \text{ is a limit point of } X\}$ and call such a set the *Cantor–Bendixson derivative* of X. Using transfinite induction we define the *iterated Cantor–Bendixson derivatives* X^α, where α is an ordinal, as follows. Starting with $X^0 = X$ we let $X^{\alpha+1} = (X^\alpha)'$ and $X^\lambda = \bigcap_{\alpha < \lambda} X^\alpha$ if λ is limit. By a classical theorem (Theorem 6.11 in [13]), if the space X is Polish (that is, separable and completely metrizable), then this iteration process "stops" at some countable ordinal. That is, for any Polish space X, there is a countable ordinal α_0 such that $X^\alpha = X^{\alpha_0}$ for all $\alpha > \alpha_0$. The set X^{α_0} is called the *perfect kernel* of X, while $X \setminus X^{\alpha_0}$ is the *scattered part*. Notice that α_0 is called the *Cantor–Bendixson rank* of X, and we denote it by $CB(X)$: in case $X^{\alpha_0} = \varnothing$, we say that X is scattered We also easily get that for a separable topological space X, X is countable if and only if $X^{CB(X)} = \varnothing$.

3   Learnability and Posets

In this section, we will discuss some results about the relation between the number of mind changes made when learning a family $\mathfrak{K}$ and structural properties of $\mathfrak{K}$. The first remark is that it is not always possible to define an upper bound of the number of mind changes. This may happen for two reasons. Either the family is not learnable at all, or the family is learnable but, at any finite stage, it is always possible to extend the copy built so far to a structure different from the one the learner is conjecturing. To study when it is possible to define such a bound, we provide the following definition.

Definition 3. *Let $\mathcal{A}$ and $\mathcal{B}$ be two structures. $\mathcal{A}$ finitely embeds in $\mathcal{B}$ (notation $\mathcal{A} \hookrightarrow_{fin} \mathcal{B}$) if for all s, $\mathcal{A} \restriction_s \hookrightarrow \mathcal{B}$.*

In general, $\hookrightarrow_{fin}$ is a preorder on $\mathfrak{K}$. In some nice cases, for example, if every structure in $\mathfrak{K}$ is finite, such relations are *partial orders* (posets). On the other hand, anti-symmetry is not guaranteed in the infinite case; we may have two infinite structures $\mathcal{A}, \mathcal{B} \in \mathfrak{K}$ such that $\mathcal{A} \hookrightarrow_{fin} \mathcal{B}$ and vice versa but $\mathcal{A} \ncong \mathcal{B}$. In this section, we will consider only families on which $\hookrightarrow_{fin}$ is a partial order, and we denote it by $(\mathfrak{K}, \hookrightarrow_{fin})$ (whenever we use this notation, we assume that $\hookrightarrow_{fin}$ is a partial order on $\mathfrak{K}$). We say that $\mathcal{A} \in \mathfrak{K}$ has *height* n, denoted by $\mathrm{height}(\mathcal{A}) = n$, if in the corresponding poset there exists a chain (i.e., a totally ordered set) of length n having $\mathcal{A}$ as maximal element but no chain of greater length has $\mathcal{A}$ as maximal element. In case the structure of the greatest height in the poset has height n, we say that $(\mathfrak{K}, \hookrightarrow_{fin})$ has height n, and we denote this by $\mathrm{height}((\mathfrak{K}, \hookrightarrow_{fin})) = n$.

Definition 4. *Let $\mathfrak{K}$ be a family of structures and suppose that $(\mathfrak{K}, \hookrightarrow_{fin})$ has height n. Let $\mathfrak{K}_{=m} = \{\mathcal{A} \in \mathfrak{K} : \mathrm{height}(\mathcal{A}) = m\}$. We say that $\mathfrak{K}$ is limit-free if*

$$(\forall m)(\forall \mathcal{A} \in \mathfrak{K}_{=m})(\forall \mathcal{S} \cong \mathcal{A})(\exists s)(\{\mathcal{B} \in \mathfrak{K} : \mathcal{S} \restriction_s \hookrightarrow \mathcal{B}\} \cap \mathfrak{K}_{=m} = \{\mathcal{A}\}).$$

In this case we say that $\mathcal{A}$ is m-minimal on $\mathcal{S} \restriction_s$.

Intuitively, a limit-free $\mathfrak{K}$ allows a learner $\mathbf{M}$ not to change its mind between two structures having the same height. Indeed, given $\mathcal{S} \in \mathrm{LD}(\mathfrak{K})$, if $\mathcal{S} \restriction t \hookrightarrow \mathcal{A}$ where $\mathrm{height}(\mathcal{A}) = n$, $\mathbf{M}$ can wait for a stage s such that $\mathcal{S} \restriction s \hookrightarrow \mathcal{A}$, and $\mathcal{A}$ is the unique structure in $\mathfrak{K}_{=m}$ for some $m \leqslant n$ where $n = \mathrm{height}((\mathfrak{K}, \hookrightarrow_{fin}))$. A trivial observation is that all finite families are clearly limit-free. For clarity, we provide an example of a non-limit-free family of graphs $\mathfrak{K}^{\mathrm{nlf}} = \{\mathcal{A}_i : i \in \mathbb{N}\}$, where:

- $\mathcal{A}_0$ is a one-way infinite line, i.e., the graph with vertices $V = \{v_j : j \in \omega\}$ and edges $E = \{(v_j, v_{j+1}) : j \in \omega\}$;
- $\mathcal{A}_{i+1}$ is a copy of C_{i+3}, i.e., the cyclic graph of $i + 3$ vertices.

We can easily notice that $\mathcal{A}_0$ witnesses that $\mathfrak{K}$ is not limit-free. Indeed, given $\mathcal{S} \in \mathrm{LD}(\mathfrak{K})$ such that $\mathcal{S} \cong \mathcal{A}_0$, for all s, $\{\mathcal{B} \in \mathfrak{K} : \mathcal{S} \restriction_s \hookrightarrow \mathcal{B}\} \cap \mathfrak{K}_{=1}$ contains infinitely many structures, i.e., $\mathcal{A}_0$ and for $i > 0$ all the $\mathcal{A}_i$'s such that $\mathcal{S} \restriction_s \hookrightarrow C_{i+3}$, which are cofinitely many. The next result (whose simple proof is omitted) gives a characterization of n-learnability for limit-free families.

Theorem 1. *Let $\mathfrak{K}$ be a limit-free family of structures. Then $\mathfrak{K}$ is n-learnable if and only if $\mathrm{height}((\mathfrak{K}, \hookrightarrow_{fin})) \leqslant n + 1$. Consequently, $\mathfrak{K}$ is proper n-learnable if and only if $\mathrm{height}((\mathfrak{K}, \hookrightarrow_{fin})) = n + 1$.*

Just considering limit free-families with $(\mathfrak{K}, \hookrightarrow_{fin})$ of different heights, we can easily derive that for any $n \in \mathbb{N}$, there is a family $\mathfrak{K}$ of structures that is proper n-learnable by a computable learner.

4   A Descriptive Set-Theoretic Characterization of n-Learnability

Before describing our results, we first give a formal definition of a reduction between equivalence relations. Let E, F be equivalence relations on $2^{\mathbb{N}}$. A *reduction* from E to F is a function $\Gamma : 2^{\mathbb{N}} \to 2^{\mathbb{N}}$ s.t. $\alpha E \beta \iff \Gamma(\alpha) F \Gamma(\beta)$, for all reals α, β. In this paper, we'll concentrate on continuous reducibility, i.e., E is *continuously reducible* to F, if there is a continuous function $\Gamma : 2^{\mathbb{N}} \to 2^{\mathbb{N}}$ reducing E to F.

Definition 5 ([3]). *A family of structures $\mathfrak{K}$ is E-learnable if there is function $\Gamma : 2^{\mathbb{N}} \to 2^{\mathbb{N}}$ which continuously reduces $\mathrm{LD}(\mathfrak{K})_{/\cong}$ to E.*

In [3] we considered several benchmark equivalence relations connecting E-learnability with the learnability notion defined in our paradigm (that recall in classical algorithmic learning theory resembles **InfEx** learnability). Among the equivalence relations we considered in the aforementioned paper, we report here the definition of E_0, the eventual agreement on reals. Given two reals $\alpha, \beta \in 2^{\mathbb{N}}$, $\alpha E_0 \beta$ if and only if $(\exists n)(\forall m > n)(\alpha(m) = \beta(m))$.

Theorem 2 (Theorem 3.1 in [3]). *A family of structures $\mathfrak{K}$ is learnable if and only if there is a continuous function $\Gamma : 2^{\mathbb{N}} \to 2^{\mathbb{N}}$ such that for all $\mathcal{A}, \mathcal{B} \in \mathrm{LD}(\mathfrak{K})$,*

$$\mathcal{A} \cong \mathcal{B} \iff \Gamma(\mathcal{A}) E_0 \Gamma(\mathcal{B}).$$

This correspondence between learnability and E_0-learnability is quite intuitive: while in our paradigm we require a learner to eventually stabilize to the correct conjecture, E_0-learnability requires that two reals identifying the same structure are mapped into two reals that eventually agree in all coordinates. In this section, after introducing Id-learnability we will study its relations with α-learnability, where α is a countable ordinal. Here, Id defines the identity on reals. That is, given two reals $\alpha, \beta \in 2^{\mathbb{N}}$, $\alpha \mathrm{Id} \beta$ if and only if $(\forall n)(\alpha(n) = \beta(n))$. The next proposition highlights the relation between Id-learnability and 0-learnability. Given $\sigma \in \mathbb{N}^{<\mathbb{N}}$ and $k \in \mathbb{N}$, we denote by σ^k the sequence obtained by the concatenation of k many σ's. The real obtained by the concatenation of infinitely many copies of σ is denoted by σ^{∞}.

Proposition 1. *Let $\mathfrak{K}$ be a family of structures. If $\mathfrak{K}$ is 0-learnable, then it is also Id-learnable. The converse is not true, i.e., there exists a family that is Id-learnable but not 0-learnable.*

Proof. The first part of the proposition is trivial. Indeed, let $\mathbf{M}$ be a learner that 0-learns $\mathfrak{K}$. Let α be a real which encodes the atomic diagram of a structure $\mathcal{S}$ isomorphic to some $\mathcal{A}$ in $\mathfrak{K}$. By definition of 0-learnability, there exists a stage s_0 such that for all $s \geqslant s_0$ $\mathbf{M}(\mathcal{S} \restriction_s) = \ulcorner \mathcal{A}_i \urcorner$ for some $i \in \omega$ and for all $t < s_0$, $\mathbf{M}(\mathcal{S} \restriction_t) = ?$. Then, we define our continuous operator Γ as $\Gamma(\alpha) = i_c^{\infty}$, where i_c is the binary translation of i. Trivially given two structures α_i, α_j identifying respectively $\mathcal{A}_i$ and $\mathcal{A}_j$ we have that $\Gamma(\alpha_i) \mathrm{Id} \Gamma(\alpha_j) \iff i = j$.

For the converse, consider the non-limit-free family $\mathfrak{K}^{\mathrm{nlf}} = \{\mathcal{A}_i : i \in \omega\}$ that we introduced in Sect. 3. Recall that $\mathcal{A}_0$ is a one-way infinite line and $\mathcal{A}_{i+1}$ is a copy of C_{i+3}, i.e., the cyclic graph of $i + 3$ vertices. A continuous reduction from $\mathrm{LD}(\mathfrak{K})_{/\cong}$ to Id is induced by a Turing operator Ψ. We give an informal description of Ψ. Let α be a real, which encodes the atomic diagram of a structure $\mathcal{B}$ isomorphic to some $\mathcal{A}_i$. Suppose that at stage s, $\alpha \restriction_s$, is isomorphic to a finite path of length s. Then $\Gamma(\alpha)(s) = 0^s$. If at some stage $s_0 > s$, $\alpha \restriction_{s_0} \cong C_{s_0}$, then $\Gamma(\alpha) = 0^{s_0-2}1^\infty$. This concludes the description of Ψ. It is clear that for every $i \geqslant 1$, we have:

$$\mathcal{B} \cong \mathcal{A}_0 \Leftrightarrow \Psi(\alpha) = 0^\infty,$$
$$\mathcal{B} \cong \mathcal{A}_i \Leftrightarrow \Psi(\alpha) = 0^{i+2}1^\infty.$$

Therefore, the family $\mathfrak{K}^{\mathrm{nlf}}$ is Id-learnable.

To complete the proof, suppose towards a contradiction that a learner $\mathbf{M}$ 0-learns $\mathfrak{K}^{\mathrm{nlf}}$. Let $\mathcal{S}$ be an isomorphic copy of $\mathcal{A}_0$ and let s be the least stage such that $\mathbf{M}(\mathcal{S} \restriction_s) \neq ?$. If $\mathbf{M}(\mathcal{S} \restriction_s) \neq \ulcorner \mathcal{A}_0 \urcorner$, $\mathbf{M}$ fails to 0-learn $\mathfrak{K}^{\mathrm{nlf}}$. Otherwise, it is not hard to build a copy $\mathcal{S}'$ of $\mathcal{A}_k$ where k is such that $\mathcal{A}_0 \restriction_s$ embeds into $\mathcal{A}_k$ and $\mathcal{S} \restriction_s = \mathcal{S}' \restriction_s$. Since $\mathbf{M}$ 0-learns $\mathfrak{K}^{\mathrm{nlf}}$, we have that $\mathbf{M}(\mathcal{S}' \restriction_s) = \ulcorner \mathcal{A}_0 \urcorner$, getting the desired contradiction. $\square$

Using non-limit-free families similar to the one used in the previous proof, it is not hard to show that there are Id-learnable families that are not n-learnable for some $n \in \omega$. On the other hand, even for $n = 1$, it is possible to define 1-learnable families that are not Id-learnable. We postpone the proof of this fact to the end of this section, when we will have a characterization of α-learnability (where α is a countable ordinal) for families that are Id-learnable. To do so, we give a "learning theoretic" characterization of the concepts coming from topology discussed in Sect. 2.2. The following definitions and results are inspired by Sects. 3.1 and 3.2 of [14]: here Lemma 1 and Theorem 3 are respectively the analogues of Lemma 3.1(1) and Theorem 3.1(1) in [14].

Let $\mathfrak{K} = \{\mathcal{A}_i : i \in \mathbb{N}\}$, and let Γ be an operator that induces a continuous reduction from $\mathrm{LD}(\mathfrak{K})$ to Id. Given $\sigma \in 2^{<\mathbb{N}}$, we define the *cone above* σ (with respect to Γ) as

$$[\sigma]_\Gamma = \{\mathcal{A}_i : \Gamma(\sigma) \sqsubseteq \mathcal{S} \cong \mathcal{A}_i\}$$

Similarly to $[\sigma]$ defined in Sect. 2.2, notice that the collection of $[\sigma]_\Gamma$ is a base for $\mathrm{LD}(\mathfrak{K})$, i.e., $\bigcup_{\sigma \in 2^{<\mathbb{N}}} [\sigma]_\Gamma \supseteq \mathrm{LD}(\mathfrak{K})$. Then for $\mathcal{A}_i \in [\sigma]_\Gamma$, let

$$CB_\Gamma(\mathcal{A}_i, \sigma) = \max\{\alpha : \Gamma(\mathcal{A}_i) \in \mathrm{range}(\Gamma)^\alpha \wedge \Gamma(\sigma) \sqsubseteq \Gamma(\mathcal{A}_i)\}$$

and

$$CB_\Gamma(\sigma) = \sup\{CB_\Gamma(\mathcal{A}_i, \sigma) : \mathcal{A}_i \in [\sigma]_\Gamma\}.$$

We say that $\mathcal{A}_i \in [\sigma]_\Gamma$ *identifies* $[\sigma]_\Gamma$ if $CB_\Gamma(\mathcal{A}_i, \sigma) = CB_\Gamma(\sigma)$. If for all $j \neq i$, $\mathcal{A}_j$ does not identify $[\sigma]_\Gamma$ we say that $\mathcal{A}_i$ *uniquely identifies* $[\sigma]_\Gamma$. Similarly to what we have done in Sect. 2.2, we say that $\mathrm{range}(\Gamma)$ is scattered, if there exists a countable ordinal α such that $\mathrm{range}(\Gamma)^\alpha = \varnothing$. Trivially, if $\sigma \sqsupseteq \tau$, then

$CB_\Gamma(\sigma) \leqslant CB_\Gamma(\tau)$. It is easy to notice that if $\mathfrak{K}$ is an Id-learnable family via some continuous operator Γ, then range(Γ) is clearly scattered. The next lemma shows a simple but useful fact that will be essential in the proof of Theorem 3.

Lemma 1. *Let $\mathfrak{K}$ be an* Id-*learnable family via some continuous operator Γ. Then for any $\mathcal{A}_i \in \mathfrak{K}$ and for every $\mathcal{S} \in \mathrm{LD}(\mathfrak{K})$ with $\mathcal{S} \cong \mathcal{A}_i$ there exists a stage s such that $\mathcal{A}_i$ uniquely identifies $[\mathcal{S} \upharpoonright_s]_\Gamma$.*

Proof. Suppose there exists $\mathcal{A}_i \in \mathfrak{K}$ and $\mathcal{S} \in \mathrm{LD}(\mathfrak{K})$ with $\mathcal{S} \cong \mathcal{A}_i$ such that for every $s \in \mathbb{N}$, there is a structure $\mathcal{A}_j \in [\mathcal{S} \upharpoonright_s]_\Gamma$, where $j \neq i$ and $CB_\Gamma(\mathcal{A}_j, \mathcal{S} \upharpoonright_s) \geqslant CB_\Gamma(\mathcal{A}_i, \mathcal{S} \upharpoonright_s) = \alpha$. Then $\mathcal{A}_i$ is not isolated in range(Γ)$^\alpha$ that, by definition, contains all structures $\mathcal{A}_j$ such that $CB_\Gamma(\mathcal{A}_j, \mathcal{S} \upharpoonright_s) \geqslant \alpha$. Hence, we have $CB_\Gamma(\mathcal{A}_i, \mathcal{S} \upharpoonright_s) \geqslant \alpha + 1$, contradiction. □

Theorem 3. *Let $\mathfrak{K}$ be an* Id-*learnable family via some continuous operator Γ. $\mathfrak{K}$ is α-learnable if and only if* range(Γ)$^{1+\alpha} = \varnothing$.

Proof. Suppose $\mathfrak{K}$ is α-learnable by a learner $\mathbf{M}$, i.e., set the mind change counter $c(\epsilon) = \alpha$. As range(Γ) is scattered, this implies that it is also non-empty (recall that the empty set is perfect by definition). This means that range(Γ)$^\alpha = \varnothing$ if and only if $\alpha > 0$. By transfinite induction we prove that if $CB_\Gamma(\epsilon) > 1 + \alpha$, then $\mathbf{M}$ does not α-learn $\mathfrak{K}$ (i.e., c is not a valid mind change counter). Suppose that for all $\beta < 1 + \alpha$ the claim holds, and consider the case for $1 + \alpha$. By contradiction, suppose that range(Γ)$^{1+\alpha} \neq \varnothing$: this means that there exists an $\mathcal{S} \in \mathrm{LD}(\mathfrak{K})$ and an s such that $CB_\Gamma(\mathcal{S} \upharpoonright_s) > 1 + \alpha$ or, equivalently, that there is a $\mathcal{A}_i \in [\mathcal{S} \upharpoonright_s]_\Gamma$ such that $CB_\Gamma(\mathcal{A}_i, \mathcal{S} \upharpoonright_s) \geqslant 1 + \alpha + 1$. We have two cases: either $\mathbf{M}(\mathcal{S} \upharpoonright_s) = \ulcorner \mathcal{A}_i \urcorner$ or $\mathbf{M}(\mathcal{S} \upharpoonright_s) \neq \ulcorner \mathcal{A}_i \urcorner$.

– Suppose $\mathbf{M}(\mathcal{S} \upharpoonright_s) = \ulcorner \mathcal{A}_i \urcorner$. Then since $\Gamma(\mathcal{A}_i)$ is not isolated in range(Γ)$^{1+\alpha}$, there is $\Gamma(\mathcal{A}_j) \in$ range(Γ)$^{1+\alpha}$ with $j \neq i$ such that $CB_\Gamma(\mathcal{A}_j, \mathcal{S} \upharpoonright_s) \geqslant 1 + \alpha$. Suppose that $\mathcal{S} \cong \mathcal{A}_j$. Since $\mathbf{M}$ learns $\mathfrak{K}$ by hypothesis, there will be a stage s' such that $\mathbf{M}(\mathcal{S} \upharpoonright_{s'}) = \ulcorner \mathcal{A}_j \urcorner$ and $\mathbf{M}(\mathcal{S} \upharpoonright_{s'}) \neq \mathbf{M}(\mathcal{S} \upharpoonright_s)$. Since this is a mind change, we will have that $c(\mathcal{S} \upharpoonright_{s'}) < c(\mathcal{S} \upharpoonright_s)$ and $c(\mathcal{S} \upharpoonright_{s'}) = \beta < 1 + \alpha$. On the other hand, $CB_\Gamma(\mathcal{A}_j, \mathcal{S} \upharpoonright_{s'}) \geqslant 1 + \alpha$ and so $CB_\Gamma(\mathcal{S} \upharpoonright_{s'}) > \beta$. By induction hypothesis for β, this is not a valid mind change counter for $\mathbf{M}$.
– Suppose $\mathbf{M}(\mathcal{S} \upharpoonright_s) \neq \ulcorner \mathcal{A}_i \urcorner$ and $\mathcal{S} \cong \mathcal{A}_i$. Since $\mathbf{M}$ learns $\mathfrak{K}$ by hypothesis, there will be a stage s' such that $\mathbf{M}(\mathcal{S} \upharpoonright_{s'}) = \ulcorner \mathcal{A}_i \urcorner$. Similarly to the first case, we get that $c(\mathcal{S} \upharpoonright_{s'}) < c(\mathcal{S} \upharpoonright_s) \leqslant 1 + \alpha$, but $CB_\Gamma(\mathcal{S} \upharpoonright_{s'}) > 1 + \alpha$, and so c is not a mind change counter for $\mathbf{M}$.

For the other direction, suppose range(Γ)$^{1+\alpha} = \varnothing$. Let $\mathbf{M}$ be a learner with mind change counter c such that $c(\epsilon) = \alpha$. Recall that if $\mathbf{M}(\sigma) \neq \mathbf{M}(\sigma^-)$ and $\mathbf{M}(\sigma^-) = ?$, this is not a mind change. Let $\mathcal{S} \in \mathrm{LD}(\mathfrak{K})$ and $s \in \mathbb{N}$. $\mathbf{M}$ is defined as follows:

$$\mathbf{M}(\mathcal{S} \upharpoonright_{s+1}) = \begin{cases} ? & \text{if } \mathcal{S} \upharpoonright_{s+1} = \epsilon \vee CB_\Gamma(\mathcal{S} \upharpoonright_{s+1}) < CB_\Gamma(\mathcal{S} \upharpoonright_s) \\ \ulcorner \mathcal{A}_i \urcorner & \text{if } CB_\Gamma(\mathcal{S} \upharpoonright_{s+1}) = CB_\Gamma(\mathcal{S} \upharpoonright_s) \text{ and } \mathcal{A}_i \\ & \quad \text{uniquely identifies } [\mathcal{S} \upharpoonright_s]_\Gamma \\ \mathbf{M}(\mathcal{S} \upharpoonright_s) & \text{if } CB_\Gamma(\mathcal{S} \upharpoonright_{s+1}) = CB_\Gamma(\mathcal{S} \upharpoonright_s) \text{ and there is no } \mathcal{A}_i \\ & \quad \text{that uniquely identifies } [\mathcal{S} \upharpoonright_s]_\Gamma \end{cases}$$

Informally, the second disjunct in the first case of $\mathbf{M}$'s definition deals with the scenario in which $\mathbf{M}$ realizes that its conjecture is wrong and changes its mind to ?. We immediately get that $\mathbf{M}$ learns $\mathfrak{K}$. Indeed, for any $\mathcal{A}_i \in \mathfrak{K}$ and for any $\mathcal{S} \in \mathrm{LD}(\mathfrak{K})$ such that $\mathcal{S} \cong \mathcal{A}_i$, by Lemma 1 there is a stage s such that for all $s' \geqslant s$, $\mathcal{A}_i$ uniquely identifies $[\mathcal{S} \upharpoonright_{s'}]_\Gamma$. So, for any $s' > s$ the second case of $\mathbf{M}$'s definition applies and $\mathbf{M}$ correctly learns $\mathcal{A}_i$. It remains to show that c is a mind change counter for $\mathbf{M}$ and $\mathfrak{K}$. We first show the following claim that, informally, states that if $\mathbf{M}$ rejects a hypothesis at a stage r, it will not output it in the future.

Claim 1. Let $\mathcal{S} \in \mathrm{LD}(\mathfrak{K})$ and $r \in \mathbb{N}$. Suppose $\mathcal{A}_i \notin [\mathcal{S} \upharpoonright_r]_\Gamma$. If $\mathbf{M}(\mathcal{S} \upharpoonright_r) \neq \ulcorner \mathcal{A}_i \urcorner$, then for all $t > r$, $\mathbf{M}(\mathcal{S} \upharpoonright_t) \neq \ulcorner \mathcal{A}_i \urcorner$.

Proof. Let $t \geqslant r$ be such that $\mathbf{M}(\mathcal{S} \upharpoonright_t) = \ulcorner \mathcal{A}_i \urcorner$. Then there is s such that $r < s \leqslant t$ such that $\mathbf{M}(\mathcal{S} \upharpoonright_{s-1}) \neq \ulcorner \mathcal{A}_i \urcorner$ but $\mathbf{M}(\mathcal{S} \upharpoonright_s) = \ulcorner \mathcal{A}_i \urcorner$. Then (as $\mathbf{M}(\mathcal{S} \upharpoonright_r) \neq \ulcorner \mathcal{A}_i \urcorner$) by the second case of $\mathbf{M}$'s definition, we have that $\mathcal{A}_i$ uniquely identifies $[\mathcal{S} \upharpoonright_s]_\Gamma$. On the other hand, $\mathcal{A}_i \notin [\mathcal{S} \upharpoonright_r]_\Gamma$ and consequently, by continuity of Γ, $\mathcal{A}_i \notin [\mathcal{S} \upharpoonright_s]_\Gamma$, contradiction. This proves the claim. □

Claim 2. Let $\mathcal{S} \in \mathrm{LD}(\mathfrak{K})$ and $s \in \mathbb{N}$. If the second case of $\mathbf{M}$'s definition applies at $\mathcal{S} \upharpoonright_{s+1}$, then there is no mind change: that is, either $\mathbf{M}(\mathcal{S} \upharpoonright_{s+1}) = \mathbf{M}(\mathcal{S} \upharpoonright_s)$ or $\mathbf{M}(\mathcal{S} \upharpoonright_s) = ?$.

Proof. Suppose that $\mathbf{M}(\mathcal{S} \upharpoonright_s) = \ulcorner \mathcal{A}_j \urcorner$ with $j \neq i$, where $\mathcal{A}_i$ uniquely identifies $[\mathcal{S} \upharpoonright_{s+1}]_\Gamma$ and $CB_\Gamma(\mathcal{S} \upharpoonright_{s+1}) = CB_\Gamma(\mathcal{S} \upharpoonright_s)$. Let $r < s + 1$ be the least stage such that $\mathbf{M}(\mathcal{S} \upharpoonright_r) = \ulcorner \mathcal{A}_j \urcorner$. The second case of $\mathbf{M}$'s definition implies that $\mathcal{A}_j$ uniquely identifies $[\mathcal{S} \upharpoonright_r]_\Gamma$. But since $\mathcal{A}_i$ uniquely identifies $[\mathcal{S} \upharpoonright_{s+1}]_\Gamma$ and $i \neq j$, we immediately get that $CB_\Gamma(\mathcal{S} \upharpoonright_{s+1}) < CB_\Gamma(\mathcal{S} \upharpoonright_r)$, and so $r < s$ as $CB_\Gamma(\mathcal{S} \upharpoonright_{s+1}) = CB_\Gamma(\mathcal{S} \upharpoonright_s)$ by the second case of $\mathbf{M}$'s definition. So $CB_\Gamma(\mathcal{S} \upharpoonright_s) < CB_\Gamma(\mathcal{S} \upharpoonright_r)$. By the first case of $\mathbf{M}$'s definition, there is a stage m with $r < m < s$ such that $\mathbf{M}(\mathcal{S} \upharpoonright_m) = ?$ and $\mathcal{A}_j \notin [\mathcal{S} \upharpoonright_m]_\Gamma$. Then the previous claim implies that $\mathbf{M}(\mathcal{S} \upharpoonright_s) \neq \ulcorner \mathcal{A}_j \urcorner$, a contradiction. The claim is proved. □

We derive that $\mathbf{M}$ changes its mind only if the first clause of $\mathbf{M}$'s definition applies (i.e., the third clause clearly does not imply a mind change, and the second one was excluded by Claim 2). As in the first part of the proof, recall that $\mathrm{range}(\Gamma)^\alpha = \varnothing$ if and only if $\alpha > 0$: this implies that for all $\mathcal{S} \in \mathrm{LD}(\mathfrak{K})$ and for all $s \in \mathbb{N}$. $CB_\Gamma(\mathcal{S} \upharpoonright_s) > 0$. So, whenever the first case of $\mathbf{M}$'s definition applies, we have that $0 < c(\mathcal{S} \upharpoonright_{s+1}) = CB_\Gamma(\mathcal{S} \upharpoonright_{s+1}) < CB_\Gamma(\mathcal{S} \upharpoonright_s) = c(\mathcal{S} \upharpoonright_s)$, and so c is a mind change counter for $\mathbf{M}$ and $\mathfrak{K}$, i.e., $\mathbf{M}$ α-learns $\mathfrak{K}$. This ends the proof of Theorem 3. □

Combining Proposition 1 and Theorem 3 we derive the following corollary that characterizes 0-learnability in terms of Id-learnability.

Corollary 1. $\mathfrak{K}$ *is 0-learnable (i.e., $\mathbf{InfFin}$-learnable) if and only if $\mathfrak{K}$ is Id-learnable via some continuous operator Γ such that* $\mathrm{range}(\Gamma)^1 = \varnothing$, *i.e., all points in* $\mathrm{range}(\Gamma)$ *are isolated.*

The last corollary shows that Id-learnability "contains" all 0-learnable families. We are now ready to show that it is not true anymore for $n > 0$. Just consider 1-learnability and let $\mathfrak{K} = \{\mathcal{A}, \mathcal{B}\}$, where $\mathcal{A}$ is isomorphic to infinitely many disjoint cycles C_3, while $\mathcal{B}$ is $\mathcal{A}$ "plus" C_4. Since $\mathfrak{K}$ is limit-free and $\mathcal{A} \hookrightarrow_{fin} \mathcal{B}$, Theorem 1 implies that $\mathfrak{K}$ is proper 1-learnable. Suppose that $\mathfrak{K}$ is Id-learnable via some continuous operator Γ. Then, as $\mathfrak{K}$ contains only two structures, the points in $\mathrm{range}(\Gamma)$ are two, and they are clearly isolated. Now Theorem 3 implies that $\mathfrak{K}$ is 0-learnable, getting the desired contradiction.

5   Learner Complexity

In this section, we show that for certain families, the complexity of the learner plays a role in the number of mind changes during the learnability process.

Theorem 4. *For any c.e. non-computable set X, there exists a countable family of graphs $\mathfrak{K}$ such that:*

- *$\mathfrak{K}$ is 0-learnable by an A-computable learner if and only if $X \leqslant_T A$;*
- *$\mathfrak{K}$ is 1-learnable by a computable learner.*

Proof. Let X be a non-computable c.e. set. We dynamically build $\mathfrak{K} = \{G_e : e \in \mathbb{N}\}$ as follows. In the construction below, when we write "add C_i to G_e" we mean that we append to some isolated vertex of G_e a copy of C_i

- *Stage 0*: for any $e \in \omega$, let G_{2e} be isomorphic to the infinite graph composed by infinitely many disjoint vertices and a copy of C_{4e} (i.e., the cyclic graph composed by $4e$ vertices). Similarly, G_{2e+1} is composed by infinitely many disjoint vertices and a copy of C_{4e+1}. Note that G_{2e} and G_{2e+1} are not isomorphic and are incomparable with respect to $\hookrightarrow_{fin}$.
- *Stage s+1*: if $e \in X_{s+1} \setminus X_s$, then
  - add C_{4e} to G_{2e+1} and C_{4e+1} to G_{2e};
  - add C_{4e+2} to G_{2e} and C_{4e+3} to G_{2e+1}.

Informally, if $e \in X_{s+1} \setminus X_s$ we first modify G_{2e} and G_{2e+1} so that they are isomorphic, and then we make them again non-isomorphic and incomparable with respect to $\hookrightarrow_{fin}$.

We first prove the first point of the theorem, starting from the right to left direction. Let A be such that $X \leqslant_T A$. We show that $\mathfrak{K}$ is 0-learnable by an A-computable learner. Let $\mathcal{S} \in \mathrm{LD}(\mathfrak{K})$ and let $s > 1$. Then the following A-computable learner clearly 0-learns $\mathfrak{K}$.

$$\mathbf{M}^A(\mathcal{S} \restriction_s) = \begin{cases} ? & \text{if } (\forall n)(C_n \not\hookrightarrow \mathcal{S} \restriction_s) \vee (e \in X \wedge C_{4e+i} \hookrightarrow \mathcal{S} \restriction_s \text{ where} \\ & i \in \{0,1\} \wedge C_{4e+j} \not\hookrightarrow \mathcal{S} \restriction_s \text{ where } j \in \{2,3\}) \\ \ulcorner G_{2e} \urcorner & \text{if } (C_{4e+2} \hookrightarrow \mathcal{S} \restriction_s) \vee (e \notin X \wedge C_{4e} \hookrightarrow \mathcal{S} \restriction_s) \\ \ulcorner G_{2e+1} \urcorner & \text{if } (C_{4e+3} \hookrightarrow \mathcal{S} \restriction_s) \vee (e \notin X \wedge C_{4e+1} \hookrightarrow \mathcal{S} \restriction_s) \end{cases}$$

Informally, $\mathbf{M}^A(\mathcal{S} \restriction_s) = ?$ if either $\mathcal{S} \restriction_s$ contains no cycle, or the cycle(s) in $\mathcal{S} \restriction_s$ allow $\mathbf{M}^A$ only to distinguish that either $\mathcal{S} \cong G_{2e}$ or $\mathcal{S} \cong G_{2e+1}$. In the first case $\mathbf{M}^A$ waits for a stage $t > s$ such that $\mathcal{S} \restriction_t$ contains some cycle (the existence of such a stage is guaranteed by $\mathfrak{K}$'s construction). In the second case, as $e \in X$ and by $\mathfrak{K}$'s construction, $\mathbf{M}^A$ knows that only one between C_{4e+2} and C_{4e+3} will be in $\mathcal{S}$ and this will allow it to output the correct conjecture, i.e., depending on the length of the cycle, the first disjunct of the second or third case of $\mathbf{M}^A$'s definition applies. Trivially, if $\mathcal{S} \restriction_s$ contains C_{4e+2} or C_{4e+3} then $\mathbf{M}^A$ immediately outputs the correct conjecture, same if $\mathcal{S} \restriction_s$ contains C_{4e} or C_{4e+1} and $e \notin X$.

For the left to right direction, assume that there exists an A-computable learner $\mathbf{M}^A$ that 0-learns $\mathfrak{K}$ but $X \nleq_T A$. We show that if it is the case, A can enumerate $\mathbb{N} \setminus X$, contradicting the fact that $X \nleq_T A$. For any $e \in \mathbb{N}$, let $\mathcal{B}_{e,n}$ be a structure isomorphic to C_{4e} and n many disjoint vertices. It is clear that for any n, $\mathcal{B}_{e,n} \hookrightarrow G_{2e}$, independently of the presence/absence of e in X. In other words, there exists $\mathcal{S} \in \mathrm{LD}(\mathfrak{K})$ such that $\mathcal{S} \cong G_{2e}$ and for any $n \in \omega$, $\mathcal{B}_{e,n} \hookrightarrow \mathcal{S}$. This means that there exists an $n \in \mathbb{N}$ such that $\mathbf{M}^A(\mathcal{B}_{e,n}) = \ulcorner G_{2e} \urcorner$ and for all $n' > n$ $\mathbf{M}^A(\mathcal{B}_{e,n'}) = \ulcorner G_{2e} \urcorner$. Let f be the following function computing the characteristic function of X:

$$f(e) = \begin{cases} 1 & \text{if } e \in X \\ 0 & \text{if } (\exists n)(\mathbf{M}^A(\mathcal{B}_{e,n}) = \ulcorner G_{2e} \urcorner \wedge n = \min_m \mathbf{M}^A(\mathcal{B}_{e,m}) \neq ?) \end{cases}$$

To show that the second case of f's definition is correct, suppose that there is n such that $\mathbf{M}^A(\mathcal{B}_{e,n}) = \ulcorner G_{2e} \urcorner \wedge n = \min_m \mathbf{M}^A(\mathcal{B}_{e,m}) \neq ?$ but $e \in X$. Then, there is some $\mathcal{S}' \in \mathrm{LD}(\mathfrak{K})$ such that $\mathcal{B}_{e,n} \hookrightarrow \mathcal{S}'$ (i.e., by $\mathfrak{K}$'s construction, $C_{4e}, C_{4e+3} \hookrightarrow \mathcal{S}'$). This means that if $\mathbf{M}^A(\mathcal{B}_{e,n}) \downarrow = \ulcorner G_{2e} \urcorner$, $\mathbf{M}^A$ needs to change its mind to $\ulcorner G_{2e+1} \urcorner$ contradicting that $\mathbf{M}^A$ 0-learns the family. We derive that f is clearly A-computable and witnesses that $X \leq_T A$ getting the desired contradiction.

It remains to show that a computable learner $\mathbf{M}$ can 1-learn the family. Let $\mathcal{S} \in \mathrm{LD}(\mathfrak{K})$ and $s > 1$:

$$\mathbf{M}(\mathcal{S} \restriction_s) = \begin{cases} ? & \text{if } (\forall n)(C_n \nhookrightarrow \mathcal{S} \restriction_s) \\ \ulcorner G_{2e} \urcorner & \text{if } (\exists n)(C_n \hookrightarrow \mathcal{S} \restriction_s \wedge (n = 4e \vee n = 4e + 2)) \\ \ulcorner G_{2e+1} \urcorner & \text{if } (\exists n)(C_n \hookrightarrow \mathcal{S} \restriction_s \wedge (n = 4e + 1 \vee n = 4e + 3)) \end{cases}$$

$\mathbf{M}$ can change its mind only in the second and the third case and this may happen at most a single time, i.e., in case $C_{4e} \hookrightarrow \mathcal{S} \restriction_s$ and there exists $s' > s$ such that $C_{4e+3} \hookrightarrow \mathcal{S} \restriction_{s'}$ (similarly, for C_{4e+1} instead of C_{4e} and C_{4e+2} instead of C_{4e+3}). This shows that $\mathfrak{K}$ is 1-learnable by $\mathbf{M}$. □

In analogy to several established notions from computable structure theory (see, e.g., [4,7]), the proof of Theorem 4 suggests the definition of *0-learning spectrum*. Indeed, for any non-computable c.e. set X we defined a family $\mathfrak{K}$ such that the oracles A for which there exists an A-computable learner that 0-learns $\mathfrak{K}$ coincide with the Turing cone above X,

$$\mathrm{Spec}_{0\text{-learn}}(\mathfrak{K}) = \{A : (\exists \mathbf{M})(\mathbf{M}^A \text{ 0-learns } \mathfrak{K})\} = \{A : X \leq_T A\}.$$

In the same spirit, it is natural to define $\mathsf{Spec}_{n\text{-learn}}(\mathfrak{K})$ as the collection of all oracles that allow us to learn $\mathfrak{K}$ with n many mind changes. We postpone the analysis of such spectra to future work.

References

1. Ambainis, A., Jain, S., Sharma, A.: Ordinal mind change complexity of language identification. In: Ben-David, S. (ed.) EuroCOLT 1997. LNCS, vol. 1208, pp. 301–315. Springer, Heidelberg (1997). https://doi.org/10.1007/3-540-62685-9_25
2. Ash, C., Knight, J.: Computable Structures and the Hyperarithmetical Hierarchy. ISSN, Elsevier Science (2000)
3. Bazhenov, N., Cipriani, V., San Mauro, L.: Learning algebraic structures with the help of Borel equivalence relations (2021). Preprint arXiv:2110.14512
4. Bazhenov, N., Fokina, E., Rossegger, D., San Mauro, L.: Degrees of bi-embeddable categoricity. Computability **10**(1), 1–16 (2021)
5. Bazhenov, N., Fokina, E., San Mauro, L.: Learning families of algebraic structures from informant. Inf. Comput. **275**, 104590 (2020). https://doi.org/10.1016/j.ic.2020.104590
6. Bazhenov, N., San Mauro, L.: On the Turing complexity of learning finite families of algebraic structures. J. Log. Comput. **31**(7), 1891–1900 (2021). https://doi.org/10.1093/logcom/exab044
7. Fokina, E.B., Kalimullin, I., Miller, R.: Degrees of categoricity of computable structures. Arch. Math. Logic **49**(1), 51–67 (2010)
8. Freivalds, R., Smith, C.: On the role of procrastination in machine learning. Inf. Comput. **107**(2), 237–271 (1993). https://doi.org/10.1006/inco.1993.1068
9. Gao, Z., Stephan, F., Wu, G., Yamamoto, A.: Learning families of closed sets in matroids. In: Dinneen, M.J., Khoussainov, B., Nies, A. (eds.) WTCS 2012. LNCS, vol. 7160, pp. 120–139. Springer, Heidelberg (2012). https://doi.org/10.1007/978-3-642-27654-5_10
10. Glymour, C.: Inductive inference in the limit. Erkenntnis **22**, 23–31 (1985). https://doi.org/10.1007/BF00269958
11. Gold, E.M.: Language identification in the limit. Inf. Control **10**(5), 447–474 (1967). https://doi.org/10.1016/S0019-9958(67)91165-5
12. Harizanov, V.S., Stephan, F.: On the learnability of vector spaces. J. Comput. Syst. Sci. **73**(1), 109–122 (2007). https://doi.org/10.1016/j.jcss.2006.09.001
13. Kechris, A.: Classical Descriptive Set Theory. Graduate Texts in Mathematics, Springer, New York (2012)
14. Luo, W., Schulte, O.: Mind change efficient learning. Inf. Comput. **204**(6), 989–1011 (2006). https://doi.org/10.1016/j.ic.2006.02.004
15. Merkle, W., Stephan, F.: Trees and learning. J. Comput. Syst. Sci. **68**(1), 134–156 (2004). https://doi.org/10.1016/j.jcss.2003.08.001
16. Putnam, H.: Trial and error predicates and the solution to a problem of Mostowski. J. Symbolic Logic **30**(1), 49–57 (1965). https://doi.org/10.2307/2270581
17. Stephan, F., Ventsov, Y.: Learning algebraic structures from text. Theor. Comput. Sci. **268**(2), 221–273 (2001). https://doi.org/10.1016/S0304-3975(00)00272-3

Well-Orders Realized by C.E. Equivalence Relations

Nikolay Bazhenov[1,2]([✉])[iD] and Maxim Zubkov[3][iD]

[1] Sobolev Institute of Mathematics, 4 Acad. Koptyug Avenue, Novosibirsk, Russia
[2] Novosibirsk State University, 2 Pirogova St., Novosibirsk, Russia
bazhenov@math.nsc.ru
[3] Kazan Federal University, 18 Kremlevskaya St., Kazan, Russia
Maxim.Zubkov@kpfu.ru
https://bazhenov.droppages.com

Abstract. We study countable linear orders realized by computably enumerable equivalence relations (ceers). A ceer E realizes a linear order L if there exists a computably enumerable binary relation $\unlhd$ respecting E such that the induced quotient structure $(\mathbb{N}/E, \unlhd)$ is isomorphic to L. In this line of research, there are many nontrivial results demonstrating complex interplay between the computability-theoretic properties of a ceer E and the isomorphism types of orders L realizable by E. For example, Gavryushkin, Khoussainov, and Stephan proved that there is a ceer E realizing only one order type—the type of $\omega + 1 + \omega^*$.

In this paper, we obtain a complete characterization of well-orders L realizable by a given ceer E for the case when E realizes some ordinal $\alpha < \omega^3$. Informally speaking, our proofs develop methods of fine-tuning the behavior of limit points of L via computability-theoretic properties of E.

Keywords: Well-order · Computable ordinal · Equivalence relation · Computable structure theory · Computably enumerable structure

1 Introduction

The paper investigates algebraic aspects of computably enumerable equivalence relations (or *ceers*, for short). Ceers and their applications in algebra constitute a classical topic in computability theory. This line of research goes back to the works of Novikov [14] and Boone [6]: independently, they built a finitely presented group with an undecidable word problem. This classical result can be re-cast in the setting of ceers as follows. Consider a finitely presented group $G = \langle X \mid R \rangle$. One can encode elements of the free group F_X (with generators X)

The work of N. Bazhenov was supported by the Russian Science Foundation (project no. 18-11-00028). The work of M. Zubkov was supported by the Russian Science Foundation (project no. 18-11-00028) and performed under the development program of the Volga Region Mathematical Center (agreement no. 075-02-2020-1478).

by their Gödel numbers. Then the word problem of the group G can be treated as a ceer that identifies two elements $a, b \in F_X$ if and only if ab^{-1} belongs to the normal subgroup of F_X generated by the relators from R. Consequently, the ceer induced by the Novikov–Boone group is non-computable.

In recent years, significant advances have been made in the studies of ceers—in particular, their computability-theoretic properties and their applications in computable structure theory. For a detailed discussion of these results, we refer the reader to, e.g., the surveys [1,17] and recent papers [2,3,7].

In this paper, we follow the approach of [11] (to be elaborated) and study algebraic structures S *realized by ceers*. Here we concentrate on the case when S is a well-order. In recent works, the approach of [11] was applied to the studies of graphs [10], linear orders [9], Boolean algebras [5], models of arithmetic and set theory [12]. The reader is referred to the survey [13] for details.

If not specified otherwise, we assume that every considered binary relation R has domain $\mathbb{N}$, i.e., the set of natural numbers. Recall that a relation R is a preorder if R is reflexive and transitive. A preorder R is an equivalence relation if R is symmetric. For an equivalence relation E and for a number $a \in \mathbb{N}$, by $[a]_E$ we denote the E-class of a. A preorder R is a *linear order* if R is antisymmetric and any two elements a and b are comparable with respect to R.

Before providing further formal definitions, we give an informal toy example. Consider the natural (lexicographic) presentation of the well-order ω^2 on the natural numbers:

$$\langle x, y \rangle \leq_{\omega^2} \langle u, v \rangle \text{ iff } (x <_{\mathbb{N}} u) \text{ or } (x = u \,\&\, y \leq_{\mathbb{N}} v),$$

where $\langle \cdot, \cdot \rangle$ is some fixed computable bijection from $\mathbb{N}^2$ onto $\mathbb{N}$, and $\leq_{\mathbb{N}}$ is the standard ordering of natural numbers.

Then, informally speaking, one can say that (a presentation of) the ordinal ω can be obtained as a quotient of the relation $\leq_{\omega^2}$, as follows:

– First, consider a new equivalence relation E:

$$(\langle x, y \rangle \, E \, \langle x', y' \rangle) \iff x = x'. \tag{1}$$

– Second, the order $\leq_{\omega^2}$ induces (in a natural way) a strict ordering $\lhd$ on the E-classes:

$$[a]_E \lhd [b]_E \iff (a \leq_{\omega^2} b) \,\&\, \neg(a \, E \, b).$$

It is clear that the quotient structure $(\mathbb{N}/E; \lhd)$ is isomorphic to $(\mathbb{N}; <_{\mathbb{N}})$.

Another intuitive way of looking at this quotient is as follows. First, one fixes the relation E from Eq. (1). Then in our new, "imaginary" universe, the relation E plays *the role of equality*: if natural numbers x and y are E-equivalent, then they are indistinguishable for us.

Following the approach of [9–11], here we are concerned with the following informal problem

$(\star)$ Which well-orders can be represented in the new E-universe?

The argument above shows that with the help of the recursive relation $\leq_{\omega^2}$, one can represent (in a formal way) the usual ordering of natural numbers.

Now we are ready to give the formal definitions, and to provide the formalization of Problem $(\star)$. We say that a binary relation R *respects* an equivalence relation E if the following holds. For all $x, x', y, y' \in \mathbb{N}$ such that $(x \, E \, x') \, \& \, (y \, E \, y') \, \& \, \neg(x \, E \, y)$, the condition $(x, y) \in R$ holds if and only if $(x', y') \in R$.

If R respects E, then one can introduce a well-defined quotient structure $\mathcal{Q}_R = (\mathbb{N}/E; R_q)$:

– The domain of $\mathcal{Q}_R$ consists of equivalence classes $[x]_E$, $x \in \mathbb{N}$.
– For $x, y \in \mathbb{N}$, we have $([x]_E, [y]_E) \in R_q$ if and only if one of the following holds: either $(x \, E \, y)$, or $\neg(x \, E \, y) \, \& \, (x, y) \in R$.

Definition 1 (see [9]). *A computably enumerable equivalence relation (ceer) E realizes a countable linear order $\mathcal{L}$ if there exists a computably enumerable binary relation R such that R respects E, and the quotient structure $\mathcal{Q}_R$ is isomorphic to $\mathcal{L}$. In this case, we say that the structure $\mathcal{Q}_R = (\mathbb{N}/E; R_q)$ is a* presentation *(or* realization*) of the order $\mathcal{L}$.*

The papers [9,11] study various problems on linear orders realized by ceers. In particular, Definition 1 induces a degree structure on ceers: if E and F are ceers, then $E \leq_{lo} F$ if and only if every linear order realized by E is also realized by F. The poset of $\leq_{lo}$-degrees contains infinite chains (Corollary 43 in [11], Theorem 3.1 in [9]) and antichains (Theorem 2.6 of [9]). This poset is not an upper semilattice (Corollary 5.4 in [9]).

In this paper we work on the following problem:

Problem 1. For a ceer E, let $Ord(E)$ denote the family of all ordinals realized by E. Provide a characterization of possible families $Ord(E)$.

Notice the following: if a ceer E has precisely m classes, where $m < \omega$, then it is clear that E can realize only one ordinal—the natural number m. Therefore, we always assume that every considered ceer has infinitely many classes. If $\alpha < \beta$ are ordinals, then we use the following notations:

$$[\alpha; \beta] = \{\gamma : \alpha \leq \gamma \leq \beta\}, \quad [\alpha; \beta) = \{\gamma : \alpha \leq \gamma < \beta\}.$$

The paper is arranged as follows. Section 2 contains necessary preliminaries and some simple useful facts. In this paper, we obtain a complete solution of Problem 1 in two particular cases. Consider a ceer E with infinitely many equivalence classes.

Theorem 1. *Suppose that $\alpha < \omega^2$ and $\alpha \in Ord(E)$. Then for some non-zero $m \in \omega$, one of the following cases holds:*

1. $Ord(E) = [\omega \cdot m; \omega_1^{CK})$;
2. $Ord(E) = [\omega \cdot m; \omega \cdot (m+1))$;
3. $Ord(E) = [\omega \cdot m + 1; \omega \cdot (m+1))$.

Each of these three cases is realizable by some ceer E.

Theorem 2. *Suppose that $\alpha < \omega^3$, $\alpha \in Ord(E)$, and $Ord(E) \cap [\omega; \omega^2) = \emptyset$. Then for some non-zero $m \in \omega$, one of the following cases holds:*

1. $Ord(E) = [\omega^2 \cdot m; \omega_1^{CK})$;
2. $Ord(E) = [\omega^2 \cdot m; \omega_1^{CK}) \setminus \{\rho + \omega : \rho$ *is an ordinal*$\}$;
3. $Ord(E) = [\omega^2 \cdot m; \omega^2 \cdot (m+1))$;
4. $Ord(E) = [\omega^2 \cdot m; \omega^2 \cdot (m+1)) \setminus \{\rho + \omega : \rho$ *is an ordinal*$\}$;
5. $Ord(E) = [\omega^2 \cdot m + 1; \omega^2 \cdot (m+1))$;
6. $Ord(E) = [\omega^2 \cdot m + 1; \omega^2 \cdot (m+1)) \setminus \{\rho + \omega : \rho$ *is an ordinal*$\}$.

Each of the six cases is realizable.

Section 3 proves Theorem 1. For reasons of space, the proof of Theorem 2 (which is more technically involved) is omitted. In order to prove Theorem 2, one has to work carefully with the classes $[x]_E$ representing limit points of an ordinal α: in some cases, we want to realize, say, an ordinal $\omega^2 \cdot m + \omega$; and in other cases, this ordinal should be "omitted".

We emphasize that the obtained theorems are fully *relativizable*: i.e., for any oracle $X \subseteq \mathbb{N}$, if an X-computably enumerable equivalence relation E realizes some infinite $\alpha < \omega^2$, then E satisfies one of the cases from Theorem 1. We strongly conjecture that the developed methods could provide a complete solution of Problem 1 for the case when some $\alpha < \omega^\omega$ belongs to $Ord(E)$.

2   Preliminaries and Simple Observations

The reader is referred to [4,8] for the background on computable structure theory. Preliminaries on countable linear orders can be found in [16]. By ω_1^{CK} we denote the least non-computable ordinal. By Id we denote the identity relation on $\mathbb{N}$.

If E and F are equivalence relations on $\mathbb{N}$, then by $E \oplus F$ we denote their *uniform join* which is defined as follows. For numbers $x, y \in \mathbb{N}$, we have $(x, y) \in E \oplus F$ if and only if either $(x = 2k) \,\&\, (y = 2\ell) \,\&\, ((k, l) \in E)$ or $(x = 2k+1) \,\&\, (y = 2\ell + 1) \,\&\, ((k, l) \in F)$.

One can also define uniform join for an arbitrary finite number of equivalences:

$$\bigoplus_{i=1}^{n+1} E_i = \left(\bigoplus_{i=1}^{n} E_i \right) \oplus E_{n+1}.$$

Definition 2. *For a c.e. set W, the ceer $E(W)$ is defined as follows:*

$$E(W) = \{(x, y) : x = y \text{ or } x, y \in W\}.$$

As usual, $(\varphi_e)_{e \in \mathbb{N}}$ denotes the standard list of all unary partial computable functions, and $W_e = \text{dom}(\varphi_e)$, for $e \in \mathbb{N}$. For the background on computability theory, we refer to [15]. Further preliminaries on ceers can be found, e.g., in the papers [1,3].

Let $\mathcal{L}$ be a linear order. An element $a \in \mathcal{L}$ is an *isolated point* if it satisfies one of the following conditions:

– a is the least element in $\mathcal{L}$ and a has an immediate successor,
– a is the greatest in $\mathcal{L}$ and a has an immediate predecessor,
– a has both immediate successor and predecessor.

If a is not an isolated point, then a is called a *limit point* of $\mathcal{L}$.

The following fact will be often used without an explicit reference:

Remark 1 (see Remark 30 in [11]*).* Suppose that a ceer E realizes a linear order $\mathcal{L}$. If a class $[x]_E$ is an isolated point in $\mathcal{L}$, then $[x]_E$ is a computable set. Furthermore, if $\mathcal{L}$ is a union of two intervals I and J such that $I <_{\mathcal{L}} J$, I has a greatest element, and J has a least element, then the sets $\{x : [x]_E \in I\}$ and $\{x : [x]_E \in J\}$ are computable.

In our proofs, we will implicitly use the fact that a c.e. relation R from Definition 1 can be always chosen as a preorder:

Proposition 1. *Let E be a ceer, and let $\mathcal{L}$ be a linear order. Then E realizes $\mathcal{L}$ if and only if there exists a c.e. preorder R with the following properties:*

1. *The relation* $\mathrm{supp}(R) = \{(x, y) : (x, y) \in R \,\&\, (y, x) \in R\}$ *is equal to E.*
2. *Consider the quotient structure $\mathcal{D}_R = (\mathbb{N}/\mathrm{supp}(R); \trianglelefteq_R)$, where $[x]_{\mathrm{supp}(R)} \trianglelefteq_R$ $[y]_{\mathrm{supp}(R)}$ iff $(x, y) \in R$. Then $\mathcal{D}_R$ is isomorphic to $\mathcal{L}$.*

Proof (sketch). ($\Leftarrow$). It is straightforward to check that the c.e. relation R satisfies all conditions from Definition 1.

($\Rightarrow$). Suppose that a c.e. relation R_1 (not necessarily preorder) satisfies Definition 1. Then one can show that a new relation $R := R_1 \cup E$ has all desired properties. $\square$

Now we give several simple facts which will be used throughout further proofs. First, recall that every hyperarithmetical ordinal has a computable copy. Hence, every ordinal realized by a ceer is computable.

Remark 2. The relation Id realizes all ordinals from the interval $[\omega; \omega_1^{CK})$.

The following two lemmas will be useful for us.

Lemma 1. *Let E be a ceer, and let α be a computable ordinal. Suppose that $\beta < \alpha$ is a successor ordinal, and γ is the ordinal such that $\alpha = \beta + \gamma$. If E realizes α, then E also realizes the ordinal $\gamma + \beta$.*

In particular, if an infinite ordinal $\alpha = \lambda + k + 1$ (where $k < \omega$) is realizable by E, then $\lambda + 1$ is also realizable by E.

Proof. Consider a presentation $(\mathbb{N}/E; \trianglelefteq)$ of the ordinal α. Find the class $[x]_E$ such that the initial segment $\{[y]_E : [y]_E \trianglelefteq [x]_E\}$ is isomorphic to β. By Remark 1, both sets
$$A = \{y : [y]_E \trianglelefteq [x]_E\} \text{ and } B = \{z : [z]_E \triangleright [x]_E\}$$
are computable. A new c.e. preorder $\sqsubseteq$ on $\mathbb{N}$ is defined as follows:

– If $x \in B$ and $y \in A$, then set $x \sqsubseteq y$.
– If $\{x, y\} \subseteq A$ or $\{x, y\} \subseteq B$, then put $x \sqsubseteq y$ if and only if $x \trianglelefteq y$.

It is not hard to show that $(\mathbb{N}/E; \sqsubseteq)$ is a presentation of well-order $\gamma + \beta$.   □

Lemma 2. *Let E and F be ceers. Suppose that $\alpha \in Ord(E)$ and $\beta \in Ord(F)$. Then $\alpha + \beta \in Ord(E \oplus F)$.*

Lemma 2 is an almost immediate corollary of the definitions. Together with Remark 2, this implies the following: if $\alpha \in Ord(E)$, then $[\alpha + \omega; \omega_1^{CK}) \subseteq Ord(E \oplus \mathrm{Id})$.

3   Proof of Theorem 1

In this section, we prove Theorem 1, i.e., we obtain a complete characterization of families $Ord(E)$ with the following additional property: there exists $\alpha < \omega^2$ such that α is realized by E. The section is arranged as follows. In Subsect. 3.1 we give a list of examples of realizable classes $Ord(E)$. Subsection 3.2 shows that this list is exhaustive.

3.1   Examples Which Can Be Realized

The first such example is obtained in the paper [11]. Recall that an infinite set $A \subseteq \mathbb{N}$ is *immune* if A does not have infinite c.e. subsets. A c.e. set W is *simple* if its complement is immune. A set A is *semirecursive* if there exists a computable function $f(x, y)$ such that for all x and y, we have $f(x, y) \in \{x, y\}$, and if $\{x, y\} \cap A \neq \emptyset$, then $f(x, y) \in A$.

Proposition 2 (Theorem 39.1 in [11]). *If W is a simple, semirecursive c.e. set, then $Ord(E(W)) = [\omega + 1; \omega \cdot 2)$.*

Proposition 2 has the following easy consequences:

Corollary 1. *Suppose that W is a simple, semirecursive c.e. set, and $2 \leq n < \omega$. Consider a ceer*

$$E_n := \bigoplus_{1 \leq i \leq n} E(W).$$

Then $Ord(E_n) = [\omega \cdot n + 1; \omega \cdot (n + 1))$.

Proof (sketch). By combining Proposition 2 with Lemma 2, it is easy to show that $[\omega \cdot n + 1; \omega \cdot (n + 1))$ is a subset of $Ord(E_n)$.

Now suppose that $\alpha \in Ord(E_n)$. Then one can obtain a decomposition $\alpha = \beta_1 + \beta_2 + \cdots + \beta_n$ such that each β_i is realizable by $E(W)$. Clearly, this implies that $\omega \cdot n + 1 \leq \alpha < \omega \cdot (n + 1)$.   □

Corollary 2. *For every non-zero $m < \omega$, there is a ceer E such that*

$$Ord(E) = [\omega \cdot m; \omega_1^{CK}).$$

Proof. Recall that we have $Ord(\text{Id}) = [\omega; \omega_1^{CK})$ (Remark 2). Hence, we can assume that $m \geq 2$. By Corollary 1, one can choose a ceer F with $Ord(F) = [\omega \cdot (m-1) + 1; \omega \cdot m)$. Now, similarly to Corollary 1, it is not hard to deduce that $Ord(F \oplus \text{Id}) = [\omega \cdot m; \omega_1^{CK})$.   □

The second series of examples is provided by the following result:

Proposition 3. *For every non-zero $n < \omega$, there is a ceer E such that $Ord(E)$ equals $[\omega \cdot n; \omega \cdot (n+1))$.*

Proof. Here we give a proof for the case of the interval $[\omega \cdot 2; \omega \cdot 3)$. The general case can be obtained via a similar argument.

We build a presentation $(\mathbb{N}/E; \preceq)$ as an isomorphic copy of the well-order $\omega \cdot 2$, while satisfying the following requirement:

The set of all E-classes cannot be split into three computable parts such that each of these parts contains infinitely many classes.

Notice that Lemma 1 immediately implies that every ordinal $\omega \cdot 2 + k$, for $1 \leq k < \omega$, is also realizable by E.

Why is the requirement above sufficient for our purposes? Towards a contradiction, assume that there exists an E-realization of some ordinal $\beta \geq \omega \cdot 3$, i.e., a c.e. preorder $\sqsubseteq$ with $(\mathbb{N}/E; \sqsubseteq) \cong \beta$.

Then this realization gives a natural splitting of $\mathbb{N}$ into three computable parts which is recovered as follows. Consider classes $[c]_E$ and $[d]_E$ which are the least and the second least limit points (with respect to $\sqsubseteq$), respectively. Let $[c_1]_E$ be the immediate successor of $[c]_E$, and let $[d_1]_E$ be the successor of $[d]_E$. Then by Remark 1, computable sets

$$U = \{x : x \sqsubseteq c\}, \quad V = \{y : c_1 \sqsubseteq y \sqsubseteq d\}, \quad W = \{z : d_1 \sqsubseteq z\}$$

form a splitting of $\mathbb{N}$. In addition, each of the sets U, V, W includes infinitely many E-classes, which contradicts our requirement.

Hence, if we satisfy the requirement, then any $\beta \geq \omega \cdot 3$ *will be not realizable* by E. The fact that the ordinals $\omega + k$, for $k < \omega$, are also not realizable by E will follow from Proposition 4 (see below) and the fact that $\omega \cdot 2 \in Ord(E)$.

Our requirement can be formally re-written as a series of requirements:

$P_{\langle i, j, k \rangle}$: For the triple (W_i, W_j, W_k) (where $i < j < k$), at least one of the following properties does not hold:

1. the sets are pairwise disjoint;
2. $W_i \cup W_j \cup W_k = \mathbb{N}$;
3. for all $\ell \in \{i, j, k\}$ and $x, y \in \mathbb{N}$, if $x \in W_\ell$ and $(y \, E \, x)$ then $y \in W_\ell$;
4. for each ℓ, W_ℓ contains infinitely many E-classes.

We describe a strategy for satisfying one requirement.

$P_{\langle i, j, k \rangle}$-STRATEGY. In the background, we construct a c.e. preorder $\preceq$ aiming for the goal $(\mathbb{N}/E; \preceq) \cong \omega \cdot 2$. So, semi-formally speaking, at a stage s, all (current) E-classes are split into two intervals $I_0[s]$ and $I_1[s]$ in a computable way. In the limit, each of these intervals will have order type ω. In addition, if a class $[x]_E$ is added to an interval I_ℓ, then it never goes to the other interval $I_{1-\ell}$.

We notice that $P_{\langle i, j, k \rangle}$ can be satisfied in a happy-go-lucky way: if we see an element x belonging to, say, $W_i \cap W_j$, then we immediately declare that the requirement is satisfied.

If $P_{\langle i, j, k \rangle}$ is not satisfied yet, then we wait until two of the sets W_i, W_j, W_k enumerate elements $x \neq y$ (say, x is enumerated into W_i, and y is enumerated into W_k) such that:

- at this stage s, we have $x \lhd_s y$ (i.e., $x \unlhd_s y$ and $y \ntrianglelefteq_s x$);
- x and y belong to the same ω-interval I_ℓ, and
- both elements are far enough from the leftmost point of the interval I_ℓ, i.e., x belongs to at least $\langle i, j, k \rangle$-th class (with respect to $\unlhd_s$) of the interval.

Then we *glue* the E-classes containing x and y, i.e., we declare that all elements z, where $[x]_E \unlhd_s [z]_E \unlhd_s [y]_E$, are E-equivalent to the element x. It is clear that if our W-sets are disjoint, then the described action forces the triple (W_i, W_j, W_k) to fail Condition (3) above.

Note that if the W-sets are pairwise disjoint and every W-set is infinite, then we will eventually find the desired pair x, y (essentially, this is the pigeonhole principle applied to the three W-sets and two ω-intervals).

If our strategy "freezes" (i.e., it waits for appropriate elements forever), then this means that one of the sets W_i, W_j, W_k includes only finitely many E-classes, i.e., Condition (4) does not hold.

Since we wait for elements, which are far enough from the leftmost point of the interval I_ℓ, this ensures that every initial segment of an ω-interval can be injured only by finitely many strategies. Each strategy acts at most one time, and, consequently, every initial segment of an ω-interval can be injured only finitely many times. Hence, a whole construction for all requirements can be handled via using a standard priority argument (even with no injuries). We leave further (standard) details to the reader. Proposition 3 is proved.   □

3.2   Why Are There No More Examples?

We recover a restriction on which families of ordinals can be realized as $Ord(E)$:

Proposition 4. *Assume that a ceer E realizes both $\alpha = \omega \cdot m + k$ and β, where $1 \leq m < \omega$, $k < \omega$, and $\beta \geq \omega \cdot (m + 1)$. Then we have $[\omega \cdot m; \omega_1^{CK}) \subseteq Ord(E)$.*

Proof. By Lemma 1, without loss of generality, we may assume that $k = 1$. We consider a presentation $\mathcal{A} = (\omega/E, \leq_A)$ for α and a presentation $\mathcal{B} = (\omega/E, \leq_B)$ for β.

(1) First, we show that the ordinal $\omega \cdot m$ is realizable by the relation E.

We choose m limit points $[x_1]_E <_B [x_2]_E <_B \cdots <_B [x_m]_E$ inside $\mathcal{B}$. They give a computable partition of $\mathbb{N}$ into $(m+1)$ intervals:

$$I_1 = \{y : [y]_E \leq_B [x_1]_E\}, \quad I_2 = \{y : [x_1]_E <_B [y]_E \leq_B [x_2]_E\},$$
$$I_3 = \{y : [x_2]_E <_B [y]_E \leq_B [x_3]_E\}, \quad \ldots,$$
$$I_m = \{y : [x_{m-1}]_E <_B [y]_E \leq_B [x_m]_E\}, \quad I_{m+1} = \{y : [y]_E >_B [x_m]_E\},$$

where each I_j includes infinitely many E-classes.

Let $[z_1]_E <_A [z_2]_E <_A \cdots <_A [z_m]_E$ be all limit points inside $\mathcal{A}$, and $[z_0]_E$ be the least $\leq_A$-element. By the pigeonhole principle, at least one of the intervals

$$J_t := \{y : [z_{t-1}]_E <_A [y]_E \leq_A [z_t]_E\}, \ 1 \leq t \leq m,$$

includes infinitely many E-classes both from I_p and from I_q, for some $p < q \leq m+1$.

Without loss of generality, we assume that J_2 includes infinitely many classes from both I_1 and I_2. Furthermore, we assume that $z_2 \notin I_1$. Then for any element $u \in \mathbb{N}$, we have $u \notin [z_2]_E$ if and only if one of the following two conditions holds:

1. $[u]_E >_A [z_2]_E$, or
2. there is an element $v \in I_1$ such that $[u]_E \leq_A [v]_E \leq_A [z_2]_E$.

This implies that the class $[z_2]_E$ is a computable set.

By recombining the $\leq_A$-intervals (notice that these intervals are computable sets, since $[z_2]_E$ is computable):

$$\{[y]_E : [y]_E \geq_A [z_2]_E\} \overset{\text{by def.}}{\trianglelefteq} \{[u]_E : [u]_E <_A [z_2]_E\},$$

we obtain that the ordinal $\omega \cdot m$ is realizable by E.

(2) Now we show that an arbitrary computable $\gamma \geq \omega \cdot (m+1)$ is also realizable by $\overline{E}$. For a non-zero $j \leq m+1$, we say that an element $x \in \mathbb{N}$ has I_j-color if $[x]_E \subseteq I_j$.

We start from the preorder $\leq_A$, and our goal is to "re-configure" the $\leq_A$-interval J_2 in an appropriate way. First, we find a computable sequence

$$z_1 <_A c_0 <_A d_0 <_A c_1 <_A d_1 <_A \cdots <_A c_\ell <_A d_\ell <_A \cdots <_A z_2$$

such that each c_i has I_1-color and each d_j has I_2-color. Note that such an alternating sequence exists. Indeed, consider an arbitrary $<_A$-increasing sequence $(c_i')_{i \in \omega}$ of I_1-colored elements inside J_2. Then for every I_2-colored element $d \notin [z_2]_E$ from J_2, there exists i such that $d <_A c_i'$: if there is no such i, then the interval J_2 will contain a limit point which is different from the points $[z_1]_E, \ldots, [z_m]_E$, and this gives a contradiction. So, informally speaking, inside J_2, the colors I_1 and I_2 alternate, and this allows to construct the needed sequence.

We proceed with the following semi-formal "surgery":

(a) If one deletes the I_1-*colored* intervals

$$C_i = (\{x \in I_1 : d_i \leq_A x \leq_A d_{i+1}\}; \leq_A), \ i \in \mathbb{N},$$

from $(\mathbb{N}/E; \leq_A)$, then the resulting structure still has order type $\omega \cdot m + 1$.

(b) Note that every C_i includes only finitely many E-classes. Since the sequence $(C_i)_{i \in \omega}$ is uniform, it is not hard to recombine these intervals is such a way that the resulting order (on the intervals) is isomorphic to a given infinite computable ordinal. Since $\gamma \geq \omega \cdot (m+1)$, this allows to appropriately "re-attach" the deleted intervals C_i, and obtain a new preorder $\sqsubseteq$ such that $(\omega/E; \sqsubseteq) \cong \gamma$.

Proposition 4 is proved. $\qquad\qquad\qquad\qquad\qquad\qquad\qquad\qquad\qquad\qquad\qquad\square$

Now we are ready to finish our main proof.

Proof (of Theorem 1). Recall that the relation E realizes some infinite ordinal less than ω^2. We choose *the least* ordinal $\alpha \in Ord(E)$. It is clear that $\alpha = \omega \cdot m + k$ for some $k < \omega$ and non-zero $m < \omega$. By Lemma 1, we deduce that $k \in \{0, 1\}$.

If there exists some $\beta \in Ord(E)$ with $\beta \geq \omega \cdot (m+1)$, then by Proposition 4, we obtain that $Ord(E) = [\omega \cdot m; \omega_1^{CK})$. Otherwise, it is obvious that $Ord(E)$ is equal either to $[\omega \cdot m; \omega \cdot (m+1))$ or to $[\omega \cdot m + 1; \omega \cdot (m+1))$. $\qquad\square$

In conclusion, we mention an interesting connection with the modern studies of natural combinatorial properties of ceers. Andrews and Sorbi [3] introduced the notions of light and dark ceers. A ceer E is *light* if there exists an infinite c.e. set $W = \{a_i : i \in \omega\}$ such that for all $i \neq j$, the elements a_i and a_j are not E-equivalent. If a ceer E is not light and it has infinitely many classes, then E is *dark*.

The methods developed in our work allow to prove the following result. Let m be a non-zero natural number, and let E be a ceer.

(a) If $Ord(E) = [\omega \cdot m; \omega_1^{CK})$, then E is light.
(b) If $Ord(E) = [\omega \cdot m + 1; \omega \cdot (m+1))$, then E is dark.
(c) There exist a light ceer E_0 and a dark ceer E_1 such that both $Ord(E_0)$ and $Ord(E_1)$ are equal to $[\omega \cdot m; \omega \cdot (m+1))$.

Acknowledgements. The authors are grateful to the anonymous reviewers for their helpful comments.

References

1. Andrews, U., Badaev, S., Sorbi, A.: A survey on universal computably enumerable equivalence relations. In: Day, A., Fellows, M., Greenberg, N., Khoussainov, B., Melnikov, A., Rosamond, F. (eds.) Computability and Complexity. LNCS, vol. 10010, pp. 418–451. Springer, Cham (2017). https://doi.org/10.1007/978-3-319-50062-1_25

2. Andrews, U., Schweber, N., Sorbi, A.: The theory of ceers computes true arithmetic. Ann. Pure Appl. Logic **171**(8), 102811 (2020). https://doi.org/10.1016/j.apal.2020.102811

3. Andrews, U., Sorbi, A.: Joins and meets in the structure of ceers. Computability **8**(3–4), 193–241 (2019). https://doi.org/10.3233/COM-180098

4. Ash, C.J., Knight, J.F.: Computable Structures and the Hyperarithmetical Hierarchy. Studies in Logic and the Foundations of Mathematics, vol. 144. Elsevier Science B.V., Amsterdam (2000)

5. Bazhenov, N., Mustafa, M., Stephan, F., Yamaleev, M.: Boolean algebras realized by C.E. equivalence relations. Sib. Elektron. Mat. Izv. **14**, 848–855 (2017). https://doi.org/10.17377/semi.2017.14.071

6. Boone, W.W.: The word problem. Proc. Natl. Acad. Sci. U.S.A. **44**(10), 1061–1065 (1958). https://doi.org/10.1073/pnas.44.10.1061

7. Delle Rose, V., San Mauro, L., Sorbi, A.: Word problems and ceers. Math. Log. Q. **66**(3), 341–354 (2020). https://doi.org/10.1002/malq.202000021

8. Ershov, Y.L., Goncharov, S.S.: Constructive Models. Kluwer Academic/Plenum Publishers, New York (2000)

9. Fokina, E., Khoussainov, B., Semukhin, P., Turetsky, D.: Linear orders realized by C.E. equivalence relations. J. Symb. Log. **81**(2), 463–482 (2016). https://doi.org/10.1017/jsl.2015.11

10. Gavruskin, A., Jain, S., Khoussainov, B., Stephan, F.: Graphs realised by R.E. equivalence relations. Ann. Pure Appl. Logic **165**(7–8), 1263–1290 (2014). https://doi.org/10.1016/j.apal.2014.04.001

11. Gavryushkin, A., Khoussainov, B., Stephan, F.: Reducibilities among equivalence relations induced by recursively enumerable structures. Theor. Comput. Sci. **612**, 137–152 (2016). https://doi.org/10.1016/j.tcs.2015.11.042

12. Godziszewski, M.T., Hamkins, J.D.: Computable quotient presentations of models of arithmetic and set theory. In: Kennedy, J., de Queiroz, R.J.G.B. (eds.) WoLLIC 2017. LNCS, vol. 10388, pp. 140–152. Springer, Heidelberg (2017). https://doi.org/10.1007/978-3-662-55386-2_10

13. Khoussainov, B.: A journey to computably enumerable structures (tutorial lectures). In: Manea, F., Miller, R.G., Nowotka, D. (eds.) CiE 2018. LNCS, vol. 10936, pp. 1–19. Springer, Cham (2018). https://doi.org/10.1007/978-3-319-94418-0_1

14. Novikov, P.S.: On the algorithmic unsolvability of the word problem in group theory. Proc. Steklov Inst. Math. **44**, 1–143 (1955). (in Russian)

15. Odifreddi, P.: Classical Recursion Theory. Studies in Logic and the Foundations of Mathematics, vol. 125. Elsevier Science B.V., Amsterdam (1992)

16. Rosenstein, J.G.: Linear Orderings. Pure and Applied Mathematics, vol. 98. Academic Press, New York (1982)

17. Sorbi, A.: Effective inseparability and its applications. In: De Mol, L., Weiermann, A., Manea, F., Fernández-Duque, D. (eds.) CiE 2021. LNCS, vol. 12813, pp. 417–423. Springer, Cham (2021). https://doi.org/10.1007/978-3-030-80049-9_41

Maximal Ideals in Countable Rings, Constructively

Ingo Blechschmidt[1] and Peter Schuster[2(✉)]

[1] Universität Augsburg, Universitätsstr. 14, 86159 Augsburg, Germany
ingo.blechschmidt@math.uni-augsburg.de
[2] Università di Verona, Strada le Grazie 15, 37134 Verona, Italy
petermichael.schuster@univr.it

Abstract. The existence of a maximal ideal in a general nontrivial commutative ring is tied together with the axiom of choice. Following Berardi, Valentini and thus Krivine but using the relative interpretation of negation (that is, as "implies $0 = 1$") we show, in constructive set theory with minimal logic, how for countable rings one can do without any kind of choice and without the usual decidability assumption that the ring is strongly discrete (membership in finitely generated ideals is decidable). By a functional recursive definition we obtain a maximal ideal in the sense that the quotient ring is a residue field (every noninvertible element is zero), and with strong discreteness even a geometric field (every element is either invertible or else zero). Krull's lemma for the related notion of prime ideal follows by passing to rings of fractions. All this equally applies to rings indexed by any well-founded set, and can be carried over to Heyting arithmetic with minimal logic. We further show how a metatheorem of Joyal and Tierney can be used to expand our treatment to arbitrary rings. Along the way we do a case study for proofs in algebra with minimal logic. An Agda formalization is available at an accompanying repository.

Let A be a commutative ring with unit. The standard way of constructing a maximal ideal of A is to apply Zorn's lemma to the set of proper ideals of A; but this method is less an actual construction and more an appeal to the transfinite.

If A is countable with enumeration $x_0, x_1, \ldots$, we can hope to provide a more explicit construction by successively adding generators to the zero ideal, skipping those which would render it improper:

$$\mathfrak{m}_0 = \{0\} \qquad \mathfrak{m}_{n+1} = \begin{cases} \mathfrak{m}_n + (x_n), & \text{if } 1 \notin \mathfrak{m}_n + (x_n), \\ \mathfrak{m}_n, & \text{else.} \end{cases}$$

A maximal ideal is then obtained in the limit as the union of the intermediate stages $\mathfrak{m}_n$. For instance, Krull in his 1929 Annals contribution [33, Hilfssatz] and books on constructive algebra [37, Lemma VI.3.2], [34, comment after Theorem VII.5.2] proceed in this fashion. A similar construction concocts Henkin models for the purpose of proving Gödel's completeness theorem for

U. Berger et al. (Eds.): CiE 2022, LNCS 13359, pp. 24–38, 2022.
https://doi.org/10.1007/978-3-031-08740-0_3

countable languages, successively adding formulas which do not render the current set inconsistent [62, Satz I.56], [17, Lemma 1.5.7], [60, Lemma III.5.4], [28, Lemma 2.1].

This procedure avoids any form of choice by virtue of being a functional recursive definition, but still requires some form of omniscience in order to carry out the case distinction. In the present text we study a variant of this construction, due to Berardi and Valentini [9], which avoids any non-constructive principles and decidability assumptions, similar to a construction which has been studied by Krivine [32, p. 410] and later Herbelin and Ilik [24, p. 11] in the context of Gödel's completeness theorem. In this generality, the resulting maximal ideal has an elusive quality to it, but useful properties can still be extracted; and not only do we recover the original construction under certain decidability assumptions, we can also exploit a relativity phenomenon of mathematical logic in order to drop, with some caveats, the assumption that A is countable.

An Agda formalization is available at an accompanying repository (https://github.com/iblech/constructive-maximal-ideals/).

Conventions. Throughout this note, we fix a ring A, and work in a constructive metatheory. In the spirit of Lombardi and Quitté [34], we employ *minimal logic* [29], where by "not φ" we mean "$\varphi \Rightarrow 1 =_A 0$", and do *not* assume any form of the axiom of choice. Consequently, by "$x \notin M$" we mean $x \in M \Rightarrow 1 =_A 0$, and a subset $M \subseteq A$ is *detachable* if and only if for all $x \in A$, either $x \in M$ or $x \notin M$. For general background on constructive mathematics, we refer to [7,8,12].

For an arbitrary subset $M \subseteq A$, not necessarily detachable, the ideal (M) generated by M is given by $\{\sum_{i=1}^{n} a_i v_i \mid n \geq 0, a_1, \ldots, a_n \in A, v_1, \ldots, v_n \in M\}$. Notice that, for every element $v \in (M)$, either $v = 0$ or M is inhabited, depending on whether $n = 0$ or $n > 0$ in $\sum_{i=1}^{n} a_i v_i$. This can also be seen from the alternative inductive generation of (M) by the following rules:

$$\frac{v = 0}{v \in (M)} \qquad \frac{v \in M}{v \in (M)} \qquad \frac{v \in (M) \quad w \in (M)}{v + w \in (M)} \qquad \frac{a \in A \quad v \in (M)}{av \in (M)}$$

Here we adhere to the paradigm of generalized inductive definitions [1,2,44].

1   A Construction

We assume that the ring A is countable, with $x_0, x_1, \ldots$ an enumeration of the elements of A. We do *not* assume that A is discrete (that is, that $x = y$ or $x \neq y$ for all elements of A) or that it is strongly discrete (that is, that finitely generated ideals of A are detachable). Up to Corollary 1.2(a) below we follow [9].

We study the following recursive construction of ideals $\mathfrak{m}_0, \mathfrak{m}_1, \ldots$ of A:

$$\mathfrak{m}_0 := \{0\} \qquad\qquad \mathfrak{m}_{n+1} := \mathfrak{m}_n + (\{x_n \mid 1 \notin \mathfrak{m}_n + (x_n)\}).$$

Finally, we set $\mathfrak{m} := \bigcup_n \mathfrak{m}_n$. The construction of $\mathfrak{m}_{n+1}$ from $\mathfrak{m}_n$ is uniquely specified, requiring no choices of any form.

The set $M_n := \{x_n \mid 1 \notin \mathfrak{m}_n + (x_n)\}$ occurring in this construction contains the element x_n if and only if $1 \notin \mathfrak{m}_n + (x_n)$; it is obtained from the singleton set $\{x_n\}$ by bounded separation. This set M_n is inhabited precisely if $1 \notin \mathfrak{m}_n + (x_n)$, in which case $\mathfrak{m}_{n+1} = \mathfrak{m}_n + (x_n)$. However, in the generality we work in, we cannot assume that M_n is empty or inhabited.

We can avoid the case distinction by the flexibility of nondetachable subsets, rendering it somewhat curious that—despite the conveyed flavor of a conjuring trick—the construction can still be used to obtain concrete positive results.

The ideal (M_n) is given by $(M_n) = \{a x_n \mid (a = 0) \lor (1 \notin \mathfrak{m}_n + (x_n))\}$.

Lemma 1.1. (a) *The subset $\mathfrak{m}$ is an ideal.*
(b) *The ideal $\mathfrak{m}$ is* proper *in the sense that $1 \notin \mathfrak{m}$.*
(c) *For every number $n \in \mathbb{N}$, the following are equivalent:*
(1) $x_n \in \mathfrak{m}_{n+1}$.   (2) $x_n \in \mathfrak{m}$.   (3) $1 \notin \mathfrak{m} + (x_n)$.   (4) $1 \notin \mathfrak{m}_n + (x_n)$.

Proof. (a) Directed unions of ideals are ideals.
(b) Assume $1 \in \mathfrak{m}$. Then $1 \in \mathfrak{m}_n$ for some number $n \geq 0$. We verify $1 = 0$ by
   induction over n. If $n = 0$, then $1 \in \mathfrak{m}_0 = \{0\}$. Hence $1 = 0$.
   If $n > 0$, then $1 = y + a x_{n-1}$ for some elements $a, y \in A$ such that $y \in \mathfrak{m}_{n-1}$
   and such that $a = 0$ or $1 \notin \mathfrak{m}_{n-1} + (x_{n-1})$. In the first case, we have $1 =$
   $y \in \mathfrak{m}_{n-1}$, hence $1 = 0$ by the induction hypothesis. In the second case we
   have $1 = 0$ by modus ponens applied to the implication $1 \notin \mathfrak{m}_{n-1} + (x_{n-1})$
   and the fact $1 \in \mathfrak{m}_{n-1} + (x_{n-1})$ (which follows directly from the equation $1 =$
   $y + a x_{n-1}$).
(c) It is clear that $(3) \Rightarrow (4) \Rightarrow (1) \Rightarrow (2)$. It remains to show that $(2) \Rightarrow (3)$.
   Assume $x_n \in \mathfrak{m}$. In order to verify $1 \notin \mathfrak{m} + (x_n)$, assume $1 \in \mathfrak{m} + (x_n)$.
   Since $\mathfrak{m} + (x_n) \subseteq \mathfrak{m}$, we have $1 \in \mathfrak{m}$. Hence $1 = 0$ by properness of $\mathfrak{m}$.

Corollary 1.2. (a) *The ideal $\mathfrak{m}$ is* maximal *in the sense that it is proper and*
   that for all elements $x \in A$, if $1 \notin \mathfrak{m} + (x)$, then $x \in \mathfrak{m}$.
(b) *The ideal $\mathfrak{m}$ is* prime *in the sense that it is proper and that for all ele-*
   ments $x, y \in A$, if $xy \in \mathfrak{m}$ and $x \notin \mathfrak{m}$, then $y \in \mathfrak{m}$.
(c) *The ideal $\mathfrak{m}$ is* radical *in the sense that for every $k \geq 0$, if $x^k \in \mathfrak{m}$, then*
   $x \in \mathfrak{m}$.

Proof. (a) Immediate by Lemma 1.1(c).
(b) This claim is true even for arbitrary maximal ideals: By maximality, it suf-
   fices to verify that $1 \notin \mathfrak{m} + (y)$. If $1 \in \mathfrak{m} + (y)$, then $x = x \cdot 1 \in (x) \cdot \mathfrak{m} + (xy) \subseteq \mathfrak{m}$
   by $xy \in \mathfrak{m}$, hence $x \in \mathfrak{m}$, thus $1 = 0$ by $x \notin \mathfrak{m}$.
(c) Let $x^k \in \mathfrak{m}$. Then $1 \notin \mathfrak{m} + (x)$, for if $1 \in \mathfrak{m} + (x)$, then also $1 = 1^k \in$
   $(\mathfrak{m} + (x))^k \subseteq \mathfrak{m} + (x^k) \subseteq \mathfrak{m}$. Hence $x \in \mathfrak{m}$ by maximality.

Remark 1.3. The ideal $\mathfrak{m}$ is double negation stable: for every ring element x,
if $\neg\neg(x \in \mathfrak{m})$, then $x \in \mathfrak{m}$. This is because by Lemma 1.1(c) membership of $\mathfrak{m}$ is
a negative condition and $\neg\neg\neg\varphi \Rightarrow \neg\varphi$ is a tautology of minimal logic.

This first-order maximality condition is equivalent [9] to the following higher-order version: For every ideal $\mathfrak{n}$ such that $1 \notin \mathfrak{n}$, if $\mathfrak{m} \subseteq \mathfrak{n}$, then $\mathfrak{m} = \mathfrak{n}$.

The quotient $A/\mathfrak{m}$ is a *residue field* in that $1 \neq 0$ and that every element which is not invertible is zero—as with the real or complex numbers in constructive mathematics.[1] Each of the latter is in fact a *Heyting field*, a residue field which also is a *local ring*: if a finite sum is invertible then one of the summands is.

Example 1.4. If we enumerate $\mathbb{Z}$ by $0, 1, -1, 2, -2, \ldots$, the ideal $\mathfrak{m}$ coincides with (2). If the enumeration starts with a prime p, the ideal $\mathfrak{m}$ coincides with (p).

Example 1.5. If A is a local ring with group of units $A^\times$, then $\mathfrak{m} = A \setminus A^\times$.

Example 1.6. We can also use an arbitrary ideal $\mathfrak{a}$ as $\mathfrak{m}_0$ instead of the zero ideal. All results in this section remain valid once "not φ" is redefined as "$\varphi \Rightarrow 1 \in \mathfrak{a}$"; the resulting ideal $\mathfrak{m}$ is then a maximal ideal above $\mathfrak{a}$; it is proper in the sense that $1 \in \mathfrak{m} \Rightarrow 1 \in \mathfrak{a}$. It can also be obtained by applying the original version of the construction in the quotient ring $A/\mathfrak{a}$ (which is again countable) and taking the inverse image of the resulting ideal along the canonical projection $A \to A/\mathfrak{a}$.

Example 1.7. Assume that A is a field. Let $f \in A[X]$ be a nonconstant monic polynomial. Since f is monic, it is not invertible; thus Example 1.6 shows that there is a maximal ideal $\mathfrak{m}$ above (f). Hence $A[X]/\mathfrak{m}$ is a field in which f has a zero, namely the equivalence class of X. Iterating this *Kronecker construction*, we obtain a splitting field of f. No assumption regarding decidability of reducibility has to be made, but in return the resulting fields are only residue fields.

If we can decide whether a finitely generated ideal contains the unit or not, we can improve on Corollary 1.2(a). For instance this is the case for strongly discrete rings such as the ring $\mathbb{Z}$, more generally for the ring of integers of every number field, and for polynomial rings over discrete fields [37, Theorem VIII.1.5].

Proposition 1.8. *Assume that for every finitely generated ideal $\mathfrak{a} \subseteq A$ we have $1 \notin \mathfrak{a}$ or $\neg(1 \notin \mathfrak{a})$. Then:*

(a) *Each ideal $\mathfrak{m}_n$ is finitely generated.*
(b) *The ideal $\mathfrak{m}$ is detachable.*

If even $1 \in \mathfrak{a}$ or $1 \notin \mathfrak{a}$ for every finitely generated ideal $\mathfrak{a} \subseteq A$, then:

---

[1] Residue fields have many of the basic properties of the fields from classical mathematics. For instance, minimal generating families of vector spaces over residue fields are linearly independent, finitely generated vector spaces do (up to $\neg\neg$) have a finite basis, monic polynomials possess splitting fields and Noether normalization is available (the proofs in [37] can be suitably adapted). The constructively rarer *geometric fields*—those kinds of fields for which every element is either invertible or zero—are required to ensure, for instance, that kernels of matrices are finite dimensional and that bilinear forms are diagonalizable.

(c) *The ideal* $\mathfrak{m}$ *is maximal in the strong sense that for every element* $x \in A$, $x \in$ $\mathfrak{m}$ *or* $1 \in \mathfrak{m} + (x)$, *which is to say that the quotient ring* $A/\mathfrak{m}$ *is a geometric field (every element is zero or invertible).*[2]

Proof. We verify claim (a) by induction. The case $n = 0$ is clear. Let $n > 0$. By the induction hypothesis, the ideal $\mathfrak{m}_{n-1}$ is finitely generated, hence so is $\mathfrak{m}_{n-1} + (x_{n-1})$. By assumption, $1 \notin \mathfrak{m}_{n-1} + (x_{n-1})$ or $\neg(1 \notin \mathfrak{m}_{n-1} + (x_{n-1}))$. In the first case $\mathfrak{m}_n = \mathfrak{m}_{n-1} + (x_{n-1})$. In the second case $\mathfrak{m}_n = \mathfrak{m}_{n-1}$. In both cases the ideal $\mathfrak{m}_n$ is finitely generated.

To verify claim (b), let an element $x_n \in A$ be given. By assumption, $1 \notin \mathfrak{m}_n + (x_n)$ or $\neg(1 \notin \mathfrak{m}_n + (x_n))$. Hence $x_n \in \mathfrak{m}$ or $x_n \notin \mathfrak{m}$ by Lemma 1.1(c).

For claim (c), let an element $x_n \in A$ be given. If $1 \in \mathfrak{m}_n + (x_n)$, then also $1 \in \mathfrak{m} + (x)$. If $1 \notin \mathfrak{m}_n + (x_n)$, then $x_n \in \mathfrak{m}$ by Lemma 1.1(c). $\square$

Remarkably, under the assumption of Proposition 1.8, the ideal $\mathfrak{m}$ is detachable even though in general it fails to be finitely generated. Usually in constructive mathematics, ideals which are not finitely generated are seldom detachable. For instance the ideal $\{x \in \mathbb{Z} \mid x = 0 \vee \varphi\} \subseteq \mathbb{Z}$ is detachable if and only if $\varphi \vee \neg\varphi$.

Remark 1.9. There is an equivalent description of the maximal ideal $\mathfrak{m}$ which uses sets G_n of generators as proxies for the intermediate ideals $\mathfrak{m}_n$:

$$G_0 := \emptyset \qquad\qquad G_{n+1} := G_n \cup \{x_n \mid 1 \notin (G_n \cup \{x_n\})\}$$

An induction establishes the relation $(G_n) = \mathfrak{m}_n$; setting $G := \bigcup_{n \in \mathbb{N}} G_n$, the analogue of Lemma 1.1(c) states that for every number $n \in \mathbb{N}$, the following are equivalent: (1) $x_n \in G_{n+1}$. (2) $x_n \in G$. (3) $1 \notin (G) + (x_n)$. (4) $1 \notin (G_n) + (x_n)$.

In particular, not only do we have that $(G) = \mathfrak{m}$, but G itself is already an ideal. This description of $\mathfrak{m}$ is in a sense more "economical" as the intermediate stages G_n are smaller (not yet being ideals), enabling arithmetization in Sect. 3.

Remark 1.10. All results in this section carry over mutatis mutandis if A is only assumed to be subcountable, that is, if we are only given a *partially defined surjection* $\mathbb{N} \rightarrowtail A$. In this case, we are given an enumeration $x_0, x_1, \ldots$ where some x_i might not be defined; we then define $\mathfrak{m}_{n+1} := \mathfrak{m}_n + (\{x_n \mid x_n \text{ is defined} \wedge 1 \notin \mathfrak{m}_n + (x_n)\})$. The generalization to the subcountable case is particularly useful in the Russian tradition of constructive mathematics as exhibited by the effective topos [6, 27, 39, 41], where many rings of interest are subcountable, including uncountable ones such as the real numbers [27, Prop. 7.2].

---

[2] This notion of a maximal ideal, together with the corresponding one of a complete theory in propositional logic, has been generalized to the concept of a complete coalition [53, 55] for an abstract inconsistency predicate.

2   On the Intersection of All Prime Ideals

Classically, Krull's lemma states that the intersection of all prime ideals is the *nilradical*, the ideal $\sqrt{(0)}$ of all nilpotent elements. In our setup, we have the following substitute concerning complements:

$$\sqrt{(0)}^c = \bigcup_{\substack{\mathfrak{p} \subseteq A \\ \mathfrak{p} \text{ prime} \\ \mathfrak{p} \neg\neg\text{-stable}}} \mathfrak{p}^c = \bigcup_{\substack{\mathfrak{p} \subseteq A \\ \mathfrak{p} \text{ prime} \\ \mathfrak{p} \text{ radical}}} \mathfrak{p}^c .$$

Lemma 2.1. *Let $x \in A$. Then there is an ideal $\mathfrak{p} \subseteq A$ which is*

1. *"x-prime" in the sense that $1 \in \mathfrak{p} \Rightarrow x \in \sqrt{(0)}$ and $ab \in \mathfrak{p} \wedge \big(b \in \mathfrak{p} \Rightarrow x \in \sqrt{(0)}\big) \Longrightarrow a \in \mathfrak{p}$, that is, prime if the negations occurring in the definition of "prime ideal" are understood as "$\varphi \Rightarrow x \in \sqrt{(0)}$",*
2. *"x-stable" in the sense that $\big((a \in \mathfrak{p} \Rightarrow x \in \sqrt{(0)}) \Rightarrow x \in \sqrt{(0)}\big) \Rightarrow a \in \mathfrak{p}$,*
3. *radical,*
4. *and such that $x \in \mathfrak{p}$ if and only if x is nilpotent.*

Proof. The localization $A[x^{-1}]$ is again countable, hence the construction of Sect. 1 can be carried out to obtain a maximal (and hence prime) ideal $\mathfrak{m} \subseteq A[x^{-1}]$. Every negation occurring in the terms "maximal ideal" and "prime ideal" refers to $1 = 0$ in $A[x^{-1}]$, which is equivalent to x being nilpotent.

The preimage of $\mathfrak{m}$ under the localization homomorphism $A \to A[x^{-1}]$ is the desired x-prime ideal.

Corollary 2.2 (Krull [33]). *Let $x \in A$ be an element which is not nilpotent. Then there is a (radical and $\neg\neg$-stable) prime ideal $\mathfrak{p} \subseteq A$ such that $x \notin \mathfrak{p}$.*

Proof. Because x is not nilpotent, the notion of an x-prime ideal and an ordinary prime ideal coincide. Hence the claim follows from Lemma 2.1.

An important part of constructive algebra is to devise tools to import proofs from classical commutative algebra into the constructive setting.[3] The following two statements are established test cases exploring the power of such tools [4, 14, 15, 40, 42, 45, 50–52, 56].

Proposition 2.3. *Let $f \in A[X]$ be a polynomial.*

1. *If f is nilpotent in $A[X]$, then all coefficients of f are nilpotent in A.*
2. *If f is invertible in $A[X]$, then all nonconstant coefficients of f are nilpotent.*

These facts have abstract classical proofs employing Krull's lemma as follows.

---

[3] Forms of Zorn's Lemma similar to Krull's Lemma feature prominently in algebra; to wit, in ordered algebra there are the Artin–Schreier theorem for fields, Levi's theorem for Abelian groups and Ribenboim's extension to modules. Dynamical algebra aside, to which we will come back later, these statements have recently gained attention from the angle of proof theory at large; see, for example, [11, 43, 46–48, 57, 66, 67].

Proof of 1. Simple induction if A is reduced; the general case reduces to this one: For every prime ideal $\mathfrak{p}$, the coefficients of f vanish over the reduced ring $A/\mathfrak{p}$. Hence they are contained in all prime ideals and are thereby nilpotent.

Proof of 2. Simple induction if A is an integral domain; the general case reduces to this one: For every prime ideal $\mathfrak{p}$, the nonconstant coefficients of f vanish over the integral domain $A/\mathfrak{p}$. Hence they are contained in all prime ideals and are thereby nilpotent.

Both statements admit direct computational proofs which do not refer to prime ideals; the challenge is not to find such proofs, but rather to imitate the two classical proofs above constructively, staying as close as possible to the original. It is remarkable that the construction of Sect. 1 meets this challenge at all, outlined as follows, despite its fundamental reliance on nondetachable subsets.

We continue assuming that A is countable: Sect. 4 indicates how this assumption can be dropped in quite general situations, while for the purposes of specific challenges such as Proposition 2.3 we could also simply pass to the countable subring generated by the polynomial coefficients or employ the method of indeterminate coefficients.

Proof (of Proposition 2.3). The first claim follows from a simple induction if A is a reduced ring. In the general case, write $f = a_n X^n + a_{n-1} X^{n-1} + \cdots + a_0$. Let $\mathfrak{p}$ be a radical a_n-prime ideal as in Lemma 2.1. Since $A/\mathfrak{p}$ is reduced, the nilpotent coefficient a_n vanishes over $A/\mathfrak{p}$. Thus $a_n \in \mathfrak{p}$, hence a_n is nilpotent. Since the polynomial $f - a_n X^n$ is again nilpotent, we can continue by induction.

The second claim follows by a simple inductive argument if A is an integral domain with double negation stable equality. In the general case, write $f = a_n X^n + \cdots + a_0$ and assume $n \geq 1$. To reduce to the integral situation, let $\mathfrak{p}$ be an a_n-prime ideal as in Lemma 2.1. With negation "$\neg\varphi$" understood as "$\varphi \Rightarrow a_n \in \sqrt{(0)}$", the quotient ring $A/\mathfrak{p}$ is an integral domain with double negation stable equality. Hence $a_n = 0$ in $A/\mathfrak{p}$, so $a_n \in \mathfrak{p}$ whereby a_n is nilpotent. The polynomial $f - a_n X^n$ is again invertible in $A[X]$ (since the group of units is closed under adding nilpotent elements) so that we can continue by induction.

Just as Corollary 2.2 is a constructive substitute for the recognition of the intersection of all prime ideals as the nilradical, the following proposition is a substitute for the classical fact that the intersection of all maximal ideals is the Jacobson radical. As is customary in constructive algebra [34, Section IX.1], by *Jacobson radical* we mean the ideal $\{x \in A \mid \forall y \in A.\ 1 - xy \in A^\times\}$.

Proposition 2.4. *Let* $x \in A$. *If* x *is* apart *from the Jacobson radical (that is,* $1 - xy \notin A^\times$ *for some element* y)*, then there is a maximal ideal* $\mathfrak{m}$ *such that* $x \notin \mathfrak{m}$.

Proof. The standard proof as in [34, Lemma IX.1.1] applies: There is an element y such that $1 - xy$ is not invertible. By Example 1.6, there is an ideal $\mathfrak{m}$

above $\mathfrak{a} := (1 - xy)$ which is maximal not only as an ideal of $A/\mathfrak{a}$ (where "$\neg\varphi$" means "$\varphi \Rightarrow 1 \in \mathfrak{a}$") but also as an ideal of A (where "$\neg\varphi$" means "$\varphi \Rightarrow 1 = 0$"). If $x \in \mathfrak{m}$, then $1 = (1 - xy) + xy \in \mathfrak{m}$; hence $x \notin \mathfrak{m}$.

The two test cases presented in Proposition 2.3 only concern prime ideals. In contrast, the following example crucially rests on the maximality of the ideal $\mathfrak{m}$.

Proposition 2.5. *Let $M \in A^{n \times m}$ be a matrix with more rows than columns. Assume that the induced linear map $A^m \to A^n$ is surjective. Then $1 = 0$.*

Proof. By passing to the quotient $A/\mathfrak{m}$, we may assume that A is a residue field. In this case the claim is standard linear algebra: If any of the matrix entries is invertible, the matrix could be transformed by elementary row and column operations to a matrix of the form $\left(\begin{smallmatrix} 1 & 0 \\ 0 & M' \end{smallmatrix}\right)$, where the induced linear map of the submatrix M' is again surjective. Thus $1 = 0$ by induction.

Hence by the residue field property all matrix entries are zero. But the vector $(1, 0, \ldots, 0) \in A^n$ still belongs to the range of $M = 0$, hence $1 = 0$ by $n > 0$.

Remark 2.6. A more significant case study is Suslin's lemma, the fundamental and originally non-constructive ingredient in his second solution of Serre's problem [61]. The classical proof, concisely recalled in Yengui's constructive account [68], reduces modulo maximal ideals. The construction of Sect. 1 offers a constructive substitute. However, since gcd computations are required in the quotient rings, it is not enough that they are residue fields; they need to be geometric fields. Hence our approach has to be combined with the technique variously known as *Friedman's trick, nontrivial exit continuation* or *baby version of Barr's theorem* in order to yield a constructive proof [5,10,21,38].

3   In Heyting Arithmetic

The construction presented in Sect. 1 crucially rests on the flexibility of nondetachable subsets: In absence of additional assumptions as in Proposition 1.8, we cannot give the ideals $\mathfrak{m}_n$ by decidable predicates $A \to \{0,1\}$—without additional hypotheses on A, membership of the ideals $\mathfrak{m}_n$ is not decidable. As such, the construction is naturally formalized in intuitionistic set theories such as CZF or IZF, which natively support such flexible subsets.

In this section, we explain how with some more care, the construction can also be carried out in much weaker foundations such as Heyting arithmetic HA. While formulation in classical Peano arithmetic PA is routine, the development in HA crucially rests on a specific feature of the construction, namely that the condition for membership is a negative condition.

To set the stage, we specify what we mean by a *ring* in the context of arithmetic. One option would be to decree that an arithmetized ring should be a single natural number coding a finite set of ring elements and the graphs of the corresponding ring operations; however, this perspective is too narrow, as we also want to work with infinite rings.

Instead, an arithmetized ring should be given by a "formulaic setoid with ring structure", that is: by a formula $A(n)$ with free variable n, singling out which natural numbers constitute representatives of the ring elements; by a formula $E(n, m)$ describing which representatives are deemed equivalent; by a formula $Z(n)$ singling out representatives of the zero element; by a formula $P(n, m, s)$ singling out representatives s of sums; and so on with the remaining data constituting a ring; such that axioms such as

$$\forall n.\, Z(n) \Rightarrow A(n) \qquad \text{"every zero representative belongs to the ring"}$$

$$\exists n.\, Z(n) \qquad \text{"there is a zero representative"}$$

$$\forall n, m.\, Z(n) \land Z(m) \Longrightarrow E(n, m) \qquad \text{"every two zero representatives are equivalent"}$$

$$\forall z, n.\, Z(z) \land A(n) \Longrightarrow P(z, n, n) \qquad \text{"zero is neutral with respect to addition"}$$

hold. This conception of arithmetized rings deviates from the usual definition in reverse mathematics [60, Definition III.5.1] to support quotients even when HA cannot verify the existence of canonical representatives of equivalence classes.

Although first-order arithmetic cannot quantify over ideals of arithmetized rings, specific ideals can be given by formulas $I(n)$ such that axioms such as

$$\forall n.\, I(n) \Rightarrow A(n) \qquad \text{"$I \subseteq A$"}$$

$$\exists n.\, Z(n) \land I(n) \qquad \text{"$0 \in I$"}$$

hold. It is in this sense that we are striving to adapt the construction of Sect. 1 to describe a maximal ideal.

In this context, we can arithmetically imitate any set-theoretic description of a single ideal as a subset cut out by an explicit first-order formula. However, for recursively defined families of ideals, we require a suitable recursion theorem: If we are given (individual formulas $M_n(x)$ indexed by numerals representing) ideals $\mathfrak{m}_0, \mathfrak{m}_1, \mathfrak{m}_2, \ldots$, we cannot generally form $\bigcup_{n \in \mathbb{N}} \mathfrak{m}_n$, as the naive formula "$\bigvee_{n \in \mathbb{N}} M_n(x)$" representing their union would have infinite length. We can take the union only if the family is *uniformly represented* by a single formula $M(n, x)$ (expressing that x represents an element of $\mathfrak{m}_n$).

This restriction is a blocking issue for arithmetizing the construction of the chain $\mathfrak{m}_0 \subseteq \mathfrak{m}_1 \subseteq \cdots$ of Sect. 1. Because $\mathfrak{m}_n$ occurs in the definition of $\mathfrak{m}_{n+1}$ in negative position, naive arithmetization results in formulas of unbounded logical complexity, suggesting that a uniform definition might not be possible.

This issue has a counterpart in type-theoretic foundations of mathematics, where the family $(\mathfrak{m}_n)_{n \in \mathbb{N}}$ cannot be given as an inductive family (failing the positivity check), and is also noted, though not resolved, in related work [24, p. 11]. The issue does not arise in the context of PA, where the law of excluded middle allows us to bound the logical complexity: We can blithely define the joint indicator function $g(n, i)$ for the sets G_n (such that $G_n = \{x_i \mid i \in \mathbb{N}, g(n, i) = 1\}$) of Remark 1.9 by the recursion

$$g(0, i) = 0$$

$$g(n + 1, i) = \begin{cases} 1, & \text{if } g(n, i) = 1 \lor (i = n \land 1 \notin (g(n, 0)x_0, \ldots, g(n, n - 1)x_{n-1}, x_n)) \\ 0, & \text{else.} \end{cases}$$

This recursion can be carried out within PA since the recursive step only references the finitely many values $g(n,0), \ldots, g(n,i)$. Heyting arithmetic, however, does not support this case distinction. The formalization of the construction in HA is only unlocked by the following direct characterization.

Lemma 3.1 *(In the situation of Remark 1.9). For every finite binary sequence* $v = [v_0, \ldots, v_{n-1}]$, *set* $\mathfrak{a}_v := (v_0 x_0, \ldots, v_{n-1} x_{n-1}, x_n)$. *Then:*

1. *For every such sequence* $v = [v_0, \ldots, v_{n-1}]$, *if* $\bigwedge_{i=0}^{n-1} (v_i = 1 \Leftrightarrow 1 \notin \mathfrak{a}_{[v_0, \ldots, v_{i-1}]})$, *then* $\mathfrak{a}_v = (G_n) + (x_n)$. *In particular, in this case* $x_n \in G$ *if and only if* $1 \notin \mathfrak{a}_v$.
2. *For every natural number* $n \in \mathbb{N}$,

$$x_n \in G \quad \Longleftrightarrow \quad \neg \exists v \in \{0,1\}^n. \, 1 \in \mathfrak{a}_v \wedge \bigwedge_{i=0}^{n-1} (v_i = 1 \Leftrightarrow 1 \notin \mathfrak{a}_{[v_0, \ldots, v_{i-1}]}).$$

Proof. The first part is by induction, employing the equivalences of Remark 1.9. The second rests on the tautology $\neg \alpha \Longleftrightarrow \neg(\alpha \wedge (\varphi \vee \neg\varphi))$:

$$x_n \in G \Longleftrightarrow \neg(1 \in (G_n) + (x_n)) \Longleftrightarrow \neg\Big(1 \in (G_n) + (x_n) \wedge \bigwedge_{i=0}^{n-1} (x_i \in G \vee x_i \notin G)\Big)$$

$$\Longleftrightarrow \neg \exists v \in \{0,1\}^n. \, \Big(1 \in (G_n) + (x_n) \wedge \bigwedge_{i=0}^{n-1} (v_i = 1 \Leftrightarrow x_i \in G)\Big)$$

$$\Longleftrightarrow \neg \exists v \in \{0,1\}^n. \, \Big(1 \in \mathfrak{a}_v \wedge \bigwedge_{i=0}^{n-1} (v_i = 1 \Leftrightarrow 1 \notin \mathfrak{a}_{[v_0, \ldots, v_{i-1}]})\Big)$$

Condition (2) is manifestly formalizable in arithmetic, uniformly in n.

4   For General Rings

The construction in Sect. 1 of a maximal ideal applies to countable rings. In absence of the axiom of choice, some restriction on the rings is required, as it is well-known that the statement that any nontrivial ring has a maximal ideal implies (over Zermelo–Fraenkel set theory ZF) the axiom of choice [3, 19, 25, 26, 58].

However, this limitation only pertains to the abstract existence of maximal ideals, not to concrete consequences of their existence. Mathematical logic teaches us by way of diverse examples to not conflate these two concerns. For instance, although ZF does not prove the axiom of choice, it does prove every theorem of ZFC pertaining only to natural numbers (by interpreting a given ZFC-proof in the constructible universe L and exploiting that the natural numbers are absolute between V and L [22, 49]); similarly, although intuitionistic Zermelo–Fraenkel set theory IZF does not prove the law of excluded middle, it does prove every Π_2^0-theorem of ZF (by the double negation translation combined with Friedman's continuation trick [20]). A similar phenomenon concerns countability, as follows.

A Metatheorem by Joyal and Tierney. Set theory teaches us that whether a given set is countable depends not only on the set itself, but is more aptly regarded as a property of the ambient universe [23]: Given any set M, there is a (non-Boolean) extension of the universe in which M becomes countable. Remarkably, the passage to such an extension preserves and reflects first-order logic. Hence we have the metatheorem that *countability assumptions from intuitionistic proofs of first-order statements can always be mechanically eliminated.*[4] Crucially, the first-order restriction is only on the form of the statements, not on the form of the proofs. These may freely employ higher-order constructs.

"First-order" statements are statements which only refer to elements, not to subsets; for instance, the statements of Proposition 2.3 are first-order and hence also hold without the countability assumption. In contrast, the statement "there is a maximal ideal" is a higher-order statement; hence we cannot eliminate countability assumptions from proofs of this statement.

The metatheorem expands the applicability of the construction of Sect. 1 and underscores the value of its intuitionistic analysis—the metatheorem cannot be applied to eliminate countability assumptions from classical proofs. Taken together, they strengthen the view of maximal ideals as convenient fictions [54, Sect. 1]. Maximal ideals can carry out their work by any of the following possibilities: (1) For countable (or well-founded) rings, no help is required. Section 1 presents an explicit construction of a maximal ideal. (2) For arbitrary rings, the existence of a maximal ideal follows from the axiom of choice. (3) Intuitionistic first-order consequences of the existence of a maximal ideal are true even if no actual maximal ideal can be constructed.

Comparison with Dynamical Algebra. The dynamical approach [34, Sect. XV.6], [15,18,69] is another technique for constructively reinterpreting, without countability assumptions, classical proofs involving maximal ideals. We sketch here how the dynamical approach is intimately connected with the technique of this section, even though it is cast in entirely different language.

---

[4] For every set M, there is a certain locale X (the *classifying locale of enumerations of M*) which is overt, positive and such that its constant sheaf $\underline{M}$ is countable in the sense of the internal language of the topos of sheaves over X. A given intuitionistic proof can then be interpreted in this topos [13,35,59]; since the constant sheaf functor preserves first-order logic (by overtness), the sheaf $\underline{M}$ inherits any first-order assumptions about M required by the proof; and since it also reflects first-order logic (by overtness and positivity), the proof's conclusion descends to M.

When we apply the construction of Sect. 1 internally in this topos, the result will be a certain sheaf of ideals; it is in that sense that every ring constructively possesses a maximal ideal. This sheaf will not be constant, hence not originate from an actual ideal of the given ring; but first-order consequences of the existence of this sheaf of ideals pass down to the ring. Details are provided by Joyal and Tierney [31, pp. 36f.], and introductions to pointfree topology and topos theory can be found in [10,30,63,64]. A predicative account on the basis of [16,36,65] is also possible. The phenomenon that size is relative also emerges in the Löwenheim–Skolem theorem.

Suppose that a given classical proof appeals to the maximality condition "$x \in \mathfrak{m}$ or $1 \in \mathfrak{m} + (x)$" ("x is zero modulo $\mathfrak{m}$ or invertible modulo $\mathfrak{m}$") only for a finite number $x_0, \ldots, x_{n-1}$ of ring elements fixed beforehand. In this case we can, even if no enumeration of all elements of A exists or is available, apply the construction in Sect. 1 to this finite enumeration and use the resulting ideal $\mathfrak{m}_n$ as a partial substitute for an intangible maximal ideal.

The tools from pointfree topology driving Joyal and Tierney's metatheorem widen the applicability of this partial substitute to cases where the inspected ring elements are not fixed beforehand, by dynamically growing the partial enumeration as the proof runs its course. If required, a continuation-passing style transform as in Remark 2.6 can upgrade the maximal ideal from only satisfying "$1 \notin \mathfrak{m} + (x)$ implies $x \in \mathfrak{m}$" to satisfying the stronger condition "$x \in \mathfrak{m}$ or $1 \in \mathfrak{m} + (x)$". Unfolding the construction of $\mathfrak{m}$ and the proof of Joyal and Tierney's metatheorem, we arrive at the dynamical method.

Acknowledgments. The present study was carried out within the project "Reducing complexity in algebra, logic, combinatorics – REDCOM" belonging to the program "Ricerca Scientifica di Eccellenza 2018" of the Fondazione Cariverona and GNSAGA of the INdAM (the opinions expressed in this paper are solely those of the authors). Important steps towards this paper were made during the Dagstuhl Seminar 21472 "Geometric Logic, Constructivisation, and Automated Theorem Proving" in November 2021. This paper would not have come to existence without the authors' numerous discussions with Daniel Wessel, and greatly benefited from astute comments of Karim Becher, Nicolas Daans, Kathrin Gimmi, Matthias Hutzler, Lukas Stoll and the three anonymous reviewers.

References

1. Aczel, P., Rathjen, M.: Notes on constructive set theory. Technical report, Institut Mittag-Leffler (2000). Report No. 40
2. Aczel, P., Rathjen, M.: Constructive set theory (2010). Book draft
3. Banaschewski, B.: A new proof that 'Krull implies Zorn'. Math. Log. Quart. **40**(4), 478–480 (1994)
4. Banaschewski, B., Vermeulen, J.: Polynomials and radical ideals. J. Pure Appl. Algebra **113**(3), 219–227 (1996)
5. Barr, M.: Toposes without points. J. Pure Appl. Algebra **5**(3), 265–280 (1974)
6. Bauer, A.: Realizability as the connection between computable and constructive mathematics (2005). http://math.andrej.com/asset/data/c2c.pdf
7. Bauer, A.: Intuitionistic mathematics and realizability in the physical world. In: Zenil, H. (ed.) A Computable Universe. World Scientific Publishing Co. (2012)
8. Bauer, A.: Five stages of accepting constructive mathematics. Bull. AMS **54**, 481–498 (2017)
9. Berardi, S., Valentini, S.: Krivine's intuitionistic proof of classical completeness (for countable languages). Ann. Pure Appl. Log. **129**(1–3), 93–106 (2004)
10. Blechschmidt, I.: Generalized spaces for constructive algebra. In: Mainzer, K., Schuster, P., Schwichtenberg, H. (eds.) Proof and Computation II, pp. 99–187. World Scientific (2021)

11. Bonacina, R., Wessel, D.: Ribenboim's order extension theorem from a constructive point of view. Algebra Universalis **81**(5), 1–6 (2020)
12. Bridges, D., Palmgren, E.: Constructive mathematics. In: Zalta, E. (ed.) The Stanford Encyclopedia of Philosophy. Metaphysics Research Lab (2018)
13. Caramello, O.: Topos-theoretic background (2014)
14. Coquand, T., Lombardi, H.: A logical approach to abstract algebra. Math. Struct. Comput. Sci **16**(5), 885–900 (2006)
15. Coste, M., Lombardi, H., Roy, M.F.: Dynamical method in algebra: effective Nullstellensätze. Ann. Pure Appl. Logic **111**(3), 203–256 (2001)
16. Crosilla, L.: Exploring predicativity. In: Mainzer, K., Schuster, P., Schwichtenberg, H. (eds.) Proof and Computation, pp. 83–108. World Scientific (2018)
17. van Dalen, D.: Logic and Structure. Universitext, Springer, Cham (2004). https://doi.org/10.1007/978-1-4471-4558-5
18. Della Dora, J., Dicrescenzo, C., Duval, D.: About a new method for computing in algebraic number fields. In: Caviness, B.F. (ed.) EUROCAL 1985. LNCS, vol. 204, pp. 289–290. Springer, Heidelberg (1985). https://doi.org/10.1007/3-540-15984-3.279
19. Erné, M.: A primrose path from Krull to Zorn. Comment. Math. Univ. Carolin. **36**(1), 123–126 (1995)
20. Friedman, H.: The consistency of classical set theory relative to a set theory with intuitionistic logic. J. Symbolic Logic **38**, 315–319 (1973)
21. Friedman, H.: Classically and intuitionistically provably recursive functions. In: Müller, G.H., Scott, D.S. (eds.) Higher Set Theory. LNM, vol. 669, pp. 21–27. Springer, Heidelberg (1978). https://doi.org/10.1007/BFb0103100
22. Gödel, K.: The consistency of the axiom of choice and of the generalized continuum-hypothesis. Proc. Natl. Acad. Sci. USA **24**(12), 556–557 (1938)
23. Hamkins, J.: The set-theoretic multiverse. Rev. Symb. Log. **5**, 416–449 (2012)
24. Herbelin, H., Ilik, D.: An analysis of the constructive content of Henkin's proof of Gödel's completeness theorem (draft) (2016)
25. Hodges, W.: Krull implies Zorn. J. Lond. Math. Soc. **19**(2), 285–287 (1979)
26. Howard, P., Rubin, J.: Consequences of the Axiom of Choice. Math. Surveys Monogr., AMS (1998)
27. Hyland, M.: The effective topos. In: Troelstra, A.S., van Dalen, D. (eds.) The L. E. J. Brouwer Centenary Symposium, pp. 165–216. North-Holland (1982)
28. Ishihara, H., Khoussainov, B., Nerode, A.: Decidable Kripke models of intuitionistic theories. Ann. Pure Appl. Logic **93**, 115–123 (1998)
29. Johansson, I.: Der Minimalkalkül, ein reduzierter intuitionistischer Formalismus. Compos. Math. **4**, 119–136 (1937)
30. Johnstone, P.T.: The point of pointless topology. Bull. AMS **8**(1), 41–53 (1983)
31. Joyal, A., Tierney, M.: An extension of the Galois theory of Grothendieck, Mem. AMS, vol. 309. AMS (1984)
32. Krivine, J.L.: Une preuve formelle et intuitionniste du théorème de complétude de la logique classique. Bull. Symb. Logic **2**, 405–421 (1996)
33. Krull, W.: Idealtheorie in Ringen ohne Endlichkeitsbedingung. Math. Ann. **101**, 729–744 (1929)
34. Lombardi, H., Quitté, C.: Commutative Algebra: Constructive Methods. AA, vol. 20. Springer, Dordrecht (2015). https://doi.org/10.1007/978-94-017-9944-7
35. Maietti, M.: Modular correspondence between dependent type theories and categories. Math. Struct. Comput. Sci. **15**(6), 1089–1149 (2005)
36. Maietti, M.: Joyal's arithmetic universes as list-arithmetic pretoposes. Theory Appl. Categ. **23**(3), 39–83 (2010)

37. Mines, R., Richman, F., Ruitenburg, W.: A Course in Constructive Algebra. Universitext, Springer, Cham (1988). https://doi.org/10.1007/978-1-4419-8640-5
38. Murthy, C.R.: Classical proofs as programs: how, what and why. In: Myers, J.P., O'Donnell, M.J. (eds.) Constructivity in CS 1991. LNCS, vol. 613, pp. 71–88. Springer, Heidelberg (1992). https://doi.org/10.1007/BFb0021084
39. van Oosten, J.: Realizability: An Introduction to its Categorical Side. Studies in Logic and the Foundations of Mathematics, vol. 152. Elsevier (2008)
40. Persson, H.: An application of the constructive spectrum of a ring. In: Type Theory and the Integrated Logic of Programs. Chalmers University, University of Gothenburg (1999)
41. Phoa, W.: An introduction to fibrations, topos theory, the effective topos and modest sets. Technical report, University of Edinburgh (1992)
42. Powell, T., Schuster, P., Wiesnet, F.: A universal algorithm for Krull's theorem. Inf. Comput. (2021)
43. Powell, T.: On the computational content of Zorn's lemma. In: LICS 2020, pp. 768–781. ACM (2020)
44. Rathjen, M.: Generalized inductive definitions in constructive set theory. In: Crosilla, L., Schuster, P. (eds.) From Sets and Types to Topology and Analysis: Towards Practicable Foundations for Constructive Mathematics, Oxford Logic Guides, vol. 48, chap. 16. Clarendon Press (2005)
45. Richman, F.: Nontrivial uses of trivial rings. Proc. AMS **103**, 1012–1014 (1988)
46. Rinaldi, D., Schuster, P.: A universal Krull-Lindenbaum theorem. J. Pure Appl. Algebra **220**, 3207–3232 (2016)
47. Rinaldi, D., Schuster, P., Wessel, D.: Eliminating disjunctions by disjunction elimination. Bull. Symb. Logic **23**(2), 181–200 (2017)
48. Rinaldi, D., Schuster, P., Wessel, D.: Eliminating disjunctions by disjunction elimination. Indag. Math. (N.S.) **29**(1), 226–259 (2018)
49. Schoenfield, J.: The problem of predicativity. In: Bar-Hillel, Y., Poznanski, E., Rabin, M., Robinson, A. (eds.) Essays on the Foundations of Mathematics, pp. 132–139. Magnes (1961)
50. Schuster, P.: Induction in algebra: a first case study. In: LICS 2012, pp. 581–585. ACM (2012)
51. Schuster, P.: Induction in algebra: a first case study. Log. Methods Comput. Sci. **9**(3:20), 1–19 (2013)
52. Schuster, P., Wessel, D.: Resolving finite indeterminacy: a definitive constructive universal prime ideal theorem. In: LICS 2020, pp. 820–830. ACM (2020)
53. Schuster, P., Wessel, D.: The computational significance of Hausdorff's maximal chain principle. In: Anselmo, M., Della Vedova, G., Manea, F., Pauly, A. (eds.) CiE 2020. LNCS, vol. 12098, pp. 239–250. Springer, Cham (2020). https://doi.org/10.1007/978-3-030-51466-2.21
54. Schuster, P., Wessel, D.: Syntax for semantics: Krull's maximal ideal theorem. In: Paul Lorenzen – Mathematician and Logician. LEUS, vol. 51, pp. 77–102. Springer, Cham (2021). https://doi.org/10.1007/978-3-030-65824-3.6
55. Schuster, P., Wessel, D.: The Jacobson radical for an inconsistency predicate. Computability (2022, forthcoming)
56. Schuster, P., Wessel, D., Yengui, I.: Dynamic evaluation of integrity and the computational content of Krull's lemma. J. Pure Appl. Algebra **226**(1) (2022)
57. Schuster, P., Wessel, D.: A general extension theorem for directed-complete partial orders. Rep. Math. Logic **53**, 79–96 (2018)
58. Scott, D.: Prime ideal theorems for rings, lattices and Boolean algebras. Bull. AMS **60**, 390 (1954)

59. Shulman, M.: Categorical logic from a categorical point of view (draft for AARMS Summer School 2016) (2016). https://mikeshulman.github.io/catlog/catlog.pdf
60. Simpson, S.: Subsystems of Second Order Arithmetic. Springer, Heidelberg (1999)
61. Suslin, A.: On the structure of the special linear group over polynomial rings. Izv. Akad. Nauk SSSR Ser. Mat. **41**, 235–252 (1977)
62. Tarski, A.: Fundamentale Begriffe der Methodologie der deduktiven Wissenschaften. I. Monatsh. Math. Phys. **37**, 361–404 (1930)
63. Vickers, S.: Locales and toposes as spaces. In: Aiello, M., Pratt-Hartmann, I., van Benthem, J. (eds.) Handbook of Spatial Logics, pp. 429–496. Springer, Heidelberg (2007). https://doi.org/10.1007/978-1-4020-5587-4.8
64. Vickers, S.: Continuity and geometric logic. J. Appl. Log. **12**(1), 14–27 (2014)
65. Vickers, S.: Sketches for arithmetic universes. J. Log. Anal. **11**(FT4), 1–56 (2016)
66. Wessel, D.: Ordering groups constructively. Comm. Alg. **47**(12), 4853–4873 (2019)
67. Wessel, D.: A note on connected reduced rings. J. Comm. Alg. **13**(4), 583–588 (2021)
68. Yengui, I.: Making the use of maximal ideals constructive. Theor. Comput. Sci. **392**, 174–178 (2008)
69. Yengui, I.: Constructive Commutative Algebra. Projective Modules Over Polynomial Rings and Dynamical Gröbner Bases. LNM, vol. 2138. Springer, Cham (2015). https://doi.org/10.1007/978-3-319-19494-3

Programming with Ordinary Differential Equations: Some First Steps Towards a Programming Language

Olivier Bournez[✉]

Ecole Polytechnique, LIX, 91128 Palaiseau Cedex, France
bournez@lix.polytechnique.fr

Abstract. Various open problems have been recently solved using Ordinary Differential Equation (ODE) programming: basically, ODEs are used to implement various algorithms, including simulation over the continuum of discrete models such as Turing machines, or simulation of discrete time algorithms working over continuous variables. Applications include: Characterization of computability and complexity classes using ODEs [1–4]; Proof of the existence of a universal (in the sense of Rubel) ODE [5]; Proof of the strong Turing completeness of biochemical reactions [6], or more generally various statements about the completeness of reachability problems (e.g. PTIME-completeness of bounded reachability) for ODEs [7].

It is rather pleasant to explain how this ODE programming technology can be used in many contexts, as ODEs are in practice a kind of universal language used by many experimental sciences, and how consequently we got to these various applications.

However, when going to say more about proofs, their authors including ourselves, often feel frustrated: Currently, the proofs are mostly based on technical lemmas and constructions done with ODEs, often mixing both the ideas behind these constructions, with numerical analysis considerations about errors and error propagation in the equations. We believe this is one factor hampering a more widespread use of this technology in other contexts.

The current article is born from an attempt to popularize this ODE programming technology to a more general public, and in particular master and even undergraduate students. We show how some constructions can be reformulated using some notations, that can be seen as a pseudo programming language. This provides a way to explain in an easier and modular way the main intuitions behind some of the constructions, focusing on the algorithm design part. We focus here, as an example, on how the proof of the universality of polynomial ODEs (a result due to [8], and fully developed in [2]) can be reformulated and presented.

1 Introduction

It has been understood quite recently that it is possible to program with Ordinary Differential Equations (ODEs). This actually was obtained as a side effect

© The Author(s), under exclusive license to Springer Nature Switzerland AG 2022
U. Berger et al. (Eds.): CiE 2022, LNCS 13359, pp. 39–51, 2022.
https://doi.org/10.1007/978-3-031-08740-0_4

from attempts to relate the computational power of analog computational models to classical computability. Refer to [9–11] for surveys on analog computation with a point of view based on computation theory aspects, or to [12–14] for surveys discussing historical and technological aspects. In particular, several authors revisited the *General Purpose Analog Computer* (GPAC) model of Shannon [15]. Following [16], this model can essentially be abstracted as corresponding to (vectorial) polynomial ordinary differential equations: That is to say, as dynamics over $\mathbb{R}^d$ corresponding to solutions of ODEs of the form $\mathbf{y}' = \mathbf{p}(\mathbf{y})$ where $\mathbf{y}(t) \in \mathbb{R}^d$ is some function of time, and $\mathbf{p} : \mathbb{R}^d \to \mathbb{R}^d$ is (componentwise) polynomial, and d is some integer. If some initial condition is added, this is also called a polynomial Initial Value Problems (pIVP).

We do not intend to repeat here the full story, but in short, two main notions of computations by pIVP have been introduced: the notion of GPAC-generated function, corresponding to the initial notion from Shannon in [15], and the notion of GPAC-computable function. This latter notion of computability is now known to be equivalent to classical computability [17]. It is also possible to talk about complexity theory in such models: It has been established that this is indeed possible, if measuring time of computation as the length of the solution [7]. This has been recently extended to space complexity in [18], or to exponential time and the Grzegorczyk hierarchy [19].

All these statements have been obtained by realizing that continuous time processes defined by ODEs, and even defined by polynomial ODEs, can simulate various discrete time processes. They hence can be used to simulate models such as Turing machines [2,20], and even some more exotic models working with a discrete time but over continuous data. This is based on various refinements of constructions done in [1–4,20]. We call this *ODE programming*, as this is indeed some kind of programing with various continuous constructions.

Forgetting analog machines or models of computation, it is important to realize that ODEs is a kind of universal language of mathematics that is used in many, if not all, experimental sciences: Physics, Biology, Chemistry, …. Consequently, once it is known that one can program with ODEs, many questions asking about universality, or computations, in experimental contexts can be solved. This is exactly what has been done by several authors, including ourselves, to solve various open problems, in various contexts such as applied maths, computer algebra, biocomputing… We do not intend here to be exhaustive about various applications, but we describe some of them.

Some Applications of ODE Programming

– **Implicit complexity: computability** Concepts such as being computable for a function over the reals (in the sense of computable analysis) can be described using ODEs only, i.e., with concepts from analysis only, and no-reference to computational models such as Turing machines.

Theorem 1 ([17]). *Let a and b be computable reals. A function $f : [a, b] \to \mathbb{R}$ is computable in the sense of computable analysis iff there exist some polynomials* *with rational coefficients* $\mathbf{p} : \mathbb{R}^{n+1} \to \mathbb{R}^n$, *some polynomial* $p_0 : \mathbb{R} \to \mathbb{R}$ *with rational coefficients, and* $n - 1$ *computable real values* $\alpha_1, ..., \alpha_{n-1}$ *such that:*

1. $(y_1, ..., y_n)$ *is the solution of the initial value problem*[1] $\mathbf{y}' = \mathbf{p}(\mathbf{y}, t)$ *with initial condition* $(\alpha_1, ..., \alpha_{n-1}, p_0(x))$ *set at time* $t_0 = 0$
2. *There are* $i, j \in \{1, ..., n\}$ *such that* $\lim_{t \to \infty} y_j(t) = 0$ *and* $|f(x) - y_i(t)| \leq y_j(t)$ *for all* $x \in [a, b]$ *and all* $t \in [0, +\infty)$.

Condition 2. basically says that some component, namely y_i is converging over time t toward $f(x)$, with error given by some other component, namely $y_j(t)$.

- **Robust complexity theory for continuous-time systems:** Defining a robust time complexity notion for continuous time systems was a well-known open problem [10], with several attempts, but with no generic solution provided. In short, the difficulty is that the naive idea of using the time variable of the ODE as a measure of "time complexity" is problematic, since time can be arbitrarily contracted in a continuous system due to the "Zeno phenomena". This was solved by establishing that the length of the solutions for pODEs provides a robust complexity, that corresponds to classical complexity [7]. This also provides some implicit characterization of PTIME, and completeness of bounded time reachability.
- **Characterization of other computability and complexity classes:** This has been extended very recently to space complexity, with a characterization of PSPACE in [18], and of EXPTIME in [19], and to the Grzegorczyk hierarchy [4].
- **A universal ordinary differential equation:** Following [21], there exists a fixed non-trivial fourth-order polynomial differential algebraic equation (DAE) $p(y, y', \ldots, y^d) = 0$ such that for any continuous positive function φ on the reals, and for any continuous positive function $\epsilon(t)$, it has a C^∞ solution with $|y(t) - \varphi(t)| < \epsilon(t)$ for all t. The question whether one can require the solution that approximates φ to be the unique solution for a given initial data was a well-known open problem [21, page 2], [22, Conjecture 6.2]. It has been solved using ODE programming.

Theorem 2 ([5], **Universal PIVP**). *There exists a fixed polynomial vector* $\mathbf{p}$ *in d variables with rational coefficients such that for any functions* $f \in C^0(\mathbb{R})$ *and* $\varepsilon \in C^0(\mathbb{R}, \mathbb{R}^{>0})$, *there exists* $\alpha \in \mathbb{R}^d$ *such that there exists a unique solution* $\mathbf{y} : \mathbb{R} \to \mathbb{R}^d$ *to* $\mathbf{y}(0) = \alpha$, $\mathbf{y}' = \mathbf{p}(\mathbf{y})$. *Furthermore, this solution satisfies that* $|y_1(t) - f(t)| \leqslant \varepsilon(t)$ *for all* $t \in \mathbb{R}$.

- **Strong Turing completeness of biochemical reactions:** Ordinary differential equations are a well-used models for modeling the dynamics of the kinetic of reactions, and in particular of biochemical reactions between proteins. Their Turing completeness was an open problem (see e.g. [23, Section 8]) solved in [6] using ODE programming.

---

[1] We suppose that $y(t)$ is defined for all $t \geq 0$. This condition is not necessarily satisfied for all polynomial ODEs, and we restrict our attention only to ODEs satisfying this condition.

However, one difficulty when one wants to present ideas of the proofs, is that currently the proofs are based on technical lemmas and constructions done with ODEs, often mixing both the ideas behind these constructions, with numerical analysis considerations about errors and error propagation in the equations. We believe this is one factor hampering a more widespread use of this technology in other contexts. This is also clearly a difficulty for newcomers in the field.

The current document is a preliminary step towards solving this, by presenting through an example a pseudo-programming language. Actually, this document follows from an attempt to popularize this ODE programming technology to a more general public, and in particular master and even undergraduate students. We show how some constructions can be reformulated using some notations, that can be seen as a pseudo programming language. This provides a way to explain in an easier and modular way the main intuitions behind some of the constructions, focusing on the algorithm design part.

From our experiments, it can be done more generally for all of the constructions of the references above. By lack of space, we only take an example, namely the main result of [8], fully developed in [2], establishing the universality of ODEs. We agree that for experts, this might be, or it is, at the end the same proofs, but we believe, that presented that way, with this pseudo-programming language the intuition is easier to grasp for newcomers. One motivation of popularizing ODE programming is that this may then help to solve other various problems in particular in experimental sciences.

We also believe that this example is good to make our reader feel what ODE programming is at the end, and the kind of techniques that are used in all the mentioned references to establish all these results.

2   Computing with pIVPs

Proving a result such as Theorem 1, is done in one direction by simulating some Turing machine using some pIVP. The purpose in this section is to provide the intuition on how this is indeed possible to do so. We believe this provides a good intuition on how this is possible to program with ODEs, and more generally solve various discrete problems in some continuous way.

Remark 1. The other direction of the theorem, that we will not discuss in this article, is obtained by proving that one can solve the involved ordinary differential equations by some numerical method, and hence a Turing machine. Notice that this is not as obvious as it may seem: All the ordinary differential equations cannot be solved easily (see famous counterexample [24]), and we use the fact that we restrict to some particular (polynomial) ordinary differential equations: See for example [25] for some conditions and methods to guarantee effectivity for more general ordinary differential equations.

Remark 2. Notice that our example of simulation of a Turing machine by an ordinary differential equation may be however misleading, as it may be thought that, as Turing machines are universal for classical computability, this is the end of the story. But, actually some results (e.g. Theorem 2) are obtained by simulating a discrete time model not directly covered by classical computability, as working over continuous variables. Understanding the suitable underlying models is a fascinating question from our point of view, which remains to be fully explored and understood.

2.1   Discrete Time Computations

Encoding a Turing Machine Configuration with a Triplet. Consider without loss of generality some Turing machine M using the ten symbols $0, 1, \ldots, 9$, where $B = 0$ is the blank symbol. Let $\ldots BBBa_{-k}a_{-k+1}\ldots a_{-1}a_0$ $a_1 \ldots a_n BBB \ldots$ denotes the content of the tape of the Turing machine M. In this representation, the head is in front of symbol a_0, and $a_i \in \{1, \ldots, 9\}$ for all i. Suppose that M has m internal states, corresponding to integers 1 to m. Such a configuration C can be encoded by some element $\gamma(C) = (y_1, y_2, q) \in \mathbb{N}^3$, by taking

$$y_1 = a_0 + a_1 10 + \cdots + a_n 10^n,$$
$$y_2 = a_{-1} + a_{-2} 10 + \cdots + a_{-k} 10^{k-1},$$

and where q denotes the internal state of M.

Let $\theta : \mathbb{N}^3 \to \mathbb{N}^3$ be the transition function of M: Function θ maps the encoding $\gamma(C)$ of a configuration C to the encoding $\gamma(C_{next})$ of its successor configuration.

Determining Next Configuration. Next step is to observe that one can construct some function $\boxed{\mathbf{f}} : \mathbb{R}^3 \to \mathbb{R}^3$ that realizes some analytic extension of θ: i.e. that coincides with θ on $\mathbb{N}^3$. To do so, the problems to solve are the following:

1. **Determine the symbol being read.** The symbol a_0 in front of the head of the machine is given by $a_0 = \mod_{10}(y_1)$, where $\mod_{10}(n)$ is the remainder of the division of integer n by 10. Since we want to consider some analytic functions, we can instead consider

$$a_0 = \omega(y_1), \tag{1}$$

where ω is some analytic extension of $\mod_{10}$. For example, it can be taken of the form

$$\omega(x) = a_0 + a_5 \cos(\pi x) + \left(\sum_{j=1}^{4} a_j \cos\left(\frac{j\pi x}{5}\right) + b_j \sin\left(\frac{j\pi x}{5}\right) \right), \tag{2}$$

where $a_0, \ldots, a_4, b_1, \ldots, b_4$ are some (computable) coefficients that can be obtained by solving some system of linear equations: write $\omega(i) = i$, for $i = 0, 1, \ldots, 9$.

2. **Determine the next state.** The function that returns the next state can be defined by a Lagrange interpolation polynomial as follows: Let $y = \omega(y_1) = a_0$ be the symbol being currently read and q the current state. Take

$$q_{next} = \sum_{i=0}^{9} \sum_{j=1}^{m} \left(\prod_{r=0, r \neq i}^{9} \frac{(y-r)}{(i-r)} \right) \left(\prod_{s=1, s \neq j}^{m} \frac{(q-s)}{(j-s)} \right) q_{i,j}, \qquad (3)$$

where $q_{i,j}$ is the state that follows symbol i and state j.

3. **Determine the symbol to be written on the tape.** The symbol to be written, s_{next}, can be obtained by some similar interpolation polynomial.

4. **Determine the direction of the move for the head.** Let h denote the direction of the move of the head, where $h = 0$ denotes a move to the left, $h = 1$ denotes a "no move", and $h = 2$ denotes a move to the right. Then, again, the "next move" h_{next} can be obtained by some interpolation polynomial.

5. **Update the tape contents.** Define functions P_1, P_2, P_3, that provides the tape contents after the head moves left, does not move, or moves right, respectively. Then, the next value of y, denoted by y_1^{next}, can be obtained by

$$y_1^{next} = P_1 \frac{(1-H)(2-H)}{2} + P_2 H(2-H) + P_3 \frac{H(H-1)}{2}, \qquad (4)$$

With $P_1 = 10 \left(y_1 + s_{next} - y \right) + \omega \left(y_2 \right)$, $P_2 = y_1 + s_{next} - y$ and $P_3 = \frac{y_1 - y}{10}$, where $H = h$ is the direction of the move given by previous item, and still $y = \omega(y_1) = a_0$. We can do something similar to get y_2^{next}.

Consequently, it is sufficient to take $\boxed{f}(y_1, y_2, q) = (y_1^{next}, y_2^{next}, q_{next})$. It follows that if one succeeds to repeat in a loop the instruction

$$\mathbf{x} \leftarrow \boxed{f}(\mathbf{x}),$$

where $\leftarrow$ denotes an assignment, that is to say replacing the value of $\mathbf{x}$ by $\boxed{f}(\mathbf{x})$, one will simulate Turing machine M: starting from $\mathbf{x}(0) = \gamma(C_0)$, encoding the initial configuration of the Turing machine M, then $\mathbf{x}(t)$ will be $\gamma(C(t))$, where $C(t)$ is the configuration of the machine at time t.

2.2   Computations with a Continuous Time

Write $instruction_1; instruction_2$ to denote the fact of doing first $instruction_1$ and then $instruction_2$. Actually, if we succeed to repeat in a loop $\mathbf{x}_2 \leftarrow \boxed{f}(\mathbf{x}); \mathbf{x} \leftarrow \mathbf{x}_2$ that would be sufficient: We will do the same, but two times slower, in the sense that starting from $\mathbf{x}(0) = \gamma(C_0)$, then now $\mathbf{x}(2t)$ will be $\gamma(C(t))$. If we want to preserve speed, it would be sufficient to repeat in a loop

$$\mathbf{x}_2 \leftarrow_{1/2} \boxed{f}(\mathbf{x}); \mathbf{x} \leftarrow_{1/2} \mathbf{x}_2 \qquad (5)$$

when $\mathbf{x} \leftarrow_{1/2} \mathbf{y}$ means an assignment done in time $1/2$, i.e. doing $\mathbf{x}(t+\frac{1}{2}) = \mathbf{y}(t)$ if executed at time t. That way, $\mathbf{x}(t)$ will still be $\gamma(C(t))$.

To do so with ODEs, one needs to be able to do this operation $\leftarrow_{1/2}$. A construction, due to Branicky in [20], is based on the following remark: One can construct some ODE that does some assignment, and even this particular assignment. More precisely, if one takes some ODE of the form

$$\mathbf{y}' = c(\mathbf{g} - \mathbf{y})^3 \phi(t), \tag{6}$$

where c is some real constant, one can check by some simple arguments from analysis, that whatever the value of $\mathbf{y}(0)$ is, the solution will converge very fast to $\mathbf{g}$. Even uniformly, in the sense that for any function $\phi(t)$ of positive integral, for any precision $\epsilon > 0$, real constant $c > 0$ can be fixed sufficient big, such that *for any $\mathbf{y}(0)$, it is certain that $\mathbf{y}(\frac{1}{2})$ is at a distance less than ϵ of $\mathbf{g}$*. In other words, looking what is written *in italic like this*, this essentially means *realizing the equivalent of assignment* $\mathbf{y} \leftarrow_{1/2} \mathbf{g}$ (possibly with some error, but less than ϵ).

Remark 3 (Notation). In order to help, we use the following notation: we write $\boxed{\mathbf{y} \leftarrow_{1/2} \mathbf{g}}_\epsilon{}'$ for $c(\mathbf{g} - \mathbf{y})^3 \phi(t)$ with the real constant c associated to that ϵ. Consequently, writing ODE

$$\mathbf{y}' = \boxed{\mathbf{y} \leftarrow_{1/2} \mathbf{g}}_\epsilon{}'$$

is the same as dynamics (6), i.e. some ODE doing $\mathbf{y} \leftarrow_{1/2} \mathbf{g}$ with an error less than ϵ.

The intuition about these notations is that $\boxed{operation}$ is about a function doing some exact operation, whereas $\boxed{operation}$ is about some function that is intending to do something similar, but possibly introducing some errors.

Once we understand this, we can solve our problem: Consider a function $\mathbf{r}$ that does some rounding componentwise, say on every component $r(x) = j$ for $x \in [j - 1/4, j + 1/4]$, for $j \in \mathbb{Z}$. We will use some function $\theta(u)$ that we will also write $\boxed{when\ u \geq 0}$. Observing that $\sin(2\pi t)$ is alternatively positive and negative, and of period 1, we consider dynamic:

$$\begin{cases} \mathbf{x}' = \boxed{when\ -\sin(2\pi t) \geq 0} \cdot \boxed{\mathbf{x} \leftarrow_{1/2} \mathbf{r}(\mathbf{x}_2)}_{1/4}{}' \\ \mathbf{x}_2' = \boxed{when\ \sin(2\pi t) \geq 0} \cdot \boxed{\mathbf{x}_2 \leftarrow_{1/2} \boxed{\mathbf{f}}(\mathbf{r}(\mathbf{x}))}_{1/4}{}' \end{cases} \tag{7}$$

with $\mathbf{x}_1(0) = \mathbf{x}_2(0) = \mathbf{x}_0$.

Written in another way, this is the dynamic:

$$\begin{cases} \mathbf{x}' = c_1 (\mathbf{r}(\mathbf{x}_2) - \mathbf{x})^3 \theta(-\sin(2\pi t)) \\ \mathbf{x}_2' = c_2 (\boxed{\mathbf{f}}(\mathbf{r}(\mathbf{x})) - \mathbf{x}_2)^3 \theta(\sin(2\pi t)) \end{cases} \tag{8}$$

We select the function $\theta(x) = \boxed{when\ x \geq 0}$ so that it is 0 for $x \leq 0$, and positive for $x > 0$ (say x^2 for $x > 0$). The idea is that $\sin(2\pi t)$ is alternatively positive for $t \in [j, j+1/2]$, then negative for $t \in [j+1/2, j]$ when t increases, where t is some integer. Consequently, $\theta(\sin(2\pi t))$ is alternatively positive and null. Consequently, $\mathbf{x}_2'$ alternates between the right hand side of ODE (6) with $\mathbf{g} = \boxed{\mathbf{f}}(\mathbf{r}(\mathbf{x}))$ (for some function ϕ) and exactly 0. In other words, alternatively $\mathbf{x}_2$ evolves in order to do $\mathbf{x}_2 \leftarrow_{1/2} \boxed{\mathbf{f}}(\mathbf{r}(\mathbf{x}))$, then stay fixed, and this process is repeated for ever.

In a symmetric way, $\mathbf{x}'$ alternates between exactly 0 and exactly the right hand side of ODE (6) with $\mathbf{g} = \mathbf{r}(\mathbf{x}_2)$ (for some function ϕ). In other words, $\mathbf{x}$ evolves between instants where it is fixed, and where one does $\mathbf{x} \leftarrow_{1/2} \mathbf{r}(\mathbf{x}_2)$).

Clearly, if one starts from a point $\mathbf{x}_0$ with integer coefficients, and since $\boxed{\mathbf{f}}$ preserves the integers, this will do exactly what intended, that is to say repeat in a loop (5): In order to get this working, it is sufficient to consider $\epsilon < 1/4$ and select c_1 and c_2 sufficiently big, by the property of the ODE (6) above.

Indeed, each time t multiple of $1/2$ is starting to do some assignment of type $\mathbf{y} \leftarrow_{1/2} \mathbf{r}(\mathbf{g})$. Actually, this does not do this exactly: $\mathbf{y}$ is not set to the precise value $\mathbf{r}(\mathbf{g})$ at next multiple of $\frac{1}{2}$, but with these hypotheses, we (by a simple induction) are always in the case where we know that $\mathbf{r}(\mathbf{g})$ has integer coordinates, and since $\epsilon < 1/4$, $\mathbf{r}(\mathbf{y})$ will indeed be the correct integer after time $\frac{1}{2}$. In other words, by recurrence, if we consider $\mathbf{r}(\mathbf{x})$ and $\mathbf{r}(\mathbf{x}_2)$ at some time multiple of $\frac{1}{2}$, this does exactly the same as repeating in a loop (5).

This works perfectly fine, and provides a way to simulate some Turing machine by some ODE, and more generally the iterations of some functions over the integers.

However, we want a stronger property: we want to simulate some Turing machine by some *analytic* dynamic. We know from the theory of analytic functions, that some analytic function that is constant in some interval is necessarily constant. Consequently, our functions θ and $\mathbf{r}$ above cannot be analytic.

The idea is then to replace ideal $\boxed{when\ u \geq 0}$ by $\boxed{when\ u \geq 0}_{\epsilon'}$ that would approximate the first.

2.3 Some Useful Functions to Correct Errors

A function such as $\sigma(x) = x - 0.2\sin(2\pi x)$ is a contraction on the vicinity of integers:

Lemma 1. *Let $n \in \mathbb{Z}$, and let $\epsilon \in [0, 1/2)$. Then there is some contracting factor $\lambda_\epsilon \in (0, 1)$ such that $\forall \delta \in [-\epsilon, \epsilon]$, $|\sigma(n + \delta) - n| < \lambda_\epsilon \delta$.*

This function can be used to do some static error correction. To help readability, we will also write $\boxed{x}$ for $\sigma(x)$. We will also write $\boxed{x}_{[n]}$ for $\sigma^{[n]}(x)$, i.e. n fold composition of function σ. We do so, as when x is close to some integer, these values are basically close to x: Just ignore rounded corners in our notations for intuition.

It is also possible to do some dynamic error correction: We construct a function $\boxed{\hookrightarrow \{0,1\}}$. It takes two arguments, $\bar{a}$ and y, and its value, that we will write $\boxed{\bar{a} \hookrightarrow \{0,1\}}_y$, values a with error at most $1/y$ when $\bar{a}$ is close to a, with $a \in \{0,1\}$ and we have some positive $y > 0$. Formally:

Lemma 2 ([2, Lemma 4.2.5]). *One can create* $\boxed{\hookrightarrow \{0,1\}} : \mathbb{R}^2 \to \mathbb{R}$ *such that for all $y > 0$, and for all $\bar{a} \in \mathbb{R}$, as soon as $|a - \bar{a}| \leq 1/4$ with $a \in \{0,1\}$, then* $\boxed{\bar{a} \hookrightarrow \{0,1\}}_y \in \left] a - \frac{1}{y}, a + \frac{1}{y} \right[$.

Proof. Consider $\boxed{x \hookrightarrow \{0,1\}}_y = \frac{1}{\pi} \arctan(4y(x - 1/2)) + \frac{1}{2}$, and observe that $\left| \frac{\pi}{2} - \arctan x \right| < \frac{1}{x}$ for $x \in (0,\infty)$ and $\left| \frac{\pi}{2} + \arctan x \right| < \frac{1}{|x|}$ for $x \in (-\infty, 0)$.

In $\boxed{x \hookrightarrow \{0,1\}}_y$, the argument x is expected to take essentially only two values. We can construct a version with 3 values, namely 0, 1 and 2.

Lemma 3 ([2, Lemma 4.2.7]). *Fix $\epsilon > 0$. One can create* $\boxed{\hookrightarrow \{0,1,2\}} : \mathbb{R}^2 \to \mathbb{R}$ *such that for all $y \geq 2$, and for all $\bar{a} \in \mathbb{R}$, as soon as $|a - \bar{a}| \leq \epsilon$ with $a \in \{0,1,2\}$, then* $\boxed{\bar{a} \hookrightarrow \{0,1,2\}}_y \in \left] a - \frac{1}{y}, a + \frac{1}{y} \right[$.

Proof. Take $\left(\left(\boxed{x}_{[d+1]} - 1 \right)^2 \hookrightarrow \{0,1\} \right)_{3y} \cdot \left(2 \cdot \boxed{x}_{[d]} / 2 \hookrightarrow \{0,1\} \right)_{3y} - 1 \right) + 1,$
where $d = 0$ if $\epsilon \leq 1/4$ and $d = \lceil -\log(4\epsilon)/\log \lambda_\epsilon \rceil$ otherwise.

2.4   And Hence, How to so with Analytic Functions?

We would like to do some dynamic close to the one of (7), but using only analytic functions. We intend to replace $\phi(t) = \theta(\sin 2\pi t) = \boxed{\text{when } \sin 2\pi t \geq 0}$ in the dynamic $\zeta(t)$, by some analytic function $\zeta : \mathbb{R} \to \mathbb{R}$.

An idea to get such a function is to consider $\zeta_\epsilon(t) = \boxed{\vartheta(t) \hookrightarrow \{0,1\}}_{1/\epsilon}$, with $\vartheta(t) = \frac{1}{2} \left(\sin^2(2\pi t) + \sin(2\pi t) \right)$. Using the notation $\boxed{\text{when } u \geq 0}_{1/\epsilon} = \boxed{u \hookrightarrow \{0,1\}}_{1/\epsilon}$, we can also write $\zeta_\epsilon(t) = \boxed{\text{when } \vartheta(t) \geq 0}_{1/\epsilon}$.

We would then like to replace dynamic (7) by something like

$$\begin{cases} \mathbf{x}' = \boxed{\text{when } \vartheta(-t) \geq 0}_{1/\epsilon} \cdot \boxed{\mathbf{x} \leftarrow_{1/2} \mathbf{r}(x_2)}_\epsilon' \\ x_2' = \boxed{\text{when } \vartheta(t) \geq 0}_{1/\epsilon} \cdot \boxed{x_2 \leftarrow_{1/2} \boxed{\mathbf{f}} (\mathbf{r}(\mathbf{x}))}_\epsilon' \end{cases} \qquad (9)$$

We however still need to get rid of functions $\mathbf{r}(r)$ doing some exact rounding, that cannot be analytic. The ideas is to consider that $\sigma^{[n]}(x) = \boxed{x}_{[n]}$ does the job, if integer n is big enough, and if $\boxed{\mathbf{f}}$ commits an error that remains small and uniform, in the vicinity of integers.

How to Control Errors on f? We basically replace $\boxed{f}$ by some function $\boxed{f}$ that is built exactly with the same ideas, but keeping errors under control.

Theorem 3 ([2, Theorem 4.4.1]). *Let* $\theta : \mathbb{N}^3 \to \mathbb{N}^3$ *be the transition function of some Turing machine. Then, given* $0 \le \epsilon < 1/2$, θ *has some analytic expansion* $\boxed{f} : \mathbb{R}^3 \to \mathbb{R}^3$ *such that*

$$\|(y_1, y_2, q) - (\overline{y}_1, \overline{y}_2, \overline{q})\| \le \kappa \Rightarrow \left\| \theta(y_1, y_2, q) - \boxed{f}(\overline{y}_1, \overline{y}_2, \overline{q}) \right\| \le \epsilon$$

where $(y_1, y_2, q) \in \mathbb{N}^3$ *encodes a configuration of* M.

Proof. To get so, using previous ideas, replace Eq. (1), by $a_0 = \overline{y} = \omega\left(\boxed{\overline{y}_1}_{[l]} \right)$, and the polynomial interpolations such as Eq. (3) to determine the next state, the next symbol and the direction of the move, by the equivalent expression where each variable has been "rounded cornered". For example, instead of (3), write

$$q_{next} = \sum_{i=0}^{9} \sum_{j=1}^{m} \left(\prod_{r=0, r\neq i}^{9} \frac{\left(\boxed{\overline{y}}_{[n]} - r \right)}{(i - r)} \right) \left(\prod_{s=1, s\neq j}^{m} \frac{\left(\boxed{\overline{q}}_{[n]} - s \right)}{(j - s)} \right) q_{i,j},$$

If l and n are chosen sufficiently big, the approximation of the interpolation will be uniform, and as small as desired.

The difficulty is on Eq. (4), since the error is not uniform if this is done in a too naive way. But actually, instead of taking $H = h$, the idea is to take some dynamic approximation sufficiently precise to correct errors.

More concretely: We still intend to define some functions $\overline{P}_1, \overline{P}_2, \overline{P}_3$, which intend to approximate the content of the tapes if the head respectively move left, don't move or move right. Let H some "sufficiently big" approximation of h, still to be determined. Then y_1^{next} can be approximated by

$$\overline{y}_1^{next} = \overline{P}_1 \frac{1}{2}(1 - H)(2 - H) + \overline{P}_2 H(2 - H) + \overline{P}_3 (-\frac{1}{2})H(1 - H), \qquad (10)$$

With $\overline{P}_1 = 10\left(\boxed{\overline{y}_1}_{[j]} + \boxed{\overline{s}_{next}}_{[j]} - \boxed{\overline{y}}_{[j]} \right) + \boxed{\omega\left(\boxed{\overline{y}_2}_{[j]} \right)}_{[j]}$, $\overline{P}_2 = \boxed{\overline{y}_1}_{[j]} + $

$\boxed{\overline{s}_{next}}_{[j]} - \boxed{\overline{y}}_{[j]}$, and $\overline{P}_3 = \dfrac{\boxed{\overline{y}_1}_{[j]} - \boxed{\overline{y}}_{[j]}}{10}$.

This is at the end, once again exactly similar to expressions in (4), but where all variables have been "rounded cornered".

The difficulty is that in that case, $\overline{P}_1$ depends on $\overline{y}_1$, which is not a bounded value. So if we take as before $\overline{H} = h = \overline{h}_{next}$, the error on term $(1 - H)(2 - H)/2$ can be arbitrarily amplified when this term is multiplied by

$\overline{P}_1$. But one can take some error proportional to $\overline{y}_1$. One can then check that $H = \boxed{\overline{h}_3 \hookrightarrow \{0,1,2\}}_{10000(\overline{y}_1+1/2)+2}$ is fine.

Use same arguments on $\overline{P}_2$ and $\overline{P}_3$ to define $|\overline{y}_1^{next} - y_1^{next}| < \epsilon$. And does something similar for the other part of the tape, to define $\overline{y}_2^{next}$ such that $|\overline{y}_2^{next} - y_2^{next}| < \epsilon$.

At the end, consider $\boxed{\mathbf{f}} : \mathbb{R}^3 \to \mathbb{R}^3$ defined by

$$\boxed{\mathbf{f}}(\overline{y}_1, \overline{y}_2, \overline{q}) = (\overline{y}_1^{next}, \overline{y}_2^{next}, \overline{q}_{next}).$$

Coming Back to the Simulation. So at the end, we have replaced the dynamic of (7) by a dynamic of the form:

$$\begin{cases} \mathbf{x}' = \boxed{when\ \vartheta(-t) \geq 0}_{1/\epsilon} \cdot \boxed{\mathbf{x} \leftarrow_{1/2} \boxed{\mathbf{x}_2}_{[n]}}_{\epsilon'}' \\ \mathbf{x}_2' = \boxed{when\ \vartheta(t) \geq 0}_{1/\epsilon} \cdot \boxed{\mathbf{x}_2 \leftarrow_{1/2} \boxed{\mathbf{f}}\left(\boxed{\mathbf{x}}_{[m]}\right)}_{\epsilon'}' \end{cases} \tag{11}$$

with $\boxed{when\ u \geq 0}_{1/\epsilon} = \boxed{u \hookrightarrow \{0,1\}}_{1/\epsilon}$.

We get consequently to some functions that are indeed analytic. It remains to check that each of the parameters n, m, ϵ, ϵ', ... can be fixed sufficiently small so that the dynamic will never leave a vicinity of the dynamic that we intend to simulate. This is basically developing all the previous arguments, without true difficulties, using basic analysis: refer to [2] for details.

2.5 Going to pODEs

The ODE that we obtained is not polynomial: It uses sin, arctan, ... for example. But it can be transformed into some pODE. The idea is that many ODEs can be transformed as such using a simple process: Introduce some variables that are needed, express their derivative in terms of already present variables, using usual relations on derivatives, and repeat this process until it terminates. It terminates in practice very quickly for usual functions.

Maybe an example is more clear than a long and formal discussion. Suppose that you want to program the equation $\begin{cases} y_1' = \sin^2 y_2 \\ y_2' = y_1 \cos y_2 - e^{e^{y_1}+t} \end{cases}$ with the initial condition $y_1(0) = 0$ and $y_2(0) = 0$.

Since y_1' is expressed as the square of the sinus of y_2, and this is not a polynomial, we introduce $y_3 = \sin y_2$, and we write $y_1' = y_3^2$ with $y_3(0) = 0$. Similarly, since $y_1 \cos y_2 - e^{e^{y_1}+t}$ is not polynomial, we introduce $y_4 = \cos y_2$ and $y_5 = e^{e^{y_1}+t}$, and we write $y_2' = y_1 y_4 - y_5$.

We then consider the derivatives of the variables that have been introduced. We compute the derivative of y_3, and we realize that this is $y_2' \cos(y_2)$. We already know y_2', and $\cos(y_2)$ is y_4. We can hence write $y_3' = y_4(y_1 y_4 - y_5)$ that is a polynomial. We now focus on the derivative of y_4 that values $-y_2' \sin(y_2)$, which can be written $y_4' = -y_3(y_1 y_4 - y_5)$. We next go to the derivative of y_5 that writes $y_5' = y_5(y_6 y_3^2 + 1)$ if we introduce $y_6 = e^{y_1}$ to keep it polynomial, writing $y_5(0) = e$. We then go to the derivative of y_6 that values $y_1' e^{y_1} = y_6 y_3^2$ which is polynomial and we write $y_6(0) = 1$.

We have obtained that we can simulate (by just projecting) the previous system by the pIVP

$$
\begin{cases}
y_1' = y_3^2 \\
y_2' = y_1 y_4 - y_5 \\
y_3' = y_4(y_1 y_4 - y_5) \\
y_4' = -y_3(y_1 y_4 - y_5) \\
y_5' = y_5(y_6 y_3^2 + 1) \\
y_6' = y_6 y_3^2
\end{cases}
\quad \text{with } \mathbf{y}(0) = (y_1, \ldots, y_6)(0) = (0, 0, 0, 1, e, 1).
$$

Coming back to previous dynamics (11): Just do the similar process on the analytic dynamic. This will necessarily terminates (from known closure properties established in [2]) and this will provide a pIVP.

Of course not all the ingredients of ODE programming are covered by this example, and we miss constructions such as using change of variables, or mixing results, etc.... by lack of space. But it is however quite representative of ODE programming technology, and of our pseudo programming language.

References

1. Hainry, E.: Modèles de calculs sur les réels. Résultats de Comparaisons. Ph.D. thesis, LORIA, 7 Décembre 2006
2. Graça, D.S.: Computability with polynomial differential equations. Ph.D. thesis, Instituto Superior Técnico (2007)
3. Pouly, A.: Continuous models of computation: from computability to complexity. Ph.D. thesis, Ecole Polytechnique and Unidersidade Do Algarve, Defended on 6 July 2015 (2015). https://pastel.archives-ouvertes.fr/tel-01223284. Prix de Thèse de l'Ecole Polyechnique 2016, Ackermann Award 2017
4. Gozzi, R.: Analog characterization of complexity classes. Ph.D. thesis, Instituto Superior Técnico, Lisbon, Portugal and University of Algarve, Faro, Portugal (2022)
5. Bournez, O., Pouly, A.: A universal ordinary differential equation. Logical Methods Comput. Sci. **16**(1) (2020)
6. Fages, F., Le Guludec, G., Bournez, O., Pouly, A.: Strong turing completeness of continuous chemical reaction networks and compilation of mixed analog-digital programs. In: Feret, J., Koeppl, H. (eds.) CMSB 2017. LNCS, vol. 10545, pp. 108–127. Springer, Cham (2017). https://doi.org/10.1007/978-3-319-67471-1_7
7. Bournez, O., Graça, D.S., Pouly, A.: Polynomial time corresponds to solutions of polynomial ordinary differential equations of polynomial length. J. ACM **64**(6), 38:1–38:76 (2017)
8. Graça, D.S., Campagnolo, M.L., Buescu, J.: Computability with polynomial differential equations. Adv. Appl. Math. **40**(3), 330–349 (2008)

9. Bournez, O., Pouly, A.: A survey on analog models of computation. In: Brattka, V., Hertling, P. (eds.) Handbook of Computability and Complexity in Analysis. TAC, pp. 173–226. Springer, Cham (2021). https://doi.org/10.1007/978-3-030-59234-9_6

10. Bournez, O., Campagnolo, M.L.: New Computational Paradigms. Changing Conceptions of What is Computable, pp. 383–423. Springer, New York (2008)

11. Orponen, P.: A survey of continuous-time computation theory. In: Du, D.Z., Ko, K.I. (eds.) Advances in Algorithms, Languages, and Complexity, pp. 209–224. Kluwer Academic Publishers (1997)

12. Ulmann, B.: Analog and Hybrid Computer Programming. De Gruyter Oldenbourg (2020)

13. Ulmann, B.: Analog Computing. Walter de Gruyter (2013)

14. MacLennan, B.J.: Analog computation. In: Meyers, R. (ed.) Encyclopedia of Complexity and Systems Science, pp. 271–294. Springer, New York (2009). https://doi.org/10.1007/978-0-387-30440-3_19

15. Shannon, C.E.: Mathematical theory of the differential analyser. J. Math. Phys. MIT **20**, 337–354 (1941)

16. Graça, D.S., Costa, J.F.: Analog computers and recursive functions over the reals. J. Complex. **19**(5), 644–664 (2003)

17. Bournez, O., Campagnolo, M.L., Graça, D.S. Hainry, E.: Polynomial differential equations compute all real computable functions on computable compact intervals. J. Complex. **23**(3), 317–335 (2007)

18. Bournez, O., Gozzi, R., Graça, D.S., Pouly, A.: A continuous characterization of PSPACE using polynomial ordinary differential equations (2022)

19. Gozzi, R., Graça, D.S.: Characterizing time computational complexity classes with polynomial differential equations (2022, submitted)

20. Branicky, M.S.: Universal computation and other capabilities of hybrid and continuous dynamical systems. Theor. Comput. Sci. **138**(1), 67–100 (1995)

21. Rubel, L.A.: A universal differential equation. Bull. Am. Math. Soc. **4**(3), 345–349 (1981)

22. Boshernitzan, M.: Universal formulae and universal differential equations. Ann. Math. **124**(2), 273–291 (1986)

23. Cook, M., Soloveichik, D., Winfree, E., Bruck, J.: Programmability of chemical reaction networks. In: Condon, A., Harel, D., Kok, J., Salomaa, A., Winfree, E. (eds.) Algorithmic Bioprocesses, pp. 543–584. Springer, Heidelberg (2009). https://doi.org/10.1007/978-3-540-88869-7_27

24. Pour-El, M.B., Richards, J.I.: A computable ordinary differential equation which possesses no computable solution. Ann. Math. Logic **17**, 61–90 (1979)

25. Collins, P., Graça, D.S.: Effective computability of solutions of ordinary differential equations the thousand monkeys approach. Electron. Notes Theor. Comput. Sci. **221**, 103–114 (2008)

A Game-Theoretic Approach for the Synthesis of Complex Systems

Véronique Bruyère(✉)

UMONS - University of Mons, 20 Place du Parc, 7000 Mons, Belgium
`Veronique.Bruyere@umons.ac.be`

Abstract. In this brief overview, we consider multi-player turn-based infinite-duration games that are played on a finite directed graph and such that each player aims at maximizing a payoff or minimizing a cost. We discuss several solution concepts and present some classical as well as some more recent results, with a focus on reachability objectives for the players.

Keywords: Computer-aided synthesis · Games played on graphs · Solution concepts

1 Introduction

Game theory is a well-developed branch of mathematics with applications to various domains like economics, biology, computer science, etc. It is the study of mathematical models of interaction and conflict between individuals and the understanding of their decisions assuming that they act rationally [44,45]. The last decades have seen a lot of research in *computer-aided synthesis* by using a game-theoretic approach. One important line of research is concerned with *reactive systems* that must continuously react to the events produced by the environment in which they evolve (daily life examples are engine control units in automotive industry, plane autopilots, medical devices, etc.). A challenging goal, called *synthesis*, is to propose techniques (models, algorithms and tools) that, given a specification for a system and a model of its environment, compute (synthesize) a *controller* of the system that enforces the specification no matter how the environment behaves. To this end, researchers have advocated the use of *two-player games played on a graph*: the vertices of the graph model the possible configurations, the system and the environment are the two players whose objectives are *antagonistic*, the infinite paths in the graph model their continuous interactions. Building a controller for the system reduces to computing a *winning strategy* in the corresponding game (if one exists) [34]. A case study

Partially supported by the PDR project *Subgame perfection in graph games* (F.R.S.-FNRS).

of synthesis is presented in [46] where it is explained how an automated lawn-mower can be controlled in a way to satisfy some qualitative and quantitative requirements when its environment is composed of the weather and a cat in the garden.

In practical situations, neither the system nor the environment are mono-lithic, and their objectives are not necessarily antagonistic: they are composed of several parts whose individual objectives must all be taken into account. For those more complex situations, it is advocated to use the model of *multi-player non-zero-sum games played on graphs*: the components are the different players, each of them aiming at satisfying their own objective. The synthesis problem is then different: winning strategies are no longer appropriate and are replaced by the concept of *equilibrium* [35]. An equilibrium models a *rational behavior* of the players: it can be seen as a contract (strategy profile) between the players that makes each player satisfied with respect to his objective and discourages him to break this contract. Different kinds of equilibria have been studied including the famous notions of *Nash equilibrium* (NE) [43] from game theory or of *subgame perfect equilibrium* (SPE) [47] more adapted to games played on graphs.

In the first part of this brief survey, we focus on the *threshold synthesis problem*: does there exist an equilibrium such that each player receives a payoff greater than a given threshold with respect to his own objective? This prob-lem is rather well understood for NEs and for classical objectives like ω-regular objectives (like avoiding a deadlock or always granting a request) or quantita-tive objectives (such as minimizing the energy consumption or guaranteeing a limited response time to a request) [17,35]. SPEs are more complex objects to study, elegant results have been recently obtained about the threshold synthesis problem for SPEs [11,12,14] but some questions remain unsolved.

In the second part of this survey, we present some interesting refinements of reactive systems proposed in the literature that avoid modeling the environment as a player with an antagonistic objective. One such refinement [31,39] mod-els the environment as several players that rationally behave by settling to an equilibrium. Two scenarios are investigated. Either the environment *cooperates* with the system, i.e., it agrees to play an equilibrium that is satisfactory for the system. Or it is *adversarial*: the environment can follow any equilibrium, and one has to synthesize a strategy for the system that is satisfactory against all these equilibria. Another refinement has been recently proposed in [20]: the environment is modeled as a single player that has several objectives. Given a strategy of the system, rationality of the environment is modeled by the fact that it only responds to this strategy in such a way to get a *Pareto-optimal* tuple of payoffs with respect to its objectives. The goal is to synthetize a strategy for the system that guarantees it to obtain a satisfactory payoff, whatever the response of the environment which ensures it a Pareto-optimal tuple of payoffs.

This survey gives a brief overview of a game-theoretic approach to computer-aided synthesis of complex systems, with a focus on results about (quantitative) reachability objectives. It is inspired by the more detailed survey [18]. The reader is referred to [7,17,35] for additional readings.

2 Games Played on Graphs

We consider multi-player turn-based games played on a finite directed graph [35]. An *arena* is a tuple $A = (\Pi, V, (V_i)_{i \in \Pi}, E, v_0)$ where Π is a finite set of *players*, V is a finite set of *vertices* and $E \subseteq V \times V$ is a set of *edges*[1], $(V_i)_{i \in \Pi}$ is a partition of V where V_i is the set of vertices controlled by player $i \in \Pi$, and v_0 is an initial vertex. A *play* is an infinite sequence $\rho = \rho_0 \rho_1 \ldots \rho_k \ldots$ of vertices such that $\rho_0 = v_0$ and $(\rho_k, \rho_{k+1}) \in E$ for all $k \in \mathbb{N}$. *Histories* are finite sequences defined in the same way. The set of plays is denoted by *Plays* and the set of histories (resp. histories ending with a vertex in V_i) by *Hist* (resp. by $Hist_i$).

Definition 1 (Game). *A game $G = (A, (\mathsf{pay}_i)_{i \in \Pi})$ is composed of an arena A and* payoff functions $\mathsf{pay}_i : Plays \to \mathbb{R}$, $i \in \Pi$, *that assign a* payoff *to every play.*

Player i prefers play ρ to play ρ' if $\mathsf{pay}_i(\rho) > \mathsf{pay}_i(\rho')$, that is, he wants to *maximize* his payoff. A particular class of games G are those equipped with *Boolean* functions $\mathsf{pay}_i : Plays \to \{0, 1\}$, $i \in \Pi$, such that a Boolean payoff is assigned to each play. The *objective* $\Omega_i = \{\rho \in Plays \mid \mathsf{pay}_i(\rho) = 1\}$ of player i is composed of his most preferred plays. Classical objectives Ω_i are ω-*regular* ones [34,35]. In this paper we focus on *reachability* objectives: each player i has a target set $U_i \subseteq V$ that he wants to reach, i.e., $\Omega_i = \{\rho = \rho_0 \rho_1 \ldots \in Plays \mid \exists k, \rho_k \in U_i\}$. We refer the reader to [34,35] for other ω-regular objectives like Büchi, co-Büchi, parity, Rabin, Streett, etc.

Other classical payoff functions are *quantitative* functions $\mathsf{pay}_i : Plays \to \mathbb{R}$ defined from a weight function $w_i : E \to \mathbb{Q}$, $i \in \Pi$ [22]. The most studied payoffs assigned to plays are the liminf (or limsup) of the weights seen along the play [22], their mean-payoff or their discounted-sum [29]. In this paper we also focus on *quantitative reachability* objectives: each player i wants to reach his target set U_i as quickly as possible (when counting the number of traversed edges[2]). In this case, it is rather a *cost* that player i wants to minimize (instead of a payoff that he wants to maximize).

A *strategy* $\sigma_i : Hist_i \to V$ for player i assigns to each history $hv \in Hist_i$ a vertex $v' = \sigma_i(hv)$ such that $(v, v') \in E$ [34,35]. Thus $\sigma_i(hv)$ is the next vertex chosen by player i (who controls vertex v, i.e., $v \in V_i$) after history hv has been played. A play ρ is *compatible* with σ_i if $\rho_{k+1} = \sigma_i(\rho_0 \ldots \rho_k)$ for all k with $\rho_k \in V_i$. The simplest strategies are the *memoryless* ones: they only depend on the last vertex of the history, i.e., $\sigma_i(hv) = \sigma_i(h'v)$ for all $hv, h'v \in Hist_i$. A *strategy profile* is a tuple $\sigma = (\sigma_i)_{i \in \Pi}$ of strategies. It determines a unique play $\langle \sigma \rangle$, called the *outcome* of σ, that starts in the initial vertex v_0 and is compatible with all strategies σ_i.

Example 2. Consider the two-player game G in Fig. 1 such that circle (resp. square) vertices are controlled by player 0 (resp. player 1). Both players have a target set: $U_0 = \{v_5, v_7, v_{10}\}$ for player 0 and $U_1 = \{v_7\}$ for player 1. Consider

---

[1] Each vertex has at least one successor in a way to avoid deadlocks.
[2] Function w_i assigns a weight of 1 to each edge.

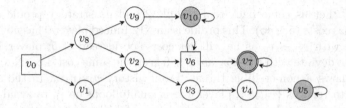

Fig. 1. A two-player game with $U_0 = \{v_5, v_7, v_{10}\}$ and $U_1 = \{v_7\}$.

the play $\rho = v_0 v_1 v_2 v_3 v_4 v_5^\omega$ looping on v_5 that visits U_0 but not U_1. In case of reachability, we thus have $(\mathsf{pay}_0(\rho), \mathsf{pay}_1(\rho)) = (1, 0)$, and in case of quantitative reachability, we have $(\mathsf{pay}_0(\rho), \mathsf{pay}_1(\rho)) = (5, +\infty)$. Consider the memoryless strategy σ_0 (resp. σ_1) such that player 0 plays $v_2 \rightarrow v_3$ and $v_8 \rightarrow v_9$ (resp. player 1 plays $v_0 \rightarrow v_1$ and $v_6 \rightarrow v_6$). The outcome of the strategy profile $\sigma = (\sigma_0, \sigma_1)$ is the play $\langle \sigma \rangle = \rho$.

3   Models of Rationality

Suppose that we have a game $G = (A, (\mathsf{pay}_i)_{i \in \Pi})$ such that each player i plays according to his strategy σ_i. The players are assumed to act *rationally* in pursuit of their preferences. This rationality is modeled as an *equilibrium* seen as a contract (strategy profile) between the players that makes each player satisfied with respect to his payoff function pay_i and discourages him to break this contract. A famous notion of equilibrium is the concept of *Nash equilibrium* (NE) [43] from game theory. Informally, a strategy profile is an NE if no player has an incentive to deviate when the other players stick to their own strategies.

Definition 3 (Nash equilibrium). *A strategy profile* $\sigma = (\sigma_i)_{i \in \Pi}$ *is a* Nash equilibrium *if* $\mathsf{pay}_i(\langle \sigma \rangle) \geq \mathsf{pay}_i(\langle \sigma_i', \sigma_{-i} \rangle)$ *for all players* $i \in \Pi$ *and all strategies* σ_i' *of player* i.

In this definition, σ_{-i} denotes the strategy profile $(\sigma_j)_{j \in \Pi \setminus \{i\}}$ of all players except player i. By using σ_i' instead σ_i, player i is not capable to strictly increase[3] his payoff.

NEs do not take into account the sequential nature of games played on graphs. Indeed after any history, the players face a new situation and may want to change their strategies. It is well-known that NEs suffer from the problem of *non-credible threat* [45]: the existence of NEs may rely on irrational strategies of some players in subgames. Another well-known concept of equilibrium from game theory is the notion the *subgame perfect equilibrium* (SPE) [47] that avoids non-credible threat: a strategy profile is an SPE if it is an NE from each history of the game.

---

[3] "stricly decrease his cost" in case of a cost function pay_i.

Example 4. Let us come back to Example 2 and its strategy profile σ whose outcome has costs $(5, +\infty)$. This profile is an NE. Indeed player 0 has no incentive to deviate with $v_2 \to v_6$ as he will get cost $+\infty$ instead of 5; player 1 has no incentive to deviate with $v_0 \to v_8$ as he will keep the same cost $+\infty$. Nevertheless this NE shows a non-credible threat. From history $v_0 v_1 v_2 v_6$, in the subgame restricted to vertices $\{v_6, v_7\}$, player 1 irrationally loops on v_6 to avoid player 0 from deviating in v_2. It would be more rational for player 1 to play $v_6 \to v_7$.

As a game may have several equilibria, it is natural to ask whether there exists one that fulfils certain requirements, like the following ones [17, 35].

Problem 5 (Threshold synthesis problem). Let G be a game and $\mu_i \in \mathbb{Q}$ be a threshold for each $i \in \Pi$. The *threshold synthesis (TS) problem* is to decide whether there exists an equilibrium $\sigma = (\sigma_i)_{i \in \Pi}$ such that $\mu_i \leq \mathsf{pay}_i(\langle \sigma \rangle)$ for all players $i \in \Pi$.

Notice that when the given bounds impose no constraint (for instance $\mu_i = 0$, $i \in \Pi$, in case of Boolean payoff functions), the decision problem can be rephrased as the *existence synthesis problem*: "decide whether there exists an equilibrium". For certain classes of games and equilibrium concepts, this problem does not need to be solved because there always exists an equilibrium for those games.

Theorem 6. *For games with (quantitative) reachability objectives,*

- *there always exists an NE (resp. SPE) [25, 33, 38, 49].*
- *the TS problem is NP-complete for NEs [15, 26] and PSpace-complete for SPEs [13, 14].*

NEs are rather well understood. There always exists an NE in all games with ω-regular objectives[4] [25, 35] and in a large class of games with quantitative payoff functions including mean-payoff and discounted-sum functions [16]. The TS problem is solved in [26, 50] for different types of ω-regular objectives. The exact complexity class for Rabin objectives is left open. The TS problem is solved in [51] for games with mean-payoff functions but is open for discounted-sum functions. The latter case is related to the challenging open *target discounted-sum problem* itself related to several open questions in mathematics and computer science [6]. For most of those results, the same general approach can be used that works as follows (see e.g. [17]). Under some general hypothesis, the plays that are NE outcomes can be *characterized* thanks to certain properties of the $n = |\Pi|$ two-player zero-sum games where one player (among the n players) is opposed to the coalition of the other players. From this characterization, it follows that there always exists an NE and that the TS problem is decidable (with known complexity class).

Whereas NEs are much studied, SPEs have received less attention and some questions are still unsolved. There always exists an SPE in games with ω-regular

---

[4] This result holds for the larger class of games with Borel Boolean objectives.

objectives [35]. It is only recently that the TS problem has been proved NP-complete for parity objectives [12] and for mean-payoff functions [11]. This problem is again related to the target discounted-sum problem for discounted-sum functions. The recent results [11,12,14] rely on a new adequate characterization of SPE outcomes more intricate than the one for NEs (see also [32]).

The TS problem for NEs and SPEs is in 3ExpTime for objectives specified by *LTL formulas* [31]. This upper bound is obtained thanks to another approach: the existence of an equilibrium satisfying the threshold is encoded into a *strategy logic* formula [24,42]. Recently, the TS problem for NEs and LTL objectives has been proved to be 2ExpTime-complete [40] by using *tree automata* techniques. Tree automata [41] allow to describe strategy profiles that are solution to the TS problem, and testing existence of a solution then reduces to tree automata non-emptiness.

Other models of rationality have been investigated. NEs capture rational behaviors when the players only care about their own payoff. The notion of *secure equilibrium* is introduced in [23] such that the players also care about the payoff of the other players. The existence of secure equilibria and the related TS problem are studied in [19,23,27]. A variant of secure equilibrium, called *Doomsday equilibrium*, is studied in [21] for games with ω-regular objectives. SPEs are immune of the problem of non-credible threats. Another concept that avoids this problem is studied in [5,28] with the concept of *admissible* strategies which are strategies not dominated by any other strategies. The algorithmic synthesis properties of this concept are studied in [4,8–10].

4   Rational Environments

In the traditional approach to *synthesis of reactive systems*, the environment is modeled by one player whose only objective is to conspire to fail the system. However, in real life, the environment can be composed of several players having objectives of their own other than to be antagonistic to the objective of the system. We here present another concept more adequate for the synthesis of reactive systems: *Stackelberg games* [48]. Those games have a specific player called the *leader* modeling the system, the other players being called *followers* and modeling the environment. The leader starts by announcing his strategy and the followers respond by playing rationally given that strategy. In case of *one* follower, his strategy can be an optimal response with respect to his own objective; in case of *several* followers, they can respond with a strategy profile that is an NE. The goal of the leader is to announce a strategy that guarantees him a payoff at least equal to some given threshold whatever the rational response of the follower(s).

We begin with the case of *several followers*, one per component of the environment. Rationality is modeled by assuming that the environment settles to an NE: each component is seen as an independent selfish individual [31,36,39].

Definition 7 (σ_0-Stackelberg profile). *Let G be a game with a specific player $0 \in \Pi$. Let σ_0 be a strategy for player 0. A σ_0-Stackelberg profile (σ_0-SP)* *is a strategy profile* $\sigma = (\sigma_0, (\sigma_i)_{i \in \Pi \setminus \{0\}})$ *such that* $\mathsf{pay}_i(\langle \sigma \rangle) \geq \mathsf{pay}_i(\langle \sigma_i', \sigma_{-i} \rangle)$ *for all players* $i \in \Pi \setminus \{0\}$ *and all strategies* σ_i' *of player* i.

In this definition, the strategy σ_0 of the leader is fixed, only deviating strategies σ_i' of the followers, i.e., with $i \neq 0$, are considered. Two variants of the TS problem are proposed in the context of Stackelberg games.

Problem 8 (Cooperative/adversarial TS problem). Let G be a game and $\mu \in \mathbb{Q}$ be a threshold.

- The *cooperative TS problem* is to decide whether there exists a strategy σ_0 for player 0 and a σ_0-SP σ such that $\mu \leq \mathsf{pay}_0(\langle \sigma \rangle)$.
- The *adversarial TS problem* is to decide whether there exists a strategy σ_0 for player 0 such that for all σ_0-SP σ, we have $\mu \leq \mathsf{pay}_0(\langle \sigma \rangle)$.

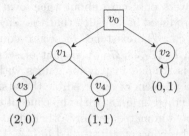

Fig. 2. A cooperative or adversarial follower.

Example 9. Consider the two-player game G in Fig. 2 such that the payoffs are indicated below each of the three plays. The leader is the player that controls the circle vertices and the (unique) follower is the other player. Suppose that the leader announces to play $v_1 \rightarrow v_4$. The follower has two possible responses that are NEs: he can either play $v_0 \rightarrow v_1$ or $v_0 \rightarrow v_2$. A cooperative follower will play $v_0 \rightarrow v_1$ that maximizes the payoff (equal to 1) of the leader. An adversarial follower will play $v_0 \rightarrow v_2$ such that the leader only gets a payoff of 0.

Every NE is a σ_0-SP. However, a solution to the cooperative TS problem is not necessarily an NE [36]. In case of Boolean payoff functions, the cooperative/adversarial TS problem is interesting only with the threshold μ equal to 1: we ask for the objective Ω_0 of the leader to be satisfied. In this case a σ_0-SP is an NE and the cooperative TS problem corresponds to the TS problem studied for NEs in Sect. 3. In case of quantitative payoff functions, the cooperative TS problem is studied in [36] for mean-payoff functions and in [30,37] for discounted-sum functions. We have the following result for the adversarial TS problem for reachability objectives.

Theorem 10 ([26]). *For games with reachability objectives, the adversarial TS problem is PSpace-complete.*

Other types of ω-regular objectives are considered in [26], the exact complexity class being left open in certain cases. The adversarial TS problem is studied in [3,30] for two-player games with mean-payoff functions. An example of a game is given in [30] such that the (unique) follower has no NE to respond to the strategy announced by the leader. Hence two notions of ϵ-best responses are proposed and studied in [3,30]. Only preliminary results are thus known; the cooperative/adversarial TS problem needs to be further investigated and extended to other kinds of equilibria. Another interesting line of research is surveyed in [1] (see references therein): it is focused on *rational verification* (instead of synthesis) seen as a refinement of *model-checking*. The model-checking problem [2] asks whether all paths in a graph satisfy some property (e.g., modeled by an LTL formula). It is proposed in [1] to limit this check to paths that are rational behaviors of multiple players, i.e., to NE outcomes. The obtained results concern NEs and objectives specified by LTL formulas. It would be interesting to investigate other types of equilibria and objectives.

We now consider the case of only *one follower* modeling the environment, however, with *several payoff functions*, one function for each component of the environment. Assume the leader has announced his strategy σ_0. After responding to σ_0 with his own strategy, the follower receives a tuple of payoffs in the corresponding outcome. Rationality of the follower is encoded by the fact that he only responds in a way to receive a *Pareto-optimal* tuple of payoffs. This setting encompasses scenarios where, for instance, several components can collaborate and agree on trade-offs. The goal of the leader is to announce a strategy that guarantees his own payoff to be larger than a given threshold, whatever the rational response of the follower [20]. Formally, we consider two-player games such that player 0 is the leader with one payoff function pay_0 and player 1 is the follower with several payoff functions $(\mathsf{pay}_i)_{i \in \{1,\dots,n\}}$. We denote by $\leq$ the component-wise partial order on the set of n-tuples of payoffs received by player 1. Given a strategy σ_0 for player 0, P_{σ_0} denotes the set of n-tuples of payoffs (for player 1) of plays compatible with σ_0 that are *Pareto-optimal* with respect to $\leq$.

Example 11. We come back to the example of Fig. 1 (thus with a single objective for player 1). Assume player 0 announces the strategy σ_0 such that $v_2 \rightarrow v_6$ and $v_8 \rightarrow v_9$. There are three compatible plays with σ_0: $v_0 v_8 v_9 v_{10}^\omega$, $v_0 v_1 v_2 v_6^\omega$ and $v_0 v_1 v_2 v_6 v_7^\omega$ with respective Boolean payoff for player 1: 0, 0, and 1. Player 1 will rationally only respond with the last play since $P_{\sigma_0} = \{1\}$.

We say that P_{σ_0} is *achievable* if it is not empty and for each $p \in P_{\sigma_0}$, there exists a play ρ compatible with σ_0 such that $p = (\mathsf{pay}_i(\rho))_{i \in \{1,\dots,n\}}$. Finite-range payoff functions (thus in particular Boolean payoff functions) always yield an achievable set P_{σ_0}. However, for games with mean-payoff functions, the set P_{σ_0} may be empty [30]. For games with Boolean payoff functions, the following Pareto-optimal TS problem is introduced and studied in [20].

Problem 12 (Pareto-optimal TS problem). Let G be a game with Boolean payoff functions and let $\mu \in \mathbb{Q}$ be a threshold. The *Pareto-optimal TS problem* is to decide whether there exists a strategy σ_0 for player 0 such that for all strategies σ_1 for player 1 such that $(\mathsf{pay}_i(\rho))_{i\in\{1,\dots,n\}} \in P_{\sigma_0}$ with $\rho = \langle(\sigma_0,\sigma_1)\rangle$, we have $\mu \leq \mathsf{pay}_0(\rho)$.

Theorem 13 ([20]). *For games with reachability objectives, the Pareto-optimal TS problem (with threshold $\mu = 1$) is NExpTime-complete.*

Few results are known about the Pareto-optimal TS problem (parity objectives are studied in [20]). For quantitative payoff functions, as the set P_{σ_0} may be empty, adequate variants of this problem need to be introduced and further studied.

References

1. Abate, A., et al.: Rational verification: game-theoretic verification of multi-agent systems. Appl. Intell. **51**(9), 6569–6584 (2021). https://doi.org/10.1007/s10489-021-02658-y
2. Baier, C., Katoen, J.: Principles of Model Checking. MIT Press, Cambridge (2008)
3. Balachander, M., Guha, S., Raskin, J.-F.: Fragility and robustness in mean-payoff adversarial Stackelberg games. In: Proceedings of CONCUR 2021. LIPIcs, vol. 203, pp. 9:1–9:17. Schloss Dagstuhl - Leibniz-Zentrum für Informatik (2021). https://doi.org/10.4230/LIPIcs.CONCUR.2021.9
4. Basset, N., Geeraerts, G., Raskin, J.-F., Sankur, O.: Admissiblity in concurrent games. In: Proceedings of ICALP 2017. LIPIcs, vol. 80, pp. 123:1–123:14. Schloss Dagstuhl - Leibniz-Zentrum für Informatik (2017). https://doi.org/10.4230/LIPIcs.ICALP.2017.123
5. Berwanger, D.: Admissibility in infinite games. In: Thomas, W., Weil, P. (eds.) STACS 2007. LNCS, vol. 4393, pp. 188–199. Springer, Heidelberg (2007). https://doi.org/10.1007/978-3-540-70918-3_17
6. Boker, U., Henzinger, T.A., Otop, J.: The target discounted-sum problem. In: Proceedings of LICS 2015, pp. 750–761. IEEE Computer Society (2015). https://doi.org/10.1109/LICS.2015.74
7. Brenguier, R., et al.: Non-zero sum games for reactive synthesis. In: Dediu, A.-H., Janoušek, J., Martín-Vide, C., Truthe, B. (eds.) LATA 2016. LNCS, vol. 9618, pp. 3–23. Springer, Cham (2016). https://doi.org/10.1007/978-3-319-30000-9_1
8. Brenguier, R., Pérez, G.A., Raskin, J.-F., Sankur, O.: Admissibility in quantitative graph games. In: Proceedings of FSTTCS 2016. LIPIcs, vol. 65, pp. 42:1–42:14. Schloss Dagstuhl - Leibniz-Zentrum für Informatik (2016). https://doi.org/10.4230/LIPIcs.FSTTCS.2016.42
9. Brenguier, R., Raskin, J.-F., Sankur, O.: Assume-admissible synthesis. Acta Inform. **54**(1), 41–83 (2016). https://doi.org/10.1007/s00236-016-0273-2
10. Brenguier, R., Raskin, J.-F., Sassolas, M.: The complexity of admissibility in omega-regular games. In: Proceedings of CSL-LICS 2014, pp. 23:1–23:10. ACM (2014).https://doi.org/10.1145/2603088.2603143
11. Brice, L., Raskin, J.-F., van den Bogaard, M.: Subgame-perfect equilibria in mean-payoff games. In: Proceedings of CONCUR 2021. LIPIcs, vol. 203, pp. 8:1–8:17. Schloss Dagstuhl - Leibniz-Zentrum für Informatik (2021). https://doi.org/10.4230/LIPIcs.CONCUR.2021.8

12. Brice, L., Raskin, J.-F., van den Bogaard, M.: On the complexity of SPEs in parity games. In: Proceedings of CSL 2022. LIPIcs, vol. 216, pp. 10:1–10:17. Schloss Dagstuhl - Leibniz-Zentrum für Informatik (2022). https://doi.org/10.4230/LIPIcs.CSL.2022.10

13. Brihaye, T., Bruyère, V., Goeminne, A., Raskin, J.-F.: Constrained existence problem for weak subgame perfect equilibria with ω-regular boolean objectives. In: Proceedings of GandALF 2018. EPTCS, vol. 277, pp. 16–29 (2018). https://doi.org/10.4204/EPTCS.277.2

14. Brihaye, T., Bruyère, V., Goeminne, A., Raskin, J.-F., van den Bogaard, M.: The complexity of subgame perfect equilibria in quantitative reachability games. Log. Methods Comput. Sci. **16**(4) (2020). https://lmcs.episciences.org/6883

15. Brihaye, T., Bruyère, V., Goeminne, A., Thomasset, N.: On relevant equilibria in reachability games. In: Filiot, E., Jungers, R., Potapov, I. (eds.) RP 2019. LNCS, vol. 11674, pp. 48–62. Springer, Cham (2019). https://doi.org/10.1007/978-3-030-30806-3_5

16. Brihaye, T., De Pril, J., Schewe, S.: Multiplayer cost games with simple nash equilibria. In: Artemov, S., Nerode, A. (eds.) LFCS 2013. LNCS, vol. 7734, pp. 59–73. Springer, Heidelberg (2013). https://doi.org/10.1007/978-3-642-35722-0_5

17. Bruyère, V.: Computer aided synthesis: a game-theoretic approach. In: Charlier, É., Leroy, J., Rigo, M. (eds.) DLT 2017. LNCS, vol. 10396, pp. 3–35. Springer, Cham (2017). https://doi.org/10.1007/978-3-319-62809-7_1

18. Bruyère, V.: Synthesis of equilibria in infinite-duration games on graphs. ACM SIGLOG News **8**(2), 4–29 (2021). https://doi.org/10.1145/3467001.3467003

19. Bruyère, V., Meunier, N., Raskin, J.-F.: Secure equilibria in weighted games. In: Proceedings of CSL-LICS 2014, pp. 26:1–26:26. ACM (2014). https://doi.org/10.1145/2603088.2603109

20. Bruyère, V., Raskin, J.-F., Tamines, C.: Stackelberg-Pareto synthesis. In: Proceedings of CONCUR 2021. LIPIcs, vol. 203, pp. 27:1–27:17. Schloss Dagstuhl - Leibniz-Zentrum für Informatik (2021). https://doi.org/10.4230/LIPIcs.CONCUR.2021.27

21. Chatterjee, K., Doyen, L., Filiot, E., Raskin, J.-F.: Doomsday equilibria for omega-regular games. Inf. Comput. **254**, 296–315 (2017). https://doi.org/10.1016/j.ic.2016.10.012

22. Chatterjee, K., Doyen, L., Henzinger, T.A.: Quantitative languages. ACM Trans. Comput. Log. **11**(4), 23:1–23:38 (2010). https://doi.org/10.1145/1805950.1805953

23. Chatterjee, K., Henzinger, T.A., Jurdzinski, M.: Games with secure equilibria. Theor. Comput. Sci. **365**(1–2), 67–82 (2006). https://doi.org/10.1016/j.tcs.2006.07.032

24. Chatterjee, K., Henzinger, T.A., Piterman, N.: Strategy logic. Inf. Comput. **208**(6), 677–693 (2010). https://doi.org/10.1016/j.ic.2009.07.004

25. Chatterjee, K., Majumdar, R., Jurdziński, M.: On Nash equilibria in stochastic games. In: Marcinkowski, J., Tarlecki, A. (eds.) CSL 2004. LNCS, vol. 3210, pp. 26–40. Springer, Heidelberg (2004). https://doi.org/10.1007/978-3-540-30124-0_6

26. Condurache, R., Filiot, E., Gentilini, R., Raskin, J.-F.: The complexity of rational synthesis. In: Proceedings of ICALP 2016. LIPIcs, vol. 55, pp. 121:1–121:15. Schloss Dagstuhl - Leibniz-Zentrum für Informatik (2016). https://doi.org/10.4230/LIPIcs.ICALP.2016.121

27. De Pril, J., Flesch, J., Kuipers, J., Schoenmakers, G., Vrieze, K.: Existence of secure equilibrium in multi-player games with perfect information. In: Csuhaj-Varjú, E., Dietzfelbinger, M., Ésik, Z. (eds.) MFCS 2014. LNCS, vol. 8635, pp. 213–225. Springer, Heidelberg (2014). https://doi.org/10.1007/978-3-662-44465-8_19

28. Faella, M.: Admissible strategies in infinite games over graphs. In: Královič, R., Niwiński, D. (eds.) MFCS 2009. LNCS, vol. 5734, pp. 307–318. Springer, Heidelberg (2009). https://doi.org/10.1007/978-3-642-03816-7_27

29. Filar, J., Vrieze, K.: Competitive Markov Decision Processes. Springer, Heidelberg (1997)

30. Filiot, E., Gentilini, R., Raskin, J.-F.: The adversarial Stackelberg value in quantitative games. In: Proceedings of ICALP 2020. LIPIcs, vol. 168, pp. 127:1–127:18. Schloss Dagstuhl - Leibniz-Zentrum für Informatik (2020). https://doi.org/10.4230/LIPIcs.ICALP.2020.127

31. Fisman, D., Kupferman, O., Lustig, Y.: Rational synthesis. In: Esparza, J., Majumdar, R. (eds.) TACAS 2010. LNCS, vol. 6015, pp. 190–204. Springer, Heidelberg (2010). https://doi.org/10.1007/978-3-642-12002-2_16

32. Flesch, J., Predtetchinski, A.: A characterization of subgame-perfect equilibrium plays in Borel games of perfect information. Math. Oper. Res. **42**(4), 1162–1179 (2017). https://doi.org/10.1287/moor.2016.0843

33. Fudenberg, D., Levine, D.: Subgame-perfect equilibria of finite- and infinite-horizon games. J. Econ. Theory **31**, 251–268 (1983)

34. Grädel, E., Thomas, W., Wilke, T. (eds.): Automata, Logics, and Infinite Games: A Guide to Current Research [Outcome of a Dagstuhl Seminar, February 2001]. Lecture Notes in Computer Science, vol. 2500. Springer, Heidelberg (2002). https://doi.org/10.1007/3-540-36387-4

35. Grädel, E., Ummels, M.: Solution concepts and algorithms for infinite multiplayer games. In: New Perspectives on Games and Interaction, vol. 4, pp. 151–178. Amsterdam University Press (2008)

36. Gupta, A., Schewe, S.: Quantitative verification in rational environments. In: Proceedings of TIME 2014, pp. 123–131. IEEE Computer Society (2014). https://doi.org/10.1109/TIME.2014.9

37. Gupta, A., Schewe, S., Wojtczak, D.: Making the best of limited memory in multiplayer discounted sum games. In: Proceedings of GandALF 2015. EPTCS, vol. 193, pp. 16–30 (2015). https://doi.org/10.4204/EPTCS.193.2

38. Harris, C.: Existence and characterization of perfect equilibrium in games of perfect information. Econometrica **53**, 613–628 (1985)

39. Kupferman, O., Perelli, G., Vardi, M.Y.: Synthesis with rational environments. Ann. Math. Artif. Intell. **78**(1), 3–20 (2016). https://doi.org/10.1007/s10472-016-9508-8

40. Kupferman, O., Shenwald, N.: The complexity of LTL rational synthesis. In: Fisman, D., Rosu, G. (eds.) TACAS 2022. LNCS, vol. 13243, pp. 25–45. Springer, Cham (2022). https://doi.org/10.1007/978-3-030-99524-9_2

41. Löding, C.: Automata on infinite trees. In: Pin, J. (ed.) Handbook of Automata Theory, pp. 265–302. European Mathematical Society Publishing House, Zürich (2021). https://doi.org/10.4171/Automata-1/8

42. Mogavero, F., Murano, A., Perelli, G., Vardi, M.Y.: Reasoning about strategies: on the model-checking problem. ACM Trans. Comput. Log. **15**(4), 34:1–34:47 (2014). https://doi.org/10.1145/2631917

43. Nash, J.F.: Equilibrium points in n-person games. In: PNAS, vol. 36, pp. 48–49. National Academy of Sciences (1950)

44. von Neumann, J., Morgenstern, O.: Theory of Games and Economic Behavior. Princeton University Press, Princeton (1944)

45. Osborne, M.J., Rubinstein, A.: A course in Game Theory. MIT Press, Cambridge (1994)

46. Randour, M.: Automated synthesis of reliable and efficient systems through game theory: a case study. CoRR abs/1204.3283 (2012). http://arxiv.org/abs/1204.3283
47. Selten, R.: Spieltheoretische Behandlung eines Oligopolmodells mit Nachfrageträgheit. Zeitschrift gesamte Staatswissenschaft 121, 301–324 and 667–689 (1965)
48. von Stackelberg, H.F.: Marktform und Gleichgewicht. Springer, Wien and Berlin (1937)
49. Ummels, M.: Rational behaviour and strategy construction in infinite multiplayer games. In: Arun-Kumar, S., Garg, N. (eds.) FSTTCS 2006. LNCS, vol. 4337, pp. 212–223. Springer, Heidelberg (2006). https://doi.org/10.1007/11944836_21
50. Ummels, M.: The complexity of Nash equilibria in infinite multiplayer games. In: Amadio, R. (ed.) FoSSaCS 2008. LNCS, vol. 4962, pp. 20–34. Springer, Heidelberg (2008). https://doi.org/10.1007/978-3-540-78499-9_3
51. Ummels, M., Wojtczak, D.: The complexity of Nash equilibria in limit-average games. In: Katoen, J.-P., König, B. (eds.) CONCUR 2011. LNCS, vol. 6901, pp. 482–496. Springer, Heidelberg (2011). https://doi.org/10.1007/978-3-642-23217-6_32

Lower Bounds on $\beta(\alpha)$

Merlin Carl[(✉)]

Institut für mathematische, naturwissenschaftliche und technische Bildung,
Abteilung für Mathematik und ihre Didaktik, Europa-Universität Flensburg,
Flensburg, Germany
merlin.carl@uni-flensburg.de

Abstract. For an ordinal α, an α-ITRM is a machine model of transfinite computability that operates on finitely many registers, each of which can contain an ordinal $\rho < \alpha$; they were introduced by Koepke in [11]. In [4], it was shown that the α-ITRM-computable subsets of α are exactly those in a level $L_{\beta(\alpha)}$ of the constructible hierarchy. It was conjectured in [4] that $\beta(\alpha)$ is the first limit of admissible ordinals above α. Here, we show that this is false; in particular, even the computational strength of ω^ω-ITRMs goes far beyond $\omega_\omega^{\mathrm{CK}}$. To this end, we prove lower bounds on this computational strength, using a strategy for iterating α-ITRM-computable operators for η many steps on α^η-ITRMs.

Keywords: Ordinal Computability · Infinite Time Register
Machines · Gandy ordinals

1 Introduction

In [11], Koepke introduced resetting α-Infinite Time Register Machines, abbreviated α-ITRMs. Such machines have finitely many registers, each of which can store a single ordinal smaller than α. Programs for α-ITRMs are just programs for classical register machines as introduced, e.g., in [7] and consist of finitely many enumerated program lines, each of which contains one of the following commands: (i) an incrementation operation, which increases the content of some register by 1, (ii) a copy instruction, which replaces the content of one register by that of another, (iii) a conditional jump, which changes the active program line to a certain value when the contents of two registers are equal and otherwise proceeds with the next program line, (iv) an oracle command, which checks whether the content of some register is contained in the oracle and changes the content of that register to 1 if that is the case and otherwise to 0.[1] For technical reasons that will become apparent below, we start the enumeration of the program lines with 1 rather than 0.

---

[1] Note that the "reset" command for replacing the content of a register by 0 can be carried out by having a register with value 0 and using the copy instruction; for this reason, it is not included here, in contrast to the account in [11].

U. Berger et al. (Eds.): CiE 2022, LNCS 13359, pp. 64–73, 2022.
https://doi.org/10.1007/978-3-031-08740-0_6

The computation of an α-ITRM then works as follows: At successor stages, we simply carry out the program as we would in a classical (finite) register machine.[2] At limit stages, the content of each register is the inferior limit of the sequence of earlier contents of this register; if this happens to be α, we say that the register "overflows" and set its content to 0.[3] The active program line is just the inferior limit of the sequence of earlier active program lines.

In [11], Koepke showed that, for $\alpha = \omega$, the subsets of α computable by such an α-ITRM are exactly those in $L_{\omega^{CK}}$. Further information on ω-ITRMs was obtained in [5] and [12]. It is also known from Koepke and Siders [13] that, when one lets α be On, i.e., when one imposes no restriction on the size of register contents, the computable sets of ordinals are exactly the constructible ones. Recently, strengthening a result in [3], it was shown in [4] that the α-ITRM-computable subsets of α coincide with those in $L_{\alpha+1}$ if and only if $L_\alpha \models ZF^-$[4]; and moreover, it was shown that, for any exponentially closed α, the α-ITRM-computable subsets of α are exactly those in $L_{\beta(\alpha)}$, where $\beta(\alpha)$ is the supremum of the α-ITRM-halting times, which coincides with the supremum of the ordinals that have α-ITRM-computable codes. To determine the computational strength of α-ITRMs for some exponentially closed ordinal α, one thus needs to determine $\beta(\alpha)$. However, except for the cases $\alpha = \omega$, $\alpha = $ On and $L_\alpha \models ZF^-$, no value of $\beta(\alpha)$ is currently known. A reasonable conjecture compatible with all results obtained in [4] was that $\beta(\alpha) = \alpha^{+\omega}$, the first limit of admissible ordinals greater than α, unless $L_\alpha \models ZF^-$, which would be the most obvious analogue of Koepke's result on ω-ITRMs.

In this paper, we will obtain lower bounds on the computational strength of α-ITRMs by showing how, when α is exponentially closed, α-ITRMs can compute transfinite (in fact $\alpha \cdot \omega$ long) iterations of β-ITRM-computable operators for $\beta < \alpha$. As a consequence, we are able to show that the conjecture mentioned above fails dramatically: In fact, for the first exponentially closed ordinal ε_0 larger than ω, we will already have $\beta(\varepsilon_0) \geq \omega_{\varepsilon_0 \cdot \omega}^{CK}$, while the next limit of admissible ordinals after ε_0 is of course still ω_ω^{CK}. This improves Corollary 48 of [4], where it was shown that $\beta(\alpha) \geq \alpha^{+\omega}$ when α is an index ordinal.

For an ordinal α, we will write α^+ to denote the smallest admissible ordinal strictly larger than α. Moreover, for $\alpha, \iota \in$ On, we recursively define $\alpha^{+0} = \alpha$, $\alpha^{+(\iota+1)} = (\alpha^{+\iota})^+$ and $\alpha^{+\iota} = \sup_{\xi < \iota} \alpha^{+\xi}$ when ι is a limit ordinal.

2   Iterations of α-ITRM-computable Operators

In [4], it was proved that, if $L_\alpha \models ZF^-$, then the supremum of the α-ITRM-clockable ordinals is α^ω. This situation, however, is rather special, and it was

---

[2] If α is a successor ordinal, the incrementation operation may lead to the register content α; in that case, the content is replaced by 0. However, only limit values of α will be considered in this paper.

[3] There is also a "weak" model for register computations on α for which the computation is undefined in this case. However, in this paper, only the strong variant will be considered.

[4] I.e., ZF set theory without the power set axiom; for the subtleties of the axiomatization, see [8].

still consistent with the results obtained in [4] that the following natural generalization of Koepke's result on the computational strength of ITRMs (see [11]) holds:

Conjecture 1. Let α be an exponentially closed ordinal. Unless $L_\alpha \models ZF^-$, we have $\beta(\alpha) = \alpha^{+\omega}$.

We will now show that this conjecture fails dramatically even for the first exponentially closed ordinal $\varepsilon_0 = \omega^{\omega^{\omega^{\cdots}}}$ greater than ω. In fact, we will show that already $\beta(\omega^\omega)$ is way bigger than ω_ω^{CK}.

Definition 1. Let α be an ordinal. We say that $F : \mathfrak{P}(\alpha) \to \mathfrak{P}(\alpha)$ is α-ITRM-computable if and only if there is an α-ITRM-program P such that, for all $x \subseteq \alpha$ and all $\iota < \alpha$, we have $P^x(\iota) \downarrow = 1$ if and only if $\iota \in F(x)$ and otherwise $P^x(\iota) \downarrow = 0$. In this situation, we also say that P computes F.

Definition 2. For each infinite ordinal α, pick an α-ITRM-computable bijection $p_\alpha : \alpha \times \alpha \to \alpha$.

Let α be an infinite ordinal, and let $F : \mathfrak{P}(\alpha) \to \mathfrak{P}(\alpha)$, $x \subseteq \alpha$. We define the iteration of F along α as follows:

- $F^0(x) = x$
- $F^{\iota+1}(x) = F(F^\iota(x))$.
- When $\delta \leq \alpha$ is a limit ordinal, then $F^\delta(x) = \{p_\alpha(\iota, \xi) : \iota < \delta, \xi < \alpha, \xi \in F^\iota(x)\}$.

In addition we also write $F^{\beta \cdot k}$ for $(F^\beta)^k$.

Lemma 1. Let α be an ordinal, and let $F : \mathfrak{P}(\alpha) \to \mathfrak{P}(\alpha)$ be an α-ITRM-computable function and let $n \in \omega$. Then F^n, the n-th iteration of F, is α-ITRM-computable.

Proof. We prove this by induction. For $n = 1$, there is nothing to show. Let Q be an α-ITRM-program that computes F and let Q_n be an α-ITRM-program that computes F^n. Then an α-ITRM-program Q_{n+1} for computing F^{n+1} works as follows: Run Q. Whenever Q makes an oracle call to ask whether $\iota \in F^n(x)$, run Q_n to evaluate this claim. When Q uses r_0 many registers and Q_n uses r_1 many registers, this can be implemented on an α-ITRM using $r_0 + r_1$ many registers.

The above iteration technique yields a new program for every iteration index n. The key for our main result is Lemma 3, a uniform version of Lemma 1, which is our next goal.

The following lemma is a standard application of ordinal arithmetic; as a coding device in infinite computability, it was already used by Koepke in [11].

Lemma 2. Let α be an ordinal, δ be a limit ordinal, $(\gamma_\iota : \iota < \delta)$ a sequence of ordinals such that $\gamma_\iota < \alpha$ for each $\iota < \delta$, and let ρ, η be arbitrary ordinals. Then $\liminf_{\iota < \delta} \alpha^{\eta+2} \cdot \rho + \alpha^\eta \cdot \gamma_\iota = \alpha^{\eta+2} \cdot \rho + \alpha^\eta \cdot \liminf_{\iota < \delta} \gamma_\iota$.

Definition 3. *Let α, β be ordinals. We say that α is exponentially closed up to β if and only if, for all $\gamma < \alpha$ and all $\iota < \beta$, we have $\gamma^\iota < \alpha$.*

The following crucial observation is similar in spirit to the iteration lemma for infinite time Blum-Shub-Smale machines, see [6], Lemma 10.

Lemma 3. *Let α be closed under ordinal multiplication, and let $F : \mathfrak{P}(\alpha) \to \mathfrak{P}(\alpha)$ be α-ITRM-computable. Moreover, let $\eta \in On$ be closed under ordinal addition. Then there is an α^η-ITRM-program $P_{iterate}$ such that, for all $\iota < \eta$, $P^x_{iterate}(\iota)$ computes $F^\iota(x)$. More precisely, for all $\iota < \eta$, $\xi < \alpha$, we will have $P^x_{iterate}(\iota, \xi) \downarrow = 1$ if and only if $\xi \in F^\iota(x)$ and $P^x_{iterate}(\iota, \xi) \downarrow = 0$, otherwise.*

Proof. Let P be an α–ITRM-program that computes F. Suppose that P uses n registers $R_1, ..., R_n$. The program $P_{iterate}$ will use registers $R'_1, ..., R'_n$ for simulating the register contents of P, a register L for storing active program lines and various auxiliar registers that will not be mentioned explictly.

The rough idea is this: When $\delta < \eta$ is a limit ordinal, the question whether $\xi \in F^\delta(x)$ can be decided by writing ξ as $\xi = p_\alpha(\xi_0, \xi_1)$ and then deciding whether $\xi_1 \in F^{\xi_0}(x)$; we will have $\xi_0 < \xi$. To compute $F^{\iota+1}(x)$ for a given $\iota < \alpha$, $P_{iterate}$ will run P in the oracle $F^\iota(x)$. This may again call P for a lower iterate etc. Since α is well-founded, however, the nesting depth will remain finite at all times. At any time of this computation, there will be a configuration $(l^\iota, r_1^\iota, ..., r_n^\iota)$ corresponding to the outermost run of P, along with finitely many configuration $(l^{\xi_1}, r_1^{\xi_1}, ..., r_n^{\xi_1})$ corresponding to the first iteration etc., up to $(l^0, r_1^0, ..., r_n^0)$ for the top iteration which works on input x directly. The program $P_{iterate}$ will store this by having $\alpha^{\iota \cdot 2} \cdot l^\iota + \alpha^{\xi_1 \cdot 2} \cdot l^1 + ... + \alpha^0 \cdot l^0$ in L and $\alpha^{\iota \cdot 2} \cdot r_i^\iota + ... + \alpha^0 \cdot r_i^0$ in R'_i. When the topmost computation terminates, it is taken off the stack and the computation "below" it is continued.

We now do it precisely. Suppose that $x \subseteq \alpha$ is given in the oracle, and that some ordinal $\iota < \eta$ is given in the first register. Our goal is to compute $F^\iota(x)$.

The computation proceeds in $\iota + 1$ many "levels", where a computation step takes place at level $\xi \le \iota$ when it belongs to an evaluation of F^ξ. When an oracle call of the form $\mathcal{O}(\zeta)$ is made in level $\xi + 1$, the computation enters level ξ; when it takes place in level δ with δ a limit ordinal and ζ is of the form $p_\alpha(\zeta_0, \zeta_1)$, the computation continues at level ζ_0 with the computation of $F^{\zeta_0}(\zeta_1)$. For the sake of convenience, we use a register S for storing the sequence $(\xi_1, ..., \xi_k)$ of currently relevant levels in the form $\alpha^{2\xi_1} + ... + \alpha^{2\xi_k}$, where, of course $\xi_1 > \xi_2 > ... > \xi_k$.

We now describe how to carry out instructions at level $\delta \le \iota$ (all contents of registers other than the ones explicitly mentioned are left unchanged). Note that δ can be reconstructed from the content of the line register L, the content of which will be of the form $\alpha^{\gamma \cdot 2} \cdot \rho + \alpha^{\delta \cdot 2} \cdot l$ with $\gamma > \delta$ and $l > 0$ (since, as we recall from the introduction, we start the enumeration of program lines with 1). The l appearing as the coefficient in this representation will be the index of a program line of P; depending on the content of this program line, the following steps are carried out:

- (Before carrying out the other steps:) When R_i contains an ordinal of the form $\alpha^{\gamma \cdot 2} \cdot \rho + \alpha^{\delta \cdot 2 + 1}$ for any $i \leq n$, replace it with $\alpha^{\gamma \cdot 2} \cdot \rho$ (this corresponds to a reset after a register overflow).
- The active program line contains the command $R_i \leftarrow R_i + 1$: Read out the content of R_i'. It will be an ordinal of the form $\alpha^{\gamma \cdot 2} \cdot \rho + \alpha^{\delta \cdot 2} \cdot r_i$ with $\gamma > \delta$; replace it with $\alpha^{\gamma \cdot 2} \cdot \rho + \alpha^{\delta \cdot 2} \cdot (r_i + 1)$. Moreover, the content of L will be an ordinal of the form $\alpha^{\gamma \cdot 2} \cdot \rho' + \alpha^{\delta \cdot 2} \cdot l$; replace it with $\alpha^{\gamma \cdot 2} \cdot \rho' + \alpha^{\delta \cdot 2} \cdot (l + 1)$.
- The active program line contains the command $\mathrm{COPY}(i, j)$: Read out the contents of R_i and R_j, which will be of the forms $\alpha^{\gamma_0 \cdot 2} \cdot \rho + \alpha^{\delta \cdot 2} \cdot r_i$ and $\alpha^{\gamma_1 \cdot 2} \cdot \rho' + \alpha^{\delta \cdot 2} \cdot r_j$, where $\delta < \gamma_0, \gamma_1$. Replace the content of R_i with $\alpha^{\gamma_0 \cdot 2} \cdot \rho + \alpha^{\delta \cdot 2} \cdot r_j$; modify the content of L as in the incrementation operation.
- The active program line contains the command IF $R_i = R_j$ GOTO l: Read out the contents of R_i and R_j, which will be of the forms $\alpha^{\gamma_0 \cdot 2} \cdot \rho + \alpha^{\delta \cdot 2} \cdot r_i$ and $\alpha^{\gamma_1 \cdot 2} \cdot \rho' + \alpha^{\delta \cdot 2} \cdot r_j$, where $\gamma_0, \gamma_1 > \delta$; moreover, let $\alpha^{\gamma_2 \cdot 2} \cdot \rho'' + \alpha^{\delta \cdot 2} \cdot l'$ be the content of L, where $\delta < \gamma_2$. If $r_i = r_j$, replace the content of L with $\alpha^{\gamma_2 \cdot 2} \cdot \rho'' + \alpha^{\delta \cdot 2} \cdot l$; if not, replace it with $\alpha^{\gamma_2 \cdot 2} \cdot \rho'' + \alpha^{\delta \cdot 2} \cdot (l' + 1)$.
- The active program line contains the oracle call $\mathcal{O}(\xi)$ and $\delta = \bar{\delta} + 1 < \iota$ is a successor ordinal: Let $\alpha^{\gamma_0 \cdot 2} \cdot \rho + \alpha^{\delta \cdot 2} \cdot r$ be the content of R_1, and let $\alpha^{\gamma_1 \cdot 2} \cdot \rho' + \alpha^{\delta \cdot 2} \cdot l$ be the content of L, where $\delta < \gamma_0, \gamma_1$. Replace the content of R_1 by $\alpha^{\gamma_0 \cdot 2} \cdot \rho + \alpha^{\delta \cdot 2} \cdot r + \alpha^{\bar{\delta} \cdot 2} \cdot \xi$ and replace the content of L by $\alpha^{\gamma_1 \cdot 2} \cdot \rho'' + \alpha^{\delta \cdot 2} \cdot l + \alpha^{\bar{\delta} \cdot 2} \cdot 1$. Also, we are now working at level $\bar{\delta}$, so we add $\alpha^{\bar{\delta} \cdot 2}$ to the content of S.
- The active program line contains the oracle call $\mathcal{O}(\xi)$ and $\delta < \iota$ is a limit ordinal: Calculate ξ_0, ξ_1 with $\xi = p_\alpha(\xi_0, \xi_1)$. If $\xi_0 \geq \delta$, return 0 and modify the content of L as in the incrementation operation. (Note that this output will be right due to the definition of the iteration at limit levels). If $\xi_0 < \delta$, we need to check whether $\xi_1 \in F^{\xi_0}(x)$. The computation will then enter level ξ_0. Thus, we add $\alpha^{\xi_0 \cdot 2}$ to the content of S. Let $\alpha^{\gamma_0 \cdot 2} \cdot \rho + \alpha^{\delta \cdot 2} \cdot r$ be the content of R_1, and let $\alpha^{\gamma_1 \cdot 2} \cdot \rho' + \alpha^{\delta \cdot 2} \cdot l$ be the content of L, where $\delta < \gamma_0, \gamma_1$. Replace the content of R_1 by $\alpha^{\gamma_0 \cdot 2} \cdot \rho + \alpha^{\delta \cdot 2} \cdot r + \alpha^{\xi_0 \cdot 2} \cdot \xi_1$ and replace the content of L by $\alpha^{\gamma_1 \cdot 2} \cdot \rho'' + \alpha^{\delta \cdot 2} \cdot l + \alpha^{\xi_0 \cdot 2} \cdot 1$.
- The active program line contains the oracle call $\mathcal{O}(\xi)$ and $\delta = 0$: This means that we are simply making a call to the given oracle, with no iterations of F applied to it. Let $\alpha^{\gamma_0 \cdot 2} \cdot \rho + \alpha^{\delta \cdot 2} \cdot r$ be the content of R_1. Check whether $\xi \in x$ (recall that x is our oracle). If yes, replace the content of R_1 by $\alpha^{\gamma_0 \cdot 2} \cdot \rho + \alpha^{\delta \cdot 2} \cdot 1$, otherwise, replace the content of R_1 by $\alpha^{\gamma_0 \cdot 2} \cdot \rho$. Modify the content of L as in the incrementation operation.
- When the coefficient of the minimal power of α in the Cantor normal form representation of the content of L is the index of a line of P that contains the "halt" command: Let R_1 contain $\alpha^{\gamma_0 \cdot 2} \cdot \rho' + \alpha^{\gamma_1 \cdot 2} \cdot r + \alpha^{\delta \cdot 2} \cdot r'$; replace it with $\alpha^{\gamma_0 \cdot 2} \cdot \rho' + \alpha^{\gamma_1 \cdot 2} \cdot r'$ (the result of the oracle call is passed down to the level that made the call).
  For $i \in \{2, ..., n\}$, let R_i contain $\alpha^{\gamma_{0,i} \cdot 2} \cdot \rho_i + \alpha^{\gamma_{1,i} \cdot 2} \cdot r_i + \alpha^{\delta \cdot 2} \cdot r_i'$; replace it with $\alpha^{\gamma_{0,i} \cdot 2} \cdot \rho_i + \alpha^{\gamma_{1,i} \cdot 2} \cdot r_i$ (the topmost layer corresponding to the now finished computation is deleted).

Also, if the content of S is $\alpha^\nu \cdot \rho + \alpha^{\delta \cdot 2}$, replace it with $\alpha^\nu \cdot \rho$ (the last entry in the sequence of currently relevant levels is deleted).

Finally, let the content of L be $\alpha^{\gamma_0 \cdot 2} \cdot \rho'' + \alpha^{\gamma_1 \cdot 2} \cdot l + \alpha^{\delta \cdot 2} \cdot l'$; replace it by $\alpha^{\gamma_0 \cdot 2} \cdot \rho'' + \alpha^{\gamma_1 \cdot 2} \cdot (l+1)$ (the active program line is increased by 1, as the oracle command has been carried out).

P_{iterate} now works on input $(\iota, \xi) \in \eta \times \alpha$ by first instantiating L with $\alpha^{\iota \cdot 2}$, R_1 with $\alpha^{\iota \cdot 2} \cdot \xi$ and R_i with 0 for $i \in \{2, 3, ..., n\}$ and then carrying out the above instructions. By additive closure of η, we will have $\gamma \cdot 2 < \eta$ whenever $\gamma < \eta$, so that all register contents generated in this procedure will be below α^η. By induction on ι and using Lemma 2, the program works as desired.

We note some important consequences of this result:

Corollary 1. *Let $\alpha > \omega$ be exponentially closed, and let $\beta < \alpha$. Moreover, let $F : \mathfrak{P}(\beta) \to \mathfrak{P}(\beta)$ be a β-ITRM-computable operator. Then:*

1. *There is an α-ITRM-program P such that, for each $x \subseteq \beta$ and each $\iota < \alpha$, $P^x(\iota)$ computes $F^\iota(x)$.*
2. *F^α, the α-th iteration of F, is α-ITRM-computable.*
3. *$F^{\alpha \cdot i}$, the $\alpha \cdot i$-th iteration of F, is α-ITRM-computable, for every $i \in \omega$.*

Proof. 1. Since $\beta^{\iota + 1} < \alpha$ by exponential closure of α, is a direct consequence of Lemma 3.
2. In order to decide whether $p_\alpha(\xi_0, \xi_1) \in F^\alpha(x)$, use the algorithm P from (1) to decide whether or not $\xi_1 \in F^{\xi_0}(x)$.
3. This is a consequence of (2) and Lemma 1.

We now extract information on $\beta(\alpha)$, for various values of α, thus, in particular, refuting the conjecture mentioned above that $\beta(\alpha) = \alpha^{+\omega}$ unless $L_\alpha \models \text{ZF}^-$.

Definition 4. *Let α be an ordinal. By recursion, we define, for $\iota \in On$: $^0\alpha = \alpha$, $^{\iota+1}\alpha = \alpha^{\iota_\alpha}$, $^\iota\alpha = \bigcup_{\xi < \iota} {}^\xi\alpha$ for ι a limit ordinal.*
As usual, we denote $^\omega\omega$ by ε_0.

Recall the following result from Koepke and Miller [12]:

Definition 5 (Cf., e.g., [14], p. 48). *Let $x \subseteq \omega$. The hyperjump of x is the set of all $i \in \omega$ such that the i-th Turing program computes a well-ordering in the oracle x. For $\iota < \varepsilon_0$, denote by $HJ^\iota(x)$ the ι-th hyperjump of x; HJ^ι denotes the ι-th hyperjump of 0.*

Theorem 6 *[See [12], Theorem 1].* *There is an ITRM-program P_{hj} such that, for each $x \subseteq \omega$, P_{hj}^x computes $HJ(x)$.*

Corollary 2.

1. *For any $n \in \omega$, the function $F_n : x \mapsto HJ_{\omega^n}(x)$, defined on $\mathfrak{P}(\omega)$, is ω^{ω^n}-ITRM-computable.*

2. For $n \in \omega$, we have $\beta(\omega^{\omega^n}) \geq \omega^{CK}_{\omega^{n+1}}$. In particular, we have $\beta(\omega^\omega) \geq \omega^{CK}_{\omega^2}$.
3. We have $\beta(\varepsilon_0) \geq \omega^{CK}_{\varepsilon_0 \cdot \omega}$.

Proof.

1. We prove this by induction. For $n = 0$, this is Theorem 6. Now suppose that $x \mapsto \mathrm{HJ}_{\omega^n}(x)$ is ω^{ω^n}-ITRM-computable, say by the program P_n. By Lemma 3, there is an $(\omega^{\omega^n})^\omega$-ITRM-program Q that computes $F_n^i(x)$ on input $i \in \omega$; note that $(\omega^{\omega^n})^\omega = \omega^{\omega^{n+1}}$. By running $Q(i,j)$ on input $p_\omega(i,j)$, we obtain an $\omega^{\omega^{n+1}}$-ITRM-program Q' that computes $F_n^\omega(x)$ in the oracle x. But F_n^ω is just F_{n+1}.
2. From (1), we have that HJ_{ω^n} is ω^{ω^n}-ITRM-computable; using Lemma 1, we obtain that $\mathrm{HJ}_{\omega^n \cdot k}$ is ω^{ω^n}-ITRM-computable for every $k \in \omega$. Therefore, a code for $\omega^{CK}_{\omega^n \cdot k}$ is ω^{ω^n}-ITRM-computable for every $k \in \omega$. Consequently, the supremum $\beta(\omega^{\omega^n})$ of the ordinals with ω^{ω^n}-ITRM-computable codes is at least $\omega^{CK}_{\omega^{n+1}}$.
3. By Theorem 6 and Corollary 1, $\mathrm{HJ}_{\varepsilon_0 \cdot k}$ is ε_0-ITRM-computable for any $k \in \omega$. Thus, $\beta(\varepsilon_0)$ is larger than $\omega^{CK}_{\varepsilon_0 \cdot k}$ for any $k \in \omega$, and thus $\beta(\varepsilon_0) \geq \omega^{CK}_{\varepsilon_0 \cdot \omega}$.

The same approach works in a much more general situation:

Definition 7. *Let us say that α is ITRM-countable if and only if there is an α-ITRM-computable bijection $f : \omega \to \alpha$. More generally, let us say that α is ITRM-effectively β-codable if and only if there is an α-ITRM-computable bijection $f : \beta \to \alpha$.*

Remark 1. In particular, α is ITRM-countable whenever α is an index (i.e., an ordinal α such that $(L_{\alpha+1} \setminus L_\alpha) \cap \mathfrak{P}(\omega) \neq \emptyset$). Note that ITRM-countability implies that there is an α-ITRM-computable real number that codes α.

Corollary 3. *Let $\alpha > \omega$ be exponentially closed and ITRM-countable. Then $\beta(\alpha) \geq \alpha^{+\alpha \cdot \omega}$.*

Proof. Let $x \subseteq \omega$ be an α-ITRM-computable code for α. By applying Corollary 8 to x and the (ω-)ITRM-program that computes hyperjumps from Theorem 6, we see that $\mathrm{HJ}^{\alpha \cdot k}(x)$ is α-ITRM-computable for every $k \in \omega$. But then, we have $\beta(\alpha) \geq \alpha^{+\alpha \cdot k}$ for every $k \in \omega$, i.e., $\beta(\alpha) \geq \alpha^{+\alpha \cdot \omega}$.

Remark 2. Note that the iteration technique just described never yields to a register overflow, so that the lower bounds just obtained in fact hold true already for the weak ("unresetting") α-ITRMs as well that were mentioned in the introduction. In the case $\alpha = \omega$, it is known that α-ITRMs are far stronger than their unresetting cousins. We do not know whether the same is true for, e.g., $\alpha = \varepsilon_0$.

2.1   Uncountable α

The lower bounds obtained from the iteration lemma above can only work when α is countable. In this section, we indicate how Abramson's and Sacks' "lifting" of results of Gostanian [9] on Gandy ordinals to the uncountable in [1] can be exploited to yield information on α-ITRM-computability for certain uncountable values of α. For the sake of brevity, simplicity and surveyability, we restrict ourselves to the case $\alpha = \aleph_\omega^+$ treated in [1]; further generalizations are deferred to later work. (The argument would equally well work for $(\aleph_\omega^L)^+$.)

In [1], the authors prove that $\aleph_\omega^+$ is Gandy, i.e., that the supremum of the $\aleph_\omega^+$-recursive ordinals is $(\aleph_\omega^+)^+$. Clearly, α-recursive sets are also α-ITRM-computable, and so this implies that $\beta(\aleph_\omega^+) \geq (\aleph_\omega^+)^+$; indeed, this much was observed in [4]. However, in order to use the strength of the iteration lemma, this is not enough: rather than being able to go from $\aleph_\omega^+$ to $(\aleph_\omega^+)^+$, we would need a uniform way – i.e., an α-ITRM-program – that allows us to go from some $x \subseteq \alpha$ that codes a well-ordering to $\omega_1^{\mathrm{CK},x}$, i.e., the smallest ordinal $\beta > \alpha$ such that $L_\beta[x]$ is admissible.

Such a program can indeed be obtained from the proof of Theorem 5 of [1] by a relativization of the construction; we will offer a brief sketch of the general strategy and the necessary adaptations.

We use the following generalization of Theorem 1 of [12]:

Definition 8 ([3], **Definition 2.3.23**). *An ordinal $\alpha > \omega$ is ITRM-singular if and only if there is an α-ITRM-computable cofinal function $f : \beta \to \alpha$ with $\beta < \alpha$.*

Lemma 4 *[See [3], Theorem 2.3.25]. If α is ITRM-singular, then there is an α-ITRM-program P_{ifs} ("ill-founded sequence") such that, for any $x \subseteq \alpha$ that codes a tree T on α, P_{ifs}^x outputs $\emptyset$ when T is well-founded and otherwise outputs an infinite branch of T.*[5]

Lemma 5. *If α is ITRM-singular, then there is an α-ITRM-program P_{wfp} ("well-founded part") such that, for any $x \subseteq \alpha$ that encodes a structure (X, E), P^x computes a subset of α that codes the well-founded part of X with respect to E.*

Proof. This follows from Lemma 4 by cutting off the given structure (X, E) below any given x and applying the well-foundedness check to determine whether there is an infinite E-decreasing sequence that starts with x.

The general strategy in [1] is the following: They define an $\aleph_\omega^+$-recursive tree T, guaranteed to have an infinite branch, whose infinite branches encode – possibly ill-founded – models of KP for which $\aleph_\omega^+$ belongs to the well-founded part. Since well-founded parts of admissible sets are known to be admissible, it follows that the height of the well-founded part of such a model must be of height at least $(\aleph_\omega^+)^+$, from which one obtains the Gandyness of $\aleph_\omega^+$.

It is not hard to modify their construction to obtain, for a given $x \subseteq \aleph_\omega^+$, a tree T_x that is uniformly $\aleph_\omega^+$-ITRM-computable in the oracle x, has at least one infinite branch and whose infinite branches encode models of KP whose

---

[5] More precisely, $P_{\mathrm{ifs}}^x(i)$ will output the i-th element of an infinite branch of T, for every $i \in \omega$.

well-founded part includes $\aleph_\omega^+$ and x. All that is required is to add, in the proof of Theorem 5 of [1], a new variable χ to the language $\mathcal{L}^*$ and the statements $\{d_\gamma \in \chi : \gamma \in x\} \cup \{d_\gamma \notin \chi : \gamma \notin \chi\}$ to the theory T^* and modify condition (viii) to demand that $(V, G) \in L_{\aleph_\omega^+}[x]$. The proof that the tree arising in this way has an infinite branch and that one obtains a model with the required properties from each infinite branch then works as in [1]. Now, by Lemma 4, we can uniformly compute a code $b \subseteq \aleph_\omega^+$ for such a branch on an $\aleph_\omega^+$-ITRM in T^*. From b, one can then easily obtain a code $m \subseteq \aleph_\omega^+$ that encodes a model of KP with $\aleph_\omega^+$ and x in its well-founded part. We can then use Lemma 5 to compute a code $w \subseteq \aleph_\omega^+$ for the well-founded part of m. Using bounded truth predicate evaluation (see, e.g., [3], Theorem 2.3.28) in m, this yields a code for the set of ordinals in m, which will be a code of an ordinal $\geq \omega_1^{\mathrm{CK},x}$.

Since this works for any $x \subseteq \aleph_\omega^+$, it is now possible to proceed as above to obtain the following:

Theorem 9. *We have* $\beta((\aleph_\omega^+)^+) \geq (\aleph_\omega^+)^{+(\aleph_\omega^+ \cdot \omega)}$.

3   Open Questions

While the above refutes a natural conjecture on the computational strength of α-ITRMs by providing some lower bounds, the value of $\beta(\alpha)$ is still unknown for any value of α unless $\alpha = \omega$ or $L_\alpha \models \mathrm{ZF}^-$. Some special cases that might be good starting points would be to determine $\beta(\omega^\omega)$, $\beta(\varepsilon_0)$, $\beta(\aleph_\omega)$ or $\beta(\omega_1^{\mathrm{CK}})$.

A crucial feature of ω-ITRMs established by Koepke and Miller in [12], the generalization of which may well shed light on the computational power of α-ITRMs, is the solvability of the bounded halting problem: Namely, for each k, the halting problem for ω-ITRMs using at most k registers is solvable on an ω-ITRM (using more than k registers). Although we are able to prove that, for each ordinal α, there is either a universal α-ITRM-program or the bounded halting problem for α-ITRMs is solvable, we are in a quite unsatisfying situation: We do not know for a single exponentially closed ordinal α except when $\alpha = \omega$ or when $L_\alpha \models \mathrm{ZF}^-$ which alternative holds. A crucial step in further work on the computational strength of α-ITRMs might be to generalize the work on the cases $\alpha = \omega$ and $L_\alpha \models \mathrm{ZF}^-$ by seeing whether the computational strength of α-ITRMs can be characterized by iterating some operator that is β-ITRM-computable for some $\beta \leq \alpha$. We also currently do not know whether there are values of α for which the lower bounds obtained in this paper are optimal. We expect that proof-theoretical considerations on iterated admissibility and inductive operators such as Jäger [10] and [2] will become relevant in further investigations.

Acknowledgements. We thank our three anonymous referees for their valuable feedback, in particular for pointing out several subtle typos.

References

1. Abramson, F.G., Sacks, G.E.: Uncountable gandy ordinals. J. London Math. Soc.-Second Ser. **2**, 387–392 (1976)
2. Buchholz, W.: Iterated inductive definitions and subsystems of analysis: recent proof-theoretical studies (1981)
3. Carl, M.: Ordinal Computability: An Introduction to Infinitary Machines. De Gruyter (2019)
4. Carl, M.: Taming Koepke's Zoo II: register machines. Ann. Pure Appl. Log. **173**, 103041 (2022)
5. Carl, M., Fischbach, T., Koepke, P., Miller, R.G., Nasfi, M., Weckbecker, G.: The basic theory of infinite time register machines. Arch. Math. Logic **49**, 249–273 (2010)
6. Carl, M., Galeotti, L.: Resetting infinite time Blum-Shub-Smale-machines. arXiv Logic (2020)
7. Cutland, N.J.: Computability: An Introduction to Recursive Function Theory (1980)
8. Gitman, V., Hamkins, J.D., Johnstone, T.A.: What is the theory ZFC without power set? Math. Log. Q. **62**, 391–406 (2016)
9. Gostanian, R.: The next admissible ordinal. Ann. Math. Log. **17**, 171–203 (1979)
10. Jäger, G.: Iterating admissibility in proof theory. Stud. Log. Found. Math. **107**, 137–146 (1982)
11. Koepke, P.: Ordinal computability. In: Ambos-Spies, K., Löwe, B., Merkle, W. (eds.) CiE 2009. LNCS, vol. 5635, pp. 280–289. Springer, Heidelberg (2009). https://doi.org/10.1007/978-3-642-03073-4_29
12. Koepke, P., Morozov, A.S.: The computational power of infinite time Blum-Shub-Smale machines. Algebra Log. **56**, 37–62 (2017)
13. Koepke, P., Siders, R.C.: Register computations on ordinals. Arch. Math. Log. **47**, 529–548 (2008)
14. Sacks, G.E.: Higher recursion theory (1990)

Proof Complexity of Monotone Branching Programs

Anupam Das[(⊠)] and Avgerinos Delkos

University of Birmingham, Birmingham, UK
a.das@bham.ac.uk, a.delkos@bham.ac.uk

Abstract. We investigate the proof complexity of systems based on positive branching programs, i.e. non-deterministic branching programs (NBPs) where, for any 0-transition between two nodes, there is also a 1-transition. Positive NBPs compute monotone Boolean functions, like negation-free circuits or formulas, but constitute a positive version of (non-uniform) **NL**, rather than **P** or $\mathbf{NC}^1$, respectively.

The proof complexity of NBPs was investigated in previous work by Buss, Das and Knop, using extension variables to represent the dag-structure, over a language of (non-deterministic) decision trees, yielding the system eLNDT. Our system eLNDT$^+$ is obtained by restricting their systems to a positive syntax, similarly to how the 'monotone sequent calculus' MLK is obtained from the usual sequent calculus LK by restricting to negation-free formulas.

Our main result is that eLNDT$^+$ polynomially simulates eLNDT over positive sequents. Our proof method is inspired by a similar result for MLK by Atserias, Galesi and Pudlák, that was recently improved to a bona fide polynomial simulation via works of Jeřábek and Buss, Kabanets, Kolokolova and Koucký. Along the way we formalise several properties of counting functions within eLNDT$^+$ by polynomial-size proofs and, as a case study, give explicit polynomial-size poofs of the propositional pigeonhole principle.

Keywords: Proof Complexity · Branching Programs · Monotone Complexity

1 Introduction

Proof complexity is the study of the size of formal proofs. This pursuit is fundamentally tied to open problems in computational complexity, in particular due the Cook-Rechow theorem [8]: $co\mathbf{NP} = \mathbf{NP}$ iff there is a 'formal' proof system that has polynomial-size proofs of each propositional tautology. This has led to what is known as 'Cook's program' for separating **P** and **NP** (see, e.g., [7,17]).

Systems of interest in proof complexity are typically motivated by analogous results from circuit complexity. For instance 'bounded depth' systems restrict proofs to formulas with a limit on the number of alternations between ∨ and

© The Author(s), under exclusive license to Springer Nature Switzerland AG 2022
U. Berger et al. (Eds.): CiE 2022, LNCS 13359, pp. 74–87, 2022.
https://doi.org/10.1007/978-3-031-08740-0_7

$\wedge$ in its formula tree, i.e. $\mathbf{AC^0}$ concepts. Indeed, Håstad's famous lower bound technique for $\mathbf{AC^0}$ [13] was lifted to the setting of proof complexity in [4], yielding lower bounds for a propositional formulation of the pigeonhole principle.

Monotone proof complexity is motivated by another famous lower bound result, namely Razborov's lower bounds on the size of negation-free circuits [22,23] (and similar ones for formulas [16]). In this regard, there has been much investigation into the negation-free fragment of Gentzen's sequent calculus, called MLK [2,3,6,14]. [3] showed a quasipolynomial simulation of LK by MLK on negation-free sequents by formalising an elegant counting argument using quasipolynomial-size negation-free counting formulae. This has recently been improved to a polynomial simulation by an intricate series of results [3,6,14], solving a question first posed in [21]. However, note the contrast with bounded depth systems: restricting negation has a different effect on computational complexity and on proof complexity.

In this work we address a similar question for the setting of *branching programs*. These are (presumably) more expressive than Boolean formulas, in that they are the non-uniform counterpart of log-space ($\mathbf{L}$), as opposed to $\mathbf{NC^1}$. They have recently been given a proof theoretic treatment in [5]. We work within that framework, only restricting to formulas representing *positive* branching programs.

Positive (or 'monotone') branching programs have been considered several times in the literature, e.g. [12,15], and are identical to Markov's 'relay-diode bipoles' from [20]. [11,12] give a general way of making a non-deterministic model of computation 'positive'; in particular, a non-deterministic branching program is positive if, whenever there is a 0-transition from a node u to a node v, there is also a 1-transition from u to v. As in the earlier work [5] we implement such a criterion by using disjunction to model nondeterminism.

Contribution. We present a formal calculus $\mathsf{eLNDT^+}$, reasoning with formula-based representations of positive branching programs, by restricting the calculus eLNDT from [5] appropriately. We consider the 'positive closures' of well-known polynomial-size 'ordered' BPs (OBDDs) for counting functions, and show that their characteristic properties admit polynomial-size proofs in $\mathsf{eLNDT^+}$.

As a case study, we show that these properties can be used to obtain polynomial-size proofs of the propositional *pigeonhole principle*, by adapting an approach of [2] for MLK. Our main result is that $\mathsf{eLNDT^+}$ in fact polynomially simulates eLNDT over positive sequents. For this we again use representations of positive NBPs for counting and small proofs of their characteristic properties. At a high level we adapt the approach of [3], but there are several additional technicalities specific to our setting. In particular, we require bespoke treatments of negative literals in eLNDT and of substitutions of (representations of) positive NBPs into (representations of) other positive NBPs.

Terminology. Throughout this work, we shall reserve the words 'monotone', 'monotonicity' etc. for *semantic* notions, i.e. as a property of Boolean functions. For (non-uniform) models of computation such as formulas, branching programs, circuits etc., we shall say 'positive' for the associated *syntactic* constraints, e.g. negation-freeness for the case of formulas or circuits. While many works simply say 'monotone' always, in particular [11,12], let us note that the distinction we make is employed by several other authors too, e.g. [1,10,18,19].

Proofs and Full Version. Proofs of all results stated in this work can be found in a preprint available at [9].

2   Preliminaries

We will use a countable set of *propositional variables*, written p, q etc., and *Boolean constants* 0 and 1, with their usual interpretations. An *assignment*, written α, β etc., is just a map from propositional variables to $\{0, 1\}$, and a *Boolean function*, f, g etc., is just a map from assignments to $\{0, 1\}$. We write $\alpha \leqslant \beta$ if, for all propositional variables p, we have $\alpha(p) \leqslant \beta(p)$. We say that a Boolean function f is *monotone* if $\alpha \leqslant \beta \implies f(\alpha) \leqslant f(\beta)$.

In proof complexity, formally, a *propositional proof system* is just a polynomial-time function P from Σ^* to the set of propositional tautologies, for Σ some finite alphabet. The idea is that P checks (efficiently) that an element $\sigma \in \Sigma^*$ correctly codes a proof in the system in which case the output $P(\sigma)$ is the tautology σ proves. Otherwise P outputs the tautology 1 by convention. We say that a propositional proof system P *polynomially simulates* a system Q if we can construct in polynomial-time, for each Q proof π of A, a P-proof of A. In practice (and throughout this work) we shall avoid specifying proof systems at such a low level, leaving such formalisation implicit.

2.1   Positive Branching Programs and Their Representations

A (non-deterministic) *branching program* (NBP) is a (rooted) directed acyclic graph G with two distinguished *sink* nodes, 0 and 1, such that:

– G has a unique root node, i.e. a unique node with in-degree 0.
– Each non-sink node v of G is labelled by a propositional variable.
– Each edge e of G is labelled by a constant 0 or 1.

Definition 1 (Positive NBPs, e.g. [12]). *An NBP is* positive *if, for every 0-edge from a node u to a node v, there is also a 1-edge from u to v.*

A *run* of a NBP G on an assignment α is a maximal path beginning at the root of G consistent with α. I.e., at a node labelled by p the run must follow an edge labelled by $\alpha(p) \in \{0, 1\}$. G *accepts* α if there is a run on α reaching the sink 1. We extend α to a map from all NBPs to $\{0, 1\}$ by setting $\alpha(G) = 1$ if G accepts α. Thus each NBP *computes* a unique Boolean function $\alpha \mapsto \alpha(G)$.

Fact 2. *A positive NBP computes a monotone Boolean function.*

Example 3 (2-out-of-4 Threshold). The 2-out-of-4 Threshold function, returning 1 if at least two of its four inputs are 1, is computed by the positive NBP on the left of Fig. 1. Here 0-edges are dotted, and 1-edges are solid; the multiple 0-leaves correspond to the same sink.

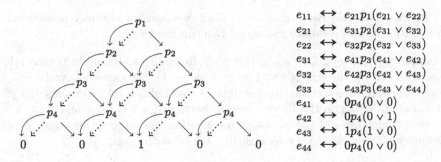

$$\begin{aligned}
e_{11} &\leftrightarrow e_{21}p_1(e_{21} \vee e_{22})\\
e_{21} &\leftrightarrow e_{31}p_2(e_{31} \vee e_{32})\\
e_{22} &\leftrightarrow e_{32}p_2(e_{32} \vee e_{33})\\
e_{31} &\leftrightarrow e_{41}p_3(e_{41} \vee e_{42})\\
e_{32} &\leftrightarrow e_{42}p_3(e_{42} \vee e_{43})\\
e_{33} &\leftrightarrow e_{43}p_3(e_{43} \vee e_{44})\\
e_{41} &\leftrightarrow 0p_4(0 \vee 0)\\
e_{42} &\leftrightarrow 0p_4(0 \vee 1)\\
e_{43} &\leftrightarrow 1p_4(1 \vee 0)\\
e_{44} &\leftrightarrow 0p_4(0 \vee 0)
\end{aligned}$$

Fig. 1. Pos. NBP for 2-out-of-4 Threshold and representation by extension axioms.

Like in [5], we shall represent (positive) NBPs in proofs by means of *extension variables*, $e_0, e_1, \ldots$ (distinguished from propositional variables). An *extended non-deterministic decision tree* formula (*eNDT* formula), written A, B etc., is generated from constants, propositional variables and extension variables by:

- If A and B are eNDT formulas then so is $(A \vee B)$.
- If A and B are eNDT formulas then so is (ApB).

Disjunction, $\vee$, has its usual semantic interpretation, while ApB should be interpreted as "if p then B else A". The role of extension variables is to 'abbreviate' complex formulas, intuitively.'naming' nodes in branching programs. Their interpretation is thus determined by additional data:

Definition 4. *A set of extension axioms $\mathcal{A}$ is a set of the form $\{e_i \leftrightarrow A_i\}_{i<n}$, where each A_i may only contain extension variables among $e_0, \ldots, e_{i-1}$.*

Thanks to the subscripting condition for $\mathcal{A}$ above we inherit a natural induction principle ('$\mathcal{A}$-induction') for formulas over $e_0, \ldots, e_{n-1}$. For instance, this means that formulas over $e_0, \ldots, e_{n-1}$ indeed compute unique Boolean functions with respect to $\mathcal{A}$:

Definition 5 (Semantics of eNDT formulas). *Satisfaction with respect to a set of extension axioms $\mathcal{A} = \{e_i \leftrightarrow A_i\}_{i<n}$, written $\vDash_{\mathcal{A}}$, is a (infix) binary relation between assignments and formulas over $e_0, \ldots, e_{n-1}$ defined as follows:*

- $\alpha \nvDash_{\mathcal{A}} 0$, $\alpha \vDash_{\mathcal{A}} 1$ and $\alpha \vDash_{\mathcal{A}} p$ if $\alpha(p) = 1$.
- $\alpha \vDash_{\mathcal{A}} A \vee B$ if $\alpha \vDash_{\mathcal{A}} A$ or $\alpha \vDash_{\mathcal{A}} B$.
- $\alpha \vDash_{\mathcal{A}} ApB$ if either $\alpha(p) = 0$ and $\alpha \vDash_{\mathcal{A}} A$, or $\alpha(p) = 1$ and $\alpha \vDash_{\mathcal{A}} B$.
- $\alpha \vDash_{\mathcal{A}} e_i$ if $\alpha \vDash_{\mathcal{A}} A_i$.

Remark 6 (Distinguishing extension variables). Note that we do not allow decisions on extension variables, i.e. formulas may not have the form Ae_iB. Otherwise we would be able to represent all Boolean circuits succinctly, cf. [5].

Definition 7 (Positive formulas). *An eNDT formula is positive if, for each subformula of the form ApB, we have $B = A \vee C$ for some C.*
A set of extension axioms $\mathcal{A} = \{e_i \leftrightarrow A_i\}_{i<n}$ is positive if each A_i is positive.

As expected, positive formulas over positive extension axioms represent positive NBPs, and so compute monotone Boolean functions.

Example 8 (2-out-of-4 Threshold, revisited). Returning to Example 3 earlier, the positive NBP on the left of Fig. 1 is represented by the extension variable e_{11} under the extension axioms on the right of Fig. 1. Each e_{ij} represents the jth node (left to right) on the ith row (top to bottom) for $1 \leqslant i \leqslant 4$ and $1 \leqslant j \leqslant i$; for well-foundedness of the extension axioms (i.e. the subscripting condition of Definition 4), note that we may identify each e_{ij} with $e_{4(4-i)+j}$.

2.2   The System eLNDT and its Positive Fragment

We now recall the system for NBPs introduced in [5]. The language of the system eLNDT comprises of just the eNDT formulas. A *sequent* is an expression $\Gamma \longrightarrow \Delta$, where Γ and Δ are multisets of eNDT formulas (' $\longrightarrow$ ' is just a syntactic delimiter). Semantically, such a sequent is interpreted as a judgement "some formula of Γ is false or some formula of Δ is true".

Definition 9 (Systems). *The system* LNDT *is given by the rules in Fig. 2. An* LNDT *derivation of* $\Gamma \longrightarrow \Delta$ *from hypotheses* $\mathcal{H} = \{\Gamma_i \longrightarrow \Delta_i\}_{i \in I}$ *is defined as expected: it is a finite list of sequents, each being either some* $\Gamma_i \longrightarrow \Delta_i$ *from* $\mathcal{H}$ *or following from previous ones by rules of* LNDT, *ending with* $\Gamma \longrightarrow \Delta$.

An eLNDT *proof is just an* LNDT *derivation from hypotheses that are a set of extension axioms* $\mathcal{A} = \{e_i \longleftrightarrow A_i\}_{i<n}$, *with* $A \longleftrightarrow B$ *construed as an abbreviation for the pair of sequents* $A \longrightarrow B$ *and* $B \longrightarrow A$. *Furthermore, we (typically) require that the conclusion of an* eLNDT *proof has no extension variables.*

The size *of a proof/derivation* P *or a formula* A, *written* $|P|$ *or* $|A|$ *respectively, is just the number of symbols occurring in it.*

Our formulation of eLNDT differs slightly from the original one in [5] in that (a) we admit Boolean constants in our language; and (b) we admit decisions only on propositional variables, not their negations. Both of these are only cosmetic, and in particular do not affect proof complexity, as observed in [5].

To define our 'positive fragment' of eLNDT notice that $Ap(A \vee B)$ is semantically equivalent to $A \vee (p \wedge B)$, which motivates the following analytic 'positive decision' rules:

$$p^+\text{-}l \, \frac{\Gamma, A \longrightarrow \Delta \quad \Gamma, p, B \longrightarrow \Delta}{\Gamma, Ap(A \vee B) \longrightarrow \Delta} \qquad p^+\text{-}r \, \frac{\Gamma \longrightarrow \Delta, A, p \quad \Gamma \longrightarrow \Delta, A, B}{\Gamma \longrightarrow \Delta, Ap(A \vee B)} \qquad (1)$$

Definition 10 (System eLNDT$^+$). *The system* eLNDT$^+$ *is defined just like* eLNDT, *except replacing the p-l and p-r rules by the positive ones above in* (1). *Moreover, all extension axioms and formulas occurring in a proof (in particular* cut*-formulas) must be positive.*

Identity, cut and structural rules:

$$\text{id}\,\frac{}{p \rightarrow p} \qquad \text{w-}l\,\frac{\Gamma \rightarrow \Delta}{\Gamma, A \rightarrow \Delta} \qquad \text{c-}l\,\frac{\Gamma, A, A \rightarrow \Delta}{\Gamma, A \rightarrow \Delta}$$

$$\text{cut}\,\frac{\Gamma \rightarrow \Delta, A \quad \Gamma, A \rightarrow \Delta}{\Gamma \rightarrow \Delta} \qquad \text{w-}r\,\frac{\Gamma \rightarrow \Delta}{\Gamma \rightarrow \Delta, A} \qquad \text{c-}r\,\frac{\Gamma \rightarrow \Delta, A, A}{\Gamma \rightarrow \Delta, A}$$

Logical rules:

$$0\,\frac{}{0 \rightarrow} \qquad \text{p-}l\,\frac{\Gamma, A \rightarrow \Delta, p \quad \Gamma, p, B \rightarrow \Delta}{\Gamma, ApB \rightarrow \Delta} \qquad \text{v-}l\,\frac{\Gamma, A \rightarrow \Delta \quad \Gamma, B \rightarrow \Delta}{\Gamma, A \vee B \rightarrow \Delta}$$

$$1\,\frac{}{\rightarrow 1} \qquad \text{p-}r\,\frac{\Gamma \rightarrow \Delta, A, p \quad \Gamma, p \rightarrow \Delta, B}{\Gamma \rightarrow \Delta, ApB} \qquad \text{v-}r\,\frac{\Gamma \rightarrow \Delta, A, B}{\Gamma \rightarrow \Delta, A \vee B}$$

Fig. 2. Rules for system (e)LNDT.

2.3 Some Basic (Meta) theorems for eLNDT$^+$

Let us first note that the set of valid positive sequents (without extension variables) is actually sufficiently expressive to be meaningful for proof complexity:

Proposition 11. *Validity of extension-free positive sequents is co**NP**-complete.*

This follows by a basic reduction from DNF validity, expressing positive terms (i.e. conjunctions of propositional variables) by recursively using the equivalence $p \wedge A \iff 0p(0 \vee A)$.

Note that our logical rules, in particular p^+-l and p^+-r, are not only sound but also invertible: the validity of the conclusion implies the validity of each premiss. A basic bottom-up proof search argument thus gives:

Proposition 12 (Soundness and completeness). eLNDT$^+$ *proves a positive sequent $\Gamma \rightarrow \Delta$ (without extension variables) iff $\bigwedge \Gamma \supset \bigvee \Delta$ is valid.*

As an example of explicit proofs in eLNDT$^+$ (and for later use) we have:

Proposition 13 (General identity). *Let $\mathcal{A} = \{e_i \leftrightarrow A_i\}_{i<n}$ be a set of positive extension axioms. There are polynomial-size eLNDT$^+$ proofs of $A \rightarrow A$, for positive formulas A containing only extension variables among $e_0, \ldots, e_{n-1}$.*

Proof. We construct proofs inductively according to the extension axiom set $\mathcal{A}$. When A is a propositional variable or Boolean constant, the required derivation is immediate by initial rule id or by the initial rules $0, 1$ along with w-l, w-r resp.

If $A = e_i$ for some $i < n$ or $A = B \vee C$, then we have proofs,[1]

$$\text{2cut}\,\frac{e_i \rightarrow A_i \quad \text{IH}\,\overline{\overline{A_i \rightarrow A_i}} \quad A_i \rightarrow e_i}{e_i \rightarrow e_i} \qquad \text{v-}r\,\frac{\text{v-}l\,\dfrac{\text{w-}r\,\dfrac{\text{IH}\,\overline{\overline{B \rightarrow B}}}{B \rightarrow B, C} \quad \text{w-}r\,\dfrac{\text{IH}\,\overline{\overline{C \rightarrow C}}}{C \rightarrow B, C}}{B \vee C \rightarrow B, C}}{B \vee C \rightarrow B \vee C}$$

---

[1] The first case exemplifies a typical argument by '$\mathcal{A}$-induction', but note also that a single cut rule between $e_i \rightarrow A_i$ and $A_i \rightarrow e_i$ would suffice.

where sequents marked IH are obtained by inductive hypothesis; other premises are extension axioms from $\mathcal{A}$. If $A = Bp(B \vee C)$ then we have the proof:

$$
\cfrac{
\cfrac{
IH \cfrac{}{B \to B}
}{
\text{w-}r \cfrac{}{B \to B}
}
\quad
\cfrac{
IH \cfrac{}{B \to B}
}{
\text{w-}r \cfrac{}{B \to B,C}
}
\;
p^{+}\text{-}r \cfrac{}{B \to Bp(B \vee C)}
\quad
\cfrac{
\text{id} \cfrac{}{p \to p}
}{
\text{w-}l,\text{w-}r \cfrac{}{p,C \to B,p}
}
\quad
\cfrac{
IH \cfrac{}{C \to C}
}{
\text{w-}l,\text{w-}r \cfrac{}{p,C \to B,C}
}
\;
p^{+}\text{-}r \cfrac{}{p,C \to Bp(B \vee C)}
}{
p^{+}\text{-}l \quad Bp(B \vee C) \to Bp(B \vee C)
}
$$

Note that we do not formally 'duplicate' the subproof corresponding to $B \to B$, we simply use it twice. Similarly, the proofs of $B \to B$ and $C \to C$ may have common subproofs corresponding to, say, the same extension variable.

To evaluate proof size note that, at each step of the argument above, we add a constant number of lines of polynomial size in A and $\mathcal{A}$. Since the total number of steps is bounded by $|A| + \sum_{i<n} |A_i|$, we obtain polynomial-size proofs overall.

Note that the result above, together with completeness, means that we can sometimes obtain polynomial-size proofs 'for free': for each valid (extension-free) sequent there is a constant-size proof by completeness, Proposition 12, and by the above result, we have polynomial-size proofs for all its 'instances' under *substitution*. E.g., by simply observing semantic validity, we immediately have:

Proposition 14 (Truth conditions). *Let $\mathcal{A} = \{e_i \leftrightarrow A_i\}_{i<n}$ be a set of positive extension axioms and let A and B be formulas over $e_0, \ldots, e_{n-1}$. There are polynomial-size* eLNDT$^+$ *proofs of the following sequents with respect to $\mathcal{A}$:*

$$Ap(A \vee B) \to A, p \quad Ap(A \vee B) \to A, B \quad A \to Ap(A \vee B) \quad p, B \to Ap(A \vee B)$$

3 Formalising Counting Arguments in eLNDT$^+$

In this work we shall make use of monotone Boolean counting functions, namely the *Threshold* functions $\mathrm{Th}_k^n : \{0,1\}^n \to \{0,1\}$ by $\mathrm{Th}_k^n(b_1, \ldots, b_n) = 1$ if at least k of $b_1, \ldots, b_n$ are 1. For a list of propositional variables $\mathbf{p} = p_1, \ldots, p_n$, we can compute the function $\mathrm{Th}_k^n(\mathbf{p})$ with polynomial-size positive NBPs as follows:

Definition 15 (Thresholds). *For each list $\mathbf{p}$ of propositional variables, and each integer k, we introduce an extension variable $t_k^{\mathbf{P}}$ and write $\mathcal{T}$ for the set of all extension axioms of the form (i.e. for all choices of p, $\mathbf{p}$ and k):*

$$t_0^{\epsilon} \leftrightarrow 1, \qquad t_k^{\epsilon} \leftrightarrow 0 \quad (if\ k \neq 0), \qquad t_k^{p\mathbf{P}} \leftrightarrow t_k^{\mathbf{P}} p(t_k^{\mathbf{P}} \vee t_{k-1}^{\mathbf{P}}) \tag{2}$$

Example 16. Revisiting Fig. 1, note that we may visualise $t_2^{p_1 p_2 p_3 p_4}$ by the program on the left. Referencing the extension axioms on the right, we may simply identify each e_{ij} with $t_{2-j+1}^{p_i \cdots p_4}$ (for $1 \leq i \leq 4$). It is not hard to see that, in general, $t_k^{\mathbf{P}}$ represents a positive NBP with number of nodes and edges quadratic in $|\mathbf{p}|$.

It turns out that eLNDT^+ admits small proofs of several characteristic properties of the Threshold functions, which we now survey. The following result is shown by induction on $|\mathbf{p}|$, appealing to Lemma 14 for all the inductive steps.

Proposition 17 ($t_k^{\mathbf{p}}$ is decreasing in k). *There are polynomial-size eLNDT^+ proofs of the following sequents over extension axioms $\mathcal{T}$:*

$$\longrightarrow t_0^{\mathbf{p}}, \qquad t_{k+1}^{\mathbf{p}} \longrightarrow t_k^{\mathbf{p}}, \qquad t_k^{\mathbf{p}} \longrightarrow \quad (if\ k > |\mathbf{p}|)$$

The next result simplifies many of our later arguments, admitting a 'direct' proof peculiar to the structure of our particular threshold programs (cf., e.g., [2,3]).

Lemma 18. *There are polynomial-size eLNDT^+ proofs over $\mathcal{T}$ of $t_k^{\mathbf{pqq}} \leftrightarrow t_k^{\mathbf{qpq}}$.*

The proof is, again, by induction on $|\mathbf{p}|$, this time using small proofs of the following 'medial' property for the inductive step:

$$\begin{aligned}
& (Aq(A \vee B))p((Aq(A \vee B)) \vee (Cq(C \vee D))) \\
\leftrightarrow \ & (Ap(A \vee C))q((Ap(A \vee C)) \vee (Bp(B \vee D)))
\end{aligned}$$

By repeatedly applying the above lemma, we obtain the following crucial result:

Theorem 19 (Symmetry). *Let π be a permutation of $\mathbf{p}$. Then there are polynomial-size eLNDT^+ proofs over $\mathcal{T}$ of $t_k^{\mathbf{p}} \leftrightarrow t_k^{\pi(\mathbf{P})}$.*

4   Case Study: The Pigeonhole Principle

As a warm up to our main result in the next section, we will show here how we may use the previous results to obtain polynomial-size proofs of the *propositional pigeonhole principle* in eLNDT^+. In our setting, this principle is encoded as:

$$\mathsf{PHP}_n := \left\{ \bigvee_{j=1}^n p_{ij} \right\}_{i=1}^{n+1} \longrightarrow \bigvee_{j=1}^n \bigvee_{i=1}^n \bigvee_{i'=i+1}^{n+1} 0p_{ij}(0 \vee p_{i'j}) \tag{3}$$

It is helpful to think of the propositional variables p_{ij} as expressing "pigeon i sits in hole j". In the RHS the formulas $0p_{ij}(0 \vee p_{i'j})$ are usually written as $p_{ij} \wedge p_{i'j}$ but, in the absence of conjunction, we adopt the current encoding.

We show that PHP_n admits small proofs in eLNDT^+ with a 'standard' high-level argument. We fix n throughout this section and write:

- $\mathbf{p}_i$ for the list $p_{i1}, \dots, p_{in}$, and just $\mathbf{p}$ for the list $\mathbf{p}_1, \dots, \mathbf{p}_{n+1}$.
- $\mathbf{p}_j^{\mathsf{T}}$ for the list $p_{1j}, \dots, p_{n+1j}$ and just $\mathbf{p}^{\mathsf{T}}$ for the list $\mathbf{p}_1^{\mathsf{T}}, \dots, \mathbf{p}_n^{\mathsf{T}}$.

The notation $\mathbf{p}^{\mathsf{T}}$ is suggestive since, construing $\mathbf{p}$ as an $(n+1) \times n$ matrix of propositional variables, $\mathbf{p}^{\mathsf{T}}$ is just the transpose $n \times (n+1)$ matrix.

Our approach towards proving PHP_n in eLNDT^+ (with small proofs) will be broken up into the three smaller steps. Writing LPHP_n and RPHP_n for the LHS and RHS, respectively, of PHP_n in (3), we will prove the following sequents:

$$\text{LPHP}_n \longrightarrow t^{\mathbf{p}}_{n+1} \quad (4) \qquad t^{\mathbf{p}}_{n+1} \longrightarrow t^{\mathbf{p}^{\mathsf{T}}}_{n+1} \quad (5) \qquad t^{\mathbf{p}^{\mathsf{T}}}_{n+1} \longrightarrow \text{RPHP}_n \quad (6)$$

Notice that, since $\mathbf{p}^{\mathsf{T}}$ is just a permutation of $\mathbf{p}$, we already have small proofs of (5) from Theorem 19, so we focus on the other two sequents. We will need:

Lemma 20 (Merging and splitting). *There are polynomial-size* eLNDT$^+$ *proofs, over extension axioms* $\mathcal{T}$, *of the following sequents:*

$$t^{\mathbf{p}}_k, t^{\mathbf{q}}_l \longrightarrow t^{\mathbf{pq}}_{k+l} \quad (7) \qquad t^{\mathbf{pq}}_{k+l} \longrightarrow t^{\mathbf{p}}_{k+1}, t^{\mathbf{q}}_l \quad (8)$$

This is again proved by induction on $|\mathbf{p}|$, appealing several times to Proposition 14. (7) yields small proofs of (4), and (8) yields small proofs of (6). Finally, (4), (5) and (6) are combined by cuts to obtain:

Theorem 21. *There are polynomial-size* eLNDT$^+$ *proofs of* PHP$_n$.

5 Positive Simulation of Non-positive Proofs

We have shown that eLNDT$^+$ can formalise basic counting arguments by giving small proofs of the pigeonhole principle. We now go further and show:

Theorem 22. eLNDT$^+$ *polynomially simulates* eLNDT *over positive sequents.*

This section is devoted to demonstrating this result, in particular defining various intermediate systems to this end. The high-level structure of the argument is similar to that of [3], but we must make several specialisations to the current setting due to the peculiarities of eNDT formulas and extension.

5.1 Positive Normal Form of eLNDT proofs

We first deal with non-positive formulas occurring in an eLNDT proof. The intuition is similar to that in [3] where negations are reduced to the variables using De Morgan duality. In our setting formulas are no longer closed under duality but, nonetheless, we are able to devise a bespoke 'positive normal form'.

First, we shall temporarily work with a presentation of eLNDT within eLNDT$^+$ by allowing *negative* literals, in order to facilitate our later translations.

Definition 23 (eLNDT$^{\pm}_{\pm}$). *For each propositional variable p we introduce a distinguished propositional variable $\overline{p}$. The system* eLNDT$^{\pm}_{\pm}$ *is defined just like* eLNDT$^+$ *but also allows positive decisions on variables $\overline{p}$. All syntactic positivity constraints remain. Furthermore,* eLNDT$^{\pm}_{\pm}$ *has additional initial sequents of the forms* $p, \overline{p} \longrightarrow$ *and* $\longrightarrow p, \overline{p}$.

Definition 24 (Positive normal form). *We define a (polynomial-time) translation from an* eLNDT *formula* A *to an* eLNDT$_-^+$ *formula* A^- *as follows:*

$$0^- := 0 \quad p^- := p \quad e_i^- := e_i \quad (A \vee B)^- := A^- \vee B^-$$
$$1^- := 1 \quad \overline{p}^- := \overline{p} \qquad\qquad (ApB)^- := 0\overline{p}(0 \vee A^-) \vee 0p(0 \vee B^-)$$

For a multiset of formulas $\Gamma = A_1, \ldots, A_n$ *we write* $\Gamma^- := A_1^-, \ldots, A_n^-$. *For a set of extension axioms* $\mathcal{A} = \{e_i \leftrightarrow A_i\}_{i<n}$, *we write* $\mathcal{A}^-$ *for* $\{e_i \leftrightarrow A_i^-\}_{i<n}$.

By induction on the length of an eLNDT proof, we obtain:

Theorem 25. *Let* P *be an* eLNDT *proof of* $\Gamma \longrightarrow \Delta$ *over extension axioms* $\mathcal{A}$. *There is an* eLNDT$_-^+$ *proof* P^- *of* $\Gamma^- \longrightarrow \Delta^-$ *over extension axioms* $\mathcal{A}^-$ *of size polynomial in* $|P|$.

The critical cases for the above theorem are the decision steps, since $\cdot^-$ commutes with everything else. For this we appeal to another 'truth lemma':

Lemma 26 (Truth for $\cdot^-$-translation). *Let* $\mathcal{A} = \{e_i \leftrightarrow A_i\}_{i<n}$ *be a set of positive extension axioms and let* A *and* B *be formulas over* $e_0, \ldots, e_{n-1}$. *There are polynomial-size* eLNDT$_-^+$ *proofs of the following sequents over* $\mathcal{A}^-$:

$$(ApB)^- \longrightarrow A^-, p \quad (ApB)^-, p \longrightarrow B^- \quad A^- \longrightarrow (ApB)^-, p \quad p, B^- \longrightarrow (ApB)^-$$

Combining the above lemma with the original truth conditions, Proposition 14, we can show, for positive extension-free formulas A, that there are polynomial-size eLNDT$_-^+$ proofs of $A^- \leftrightarrow A$. This is established by direct structural induction on A (which has no extension variables), and thus yields:

Corollary 27. eLNDT$_-^+$ *polynomially simulates* eLNDT, *over positive sequents.*

5.2 Generalised Counting Formulas

[3] relies heavily on substitution of formulas for variables in proofs of LK. Being based on usual Boolean formulae, this is entirely unproblematic in that setting, but for us causes low-level difficulties due to the restrictions of our syntax.

Our aim is to 'replace' negative literals in an eLNDT$_-^+$ proof by certain threshold formulas from Definition 15. However, if a literal occurs as a decision variable, then we cannot directly substitute an extension variable for it, since the syntax of eLNDT (crucially) does not allow this. To handle this, we introduce a generalisation of our previous threshold extension variables and axioms below that accounts for all such substitution situations. To maintain well-foundedness of sets of extension axioms, cf. Definition 4, these extension variables should be considered defined mutually inductively with eNDT formulas themselves. We shall gloss over the details of this technicality in what follows.

Definition 28 (Threshold decisions). *We introduce extension variables* $[At_k^{\mathbf{P}}{}_{(A\vee B)}]$ *for each list* $\mathbf{p}$ *of propositional variables, integer* k*, and formulas* A, B*. We extend* $\mathcal{T}$ *to include all extension axioms of the following form:*

$$
\begin{aligned}
[At_0^{\epsilon}{}_{(A\vee B)}] &\leftrightarrow A \vee B \\
[At_k^{\epsilon}{}_{(A\vee B)}] &\leftrightarrow A &&\text{if } k \neq 0 \qquad (9)\\
[At_k^{p\mathbf{P}}{}_{(A\vee B)}] &\leftrightarrow [At_k^{\mathbf{P}}{}_{(A\vee B)}]p([At_k^{\mathbf{P}}{}_{(A\vee B)}] \vee [At_{k-1}^{\mathbf{P}}{}_{(A\vee B)}])
\end{aligned}
$$

Despite the notation, $[At_k^{\mathbf{P}}{}_{(A\vee B)}]$ is, formally speaking, a single extension variable, not a decision on the extension variable $t_k^{\mathbf{P}}$ which, recall, our syntax does not permit. However the notation is suggestive, justified by the following counterpart of the truth conditions from Proposition 14 (proved by induction on $|\mathbf{p}|$):

Proposition 29 (Truth). *There are polynomial size* eLNDT$^+$ *proofs over* $\mathcal{T}$ *of:*

$$
[At_k^{\mathbf{P}}{}_{(A\vee B)}] \longrightarrow A, t_k^{\mathbf{P}} \quad [At_k^{\mathbf{P}}{}_{(A\vee B)}] \longrightarrow A, B \quad A \longrightarrow [At_k^{\mathbf{P}}{}_{(A\vee B)}] \quad t_k^{\mathbf{P}}, B \longrightarrow [At_k^{\mathbf{P}}{}_{(A\vee B)}]
$$

5.3 'Substituting' Thresholds for Negative Literals

For the remainder of this section we work with a fixed eLNDT$^+_-$ proof P, over extension axioms $\mathcal{A} = \{e_i \leftrightarrow A_i(e_0, \dots, e_{i-1})\}_{i<n}$, of a positive sequent $\Gamma \longrightarrow \Delta$, with propositional variables among $\mathbf{p} = p_0, \dots, p_{m-1}$ and extension variables among $\mathbf{e} = e_0, \dots, e_{n-1}$. Recall we are only concerned with the provable *positive* sequents of eLNDT, so our consideration of eLNDT$^+_-$ here suffices by Corollary 27.

Throughout this section, we write $\mathbf{p}_i$ for $p_0, \dots, p_{i-1}, p_{i+1}, \dots, p_{m-1}$, i.e. just $\mathbf{p}$ with p_i removed. We will need to define a family of intermediary systems eLNDT$^+_k(P)$, for each $k \geq 0$. Before that, we introduce the following translation:

Definition 30 ('Substituting' thresholds). *We define a (polynomial-time) translation from an* eLNDT$^+_-$ *formula A (over $\mathbf{p}$, $\overline{\mathbf{p}}$ and $\mathbf{e}$) to an* eLNDT$^+$ *formula A^k (over $\mathbf{p}$, some extension variables $\mathbf{e}^k$ and extension variables from $\mathcal{T}$) by:*

- $0^k := 0$, $1^k := 1$ *and* $p_i^k := p_i$ — $(A \vee B)^k := A^k \vee B^k$
- $\overline{p}_i^k := t_k^{p_i}$ — $(Ap_i(A \vee B))^k := A^k p_i(A^k \vee B^k)$
- e_i^k *is a fresh extension variable.* — $(A\overline{p}_i(A \vee B))^k := [A^k t_k^{p[0/p_i]}{}_{(A^k \vee B^k)}]$

Also $\mathcal{A}^k := \{e_i^k \leftrightarrow A_i^k(e_0^k, \dots, e_{i-1}^k)\}_{i<n}$*, and* $\{B_1, \dots, B_l\}^k := B_1^k, \dots, B_l^k$*.*

While this translation, and the threshold decisions themselves, may seem syntactically heavy, at the level of branching programs the idea is simple: the NBP represented by A^k is obtained by substituting the NBP represented by $t_k^{p_i}$ for each node labelled by $\overline{p}_i$ in the NBP represented by A. This may be visualised:

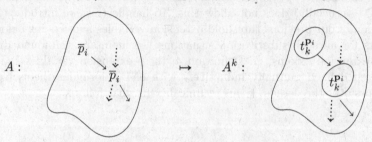

Our systems $\mathsf{eLNDT}_k^+(P)$ are parametrised by the choice of $k \geq 0$, and are peculiar to $\mathcal{A}$, $\mathbf{p}$ and P we fixed at the beginning of this subsection:

Definition 31. $\mathsf{eLNDT}_k^+(P)$ *is defined just like* eLNDT^+, *but has extra initial sequents* $p_i, t_k^{\mathbf{p}_i} \longrightarrow$ *and* $\longrightarrow p_i, t_k^{\mathbf{p}_i}$, *and only uses extension axioms* $\mathcal{T} \cup \mathcal{A}^k$.

By replacing every formula A in P by A^k and locally repairing the proof:

Lemma 32. *There is a* $\mathsf{eLNDT}_k^+(P)$ *proof* P^k *of* $\Gamma \longrightarrow \Delta$ *of size polynomial in* $|P|$.

The critical cases for this result are positive decisions on negative literals, for which we appeal to the previously given truth conditions, Proposition 29.

5.4   Putting It All Together

In this section we stitch together the proofs obtained in each $\mathsf{eLNDT}_k^+(P)$ for $0 \leqslant k \leqslant m + 1$ to obtain our main simulation result. Before this we will need the following result, proved by directly applying Lemmas 18 and 20.

Proposition 33. *For* $k \geq 0$, *there are polynomial size* eLNDT^+ *proofs over* $\mathcal{T}$ *of:*

$$p_i, t_k^{\mathbf{p}_i} \longrightarrow t_{k+1}^{\mathbf{P}} \qquad (10) \qquad\qquad t_k^{\mathbf{P}} \longrightarrow p_i, t_k^{\mathbf{p}_i} \qquad (11)$$

By adding $t_k^{\mathbf{P}}$ to the LHS and $t_{k+1}^{\mathbf{P}}$ to the RHS of each sequent in P^k from Lemma 32, replacing the additional initial sequents of $\mathsf{eLNDT}_k^+(P)$ from Definition 31 by (10) and (11) resp., we obtain:

Lemma 34. *For* $k \geq 0$, *there are polynomial size* eLNDT^+ *proofs over extension axioms* $\mathcal{T} \cup \mathcal{A}^k$ *of* $t_k^{\mathbf{P}}, \Gamma \longrightarrow \Delta, t_{k+1}^{\mathbf{P}}$

We may now assemble the proof of our main result:

Proof (of Theorem 22). By Corollary 27, without loss of generality let P be an eLNDT_-^+ proof of a positive sequent $\Gamma \longrightarrow \Delta$ over extension axioms $\mathcal{A}$. By Lemma 34 we construct, for each $k \leqslant n + 1$, polynomial-size proofs of $t_k^{\mathbf{P}}, \Gamma \longrightarrow \Delta, t_{k+1}^{\mathbf{P}}$, over $\mathcal{T} \cup \mathcal{A}^k$, and we simply cut them all together as follows:

$$\cfrac{\overset{\text{Prop. 17}}{\longrightarrow t_0^{\mathbf{P}}} \quad \overset{\text{Lem. 34}}{t_0^{\mathbf{P}}, \Gamma \longrightarrow \Delta, t_1^{\mathbf{P}}} \quad \cdots \quad \overset{\text{Lem. 34}}{t_m^{\mathbf{P}}, \Gamma \longrightarrow \Delta, t_{m+1}^{\mathbf{P}}} \quad \overset{\text{Prop. 17}}{t_{m+1}^{\mathbf{P}} \longrightarrow}}{\Gamma \longrightarrow \Delta} {\scriptstyle (m+2)\mathrm{cut}}$$

The resulting proof is indeed an eLNDT^+ proof of the required sequent, in particular over extension axioms $\mathcal{T} \cup \mathcal{A}^0 \cup \mathcal{A}^1 \cup \cdots \cup \mathcal{A}^{m+1}$.

Acknowledgments. This work was supported by a UKRI Future Leaders Fellowship, 'Structure vs Invariants in Proofs', project reference MR/S035540/1.

References

1. Ajtai, M., Gurevich, Y.: Monotone versus positive. J. ACM **34**(4), 1004–1015 (1987). https://doi.org/10.1145/31846.31852
2. Atserias, A., Galesi, N., Gavaldá, R.: Monotone proofs of the pigeon hole principle. In: Montanari, U., Rolim, J.D.P., Welzl, E. (eds.) ICALP 2000. LNCS, vol. 1853, pp. 151–162. Springer, Heidelberg (2000). https://doi.org/10.1007/3-540-45022-X_13
3. Atserias, A., Galesi, N., Pudlák, P.: Monotone simulations of non-monotone proofs. J. Comput. Syst. Sci. **65**(4), 626–638 (2002). https://doi.org/10.1016/S0022-0000(02)00020-X
4. Beame, P., Impagliazzo, R., Krajícek, J., Pitassi, T., Pudlák, P., Woods, A.R.: Exponential lower bounds for the pigeonhole principle. In: 24th Annual ACM STOC (1992). https://doi.org/10.1145/129712.129733
5. Buss, S., Das, A., Knop, A.: Proof complexity of systems of (non-deterministic) decision trees and branching programs. In: 28th Annual CSL. LIPIcs (2020). http://arxiv.org/abs/1910.08503
6. Buss, S., Kabanets, V., Kolokolova, A., Koucký, M.: Expander construction in VNC1. In: 8th ITCS Conference (2017). https://doi.org/10.4230/LIPIcs.ITCS.2017.31
7. Buss, S.R.: Towards NP-P via proof complexity and search. Ann. Pure Appl. Log. **163**, 906–917 (2012). https://doi.org/10.1016/j.apal.2011.09.009
8. Cook, S.A., Reckhow, R.A.: The relative efficiency of propositional proof systems. J. Symb. Log. **44**(1), 36–50 (1979). https://doi.org/10.2307/2273702
9. Das, A., Delkos, A.: Proof complexity of positive branching programs. CoRR (2021). https://arxiv.org/abs/2102.06673
10. Das, A., Oitavem, I.: A recursion-theoretic characterisation of the positive polynomial-time functions. In: 26th Annual CSL. LIPIcs (2018). http://drops.dagstuhl.de/opus/volltexte/2018/9685
11. Grigni, M.: Structure in monotone complexity. Ph.D. thesis (1991). http://www.mathcs.emory.edu/~mic/papers/Thesis.ps.gz
12. Grigni, M., Sipser, M.: Monotone complexity. In: LMS Symposium on Boolean Function Complexity (1992). https://citeseerx.ist.psu.edu/viewdoc/download?doi=10.1.1.72.7667&rep=rep1&type=pdf
13. Håstad, J.: Almost optimal lower bounds for small depth circuits. In: 18th Annual ACM STOC (1986). https://doi.org/10.1145/12130.12132
14. Jerábek, E.: A sorting network in bounded arithmetic. Ann. Pure Appl. Log. **162**, 341–355 (2011). https://doi.org/10.1016/j.apal.2010.10.002
15. Karchmer, M., Wigderson, A.: On span programs. In: 8th Annual SCT Conference (1993). https://doi.org/10.1109/SCT.1993.336536
16. Karchmer, M., Wigderson, A.: Monotone circuits for connectivity require super-logarithmic depth. In: 20th Annual ACM STOC (1988). https://doi.org/10.1145/62212.62265
17. Krajícek, J.: The Cook-Reckhow definition. CoRR (2019). http://arxiv.org/abs/1909.03691
18. Lautemann, C., Schwentick, T., Stewart, I.: Positive versions of polynomial time. Inf. Comput. **147**, 145–170 (1998). https://doi.org/10.1006/inco.1998.2742
19. Lautemann, C., Schwentick, T., Stewart, I.A.: On positive P. In: 11th Annual IEEE CCC (1996). https://doi.org/10.1109/CCC.1996.507678

20. Markov, A.A.: Minimal relay-diode bipoles for monotonic symmetric functions. Probl. Kibernetiki **8**, 117–121 (1962)
21. Pudlák, P., Buss, S.R.: How to lie without being (easily) convicted and the length of proofs in propositional calculus. In: 3rd Annual CSL. LIPIcs (1994). https://doi.org/10.1007/BFb0022253
22. Razborov, A.A.: Lower bounds for the monotone complexity of some boolean functions. In: Soviet Mathematics Doklady (1985). http://people.cs.uchicago.edu/~razborov/files/clique.pdf
23. Razborov, A.A.: Lower bounds on monotone complexity of the logical permanent. Math. Notes Acad. Sci. USSR (1985). https://link.springer.com/article/10.1007

Enumerating Classes of Effective Quasi-Polish Spaces

Matthew de Brecht[1], Takayuki Kihara[2], and Victor Selivanov[3]($\boxtimes$) ⓘ

[1] Graduate School of Human and Environmental Studies, Kyoto University, Kyoto, Japan
matthew@i.h.kyoto-u.ac.jp

[2] Department of Mathematical Informatics, Graduate School of Informatics, Nagoya University, Nagoya, Japan
kihara@i.nagoya-u.ac.jp

[3] A.P. Ershov Institute of Informatics Systems SB RAS, Novosibirsk, Russia
vseliv@iis.nsk.su

Abstract. We discuss ideal presentations of effective quasi-Polish spaces and some of their subclasses. Based on this, we introduce and study natural numberings of these classes, in analogy with the numberings of classes of algebraic structures popular in computability theory. We estimate the complexity of (effective) homeomorphism w.r.t. these numberings, and of some natural index sets. In particular, we give precise characterizations of the complexity of certain classes related to separation axioms.

Keywords: Effective quasi-Polish space · effective Polish space · effective domain · c.e. transitive relation · c.e. preorder · numbering · index set · effective descriptive set theory · separation axioms

1 Introduction

The investigation of computability in topological structures (which is currently a hot topic in computability theory) is less straightforward than the investigation of computability in countable algebraic structures [2, 7]. A reason is that it is not clear how to capture the computability issues for a topological space (even if the space is Polish) by a single countable algebraic structure. Nevertheless, people often look for analogues of well-developed notions and methods of the computable structure theory in the topological context. For instance, analogues of computable categoricity turned out fruitful also in the study of computable

M. de Brecht—De Brecht's research was supported by JSPS KAKENHI Grant Number 18K11166.

T. Kihara—Kihara's research was partially supported by JSPS KAKENHI Grant Numbers 19K03602 and 21H03392, and the JSPS-RFBR Bilateral Joint Research Project JPJSBP120204809.

V. Selivanov—Selivanov's research was supported by the RFBR-JSPS Bilateral Joint Research Project 20-51-50001.

U. Berger et al. (Eds.): CiE 2022, LNCS 13359, pp. 88–102, 2022.
https://doi.org/10.1007/978-3-031-08740-0_8

metric spaces and Banach spaces (see e.g. [18,19]), and analogues of degree spectra turned out interesting also for topological spaces [12,14,22].

In this paper, we introduce some natural numberings of classes of effective quasi-Polish (EQP-) spaces and initiate their investigation in analogy with numberings of classes of algebraic structures popular in computable structure theory (see e.g. [8–11,20] and references therein). Quasi-Polish spaces [3] are a class of well-behaved countably based spaces that includes many spaces of interest in analysis and theoretical computer science, such as Polish spaces and ω-continuous domains. The study of effective versions of quasi-Polish spaces was initiated in [16,21] and recently continued in [4,6,13]. Theorem 11 in [6] characterises the EQP-spaces (called there precomputable QP-spaces) as the spaces of ideals of c.e. transitive relations on ω (see also Theorem 3 in [4] for a more direct proof). This characterisation is very much in the spirit of domain theory where similar characterisations of computable domains are important. It is a basic technical tool of our paper because it enables to deduce precise complexity estimates for (the index sets of) several natural classes of EQP-spaces. These estimates are the main technical results of this paper but we also establish some facts on the complexity of (effective) homeomorphism.

After recalling some preliminaries in the next section, we discuss in Sect. 3 natural numberings of some classes of c.e. binary relations on ω and of the corresponding classes of EQP-spaces (some of which were considered in [22]). In Sect. 4 we estimate the complexity of (effective) homeomorphism in the introduced numberings in parallel to the similar question for algebraic structures (see e.g. [8,9,11]). In Sect. 5 we establish precise estimates of index sets of some popular classes of spaces related to separation axioms, which are certainly the main technical results of this paper.

2   Preliminaries

Here we recall some notation, notions and facts used throughout the paper. More special information is recalled in the corresponding sections below.

We use standard set-theoretical notation, in particular, Y^X is the set of functions from X to Y, and $P(X)$ is the class of subsets of a set X. All (topological) spaces in this paper are countably based T_0 (cb$_0$-spaces, for short). We denote the homeomorphism relation by $\simeq$. An *effective space* is a pair (X, β) where X is a cb$_0$-space, and $\beta : \omega \to P(X)$ is a numbering of a base in X such that there is a uniformly c.e. sequence $\{A_{ij}\}$ of c.e. sets with $\beta(i) \cap \beta(j) = \bigcup \beta(A_{ij})$ where $\beta(A_{ij})$ is the image of A_{ij} under β. We simplify (X, β) to X if β is clear from the context.

The effective space (X, β) is *c.e. (or overt)* if the set $\{n \mid \beta(n) \neq \varnothing\}$ is c.e. A subspace of a c.e. space is not necessarily c.e. Among the effective spaces are: the discrete space $\mathbb{N}$ of natural numbers, the Euclidean spaces $\mathbb{R}^n$, the Scott domain $P\omega$ (the powerset of the natural numbers with the Scott-topology; see [1] for information about domains), the Baire space $\mathcal{N} = \mathbb{N}^{\mathbb{N}}$, the Hilbert cube $[0, 1]^\omega$; all these spaces come with natural numberings of bases. With any effective space (X, β) we associate the *canonical embedding* $e : X \to P\omega$ defined by $e(x) = \{n \mid$

$x \in \beta(n)\}$. The canonical embedding is a computable homeomorphism between X and the subspace $e(X)$ of $P\omega$.

In any effective space X, one can define effective versions of classical hierarchies (see e.g. [21]), in particular the effective Borel hierarchy $\{\Sigma^0_{1+n}(X)\}_{n<\omega}$ and the effective Luzin hierarchy $\{\Sigma^1_n(X)\}_{n<\omega}$. For $X = \omega$, these coincide resp. with the arithmetical and analytical hierarchies.

An effective space is *effective Polish* (resp. *effective quasi-Polish*, abbreviated as EQP) if it is effectively homeomorphic to a Π^0_2-subspace of the Hilbert cube (resp. the Scott domain). Note that EQP-spaces are called in [6] precomputable QP-spaces, while c.e. EQP-spaces are called computable QP-spaces. All the aforementioned examples of spaces are c.e. EQP-spaces. Moreover, all computable Polish spaces and all computable ω-continuous domains (see e.g. [21]) are c.e. EQP-spaces. However, an effective Polish space is not necessarily computable Polish (nor even Δ^1_1-computable Polish; for example, consider a Π^0_1 subspace P of $\mathbb{N}^{\mathbb{N}}$ with no Δ^1_1 elements. If P were Δ^1_1-overt, P would have a Δ^1_1 element). The relation of effective homeomorphism between effective spaces will be denoted by $\simeq_e$. Note that if $(X, \beta) \simeq_e (Y, \gamma)$ then $X \simeq Y$. All classes of effective spaces considered below will be closed under $\simeq_e$.

We use standard terminology about binary relations and about domains (see e.g. [1,22]). In particular, an *ideal* of $(S; \rho)$ is a directed lower subset of S. By *interpolable* relations we mean transitive relations $\prec$ on S such that any initial segment $\{x \mid x \prec y\}$, $y \in S$, is directed.

We conclude this section with recalling the basic fact established in Theorem 11 [6] (see also Theorem 3 in [4] for additional details). Let $\prec$ be a transitive relation on ω. We consider the set $I(\prec)$ of all ideals of $\prec$ as a topological space with the topology induced by the Scott topology on $P\omega$. More precisely, the sets $[n]_\prec = \{I \in I(\prec) \mid n \in I\}$ for $n \in \omega$ form a basis of the topology and not just a subbasis. As shown in [6], such spaces of ideals are closely related to QP-spaces, namely: a space X is quasi-Polish iff it is homeomorphic to $I(\prec)$ for some transitive relation $\prec$ on ω. Moreover, an effective space (X, ξ) is EQP iff it is computably homeomorphic to $I(\prec)$ for some transitive c.e. relation $\prec$ on ω.

3   Enumerating Classes of Spaces

Here we introduce and study numberings of some classes of relations on ω and of EQP-spaces. Some natural numberings of spaces may be defined directly from the definitions of Sect. 2. For any effective space X, let π_X be the standard numbering of Π^0_2-subspaces of X. In the particular case $X = P\omega$ we obtain the numbering $\pi = \pi_X$ of all (up to $\simeq_e$) EQP-spaces. In the particular case $X = [0,1]^\omega$, π_X is a numbering of all effective Polish spaces (because, up to homeomorphism, Polish spaces are precisely the Π^0_2-subspaces of the Hilbert cube, see e.g. Theorem 4.14 in [15]); setting $\mu(n) = e(\pi_X(n))$, where e is the canonical embedding of $[0,1]^\omega$ into $P\omega$, we obtain a numbering μ of effective Polish spaces realised as Π^0_2-subspaces of $P\omega$.

Other natural numberings of spaces are defined using the ideal representations. We first define some numberings of classes of relations on ω. Setting

$V_n = \{(i,j) \mid \langle i,j \rangle \in W_n\}$, we obtain a standard computable numbering $\{V_n\}$ of the class $\mathbf{E}$ of all c.e. binary relations on ω. Let $\mathbf{T}, \mathbf{I}, \mathbf{P}, \mathbf{O}$ be the classes of all transitive c.e. relations, all interpolable c.e. relations, all c.e. preorders, and all c.e. partial orders on ω, respectively.

Proposition 1.

(1) There is a computable function t such that: $V_{t(n)} \in \mathbf{T}$, $V_n \in \mathbf{T}$ implies $V_n = V_{t(n)}$, and $V_m = V_n$ implies $V_{t(m)} = V_{t(n)}$.

(2) There is a computable function p such that: $V_{p(n)} \in \mathbf{P}$, $V_n \in \mathbf{P}$ implies $V_n = V_{p(n)}$, and $V_m = V_n$ implies $V_{p(m)} = V_{p(n)}$.

(3) There is a computable function o such that: $V_{o(n)} \in \mathbf{O}$, and $V_n \in \mathbf{O}$ implies $V_n = V_{o(n)}$.

Proof.

(1) As t we can take arbitrary computable function such that $V_{t(n)}$ is the transitive closure of V_n (such a function obviously exists).

(2) As p we can take arbitrary computable function such that $V_{p(n)}$ is the reflexive transitive closure of V_n (such a function obviously exists).

(3) Given a computable step-wise enumeration of $\{V_{p(n)}\}$, it is straightforward to construct a computable sequence $\{A_n\}$ of c.e. partial orders on ω such that: $A_n \subseteq V_{p(n)}$; if $V_{p(n)}$ is a partial order then $A_n = V_{p(n)}$; if $V_{p(n)}$ is not a partial order then almost all elements of A_n are pairwise incomparable. As o we can take arbitrary computable function such that $V_{o(n)} = A_n$. □

We thank an anonymous referee for showing that there is no function o as in item (3) with the additional property that $V_m = V_n$ implies $V_{o(m)} = V_{o(n)}$.

Corollary 1. *The classes $\mathbf{T}, \mathbf{P}, \mathbf{O}$ have computable numberings, namely the numberings $\{V_{t(n)}\}$, $\{V_{p(n)}\}$, $\{V_{o(n)}\}$, respectively.*

We do not know whether the class $\mathbf{I}$ has a computable numbering but we can define a natural non-computable one $\{V_{i(n)}\}$ where i is the $\varnothing''$-computable function which enumerates the Π_2^0-set $\{m \mid V_{t(m)} \in \mathbf{I}\}$ in the increasing order. Let also j, c be $\varnothing''$-computable functions which enumerate the Σ_3^0-sets $\{m \mid V_{t(m)}$ is computable$\}$ and $\{m \mid V_{p(m)}$ is computable$\}$, respectively.

Theorem 11 in [6], Corollary 1, and Propositions 3, 4 in [22] imply that $\{I(V_{t(n)})\}$, $\{I(V_{p(n)})\}$, $\{I(V_{o(n)})\}$, $\{I(V_{c(n)})\}$ are numberings of all (up to $\simeq_e$) EQP-spaces, positive algebraic domains, c.e. algebraic domains, and computable algebraic domains, respectively (see [22] for precise definitions and a discussion of these classes of domains); we sometimes denote these numberings by $\iota, \alpha, \beta, \gamma$, respectively. Sequences $\{I(V_{i(n)})\}$ and $\{I(V_{j(n)})\}$ are numberings of natural classes of ω-continuous domains, which we also denote by δ and ε, respectively. Below is a summary of the introduced numberings.

- μ: Standard numbering of Π_2^0-subspaces of $[0,1]^\omega$.
- π: Standard numbering of Π_2^0-subspaces of $\mathcal{P}\omega$.

- ι: Numbering of EQP-spaces derived from the computable numbering $\{V_{t(n)}\}$ of c.e. transitive relations ($\mathbf{T}$).
- α: Numbering of positive algebraic domains derived from the computable numbering $\{V_{p(n)}\}$ of c.e. preorders ($\mathbf{P}$).
- β: Numbering of c.e. algebraic domains derived from the computable numbering $\{V_{o(n)}\}$ of c.e. partial orders ($\mathbf{O}$).
- γ: Numbering of computable algebraic domains derived from the $\varnothing''$-computable numbering of computable partial orders.
- δ: Numbering of ω-continuous domains derived from the $\varnothing''$-computable numbering $\{I(V_{i(n)})\}$ of interpolable c.e. relations ($\mathbf{I}$).
- ε: Numbering of ω-continuous domains derived from the $\varnothing''$-computable numbering $\{I(V_{j(n)})\}$ of interpolable computable relations.

The next proposition compares the introduced numberings under the following preorder on the numberings of effective spaces: $\nu \leqslant_e \nu'$, if $\nu(n) \simeq_e \nu'(f(n))$ for some computable function f; let $\equiv_e$ be the equivalence relation induced by $\leqslant_e$. For an oracle h, let $\leqslant_e^h$ and $\equiv_e^h$ be the h-relativizations of $\leqslant_e$ and $\equiv_e$, respectively. The presence of oracles in some of the reductions below is explained by the fact that numberings $\gamma, \delta, \varepsilon$ are defined in a less constructive way than the other numberings.

Proposition 2. *We have:* $\mu \leqslant_e \pi \equiv_e \iota$, $\beta \leqslant_e \alpha \leqslant_e \iota$, $\varepsilon \leqslant_e^{\varnothing''} \delta \leqslant_e^{\varnothing''} \iota$, *and* $\gamma \leqslant_e^{\varnothing''} \alpha$. *The binary operations of product and coproduct are represented by computable functions in any of the numberings* $\mu, \pi, \iota, \alpha, \gamma$ *(again, up to* $\equiv_e$*).*

Proof. The relation $\pi \equiv_e \iota$ follows from the effectivity of proofs of Theorem 11 in [6] and Theorem 3 in [4]. The relation $\mu \leqslant_e \pi$ follows from Theorem 1 in [13] because the Hilbert cube is a computable Polish space. The remaining relations follow from the definition of the numbering and of functions i, j, c, and from Proposition 1. The assertion about product and coproduct is checked in a straightforward way, similar to Sects. 3.1 and 3.2 in [4]. $\qquad\square$

One could hope to find new interesting classes of EQP-spaces by restricting the general transitive relations. We conclude this section by showing that we get computably equivalent numberings of EQP-spaces based on computable strict partial orders instead of all c.e. transitive relations.

Proposition 3. *There is a computable function s such that $V_{s(n)}$ is a computable strict partial order and $I(V_{t(n)}) \simeq_e I(V_{s(n)})$ for each $n \in \omega$.*

Proof. We write $\prec_n$ for the relation $V_{t(n)}$. Let $\prec_n^{(k)}$ be a computable relation satisfying $\forall n, x, y(x \prec_n y \leftrightarrow \exists k(x \prec_n^{(k)} y))$, and let $\{F_i\}$ be a computable enumeration of all non-empty finite subsets of ω. Then there is a computable function s such that $s(n)$ is an index for the relation $\sqsubset_n$ defined as $\langle i, l \rangle \sqsubset_n \langle j, m \rangle$ iff the following all hold: (1) $F_i \subseteq F_j$, (2) $l < m$, (3) $\forall x \leqslant m, \forall k \leqslant m(x \prec_n^{(k)} y \to x \in F_j)$, (4) $\exists y \in F_j, \forall x \in F_i, \exists k \leqslant m(x \prec_n^{(k)} y)$. The relation $\sqsubset_n$ is computable, irreflexive, and transitive, hence it is a computable strict partial order. One then checks that the functions $f: I(\prec_n) \to I(\sqsubset_n)$ and $g: I(\sqsubset_n) \to I(\prec_n)$, defined as $f(I) = \{\langle j, m \rangle \mid F_j \subseteq I \wedge m \in \omega\}$ and $g(I) = \bigcup_{\langle j,m \rangle \in I} F_j$, are computable inverses of each other. We omit the details.   □

4   Complexity of (Effective) Homeomorphism

Here we estimate the complexity of (effective) homeomorphism relations $\simeq_e$ and $\simeq$ in the introduced numberings and deduce some corollaries. Similar questions for algebraic structures were studied in detail (see e.g. [8,9,11]). In the next theorem we collect some estimates which for the classes of domains resemble the corresponding estimates for algebraic structures[1], while for Polish and quasi-Polish spaces are apparently higher.

To obtain the estimate for ι, we employ the representation of computable functions $f: I(\prec_1) \to I(\prec_2)$ between spaces of ideals, where $\prec_1, \prec_2 \in \mathbf{T}$, established in [4], Theorem 2. We associate with any $R \subseteq \mathbb{N} \times \mathbb{N}$ a partial function $\ulcorner R \urcorner$ from $I(\prec_1)$ to $I(\prec_2)$ as follows: $\ulcorner R \urcorner (I) = \{n \in \mathbb{N} \mid \exists m \in I(mRn)\}$, $dom(\ulcorner R \urcorner) = \{I \in I(\prec_1) \mid \ulcorner R \urcorner (I) \in I(\prec_2)\}$. By Theorem 2 in [4], a function $f: I(\prec_1) \to I(\prec_2)$ is computable iff $f = \ulcorner R \urcorner$ for some c.e. binary relation R.

For the case $\prec_1, \prec_2 \in \mathbf{I}$ of domains, the above representation may be simplified using the effective version of results in Sect. 2.2.6 of [1] (see Definition 2.2.27 and Theorem 2.2.28). Namely, the computable functions $f: I(\prec_1) \to I(\prec_2)$ coincide with the functions $\ulcorner R \urcorner$ where R is a binary c.e. relation on ω satisfying the following conditions: if aRb and $a \prec_1 a'$ then $a'Rb$; if aRb and $b' \prec_2 b$ then aRb'; for any a there is b with aRb; for all a, b, b' with aRb, aRb' there is b'' with $b \prec_2 b'', b' \prec_2 b''$, and aRb''; if aRb then $a'Rb$ for some $a' \prec_1 a$. Conjunction of these conditions is denoted as $mor(R, \prec_1, \prec_2)$ (meaning "R is a morphism from $\prec_1$ to $\prec_2$"). We note that $\ulcorner R \urcorner = id_{I(\prec_1)}$ iff $aRb \leftrightarrow b \prec_1 a$.

Theorem 1.

(1) Let $\nu \in \{\alpha, \beta, \gamma, \delta, \varepsilon\}$. Then the relations $\nu(m) \simeq_e \nu(n)$ and $\nu(m) \simeq \nu(n)$ are Σ_3^0-complete and Σ_1^1-complete sets, respectively. Moreover, they are resp. Σ_3^0- and Σ_1^1-complete equivalence relations under the computable reducibility of equivalence relations.

(2) Let $\nu \in \{\iota, \mu\}$. The relations $\nu(m) \simeq_e \nu(n)$ and $\nu(m) \simeq \nu(n)$ are Π_1^1 and Σ_2^1, respectively.

Proof. 1. First we prove the upper bounds. For $\nu = \alpha$, it is easy to see (cf. proof of Theorem 2 in [22]) that $\alpha(m) \simeq_e \alpha(n)$ iff $(\omega; V_{p(m)}) \simeq_e (\omega; V_{p(n)})$ iff

$$\exists k, l \forall x, y (\varphi_k(x) \downarrow \wedge \varphi_l(x) \downarrow \wedge (x V_{p(m)} y \leftrightarrow \varphi_k(x) V_{p(n)} \varphi_k(y)) \wedge (x V_{p(n)} y \leftrightarrow$$
$$\varphi_l(x) V_{p(m)} \varphi_l(y)) \wedge x V_{p(m)} \varphi_l(\varphi_k(x)) V_{p(m)} x \wedge y V_{p(n)} \varphi_k(\varphi_l(y) V_{p(n)} y)),$$

hence the relation is Σ_3^0. For the relation $\simeq$ we only have to add the functional quantifier $\exists h$ in the beginning of the above formula and relativize φ to the oracle h; this yields the desired estimate Σ_1^1.

---

[1] We thank Nikolay Bazhenov for the related bibliographical hints.

The above argument works for $\nu = \beta$ if we just replace p by o. For $\nu = \gamma$, we also replace p by c; it is easy to see that the $\varnothing''$-computability of c does not damage the estimate Σ_3^0 and (trivially) the estimate Σ_1^1.

For $\nu = \delta$, we use the representation of computable functions between ideal spaces described before the formulation of the theorem: $\delta(m) \simeq_e \delta(n)$ iff

$$\exists k, l, x, y(x = i(m) \wedge y = i(n) \wedge mor(V_k, V_x, V_y) \wedge mor(V_l, V_y, V_x) \wedge$$
$$\forall a, b(a(V_l \circ V_k)b \leftrightarrow bV_x a) \wedge \forall a, b(a(V_k \circ V_l)b \leftrightarrow bV_y a)).$$

Since i is $\varnothing''$-computable, the first two conjuncts in the main parenthesis are Σ_3^0. Since V_x is c.e., the same holds for the third and fourth conjuncts, while the fifth and sixth conjuncts are Π_2^0. This concludes the estimate for $\simeq_e$. For the relation $\simeq$ we only have to add the functional quantifier $\exists h$ in the beginning of the above formula and replace V_k, V_l by V_k^h, V_l^h; this yields the desired estimate Σ_1^1. The above argument (with j in place of i) works for $\nu = \varepsilon$.

Now we prove the lower bounds. By Theorem 4.7(a) in [11], for any Σ_3^0 set A there are computable sequences $\{L_k\}, \{M_k\}$ of computable linear orders on ω such that $k \in A$ iff $L_k \simeq_e M_k$. By the definition of ideal spaces, $L_k \simeq_e M_k$ iff $I(L_k) \simeq_e I(M_k)$ iff $A \leqslant_m \{\langle k, l \rangle \mid \nu(k) \simeq_e \nu(l)\}$ for every $\nu \in \{\alpha, \beta, \gamma, \delta, \varepsilon\}$, concluding the proof for Σ_3^0.

By Theorem 4.4(d) in [11], for any Σ_1^1 set A there are computable sequences $\{L_k\}, \{M_k\}$ of computable linear orders on ω such that $k \in A$ iff $L_k \simeq M_k$. Repeating the argument of the previous paragraph, we obtain the proof for Σ_1^1.

It remains to show that $\simeq_e$ and $\simeq$ are also complete as equivalence relations. As follows from Proposition 4 in [9], for any Σ_3^0 equivalence relation A on ω there is a computable sequence $\{L_k\}$ of computable partial orders on ω such that kAl iff $L_k \simeq_e L_l$ which proves the Σ_3^0 completeness for every $\nu \in \{\alpha, \beta, \gamma, \delta, \varepsilon\}$. By Theorem 5 in [8], for any Σ_1^1 equivalence relation A on ω there is a computable sequence $\{L_k\}$ of computable linear orders on ω such that kAl iff $L_k \simeq L_l$. This proves the Σ_1^1 completeness for every $\nu \in \{\alpha, \beta, \gamma, \delta, \varepsilon\}$.

2. By Proposition 2, we can use ι instead of π. Denoting the relation $V_{t(n)}$ in Proposition 1 by $\prec_n$, we obtain: $\iota(m) \simeq_e \iota(n)$ iff $I(\prec_m) \simeq_e I(\prec_n)$ iff

$$\exists k, l(\ulcorner V_k \urcorner : I(\prec_m) \to I(\prec_n) \wedge \ulcorner V_l \urcorner : I(\prec_n) \to I(\prec_m) \wedge$$
$$\ulcorner V_l \urcorner \circ \ulcorner V_k \urcorner = id_{I(\prec_m)} \wedge \ulcorner V_k \urcorner \circ \ulcorner V_l \urcorner = id_{I(\prec_n)}),$$

hence it suffices to check that the relation $\ulcorner V_l \urcorner \circ \ulcorner V_k \urcorner = id_{I(\prec_m)}$ is Π_1^1. Since it is equivalent to $\forall I \in I(\prec_m)(\ulcorner V_j \urcorner(\ulcorner V_i \urcorner(I)) = I)$, this follows from the definition of $\ulcorner R \urcorner(I)$.

The second assertion is a straightforward relativization of the first one. Indeed, $\iota(m) \simeq \iota(n)$ iff $I(\prec_m) \simeq I(\prec_n)$ iff

$$\exists R, S \subseteq \mathbb{N}^2(\ulcorner R \urcorner : I(\prec_m) \to I(\prec_n) \wedge \ulcorner S \urcorner : I(\prec_n) \to I(\prec_m) \wedge$$
$$\ulcorner S \urcorner \circ \ulcorner R \urcorner = id_{I(\prec_m)} \wedge \ulcorner R \urcorner \circ \ulcorner S \urcorner = id_{I(\prec_n)}),$$

hence the relation is Σ_2^1. $\square$

We do not currently know whether the estimates in item 2 of the above theorem are precise. From the effective Stone duality developed in [12,14] it follows that the homeomorphism relation between computable compact Polish spaces is Σ_1^1-complete, as it was noticed in a recent communication of the third author with Alexander Melnikov (see Corollary 4.28 in [5]). But for computable Polish spaces the question remains open.

As a corollary of Theorem 1 and Proposition 2, we obtain upper bounds for ι-index sets of some natural classes of spaces.

Corollary 2. *Let $\nu \in \{\mu, \alpha, \beta, \gamma, \delta, \varepsilon\}$. Then $\{n \mid \exists m(\iota(n) \simeq_e \nu(m))\}$ is Π_1^1 and $\{n \mid \exists m(\iota(n) \simeq \nu(m))\}$ is Σ_2^1.*

In particular, the problem of deciding whether a given effective quasi-Polish space is effectively homeomorphic to a metrizable space (a c.e. domain, c.e. algebraic domain, etc.) is Π_1^1. For the homeomorphism problem, it is Σ_2^1. In the next section we show that the estimate for metrizable spaces can be improved.

5   Complexity of Separation Axioms

Here we discuss some classes of spaces related to separation axioms. Let $\mathcal{T}_1, \mathcal{T}_2, \mathcal{R}, \mathcal{M}$ be the classes of T_1-, T_2-, regular, and metrisable spaces, respectively. Let $\{D_n\}$ be the standard numbering of finite subsets of ω, then the sets $\check{D}_n = \{A \subseteq \omega \mid D_n \subseteq A\}$ form the standard basis of the Scott topology on $P\omega$.

Proposition 4. *The π-index set of any of the classes $\mathcal{T}_1$, $\mathcal{T}_2$, $\mathcal{R}$, $\mathcal{M}$ is Π_1^1.*

Proof. By the definition of a T_1-space, $\pi(m) \in \mathcal{T}_1$ iff $\forall x, y \in \pi(m)(x \neq y \rightarrow \exists n(x \in \check{D}_n \not\ni y))$. Since $\pi(m) \in \Pi_2^0(P\omega)$, we get $\pi^{-1}(\mathcal{T}_1) \in \Pi_1^1$.

By the definition of a T_2-space, $\pi(m) \in \mathcal{T}_2$ iff

$$\forall x, y \in \pi(m)(x \neq y \rightarrow \exists i, j(x \in \check{D}_i \wedge y \in \check{D}_j \wedge \check{D}_i \cap \check{D}_j \cap \pi(m) = \varnothing)).$$

Since $\check{D}_i \cap \check{D}_j \cap \pi(m) = \varnothing$ iff $\forall z \in \pi(m)(z \notin \check{D}_i \vee z \notin \check{D}_j)$, we have $\pi^{-1}(\mathcal{T}_2) \in \Pi_1^1$.

Recall that X is regular iff for every $x \in X$ and every basic neighborhood U of x there is a basic neighborhood V of x such that the closure $Cl(V)$ of V in X is contained in U. For $X = \pi(m)$ this reads: $\pi(m) \in \mathcal{R}$ iff $\forall x \in \pi(m)\forall i(x \in \check{D}_i \rightarrow \exists j(x \in \check{D}_j \wedge Cl(\check{D}_j \cap \pi(m)) \subseteq \check{D}_i))$. Thus, it suffices to check that the relation $\forall y(y \in Cl(\check{D}_j \cap \pi(m)) \rightarrow y \in \check{D}_i)$ is Π_1^1, and for this it suffices to check that the relation $y \in Cl(\check{D}_j \cap \pi(m))$ is Σ_1^1. The relation is equivalent to $\forall k(y \in \check{D}_k \cap \pi(m) \rightarrow \exists z \in \check{D}_j \cap \pi(m)(z \in \check{D}_k))$, hence it is indeed Σ_1^1.

By the Urysohn metrisation theorem we have $\mathcal{M} = \mathcal{T}_1 \cap \mathcal{R}$, hence the estimate Π_1^1 for $\pi^{-1}(\mathcal{M})$ follows from the previous ones. Note that the upper bound Σ_2^1 of $\pi^{-1}(\mathcal{M})$ in Corollary 2 (without using the Urysohn theorem) is much worse.   □

Next we show that the upper bounds of Proposition 4 are optimal. Our proofs below demonstrate that the ideal characterisations provide useful tools for such kind of results. Recall that the following implications hold for cb$_0$-spaces:

$$\text{metrizable} \iff \text{regular} \implies \text{Hausdorff} \implies T_1 \implies T_0.$$

We start with the following Π_1^1-completeness result with respect to the numbering ι (i.e., the numbering of all effective quasi-Polish spaces induced from the standard numbering of c.e. transitive relations), where recall $\iota \equiv_e \pi$ from Proposition 2.

Theorem 2. *Let $F \subseteq \omega$ be a Π_1^1 set. Then, there exists a computable function which, given $p \in \omega$, returns an ι-index of a c.e. EQP-space X such that*

$$\begin{cases} X \text{ is metrizable} & \text{if } p \in F, \\ X \text{ is not } T_1 & \text{if } p \notin F. \end{cases}$$

Proof. Recall that the set of indices of well-founded computable trees is Π_1^1 complete. Hence, instead of a Π_1^1 set, we consider computable trees. Let $T \subseteq \omega^{<\omega}$ be a computable tree. Our space X will be $\{I_x : x \in \omega^\omega\} \cup \{J_x : x \in [T]\}$ equipped with the specialization order $J_x \leqslant I_x$, where $[T]$ is the set of all infinite paths through T. The discussion from here on is to write down this space X as an ideal space.

For each $\sigma \in \omega^{<\omega}$, we prepare for a new symbol $\underline{\sigma}$. Let $|\sigma|$ be the length of σ, and put $|\underline{\sigma}| = |\sigma|$. If σ is nonempty, i.e., $|\sigma| > 0$, we denote by σ^- the immediate predecessor of σ. We define a computable binary relation $\prec$ on the set $|\prec| := \{\sigma, \underline{\sigma} : \sigma \in \omega^{<\omega}\}$ as follows: If $\sigma \in \omega^\omega$ is nonempty, enumerate $\sigma^- \prec \sigma$, $\underline{\sigma^-} \prec \underline{\sigma}$, and $\sigma \prec \underline{\sigma}$. If $\sigma \notin T$ then we also enumerate $\underline{\sigma^-} \prec \sigma$. Then consider its transitive closure and define $X = I(\prec)$.

Note that if $a \prec b$ then either $|a| < |b|$ or $a = \sigma$ and $b = \underline{\sigma}$ for some $\sigma \in \omega^{<\omega}$. If I is an ideal of $\prec$, then for any $a \in I$ one can use directedness of I twice to obtain $b, c \in I$ such that $a \prec b \prec c$. Then, by the property of $\prec$ mentioned above, we have $|a| < |c|$. Therefore, any ideal contains arbitrarily long strings. Moreover, as no pair of incomparable strings has an upper bound, in order for a set to be directed, all of its members must be comparable. This means that for any ideal I of $\prec$ there exists an infinite string $x \in \omega^\omega$ such that I consists only of the initial segments of x or those underlined in them. In other words, I is the $\prec$-downward closure of $\{\sigma : \sigma \subset x\}$ or $\{\underline{\sigma} : \sigma \subset x\}$, where we mean by $\sigma \subset x$ that σ is an initial segment of x.

If x is an infinite path through T, then the downward closure of $\{\sigma : \sigma \subset x\}$ is $J_x = \{\sigma : \sigma \subset x\}$, and the downward closure of $\{\underline{\sigma} : \sigma \subset x\}$ is $I_x = \{\sigma, \underline{\sigma} : \sigma \subset x\}$. Both I_x and J_x are ideals, and since $J_x \subseteq I_x$, obviously $J_x \in [\tau]_\prec$ implies $I_x \in [\tau]_\prec$, so $J_x \leqslant_X I_x$, where recall that $[n]_\prec = \{I \in I(\prec) : n \in I\}$ is a basic open set, and $\leqslant_X$ is the specialization order. Hence, if T is not well-founded, then X is not T_1. If T is well-founded, then any $x \in \omega^\omega$ has an initial segment $\sigma \notin T$, and for any such σ we have $\sigma^- \prec \underline{\sigma^-} \prec \sigma \prec \underline{\sigma} \prec \dots$. Hence, $\{\sigma : \sigma \subset x\}$ and $\{\underline{\sigma} : \sigma \subset x\}$ have the same downward closure $I_x = \{\sigma, \underline{\sigma} : \sigma \subset x\}$. Therefore, any ideal is of the form I_x for some $x \in \omega^\omega$. Thus, we have $X = \{I_x : x \in \omega^\omega\}$, which is homeomorphic to Baire space ω^ω. This is because, as $|\prec| = \{\sigma, \underline{\sigma} : \sigma \in \omega^{<\omega}\}$ is the underlying set of the binary relation $\prec$, the set $\{[\sigma]_\prec, [\underline{\sigma}]_\prec : \sigma \in \omega^{<\omega}\}$ yields the topology on X by definition, and the above argument shows $X \cap [\sigma]_\prec = X \cap [\underline{\sigma}]_\prec = \{I_x : \sigma \subset x\}$. In particular, X is metrizable.

For overtness, given $\sigma \in \omega^{<\omega}$, if x extends σ then $I_x = \{\sigma, \underline{\sigma} : \sigma \subset x\}$ is an ideal of $\prec$ as seen above, and contains both σ and $\underline{\sigma}$; hence $I_x \in [\sigma]_\prec$ and $I_x \in [\underline{\sigma}]_\prec$. This means that $X \cap [\tau]_\prec \neq \emptyset$ for any $\tau \in |\prec|$. In particular, X is overt.   □

Theorem 2 shows that, for any $i \in \{1, 2, 3\}$, the ι-index set of all c.e. EQP T_i-spaces is Π_1^1-complete, where a second countable T_0 space is T_3 if and only if it is metrizable. This result can be further extended as follows.

Theorem 3. *Let* $M \subseteq H \subseteq F \subseteq \omega$ *be* Π_1^1 *sets. Then, there exists a computable function which, given* $p \in \omega$, *returns an* ι*-index of a c.e. EQP-space* X *such that*

$$
\begin{cases}
X \text{ is metrizable} & \text{if } p \in M, \\
X \text{ is Hausdorff, but not metrizable} & \text{if } p \in H \backslash M, \\
X \text{ is } T_1, \text{ but not Hausdorff} & \text{if } p \in F \backslash H, \\
X \text{ is not } T_1 & \text{if } p \notin F.
\end{cases}
$$

This means that every tuple (M, H, F) of Π_1^1-sets such that $M \subseteq H \subseteq F$ uniformly m-reduces to $(\iota^{-1}(\mathcal{M}), \iota^{-1}(\mathcal{T}_2), \iota^{-1}(\mathcal{T}_1))$. Let us decompose the proof of Theorem 3 into a few lemmas.

Lemma 1. *Let* $H \subseteq \omega$ *be a* Π_1^1 *set. Then, there exists a computable function which, given* $p \in \omega$, *returns an* ι*-index of a c.e. EQP-space* X *such that*

$$
\begin{cases}
X \text{ is metrizable} & \text{if } p \in H, \\
X \text{ is } T_1, \text{ but not Hausdorff} & \text{if } p \notin H.
\end{cases}
$$

Proof. First, one specific example of a second countable T_1 topology which is not Hausdorff is called a telophase topology [23, II.73]. Here, our construction is closer to the one in [17], which adds an inseparable pair of points at infinity to ω than the one in [23, II.73], which adds a new point 1^* to $[0, 1]$ where $(1, 1^*)$ forms an inseparable pair. In our construction, a tree $T \subseteq \omega^{<\omega}$ is first given. For $x \in \omega^\omega$, if x is an infinite path through T then we add an inseparable pair (I_x, I_x^*) of points at infinity to the discrete space $\omega^{<\omega}$. If x is not an infinite path through T then we add a single point J_x at infinity to $\omega^{<\omega}$.

Formally, given a tree $T \subseteq \omega^{<\omega}$, we consider the following specific presentation $\prec$ of a telophase topology: For each $\sigma \in \omega^{<\omega}$, we prepare for symbols $\underline{\sigma}$, $[\sigma, \infty]$, and $[\sigma, \infty^*]$. We define a computable binary relation $\prec$ on the set $|\prec| := \{\underline{\sigma}, [\sigma, \infty], [\sigma, \infty^*] : \sigma \in \omega^{<\omega}\}$. If σ is nonempty, we denote by σ^- the immediate predecessor of σ, and enumerate $[\sigma^-, o] \prec [\sigma, o] \prec \underline{\sigma} \prec \underline{\sigma}$ for each $o \in \{\infty, \infty^*\}$. If $\sigma \notin T$, we also enumerate $[\sigma^-, \infty^*] \prec [\sigma, \infty] \prec [\sigma, \infty^*]$. Then consider its transitive closure and define $X = I(\prec)$.

First, since $\underline{\sigma} \prec \underline{\sigma}$, the $\prec$-downward closure of $\{\underline{\sigma}\}$ forms an ideal. This is $I_\sigma = \{\underline{\sigma}\} \cup \{[\tau, \infty], [\tau, \infty^*] : \tau \subseteq \sigma\}$, where we mean by $\tau \subseteq \sigma$ that τ is an initial segment of σ. Note that the subspace $Y = \{I_\sigma : \sigma \in \omega^{<\omega}\}$ of X is discrete since $Y \cap [\underline{\sigma}]_\prec = \{I_\sigma\}$. For any $a \notin I_\sigma$, a and $\underline{\sigma}$ have no common upper bound, so I_σ is the unique ideal containing $\underline{\sigma}$. If an ideal I does not contain $\underline{\sigma}$ for any $\sigma \in \omega^{<\omega}$, then as in the proof of Theorem 2, one can see that I contains $[\sigma, \infty]$ or $[\sigma, \infty^*]$ for an arbitrarily long string σ. Moreover, as no pair of incomparable strings has an upper bound, in order for a set to be directed, all of its members must be comparable. This means that for any such ideal I of $<$ there exists an infinite string $x \in \omega^\omega$ such that I consists only of $[\sigma, \infty]$ or $[\sigma, \infty^*]$ for initial segments σ of x. In other words, such an I is the $<$-downward closure of $\{[\sigma, \infty] : \sigma \subset x\}$ or $\{[\sigma, \infty^*] : \sigma \subset x\}$.

If x is an infinite path through T, then both $I_x = \{[\sigma, \infty] : \sigma \subset x\}$ and $I_x^* = \{[\sigma, \infty^*] : \sigma \subset x\}$ are downward closed. Hence, any ideal is of the form I_σ, I_x or I_x^*. We claim that the latter two ideals as points cannot be separated by disjoint open sets. This is because any basic open sets containing I_x and I_x^* are of the form $[[\sigma, \infty]]_<$ for some $\sigma \subset x$ and $[[\tau, \infty^*]]_<$ for some $\tau \subset x$ respectively. However, $[[\sigma, \infty]]_<$ and $[[\tau, \infty^*]]_<$ always have an intersection I_ρ, where ρ is a common extension of σ and τ. Hence, X is not Hausdorff. If x is not an infinite path through T, then as in the proof of Theorem 3, one can see that both $\{[\sigma, \infty] : \sigma \subset x\}$ and $\{[\sigma, \infty^*] : \sigma \subset x\}$ have the same downward closure $J_x = \{[\sigma, \infty], [\sigma, \infty^*] : \sigma \subset x\}$. In any case, no two ideals are comparable by $\subseteq$, so X is T_1. Hence, if T is ill-founded, then X is T_1, but not Hausdorff.

If T is well-founded, then as seen above, any ideal is of the form I_σ or J_x; that is, $X = \{I_\sigma : \sigma \in \omega^{<\omega}\} \cup \{J_x : x \in \omega^\omega\}$. We claim that X is homeomorphic to the Polish space $\omega^{\leq\omega} := \omega^{<\omega} \cup \omega^\omega$ whose topology is generated from $\{\sigma : \sigma \in \omega^{<\omega}\}$ and $[\sigma] = \{x \in \omega^{\leq\omega} : x \text{ extends } \sigma\}$. This is because, as $|<| = \{\underline{\sigma}, [\sigma, \infty], [\sigma, \infty^*] : \sigma \in \omega^{<\omega}\}$ is the underlying set of the binary relation $<$, the set $\{[\underline{\sigma}]_<, [[\sigma, \infty]]_<, [[\sigma, \infty^*]]_< : \sigma \in \omega^{<\omega}\}$ yields the topology on X by definition, and the above argument shows $X \cap [[\sigma, \infty]]_< = X \cap [[\sigma, \infty^*]]_< = \{I_\tau : \tau \subseteq \sigma\} \cup \{J_x : \sigma \subset x\}$. Hence, the union of the map $\sigma \mapsto I_\sigma$ and the map $x \mapsto J_x$ gives a homeomorphism between $\omega^{\leq\omega}$ and X. In particular, X is metrizable.

For overtness, given $\sigma \in \omega^{<\omega}$, we have $I_\sigma \in [\sigma]_<$, and if x extends σ then $I_x, J_x \in [[\sigma, \infty]]_<$ and $I_x^*, J_x \in [[\sigma, \infty^*]]_<$. This means that $X \cap [\tau]_< \neq \varnothing$ for any $\tau \in |<|$. In particular, X is overt. $\qquad\square$

Lemma 2. *Let $M \subseteq \omega$ be a Π_1^1 set. Then, there exists a computable function which, given $p \in \omega$, returns an ι-index of a c.e. EQP-space X such that*

$$\begin{cases} X \text{ is metrizable} & \text{if } p \in M, \\ X \text{ is Hausdorff, but not metrizable} & \text{if } p \notin M. \end{cases}$$

Proof. First, one specific example of a second countable Hausdorff topology which is not metrizable is called a double origin topology [23, II.74]. It is like a Euclidean plane with two origins, which cannot be separated by closed neighborhoods (that cause non-metrizability). Here, our construction is closer to the one in [17], which is quasi-Polish, while the example in [23, II.74] is not quasi-Polish. In our construction, a tree $T \subseteq \omega^{<\omega}$ is first given. The base plane of our space is the discrete space $\omega \times (\omega^{<\omega} \sqcup \omega^{<\omega})$. For each $x \in \omega^\omega$, the points $I_{n,x} = (n, x)$ and (∞, x) may be added. Here, if x is an infinite path through T then two points

J_x^+ and J_x^- corresponding to (∞, x) are added, and these cannot be separated by closed neighborhoods. Indeed, the intersection of any two closed neighborhoods containing J_x^+ and J_x^- respectively contains $I_{n,x}$ for an arbitrary large n. If x is not an infinite path through T then the plane is folded in half with the abscissa $\{I_{n,x} : n \in \omega\}$ as the fold line, and then J_x^+ is identified with J_x^-.

Formally, given a tree $T \subseteq \omega^{<\omega}$, we consider the following specific presentation $\prec$ of a telophase topology: For each $n \in \omega$ and $\sigma \in \omega^{<\omega}$, we prepare for symbols (n, σ), $(n, \underline{\sigma})$, $(n, \sigma^{\pm})$, $[n, \sigma]$ and $[n, \underline{\sigma}]$. We define a computable binary relation $\prec$ on the set

$$|\prec| := \{(n, \sigma), (n, \underline{\sigma}), (n, \sigma^{\pm}), [n, \sigma], [n, \underline{\sigma}] : n \in \omega \text{ and } \sigma \in \omega^{<\omega}\}.$$

For any $m < n$, put the following:

$$[m, \sigma] \prec [n, \sigma] \prec (n, \sigma) \prec (n, \sigma),$$
$$[m, \underline{\sigma}] \prec [n, \underline{\sigma}] \prec (n, \underline{\sigma}) \prec (n, \underline{\sigma}).$$

If τ is a proper initial segment of σ, put the following:

$$(n, \tau^{\pm}) \prec (n, \sigma^{\pm}), \quad (n, \sigma^{\pm}) \prec (n, \sigma), \quad (n, \sigma^{\pm}) \prec (n, \underline{\sigma}).$$

If $m < n$ and τ is a proper initial segment of σ, put the following:

$$[m, \tau] \prec [n, \sigma], \quad [m, \underline{\tau}] \prec [n, \underline{\sigma}].$$

If $\sigma \notin T$, $m < n$, and τ is a proper initial segment of σ, then we also put the following:

$$[m, \tau] \prec [n, \underline{\sigma}] \prec [n, \sigma], \quad (n, \sigma) \prec (n, \underline{\sigma}) \prec (n, \sigma).$$

Then consider its transitive closure and define $X = I(\prec)$. For a directed set D, let $\downarrow D$ denote the $\prec$-downward closure of D. As in the previous proofs, one can see that any ideal of $\prec$ is one of the following forms:

$$I_{n,\sigma} = \downarrow\{(n, \sigma)\}, \quad I_{n,\underline{\sigma}} = \downarrow\{(n, \underline{\sigma})\}, \quad I_{n,x} = \downarrow\{(n, \sigma^{\pm}) : \sigma \subset x\},$$
$$J_x^+ = \downarrow\{[n, \sigma] : n \in \omega \text{ and } \sigma \subset x\}, \quad J_x^- = \downarrow\{[n, \underline{\sigma}] : n \in \omega \text{ and } \sigma \subset x\}.$$

If x is not an infinite path through T, then it is easy to see that $I_{n,\sigma} = I_{n,\underline{\sigma}}$ and $J_x^+ = J_x^-$. We claim that X is Hausdorff. First, to see $I_{n,\sigma}$ and $I_{m,\tau}$ are separated for $n \neq m$ or $\sigma \neq \tau$ where $\sigma, \tau \in \omega^{<\omega}$, note that (n, σ) and (m, τ) have no common upper bound, so $[(n, \sigma)]_{\prec}$ and $[(m, \tau)]_{\prec}$ have no intersection. Thus, the points $I_{n,\sigma}$ and $I_{m,\tau}$ are separated by $[(n, \sigma)]_{\prec}$ and $[(m, \tau)]_{\prec}$. Similarly, one can see that $I_{n,\sigma}$ and $I_{n,\underline{\tau}}$ are separated. If $\sigma \in T$ then $I_{n,\sigma}$ and $I_{n,\underline{\sigma}}$ are separated, and if $\sigma \notin T$ then $I_{n,\sigma} = I_{n,\underline{\sigma}}$. If $m > n$ then $(n, \sigma^{\pm})$ and $[m, \sigma]$ have no common upper bound, so $[(n, \sigma^{\pm})]_{\prec}$ and $[(m, \sigma)]_{\prec}$ have no intersection. Thus, $I_{n,x}$ and J_x^+ are separated by them. In a similar manner, one can easily separate pairs $(I_{n,x}, J_y^-)$, $(I_{n,\sigma}, J_x^+)$, $(I_{n,\sigma}, I_{n,x})$, etc. If x is an infinite path through T, then $[n, \sigma]$ and $[n, \underline{\sigma}]$ have no common upper bound, so $[[n, \sigma]]_{\prec}$ and $[[n, \underline{\sigma}]]_{\prec}$

have no intersection. Thus, J_x^+ and J_x^- are separated by them. If x is not an infinite path through T, then $J_x^+ = J_x^-$. This concludes that X is Hausdorff.

If x is an infinite path through T, we claim that J_x^+ and J_x^- cannot be separated by closed neighborhoods. Indeed, we show that any closed neighborhood of J_x^+ or J_x^- contains $I_{n,x}$ for some $n \in \omega$. To see this, consider an open neighborhood $[[n, \sigma]]_<$ of J_x^+. Then, for any $m \geqslant n$, $[(m, \sigma^\pm)]_<$ is an open neighborhood of $I_{m,x}$. Since $m \geqslant n$, (m, σ) is a common upper bound of $[n, \sigma]$ and $(m, \sigma^\pm)$, so we have $I_{m,\sigma} \in [(m, \sigma)]_< \subseteq [[n, \sigma]]_< \cap [(m, \sigma^\pm)]_<$. Hence, any open neighborhood of $I_{m,x}$ intersects with $[[n, \sigma]]_<$, and this means that the closure of $[[n, \sigma]]_<$ contains $I_{m,x}$ for any $m \geqslant n$. Similarly, the closure of $[[n, \underline{\sigma}]]_<$ contains $I_{m,x}$ for any $m \geqslant n$. This verifies the claim. In particular, if T is ill-founded, then such an x exists, so X is not metrizable.

If T is well-founded, then $I_{n,\sigma} = I_{n,\underline{\sigma}}$ and $J_x^+ = J_x^-$. Hence,

$$X = \{I_{n,\sigma} : n \in \omega \text{ and } \sigma \in \omega^{<\omega}\} \cup \{I_{n,x} : n \in \omega \text{ and } x \in \omega^\omega\} \cup \{J_x^+ : x \in \omega^\omega\}.$$

We claim that X is embedded into the Polish space $Z = (\omega + 1) \times \omega^{\leqslant \omega}$, where $\omega + 1$ is the one point compactification of ω, and $\omega^{\leqslant \omega}$ endowed with the Polish topology as in the proof of Lemma 1. Indeed, the union of the maps $\langle n, \sigma \rangle \mapsto I_{n,\sigma}$, $\langle n, x \rangle \mapsto I_{n,x}$, and $\langle \omega, x \rangle \mapsto J_x^+$ gives a homeomorphism between $(\omega \times \omega^{\leqslant \omega}) \cup (\{\omega\} \times \omega^\omega) \subseteq Z$ and X. This is because we have $[(n, \sigma)]_< = \{I_{n,\sigma}\}$, and if T has no infinite path extending σ, then we have $[(n, \sigma^\pm)]_< = \{I_{n,\tau} : \sigma \subseteq \tau\} \cup \{I_{n,x} : \sigma \subset x\}$, and $[[n, \sigma]]_< = \{I_{m,\tau} : n \leqslant m, \sigma \subseteq \tau\} \cup \{I_{n,x} : n \leqslant m, \sigma \subset x\} \cup \{J_x^+ : \sigma \subset x\}$. This means that the basic open set $[(n, \sigma)]_<$ in X corresponds to the basic open set $\{\langle n, \sigma \rangle\}$ in Z, the basic open set $[(n, \sigma^\pm)]_<$ in X corresponds to the basic open set $\{n\} \times \{x \in \omega^{\leqslant \omega} : \sigma \subset x\}$ in Z, and the basic open set $[[n, \sigma]]_<$ in X corresponds to the basic open set $\{m \in \omega + 1 : m \geqslant n\} \times \{x \in \omega^{\leqslant \omega} : \sigma \subset x\}$ in Z. Hence, if T is well-founded, then X is metrizable. Overtness of X is obvious as before.   □

Remark 1. Our proof of Lemma 2 actually gives a metrizable space if $p \in M$, and a Hausdorff but not $T_{2.5}$ space if $p \notin M$. On the other hand, an anonymous referee suggested an alternative proof of Lemma 2, which gives a metrizable space if $p \in M$, and a $T_{2.5}$ (indeed, submetrizable) but not metrizable space if $p \notin M$: It is the product space $\omega^\omega \times [0, 1]^2$ with $C = [T] \times \{(x, y) : x = 0 \text{ and } y > 0\}$ added to the topology as a closed set. Taken together, Theorem 3 is more complete: Every tuple (M, U, H, F) of Π_1^1-sets such that $M \subseteq U \subseteq H \subseteq F$ uniformly m-reduces to $(\iota^{-1}(\mathcal{M}), \iota^{-1}(\mathcal{T}_{2.5}), \iota^{-1}(\mathcal{T}_2), \iota^{-1}(\mathcal{T}_1))$.

Proof of Theorem 3. Let $M \subseteq H \subseteq F \subseteq \omega$ be Π_1^1 sets. Let X_F, X_H and X_M be c.e. EQP-spaces obtained by Theorem 2, Lemma 1 and Lemma 2. Then, consider the disjoint union of these spaces, i.e., $X = (\{0\} \times X_F) \cup (\{1\} \times X_H) \cup (\{2\} \times X_M)$. If $p \in M$ then all of these spaces are metrizable, so X is metrizable. If $p \in H \backslash M$, then X_F and X_H are metrizable, and X_M is Hausdorff, but not metrizable. Therefore, X is Hausdorff, but not metrizable. If $p \in F \backslash H$, then X_F is metrizable, X_H is T_1, but not Hausdorff, and X_M is Hausdorff. Therefore, X is T_1, but not Hausdorff. If $p \notin F$, then X_F is not T_1. Thus, X is not T_1.   □

Acknowledgement. The authors are grateful to anonymous referees for the careful reading and valuable suggestions.

References

1. Abramsky S., Jung, A.: Domain theory. In: Handbook of Logic in Computer Science, vol. 3, pp. 1–168. Oxford (1994)
2. Ash, C., Knight, J.: Computable Structures and the Hyperarithmetical Hierarchy. Studies in Logic and the Foundations of Mathematics, vol. 144. North-Holland Publishing Co., Amsterdam (2000)
3. de Brecht, M.: Quasi-Polish spaces. Ann. Pure Appl. Logic **164**, 356–381 (2013)
4. de Brecht, M.: Some notes on spaces of ideals and computable topology. In: Anselmo, M., Della Vedova, G., Manea, F., Pauly, A. (eds.) CiE 2020. LNCS, vol. 12098, pp. 26–37. Springer, Cham (2020). https://doi.org/10.1007/978-3-030-51466-2_3
5. Downey R., Melnikov A.G.: Effectively compact spaces. Unpublished manuscript
6. de Brecht, M., Pauly, A., Schröder, M.: Overt choice. Computability **9**(3–4), 169–191 (2020)
7. Ershov, Y.L., Goncharov, S.S.: Constructive Models. Plenum, New York (1999)
8. Fokina, E.D., Friedman, S.D., Harizanov, V., Knight, J.F., McCoy, C., Montalban, A.: Isomrphism relations on computable structures. J. Symb. Log. **77**(1), 122–132 (2012)
9. Fokina, E., Friedman, S., Nies, A.: Equivalence relations that are Σ^0_3 complete for computable reducibility. In: Ong, L., de Queiroz, R. (eds.) WoLLIC 2012. LNCS, vol. 7456, pp. 26–33. Springer, Heidelberg (2012). https://doi.org/10.1007/978-3-642-32621-9_2
10. Fokina, E.B., Harizanov, V., Melnikov, A.: Computable model theory. In: Turing's Legacy: Developments From Turing's Ideas in Logic. Lecture Notes Logic, vol. 42, pp. 124–194. Association for Symbolic Logic, La Jolla (2014)
11. Goncharov S.S., Knight J.: Computable structure and antistructure theorems. Algebra Logika **41**(6), 639–681, 757 (2002)
12. Hoyrup, M., Kihara, T., Selivanov, V. Degree spectra of homeomorphism types of Polish spaces. Arxiv 2004.06872v1 (2020)
13. Hoyrup, M., Rojas, C., Selivanov, V., Stull, D.M.: Computability on Quasi-Polish spaces. In: Hospodár, M., Jirásková, G., Konstantinidis, S. (eds.) DCFS 2019. LNCS, vol. 11612, pp. 171–183. Springer, Cham (2019). https://doi.org/10.1007/978-3-030-23247-4_13
14. Harrison-Trainor M., Melnikov A., Ng K.M.: Computability of Polish spaces up to homeomorphism. J. Symb. Log. **85**(4), 1–25 (2020)
15. Kechris, A.S.: Classical Descriptive Set Theory. Graduate Texts in Mathematics, vol. 156. Springer, New York (1995). https://doi.org/10.1007/978-1-4612-4190-4
16. Korovina, M., Kudinov, O.: On higher effective descriptive set theory. In: Kari, J., Manea, F., Petre, I. (eds.) CiE 2017. LNCS, vol. 10307, pp. 282–291. Springer, Cham (2017). https://doi.org/10.1007/978-3-319-58741-7_27
17. Kihara, T., Ng, K.M., Pauly, A.: Enumeration degrees and nonmetrizable topology. Submitted. arXiv:1904.04107
18. McNicholl, T.H., Stull, D.M.: The isometry degree of a computable copy of ℓ^{p1}. Computability **8**(2), 179–189 (2019)
19. Melnikov, A.G.: Computably isometric spaces. J. Symb. Log. **78**(4), 1055–1085 (2013)

20. Selivanov, V.L.: Positive structures. In: Barry Cooper, B., Goncharov, S.S. (eds.) Computability and Models, Perspectives East and West, pp. 321–350. Kluwer Academic/Plenum Publishers, New York (2003)

21. Selivanov, V.L.: Towards the effective descriptive set theory. In: Beckmann, A., Mitrana, V., Soskova, M. (eds.) CiE 2015. LNCS, vol. 9136, pp. 324–333. Springer, Cham (2015). https://doi.org/10.1007/978-3-319-20028-6_33

22. Selivanov, V.: On degree spectra of topological spaces. Lobachevskii J. Math. **41**(2), 252–259 (2020)

23. Steen, L.A., Seebach, J.A.: Counterexamples in Topology. Springer, New York (1978). https://doi.org/10.1007/978-1-4612-6290-9. Reprinted by Dover Publications, New York, 1995

Maps of Restrictions for Behaviourally Correct Learning

Vanja Doskoč[(⊠)] and Timo Kötzing

Hasso Plattner Institute, University of Potsdam, Potsdam, Germany
{vanja.doskoc,timo.koetzing}@hpi.de

Abstract. In *language learning in the limit*, we study computable devices (learners) learning formal languages. We consider learning tasks paired with restrictions regarding, for example, the hypotheses made by the learners. We compare such restrictions with each other in order to study their impact and depict the results in overviews, the so-called *maps*. In the case of *explanatory* learning, the literature already provides various maps.

On the other hand, in the case of *behaviourally correct* learning, only partial results are known. In this work, we complete these results and provide full behaviourally correct maps for different types of data presentation. In particular, in all studied settings, we observe that monotone learning implies non-U-shaped learning and that cautiousness, semantic conservativeness and weak monotonicity are equally powerful.

Keywords: Language Learning in the Limit · Behaviourally Correct Learning · Learning Restrictions · Map

1 Introduction

Motivation. In his seminal work, Gold [10] introduced the *language learning in the limit* framework. Here, a learner (a computable function) successively receives positive information about a target language (a subset of the natural numbers). With each new datum, the learner produces a conjecture which language it believes to be presented. Once these guesses converge to a *single*, correct explanation of the target language, we say that the learner successfully learned the target language.

This is known as *explanatory* learning and denoted as[1] **TxtGEx**. We focus on the semantic version thereof, namely *behaviourally correct* learning [5,21], denoted as **TxtGBc**. Here, almost all conjectures of the learner have to be correct (but do not need to be syntactically identical). Naturally, each single language may be learned by a learner which always suggests (a conjecture for) this language. Thus, we focus on learning classes of languages learnable by a single learner.

---

[1] Particularly, a *text* (**Txt**) provides positive information about the target language, from which *Gold-style* (**G**) learners then infer their conjectures. Lastly, **Ex** for stands for explanatory learning.

U. Berger et al. (Eds.): CiE 2022, LNCS 13359, pp. 103–114, 2022.
https://doi.org/10.1007/978-3-031-08740-0_9

These learning criteria are extended or altered to study the impact of certain restrictions. These may limit which hypotheses are allowed, for example requiring them to follow a monotone behaviour or by constraining when changes of conjectures are allowed, or the data representation, for example, by leaving out information on the order the data is presented. An overview of the studied restrictions can be found in Sect. 2. A particular branch of study focuses on the pairwise relation between such restrictions. The findings are then depicted in overviews, so-called *maps*. The literature already provides maps of explanatory learners with various modes of data representation [11,15,16]. However, for behaviourally correct learning only partial results on the pairwise interaction of different restrictions are known so far [2,7–9,12,17].

Our Contribution. In this work, we provide the missing relations. This way, we obtain a full picture regarding the pairwise relation of the studied restrictions. We provide the collected findings in Fig. 1. In particular, we observe in all studied settings that classes of languages that can be learned by learners which never discard correctly conjectured elements, that is, monotone learners, can also be learned by learners which never change their mind from a correct guess, that is, non-U-shaped learners. These results are presented in Lemma 1 and Theorems 3 and 5. Furthermore, we find that learners which base their guess solely on the set of elements presented change their mind only when witnessing inconsistent information, see Theorem 2. We note that analogous results hold in the explanatory setting [14–16]. However, one difference between these settings is that neither learners which may change their mind only when inconsistent, nor learners which never fall back to a proper subset of a previous guess depend on the order or amount of data presented, see Theorem 2.

Another contribution of this work pertains to normal forms of learners. Particularly interesting are *strongly* **Bc**-*locking* learners [15]. These learners have, on each text for a target language, a **Bc**-*locking sequence*, that is, a sequence which contains enough information for the learner to be correct and never change its mind any more regardless what information from the target language it receives [3,12]. With Theorem 4, we complete the literature by showing that for all considered restrictions the learners may be assumed strongly **Bc**-locking.

Future Work. We leave studying one important restriction to future work: decisiveness [20]. Here, a learner may never get back to a previous, rejected hypothesis. In particular, it is open to resolve whether each class of languages a monotone learner learns can be learned decisively. We note that Theorem 2 shows that decisiveness is no restriction for learners which base their hypotheses solely on the set of elements, that is, set-driven learners.

The impact of the data presented during learning varies depending on the studied restriction [6–8,17]. For example, cautious or semantically conservative learners do not rely on the order or amount of data presented while monotone learners do. Future work may resolve how the provided data impacts decisive and non-U-shaped learners.

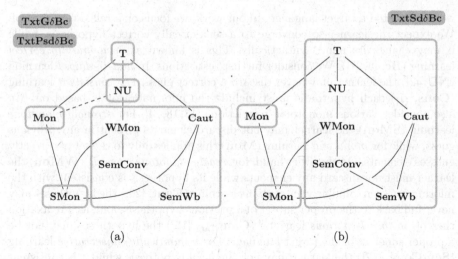

Fig. 1. A depiction of the relation between the studied restrictions (compare Sect. 2) for Gold-style and partially set-driven (see Fig. (a)) as well as set-driven learning (see Fig. (b)). Solid and dashed lines imply trivial and non-trivial inclusions (both bottom-to-top), respectively. Greyly edged areas illustrate a collapse of the enclosed learning criteria. There are no further collapses.

Structure of the Work. This work is structured as follows. In Sect. 2, we shortly discuss important concepts for this work. In the remaining sections, we discuss the initial situation for the respective studied mode of data representation and provide our results to complete the particular map. Missing proofs and the full preliminaries can be found in the full version[2] of this paper.

2   Language Learning in the Limit

In this section, we shortly introduce important concepts for language learning in the limit. We learn languages $L \subseteq \mathbb{N}$ (recursively enumerable sets) using learners (computable functions). Hereby, information about the target language is successively provided by texts (lists containing all and only the positive information about the target language). An *interaction operator* β provides the learner with the information to make its guess. In this work, we consider the interaction operators **Sd** for set-driven learning [23], which provides the learner only with the set of elements, **Psd** for partially set-driven learning [3,22], where the learners additionally receive a counter of the total elements presented so far, and **G** for Gold-style learning [10], where the learners also obtain information on the order the elements are presented in.

We consider the following learning criteria. Initially, for *explanatory* learning (**Ex**, [10]) the learner is expected to converge to a single, correct hypothesis

[2] https://hpi.de/fileadmin/user_upload/fachgebiete/friedrich/documents/Doskoc/CiE_DoskocKoetzing_BCMaps.pdf.

when presented a target language. In our work, we focus on a relaxation thereof: We expect the learner to converge to a semantically correct hypothesis, while it may change its mind syntactically. This is known as *behaviourally correct* learning (**Bc**, [5,21]). We consider further restrictions. In *non-U-shaped* learning (**NU**, [2]) the learner may never discard a correct guess. For *consistent* learning (**Cons**, [1]) each hypothesis must include the information it is based on. We also consider various monotonic restrictions [13,18,24]. For *strongly monotone* learning (**SMon**) the learner may not discard elements present in any previous guess, while for *monotone* learning (**Mon**) this applies only to the set of correctly guesses elements. On the other hand, for *weakly monotone* learning (**WMon**) the learner must not discard any elements while its hypothesis is consistent with the information seen. Similarly, in *cautious* learning (**Caut**, [20]) the hypotheses may never fall back to the proper subset of a previous hypothesis, and, as a relaxation thereof, in *target-cautious* learning (**Caut**$_{\text{Tar}}$, [15]) the hypotheses may not be a proper superset of the target language. For *semantically conservative* learning (**SemConv**, [17]) the learner may not change a hypothesis while it is consistent with the data given. Lastly, in *semantically witness-based* learning (**SemWb**, [17]) the learner must justify each mind change. We combine any two restrictions δ and δ' by intersecting them and denote this as $\delta\delta'$. With **T** we denote the absence of a learning restriction.

In this work, we denote a *learning criterion* as **Txt**$\beta\delta$. Here, **Txt** signalizes that we are learning from text, β indicates the interaction operator and δ is the restriction required to hold on all texts belonging to some target language. Given a learner h, we write **Txt**$\beta\delta(h)$ for the set of all languages h **Txt**$\beta\delta$-learns. The set of, for all learners h', all **Txt**$\beta\delta(h')$ is denoted as [**Txt**$\beta\delta$] and referred to as *learning power* of **Txt**$\beta\delta$-learners. Note that we solely consider total learners, as all behaviourally correct learners may be assumed total [17].

Certain sequences may contain especially valuable information for learners. A **Bc**-*locking sequence* contains sufficient information on the target language so that the learner does not change its mind (semantically) from a correct hypothesis any more, regardless what information from the target language it witnesses [3,12]. It is known that *every* **Bc**-learner has a **Bc**-locking sequence [3], however, there are learners and texts where no initial sequence of the text is a **Bc**-locking sequence [3]. We call a learner h *strongly* **Bc**-*locking* if every text of every language it learns contains an initial sequence serving as a **Bc**-locking sequence [15–17].

3   Set-Driven Map

In set-driven learning, unrestricted learners may be assumed cautious and consistent at the same time [8]. Furthermore, semantically conservative and semantically witness-based learners may be assumed consistent and equally powerful [17]. As a matter of fact, they are even as powerful as their Gold-style counterpart [7]. In this section we show that all of these learners are equal regarding their learning power. In particular, we exploit two known concepts. First, we use the same approach as when showing that set-driven learners may be assumed target-cautious [8] to show that without loss of generality they are also non-U-shaped, see Lemma 1. Using this, we can obtain semantically conservative learners (see Theorem 2) in a similar fashion as when making semantically conservative learners so *everywhere* [7]. In particular, we can override wrong hypotheses of the learners using witnessing elements (as, by target-cautious learning, incorrect guesses cannot overgeneralize the target language) and right hypotheses are never discarded (by non-U-shaped learning).

Lemma 1. *Every* **TxtSdBc***-learner* h *may be assumed to be target-cautious* (**Caut$_{Tar}$**), *non-U-shaped* (**NU**) *and consistent* (**Cons**) *simultaneously.*

Theorem 2. *We have that*

$$[\textbf{TxtSdBc}] = [\textbf{TxtSdCautBc}] = [\textbf{TxtGCautBc}]$$
$$= [\textbf{TxtSdSemWbBc}] = [\textbf{TxtGSemWbBc}].$$

Now, the set-driven map is completed, as monotone learning is a restriction, but strictly more powerful than strongly monotone learning [12].

4 Partially Set-Driven Map

Theorem 2 already shows that semantically conservative, semantically witness-based, cautious and weakly monotone learning coincide in the partially set-driven setting. However, these restrictions are known to be restrictive [12,17]. Furthermore, they are known to be incomparable to monotone learning [12], while both are more powerful than strongly monotone learning [12]. Non-U-shaped learning separates from the mentioned restrictions [12,17]. However, non-U-shaped learning is a restriction for Gold-style learners [2,9] and, equivalently, for partially set-driven learners [8]. Note that for explanatory learners this is not the case [4].

We complete this map by showing that monotone learning implies non-U-shaped learning, see Theorem 3. In particular, we create a new hypothesis by adding all information obtainable by some future hypothesis generated from all seen elements. If this generates a correct hypothesis, no future hypotheses may be wrong, as otherwise the current hypothesis must contain further elements.

Theorem 3. *We have that* $[\textbf{TxtPsdMonBc}] \subseteq [\textbf{TxtPsdNUBc}]$.

Proof. Let h be a **TxtPsdMonBc**-learner. Note that h is, without loss of generality, strongly **Bc**-locking [17]. Let furthermore $\mathcal{L} = \textbf{TxtPsdMonBc}(h)$. We provide a **TxtPsdNUBc**-learner h' which learns $\mathcal{L}$. For all finite sets $D \subseteq \mathbb{N}$, all $t < \infty$ and all $s \in \mathbb{N}_{\geq 1}$, define

$$W^0_{h'(D,t)} = D,$$

$$W^s_{h'(D,t)} = \bigcup_{\substack{(D',t') \text{ with} \\ (D,t) \preceq (D',t') \preceq (W^{s-1}_{h'(D,t)}, t+s)}} W^{s-1}_{h(D',t')}.$$

Finally, $W_{h'(D,t)} = \bigcup_{s \in \mathbb{N}} W^s_{h'(D,t)}$. Intuitively, the learner h' produces its hypothesis on (D,t) iteratively. At stage s, $W^s_{h'(D,t)}$ enumerates all elements witnessed by the learner h on some hypothesis extending (D,t) using elements witnessed so far, that is, elements in $W^{s-1}_{h'(D,t)}$.

We show that h' **TxtPsdNUBc**-learns $\mathcal{L}$. Let $L \in \mathcal{L}$ and $T \in \textbf{Txt}(L)$. We provide a proof in two steps.

1. We first show that there exists an n_0 such that $W_{h'(\text{content}(T[n_0]),n_0)} = L$.
2. Afterwards, we show that, for all n, whenever $W_{h'(\text{content}(T[n]),n)} = L$ we have, for all $n' > n$, also $W_{h'(\text{content}(T[n']),n')} = L$.

For the first, let n_0 be such that $(D,t) := (\text{content}(T[n_0]), n_0)$ is a **Bc**-locking information for h on L. Then, by definition of h', we have $W_{h'(D,t)} \supseteq W_{h(D,t)} = L$. For the other direction, we show that for all $s \in \mathbb{N}$ we have $W^s_{h'(D,t)} \subseteq L$ by induction on s. We get the statement for $s = 0$ immediately. Assuming it holds for $s \in \mathbb{N}$, we show it for $s + 1$. Since $W^s_{h'(D,t)} \subseteq L$, we have that (D',t') with $(D,t) \preceq (D',t') \preceq (W^s_{h'(D,t)}, t+s+1)$ is also a **Bc**-locking information for h on L. In particular, we have $W_{h(D',t')} = L$. This results in

$$W^{s+1}_{h'(D,t)} = \bigcup_{\substack{(D',t') \text{ with} \\ (D,t) \preceq (D',t') \preceq (W^s_{h'(D,t)}, t+s+1)}} W^s_{h(D',t')} \subseteq L.$$

For the second claim, let $n \in \mathbb{N}$ and $(D,t) := (\text{content}(T[n]), n)$ be such that $W_{h'(D,t)} = L$, let $n' \geq n$ and $(D'',t'') := (\text{content}(T[n']), n')$. Note that $D \subseteq D'' \subseteq L$ and $t'' \geq t$. We show that $W_{h'(D'',t'')} = L$. First, note that (D'',t'') will eventually be considered when enumerating $W_{h'(D,t)}$, that is, there exists an $s \in \mathbb{N}$ such that $(D'',t'') \preceq (W^{s-1}_{h'(D,t)}, t+s)$. Hence,

$$W_{h'(D'',t'')} = \bigcup_{s \in \mathbb{N}} \bigcup_{\substack{(D',t') \text{ with} \\ (D'',t'') \preceq (D',t') \preceq (W^{s-1}_{h'(D'',t'')}, t+s)}} W^{s-1}_{h(D',t')}$$

$$\subseteq \bigcup_{s \in \mathbb{N}} \bigcup_{\substack{(D',t') \text{ with} \\ (D,t) \preceq (D',t') \preceq (W^{s-1}_{h'(D,t)}, t+s)}} W^{s-1}_{h(D',t')} = W_{h'(D,t)} = L.$$

Secondly, we show that for each $x \in L = W_{h'(D,t)}$ we also have $x \in W_{h'(D'',t'')}$. We show (by induction on s) that $W^s_{h'(D,t)} \subseteq W_{h'(D'',t'')}$. For $s = 0$ we have $W^s_{h'(D,t)} = D \subseteq D'' = W^0_{h'(D'',t'')} \subseteq W_{h'(D'',t'')}$. Let the statement be fulfilled until s. At step $s + 1$, we distinguish the following cases.

1. Case: If $W^s_{h'(D,t)} = W^{s+1}_{h'(D,t)}$, that is, no new element is enumerated, the statement of the induction step is true immediately.
2. Case: If $W^s_{h'(D,t)} \subsetneq W^{s+1}_{h'(D,t)}$, let $x \in W^{s+1}_{h'(D,t)} \setminus W^s_{h'(D,t)}$. Note that $x \in L$. Let $(\tilde{D}, \tilde{t})$, with $(D,t) \preceq (\tilde{D}, \tilde{t}) \preceq (W^s_{h'(D,t)}, t+s)$, be the information on which x was witnessed, that is, $x \in W_{h(\tilde{D},\tilde{t})}$. By $W^s_{h'(D,t)} \subseteq W_{h'(D'',t'')}$ (the induction

assumption), there exists s'' such that $(\tilde{D}, \tilde{t}) \preceq (W_{h'(D'',t'')}^{s''}, t'' + s'')$. Since h is monotone and $x \in L$ we have

$$x \in W_{h(W_{h'(D'',t'')}^{s''}, t'' + s'')} \overset{\text{def. of } h'}{\subseteq} W_{h'(D'',t'')}.$$

Altogether, we get the desired result.   □

5   Gold-Style Learning Map

The overall situation for Gold-style learning is basically analogous to the initial situation for partially set-driven learning as discussed in Sect. 4, compare the literature [2,9,12,17] and Theorem 2. We complete the map by showing that monotone learning implies non-U-shaped learning, see 5.

We aim to employ a similar approach as for the partially set-driven case. To that end, we have to overcome two obstacles. Firstly, we show that monotone Gold-style learners are strongly **Bc**-locking, see Theorem 4. In particular, this shows that *all* restrictions studied in this paper allow for strongly **Bc**-locking learning [4,17]. Secondly, Gold-style learners infer from sequences, meaning that extensions considered at a certain step do not necessarily have to be considered in later steps (as opposed to partially set-driven learning). We circumvent this by also enumerating elements from previous guesses on which the learner shows a monotone behaviour, as they are likely part of the target language.

Theorem 4. *Any* **TxtGMonBc***-learner may be assumed strongly* **Bc***-locking.*

Proof. This proof is inspired by the proof based on private communication with Sanjay Jain where, for certain restrictions δ, [**TxtPsdδBc**] = [**TxtGδBc**] is shown [8, Thm. 10]. Let h be a learner and let $\mathcal{L} = $ **TxtGMonBc**(h). We provide a strongly **Bc**-locking **TxtGMonBc**-learner h' for $\mathcal{L}$ as follows. For two finite sequences σ, σ', define the auxiliary function g as

$$W_{g(\sigma',\sigma)} = \bigcap_{\tau \in \text{content}(\sigma)_{\#}^{\leq|\sigma|}} W_{h(\sigma'\tau)} \cap \bigcap_{\substack{\sigma'' \leq \sigma', \\ \sigma'' \in \text{content}(\sigma')_{\#}^{*}}} \bigcup_{\tau'' \in \text{content}(\sigma')_{\#}^{*}} W_{h(\sigma''\tau'')}.$$

Then, define the learner h' on finite sequences σ as

$$W_{h'(\sigma)} = \bigcup_{\sigma' \subseteq \sigma} W_{g(\sigma',\sigma)}.$$

The intuition is the following. With the function g, we search for minimal **Bc**-locking sequences [8]. To ensure that g eventually only contains elements from the target language, we extend the left hand intersection to be based on σ. However, as σ contains more and more information, additional sequences are also considered in the right hand intersection. This may lead to already enumerated elements being discarded (even if they belong to a target language). To prevent this, we take the union over all possible $W_{g(\sigma',\sigma)}$.

We formally show that h' has the desired properties. First, we show that h' is **Mon**. Let $L \in \mathcal{L}$ and $\sigma_1, \sigma_2 \in L_\#^*$ with $\sigma_1 \subseteq \sigma_2$. We show that for all $x \in \mathbb{N}$

$$x \in W_{h'(\sigma_1)} \cap L \Rightarrow x \in W_{h'(\sigma_2)} \cap L.$$

As $x \in W_{h'(\sigma_1)}$, there exists $\sigma_1' \subseteq \sigma_1$ such that $x \in W_{g(\sigma_1', \sigma_1)}$, that is,

$$x \in \bigcap_{\tau \in \text{content}(\sigma_1)_\#^{\leq |\sigma_1|}} W_{h(\sigma_1' \tau)} \cap \bigcap_{\substack{\sigma'' \leq \sigma_1', \\ \sigma'' \in \text{content}(\sigma_1')_\#^*}} \bigcup_{\tau'' \in \text{content}(\sigma_1')_\#^*} W_{h(\sigma'' \tau'')}. \tag{1}$$

In particular, $x \in W_{h(\sigma_1')}$. We show that $x \in W_{g(\sigma_1', \sigma_2)}$. By monotonicity of h, we have that

$$x \in \bigcap_{\tau \in \text{content}(\sigma_2)_\#^{\leq |\sigma_2|}} W_{h(\sigma_1' \tau)}.$$

As the right hand intersection in Eq. (1) (of which x is an element) does not depend on σ_1, we have that

$$x \in \bigcap_{\tau \in \text{content}(\sigma_2)_\#^{\leq |\sigma_2|}} W_{h(\sigma_1' \tau)} \cap \bigcap_{\substack{\sigma'' \leq \sigma_1', \\ \sigma'' \in \text{content}(\sigma_1')_\#^*}} \bigcup_{\tau'' \in \text{content}(\sigma_1')_\#^*} W_{h(\sigma'' \tau'')}$$

$$= W_{g(\sigma_1', \sigma_2)}.$$

By definition of h' and since $\sigma_1' \subseteq \sigma_1 \subseteq \sigma_2$, we have

$$W_{g(\sigma_1', \sigma_2)} \subseteq \bigcup_{\sigma' \subseteq \sigma_2} W_{g(\sigma', \sigma_2)} = W_{h'(\sigma_2)}.$$

Thus, $x \in W_{h'(\sigma_2)} \cap L$.

We now show that h' is strongly **Bc**-locking (and thus also **Bc**-learns $\mathcal{L}$). Let $L \in \mathcal{L}$ and $T \in \textbf{Txt}(L)$. Let $\sigma_0 \in L_\#^*$ be the $\leq$-minimal **Bc**-locking sequence for h on L [3]. For each $\sigma' < \sigma_0$ with $\text{content}(\sigma') \subseteq L$, let $\tau_{\sigma'} \in L_\#^*$ be such that $\sigma' \tau_{\sigma'}$ is a **Bc**-locking sequence for h on L [19]. Let n_0 be such that h converges on $T[n_0]$, that is, for all $n' \geq n_0$, $W_{h(T[n])} = L$. Let $n_1 \geq n_0$ be such that

- $\sigma_0 \leq T[n_1]$,
- $\sigma_0 \in \text{content}(T[n_1])_\#^*$, and
- for all $\sigma' < \sigma_0$ such that $\text{content}(\sigma') \subseteq L$, we have that $\text{content}(\sigma' \tau_{\sigma'}) \subseteq \text{content}(T[n_1])$ and $|\tau_{\sigma'}| \leq n_1$.

To show that $\sigma_1 := T[n_1]$ is a **Bc**-locking sequence for h' on L, we show that, for any $\rho \in L_\#^*$, $\sigma_1 {}^\frown \rho =: \sigma_1 \rho$ is a correct guess, that is, $W_{h'(\sigma_1 \rho)} = L$. Let $\rho \in L_\#^*$. We prove each direction of $W_{h'(\sigma_1 \rho)} = L$ separately.

1.C.: $W_{h'(\sigma_1 \rho)} \subseteq L$: Let $x \in W_{h'(\sigma_1 \rho)}$. Then there exists $\sigma' \subseteq \sigma_1 \rho$ such that $x \in W_{g(\sigma', \sigma_1 \rho)}$. In particular,

$$x \in \bigcap_{\tau \in \text{content}(\sigma_1 \rho)_\#^{\leq |\sigma_1 \rho|}} W_{h(\sigma' \tau)} \cap \bigcap_{\substack{\sigma'' \leq \sigma', \\ \sigma'' \in \text{content}(\sigma')_\#^*}} \bigcup_{\tau'' \in \text{content}(\sigma')_\#^*} W_{h(\sigma'' \tau'')}. \tag{2}$$

We distinguish based on the relation between σ' and σ_1.

1.1.C.: If $\sigma' \subseteq \sigma_1$, then there exists $\tau \in \text{content}(\sigma_1\rho)_{\#}^{\leq|\sigma_1\rho|}$ such that $\sigma'\tau = \sigma_1$. As $h(\sigma_1)$ is a correct guess and $W_{h(\sigma_1)}$ is considered in the left hand intersection of Eq. (2), we have that $x \in L$.

1.2.C.: If $\sigma' \supsetneq \sigma_1$, we have $\sigma_0 \leq \sigma_1 \subseteq \sigma'$ and $\sigma_0 \in \text{content}(\sigma_1)_{\#}^* \subseteq \text{content}(\sigma')_{\#}^*$. Thus, σ_0 is considered in the right hand intersection of Eq. (2). Since, for any $\tau \in L_{\#}^*$, we have $W_{h(\sigma_0\tau)} = L$, we get $x \in W_{h(\sigma_0\tau)} = L$.

2.C.: $L \subseteq W_{h'(\sigma_1\rho)}$: Let $x \in L$. We show that $x \in W_{g(\sigma_1,\sigma_1\rho)}$. As h is monotone, $\sigma_1 \subseteq \sigma_1\rho$ and h converges on σ_1, we have

$$x \in \bigcap_{\tau \in \text{content}(\sigma_1)_{\#}^*} W_{h(\sigma_1 \frown \tau)}.$$

Moreover, by choice of n_1, we have, for all $\sigma'' \leq \sigma_1$ with $\sigma'' \in \text{content}(\sigma_1)_{\#}^*$, that $\tau_{\sigma''}'' \in \text{content}(\sigma_1)_{\#}^*$. As $\sigma''\tau_{\sigma''}''$ is a **Bc**-locking sequence for h on L, we get $x \in W_{h(\sigma''\tau_{\sigma''}'')}$. Hence,

$$x \in \bigcap_{\substack{\sigma'' \leq \sigma_1, \\ \sigma'' \in \text{content}(\sigma_1)_{\#}^*}} \bigcup_{\tau'' \in \text{content}(\sigma_1)_{\#}^*} W_{h(\sigma''\tau'')}.$$

Altogether, $x \in W_{g(\sigma_1,\sigma_1\rho)} \subseteq W_{h'(\sigma_1\rho)}$.

In the end, we have $W_{h'(\sigma_1\rho)} = L$, which concludes the proof. $\qquad\square$

Theorem 5. *We have that* $[\textbf{TxtGMonBc}] \subseteq [\textbf{TxtGNUBc}]$.

Proof. Let h be a **TxtGMonBc**-learner. Without loss of generality, h may be assumed strongly **Bc**-locking, see Theorem 4. Let $\mathcal{L} = \textbf{TxtGMonBc}(h)$. We provide a learner h' which **TxtGNUBc**-learns $\mathcal{L}$. To do so, we employ both a *forward enumeration strategy* (via sets $F_{\sigma,s}$) as well as a *backward search strategy* (via sets $B_{\sigma,s}$). For a finite sequence σ and computation step $s \in \mathbb{N}$ we define $F_{\sigma,s}$ (forward enumeration set) and $B_{\sigma,s}$ (backwards search set) as follows. Let $F_{\sigma,0} = B_{\sigma,0} = \text{content}(\sigma)$. Furthermore, let

$$F_{\sigma,s+1} = F_{\sigma,s} \cup \bigcup_{\tau \in (F_{\sigma,s} \cup B_{\sigma,s})_{\#}^{\leq s}} W_{h(\sigma\tau)}^s.$$

Intuitively, $F_{\sigma,s+1}$ contains all elements enumerated by some possible future guess, that is, for $\tau \in (F_{\sigma,s} \cup B_{\sigma,s})_{\#}^{\leq s}$, $W_{h(\sigma\tau)}$. Note that this is a similar approach as in the **Psd**-case, see the proof of Theorem 3. However, as opposed to partially set-driven learning, this alone does not suffice. In particular, $F_{\sigma,s}$ may consider $\sigma \frown \tau$ and $\sigma \frown \tau'$, where $\tau \neq \tau'$, in its enumeration, but, for a later hypothesis σ', $F_{\sigma',s}$ cannot consider both, as σ' cannot extend both $\sigma \frown \tau$ and $\sigma \frown \tau'$. To circumvent this, we need the backwards search set $B_{\sigma,s}$.

To define $B_{\sigma,s}$, we introduce the following auxiliary predicate and function. Given a learner h (we omit using Gödel numbers in favour of readability), finite sequences σ and ρ, an element $x \in \mathbb{N}$ and a counter $s \in \mathbb{N}$, we define

$$\textbf{MonBeh}(h, \rho, x, s, \sigma) \Leftrightarrow \forall \tau \in \text{content}(\sigma)^{\leq s+|\sigma|} : x \in W_{h(\rho \frown \tau)}.$$

Intuitively, $\mathbf{MonBeh}(h, \rho, x, s, \sigma)$ checks whether h, starting on information ρ, exhibits a monotonic behaviour regarding the element x. We further introduce a function which gives us the newly enumerated element by some hypothesis. In particular, let $\tilde{x} := \mathbf{nextEl}(h', \sigma', \sigma, s)$ be the element enumerated next by $F_{\sigma', s}$ which is not yet in $W_{h'(\sigma)}$. Furthermore, let $\tilde{\sigma} := \sigma'^\frown \tau$ be the (minimal) sequence on which $\tilde{x}$ has been seen for the first time inside $F_{\sigma', s}$. We define the backwards search set as, for finite sequences σ, σ'' and $s \in \mathbb{N}$,

$$B_{\sigma, 0, \sigma''} = \text{content}(\sigma''),$$

$$B_{\sigma, s+1, \sigma''} = B_{\sigma, s, \sigma''} \cup \begin{cases} \{\tilde{x}\}, & \text{for } \tilde{x} = \mathbf{nextEl}(h', \sigma'', \sigma, s) \text{ via } \tilde{\sigma} \text{ if} \\ & \quad \mathbf{MonBeh}(h', \tilde{\sigma}, \tilde{x}, s, \sigma), \\ \emptyset, & \text{else.} \end{cases}$$

$$B_{\sigma, s+1} = B_{\sigma, s} \cup \bigcup_{\sigma'' \subsetneq \sigma} B_{\sigma, s, \sigma''}.$$

Note that $\bigcup_{s \in \mathbb{N}} B_{\sigma, s, \sigma''} \subseteq \bigcup_{s \in \mathbb{N}} F_{\sigma'', s}$. The idea behind the backwards search is based on the following observation. Given two sequences $\sigma' \subseteq \sigma$, let x be the first element enumerated by $F_{\sigma', s}$ (which is not in content(σ')). If x is an element of the target language, it will eventually be enumerated in $F_{\sigma, s}$ as well (as it has to appear in $W_{h(\sigma)}$ by monotonicity of h). However, further enumerations may not be similar, as $F_{\sigma', s}$ may build its further hypotheses on $\sigma'^\frown x$, which in general is no subsequence of σ. With the backwards search, we check for such elements and enumerate them in case the learner h shows a monotonic behaviour regarding them. In the end, we define the learner h' as

$$W_{h'(\sigma)} = \bigcup_{s \in \mathbb{N}} B_{\sigma, s} \cup F_{\sigma, s}.$$

We show that h' $\mathbf{TxtGNUBc}$-learns $\mathcal{L}$. Let $L \in \mathcal{L}$ and $T \in \mathbf{Txt}(L)$. First, we show $\mathbf{Bc}$-convergence and afterwards that h' is $\mathbf{NU}$. To that end, let n_0 be such that $T[n_0]$ is a $\mathbf{Bc}$-locking sequence for h on L (this exists by Theorem 4). For each $n < n_0$, let $\tilde{x}_n = \mathbf{nextEl}(h', T[n], T[n_0], s)$ (via $\tilde{\sigma}_n$) be the first newly enumerated element not in L (if such exists). Then, let Let $n_1 \geq n_0$ be such that, for $n < n_0$, for each $\tilde{\sigma}_n$ there exists a $\tau \in \text{content}(T[n_1])_{\#}^{\leq |T[n_1]|}$ such that $h(\tilde{\sigma}_n^\frown \tau)$ is a correct guess. In particular, $\mathbf{MonBeh}(h, \tilde{\sigma}, \tilde{x}, s, T[n_1])$ fails and, therefore, no $B_{T[n_1], s, T[n]}$ contains elements which are not in L.

Also, for $n \geq n_0$, $B_{T[n_1], s, T[n]}$ only contains elements in L (as $T[n_0]$ is a $\mathbf{Bc}$-locking sequence). Hence, for $n \geq n_1$, we have

$$\bigcup_{s \in \mathbb{N}} B_{T[n], s} \subseteq L.$$

In particular, as $T[n]$ is also a $\mathbf{Bc}$-locking sequence, we get

$$\bigcup_{s \in \mathbb{N}} F_{T[n], s} = L.$$

Thus, $W_{h'(T[n])} = L$.

It remains to be shown that h' is **NU**. Let n be minimal such that $W_{h'(T[n])} = L$. We show that, for $n' \geq n$, we have $W_{h'(T[n'])} = L$ as well. Note that by definition of the backwards search sets, for $\tilde{n} \leq n$, we have

$$\bigcup_{s \in \mathbb{N}} B_{T[n],s,T[\tilde{n}]} \supseteq \bigcup_{s \in \mathbb{N}} B_{T[n'],s,T[\tilde{n}]}.$$

Furthermore,

$$\bigcup_{s \in \mathbb{N}} F_{T[n],s} \supseteq \bigcup_{s \in \mathbb{N}} F_{T[n'],s} \cup \bigcup_{\substack{\tilde{n} \in \mathbb{N}, \\ n \leq \tilde{n} \leq n'}} \bigcup_{s \in \mathbb{N}} B_{T[n'],s,T[\tilde{n}]},$$

as, firstly, $T[n']$ is a candidate within, from some s onwards, $F_{T[n],s}$ and, secondly, the backwards search set $\bigcup_{s \in \mathbb{N}} B_{T[n'],s,T[\tilde{n}]}$ can only enumerate as much as the forward enumeration set $\bigcup_{s \in \mathbb{N}} F_{T[\tilde{n}],s}$. Thus, $W_{h'(T[n'])} \subseteq W_{h'(T[n])} = L$. Next we show that each element $x \in W_{h'(T[n])}$ will be enumerated in $W_{h'(T[n'])}$. We show this by case distinction depending how x is enumerated in $W_{h'(T[n])}$.

1.C.: For some s', the element x is enumerated in $F_{T[n],s'}$. Then, we get $x \in \bigcup_{s \in \mathbb{N}} B_{T[n],s,T[n']}$ as the **MonBeh** check passes for elements in L.

2.C.: For some s' and $\tilde{n} \leq n$, we have $x \in B_{T[\tilde{n}],s',T[n]}$. Then, x is also enumerated in $\bigcup_{s \in \mathbb{N}} B_{T[\tilde{n}],s,T[n']}$ as the **MonBeh** check passes for elements in L.

Thus, $W_{h'(T[n'])} \supseteq L$ and, altogether, $W_{h'(T[n'])} = L$. $\qquad\square$

References

1. Angluin, D.: Inductive inference of formal languages from positive data. Inf. Control **45**, 117–135 (1980)
2. Baliga, G., Case, J., Merkle, W., Stephan, F., Wiehagen, R.: When unlearning helps. Inf. Comput. **206**, 694–709 (2008)
3. Blum, L., Blum, M.: Toward a mathematical theory of inductive inference. Inf. Control **28**, 125–155 (1975)
4. Case, J., Kötzing, T.: Strongly non-U-shaped language learning results by general techniques. Inf. Comput. **251**, 1–15 (2016)
5. Case, J., Lynes, C.: Machine inductive inference and language identification. In: Nielsen, M., Schmidt, E.M. (eds.) ICALP 1982. LNCS, vol. 140, pp. 107–115. Springer, Heidelberg (1982). https://doi.org/10.1007/BFb0012761
6. Doskoč, V., Kötzing, T.: Mapping monotonic restrictions in inductive inference. In: De Mol, L., Weiermann, A., Manea, F., Fernández-Duque, D. (eds.) CiE 2021. LNCS, vol. 12813, pp. 146–157. Springer, Cham (2021). https://doi.org/10.1007/978-3-030-80049-9_13
7. Doskoč, V., Kötzing, T.: Normal forms for semantically witness-based learners in inductive inference. In: De Mol, L., Weiermann, A., Manea, F., Fernández-Duque, D. (eds.) CiE 2021. LNCS, vol. 12813, pp. 158–168. Springer, Cham (2021). https://doi.org/10.1007/978-3-030-80049-9_14
8. Doskoč, V., Kötzing, T.: Cautious limit learning. In: Algorithmic Learning Theory (ALT), pp. 117:251–117:276 (2020)

9. Fulk, M.A., Jain, S., Osherson, D.N.: Open problems in "systems that learn". J. Comput. Syst. Sci. **49**(3), 589–604 (1994)

10. Gold, E.M.: Language identification in the limit. Inf. Control **10**, 447–474 (1967)

11. Jain, S., Kötzing, T., Ma, J., Stephan, F.: On the role of update constraints and text-types in iterative learning. Inf. Comput. **247**, 152–168 (2016)

12. Jain, S., Osherson, D., Royer, J.S., Sharma, A.: Systems that Learn: An Introduction to Learning Theory, 2nd edn. MIT Press, Cambridge (1999)

13. Jantke, K.: Monotonic and non-monotonic inductive inference. N. Gener. Comput. **8**, 349–360 (1991)

14. Kinber, E.B., Stephan, F.: Language learning from texts: mindchanges, limited memory, and monotonicity. Inf. Comput. **123**, 224–241 (1995)

15. Kötzing, T., Palenta, R.: A map of update constraints in inductive inference. Theoret. Comput. Sci. **650**, 4–24 (2016)

16. Kötzing, T., Schirneck, M.: Towards an atlas of computational learning theory. In: Symposium on Theoretical Aspects of Computer Science (STACS), pp. 47:1–47:13 (2016)

17. Kötzing, T., Schirneck, M., Seidel, K.: Normal forms in semantic language identification. In: Algorithmic Learning Theory (ALT), pp. 76:493–76:516 (2017)

18. Lange, S., Zeugmann, T.: Monotonic versus non-monotonic language learning. In: Brewka, G., Jantke, K.P., Schmitt, P.H. (eds.) NIL 1991. LNCS, vol. 659, pp. 254–269. Springer, Heidelberg (1993). https://doi.org/10.1007/BFb0030397

19. Osherson, D., Stob, M., Weinstein, S.: Systems that Learn: An Introduction to Learning Theory for Cognitive and Computer Scientists. MIT Press, Cambridge (1986)

20. Osherson, D.N., Stob, M., Weinstein, S.: Learning strategies. Inf. Control **53**, 32–51 (1982)

21. Osherson, D.N., Weinstein, S.: Criteria of language learning. Inf. Control **52**, 123–138 (1982)

22. Schäfer-Richter, G.: Über eingabeabhängigkeit und komplexität von inferenzstrategien. Ph.D. thesis, RWTH Aachen University, Germany (1984)

23. Wexler, K., Culicover, P.W.: Formal Principles of Language Acquisition. MIT Press, Cambridge (1980)

24. Wiehagen, R.: A thesis in inductive inference. In: Dix, J., Jantke, K.P., Schmitt, P.H. (eds.) NIL 1990. LNCS, vol. 543, pp. 184–207. Springer, Heidelberg (1991). https://doi.org/10.1007/BFb0023324

An Extension of the Equivalence Between Brouwer's Fan Theorem and Weak König's Lemma with a Uniqueness Hypothesis

Makoto Fujiwara[✉][iD]

Department of Applied Mathematics, Faculty of Science Division I, Tokyo University of Science, 1-3 Kagurazaka, Shinjuku-ku, Tokyo 162-8601, Japan
makotofujiwara@rs.tus.ac.jp

Abstract. Generalizing Schwichtenberg's arguments [J. Univ. Comput. Sci. $11(12)$, 2086–2095 (2005)], we show that bounded König's lemma with a uniqueness hypothesis is equivalent to the decidable fan theorem for bounded spreads over the intuitionistic counterpart EL_0 of RCA_0 in classical reverse mathematics. Then it follows that bounded König's lemma with the uniqueness hypothesis is equivalent to weak König's lemma with the uniqueness hypothesis over EL_0.

Keywords: Weak König's lemma · Bounded König's lemma · Uniqueness hypothesis · The decidable fan theorem · Constructive reverse mathematics

1 Introduction

Reverse mathematics is a research program in foundations of mathematics initiated by Friedman in 1970's and developed extensively by Simpson and others in 1980's and thereafter. In reverse mathematics, for each theorem in ordinary (non-set-theoretic) mathematics, one seeks an equivalent axiom over some weak theory which does not prove the theorem. As summarized in Simpson's book [9], reverse mathematics has been systematically developed mainly over a subsystem RCA_0 of second-order arithmetic based on classical logic. The base theory for reverse mathematical investigation, however, is not necessarily RCA_0. Some constructivists (who accept only "constructive" reasoning in proofs) have investigated the interrelation between non-constructive principles over some constructive theory based on intuitionistic logic. The research of this kind is called *constructive reverse mathematics* (cf. [5]). In particular, constructive reverse mathematics over the intuitionistic counterpart EL_0 of RCA_0 can be seen as a fine-grained analysis of classical reverse mathematics (a la Friedman and Simpson).

Weak König's lemma WKL, which states that every infinite binary tree has an infinite path, plays a crucial role in classical reverse mathematics [9]. On the

U. Berger et al. (Eds.): CiE 2022, LNCS 13359, pp. 115–124, 2022.
https://doi.org/10.1007/978-3-031-08740-0_10

other hand, Brouwer's fan theorem $\mathrm{FAN_D(T_{01})}$ from intuitionistic mathematics is a sort of contrapositive of WKL. In the context of constructive reverse mathematics, both of WKL and $\mathrm{FAN_D(T_{01})}$ has been studied extensively. In particular, as shown in [6], WKL implies $\mathrm{FAN_D(T_{01})}$ over the intuitionistic counterpart $\mathrm{EL_0}$ of $\mathrm{RCA_0}$. In contrast, the converse direction is not the case. Then Berger and Ishihara [1] showed that weak König's lemma with a uniqueness hypothesis WKL! is equivalent to $\mathrm{FAN_D(T_{01})}$ in the context of Bishop's constructive mathematics (which accepts the use of the full countable choice scheme and the full induction scheme). In [1], however, the equivalence between WKL! and $\mathrm{FAN_D(T_{01})}$ is a consequence from a circle of implications. Later, Schwichtenberg [8] gave a direct proof of the equivalence (the originality is in the proof of $\mathrm{FAN_D(T_{01})} \to$ WKL!) and formalize the proof in the Minlog proof assistant. More recently, Moschovakis [7] studied weak König's lemma with another uniqueness hypothesis WKL!!.

Bounded König's lemma BKL, which states that every infinite bounded tree has an infinite path, is a generalization of WKL. In classical reverse mathematics, BKL is known to be equivalent to WKL over $\mathrm{RCA_0}$ (see [9, Lemma IV.1.4.]), and frequently used in showing that WKL is enough (as an axiom) to prove a mathematical assertion on a compactness property. The equivalence between WKL and BKL is trivial over a theory containing the countable choice scheme (as Bishop's constructive mathematics), but not so over $\mathrm{RCA_0}$ or $\mathrm{EL_0}$ since they contain only a restriction of the countable choice scheme. The proof of WKL $\to$ BKL over $\mathrm{RCA_0}$ in [9, Lemma IV.1.4] provides an effective translation from an infinite bounded tree into an infinite binary tree such as an infinite path of the binary tree entails an infinite path of the original bounded tree constructively.[1]

Recently, the author [4] studied several variations of König's lemma and the decidable fan theorem over $\mathrm{EL_0}$ (with some additional induction scheme for some case). In [4], he introduced unique variants BKL! and BKL!! of bounded König's lemma, and showed that the uniqueness condition on BKL!! is preserved (constructively) by the effective translation from an infinite bounded tree into an infinite binary tree in [9, Lemma IV.1.4], and hence, it follows that WKL!! implies BKL!! over $\mathrm{EL_0}$ (see [4, Lemma 4.26]). However, this seems not to be the case for BKL!. Thus it is non-trivial whether BKL! is equivalent to WKL! over $\mathrm{EL_0}$. On the other hand, since the two uniqueness hypotheses are equivalent in the presence of Markov's non-constructive principle MP (see [4, Lemma 4.25]), it follows that BKL! is equivalent to WKL! over $\mathrm{EL_0 + MP}$.

In this article, we extend the constructive equivalence between WKL! and $\mathrm{FAN_D(T_{01})}$ for binary trees [1,8] to the corresponding equivalence for arbitrary bounded trees (see Theorem 1). For this purpose, we generalize Schwichtenberg's arguments for binary trees in [8] to arbitrary bounded trees. Another advantage of our results over [1,8] is in that all of our arguments are developed inside the weak intuitionistic theory $\mathrm{EL_0}$. Then it follows from our results that BKL! is equivalent to WKL! over $\mathrm{EL_0}$ (see Corollary 1).

---

[1] An analogous translation can be found already in [11, Sect. 4.7.5].

2   Preparation

We work in the same framework as [4]. Our base theory $\mathsf{EL_0}$ is a subsystem of intuitionistic analysis EL [10, Sect. 1.9.10], which has two-sorted variables (one is for natural numbers and another is for functions over natural numbers) in its language. Note that the subscript 0 of $\mathsf{EL_0}$ denotes the restriction of the induction axiom schema to quantifier-free predicates in this context. In addition, $\mathsf{EL_0}$ contains the number-number choice scheme for quantifier-free predicates

$$\mathrm{QF\text{-}AC}^{0,0} : \forall x^{\mathbb{N}} \exists y^{\mathbb{N}} A_{\mathrm{qf}}(x, y) \rightarrow \exists f^{\mathbb{N} \rightarrow \mathbb{N}} \forall x A_{\mathrm{qf}}(x, f(x))$$

where A_{qf} is quantifier-free. In fact, $\mathsf{EL_0}$ augmented with the law-of-excluded-middle LEM is equivalent to the most popular base theory $\mathsf{RCA_0}$ of classical reverse mathematics [9]. To explore the relation with classical reverse mathematics, constructive reverse mathematics has been recently carried out over $\mathsf{EL_0}$ (cf. [2,4]). See [3, Sect. 2.2.1] for the description of $\mathsf{EL_0}$.

Notation. We use the same notation as in [4]. We indicate the types of variables by their superscripts ($\mathbb{N}$ or $\mathbb{N}^{\mathbb{N}}$) but often suppress them when they are clear from the context. In particular, the letters x, i, j, k, m, n range over objects of type $\mathbb{N}$ (a type for natural numbers), the letters f, g, h, p, q range over objects of type $\mathbb{N}^{\mathbb{N}}$, which is also denoted by $\mathbb{N} \rightarrow \mathbb{N}$ (a type for functions from natural numbers to natural numbers). We assume a fixed bijective coding of finite sequences of objects of type $\mathbb{N}$ defined by the bijective pairing function (see e.g. [10, Sect. 1.3.9]). The letters u, v, b range over the set $\mathbb{N}^*$ of (the codes of) finite sequences of objects of type $\mathbb{N}$. Under the fixed coding, inside $\mathsf{EL_0}$, we identify an element in $\mathbb{N}^*$ with its code (an object of type $\mathbb{N}$), and identify a subset of $\mathbb{N}^*$ with the characteristic function of the corresponding subset of the codes. A finite sequence consisting of $x_0, \ldots, x_k$ is denoted by $\langle x_0, \ldots, x_k \rangle$. The concatenation of finite sequences u and v is denoted by $u * v$. The length of a finite sequence u is denoted by $|u|$, and if $x < |u|$, then u_x denotes the x-th entry of u. We write $u \preceq v$ if u is an initial segment of v. For g of type $\mathbb{N} \rightarrow \mathbb{N}$, $\overline{g}n$ denotes the initial segment of g of length n, especially, $\overline{g}0 = \langle \rangle$. If u is a finite sequence, then $\widehat{u}$ denotes the infinite sequence (of type $\mathbb{N} \rightarrow \mathbb{N}$) $u * (\lambda x.0)$, and $\overline{u}n$ denotes the initial segment of u of length n for $n \leq |u|$. We use the notation A_{qf} for quantifier-free predicates.

We also recall the following notions on trees: $T \subseteq \mathbb{N}^*$ is a **tree** if $\forall u, v \in \mathbb{N}^* (u * v \in T \rightarrow u \in T)$. A tree T is **infinite** if $\forall i^{\mathbb{N}} \exists u \in \mathbb{N}^*(|u| = i \wedge u \in T)$. A **height-wise bounding function** of a tree T is a function $h^{\mathbb{N} \rightarrow \mathbb{N}}$ such that $\forall u \in T \forall j < |u| (u_j \leq h(j))$. A tree T is **bounded** if T has a height-wise bounding function. A **binary** tree is a bounded tree with height-wise bounding function $h := \lambda x.1$. A **path** through a tree T is a function $p^{\mathbb{N} \rightarrow \mathbb{N}}$ such that $\forall i (\overline{p}i \in T)$. $T \subseteq \mathbb{N}^*$ is a **bounded spread** if T is an inhabited (i.e., $\langle \rangle \in T$) bounded tree such that $\forall u \in T \exists x^{\mathbb{N}}(u * \langle x \rangle \in T)$. A tree T **does not have two paths** if

$$\forall p^{\mathbb{N} \rightarrow \mathbb{N}}, q^{\mathbb{N} \rightarrow \mathbb{N}} \left(\exists n(p(n) \neq q(n)) \rightarrow \exists n (\overline{p}n \notin T) \vee \exists n (\overline{q}n \notin T) \right). \tag{1}$$

A tree T **has at most one path** if

$$\forall p^{\mathbb{N}\to\mathbb{N}}, q^{\mathbb{N}\to\mathbb{N}} \left(\forall n\,(\overline{p}n \in T) \wedge \forall n\,(\overline{q}n \in T) \to \forall n(p(n) = q(n))\right). \tag{2}$$

Uniqueness conditions (1) and (2) for binary trees were studied in [1,8] and [7] respectively, and they have been generalized for arbitrary finitely-branching trees recently in [4]. Of course, conditions (1) and (2) are equivalent over classical logic. In contrast, over intuitionistic logic, condition (1) implies condition (2), but not vice versa. See [4, Sect. 4.2.1] for more information about conditions (1) and (2).

Using these notions made in EL_0, our principles are defined as follows:

Definition 1. *Bounded König's lemma with a uniqueness hypothesis* BKL! *states that for any infinite bounded tree T which does not have two paths, there exists a path through T. Formally,* BKL! *is formalized in terms of EL_0 as follows (where we still use the informal description of the inequalities and the negations of equality for readability):*

$$\forall f^{\mathbb{N}^{\mathbb{N}}}, h^{\mathbb{N}^{\mathbb{N}}} \left(\begin{array}{l} \forall u^{\mathbb{N}}(f(u) = 0 \to \forall j < |u|(u_j \leq h(j))) \\ \wedge\, \forall u^{\mathbb{N}}, v^{\mathbb{N}}(f(u * v) = 0 \to f(u) = 0) \\ \wedge\, \forall i^{\mathbb{N}}\exists u^{\mathbb{N}}(|u| = i \wedge f(u) = 0) \\ \wedge\, \forall p^{\mathbb{N}^{\mathbb{N}}}, q^{\mathbb{N}^{\mathbb{N}}} \left(\begin{array}{l} \exists n^{\mathbb{N}}(p(n) \neq q(n)) \\ \to \exists n^{\mathbb{N}}\,(f\,(\overline{p}n) \neq 0) \vee \exists n^{\mathbb{N}}\,(f\,(\overline{q}n) \neq 0) \end{array} \right) \\ \to \exists p^{\mathbb{N}^{\mathbb{N}}}\forall n^{\mathbb{N}} f(\overline{p}n) = 0 \end{array} \right). \tag{3}$$

In particular, trees are encoded by their characteristic functions in EL_0. Weak König's lemma with a uniqueness hypothesis WKL! *is a particular instance of* BKL! *for $h := \lambda x.1$ in (3) (cf. [4, Sect. 4.2.1]). The bounded decidable fan theorem* BFAN_D *states that for any quantifier-free predicate (which is decidable in EL_0) A_{qf} and any bounded spread $T \subseteq \mathbb{N}^*$,*

$$\forall p \in T \exists m^{\mathbb{N}} A_{\mathrm{qf}}\,(\overline{p}m) \to \exists n^{\mathbb{N}}\forall p \in T \exists m \leq n A_{\mathrm{qf}}\,(\overline{p}m), \tag{4}$$

where $p \in T$ means $\forall i^{\mathbb{N}}\,(\overline{p}i \in T)$. Formally, BFAN_D *is formalized in terms of EL_0 as follows (where we still use some informal description as before):*

$$\forall g^{\mathbb{N}^{\mathbb{N}}}, f^{\mathbb{N}^{\mathbb{N}}}, h^{\mathbb{N}^{\mathbb{N}}} \left(\begin{array}{l} \forall u^{\mathbb{N}}(f(u) = 0 \to \forall j < |u|(u_j \leq h(j))) \\ \wedge\, \forall u^{\mathbb{N}}, v^{\mathbb{N}}(f(u * v) = 0 \to f(u) = 0) \\ \wedge\, f\,(\langle\rangle) = 0 \wedge \forall u^{\mathbb{N}}\,(f(u) = 0 \to \exists x^{\mathbb{N}}\,(f(u * \langle x \rangle) = 0)) \\ \wedge\, \forall p^{\mathbb{N}^{\mathbb{N}}}\,(\forall i^{\mathbb{N}}(f\,(\overline{p}i) = 0) \to \exists m^{\mathbb{N}}(g\,(\overline{p}m) = 0)) \\ \to \exists n^{\mathbb{N}}\forall p^{\mathbb{N}^{\mathbb{N}}}\,(\forall i^{\mathbb{N}}(f\,(\overline{p}i) = 0) \to \exists m \leq n(g\,(\overline{p}m) = 0)) \end{array} \right). \tag{5}$$

The binary decidable fan theorem $\mathsf{FAN}_D(\mathsf{T}_{01})$ *is a particular instance of* BFAN_D *for $h := \lambda x.1$ in (5).*

In this paper, we prefer the informal (or semi-formal) description for readability. Our informal description can be translated into the formal description in EL_0 in a straightforward way. The following arguments were already established in [4]:

Lemma 1 (cf. [4, Lemma 4.5]). $EL_0 + FAN_D(T_{01}) \vdash BFAN_D$.

Lemma 2 (cf. [4, Proposition 4.12]). EL_0 *proves that for a bounded tree* T^h *with* $h^{N \to N}$ *as its height-wise bounding function,* T^h *does not have two paths if and only if* T^h *satisfies the following:*

$$\forall p, q \in \{f^{N \to N} \mid \forall i^N (f(i) \le h(i))\} \left(\begin{array}{l} \exists n (p(n) \ne q(n)) \\ \to \exists n (\overline{p}n \notin T^h) \vee \exists n (\overline{q}n \notin T^h) \end{array} \right). \quad (6)$$

3   Results

Proposition 1. $EL_0 \vdash WKL! \leftrightarrow FAN_D(T_{01})$.

Proof. Inside EL_0, one can formalize the proof of the equivalence between (an equivalent of) WKL! and $FAN_D(T_{01})$ in [8] (cf. the proof of Theorem 1 below). $\qquad\square$

Lemma 3. EL_0 *proves that a bounded tree* T^h *with* $h^{N \to N}$ *as its height-wise bounding function satisfies*

$$\forall u \in T^h \left(u \le \overline{h} (|u|) \right).$$

Proof. Fix $u \in T^h$. In EL_0, one can show $\forall j^N \left(j \le |u| \to \overline{u}j \le \overline{h}j \right)$ by induction on j. Then, taking $|u|$ as j, we have $u = \overline{u} (|u|) \le \overline{h} (|u|)$. $\qquad\square$

Lemma 4. $EL_0 \vdash BKL! \to BFAN_D$.

Proof. We recast the proof of that WKL! implies $FAN_D(T_{01})$ in [1] (and [8]).

Let $T \subseteq N^*$ be a bounded fan with $h^{N \to N}$ as its height-wise bounding function. For showing the decidable fan theorem for T, it suffices to show (4) for a bounded fan $N^*_{\le h} := \{u \in N^* \mid \forall i < |u| (u_i \le h(i))\}$ which contains T (cf. [4, Remark 4.4]). Let A_{qf} be a quantifier-free predicate on N^* such that $\forall q \in N^*_{\le h} \exists j A_{qf} (\overline{q}j)$, where $q \in N^*_{\le h}$ means $\forall i^N \left(\overline{q}i \in N^*_{\le h} \right)$ as in (4). In EL_0, take (the characteristic function of) $B \subseteq N^*$ as

$$B = \{u \in N^* \mid \exists j \le |u| A_{qf} (\overline{u}j)\}.$$

Then we have

$$\forall q \in N^*_{\le h} \exists n (\overline{q}n \in B). \quad (7)$$

Now we say that n^N is *big for* B *in* $N^*_{\le h}$ if $u \in B$ for all $u \in N^*_{\le h}$ such that $|u| = n$. Note that the predicate "n is big for B in $N^*_{\le h}$" is decidable by Lemma 3. In EL_0 (which contains $QF\text{-}AC^{0,0}$), define a function $f^{N \to N^*}$ such that

- if n is not big for B in $N^*_{\le h}$, $f(n)$ is the least element (as code) in $\{u \in N^*_{\le h} \setminus B \mid |u| = n\}$;

– if n is big for B in $\mathbb{N}^*_{\leq h}$, $f(n) = f(k) * 0^{n-k}$ with the greatest $k < n$ such that k is not big for B in $\mathbb{N}^*_{\leq h}$, where 0^{n-k} denotes the finite sequence $\langle 0, \ldots, 0 \rangle$ of length $n - k$.

Put

$$T^h := \left(\mathbb{N}^*_{\leq h} \setminus B \right) \cup \left\{ f(n) \in \mathbb{N}^*_{\leq h} \mid n^{\mathbb{N}} \text{ is big for } B \text{ in } \mathbb{N}^*_{\leq h} \right\}.$$

Note that $|f(n)| = n$ and $f(n) \in T^h \subseteq \mathbb{N}^*_{\leq h}$ for all $n^{\mathbb{N}}$. If $u * v \in T^h$, then $u \in T^h$ since B is upward closed. Thus T^h is an infinite tree with h as its height-wise bounding function. To show (6) in Lemma 2, assume that $q', q'' \in \{ f^{\mathbb{N} \to \mathbb{N}} \mid \forall i^{\mathbb{N}} (f(i) \leq h(i)) \}$ satisfy $q'(n) \neq q''(n)$ for some $n^{\mathbb{N}}$. By (7), there exist n' and n'' such that $\overline{q'}n' \in B$ and $\overline{q''}n'' \in B$. Put $n_0 := \max\{n + 1, n', n''\}$. Since B is upward closed, we have $\overline{q'}n_0 \neq \overline{q''}n_0$, $\overline{q'}n_0 \in B$ and $\overline{q''}n_0 \in B$. If $\overline{q'}n_0 \in T^h$ and $\overline{q''}n_0 \in T^h$, by the definition of T^h, we have that n_0 is big for B in $\mathbb{N}^*_{\leq h}$ and $\overline{q'}n_0 = f(n_0) = \overline{q''}n_0$, which contradicts $\overline{q'}n_0 \neq \overline{q''}n_0$. Thus we have $\overline{q'}n_0 \notin T^h$ or $\overline{q''}n_0 \notin T^h$. Then, by Lemma 2, it follows that T^h does not have two paths.

By BKL!, there exists a path $p^{\mathbb{N} \to \mathbb{N}}$ through T^h. Since $p \in T^h$ (in the same sense as in (4)), by (7), there exists $n_1^{\mathbb{N}}$ such that $\overline{p}n_1 \in B$. Since p is a path through T^h, we have that n_1 is big for B in $\mathbb{N}^*_{\leq h}$. Then, for all $q \in \mathbb{N}^*_{\leq h}$, we have $\overline{q}n_1 \in B$, and hence, there exists $j \leq n_1$ such that $A_{\text{qf}}(\overline{q}j)$. Thus we have shown $\forall q \in \mathbb{N}^*_{\leq h} \exists j \leq n_1 A_{\text{qf}}(\overline{q}j)$.   □

For the converse direction of Lemma 4, we use the product type $\mathbb{N} \times \mathbb{N}$. Since there is a bijective pairing function in EL_0, one can encode objects of type $\mathbb{N} \times \mathbb{N}$ or $(\mathbb{N} \times \mathbb{N})^*$ (the type for the finite sequences of elements of type $\mathbb{N} \times \mathbb{N}$) into objects of type $\mathbb{N}$ in EL_0. To make our arguments absolutely clear, we fix a pairing function $\pi : \mathbb{N} \times \mathbb{N} \to \mathbb{N}$ with its inverses $\pi^l, \pi^r : \mathbb{N} \to \mathbb{N}$ such that $\pi^l(x, y) = x, \pi^r(x, y) = y$ and $\pi \left(\pi^l(z), \pi^r(z) \right) = z$ for all $x, y, z \in \mathbb{N}$ (see e.g. [10, Sect. 1.3.9]).

Notation. In what follows, we employ the following notation:

– For $h \in \mathbb{N}^{\mathbb{N}}$,
  • $u \in (\mathbb{N} \times \mathbb{N})^*_{\leq h}$ denotes $u \in (\mathbb{N} \times \mathbb{N})^*$ and $\forall i < |u|(\pi^l(u_i) \leq h(i) \wedge \pi^r(u_i) \leq h(i))$;
  • $f \in (\mathbb{N} \times \mathbb{N})^{\mathbb{N}}_{\leq h}$ denotes $f \in (\mathbb{N} \times \mathbb{N})^{\mathbb{N}}$ and $\forall i(\pi^l(f(i)) \leq h(i) \wedge \pi^r(f(i)) \leq h(i))$.
– For $f \in \mathbb{N} \to (\mathbb{N} \times \mathbb{N})$, f^l and f^r denote the functions $\lambda i. \pi^l(f(i))$ and $\lambda i. \pi^r(f(i))$ respectively.
– For $u \in (\mathbb{N} \times \mathbb{N})^*$, $u^l \equiv u^r \equiv \langle \rangle$ if u is an empty sequence, otherwise, u^l and u^r denote the sequences $\langle \pi^l(u_0), \pi^l(u_1), \ldots, \pi^l(u_{|u|-1}) \rangle$ and $\langle \pi^r(u_0), \pi^r(u_1), \ldots, \pi^r(u_{|u|-1}) \rangle$ respectively.
– For $u \in \mathbb{N}^*$ such that $|u| = 2j > 0$, u^{even} and u^{odd} denote the sequences $\langle u_0, u_2, \ldots, u_{2j-2} \rangle$ and $\langle u_1, u_3, \ldots, u_{2j-1} \rangle$ respectively.
– For $u \in \mathbb{N}^*$ such that $|u| = 2j > 0$, $\widetilde{u}$ denotes the finite sequence in $(\mathbb{N} \times \mathbb{N})^j$ (of length j) such that $(\widetilde{u})_i = \pi \left((u^{even})_i, (u^{odd})_i \right)$ for all $i < j$.

- For $h \in \mathbb{N}^{\mathbb{N}}$, $\tilde{h}$ denotes the function in $\mathbb{N}^{\mathbb{N}}$ such that $\tilde{h}(2i) = \tilde{h}(2i+1) = h(i)$ for all $i \in \mathbb{N}$.

Lemma 5. $\mathrm{EL_0 + BFAN_D}$ *proves that for all* $h^{\mathbb{N}\to\mathbb{N}}$, $n^{\mathbb{N}}$ *and* $X \subseteq (\mathbb{N} \times \mathbb{N})^*_{\leq h}$, *if*

$$\forall u \in (\mathbb{N} \times \mathbb{N})^*_{\leq h} \, \forall j < |u| \, (\overline{u}j \in X \to u \in X) \tag{8}$$

and

$$\forall f \in (\mathbb{N} \times \mathbb{N})^{\mathbb{N}}_{\leq h} \left(\overline{f^l}n \neq \overline{f^r}n \to \exists m^{\mathbb{N}} \left(\overline{f}m \in X \right) \right), \tag{9}$$

then

$$\exists k^{\mathbb{N}} \forall f \in (\mathbb{N} \times \mathbb{N})^{\mathbb{N}}_{\leq h} \left(\overline{f^l}n \neq \overline{f^r}n \to \overline{f}k \in X \right). \tag{10}$$

Proof. Fix $h^{\mathbb{N}\to\mathbb{N}}$, $n^{\mathbb{N}}$ and $X \subseteq (\mathbb{N} \times \mathbb{N})^*_{\leq h}$ which satisfy (8) and (9). Without loss of generality, assume $n > 0$. Consider the following decidable predicate on $\mathbb{N}^*$:

$$A_{\mathrm{qf}}(u) :\equiv \exists j \leq |u| \left(j \geq n \wedge |u| = 2j \wedge \left(\widetilde{u^{even}}n \neq \widetilde{u^{odd}}n \to \tilde{u} \in X \right) \right).$$

Note that

$$T^{\tilde{h}} := \left\{ u \in \mathbb{N}^* \mid \forall i < |u| \left(u_i \leq \tilde{h}(i) \right) \right\}$$

is a bounded fan with $\tilde{h}$ as its height-wise bounding function.

We claim that for any q in $T^{\tilde{h}}$ (in the same sense as in (4)), there exists $m^{\mathbb{N}}$ such that $A_{\mathrm{qf}}(\overline{q}m)$ holds. For given $q \in T^{\tilde{h}}$, put $q' := \lambda i.q(2i)$ and $q'' := \lambda i.q(2i+1)$. Then, by the definition of $T^{\tilde{h}}$, we have that $q'(i) \leq h(i)$ and $q''(i) \leq h(i)$ for all $i^{\mathbb{N}}$. Now either $\overline{q'}n = \overline{q''}n$ or $\overline{q'}n \neq \overline{q''}n$. In the former case, we trivially have $A_{\mathrm{qf}}(\overline{q}(2n))$. In the latter case, by (9), there exists $m^{\mathbb{N}}$ such that $\overline{q'''}m \in X$ where $q''' \in (\mathbb{N} \times \mathbb{N})^{\mathbb{N}}_{\leq h}$ is defined as $q'''(i) = \pi(q'(i), q''(i))$. Put $m' := \max\{n, m\}$. Then, by (8), we have $\overline{q'''}m' \in X$. Since $\widetilde{\overline{q}(2m')} = \overline{q'''}m'$, we have $A_{\mathrm{qf}}(\overline{q}(2m'))$ in a straightforward way.

Then, by $\mathrm{BFAN_D}$, there exists $k \in \mathbb{N}$ such that $\forall q \in T^{\tilde{h}} \exists m \leq k A_{\mathrm{qf}}(\overline{q}m)$. In the following, we show that this k is a desired witness of (10). Fix $f \in (\mathbb{N} \times \mathbb{N})^{\mathbb{N}}_{\leq h}$ such that $\overline{f^l}n \neq \overline{f^r}n$. Define $f' \in \mathbb{N} \to \mathbb{N}$ as $f'(2i) = f^l(i)$ and $f'(2i+1) = f^r(i)$. Since $f \in (\mathbb{N} \times \mathbb{N})^{\mathbb{N}}_{\leq h}$, we have that $f'(i) \leq \tilde{h}(i)$ for all $i^{\mathbb{N}}$, and hence, $f' \in T^{\tilde{h}}$ (in the same sense as in (4)). Then there exists $n' \leq k$ such that $A_{\mathrm{qf}}(\overline{f'}n')$, namely, there exists $j' < n'$ such that

$$n' \geq 2n \wedge n' = 2j' \wedge \left(\overline{(\overline{f'}n')}^{even}n \neq \overline{(\overline{f'}n')}^{odd}n \to \widetilde{\overline{f'}n'} \in X \right). \tag{11}$$

By the definitions, we have $\overline{(\overline{f'}n')}^{even}n = \overline{f^l}n$ and $\overline{(\overline{f'}n')}^{odd}n = \overline{f^r}n$, and hence, $\overline{(\overline{f'}n')}^{even}n \neq \overline{(\overline{f'}n')}^{odd}n$. By (11), we have $\widetilde{\overline{f'}n'} \in X$, and hence, $\overline{f}j' \in X$. Since $j' < n' \leq k$, by (8), we have $\overline{f}k \in X$. $\qquad\square$

Lemma 6. $\mathrm{EL}_0 + \mathrm{BFAN}_\mathrm{D}$ *proves that a bounded tree T not having two paths satisfies the following:*

$$\forall n^\mathrm{N} \exists k \geq n \forall u, v \in T \left(|u| = |v| = k \to \overline{u}n = \overline{v}n \right). \tag{12}$$

Proof. Let T^h be a bounded tree with $h^{\mathrm{N} \to \mathrm{N}}$ as its height-wise bounding function. Fix n^N. Put

$$X := \left\{ u \in (\mathbb{N} \times \mathbb{N})^*_{\leq h} \mid \neg \left(u^l \in T^h \wedge u^r \in T^h \right) \right\}.$$

In what follows, we show that (8) and (9) in Lemma 5 hold for these h, n and X.

For verifying (8), fix $v \in (\mathbb{N} \times \mathbb{N})^*_{\leq h}$ and $j < |v|$ such that $\overline{v}j \in X$. Since X is decidable in EL_0, it suffices to show $\neg\neg (v \in X)$. Assume $v \notin X$. Since our tree T^h is decidable in EL_0, we have $v^l \in T^h$ and $v^r \in T^h$. Then, since T^h is a tree, we have $(\overline{v}j)^l \in T^h$ and $(\overline{v}j)^r \in T^h$, which contradicts $\overline{v}j \in X$. Thus we have shown $v \in X$.

For verifying (9), fix $f \in (\mathbb{N} \times \mathbb{N})^\mathrm{N}_{\leq h}$ such that $\overline{f^l}n \neq \overline{f^r}n$. Since T^h does not have two paths, there exists m^N such that $\overline{f^l}m \notin T^h$ or $\overline{f^r}m \notin T^h$. In either case, we have $\overline{f}m \in X$ in a straightforward way.

Then, by Lemma 5, there exists k^N which satisfies (10). Put $k' := \max\{n, k\}$. We show that this k' is our desired witness. Fix u and v in T^h such that $|u| = |v| = k'$. Assume $\overline{u}n \neq \overline{v}n$. Take $\widehat{u}$ and $\widehat{v}$, which are trivially in $(\mathbb{N} \times \mathbb{N})^\mathrm{N}_{\leq h}$. Define $f \in (\mathbb{N} \times \mathbb{N})^\mathrm{N}$ as $f(i) = (\widehat{u}(i), \widehat{v}(i))$. Since $\overline{f^l}\,n = \overline{\widehat{u}}n = \overline{u}n \neq \overline{v}n = \overline{\widehat{v}}n = \overline{f^r}\,n$, by (10) and (8), we have $\overline{f}\,k' \in X$. On the other hand, $(\overline{f}\,k')^l = \overline{\widehat{u}}k' = u \in T^h$ and $(\overline{f}\,k')^r = \overline{\widehat{v}}k' = v \in T^h$, which is a contradiction. Thus we have shown $\neg\neg (\overline{u}n = \overline{v}n)$, and hence, $\overline{u}n = \overline{v}n$ follows. $\square$

Lemma 7. $\mathrm{EL}_0 + \mathrm{BFAN}_\mathrm{D} \vdash \mathrm{BKL}!$.

Proof. Let T^h be an infinite bounded tree T^h with $h^{\mathrm{N} \to \mathrm{N}}$ as its height-wise bounding function. By Lemma 6, we have (12) for this T^h. By Lemma 3, any $u \in T^h$ of length k is bounded by $\overline{h}k$. Then, using $\mathrm{QF\text{-}AC}^{0,0}$ in EL_0, we have that there exists $f^{\mathrm{N} \to \mathrm{N}}$ such that

$$\forall n^\mathrm{N} \left(f(n) \geq n \wedge \forall u, v \in T^h \left(|u| = |v| = f(n) \to \overline{u}n = \overline{v}n \right) \right). \tag{13}$$

Without loss of generality, assume that f is monotone, namely,

$$\forall i^\mathrm{N}, j^\mathrm{N} \left(i \leq j \to f(i) \leq f(j) \right).$$

Since T^h is infinite, by $\mathrm{QF\text{-}AC}^{0,0}$, there exists $g^{\mathrm{N} \to \mathrm{N}}$ such that

$$\forall n^\mathrm{N} \left(g(n) \in T^h \wedge |g(n)| = n \right).$$

Put $b_n := \overline{g\left(f(n)\right)}\,n$, and define $p \in \mathbb{N}^\mathrm{N}$ as $p(n) := (b_{n+1})_n$. In what follows, we show that this p is a path through T^h. Since $b_n \in T^h$ for all n^N, it suffices to show that $\overline{p}n = b_n$ for all n^N.

For this purpose, we first claim that $b_n = \overline{b_{n+1}}\, n$ for all $n^{\mathbb{N}}$. Fix $n^{\mathbb{N}}$. Since both of $g(f(n))$ and $\overline{g\,(f(n+1))}(f(n))$ are in T^h and of length $f(n)$, by (13), we have

$$b_n = \overline{g\,(f(n))}\, n = \overline{\overline{g\,(f(n+1))}\,(f(n))}\, n$$

$$= \overline{g\,(f(n+1))}\, n = \overline{g\,(f(n+1))}\,(n+1)\, n = \overline{b_{n+1}}\, n.$$

Now we show $\forall n^{\mathbb{N}}\,(\overline{p}n = b_n)$ by induction on n. The base case is trivial. For the induction step, assume that $\overline{p}n = b_n$. Then, using the above claim, we have

$$\overline{p}(n+1) = \overline{p}n * \langle p(n)\rangle = b_n * \langle p(n)\rangle = b_n * \langle (b_{n+1})_n\rangle = \overline{b_{n+1}}\, n * \langle (b_{n+1})_n\rangle = b_{n+1}.$$

$\square$

Theorem 1. $\text{EL}_0 \vdash \text{BKL!} \leftrightarrow \text{BFAN}_D$.

Proof. By Lemma 4 and Lemma 7. $\square$

Corollary 1. $\text{EL}_0 \vdash \text{BKL!} \leftrightarrow \text{WKL!}$.

Proof. Immediate from Theorem 1, the fact that BFAN_D implies $\text{FAN}_D(T_{01})$, Lemma 1 and Proposition 1. $\square$

Question 1. Is there a direct proof of WKL! $\to$ BKL!? Here, a "direct" proof means a proof with an effective translation from an infinite bounded tree into an infinite binary tree which preserves condition (1) such as an infinite path of the binary tree entails an infinite path of the original bounded tree constructively.

Acknowledgements. The author thanks Helmut Schwichtenberg for helpful discussion. This work is supported by JSPS KAKENHI Grant Numbers JP19J01239 and JP20K14354.

References

1. Berger, J., Ishihara, H.: Brouwer's fan theorem and unique existence in constructive analysis. Math. Log. Q. **51**(4), 360–364 (2005). https://doi.org/10.1002/malq.200410038
2. Berger, J., Ishihara, H., Kihara, T., Nemoto, T.: The binary expansion and the intermediate value theorem in constructive reverse mathematics. Arch. Math. Logic **58**(1–2), 203–217 (2019). https://doi.org/10.1007/s00153-018-0627-2
3. Fujiwara, M.: Intuitionistic and uniform provability in reverse mathematics. Ph.D. thesis, Tohoku University (2015)
4. Fujiwara, M.: König's lemma, weak König's lemma, and the decidable fan theorem. Math. Log. Q. **67**(2), 241–257 (2021). https://doi.org/10.1002/malq.202000020
5. Ishihara, H.: Constructive reverse mathematics: compactness properties. In: From Sets and Types to Topology and Analysis, Oxford Logic Guides, vol. 48, pp. 245–267. Oxford University Press, Oxford (2005). https://doi.org/10.1093/acprof:oso/9780198566519.003.0016

6. Ishihara, H.: Weak König's lemma implies Brouwer's fan theorem: a direct proof. Notre Dame J. Formal Logic **47**(2), 249–252 (2006). https://doi.org/10.1305/ndjfl/1153858649

7. Moschovakis, J.R.: Another unique weak König's lemma. In: Berger, U., Diener, H., Schuster, P., Monika, S. (eds.) Logic, Construction, Computation, pp. 343–352. Ontos Mathematical Logic, De Gruyter, Berlin (2012). https://doi.org/10.1515/9783110324921.343

8. Schwichtenberg, H.: A direct proof of the equivalence between Brouwer's fan theorem and König's lemma with a uniqueness hypothesis. J. Univ. Comput. Sci. **11**(12), 2086–2095 (2005)

9. Simpson, S.G.: Subsystems of Second Order Arithmetic, 2nd edn. Perspectives in Logic, Cambridge University Press, Cambridge (2009)

10. Troelstra, A.S. (ed.): Metamathematical investigation of intuitionistic arithmetic and analysis. Lecture Notes in Mathematics, vol. 344. Springer-Verlag, Berlin (1973)

11. Troelstra, A.S., van Dalen, D.: Constructivism in mathematics, an introduction. vol. I, Studies in Logic and the Foundations of Mathematics, vol. 121. North Holland, Amsterdam (1988)

Defining Long Words Succinctly in FO and MSO

Lauri Hella(ID) and Miikka Vilander(✉)(ID)

Tampere University, 33100 Tampere, Finland
miikka.vilander@tuni.fi

Abstract. We consider the length of the longest word definable in FO and MSO via a formula of size n. For both logics we obtain as an upper bound for this number an exponential tower of height linear in n. We prove this by counting types with respect to a fixed quantifier rank. As lower bounds we obtain for both FO and MSO an exponential tower of height in the order of a rational power of n. We show these lower bounds by giving concrete formulas defining word representations of levels of the cumulative hierarchy of sets. In addition, we consider the Löwenheim-Skolem and Hanf numbers of these logics on words and obtain similar bounds for these as well.

Keywords: Logic on words · Monadic second-order logic · Succinctness

1 Introduction

We consider the succinctness of defining words. More precisely, if we allow formulas of size up to n in some logic, we want to know the length of the longest word definable by such formulas.

This question is not very interesting for all formalisms. An example where this is the case is given by regular expressions. There is no smaller regular expression that defines a word than the word itself. This result is spelled out at least in the survey [3]. However, the situation is completely different for monadic second-order logic MSO over words with linear order and unary predicates for the letters. Even though MSO has the same expressive power as regular expressions over words, it is well-known that MSO is non-elementarily more succinct. This follows from the results in the PhD thesis [12] of Stockmeyer. In fact, he proved that the problem whether the language defined by a given star-free generalized regular expression has non-empty complement is of non-elementary complexity with respect to the length of the expression. Since star-free generalized expressions can be polynomially translated into first-order logic FO, it follows that already FO is non-elementarily more succinct than regular expressions. In the article [11], Reinhardt

M. Vilander acknowledges the financial support of the Academy of Finland project *Explaining AI via Logic* (XAILOG), project number 345612.

U. Berger et al. (Eds.): CiE 2022, LNCS 13359, pp. 125–138, 2022.
https://doi.org/10.1007/978-3-031-08740-0_11

uses a variation of Stockmeyer's method for proving similar non-elementary succinctness gaps between finite automata and the logics MSO and FO.

In this paper our focus is in the definability of words in MSO and FO. As far as we know, this aspect of succinctness has not been considered previously in the context of words. We show that these logics can define words of non-elementary length via formulas of polynomial size.

In order to argue about definability via formulas of bounded size, we define the size n fragments $FO[n]$ and $MSO[n]$ that include only formulas of size up to n. We also define similar quantifier rank k fragments FO_k and MSO_k and use them to prove our upper bounds. Both of these types of fragments are essentially finite in the sense that they contain only a finite number of non-equivalent formulas. We call the length of the longest word definable in a fragment the definability number of that fragment. Using this concept, our initial question is reframed as studying the definability numbers of $FO[n]$ and $MSO[n]$.

The definability number of a fragment is closely related to the Löwenheim-Skolem and Hanf numbers of the fragment. The Löwenheim-Skolem number of a fragment is the smallest number m such that each satisfiable formula in the fragment has a model of size at most m. The Hanf number is the smallest number l such that any formula with a model of size greater than l has arbitrarily large models. These were originally defined for extensions of first-order logic in the context of model theory of infinite structures, but they are also meaningful in the context of finite structures. For a survey on Löwenheim-Skolem and Hanf numbers both on infinite and finite structures see [1]. For previous research on finite Löwenheim-Skolem type results see [4] and [5].

Aside from what we have already mentioned, related work includes the article [9] of Pikhurko and Verbitsky, where they consider the complexity of single finite structures. They study the minimal quantifier rank in FO of both defining a single finite structure and separating it from other structures of the same size. In [8] the same authors and Spencer consider quantifier rank and formula size required to define single graphs in FO. The survey [10] by Pikhurko and Verbitsky covers the above work and more on the logical complexity of single graphs in FO. By logical complexity they mean minimal quantifier rank, number of variables and length of a defining formula as functions of the size of the graph. They give an extensive account of these measures and relate them to each other, the Ehrenfeucht-Fraïssé game and the Weisfeiler-Lehman algorithm. An important difference between our approach and theirs is that we take formula size as the parameter and look for the longest definable word, whereas they do the opposite.

Our contributions are upper and lower bounds for the definability, Löwenheim-Skolem and Hanf numbers of the size n fragments of FO and MSO on words. The upper bounds in Sect. 3 are obtained by counting types with respect to the quantifier rank $n/2$ fragment. The upper bounds for both FO and MSO are exponential towers of height $n/2 + \log^*(t) + 1$ where t is a polynomial term. The lower bounds in Sects. 4 and 5 are given by concrete polynomial size formulas that define words of non-elementary length based on the cumulative hierarchy of sets. The lower bounds are exponential towers of height $\sqrt[5]{n/c}$ for FO and $\sqrt{n/c}$ for MSO, respectively.

An anonymous referee pointed out that lower bounds similar to ours can be obtained by adapting the method used by Reinhardt in [11], which in turn is based on the work of Stockmeyer [12]. However, our formulas are based on the cumulative hierarchy of sets instead of the binary counters used in Stockmeyer and Reinhardt. Furthermore, we emphasize defining single words and relate the bounds to Löwenheim-Skolem and Hanf numbers.

Note that our results only apply in the context of words. If finite structures over arbitrary finite vocabularies are allowed, then there are no computable upper bounds for the Löwenheim-Skolem or Hanf numbers of the size n fragments of FO. For the Löwenheim-Skolem number, this follows from Trakhtenbrot's theorem[1] (see, e.g., [7]), and for the Hanf number, this follows from a result of Grohe in [4]. Clearly the same applies for the size n fragments of MSO as well.

2   Preliminaries

The logics we consider in this paper are first-order logic FO and monadic second-order logic MSO and their (typically finite) fragments. The syntax and semantics of these are standard and well-known. Due to space restrictions we will not present them here, instead directing the reader to [2] and [7].

In terms of structures we limit our consideration to words of the two letter alphabet $\Sigma = \{l, r\}$. We have chosen to use letters for readability but intuitively the l stands for the left brace { and r for the right brace }. We use these later to encode sets as words. The empty set would be encoded as lr, or {}.

When we say that a word satisfies a logical sentence, we mean the natural corresponding word model does. A word model is a finite structure with linear order and unary predicates P_l and P_r for the two symbols. Since we only consider words over the two letter alphabet Σ, we will tacitly assume that all formulas of MSO are in the vocabulary $\{<, P_l, P_r\}$ of the corresponding word models (and similarly for FO-formulas).

Definition 1. *The size* $\mathrm{sz}(\varphi)$ *of a formula* $\varphi \in$ MSO *is defined recursively as follows:*

- $\mathrm{sz}(\varphi) = 1$ *for atomic* φ,
- $\mathrm{sz}(\neg\psi) = \mathrm{sz}(\psi) + 1$,
- $\mathrm{sz}(\psi \wedge \theta) = \mathrm{sz}(\psi \vee \theta) = \mathrm{sz}(\psi) + \mathrm{sz}(\theta) + 1$,
- $\mathrm{sz}(\exists x \psi) = \mathrm{sz}(\forall x \psi) = \mathrm{sz}(\exists U \psi) = \mathrm{sz}(\forall U \psi) = \mathrm{sz}(\psi) + 1$.

For $n \in \mathbb{N}$ *the size* n *fragment of* MSO, *denoted* MSO$[n]$, *consists of the formulas of* MSO *with size at most* n. *Size as well as size* n *fragments are defined in the same way for* FO.

Definition 2. *The quantifier rank* $\mathrm{qr}(\varphi)$ *of a formula* $\varphi \in$ MSO *is defined recursively as follows:*

---

[1] Trakhtenbrot's theorem states that the finite satisfiability problem of FO is undecidable. Hence there cannot exist any computable upper bound for the size of models that need to be checked to see whether a given formula is satisfiable.

- $\mathrm{qr}(\varphi) = 0$ *for atomic* φ,
- $\mathrm{qr}(\neg\psi) = \mathrm{qr}(\psi)$,
- $\mathrm{qr}(\psi \wedge \theta) = \mathrm{qr}(\psi \vee \theta) = \max\{\mathrm{qr}(\psi), \mathrm{qr}(\theta)\}$,
- $\mathrm{qr}(\exists x\psi) = \mathrm{qr}(\forall x\psi) = \mathrm{qr}(\exists U\psi) = \mathrm{qr}(\forall U\psi) = \mathrm{qr}(\psi) + 1$.

For $k \in \mathbb{N}$, *the quantifier rank* k *fragment of* MSO, *denoted* MSO_k, *consists of the formulas* $\varphi \in$ MSO *with* $\mathrm{qr}(\varphi) \leq k$. *The quantifier rank* k *fragment of* FO *is defined in the same way and denoted* FO_k.

Note that both size n fragments and quantifier rank k fragments are essentially finite in the sense that they contain only finitely many non-equivalent formulas.

Definition 3. *For each (finite) fragment* L *of* MSO *or* FO, *we define the relation* $\equiv_L$ *on* Σ-*words as*

$$w \equiv_L v, \ \text{if } w \text{ and } v \text{ agree on all } L\text{-sentences.}$$

Clearly $\equiv_L$ is an equivalence relation. We denote the set of equivalence classes of $\equiv_L$ by $\Sigma^* / \equiv_L$ and define a notation for the number of these classes.

Definition 4. *For each (finite) fragment* L *of* MSO *or* FO, *we denote the number of equivalence classes of* $\equiv_L$ *by* N_L, *i.e.*

$$N_L := |\Sigma^* / \equiv_L|.$$

Note that each equivalence class of $\equiv_L$ is uniquely determined by a subset $\mathrm{tp}_L(w) = \{\varphi \in L \mid w \models \varphi\}$ of L sentences, which we call the L-type of w. Thus, N_L is the number of L-types. In the case $L = \mathrm{MSO}_k$ or $L = \mathrm{FO}_k$, we talk about quantifier rank k types.

Definition 5. *We say that a sentence* $\varphi \in$ MSO *defines a word* $w \in \Sigma^+$ *if* $w \models \varphi$ *and* $v \nvDash \varphi$ *for all* $v \in \Sigma^+ \setminus \{w\}$.

For a fragment L *of* MSO *or* FO, *we denote by* $\mathrm{Def}(L)$ *the set of words definable in* L, *i.e.*

$$\mathrm{Def}(L) := \{w \in \Sigma^+ \mid \text{there is } \varphi \in L \text{ s.t. } \varphi \text{ defines } w\}.$$

In order to discuss words of non-elementary length and make our bounds precise, we define the exponential tower function twr for the positive reals as well as the, essentially inverse, iterated logarithm function $\log^*$.

Definition 6. *The exponential tower function* tower $: \mathbb{N} \to \mathbb{N}$ *is defined recursively by setting* tower$(0) := 1$ *and* tower$(n+1) := 2^{\mathrm{tower}(n)}$. *We extend this definition to a function* twr $: [0, \infty[\to \mathbb{N}$ *by setting* twr$(x) = $ tower$(\lceil x \rceil)$. *The iterated logarithm function* $\log^* : [1, \infty[\to \mathbb{N}$ *is defined by setting* $\log^*(x)$ *as the smallest* $m \in \mathbb{N}$ *that has* tower$(m) \geq x$.

2.1   Definability, Löwenheim-Skolem and Hanf Numbers

Löwenheim-Skolem and Hanf numbers were originally introduced for studying the behaviour of extensions of first-order logic on infinite structures. See the article [1] of Ebbinghaus for a nice survey on the infinite case. As observed in [4], with suitable modifications, it is possible to give meaningful definitions for these numbers also on finite structures. We will now give such definitions for finite fragments L of FO and MSO, and in addition, we introduce the closely related definability number of L.

Let φ be a sentence in MSO over Σ-words. If it has a model, we denote by $\mu(\varphi)$ the minimal length of a model of φ: $\mu(\varphi) = \min\{|w| \mid w \in \Sigma^+, w \models \varphi\}$. If φ has no models, we stipulate $\mu(\varphi) = 0$. Furthermore, we denote by $\nu(\varphi)$ the maximum length of a model of φ, assuming the maximum is well-defined. If the maximum is not defined, i.e., if φ has no models or has arbitrarily long models, we stipulate $\nu(\varphi) = 0$.

Definition 7. *Let L be a finite fragment of* MSO *or* FO *with* $\mathrm{Def}(L) \neq \emptyset$.
  (a) The definability number of L is
    $$\mathrm{DN}(L) = \max\{|w| \mid w \in \Sigma^+, w \in \mathrm{Def}(L)\}.$$
  (b) The Löwenheim-Skolem number of L is $\mathrm{LS}(L) = \max\{\mu(\varphi) \mid \varphi \in L\}$.
  (c) The Hanf number of L is $\mathrm{H}(L) = \max\{\nu(\varphi) \mid \varphi \in L\}$.

Thus, $\mathrm{DN}(L)$ is the length of the longest L-definable word. Note further that $\mathrm{LS}(L)$ is the smallest number m such that every $\varphi \in L$ that has a model, has a model of length at most m. Similarly $\mathrm{H}(L)$ is the smallest number ℓ such that if $\varphi \in L$ has a model of length greater than ℓ, then it has arbitrarily long models.

Since every sentence φ of MSO defines a regular language over Σ, and there is an effective translation from MSO to equivalent finite automata, it is clear that we can compute the numbers $\mu(\varphi)$ and $\nu(\varphi)$ from φ. Consequently, for any finite fragment L of MSO, $\mathrm{LS}(L)$ and $\mathrm{H}(L)$ can be computed from L.

As we mentioned in the Introduction, $\mathrm{LS}(\mathrm{FO}[n])$ and $\mathrm{H}(\mathrm{FO}[n])$ are not computable from n if we consider arbitrary finite models instead of words. Clearly the same holds also for the fragments FO_k, $\mathrm{MSO}[n]$ and MSO_k.

It follows immediately from Definition 7 that the definability number of any finite fragment of MSO is bounded above by its Löwenheim-Skolem number and its Hanf number:

Proposition 1. *If L is a finite fragment of* MSO, *then* $\mathrm{DN}(L) \leq \mathrm{LS}(L), \mathrm{H}(L)$.

Proof. It suffices to observe that if $w \in \mathrm{Def}(L)$, then $\mu(\varphi) = \nu(\varphi) = |w|$, where $\varphi \in L$ is the sentence that defines w.

Note that all three cases for the relationship between $\mathrm{LS}(L)$ and $\mathrm{H}(L)$ are possible. Indeed, if L consists of existential first-order sentences, then any $\varphi \in L$ that has a model, has arbitrarily long models, whence $\mathrm{H}(L) = 0$. Clearly $\mathrm{LS}(L)$ can be arbitrarily large for such an L. On the other hand, if L consists of universal first-order sentences, then any satisfiable $\varphi \in L$ has a model of length 1, whence $\mathrm{LS}(L) \leq 1$. If L contains, e.g., the sentence $\forall x_0 \ldots \forall x_\ell \bigvee_{i<j\leq\ell} x_i = x_j$ for $\ell > 1$, then $\mathrm{H}(L) \geq \ell > \mathrm{LS}(L)$. Finally, combining existential and universal sentences it is easy to construct a finite fragment L of FO such that $\mathrm{LS}(L) = \mathrm{H}(L)$.

3   Upper Bounds for the Length of Definable Words

3.1   Definability and Types

It is well-known that equivalence of words up to a quantifier rank is preserved in catenation:

Theorem 1. *Let $L \in \{\mathrm{FO}_k, \mathrm{MSO}_k\}$ for some $k \in \mathbb{N}$. Assume that $v, v', w, w' \in \Sigma^+$ are words such that $v \equiv_L v'$ and $w \equiv_L w'$. Then $vw \equiv_L v'w'$.*

Proof. The claim is proved by a straightforward Ehrenfeucht-Fraïssé game argument (see Proposition 2.1.4 in [2]).

Using Theorem 1, we get the following upper bounds for the numbers $\mu(\varphi)$ and $\nu(\varphi)$ in terms of the quantifier rank of φ:

Proposition 2. *Let $L \in \{\mathrm{FO}_k, \mathrm{MSO}_k\}$ for some $k \in \mathbb{N}$. If φ is a sentence of L, then $\mu(\varphi), \nu(\varphi) \leq N_L$.*

Proof. If $|w| \leq N_L$ for all words $w \in \Sigma^+$ such that $w \models \varphi$, the claim is trivial. Assume then that $w \models \varphi$ and $|w| > N_L$. Then there are two initial segments u and u' of w such that $|u| < |u'|$ and $u \equiv_L u'$. Let v and v' be the corresponding end segments, i.e., $w = uv = u'v'$. Then by Theorem 1, $uv' \equiv_L u'v' = w$, and similarly $u'v \equiv_L uv = w$, whence $uv' \models \varphi$ and $u'v \models \varphi$.

Since $|uv'| < |w|$, we see that w is not the shortest word satisfying φ. The argument applies to any word w with $|w| > N_L$, whence we conclude that $\mu(\varphi) \leq N_L$. On the other hand $|u'v| > |w|$, whence w is neither the longest word satisfying φ. Applying this argument repeatedly, we see that φ is satisfied in arbitrarily long words, whence $\nu(\varphi) = 0 \leq N_L$.

From Propositions 1 and 2 we immediately obtain the following upper bound for the definability numbers of quantifier rank fragments of MSO:

Corollary 1. *Let $k \in \mathbb{N}$ and $L \in \{\mathrm{FO}_k, \mathrm{MSO}_k\}$. Then $\mathrm{LS}(L), \mathrm{H}(L) \leq N_L$, and consequently $\mathrm{DN}(L) \leq N_L$.*

This N_L upper bound for the definability, Löwenheim-Skolem and Hanf numbers shows that the quantifier rank fragments L of FO and MSO behave quite tamely on words: Clearly every type $\mathrm{tp}_L(w)$ is definable by a sentence of L, whence the number of non-equivalent sentences in L is 2^{N_L}. Thus, any collection of representatives of non-equivalent sentences of L necessarily contains sentences of size close to N_L. But in spite of this, it is not possible to define words that are longer than N_L by sentences of L.

This shows that quantifier rank is not a good starting point if we want to prove interesting succinctness results for definability. Hence we turn our attention to the size n fragments $\mathrm{FO}[n]$ and $\mathrm{MSO}[n]$. Note first that for any $n \in \mathbb{N}$, $\mathrm{FO}[n]$ is trivially contained in FO_n, and similarly, $\mathrm{MSO}[n]$ is contained in MSO_n. A simple argument shows that this can be improved by a factor of 2:

Lemma 1. *For any $n \in \mathbb{N}$, $\mathrm{FO}[2n] \leq \mathrm{FO}_n$ and $\mathrm{MSO}[2n] \leq \mathrm{MSO}_n$.*

Proof. (Idea) Any sentence φ with quantifier rank n is equivalent to one with smaller quantifier rank unless it contains atomic formulas of the form $x < y$ mentioning each quantified variable, and more than one of them at least twice. Counting the quantifiers, the atomic formulas, and the connectives needed, we see that $\mathrm{sz}(\varphi) \geq 2n$.

Note that we have not tried to be optimal in the formulation of Lemma 1. We believe that with a more careful analysis, $2n$ could be replaced with $3n$, and possibly with an even larger number.

Corollary 2. *For any $n \in \mathbb{N}$, $\mathrm{DN}(\mathrm{FO}[2n]), \mathrm{LS}(\mathrm{FO}[2n]), \mathrm{H}(\mathrm{FO}[2n]) \leq N_{\mathrm{FO}_n}$ and $\mathrm{DN}(\mathrm{MSO}[2n]), \mathrm{LS}(\mathrm{MSO}[2n]), \mathrm{H}(\mathrm{MSO}[2n]) \leq N_{\mathrm{MSO}_n}$.*

3.2 Number of Types

As we have seen in the previous section, the numbers of FO_k-types and MSO_k-types give upper bounds for the corresponding definbability, Löwenheim-Skolem and Hanf-numbers. It is well known that on finite relational structures, for FO_k this number is bound above by an exponential tower of height $k + 1$ with a polynomial, that depends on the vocabulary, on top (see, e.g., [10] for the case of graphs). It is straightforward to generalize this type of upper bound to MSO_k. On the class of Σ-words, we can prove the following explicit upper bounds. For the proof of this result, see the Appendix in the pre-print [6].

Theorem 2. *For any $k \in \mathbb{N}$, $N_{\mathrm{FO}_k} \leq \mathrm{twr}(k + \log^*(k^2 + k) + 1)$ and $N_{\mathrm{MSO}_k} \leq \mathrm{twr}(k + \log^*((k + 1)^2) + 1)$.*

By Corollary 1, we obtain the same upper bounds for the definability, Löwenheim-Skolem and Hanf numbers of the quantifier rank fragments.

Corollary 3. *For any $k \in \mathbb{N}$,*
$\mathrm{DN}(\mathrm{FO}_k), \mathrm{LS}(\mathrm{FO}_k), \mathrm{H}(\mathrm{FO}_k) \leq \mathrm{twr}(k + \log^*(k^2 + k) + 1)$ *and*
$\mathrm{DN}(\mathrm{MSO}_k), \mathrm{LS}(\mathrm{MSO}_k), \mathrm{H}(\mathrm{MSO}_k) \leq \mathrm{twr}(k + \log^*((k + 1)^2) + 1)$.

As we discussed after Corollary 1, from the point of view of succinctness it is more interesting to consider the definability numbers of the size fragments of FO and MSO than those of the quantifier rank fragments. Using Corollary 2, we obtain the following upper bounds for $\mathrm{FO}[n]$ and $\mathrm{MSO}[n]$.

Corollary 4. *For any $n \in \mathbb{N}$,*
$\mathrm{DN}(\mathrm{FO}[n]), \mathrm{LS}(\mathrm{FO}[n]), \mathrm{H}(\mathrm{FO}[n]) \leq \mathrm{twr}(n/2 + \log^*((n/2)^2 + n/2) + 1)$ *and*
$\mathrm{DN}(\mathrm{MSO}[n]), \mathrm{LS}(\mathrm{MSO}[n]), \mathrm{H}(\mathrm{MSO}[n]) \leq \mathrm{twr}(n/2 + \log^*((n/2 + 1)^2) + 1)$.

In the next two sections we will prove lower bounds for the definability numbers of $\mathrm{FO}[n]$ and $\mathrm{MSO}[n]$ by providing explicit polynomial size sentences that define words that are of exponential tower length.

4   Lower Bounds for FO

In order to obtain a lower bound for $DN(FO[n])$ we need a relatively small FO-formula that defines a long word. The long word we define has to do with the cumulative hierarchy of finite sets.

The finite levels V_i of the cumulative hierarchy are defined by $V_0 = \emptyset$ and $V_{i+1} = \mathcal{P}(V_i)$. We represent finite sets as words using only braces { and } in a straightforward fashion. For example V_0 is encoded as {} and V_1 as {{}}. V_2 has two possible encodings: {{}{{}}} and {{{}}{}}. It is well known that $|V_{i+1}| = \mathrm{twr}(i)$. Thus the encodings of V_{i+1} have length at least $\mathrm{twr}(i)$. We will define one such word via an FO-formula of polynomial size with respect to i.

For readability, we define $L(x) := P_l(x)$ and $R(x) := P_r(x)$ that say x is a left or right brace, respectively. We also define $S(x, y) := x < y \land \neg\exists z(x < z < y)$ that says y is the successor of x.

As each set in the encoding can be identified by its outermost braces, the formula mostly operates on pairs of variables. For readability we adopt the convention $\overline{x} := (x_1, x_2)$, and similarly for different letters, to denote these pairs. To ensure that our formula defines a single encoding of V_i, we also define a linear order on encoded sets and require that the elements are in that order.

We define our formula recursively in terms of many subformulas. We briefly list the meanings and approximate sizes of each subformula involved:

- $\mathsf{core}(\overline{x}, \theta(s, t))$: the common core formula used in the formulas set_i and oset_i defined below. States that every brace y between x_1 and x_2 has a pair z such that the pair satisfies θ. In practice, θ will be another step of a similar recursion. The variables s and t are used to deal with both cases $y < z$ and $z < y$ at once, making the formula smaller.

$$
\begin{aligned}
\mathsf{core}(\overline{x}, \theta(s,t)) := {}& x_1 < x_2 \land L(x_1) \land R(x_2) \\
& \land \forall y(x_1 < y < x_2 \to \exists z(x_1 < z < x_2 \land y \neq z \\
& \land \exists s \exists t((y < z \to (s = y \land t = z)) \\
& \land (z < y \to (s = z \land t = y)) \land \theta(s,t))))
\end{aligned}
$$

- $\mathsf{set}_i(\overline{x})$: $\overline{x}$ correctly encodes a set in V_i, possibly with repetition. Size linear in i.

$$
\begin{aligned}
\mathsf{set}_0(\overline{x}) &:= L(x_1) \land R(x_2) \land S(x_1, x_2) \\
\mathsf{set}_{i+1}(\overline{x}) &:= \mathsf{core}(\overline{x}, \mathsf{set}_i(s, t))
\end{aligned}
$$

- $\overline{x} \in_i \overline{y}$: $\overline{x}$ is an element of $\overline{y}$. Size linear in i. Assumes that $\overline{x}$ encodes a set in V_i and $\overline{y}$ encodes a set in V_{i+1}. The part with $\overline{z}$ is used to ensure that $\overline{x}$ is an element of $\overline{y}$ and not for example an element of an element.

$$
\overline{x} \in_i \overline{y} := y_1 < x_1 < x_2 < y_2 \land \neg\exists \overline{z}(\mathsf{set}_i(\overline{z}) \land y_1 < z_1 < x_1 \land x_2 < z_2 < y_2)
$$

- $\overline{x} \sim_i \overline{y}$: $\overline{x}$ and $\overline{y}$ encode the same set, possibly in a different order. Size $\mathcal{O}(i^2)$. Assumes $\overline{x}$ and $\overline{y}$ encode sets in V_i. The two implications on the second line are used to deal with the symmetry of $\overline{x}$ and $\overline{y}$ at once, making the formula smaller.

$$\overline{x} \sim_0 \overline{y} := \top$$
$$\overline{x} \sim_{i+1} \overline{y} := \forall \overline{a}(\mathsf{set}_i(\overline{a}) \to \exists \overline{b}(\mathsf{set}_i(\overline{b})$$
$$\wedge\, (\overline{a} \in_i \overline{x} \to \overline{b} \in_i \overline{y}) \wedge (\overline{a} \in_i \overline{y} \to \overline{b} \in_i \overline{x}) \wedge \overline{a} \sim_i \overline{b}))$$

– $\overline{x} \prec_i \overline{y}$: the $\prec_{i-1}$-greatest element of the symmetric difference of $\overline{x}$ and $\overline{y}$ is in $\overline{y}$. Size $\mathcal{O}(i^3)$. Defines a linear order for encoded sets in V_i. The set $\overline{z}$ is in $\overline{y}$, is not in $\overline{x}$ and is larger than any $\overline{a}$ in $\overline{x}$.

$$\overline{x} \prec_0 \overline{y} := \bot$$
$$\overline{x} \prec_{i+1} \overline{y} := \exists \overline{z}(\mathsf{set}_i(\overline{z}) \wedge \overline{z} \in_i \overline{y} \wedge \forall \overline{a}((\mathsf{set}_i(\overline{a}) \wedge \overline{a} \in_i \overline{x})$$
$$\to(\overline{a} \approx_i \overline{z} \wedge (\forall \overline{b}((\mathsf{set}_i(\overline{b}) \wedge \overline{b} \in_i \overline{y}) \to \overline{a} \approx_i \overline{b}) \to \overline{a} \prec_i \overline{z}))))$$

– $\mathsf{oset}_i(\overline{x})$: $\overline{x}$ correctly encodes a set in V_i with no repetition and with the elements in the linear order given by the formula $\overline{x} \prec_i \overline{y}$. Size $\mathcal{O}(i^4)$. Ensures that only a singular word satisfies our formula.

$$\mathsf{oset}_0(\overline{x}) := L(x_1) \wedge R(x_2) \wedge S(x_1, x_2)$$
$$\mathsf{oset}_{i+1}(\overline{x}) := \mathsf{core}(\overline{x}, \mathsf{oset}_i(s,t)) \wedge \forall \overline{a} \forall \overline{b}((\mathsf{set}_i(\overline{a}) \wedge \mathsf{set}_i(\overline{b})$$
$$\wedge\, \overline{a} \in_i \overline{x} \wedge \overline{b} \in_i \overline{x} \wedge a_1 < b_1) \to \overline{a} \prec_i \overline{b})$$

– $\mathsf{add}_i(\overline{x}, \overline{y}, \overline{z})$: States that $\overline{x} = \overline{y} \cup \{\overline{z}\}$. Size $\mathcal{O}(i^2)$. Assumes $\overline{x}$ and $\overline{y}$ encode sets in V_i and $\overline{z}$ encodes a set in V_{i-1}. The first line states that $\overline{y} \subseteq \overline{x}$, the second line states $\overline{z} \in \overline{x}$ and the two final lines state $\overline{x} \setminus \{\overline{z}\} \subseteq \overline{y}$.

$$\mathsf{add}_{i+1}(\overline{x}, \overline{y}, \overline{z}) := \forall \overline{a}((\mathsf{set}_i(\overline{a}) \wedge \overline{a} \in_i \overline{y}) \to \exists \overline{b}(\mathsf{set}_i(\overline{b}) \wedge \overline{b} \in_i \overline{x} \wedge \overline{a} \sim_i \overline{b}))$$
$$\wedge\, \exists \overline{c}(\mathsf{set}_i(\overline{c}) \wedge \overline{c} \in_i \overline{x} \wedge \overline{c} \sim_i \overline{z})$$
$$\wedge\, \forall \overline{d}((\mathsf{set}_i(\overline{d}) \wedge \overline{d} \in_i \overline{x} \wedge d_1 \neq c_1)$$
$$\to \exists \overline{e}(\mathsf{set}_i(\overline{e}) \wedge \overline{e} \in_i \overline{y} \wedge \overline{e} \sim_i \overline{d})))$$

– $V_i(\overline{x})$: $\overline{x}$ encodes the set V_i. Size $\mathcal{O}(i^5)$. States that $\overline{x}$ is an ordered encoding, $\emptyset \in \overline{x}$, $V_{i-1} \in \overline{x}$ and for all $\overline{c} \in \overline{x}$ and $\overline{d} \in V_{i-1}$, we have $\overline{c} \cup \{\overline{d}\} \in \overline{x}$.

$$V_0(\overline{x}) := \mathsf{set}_0(\overline{x})$$
$$V_{i+1}(\overline{x}) := \mathsf{oset}_{i+1}(\overline{x}) \wedge \exists \overline{a}(V_0(\overline{a}) \wedge S(x_1, a_1)) \wedge \exists \overline{b}(V_i(\overline{b}) \wedge S(b_2, x_2)$$
$$\wedge\, \forall \overline{c} \forall \overline{d}((\mathsf{set}_i(\overline{c}) \wedge \overline{c} \in_i \overline{x} \wedge \mathsf{set}_{i-1}(\overline{d}) \wedge \overline{d} \in_{i-1} \overline{b})$$
$$\to \exists \overline{e}(\mathsf{set}_i(\overline{e}) \wedge \overline{e} \in_i \overline{x} \wedge \mathsf{add}_i(\overline{e}, \overline{c}, \overline{d}))))$$

– ψ_i: the entire word is the ordered encoding of the set V_i. Size $\mathcal{O}(i^5)$.

$$\psi_i := \exists x \exists y \forall z (x \leq z \wedge z \leq y \wedge V_i(x, y))$$

The formula ψ_{i+1} defines a word w that, as an encoding of the set V_{i+1}, has length at least $\mathrm{twr}(i)$. The size of ψ_{i+1} is $\mathcal{O}((i+1)^5)$ and thus $\mathcal{O}(i^5)$. Let c be a constant such that $\mathrm{sz}(\psi_{i+1}) \leq c \cdot i^5$ so $w \in \mathrm{Def}(\mathrm{FO}[c \cdot i^5])$. As we want to relate the length of w to the size of ψ_i, we set $n = c \cdot i^5$ and obtain the following result:

Theorem 3. *For some constant $c \in \mathbb{N}$ there are infinitely many $n \in \mathbb{N}$ satisfying*

$$\mathrm{DN}(\mathrm{FO}[n]) \geq \mathrm{twr}(\sqrt[5]{n/c}).$$

Proposition 1 immediately gives the same bound for the Hanf number.

Corollary 5. *For some constant $c \in \mathbb{N}$ there are infinitely many $n \in \mathbb{N}$ satisfying*

$$\mathrm{H}(\mathrm{FO}[n]) \geq \mathrm{twr}(\sqrt[5]{n/c}).$$

By omitting the subformula $\mathtt{oset}_{i+1}$ from the above we get a formula of size $\mathcal{O}(i^3)$ that is no longer satisfied by only one word but still only has large models. With this formula we obtain a lower bound for the Löwenheim-Skolem number.

Corollary 6. *For some $c \in \mathbb{N}$ there are arbitrarily large $n \in \mathbb{N}$ satisfying*

$$\mathrm{LS}(\mathrm{FO}[n]) \geq \mathrm{twr}(\sqrt[3]{n/c}).$$

5   Lower Bounds for MSO

In this section, we define a similar formula for MSO as we did above for FO. The formula again defines an encoding of V_i but for MSO our formula is of size $\mathcal{O}(i^2)$ compared to the $\mathcal{O}(i^5)$ of FO. We achieve this by quantifying a partition of so called levels for the braces and thus the encoded sets and using a different method to define only a single encoding.

The level of the entire encoded set will be equal to the maximum depth of braces inside the set. The level of an element of a set will always be one less than the level of the parent set. This means that there will be instances of the same set with different levels in our encoding. For example in the encoding $\{\{\}\{\{\}\}\}$ the outermost braces are level 2, both of the elements are level 1 and the empty set in the second element is level 0.

We again define our formula in terms of many subformulas and briefly list the meaning and size of each subformula:

- $\mathtt{set}_i(\overline{x})$: $\overline{x}$ encodes a set of level i. Size constant. Here we only require that there are no braces of the same level between x_1 and x_2, leaving the rest to the formula $\mathtt{levels}_i$ below.

$$\mathtt{set}_0(\overline{x}) := S(x_1, x_2) \wedge L(x_1) \wedge R(x_2) \wedge D_0(x_1) \wedge D_0(x_2)$$
$$\mathtt{set}_i(\overline{x}) := x_1 < x_2 \wedge L(x_1) \wedge R(x_2) \wedge D_i(x_1) \wedge D_i(x_2)$$
$$\wedge\, \forall y(x_1 < y < x_2 \to \neg D_i(y))$$

- `levels`$_i$: The relations D_j define the levels of sets as intended and there are no odd braces without pairs. Size $\mathcal{O}(i^2)$. States that every brace has a level, no brace has two different levels, every set encloses only braces of lower levels and every brace has a pair of the same level to form a set.

$$\text{levels}_i := \forall x(\bigvee_{j=0}^{i} D_j(x) \wedge \bigwedge_{\substack{j,k\in\{0,\dots,i\}\\ j\neq k}} \neg(D_j(x) \wedge D_k(x))$$

$$\wedge \forall \overline{x}(\bigwedge_{j=0}^{i}(\text{set}_j(\overline{x}) \to \forall y(x_1 < y < x_2 \to \bigvee_{k=0}^{j-1} D_k(y))))$$

$$\wedge \forall x_1(\bigwedge_{j=0}^{i}((L(x_1) \wedge D_j(x_1)) \to \exists x_2 \text{set}_j(x_1,x_2))$$

$$\wedge \bigwedge_{j=0}^{i}(R(x_1) \wedge D_j(x_1)) \to \exists x_2 \text{set}_j(x_2,x_1))$$

- $\overline{x} \in \overline{y}$: $\overline{x}$ is an element of $\overline{y}$. Size constant. Assumes $\overline{x}$ encodes a set of level i and $\overline{y}$ encodes a set of level $i-1$.

$$\overline{x} \in \overline{y} := y_1 < x_1 \wedge x_2 < y_2$$

- $\overline{x} \sim_i \overline{y}$: $\overline{x}$ and $\overline{y}$ encode the same set. Size linear in i. Assumes $\overline{x}$ and $\overline{y}$ encode sets of level i. Similar to the FO case.

$$\overline{x} \sim_0 \overline{y} := \top$$
$$\overline{x} \sim_{i+1} \overline{y} := \forall \overline{a}(\text{set}_i(\overline{a}) \to \exists \overline{b}(\text{set}_i(\overline{b})$$
$$\wedge (\overline{a} \in \overline{x} \to \overline{b} \in \overline{y}) \wedge (\overline{a} \in \overline{y} \to \overline{b} \in \overline{x}) \wedge \overline{a} \sim_i \overline{b}))$$

- $\text{add}_i(\overline{x},\overline{y},\overline{z})$: States that $\overline{x} = \overline{y}\cup\{\overline{z}\}$. Size linear in i. Assumes $\overline{x}$ and $\overline{y}$ encode sets of level i and $\overline{z}$ encodes a set of level $i-1$. Similar to the FO case.

$$\text{add}_{i+1}(\overline{x},\overline{y},\overline{z}) := \forall \overline{a}((\text{set}_i(\overline{a}) \wedge \overline{a} \in \overline{y}) \to \exists \overline{b}(\text{set}_i(\overline{b}) \wedge \overline{b} \in \overline{x} \wedge \overline{a} \sim_i \overline{b}))$$
$$\wedge \exists \overline{c}(\text{set}_i(\overline{c}) \wedge \overline{c} \in \overline{x} \wedge \overline{c} \sim_i \overline{z}$$
$$\wedge \forall \overline{d}((\text{set}_i(\overline{d}) \wedge \overline{d} \in \overline{x} \wedge d_1 \neq c_1)$$
$$\to \exists \overline{e}(\text{set}_i(\overline{e}) \wedge \overline{e} \in \overline{y} \wedge \overline{e} \sim_i \overline{d})))$$

- $V_i(\overline{x})$: $\overline{x}$ encodes the set V_i. Size $\mathcal{O}(i^2)$. Assumes the level partition is given. Similar to the FO case with no ordering.

$$V_0(\overline{x}) := \text{set}_0(\overline{x})$$
$$V_{i+1}(\overline{x}) := \text{set}_{i+1}(\overline{x}) \wedge \exists \overline{a}(\text{set}_i(\overline{a}) \wedge \overline{a} \in \overline{x} \wedge S(a_1,a_2))$$
$$\wedge \exists \overline{b}(V_i(\overline{b}) \wedge \overline{b} \in \overline{x} \wedge \forall \overline{c}\forall \overline{d}((\text{set}_i(\overline{c}) \wedge \overline{c} \in \overline{x} \wedge \text{set}_{i-1}(\overline{d}) \wedge \overline{d} \in \overline{b})$$
$$\to \exists \overline{e}(\text{set}_i(\overline{e}) \wedge \overline{e} \in \overline{x} \wedge \text{add}_i(\overline{e},\overline{c},\overline{d})))$$

– $\varphi_i(x, y)$: Quantifies the level partition and states the subword from x to y encodes V_i. Size $\mathcal{O}(i^2)$.

$$\varphi_i(x, y) := \exists D_0 \ldots \exists D_i(\texttt{levels}_i \wedge V_i(x, y)))$$

We now have a formula $\varphi_i(x, y)$ that says the subword from x to y encodes the set V_i. There are still multiple words that satisfy this formula, since different orders of the sets and even repetition are still allowed. To pick out only one such word, we use a lexicographic order, where a shorter word always precedes a longer one.

Let φ_i' be the formula obtained from φ_i by replacing each occurrence of $L(x)$ with $P_1(x)$ and $R(x)$ with $P_2(x)$. We define the final formula ψ_i of size $\mathcal{O}(i^2)$ that says the entire word model is the least word in the lexicographic order that satisfies the property of φ_i. We check that no lexicographically smaller word satisfies φ_i by quantifying the word under consideration on top of the same word model using the variables P_1 and P_2 for the two letters. We first ensure that P_1 and P_2 partition the model and then use y' as the cut-off point for the possibly shorter word we want to quantify. If $y' = y$ we check the lexicographic order with z as the first different symbol. Finally we state that the quantified word does not satisfy φ_i.

$$\begin{aligned}
\psi_i := {}& \exists x \exists y (\forall z (x \leq z \wedge z \leq y) \wedge \varphi_i(x, y) \\
& \wedge \forall P_1 \forall P_2 (\forall z ((P_1(z) \vee P_2(z)) \wedge \neg (P_1(z) \wedge P_2(z)))) \\
& \wedge \forall y' ((y' < y \vee \exists z (\forall a (a < z \to (L(a) \leftrightarrow P_1(a) \wedge R(a) \leftrightarrow P_2(a))) \\
& \wedge (P_1(z) \wedge R(z))) \to \neg \varphi_i'(x, y'))))
\end{aligned}$$

We have used the lexicographic order here to select only one of the possible words that satisfy our property. Note that this can be done for any property. The size of such a formula will depend polynomially on the size of the alphabet, as well as linearly on the size of the formula defining the property in question.

We obtain the lower bound for the definability number as in the FO case.

Theorem 4. *For some constant $c \in \mathbb{N}$ there are infinitely many $n \in \mathbb{N}$ satisfying*

$$\mathrm{DN}(\mathrm{MSO}[n]) \geq \mathrm{twr}(\sqrt{n/c}).$$

We get the same bounds for $\mathrm{LS}(\mathrm{MSO}[n])$ and $\mathrm{H}(\mathrm{MSO}[n])$ via Proposition 1.

Corollary 7. *For some constant $c \in \mathbb{N}$ there are infinitely many $n \in \mathbb{N}$ satisfying*

$$\mathrm{LS}(\mathrm{MSO}[n]), \mathrm{H}(\mathrm{MSO}[n]) \geq \mathrm{twr}(\sqrt{n/c}).$$

6 Conclusion

We considered the definability number, the Löwenheim-Skolem number and the Hanf number on words in the size n fragments of first-order logic and monadic second-order logic. We obtained exponential towers of various heights as upper and lower bounds for each of these numbers.

For FO, we obtained the bounds

$$\mathrm{twr}(\sqrt[5]{n/c}) \leq \mathrm{DN}(\mathrm{FO}[n]) \leq \mathrm{twr}(n/2 + \log^*((n/2)^2 + n/2) + 1)$$

for some constant c. As corollaries, we obtained the same bounds for $\mathrm{LS}(\mathrm{FO}[n])$ and $\mathrm{H}(\mathrm{FO}[n])$. In addition, by modifying the formula we used for the lower bounds, we obtained a slightly better lower bound of $\mathrm{twr}(\sqrt[3]{n/c})$ for $\mathrm{LS}(\mathrm{FO}[n])$.

In the case of MSO, the bounds are similarly

$$\mathrm{twr}(\sqrt{n/c}) \leq \mathrm{DN}(\mathrm{MSO}[n]) \leq \mathrm{twr}(n/2 + \log^*((n/2 + 1)^2) + 1)$$

for a different constant c. We again immediately obtained the same bounds for $\mathrm{LS}(\mathrm{MSO}[n])$ and $\mathrm{H}(\mathrm{MSO}[n])$.

The gaps between the lower bounds and upper bounds we have proved are quite big. In absolute terms, they are actually huge, as each upper bound is non-elementary with respect to the corresponding lower bound. However, it is more fair to do the comparison in the iterated logarithmic scale, which reduces the gap to be only polynomial. Nevertheless, a natural task for future research is to look for tighter lower and upper bounds.

Finally, we remark that the technique for proving an exponential tower upper bound for the number of types in the quantifier rank fragments of some logic $\mathcal{L}$ is completely generic: it works in the same way irrespective of the type of quantifiers allowed in $\mathcal{L}$. Thus, it can be applied for example in the case where $\mathcal{L}$ is the extension of FO with some generalized quantifier (or a finite set of generalized quantifiers). Assuming further that the quantifier rank fragments L of $\mathcal{L}$ satisfy Theorem 1, we can obtain this way an exponential tower upper bound for the numbers $\mathrm{DN}(L)$, $\mathrm{LS}(L)$ and $\mathrm{H}(L)$. On the other hand, note that if the quantifier rank fragments L satisfy Theorem 1, then each $\equiv_L$ is an invariant equivalence relation, whence $\mathcal{L}$ can only define regular languages. Therefore it seems that our technique for proving upper bounds cannot be used for logics with expressive power beyond regular languages.

References

1. Ebbinghaus, H.D.: Löwenheim-Skolem theorems. In: Gabbay, D., Thagard, P., Woods, J., Jacquette, D. (eds.) Philosophy of Logic, Handbook of the Philosophy of Science. Elsevier Science (2006)
2. Ebbinghaus, H., Flum, J.: Finite model theory. Perspectives in Mathematical Logic, Springer, Germany (1995)
3. Ellul, K., Krawetz, B., Shallit, J., Wang, M.W.: Regular expressions: new results and open problems. J. Autom. Lang. Comb. **10**(4), 407–437 (2005). https://doi.org/10.25596/jalc-2005-407
4. Grohe, M.: Some remarks on finite Löwenheim-Skolem theorems. Math. Log. Q. **42**, 569–571 (1996). https://doi.org/10.1002/malq.19960420145

5. Grohe, M.: Large finite structures with few L^k-types. Inf. Comput. **179**(2), 250–278 (2002). https://doi.org/10.1006/inco.2002.2954
6. Hella, L., Vilander, M.: Defining long words succinctly in FO and MSO (2022). https://doi.org/10.48550/arxiv.2202.10180, pre-print
7. Libkin, L.: Elements of finite model theory. Texts in Theoretical Computer Science. An EATCS Series, Springer (2004). https://doi.org/10.1007/978-3-662-07003-1
8. Pikhurko, O., Spencer, J., Verbitsky, O.: Succinct definitions in the first order theory of graphs. Ann. Pure Appl. Log. **139**(1–3), 74–109 (2006). https://doi.org/10.1016/j.apal.2005.04.003
9. Pikhurko, O., Verbitsky, O.: Descriptive complexity of finite structures: saving the quantifier rank. J. Symb. Log. **70**(2), 419–450 (2005). https://doi.org/10.2178/jsl/1120224721
10. Pikhurko, O., Verbitsky, O.: Logical complexity of graphs: a survey. In: Grohe, M., Makowsky, J.A. (eds.) Model Theoretic Methods in Finite Combinatorics - AMS-ASL Joint Special Session, Washington, DC, 5–8 January 2009. Contemporary Mathematics, vol. 558, pp. 129–180. American Mathematical Society (2009)
11. Reinhardt, K.: The complexity of translating logic to finite automata. In: Grädel, E., Thomas, W., Wilke, T. (eds.) Automata Logics, and Infinite Games. LNCS, vol. 2500, pp. 231–238. Springer, Heidelberg (2002). https://doi.org/10.1007/3-540-36387-4_13
12. Stockmeyer, L.J.: The complexity of decision problems in automata theory and logic. Ph.D. thesis, Massachusetts Institute of Technology (1974)

Processing Natural Language with Biomolecules: Where Linguistics, Biology and Computation Meet

M. Dolores Jiménez López[✉] [iD]

Universitat Rovira i Virgili, 43002 Tarragona, Spain
mariadolores.jimenez@urv.cat

Abstract. The explanation, formal modelling and processing of language remain a challenge. Natural language is a hard problem not only for linguistics that has not yet provided universal accepted theories about how language is acquired and processed, but also for computer science that has not found a satisfactory computational model for processing natural language. The interplay between linguistics, biology and computation can provide a new paradigm where challenges in the area of natural language can be afforded in a different way and where new models can be devised. In this paper, we present the challenges and opportunities of applying computing with biomolecules to natural language processing. We present a state-of-the-art of the interchange of methods between linguistics, biology and computation and show how computer science can provide the theoretical tools and formalisms to transfer biological concepts to natural language in order to improve language processing.

Keywords: Natural language · Computing with biomolecules · Bio-inspired models

1 Introduction

The main goal of this paper is to highlight the benefits of the interdisciplinarity among linguistics, biology and computation. The area of convergence between those three disciplines is given rise to the emergence of new scientific paradigms. This paper is placed in the confluence of these three theories, highlighting the relevance of the biological approach with formal/computational methods for explaining linguistic issues.

Linguistics has still the challenge to understand how natural language is acquired, produced and processed. Up to now, linguistics has not been able to solve these challenges, partly, because of the fail in the models adopted. Biology has become a pilot science, so that many disciplines have formulated their theories under models taken from biology. Computer science has become a bioinspired field thanks to the great development of natural computing (evolutionary algorithms, neural networks, molecular computing, quantum computing...).

U. Berger et al. (Eds.): CiE 2022, LNCS 13359, pp. 139–150, 2022.
https://doi.org/10.1007/978-3-031-08740-0_12

In the case of linguistics, despite the fact that several attempts of establishing structural parallelisms between DNA sequences and verbal language have been performed [24, 25, 31], linguists have not attempted to construct a new paradigm taking advantage of the developments in molecular biology. In this paper, we claim that the application of molecular computing to linguistics may provide a new model to reconstruct language description with molecular methods; define a formalization that can be implemented and may be able to describe and predict the behavior of linguistic structures and offer a method of language manipulation that can be useful for natural langauge processing.

2   The Interplay Between Linguistics, Biology and Computation

The interplay between biology, linguistics and computation is not something new. There has been a long tradition of interchanging methods in biology and natural/formal language theory.

Regarding the interchange of methods *from computer science to biology*, by taking into account the communicative consideration of the genetic code, molecular biology has taken several models from formal language theory in order to explain the structure and working of DNA. Such attempts have been focused in the design of grammar-based approaches to define combinatorics in protein and DNA sequences and the application of generativist approaches to the analysis of the genetic code. From this interchange of methods several models have been developed such as Pawlak dependency grammars as an approach in the study of protein formation [37]; stochastic context-free grammars for modeling RNA [44]; definite clause grammars and cut grammars to investigate gene structure and mutations and rearrangement [47]; and tree-adjoining grammars for predicting RNA structure of biological data [54].

Among the influence of *linguistic models in biology*, we can refer to Watson's understanding of heredity as a form of communication [55]; Asimov's idea that nucleotide bases are letters and form an alphabet [2]; Jakobson's ideas about taking the nucleotide bases as phonemes of the genetic code or about the binary oppositions in phonemes and in the nucleic code [23]. Moreover, some authors have achieved quite successful results in the description of the structure of genes by means of formal grammars [10, 47]. Linguistics and molecular biology are also related by computer science in scientific programs like NLP for biology [50].

Biological ideas have been applied *in linguistics* as shown in theories such as the *tree model* proposed by Schleicher [45]; the *wave model* due to Schmidt [46]; the *geometric network model* proposed by Forster [16]; the naturalistic metaphor in linguistics defended by Jakobson [23, 24]; or the biological-evolutionary model for language change [11].

Finally, the use of *biological models* is frequent *in computation*, as shown in theories like neural networks [21], cellular automata [34], evolutionary computing [20] and ant colonies [12]. Using DNA and cell biology as a support for computation is the basic idea of molecular computing, natural computing and DNA computing.

3   Formal Language Theory and Linguistics

In order to understand the role of formal language theory in linguistics, we have to go back to the origins of this field. The area of formal languages emerged as an interdisciplinary area in the middle of the 20th çentury, relating *mathematics* and *linguistics.*

In the area of mathematics, the key names are A. Thue, E. Post and A. Turing. Thue [51,52] and Post [38] introduced the formal notion of a rewriting system, while Turing [53] introduced the general idea of finding models of computing where the power of a model could be described by the complexity of the language it generates/accepts. Building on the work by Thue, Turing and Post, Noam Chomsky started in the 1950s s the study of grammars and the grammatical structure of a language. Chomsky's goal was to give a precise characterization of the structure of natural languages. He wanted to define the syntax of languages using simple and precise mathematical rules. In order to reach this goal, he introduced his grammar hierarchy as a tool for modelling natural languages.

The view of natural languages as formal languages played a significant role in the development of linguistics in the second half of the 20th century. In fact, the view of languages as sets of strings underlay the early development of generative grammar [35]. It was a period dominated by the interest on syntax, and the formalism introduced by Chomsky was considered a good mathematical approach to solve the problem of approaching natural language from a formal point of view.

We can say that the 'golden period' of the relationship between linguistics and formal language theory was from the 60s to the 80s. At that time, there was a big activity in the application of formal language models to natural language issues. The debate about the context-freeness of natural language and the proposal of new models in the area of formal language to better describe natural language were the central core of linguistics in those decades of the 20th century. In that period, books on mathematical and formal linguistics always reported on the advances in the field of formal language theory by including chapters dedicated to the hierarchy of languages and grammars introduced by Chomsky and by introducing the new models that were proposed. An example of this can be the classical book on mathematical linguistics by Barbara Partee, Alice ter Meulen and Robert E. Wall [36].

Currently, the situation depicted above has drastically changed. The following quotation by Levelt [29] summarizes the current influence of formal languages in linguistics:

> Any linguist reading an introduction to this field some 30 or 40 years ago felt at home right away. [...] Nowadays, an interested linguist or psycholinguist opening any text or handbook on formal language can no longer see the wood for the trees. Not only are linguistic applications in the small minority, but it also by no means evident which formal, mathematical tools are really required for natural language applications.

From the 60s to the 80s, linguistics was the central application of formal language theory and linguists were very much interested in applying formal language models to the formalization of natural language. On the contrary, from the 90s, the interest of linguistics in formal languages seems to have disappeared and formal language theorists have found innumerable applications of their theory different from linguistics.

The reasons that explain this separation of linguistics from formal language theory could be very different; among them we stress the following ones:

1. Problems that linguists found when trying to describe natural language by the classical theory of formal languages. For example, the difficulty of locating natural language in the Chomsky hierarchy and, therefore, the necessity of defining different new formalisms.
2. The growing interest on less theoretical/formal areas of linguistics –as *cognitive linguistics* [17]– and, therefore, the need for looking for more natural computational systems to give account of natural language processing. Rewriting methods used in natural language approaches based on formal languages seemed to be not very adequate, from a cognitive perspective, to account for the processing of language.
3. The importance gained in the field of linguistics of subdisciplines such as *semantics* [28], *pragmatics* [22] or *sociolinguistics* [3]. Formal language theory was very useful in linguistics when the main interest of this discipline was to describe the syntax of a natural language. When linguists tried to approach dynamical parts of natural language that depends on the context of use, classical models of formal languages became too rigid.

Those problems were related to the first generation of formal languages based on rewriting systems. Models proposed from the 90s in the area of formal language theory may solve those classic problems. However, the divorce between the theory of formal languages and linguistics, due to initial difficulties, has led to a lack of communication between researchers of both disciplines that has prevented linguists to have access to new models proposed in the field of formal languages. In fact, if we have a look at recent books on mathematical linguistics –as the one published by Kornai [27]– we will see that they do not report on the models defined in the field of formal language theory from the 90s. Biological-inspired methods are quite recent and have been introduced in a period when linguistics and formal languages were two separated disciplines.

Summing up, the current situation of the relationship between linguistics and formal language theory is one in which there is no relation at all. Linguistics is working on informally or seminformally theories of natural language. Natural language processing prefers statistical methods to formal models. And formal language theory has a wide-range of applications being linguistics out of its interests.

3.1   Natural Computing and Linguistics

Natural computing has become one of the most extended frameworks where new models for formal language theory have been developed.

One of the most developed lines of research in natural computing is *molecular computing*, a model based on molecular biology, which arose mainly after Adleman's work [1]. An active area in molecular computing is DNA computing [41], inspired by the way DNA perform operations to generate, replicate or change the configuration of the strings. *Splicing systems* or *H systems* –introduced by Tom Head [19]– represent a model for DNA computation that is part of formal language theory. H systems can be viewed as a development in formal language theory that provides new generative devices that allow close simulation of molecular recombination processes by corresponding generative processes acting on strings.

Systems biology and cellular biology have achieved an important development. These advances have provided new models for computer science. One of them is *cellular computing*, that emphasizes the concept of microbiological populations as well as the equilibrium of the devices and the relationships between the elements. *P systems* or *membrane systems* [40] can be considered an example of this emerging paradigm. Membrane systems consist of multisets of objects placed in the compartments defined by the membrane structure that delimits the system from its environment.

On the other hand, natural computing has evolved from the first numeric models –like neural networks– to symbolic models which are closer to multi-agent systems. *Networks of evolutionary processors* (NEPs) [8] are inspired by both, bio cellular models and basic structures for parallel and distributed symbolic processing. NEPs can be defined as systems consisting of several devices whose communication is regulated by an underlying graph. Such devices, which are an abstract formalization of cells, are described by a set of words evolving by mutations, according to some predefined rules. The cellular basis of the NEPs relate them with P systems, especially with tissue P systems [32], a theory in the area of membrane computing whose biological referent is the structure and behaviour of multicellular organisms. In tissue P systems, cells form a multitude of different associations performing various functions. NEPs could be linked to systems biology as well, because the model aims to develop a holistic theory where the behaviour of each agent can influence the environment and the other agents.

Those bioinspired developments of formal language theory are quite recent and have been seldom considered in the literature of formal methods in linguistics, despite the fact that due to their features they may be suitable for modelling natural language providing an integrative path for biology, computer science and natural language processing.

4   From Linguistics to Biology and Back Through Computation

Formalization is a key point of the models we have to propose in pursuit of understanding natural language. However to find the right formal model is often very hard [27].

Looking at the bioinspired formal languages reported in the previous section, one realizes that these models can be applied to problems different from syntax – that is the classical area where formal models have been used. Biological inspired frameworks can deal with key problems in the formal approach to language. Non-standard models in formal languages may cover the whole range of linguistic disciplines, from phonology to pragmatics. Here are some examples of those possible applications.

DNA computing and NEPs can be good solutions for *syntax*. Application of molecular computing methods to natural language syntax gives rise to *molecular syntax* [4]. Molecular syntax takes as a model the two types of mechanisms used in biology in order to modify or generate DNA sequences: *mutations* and *splicing*. From a linguistic point of view, the main difference between mutations and splicing is that mutations refer to changes performed in a linguistic string, being this a phrase, sentence or text, while splicing is a process carried out involving two or more linguistic sequences. Therefore, whereas mutations are more suitable to explain different configurations in a simple linguistic string, splicing can account for complexity and is a good framework for approaching syntax. Splicing is defined as the operation which consists of splitting up two strings in an arbitrary way and sticking the left side of the first one to the right side of the second, and the left side of the second one to the right side of the first one. Syntactic complexity can be generated by the technique of cutting and pasting lineal structures. Combining elementary rules in genetic processes –cut, paste, delete, move– most of the complex syntactic structures of natural language can be obtained.

Three features of NEPs are crucial for their application to language processing and, especially, to parsing technologies: NEPs are *specialized, modular* communicating systems that work in *parallel*. Adopting these characteristics in the modelling of a parser may improve its efficiency and decrease the complexity. In [6], an application of NEPs for the analysis and recognition of sentences of natural language is presented. In this NEPs parsing application, each processor is specialized in the processing of different syntactic patterns. Modularity and specialisation allow designing processors which only accept, recognize and label a single type of syntactic phrases or functions. By parallelism, all lexical items are analyzed at the same time, and afterwards, grammatical units may be packed in different processors. The system performs two main tasks: a) to recognize correct strings, and b) to provide an output with labelled elements that give account of the syntactic structure of the input sentence.

Membrane systems can solve issues in *semantics* and *pragmatics*. Formalizing semantics and pragmatics is one of the most challenging works in linguistics, specially because the system in semantics/pragmatics is very interactive and constantly evolving. The most important intuition for translating membrane systems to semantics and pragmatics is that membranes can be understood as *contexts*. Contexts may be different words, persons, social groups, historical periods, languages. They can accept, reject, or produce changes in elements they have inside. Moreover, contexts/membranes and their rules evolve, that is, change, appear, vanish, etc. Therefore, membranes and elements of the system are constantly interacting. Some ideas of applications of membrane systems to linguistic issues can be found in [5].

Besides those general applications, there are many challenges in contemporary linguistics to which bioinspired formal language theory can help to find a solution. We highlight the following ones:

1. *Context formalization.* Context formalization is one of the most important areas of research that need to be improved in linguistics. Context-dependency is a core notion in linguistics. Natural language processing depends on the relationship between the utterances produced and the context in which they are interpreted. In traditional linguistics, context is conceived of as comprising the immediate features of a speech situation in which an expression is uttered, such as time, location, speaker, hearer and preceding discourse [14]. However, context is a much wider notion. According to Fetzer [15], context is conceived as a frame whose job is to frame content by delimiting that content; context is a dynamic construct which is interactionally organized in and through the process of communication; context is the common ground or background information which participants take for granted in interaction. Although most scholars would accept that the notion of context is fundamental for linguistics, in general, robust theories of context are lacking. In recent years, a renewed interest in approaching the notion of context has been observed [14,15]. *Membrane theory* or *NEPs* are good candidates to help in the problem of context formalization in linguistics. Those frameworks provide models in which contexts are an important element which is already formalized and can give to linguistics the theoretical tools needed.

2. *Models for dealing with interaction/interfaces among linguistic modules in a grammar.* The modular conception of language and the classical notion of linguistic level caused the specialization of linguists in a concrete module of natural language (syntax, morphology, phonology, semantics, etc.) forgetting the need to address the interaction between the various components that make up the grammar of a language. Linguistic research in recent years has highlighted the need to address the relationships between the different modules of grammar. The description of the interfaces between phonetics, phonology, morphology, syntax, semantics and pragmatics make up a new area of research in current linguistics [42]. We need formal models to address this interaction among language modules. Language interfaces formalization is a problem for hierarchical and sequential language models. However, this formalization does not pose any problem in models that formalize the ideas of parallelism, interaction, distribution and cooperation.

3. *Formalization of the notion of evolution.* An important problem in the formalization of natural language is its dynamicity, its changing nature. Evolution is a key notion in Evolutionary Linguistics, a discipline that aims to identify when, where, and how human language originates, changes, and dies out [18]. According to Smith [48], computational simulations have been at the heart of the field of evolutionary linguistics for the past two decades, and these are now being extended and complemented in a number of directions, through formal mathematical models, language-ready robotic agents, and experimental simulations in the laboratory. In this search of mathematical/formal models to capture the dynamics of natural language, bioinspired models in formal language can be useful. *NEPs*, for example, offer enough flexibility to model any change at any moment in any part of the system, being able of formalizing evolution in a highly pertinent way.

4. *Definition of parallel models for language processing.* Natural language processing has been traditionally studied from a linear and sequential point of view. In opposition to this view, some linguistic theories, like *autolexical syntax* [43], are defined by their authors as parallel, indicating that natural language expressions are organized along a number of simultaneous informational dimensions. Language production is understood as a parallel process [33]. Moreover, the multimodal approach to communication, where not just production, but also gestures, vision and supra-segmental features of sounds have to be tackled, refers to a parallel way of processing. In order to define parallel models for language processing, *NEPs* offer good mathematical tools.

5. *Frameworks for dealing with different levels of grammaticality.* Linguistics has always presented the notion of grammaticality discretely. Despite those ideas, it seems quite obvious that humans do not process language in discrete terms but gradually. In fact, in recent years, some linguistic theories have arisen that seek to account for different levels of grammaticality [7,9,13,26,30,39,49]. In general, the models that advocate for the idea of fuzzy grammaticality do not provide a formal definition of the concept. Therefore, we need formal models for capturing this essential idea in natural language processing. We think that bio-inspired formal languages can also help in this linguistic issue.

The above topics are just some of the current challenges in linguistics that could be better solved by using bio-inspired formal language theory. The full development of formal theories that tackle the above issues may help in the better description and formalization of natural language and this advance will have great importance in the field of artificial intelligence that still having the challenge of making computers speak in a 'natural' way.

5   Conclusions

Language is one of the most challenging issues that remain to be explained. The careless look at natural language approaches proposed up to now shows several facts that somehow invite to the search of new formalisms to account in a simpler and more natural way for natural languages. The fact that 1) natural language sentences cannot be placed in any of the families of the Chomsky hierarchy in which current computational models are basically based or 2) the idea that rewriting methods used in a large number of natural language approaches seem to be not very adequate, from a cognitive perspective, to account for the processing of language lead us to look for a more *natural* computational system to give a *formal* account of natural languages.

The idea of using biocomputing models in the description of natural language is backed up both by a long tradition of interchanging methods between biology and natural/formal language theory and by several analogies between natural and genetic languages.

In this paper, we have focused our attention in the role of formal language theory in linguistics. However, the interdisciplinarity we speak about is bidirectional, this is, we think that models in formal language theory can benefit from linguistic theories as well. Therefore, we would like to call the attention of researchers working in formal language theory about the possibilities that the human processing of language offers as motivation/inspiration for new frameworks in the field of formal languages. As the following quotation emphasizes, formal language theory can benefit from going back to its origins and having again natural language as a model:

> Besides improving our understanding of natural language, a worthy goal in itself, the formalization opened the door to the modern theory of computer languages and their compilers. This is not to say that every advance in formalizing linguistic theory is likely to have a similarly spectacular payoff, but clearly the informal theory remains a treasure-house inasmuch as it captures important insights about natural language. While not entirely comparable to biological systems in age and depth, natural language embodies a significant amount of evolutionary optimization, and artificial communication systems can benefit for these developments only to the extent that the informal insights are capture by formal methods [27].

Summing up, to promote the relationship between linguistics and formal language theory may be fruitful to both research areas. Linguistics would find in formal language theory the mathematical tools for presenting its theories in a rigorous fashion contributing to better understanding natural language. Formal language theory would find in linguistics a 'natural' inspiration for defining new models that could become the theoretical basis for future computational systems that will, for sure, improve our interaction with computers.

References

1. Adleman, L.: Molecular computation of solutions to combinatorial problems. Science **226**, 1021–1024 (1994)
2. Asimov, I.: Il Codice Genetico. Einaudi, Torino (1968)

3. Bayley, R., Cameron, R., Lucas, C.: The Oxford Handbook of Sociolinguistics. Oxford University Press, Oxford (2013)
4. Bel-Enguix, G., Jiménez-López, M.D.: Byosyntax. an overview. Fundam. Inform. **64**, 1–12 (2005)
5. Enguix, G.B., Jiménez-López, M.D.: Linguistic membrane systems and applications. In: Ciobanu, G., Păun, G., Pérez-Jiménez, M.J. (eds.) Applications of Membrane Computing, pp. 347–388. Springer, Berlin (2005). https://doi.org/10.1007/3-540-29937-8_13
6. Bel-Enguix, G., Jiménez-López, M.D., Mercas, R., Perekrestenko, A.: Networks of evolutionary processors as natural language parsers. In: Proceedings of the First International Conference on Agents and Artificial Intelligence, pp. 619–625. INSTICC, Oporto (2009)
7. Blache, P., Balfourier, J.: Property grammars: a flexible constraint-based approach to parsing. In: Proceedings of Seventh International Workshop on Parsing Technologies. Tsinghua University Press, Beijing (2001)
8. Castellanos, J., Martín-Vide, C., Mitrana, V., Sempere, J.: Networks of evolutionary processors. Acta Informatica **39**, 517–529 (2003). https://doi.org/10.1007/s00236-003-0114-y
9. Clark, A., Giorgolo, G., Lappin, S.: Towards a statistical model of grammaticality. In: Proceedings of the 35th Annual Conference of the Cognitive Science Society (2013)
10. Collado-Vides, J.: Towards a grammatical paradigm for the study of the regulation of gene expression. In: Theoretical Biology. Epigenetic and Evolutionary Order from Complex Systems. Edinburgh University Press, Edinburgh (1989)
11. Croft, W.: Explaining Language Change: An Evolutionary Approach. Longman, Singapore (2000)
12. Dorigo, M., Stützle, T.: Ant Colony Optimization. MIT Press/Bradford Books, Cambridge, MA (2004)
13. Duchier, D., Prost, J.-P., Dao, T.-B.-H.: A model-theoretic framework for grammaticality judgements. In: de Groote, P., Egg, M., Kallmeyer, L. (eds.) FG 2009. LNCS (LNAI), vol. 5591, pp. 17–30. Springer, Heidelberg (2011). https://doi.org/10.1007/978-3-642-20169-1_2
14. Fetzer, A.: Recontextualizing Context: Grammaticality Meets Appropriateness. John Benjamins, Amsterdam (2004)
15. Fetzer, A.: Context and Appropriateness: Micro Meets Macro. John Benjamins, Amsterdam (2007)
16. Forster, P.: Network analysis of word lists. In: Third International Conference on Quantitative Linguistics, pp. 184–186. Research Institute for the Languages of Finland, Helsinki (1997)
17. Geeraerts, D., Cuyckens, H.: The Oxford Handbook of Cognitive Linguistics. Oxford University Press, Oxford (2010)
18. Gong, T., Shuai, L., Zhang, M.: Modelling language evolution: examples and predictions. Phys. Life Rev. **11**(2), 280–302 (2014)
19. Head, T.: Formal language theory and DNA: an analysis of the generative capacity of specific recombination behaviors. Bull. Math. Biol. **49**, 737–759 (1987). https://doi.org/10.1007/BF02481771
20. Holland, J.: Adaptation in Natural and Artificial Systems. University of Michigan Press, Michigan (1975)
21. Hopfiel, H.: Neural networks and physical systems with emergent collective computational abilities. In: Proceedings of the National Academy of Sciences-USA, vol. 79, p. 2554. National Academy of Sciences (1982)

22. Horn, L., Ward, G.: The Handbook of Pragmatics. Blackwell, Oxford (2005)
23. Jakobson, R.: Linguistics. In: Main Trends of Research in the Social and Human Sciences, pp. 419–463. Mouton, Paris (1970)
24. Jakobson, R.: Essais de Linguistique Générale. 2, Rapports Internes et Externes du Language. Les Éditions de Minuit, Paris (1973)
25. Ji, S.: Microsemiotics of DNA. Semiotica **138**(1/4), 15–42 (2002)
26. Keller, F.: Gradience in grammar: experimental and computational aspects of degrees of grammaticality. Ph.D. thesis, University of Edinburgh (2000)
27. Kornai, A.: Speech and handwriting. In: Mathematical Linguistics. AIKP, pp. 219–246. Springer, London (2008). https://doi.org/10.1007/978-1-84628-986-6_9
28. Lappin, S.: The Handbook of Contemporary Semantic Theory. Blackwell, Oxford (1997)
29. Levelt, W.: Formal Grammars in Linguistics and Psycholinguistics. Jonh Benjamins, Amsterdam (2008)
30. Manning, C.: Probabilistic approaches to syntax. In: Probability Theory in Linguistics, pp. 289–342. MIT Press, Cambridge (2003)
31. Marcus, S.: Language at the Crossroad of Computation and Biology. In: Computing with Bio-Molecules, pp. 1–35. Springer, Singapore (1998)
32. Martín-Vide, C., Pazos, J., Păun, G., Rodríguez-Patón, A.: A new class of symbolic abstract neural nets: tissue P systems. In: Ibarra, O.H., Zhang, L. (eds.) COCOON 2002. LNCS, vol. 2387, pp. 290–299. Springer, Heidelberg (2002). https://doi.org/10.1007/3-540-45655-4_32
33. Melinger, A., Branigan, H., Pickering, M.: Parallel processing in language production. Lang. Cogn. Neurosci. **29**(6), 663–683 (2014)
34. von Neumann, J.: The Theory of Self-Reproducing Automata. University of Illinois Press, Urbana, IL (1968)
35. Newmeyer, F.: Generative Linguistics: An Historical Perspective. Routledge, London (1997)
36. Partee, B., ter Meulen, A., Wall, R.: Mathematical Methods in Linguistics. Kluwer, Drodrecht (1993)
37. Pawlak, Z.: Gramatyka i Matematika. Panstwowe Zakady Wydawnietw Szkolnych, Warzsawa (1998)
38. Post, E.: Finite combinatory processes-formulation. J. Symbolic Logic **1**, 103–105 (1936)
39. Prince, A., Smolensky, P.: Optimality theory: constraint interaction in generative grammar. Technical report, Rutgers University (1993)
40. Păun, G.: Computing with membranes. J. Comput. Syst. Sci. **61**, 108–143 (2000)
41. Păun, G., Rozenberg, G., Salomaa, A.: DNA Computing. New Computing Paradigms. Springer, Berlin (1998)
42. Ramchand, G., Reiss, C.: The Oxford Handbook of Linguistic Interfaces. Oxford University Press, Oxford (2007)
43. Sadock, J.: Autolexical Syntax. A Theory of Parallel Grammatical Representations. University of Chicago Press, Chicago (1991)
44. Sakakibara, Y., Brown, M., Underwood, R., Mian, I.S., Haussler, D.: Stochastic context-free grammars for modeling RNA. In: Proceedings of the 27th Hawaii International Conference on System Sciences, pp. 284–293. IEEE Computer Society Press, Honolulu (1994)
45. Schleicher, A.: Die Darwinsche Theorie Und Die Sprachwissenschaft. Böhlau, Weimar (1863)
46. Schmidt, J.: Die Verwantschaftsverhältnisse Der Indogermanischen Sprachen. Böhlau, Weimar (1872)

47. Searls, D.: Investigating the linguistics of DNA with definite clause grammars. In: Logic Programming: Proceedings of the North American Conference on Logic Programming, vol. 1. Association for Logic Programming (1989)

48. Smith, A.: Models of language evolution and change. Wiley Interdisc. Rev.: Cogn. Sci. **5**(3), 281–293 (2014)

49. Smolensky, P., Legendre, G.: The Harmonic Mind: From Neural Computation to Optimality-Theoretic Grammar. MIT Press, Cambridge (2006)

50. Tateisi, Y., Ohta, T., Tsujii, J.: Annotation of predicate-argument structure on molecular biology text. In: Proceedings of the Workshop on the 1st International Joint Conference on Natural Language Processing (IJCNLP) (2004)

51. Thue, A.: Über unendliche zeichenreihen. Norske Vid. Selsk. Skr., I Mat. Nat. Kl., Kristiania vol. 7, pp. 1–22 (1906)

52. Thue, A.: Über die gegenseitige lage gleicher teile gewisser zeichenreihen. Norske Vid. Selsk. Skr., I Mat. Nat. Kl., Kristiania, vol. 1, pp. 1–67 (1912)

53. Turing, A.M.: On computable numbers with an application to the entscheidungsproblem. In: Proceedings London Mathematical Society, vol. 2/42 (1937)

54. Uemura, Y., Hasegawa, A., Kobayashi, S., Yokomori, T.: Tree adjoining grammars for RNA structure prediction. Theor. Comput. Sci. **210**(2), 277–303 (1999)

55. Watson, J.: Biologie Moléculaire du Gène. Ediscience, Paris (1968)

Strong Medvedev Reducibilities and the KL-Randomness Problem

Bjørn Kjos-Hanssen[(⊠)] and David J. Webb

University of Hawai'i at Mānoa, Honolulu, HI 96822, USA
{bjoern.kjos-hanssen,dwebb42}@hawaii.edu
http://math.hawaii.edu/wordpress/bjoern/

Abstract. While it is not known whether each real that is Kolmogorov-Loveland random is Martin-Löf random, i.e., whether KLR ⊆ MLR, Kjos-Hanssen and Webb (2021) showed that MLR is truth-table Medvedev reducible ($\leq_{s,tt}$) to KLR. They did this by studying a natural class Either (MLR) and showing that MLR $\leq_{s,tt}$ Either (MLR) ⊇ KLR. We show that Degtev's stronger reducibilities (positive and linear) do not suffice for the reduction of MLR to Either (MLR), and some related results.

Keywords: Martin-Löf Randomness · Medvedev reducibility · truth-table reducibility

1 Introduction

The theory of algorithmic randomness attempts to study randomness of not just random variables, but individual outcomes. The idea is to use computability theory and declare that an outcome is random if it "looks random to any computer". This can be made precise in several ways (with notions such as Martin-Löf randomness and Schnorr randomness), whose interrelation is for the most part well understood [DH10, Nie09]. However, a remaining major open problem of algorithmic randomness asks whether each Kolmogorov–Loveland random (KL-random) real is Martin-Löf random (ML-random).

It is known that one can compute an ML-random real from a KL-random real [MMN+06] and even uniformly so [KHW21]. This uniform computation succeeds in an environment of uncertainty, however: one of the two halves of the KL-random real is already ML-random and we can uniformly stitch together a ML-random without knowing which half. In this article we pursue this uncertainty and are concerned with uniform reducibility when information has been hidden in a sense. Namely, for any class of reals $\mathcal{C} \subseteq 2^\omega$, we write

Bjørn Kjos-Hanssen—This work was partially supported by a grant from the Simons Foundation (#704836 to Bjørn Kjos-Hanssen). The authors would like to thank Reviewer 2 for Theorem 5. The second author would also like to thank Carl Eadler for pointing him towards results about Karnaugh maps, which were helpful in thinking about Theorem 4.

U. Berger et al. (Eds.): CiE 2022, LNCS 13359, pp. 151–161, 2022.
https://doi.org/10.1007/978-3-031-08740-0_13

$$\text{Either}(\mathcal{C}) = \{A \oplus B : A \in \mathcal{C} \text{ or } B \in \mathcal{C}\},$$

where $A \oplus B$ is the computability-theoretic join:

$$A \oplus B = \{2k \mid k \in A\} \cup \{2k + 1 \mid k \in B\}.$$

For notation, we often refer to 'even' bits of such a real as those coming from A, and 'odd' bits coming from B.

An element of Either$(\mathcal{C})$ has an element of $\mathcal{C}$ available within it, although in a hidden way. We are not aware of the Either operator being studied in the literature, although Higuchi and Kihara [HK14b, Lemma 4] (see also [HK14a]) considered the somewhat more general operation $f(\mathcal{C}, \mathcal{D}) = (2^\omega \oplus \mathcal{C}) \cup (\mathcal{D} \oplus 2^\omega)$.

A real A is Martin-Löf random iff there is a positive constant c so that for any n, the Kolmogorov complexity of the first n bits of A is at least $n - c$, (that is, $\forall n, \ K(A_i \restriction n) \geq n - c$).

This is one of several equivalent definitions – for instance, A is Martin-Löf random $(A \in \text{MLR})$ iff no c.e. martingale succeeds on it. In contrast, A is Kolomogorov-Loveland random $(A \in \text{KLR})$ iff no computable nonmonotonic betting strategy succeeds on it.

As MLR $\subseteq$ KLR, KLR is trivially Medvedev reducible to MLR. In [KHW21], Either is implicitly used to show the reverse, that MLR is Medvedev reducible to KLR. For a reducibility r, such as $r = tt$ (truth-table, Definition 1) or $r = T$ (Turing), let $\leq_{s,r}$ denote strong (Medvedev) reducibility using r-reductions, and $\leq_{w,r}$ the corresponding weak (Muchnik) reducibility.

Theorem 1. MLR $\leq_{s,tt}$ Either(MLR).

Proof. [KHW21, Theorem 2] shows that MLR $\leq_{s,tt}$ KLR. The proof demonstrates that MLR $\leq_{s,tt}$ Either(MLR) and notes, by citation to [MMN+06], that KLR $\subseteq$ Either(MLR). □

In fact, the proof shows that the two are truth-table Medvedev equivalent. A natural question is whether they are Medvedev equivalent under any stronger reducibility.

Let $\text{DIM}_{1/2}$ be the class of all reals of effective Hausdorff dimension $1/2$. Theorem 1 is a counterpoint to Miller's result MLR $\not\leq_{w,T}$ $\text{DIM}_{1,2}$ [Mil11], since MLR $\not\leq_{s,tt}$ $\text{DIM}_{1,2} \supseteq$ Either(MLR).

Definition 1. *Let $\{\sigma_n \mid n \in \omega\}$ be a uniformly computable list of all the finite propositional formulas in variables $v_1, v_2, \ldots$. Let the variables in σ_n be $v_{n_1}, \ldots, v_{n_d}$ where d depends on n. We say that $X \models \sigma_n$ if σ_n is true with $X(n_1), \ldots, X(n_d)$ substituted for $v_{n_1}, \ldots, v_{n_d}$. A reduction Φ^X is a* **truth-table** *reduction if there is a computable function f such that for each n and X, $n \in \Phi^X$ iff $X \models \sigma_{f(n)}$.*

For two classes of reals $\mathcal{C}, \mathcal{D}$, we write $\mathcal{C} \leq_{s,*} \mathcal{D}$ to mean that there is a $*$-reduction Φ such that $\Phi^D \in \mathcal{C}$ for each $D \in \mathcal{D}$, where $*$ is a subscript in Table 1.

As shown in Fig. 1, the next three candidates to strengthen the result (by weakening the notion of reduction under consideration) are the positive, linear, and bounded truth-table reducibilties. Unfortunately, any proof technique using Either will no longer work, as for these weaker reducibilities, MLR is not Medvedev reducible to Either (MLR).

2 The Failure of Weaker Reducibilities

When discussing the variables in a table $\sigma_{f(n)}$, we say that a variable is of a certain parity if its index is of that parity, i.e. n_2 is an even variable. As our reductions operate on 2^ω, we identify the values $X(n_i)$ with truth values as $1 = \top$ and $0 = \bot$.

Definition 2. *A truth-table reduction Φ^X is a **positive** reduction if the only connectives in each $\sigma_f(n)$ are $\vee$ and $\wedge$.*

Theorem 2. MLR $\not\leq_{s,p}$ Either(MLR).

Proof. Let Φ^X be a positive reduction. By definition, for each input n, $\sigma_{f(n)}$ can be written in conjunctive normal form: $\sigma_{f(n)} = \bigwedge_{k=1}^{t_n} \bigvee_{i=1}^{m_k} v_{f(n),i,k}$. We say that a clause of $\sigma_{f(n)}$ is a disjunct $\bigvee_{i=1}^{m_k} v_{f(n),i,k}$. There are two cases to consider:

Case 1: There is a parity such that there are infinitely many n such that every clause of $\sigma_{f(n)}$ contains a variable.

Without loss of generality, consider the even case. Let $A = \omega \oplus R$ for R an arbitrary random real. Each $\bigvee_{i=1}^{m_k} v_{n,i,k}$ that contains an even variable is true. So for the infinitely many n whose disjunctions all query an even variable, $\sigma_{f(n)} = \bigwedge_{k=1}^{t_n} \top = \top$. As these infinitely many n can be found computably, Φ^A is not immune, and so not random.

Case 2: For either parity, for almost all inputs n, there is a clause of $\sigma_{f(n)}$ containing only variables of that parity.

Set $A = R \oplus \emptyset$ for an arbitrary random real R. For almost all inputs, some clause is a disjunction of $\bot$, so that the entire conjunction is false. Thus Φ^A is cofinitely often 0, and hence computable, and so not random. $\square$

Table 1. Correspondences between reducibilities and sets in Post's lattice. Here $+$ is addition mod 2 (also commonly written XOR). Note that while a *btt* reduction can use any connectives, there is a bound c on how many variables each $\sigma_{f(n)}$ can have, hence if $c = 1$ the only connective available is $\neg$.

Reducibility	Subscript	Connectives
Truth table	tt	any
Bounded tt	btt	any
$btt(1)$	$btt(1)$	$\{\neg\}$
Linear	ℓ	$\{+\}$
Positive	p	$\{\wedge, \vee\}$
Conjunctive	c	$\{\wedge\}$
Disjunctive	d	$\{\vee\}$
Many-one	m	none

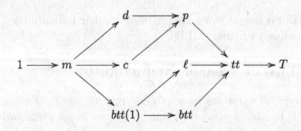

Fig. 1. [Odi99] The relationships between reducibilities in Table 1, which themselves are between $\leq_1$ and $\leq_T$. Here $x \to y$ indicates that if two reals A and B enjoy $A \leq_x B$, then also $A \leq_y B$.

Remark 1. The proof of Theorem 2 also applies to randomness over 3^ω (and beyond). To see this, we consider the alphabet $\{0, 1, 2\}$ and let each $p(j)$ be an identity function and $\vee, \wedge$ be the maximum and minimum under the ordering $0 < 1 < 2$.

Definition 3. *A truth-table reduction Φ^X is a **linear** reduction if each $\sigma_{f(n)}$ is of the form $\sigma_{f(n)} = \sum_{k=1}^{t_n} v_{f(n),k}$ or $\sigma_{f(n)} = 1 + \sum_{k=1}^{t_n} v_{f(n),k}$ where addition is mod 2.*

Theorem 3. MLR $\not\leq_{s,\ell}$ Either(MLR).

Proof. We may assume that Φ infinitely often queries a bit that it has not queried before (else Φ^A is always computable). Without loss of generality, suppose Φ infinitely often queries an even bit it has not queried before. We construct A in stages, beginning with $A_0 = \emptyset \oplus R$ for R an arbitrary random real.

For the infinitely many n_i that query an unqueried even bit, let v_i be the least such bit. Then at stage $s+1$, set $v_i = 1$ if $\Phi^{A_s}(n_i) = 0$. Changing a single bit in a linear $\sigma_{f(n_i)}$ changes the output of $\sigma_{f(n_i)}$, so that $\Phi^A(n) = \Phi^{A_{s+1}}(n_i) = 1$.

As these n_i form a computable set, Φ^A fails to be immune, and so cannot be random. $\qquad\square$

Definition 4. *A truth-table reduction Φ^X is a **bounded truth-table** reduction if there is a c such that there are most c variables in each $\sigma_{f(n)}$ (in particular we say it is a btt(c) reduction).*

Theorem 4. MLR $\not\leq_{s,btt}$ Either(MLR).

Proof. Suppose that Φ is a btt-reduction from Either(MLR) to MLR and let c be its bound on the number of oracle bits queried. We proceed by induction on c, working to show that an $X = X_0 \oplus X_1$ exists with X_0 or X_1 ML-random, for which Φ^X is not bi-immune.

Base for the induction (c = 1). As btt(1) reductions are linear, it is enough to appeal to Theorem 3. But as a warmup for what follows, we shall prove this case directly. Let Φ be a btt(1) reduction. Here $\Phi^X(n) = f_n(X(q(n))$ where

$f_n : \{0,1\} \to \{0,1\}$, $q : \omega \to \omega$ is computable, and $\{f_n\}_{n \in \omega}$ is computable. (If no bits are queried on input n, let f_n be the appropriate constant function.)

If for infinitely many n, f_n is the constant function 1 or 0, and the claim is obvious.

Instead, suppose f_n is only constant finitely often, i.e. $f_n(x) = x$ or $f_n(x) = 1 - x$ cofinitely often. Without loss of generality, there are infinitely many n such that $q(n)$ is even. Let $X = \emptyset \oplus R$, where R is an arbitrary ML-random set.

As $X(q(n)) = 0$ and $f(x)$ is either identity or $1 - x$ infinitely often, there is an infinite computable subset of either Φ^X or $\overline{\Phi^X}$ so Φ^X is not bi-immune.

Induction Step. Assume the $c - 1$ case, and consider a $btt(c)$ reduction Φ.

Now there are uniformly computable finite sets $Q(n) = \{q_1(n), \ldots, q_{d_n}(n)\}$ and Boolean functions $f_n : \{0,1\}^{d_n} \to \{0,1\}$ such that for all n, $\Phi^X(n) = f_n(X(q_1(n)), \ldots, X(q_{d_n}(n)))$ and $d_n \leq c$.

Consider the greedy algorithm that tries to find a collection of pairwise disjoint $Q(n_i)$ as follows:

- $n_0 = 0$.
- n_{i+1} is the least n such that $Q(n) \cap \bigcup_{k < i} Q(n_k) = \emptyset$.

If this algorithm cannot find an infinite sequence, let i be least such that n_{i+1} is undefined, and define $H = \bigcup_{k \leq i} Q(n_k)$. It must be that for $n > n_i$ no intersection $Q(n) \cap H$ is empty. Thus there are finitely many bits that are in infinitely many of these intersections, and so are queried infinitely often. We will "hard code" the bits of H as 0 in a new function $\hat{\Phi}$.

To that end, define $\hat{Q}(n) = Q(n) \setminus H$, and let $\hat{f}$ be the function that outputs the same truth tables as f, but for all $n \in H$, v_n is replaced with $\perp$. List the elements of $\hat{Q}$ in increasing order as $\{\hat{q}_1(n), \ldots, \hat{q}_{e_n}(n)\}$. Now if $X \cap H = \emptyset$, any $q_i(n) \in H$ have $X(q_i(n)) = 0$, so that $\Phi^X = \hat{\Phi}^X$, as for every n,

$$f(X(q_1(n)), \ldots X(q_{d_n}(n))) = \hat{f}_n(X(\hat{q}_1(n)), \ldots, X(\hat{q}_{e_n}(n))).$$

As Q and the f_n are uniformly computable and H is finite, $\hat{Q}$ and the $\hat{f}_n$ are also uniformly computable. As no intersection $Q(n) \cap H$ was empty, $e_n < d_n \leq c$. So $\hat{Q}$ and the $\hat{f}_n$ define a $btt(c-1)$-reduction. By the induction hypothesis, there is a real $A \in \text{Either}(\text{MLR})$ such that $\hat{\Phi}^A$ is not random. Either(MLR) is closed under finite differences (as MLR is), so the set $B = A \setminus H$ witnesses $\Phi^B = \hat{\Phi}^A$, and Φ^B is not random as desired.

This leaves the case where the algorithm enumerates a sequence of pairwise disjoint $Q(n_i)$.

Say that a collection of bits $C(n) \subseteq Q(n)$ can *control* the computation $\Phi^X(n)$ if there is a way to assign the bits in C_n so that $\Phi^X(n)$ is the same no matter what the other bits in $Q(n)$ are. For example, $(a \wedge b) \vee c$ can be controlled by $\{a, b\}$, by setting $a = b = 1$. Note that if the bits in $C(n)$ are assigned appropriately, $\Phi^X(n)$ is the same regardless of what the rest of X looks like.

Suppose now that there are infinitely many n_i such that some $C(n_i)$ containing only even bits controls $\Phi^X(n_i)$. Collect these n_i into a set E. Let X_1 be an arbitrary ML-random set. As there are infinitely many n_i, and it is computable to determine whether an assignment of bits controls $\Phi^X(n)$, E is an infinite computable set. For $n \in E$, we can assign the bits in $Q(n)$ to control $\Phi^X(n)$, as the $Q(n)$ are mutually disjoint. Now one of the sets

$$\{n \in E \mid \Phi^X(n) = 0\} \qquad \text{or} \qquad \{n \in E \mid \Phi^X(n) = 1\}$$

is infinite. Both are computable, so in either case Φ^X is not bi-immune.

Now suppose that cofinitely many of the n_i cannot be controlled by their even bits. Here let X_0 be an arbitrary ML-random set. For sufficiently large n_i, no matter the values of the even bits in $Q(n_i)$, there is a way to assign the odd bits so that $\Phi^X(n_i) = 1$. By pairwise disjointness, we can assign the odd bits of $\bigcup Q(n_i)$ as needed to ensure this, and assign the rest of the odd bits of X however we wish. Now the n_i witness the failure of Φ^X to be immune. $\square$

3   Arbitrarily Many Columns

It is worth considering direct sums with more than two summands. In this new setting, we first prove the analog of Theorem 2 of [KHW21] for more than two columns, before sketching the modifications necessary to prove analogues of Theorems 2 to 4.

Recall that the infinite direct sum $\bigoplus_{i=0}^{\omega} A_i$ is defined as $\{\langle i, n \rangle \mid n \in A_i\}$, where $\langle \cdot, \cdot \rangle : \omega^2 \to \omega$ is a fixed computable bijection.

Definition 5. *For each $\mathcal{C} \subseteq 2^{\omega}$ and ordinal $\alpha \leq \omega$, define*

$$\mathrm{Some}(\mathcal{C}, \alpha) = \left\{ \bigoplus_{i=0}^{\alpha} A_i \in 2^{\omega} \;\middle|\; \exists i \; A_i \in \mathcal{C} \right\},$$

$$\mathrm{Many}(\mathcal{C}) = \left\{ \bigoplus_{i=0}^{\omega} A_i \in 2^{\omega} \;\middle|\; \exists^{\infty} i \; A_i \in \mathcal{C} \right\}.$$

These represent different ways to generalize $\mathrm{Either}(\mathcal{C})$ to the infinite setting: we may know that some possibly finite number of columns A_i are in $\mathcal{C}$, or that infinitely many columns are in $\mathcal{C}$. If $\alpha = \omega$, these notions are m-equivalent, so we can restrict our attention to $\mathrm{Some}(\mathrm{MLR}, \alpha)$ without loss of generality:

Theorem 5 (due to Reviewer 2). $\mathrm{Some}(\mathcal{C}, \omega) \equiv_{s,m} \mathrm{Many}(\mathcal{C})$.

Proof. The $\leq_{s,m}$ direction follows from the inclusion $\mathrm{Many}(\mathcal{C}) \subseteq \mathrm{Some}(\mathcal{C}, \omega)$.

For $\geq_{s,m}$, let $B \in \mathrm{Some}(\mathcal{C}, \omega)$ and define A by:

$$\langle \langle i, j \rangle, n \rangle \in A \iff \langle i, n \rangle \in B$$

Then $A \leq_m B$ and $A \in \mathrm{Many}(\mathcal{C})$, so that $\mathrm{Some}(\mathcal{C}, \omega) \geq_{s,m} \mathrm{Many}(\mathcal{C})$. $\square$

3.1 Truth-Table Reducibility

Recall that a real A is Martin-Löf random iff there is a positive constant c (the randomness deficiency) so that for any n, $K(A_i \upharpoonright n) \geq n - c$. Let $K_s(\sigma)$ be a computable, non-increasing approximation of $K(\sigma)$ at stages $s \in \omega$.

Theorem 6. *For all ordinals $\alpha \leq \omega$, MLR $\leq_{s,tt}$ Some(MLR, α).*

Proof. Given a set $A = \bigoplus_{i=0}^{\alpha} A_i$, we start by outputting bits from A_0, switching to the next A_i whenever we notice that the smallest possible randomness deficiency increases. This constant c depends on s and changes at stage $s + 1$ if

$$(\exists n \leq s + 1) \quad K_{s+1}(A_i \upharpoonright n) < n - c_s. \tag{1}$$

In detail, fix a map $\pi : \omega \to \alpha$ so that for all y, the preimage $\pi^{-1}(\{y\})$ is infinite. Let $n(0) = 0$, and if Eq. (1) occurs at stage s, set $n(s + 1) = n(s) + 1$, otherwise $n(s + 1) = n(s)$. Finally, define $A(s) = A_{\pi(n(s))}(s)$.

As some A_i is in MLR, switching will only occur finitely often. So there is an stage s such that for all larger t, $A(t) = A_i(t)$. Thus our output will have an infinite tail that is ML-random, and hence will itself be ML-random.

To guarantee that this is a truth-table reduction, we must check that this procedure always halts. But this is immediate, as Eq. (1) is computable for all $s \in \omega$ and $A_i \in 2^\omega$.   □

3.2 Positive Reducibility

We say that a variable is from a certain column if its index codes a location in that column, i.e. n_k is from A_i if $k = \langle i, n \rangle$ for some n.

Theorem 7. *For all $\alpha \leq \omega$, MLR $\not\leq_{s,p}$ Some(MLR, α).*

Proof. Let Φ^X be a positive reduction. Assume each $\sigma_{f(n)}$ is written in conjunctive normal form. We sketch the necessary changes to the proof of Theorem 2:

Case 1: There is an i such that there are infinitely many n such that every clause of $\sigma_f(n)$ contains a variable from A_i.

Without loss of generality, let that column be $A_0 = \omega$. The remaining A_i can be arbitrary, as long as one of them is random.

Case 2: For all i, for almost all n, there is a clause in $\sigma_f(n)$ that contains no variables from A_i.

In particular this holds for $i = 0$, so let $A_0 \in$ MLR and the remaining $A_i = \emptyset$.   □

3.3 Linear Reducibility

Theorem 8. *For all $\alpha \leq \omega$, MLR $\not\leq_{s,\ell}$ Some(MLR, α).*

Proof. We may assume that Φ infinitely often queries a bit it has not queried before (else Φ^A is always computable). If there is an i such that Φ infinitely often queries a bit of A_i it has not queried before, the stage construction from Theorem 3 can be carried out with A_i standing in for A_0, and some other $A_j \in \mathrm{MLR}$.

That case always occurs for $\alpha < \omega$, but may not when $\alpha = \omega$. That is, it may the the case that Φ only queries finitely many bits of each A_i. Letting each A_i be random, these bits may be set to 0 without affecting the randomness of any given column, so we could set $A_0 \in \mathrm{MLR}$ while other $A_i = \emptyset$. $\square$

3.4   Bounded Truth-Table Reducibility

As $btt(1)$ reductions are linear, Theorem 8 provides the base case for induction arguments in the vein of Theorem 4. So for each theorem, we can focus our attention on the induction step:

Theorem 9. *For all $\alpha \leq \omega$, $\mathrm{Many}(\mathrm{MLR}) \not\leq_{s,btt} \mathrm{Some}(\mathrm{MLR}, \alpha)$.*

Proof. In the induction step, the case where the greedy algorithm fails is unchanged. Instead, consider the case where the algorithm enumerates a sequence of pairwise disjoint $Q(n_i)$. If there is a column A_j such that there are infinitely many n_i such that some $C(n_i)$ containing only bits from A_j controls $\Phi^X(n)$, then we proceed as in Theorem 4: start with some other $A_k \in \mathrm{MLR}$ while the remaining columns are empty. We can then set the bits in each $Q(n_i)$ to control $\Phi^X(n_i)$ to guarantee that Φ^X is not bi-immune. This only changes bits in A_j, not A_k, so the final $A \in \mathrm{Some}(\mathrm{MLR}, \alpha)$.

This leaves the case where for each A_j, cofinitely many of the n_i cannot be controlled by their bits in A_j. Here put $A_0 \in \mathrm{MLR}$ and assign bits to the other columns as in Theorem 4. $\square$

4   On the Medvedev m-reducibility of MLR to (a.e.-)KLR

Let μ denote the Lebesgue fair-coin measure on 2^ω. It enjoys the familiar probabilistic properties such as Lemma 1:

Lemma 1. *Let $\mathcal{C}, \mathcal{D} \subseteq 2^\omega$. If $\mu(\mathcal{C}) = 1$ and $\mu(\mathcal{D}) = 1$ then $\mu(\mathcal{C} \cap \mathcal{D}) = 1$.*

Given a randomness notion $\mathcal{C}$, we say that a set A is *almost everywhere $\mathcal{C}$-random*[1] if $\mu\{B \mid A \in \mathcal{C}^B\} = 1$. The following is an easy corollary of van Lambalgen's theorem:

Theorem 10. a.e.-MLR = MLR.

Proof. The $\subseteq$ direction is immediate – if A is random relative to some oracle, it is random relative to having no oracle, so $A \in \mathrm{MLR}$. For the reverse, let $A \in \mathrm{MLR}$. If $B \in \mathrm{MLR}^A$, then $A \in \mathrm{MLR}^B$ by van Lambalgen's theorem. Thus $\mu\{B \mid A \in \mathrm{MLR}^B\} \geq \mu(\mathrm{MLR}^A) = 1$, so that $A \in$ a.e.-MLR.

---

[1] This notion was previously defined for the class of computable randoms in [BDRS22].

The corresponding theorem for a.e.-KLR and KLR is an open question, and in fact whether KLR satisfies a version of van Lambalgen's theorem is also open [DGT13]. The situation can be summarized as follows:

$$\text{a.e.-MLR} = \text{MLR} \subseteq \text{a.e.-KLR} \subseteq \text{KLR}.$$

Here we investigate possible connections between MLR and a.e.-KLR.

Write $f : A \to B$ to indicate that f is a total function from A to B. No confusion is likely if, in addition to the Lebesgue measure on 2^ω, μ also denotes the least number operator as follows: for an arithmetic predicate $R(k)$, $\mu k(R(k))$ is the least k such that $R(k)$ is true.

Let $f : \omega \to \omega$ with range $f[w]$, and define $f^{\mathrm{inv}} : f[\omega] \to \omega$ by $f^{\mathrm{inv}}(n) = \mu m(f(m) = n)$. Let $g : \omega \to \omega$ be defined by $g(0) = f(0)$, and

$$g(n + 1) = f(\mu k(f(k) > g(n))).$$

If f is unbounded then $g : \omega \to \omega$ is total. If in addition f is Δ_1^0, then so is g. In fact, if f is unbounded and Δ_1^0 then $g[\omega]$ is infinite and Δ_1^0.

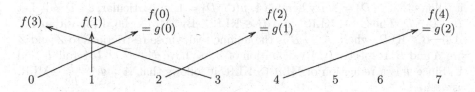

Fig. 2. An example of the behaviors of f and g in Lemma 2.

Lemma 2. Let $A \in 2^\omega$ and let $f : \omega \to \omega$ be an unbounded Δ_1^0 function. Define g by

$$g(n + 1) = f(\mu k(f(k) > g(n))).$$

Then we have the implication $A \circ f \in \text{MLR} \implies A \circ g \in \text{MLR}$.

Proof. Suppose that $A \circ g \notin \text{MLR}$. Then A is Martin-Löf null, i.e., there is some uniformly Σ_1^0 class $\{U_n\}_{n\in\omega}$ with $\mu(U_n) \leq 2^{-n}$ such that $A \circ g \in \bigcap_{n\in\omega} U_n$. Note that $f^{\mathrm{inv}} \circ g : \omega \to \omega$ is total and strictly increasing. Also, $f \circ f^{\mathrm{inv}}$ is the identity function on $f[\omega] \supseteq g[\omega]$.

Thus

$$A \circ g = A \circ f \circ f^{\mathrm{inv}} \circ g$$

and we have

$$A \circ f \in V_n := \{B \mid B \circ f^{\mathrm{inv}} \circ g \in U_n\}$$

The sets V_n are also Σ_1^0 uniformly in n, and $\mu(V_n) \leq 2^{-n}$. Thus $A \circ f \notin \text{MLR}$.

Lemma 3. If C is a class of reals and $\text{MLR} \leq_{s,m} C$, then there is a 1-reduction $A \mapsto \Psi^A = A \circ g$, of MLR to C, such that g is strictly increasing and has computable range.

Proof. Suppose $\Phi^A(n) = A \circ f(n)$ for all A and n, where $A \in \mathcal{C} \implies \Phi^A \in \mathrm{MLR}$ for all A and $f : \omega \to \omega$ is Δ_1^0. Since there is no computable element of MLR, it follows that f is unbounded.

Let $\Psi^A(n) = A \circ g(n)$ with g as in Lemma 2. Then we have

$$A \in \mathcal{C} \implies \Phi^A \in \mathrm{MLR} \implies \Psi^A \in \mathrm{MLR},$$

as desired.

Theorem 11. *If* $\mathrm{MLR} \leq_{s,m} \mathrm{KLR}$ *then* a.e.-$\mathrm{KLR} = \mathrm{MLR}$.

Proof. Assume that $\mathrm{MLR} \leq_{s,m} \mathrm{KLR}$. By Lemma 3, we have in fact a 1-reduction Φ given by $\Phi^A(n) = A(f(n))$ for an injective and strictly increasing computable f with computable range Z.

Let $A \in$ a.e.-KLR. Consider the following classes of reals:

$$\mathcal{C} = \{B \mid A \in \mathrm{KLR}^B\}$$
$$\mathcal{D} = \{B \mid B \in \mathrm{KLR}^A\}$$
$$\mathcal{E} = \{B \mid B \in \mathrm{MLR}^A\}$$

Since $A \in$ a.e.-KLR, $\mu(\mathcal{C}) = 1$. It is well-known that $\mu(\mathcal{E}) = 1$. Since $\mathcal{D} \supseteq \mathcal{E}$, it follows that $\mu(\mathcal{D}) = 1$. By Lemma 1, $\mu(\mathcal{C} \cap \mathcal{D}) = 1$; in particular, $\mathcal{C} \cap \mathcal{D} \neq \emptyset$. Let $B \in \mathcal{C} \cap \mathcal{D}$. Thus $A \in \mathrm{KLR}^B$ and $B \in \mathrm{KLR}^A$. By [MMN+06, Proposition 11], $A \oplus_Z B \in \mathrm{KLR}$, where $A \oplus_Z B$ is the unique real whose restrictions to $\overline{Z}$ and Z are A and B, respectively. By definition of Z, we have $\Phi^{U \oplus_Z V} = U$ for all U and V. Since Φ is a reduction of MLR to KLR, it follows that $A = \Phi^{A \oplus_Z B} \in \mathrm{MLR}$, as desired.

Theorem 12. *Let* Z *be an infinite computable set and let* A, B, X *be sets. If* $A \in \mathrm{KLR}^{B \oplus X}$ *and* $B \in \mathrm{KLR}^{A \oplus X}$ *then* $A \oplus_Z B \in \mathrm{KLR}^X$.

Proof. Relativization of [MMN+06, Proposition 11].

We can relativize to obtain the following conditional result, a strengthening of Theorem 11:

Theorem 13. *If* $\mathrm{MLR} \leq_{s,m}$ a.e.-KLR *then* $\mathrm{MLR} =$ a.e.-KLR.

Proof. Assume $\mathrm{MLR} \leq_{s,m}$ a.e.-KLR as witnessed by a reduction Φ, and let $A \in$ a.e.-KLR. Let Z be as in the proof of Theorem 11.

By definition of a.e.-KLR, for almost all (B, X), $A \in \mathrm{KLR}^{B \oplus X}$. Moreover, for almost all (B, X), $B \in \mathrm{MLR}^{A \oplus X} \subseteq \mathrm{KLR}^{A \oplus X}$.

Therefore

$$\mu\{(B, X) \mid A \oplus_Z B \in \mathrm{KLR}^X\} = 1$$

by Theorem 12. By Fubini's Theorem this implies

$$\mu\{B \mid \mu\{X \mid A \oplus B \in \mathrm{KLR}^X\} = 1\} = 1.$$

Since measure-one sets are nonempty, there exists a set B such that

$$\mu\{X \mid A \oplus B \in \mathrm{KLR}^X\} = 1,$$

i.e., $A \oplus B \in$ a.e.-KLR. By assumption on Φ, $A = \Phi^{A \oplus_Z B} \in \mathrm{MLR}$, as desired.

We can also strengthen these results to work for $btt(1)$-reducibility instead of m-reducibility.

If an analogue of Van Lambalgen's theorem holds for KLR (as it does for MLR), then the two theorems have the same content, as KLR = a.e.-KLR.

References

BDRS22. Bienvenu, L., Rose, V.D., Steifer, T.: Probabilistic vs deterministic gamblers. In: 39th International Symposium on Theoretical Aspects of Computer Science (STACS 2022), pp. 11:1–11:13. Schloss Dagstuhl - Leibniz-Zentrum für Informatik (2022)

DGT13. Diamondstone, D., Greenberg, N., Turetsky, D.: A van Lambalgen theorem for Demuth randomness. In Proceedings of the 12th Asian Logic Colloquium, pp, 115–124. World Scientific (2013)

DH10. Downey, R.G., Hirschfeldt, D.R.: Algorithmic Randomness and Complexity. Theory and Applications of Computability. Springer, New York (2010)

HK14a. Higuchi, K., Kihara, T.: Inside the Muchnik degrees I: discontinuity, learnability and constructivism. Ann. Pure Appl. Logic **165**(5), 1058–1114 (2014)

HK14b. Higuchi, K., Kihara, T.: Inside the Muchnik degrees II: the degree structures induced by the arithmetical hierarchy of countably continuous functions. Ann. Pure Appl. Logic **165**(6), 1201–1241 (2014)

KHW21. Kjos-Hanssen, B., Webb, D.J.: KL-randomness and effective dimension under strong reducibility. In: De Mol, L., Weiermann, A., Manea, F., Fernández-Duque, D. (eds.) CiE 2021. LNCS, vol. 12813, pp. 457–468. Springer, Cham (2021). https://doi.org/10.1007/978-3-030-80049-9_45

Mil11. Miller, J.S.: Extracting information is hard: a Turing degree of non-integral effective hausdorff dimension. Adv. Math. **226**(1), 373–384 (2011)

MMN+06. Merkle, W., Miller, J.S., Nies, A., Reimann, J., Stephan, F.: Kolmogorov-Loveland randomness and stochasticity. Ann. Pure Appl. Logic **138**(1–3), 183–210 (2006)

Nie09. Nies, A.: Computability and Randomness, vol. 51. Oxford Logic Guides. Oxford University Press, Oxford (2009)

Odi99. Odifreddi, P.: Reducibilities, Chapter 3. In: Handbook of Computability Theory. Studies in Logic and the Foundations of Mathematics, vol. 140, pp. 89–119. Elsevier (1999)

On the Necessity of Some Topological Spaces

Robert S. Lubarsky[⌧]

Department of Mathematical Sciences, Florida Atlantic University,
Boca Raton, FL 33431, USA
Robert.Lubarsky@alum.mit.edu

Abstract. Topological models are sometimes used to prove independence results in constructive mathematics. Here we show that some of the topologies that have been used are necessary for those results.

Keywords: constructive mathematics · topological models

1 Introduction

The motivation behind reverse math is the foundational question whether, if a certain method, broadly understood, is used to prove a theorem, that method is in some sense necessary. The cleanest kind of result, when the "method" is a hypothesis, is that the theorem implies the hypothesis. A similar kind of result obtains when the "method" in question is the use of a certain object, and you show that any procedure which ends in that theorem must use that object. That is the goal of this work.

The framework we will be using is topological models for constructive mathematics. (A brief introduction to topological models, with references, is given in a sub-section at the end of this introduction.) If you want an independence result, like ϕ does not imply ψ, then you could show this by developing a topological space T such that the model built over T satisfies ϕ and not ψ. What we would like to show here is that if the model built over any space U similarly satisfies ϕ and not ψ then U in some sense induces T. This is familiar from forcing: if G is $\mathbb{P}$-generic, and $H \in V[G]$ is $\mathbb{Q}$-generic, then (the complete Boolean algebra generated by) $\mathbb{Q}$ is a sub-algebra of (the cBa generated by) $\mathbb{P}$ (see for instance [8], 15.42–15.45). What corresponds to a cBa $\mathbb{P}$ in our setting is the complete Heyting algebra of the open sets of U. So the way T sits inside of U should be so that the opens of T are a sub-cHa of those of U.

One way this could happen is if U is $T \times V$. (That could be the case for instance if ϕ is made true by the existence of an object generic over T. A generic for U is a pair of generics for T and V.) Then T is a quotient space of U. Or if U is the disjoint union $T \uplus V$ (which could be the case if forcing with V also satisfies ϕ), in which case T is a subspace of U.

U. Berger et al. (Eds.): CiE 2022, LNCS 13359, pp. 162–171, 2022.
https://doi.org/10.1007/978-3-031-08740-0_14

A limitation of the efforts here is that we consider only topological models. A slight extension would include arbitrary Heyting-valued models, accounting for Heyting algebras that are not spatial. More broadly than that, there are other constructions of constructive models, such as realizability and Kripke models. Moreover, these various methods can be mixed and matched, such as a Kripke model built using cHa extensions of a realizability model. They are all instances of Krivine's classical realizability [9,10], a construction method that covers all of those mentioned thus far, classical forcing included. That could be a setting in which one could hope to show that any construction which has a given property must of necessity contain a certain core. It is not clear that such will always be possible. For instance, the two known models separating Decidable Fan from c-Fan [1,13] are very different from each other, making it unclear that in that case there is a common core to that separation. No doubt in other cases there is a common core. This is all left for future work.

Regarding the meta-theory used here, if push comes to shove it is taken to be ZFC. To illustrate why, at one point we come up with an ultrafilter, which is known to require a certain amount of Choice. There are constructive work-arounds to ultrafilters, so no doubt matters could be re-formulated and done more carefully to stay within constructive set theory. That is not the purpose of this paper.

This section continues with a brief introduction to topological models in general, and a summary of the principles we will be analyzing. Each of the next three sections extracts a topological consequence from a separation of those principles. The final section suggests some possibilities for future work along these lines, especially in connection with BD-N.

Thanks are to be given to Matt Hendtlass, who was the inspiration for this work. He came up with the idea for this project, and proved the chronologically first theorem, Theorem 2 here. May he come back!

1.1   Topological Models

Forcing in set theory can be described as Boolean-valued models, built over complete Boolean algebras. The reason that Boolean algebras are used here is that they exactly characterize classical logic. If what you want is instead constructive logic, the appropriate structures are Heyting algebras. Heyting-valued models, built over complete Heyting algebras (cHa's), can be developed just like Boolean-valued models. The open sets of a topological space form a cHa; the Heyting-valued model built over such a cHa is called a topological model. The opens of a topological space form what is called a spatial Heyting algebra; not every cHa is spatial. Although there is a prior history of topological semantics, Heyting-valued semantics for set theory were fully developed in [3]; a more recent and perhaps more accessible account for topological models is given in [4], which also contains most of the independence proofs referenced in this paper. To help make this current work more self-contained, the basic definitions of these models from the latter paper are given below.

Topological models are Heyting valued models where the complete Heyting algebra is the lattice of opens $\mathcal{O}_T$ of a topological space T. Meet and join in $\mathcal{O}_T$ are given by intersection and union respectively, while the psuedo-complement $\rightarrow$ is defined by

$$\mathcal{U} \rightarrow \mathcal{V} \equiv (-\mathcal{U} \cup \mathcal{V})^\circ,$$

where $-\mathcal{U}$ denotes the complement of $\mathcal{U}$ in T and $\mathcal{W}^\circ$ denotes the interior of $\mathcal{W}$. The *full topological model* over T consists of the class of *names* or *terms*, defined inductively by

$$V_\alpha(T) = \mathcal{P}\left(\bigcup\{V_\nu(T) \times \mathcal{O}_T : \nu \in \alpha\}\right),$$
$$V(T) = \bigcup_{\alpha \in \mathrm{ORD}} V_\alpha(T).$$

Given $\sigma \in V_\alpha(T)$, the meaning of $\langle \tau, \mathcal{U} \rangle \in \sigma$ is that $\mathcal{U}$ is the degree of truth, or truth-value, of τ being in σ. (Of course, the ultimate value of $\tau \in \sigma$ might be greater than $\mathcal{U}$, depending on what else is in σ.) The idea of the full model is to throw in absolutely everything you can. We will have occasion to look at sub-models of the full model. An embedding $\check{\ }$ of the ground model V into $V(T)$ is defined inductively by

$$\check{a} = \{< \check{b}, T >: b \in a\}.$$

The truth value of any proposition A, with parameters from $V(T)$, is an open subset of T and is denoted by $[\![A]\!]$. To say that a proposition A is *true*, or *satisfied*, in a topological model M_T over T means $[\![A]\!] = T$, otherwise A is said to fail in M_T. Being false in M_T is a stronger property: A is said to be *false* in M_T if M_T satisfies $\neg A$, or equivalently $[\![A]\!] = \emptyset$. We freely switch between truth value notation $[\![\cdot]\!]$ for topological models and forcing notation: a point $x \in T$ *forces* a formula A, written $x \Vdash A$, if and only if $x \in [\![A]\!]$, and, for an open subset $\mathcal{U}$ of T, $\mathcal{U} \Vdash A$ if and only if $\mathcal{U} \subset [\![A]\!]$.

A particularly important object, the *generic*, in a topological model M_T is described by the name

$$G = \{< \check{\mathcal{U}}, \mathcal{U} >: \mathcal{U} \in \mathcal{O}_T\}.$$

Strictly speaking, the generic contains as its members open sets from the ground model, being characterised by

$$\mathcal{U} \Vdash \check{\mathcal{U}} \in G$$

for all $\mathcal{U} \in \mathcal{O}_T$. In practice though, it is more useful to think of the generic as a new element of the topological space over which we are forcing. A point in a Hausdorff space is determined by its open neighborhoods, and so could be thought of as the set consisting of all of those neighborhoods. Similarly, in the other direction, $\check{\mathcal{U}} \in G$ can fruitfully be thought of as $G \in \mathcal{U}$. Of course, since G is not in the ground model, $G \in \check{\mathcal{U}}$ is just false. Instead, one may think of $\mathcal{U}$

as being given by a description, and then "$G \in \mathcal{U}$" would mean that G satisfies this description, as interpreted in the extension. For instance, if $\mathcal{T}$ is the reals, then $\mathcal{U}$ might be the interval (p, q) with rational endpoints; G could be thought of as a generic real number, and $\mathcal{U} \in G$ could be read as meaning $p < G < q$.

IZF, Intuitionistic ZF, is a ZF-style axiomatization of set theory using constructive logic, which is equivalent with ZF under classical logic.

Theorem 1. *(Grayson) Topological models preserve IZF; that is, IZF proves that the full topological model $V(\mathcal{T})$ satisfies the axioms of IZF.*

1.2 Summary of Constructive Principles

- BD-N: Every countable, pseudo-bounded set of natural numbers is bounded.
- LLPO, the Lesser Limited Principle of Omniscience: Every binary sequence with at most one 1 has either all the even slots 0 or all the odds 0.
- LPO, the Limited Principle of Omniscience: Every binary sequence is either all 0s or has a 1 in it.
- MP, Markov's Principle: If it is impossible for every value in a binary sequence to be 0, then there is one value which is 1.
- WLEM, the Weak Law of the Excluded Middle: For any proposition A, either $\neg A$ or $\neg\neg A$.
- WLEM$_\omega$: For any countable sequence of propositions, if it is impossible that for any distinct pair of them both are true, then one of them must be false;
  $\neg \bigvee_{i,j \in \omega, i \neq j} A_i \wedge A_j \rightarrow \bigvee_i \neg A_i$.
- WMP, Weak Markov's Principle:

$$\forall \gamma \, [\forall \beta \, (\neg\neg\exists n \, (\beta(n) = 1) \vee \neg\neg\exists n \, (\gamma(n) = 1 \wedge \beta(n) = 0)) \rightarrow \exists n \, \gamma(n) = 1].$$

2 The Coarse Topology on ω^+

The first example we will consider may as well be the simplest. Let ω^+ be $\omega \cup \{*\}$. We extend the discrete topology on ω (under which every set is open) in the coarsest possible way to ω^+ by letting the entire space be the only open neighborhood of $*$. When we refer to ω^+ as a topological space, we mean this *coarse topology*.

The Limited Principle of Omniscience, LPO, states that every binary sequence is either all 0s or has a 1 in it. A weakening of the Weak Law of the Excluded Middle, WLEM$_\omega$ is the assertion that, for any countable sequence of propositions, if it is impossible that for any distinct pair of them both are true, then one of them must be false.

It is shown in [4], Theorem 4.1, that LPO does not imply WLEM$_\omega$, by showing that in the topological model over ω^+ LPO holds while $*$ does not force WLEM$_\omega$ (meaning no neighborhood of $*$ forces as much). We show that any topological space with a point not forcing WLEM$_\omega$ induces ω^+.

Theorem 2. *If $x \in \mathcal{T}$ and $x \not\Vdash WLEM_\omega$ then a quotient space of $\mathcal{T}$ is isomorphic to ω^+.*

Proof. By the failure of WLEM$_\omega$ at x, there is a neighborhood $\mathcal{O}$ of x and a sequence of A_i $(i \in \omega)$ of propositions such that $\mathcal{O}$ forces that no pair A_i, A_j $(i \neq j)$ are both true, but $\mathcal{O}$ does not force that one is false. Without loss of generality we take each open set $[\![A_i]\!]$, which is best thought of as the truth value of A_i, to be a subset of $\mathcal{O}$, since we could replace $[\![A_i]\!]$ by $[\![A_i]\!] \cap \mathcal{O}$. Since $\mathcal{O}$ forces no pair to be true, $[\![A_i]\!] \cap [\![A_j]\!] = \emptyset$. Since $\mathcal{O}$ does not force one to be false, the union $\bigcup_i [\![\neg A_i]\!]$ is not all of $\mathcal{O}$. So there is some point, let's call it ∞, which is in no $[\![\neg A_i]\!]$. That means that ∞ is in the closure of each $[\![A_i]\!]$. Furthermore, ∞ is in no $[\![A_i]\!]$, since the closure of $[\![A_j]\!]$ is the smallest closed set containing $[\![A_j]\!]$, and one such closed set is the complement of $[\![A_i]\!]$. So ∞ is in the boundary of each $[\![A_i]\!]$. Take the quotient space that sends all of $[\![A_i]\!]$ to one point, call it i, and everything not in any $[\![A_i]\!]$ to $*$. Notice that ∞ goes to $*$. In the quotient topology, each i is open, because its inverse image is $[\![A_i]\!]$. Now consider a set X containing $*$ and missing some i. The inverse image of X contains ∞, which is in the boundary of $[\![A_i]\!]$, yet is disjoint from $[\![A_i]\!]$, and so is not open. That yields that the only possible open neighborhood of $*$ cannot miss any i. Trivially, the inverse image of the entire quotient is all of $\mathcal{T}$, and so the quotient space is open. Hence the quotient space is ω^+.   □

3   The Necessity of Ultrafilters

Theorem 5.1 of [4] is that WLEM does not imply WMP, Weak Markov's Principle. The topological model that is used for this is based on a non-principal ultrafilter of ω. This is unsettling, because the existence of ultrafilters needs some amount of Choice, but the independence of WMP from WLEM should not depend on Choice. Are the ultrafilters just a trick which happens to work? Or are they somehow fundamental to the questions at hand?

   In the following, we will work with LLPO, which follows from WLEM, and LPO, from which WMP follows. LLPO, the Lesser Limited Principle of Omniscience, states that every binary sequence with at most one 1 has either all the even slots 0 or all the odds 0. The construction that WLEM does not imply WMP yields trivially that LLPO does not imply LPO.

Lemma 1. *A point x in a topological space $\mathcal{T}$ does not force LPO if and only if there exists a sequence $(C_n)_{n \in \omega}$ of clopen subsets of $\mathcal{T}$ such that*

$$x \notin \left(\bigcap_{n \in \omega} C_n\right)^{\circ} \cup \bigcup_{n \in \omega} -C_n.$$

Proof. Let α be a counterexample to LPO at x. (Without loss of generality, $\mathcal{T} \Vdash \alpha \in 2^\omega$.) Let C_n be $[\![\alpha(n) = 0]\!]$. Then $\left(\bigcap_{n \in \omega} C_n\right)^{\circ} \Vdash \forall n\ \alpha(n) = 0$, while $\bigcup_{n \in \omega} -C_n \Vdash \exists n\ \alpha(n) = 1$; whence x is in neither of these sets.

   In the other direction, given such a sequence C_n, define α to be the term such that $[\![\alpha(n) = 0]\!] = C_n$.   □

We will call a topological space an *ultrafilter topology on* ω if (up to home-omorphism) the underlying set is $\omega \cup \{*\}$, the subspace ω carries the discrete topology, and for some ultrafilter $\mathcal{U}$, the neighborhoods of $*$ are of the form $\{*\} \cup u$ where $u \in \mathcal{U}$.

Theorem 3. *If* $x \in \mathcal{T}$ *forces LLPO and not LPO, then a subset of* $\mathcal{T}$ *has a quotient space with an ultrafilter topology on* ω.

Proof. Since x does not force LPO, let $\mathcal{C}_n$ be a sequence of clopens as in the previous lemma. Without loss of generality we can take $\mathcal{C}_0$ to be $\mathcal{T}$ and the sequence to be strictly decreasing: $\mathcal{C}_0 \supsetneq \mathcal{C}_1 \supsetneq \ldots$. Of course, $\bigcap_{n \in \omega} \mathcal{C}_n$ has a non-empty boundary, because it contains x in particular. In the following construction, anything else in the boundary might be trouble (an example follows the proof). So consider the subspace of $\mathcal{T}$ with those other points removed. In other words, we want $\bigcap_{n \in \omega} \mathcal{C}_n \backslash \{x\}$ to be open. We recycle notation, and call this subspace $\mathcal{T}$ also.

Let $\mathcal{O}_n$ be $\mathcal{C}_n \backslash \mathcal{C}_{n+1}$. Notice $\bigcup_{n \in \omega} \mathcal{O}_n = \mathcal{T} \backslash \bigcap_{n \in \omega} \mathcal{C}_n$. Let f send $\mathcal{O}_n$ to n and $\bigcap_{n \in \omega} \mathcal{C}_n$ to $*$. We claim that the induced quotient topology on $\omega \cup \{*\}$ is an ultrafilter topology.

For starters, ω carries the discrete topology, because each $\mathcal{O}_n$ is (clopen and therefore in particular) open. As for neighborhoods of $*$, first, $\{*\} \cup \omega$ is open because its inverse image is all of $\mathcal{T}$. Also, $\{*\}$ is not open because its inverse image is $\bigcap_{n \in \omega} \mathcal{C}_n$, which contains x as a member, but x is not in the interior. As for closure under intersection, if the inverse images of both $\{*\} \cup u$ and $\{*\} \cup v$ are open, then the inverse image of $\{*\} \cup (u \cap v)$ is open, being the intersection of two open sets.

Finally, suppose $v = \omega \backslash u$. We must show the inverse image of either $\{*\} \cup u$ or $\{*\} \cup v$ is open. We can safely assume both u and v are infinite. Let g and h enumerate u and v respectively. Let α be such that $[\![\alpha(2n) = 1]\!] = \mathcal{O}_{g(n)}$ and $[\![\alpha(2n+1) = 1]\!] = \mathcal{O}_{h(n)}$. Since x forces LLPO, some neighborhood of x, say $\mathcal{N}$, forces either all of α's even entries or all of α's odds to be 0. Say it's the evens. Then $\mathcal{N}$ is a subset of the inverse image of $\{*\} \cup v$. Hence the latter set is itself open, being the union of $\mathcal{N}$ with the open sets $\mathcal{O}_{h(n)}$ and $\left(\bigcap_{n \in \omega} \mathcal{C}_n \right)^{\circ}$. $\qquad \square$

To see why we had to throw the boundary points away, consider the following variant of the ultrafilter topology on ω. The underlying set is $\omega \cup \{*, \perp\}$, the neighborhoods of $*$ are as before, and the neighborhoods of $\perp$ include $*$ and a cofinite subset of ω. If $\perp$ is not thrown away, the ultrafilter is obscured.

4 The Necessity of Non-ultra Filters

While the previous section focused on ultrafilters, some of the constructions of [4], while being based on filters, pointedly do not use maximal filters. This is clearest in the one model of Theorem 5.6 (WMP does not imply $\mathrm{MP}_{\omega}^{\vee}$) which uses the Fréchet filter. There are, however, other models presented there, namely in Theorems 5.2, 5.7, and 5.8, which look a bit different from each other, while all ultimately using non-maximal (a.k.a. non-ultra) filters, even though that latter fact is not flagged there. Is there a commonality that binds them all together?

In the following, we will need:

- MP (Markov's Principle): If it is impossible for all terms of α to be zero, then there exists an n such that $\alpha(n) = 1$.

We will also need:

- WMP (Weak Markov's Principle):

$$\forall \gamma \, [\forall \beta \, (\neg\neg\exists n \, (\beta(n) = 1) \vee \neg\neg\exists n \, (\gamma(n) = 1 \wedge \beta(n) = 0)) \rightarrow \exists n \, \gamma(n) = 1].$$

(The aforementioned $MP_\omega^\vee$ is a weakening of MP which we will not use here.)

Theorem 4. *At a point ∞ in a topological space T, if $\infty \Vdash WMP$ and $\infty \nVdash MP$ then it is dense at ∞ that there is a quotient space which is homeomorphic to a non-principal non-ultra filter topology on ω.*

(To say that property P holds densely at point x means that every open set containing x has an open subset satisfying P. For $\mathcal{F}$ a filter on ω, the induced filter topology on $\omega \cup \{*\}$ is discrete on ω and has as neighborhoods of $*$ all sets of the form $u \cup \{*\}$ for $u \in \mathcal{F}$.)

Proof. $\infty \nVdash$ MP iff for all $\mathcal{O}$ containing ∞, $\mathcal{O} \nVdash$ MP. Unpacking the definition of $\Vdash$, we get that for some $\hat{\mathcal{O}} \subseteq \mathcal{O}$ and α, $\hat{\mathcal{O}} \Vdash \alpha$ is a binary sequence, $\hat{\mathcal{O}} \Vdash \neg\forall n \, \alpha(n) = 0$, yet $\hat{\mathcal{O}} \nVdash \exists n \, \alpha(n) = 1$. Working within $\hat{\mathcal{O}}$, let $\mathcal{C}_n$ be $[\![\alpha(n) = 0]\!]$. Since α is forced not to be the 0 sequence, $\bigcap_{n \in \omega} \mathcal{C}_n$ has an empty interior. At the same time, $\bigcap_{n \in \omega} \mathcal{C}_n$ is non-empty, as follows. If that intersection were empty, then each $x \in \hat{\mathcal{O}}$ is in the complement of some $\mathcal{C}_n$. Each $\mathcal{C}_n$ is clopen, so this complement is open, and forces $\exists n \, \alpha(n) = 1$. Hence $\hat{\mathcal{O}}$ is covered by open sets each forcing $\exists n \, \alpha(n) = 1$, and so $\hat{\mathcal{O}}$ forces the same. This contradicts the choice of $\hat{\mathcal{O}}$ and α.

Let $\mathcal{O}_n$ be $(\hat{\mathcal{O}} \backslash \mathcal{C}_n) \backslash (\bigcup_{k<n} \mathcal{O}_k)$. Because each $\mathcal{C}_n$ is clopen, so is each $\mathcal{O}_n$. Notice that $\mathcal{O}_n$ is the truth-value of "n is the first place where α is 1;" as is often the case, once we have an occurrence of 1 in α our work is done, and it's easier to focus on the first such occurrence. If only finitely many of the $\mathcal{O}_n$'s were non-empty, then their union $\bigcup_n \mathcal{O}_n$ would be a union of finitely many clopen sets, hence itself clopen. That would make the complement of $\bigcup_n \mathcal{O}_n$ also clopen. But that complement is $\bigcap_n \mathcal{C}_n$, which we have seen is non-empty with empty interior, and so cannot be clopen. We conclude that infinitely many of the $\mathcal{O}_n$'s are non-empty. By thinning the sequence of $\mathcal{O}_n$'s by eliminating those that are empty, we can assume without loss of generality that each $\mathcal{O}_n$ is non-empty.

Consider the function f which sends each point in $\mathcal{O}_n$ to n and the rest of $\hat{\mathcal{O}}$ to $*$. This epimorphism induces a corresponding quotient space topology on $\omega \cup \{*\}$. Because each $\mathcal{O}_n$ is clopen, the quotient topology on ω is the discrete topology. We need only concern ourselves with neighborhoods of $*$.

Toward this end, let $\mathcal{F}$ be $\{u \subseteq \omega \mid u \cup \{*\}$ is open in the quotient topology$\}$, meaning that its inverse image under f is open in $\hat{\mathcal{O}}$. We will show first that $\mathcal{F}$ is a non-principal filter.

For starters, $\emptyset \notin \mathcal{F}$, because the inverse image of $*$ is $\bigcap_n \mathcal{C}_n$, which is not open. Also, $\mathcal{F}$ is closed upwards: if $v \supseteq u \in \mathcal{F}$, then the inverse image of $v \cup \{*\}$ is the union of the inverse image of $u \cup \{*\}$ with some open sets. Furthermore, $\mathcal{F}$ is closed under intersections, because the inverse image of an intersection is the intersection of the inverse images, and the intersection of open sets is open. Hence $\mathcal{F}$ is a filter. Because each $\mathcal{O}_n$ is clopen, $\mathcal{F}$ contains each co-finite set, and so is not principal.

The construction above could be applied to any open $\mathcal{O}' \subseteq \hat{\mathcal{O}}$ as long as $\mathcal{O}'$ contains some point from $\bigcap_n \mathcal{C}_n$ (by considering the sequence $\mathcal{O}' \cap \mathcal{O}_n$). If there is some such $\mathcal{O}'$ where the induced filter $\mathcal{F}$ is not an ultrafilter then we are done. Hence assume there is no such, which we will call the ultrafilter assumption, toward a contradiction.

Let γ be such that $[\![\gamma(n) = 1]\!] = \mathcal{O}_n$. Effectively, γ is α up until the first 1, and then 0 thereafter. Because WMP was forced by $\mathcal{O}$, we can apply WMP to γ. We will show that $\hat{\mathcal{O}}$ forces the hypothesis of WMP, so that $\hat{\mathcal{O}}$ forces γ to have a 1 somewhere. Then $\hat{\mathcal{O}}$ will force α to have a 1 somewhere, the desired contradiction.

So let $\bar{\mathcal{O}} \subseteq \hat{\mathcal{O}}$ force β to be a binary sequence. Let $\bar{\beta}$ be such that $[\![\bar{\beta}(n) = 1]\!] = [\![\beta(n) = 1]\!] \cap \mathcal{O}_n$. The purpose of $\bar{\beta}$ is that, if anything, it is even more difficult to verify the hypothesis of WMP on $\bar{\beta}$ than it is on β. After all, the value at any n of $[\![\bar{\beta}(n) = 1]\!]$ is a subset of that of $[\![\beta(n) = 1]\!]$, so it is more difficult to make the first disjunct true for $\bar{\beta}$ than for β. Regarding the second disjunct, the value $[\![\beta(n) = 1 \wedge \bar{\beta}(n) = 0]\!]$ is disjoint from $\mathcal{O}_n$, meaning $[\![\beta(n) = 1 \wedge \bar{\beta}(n) = 0]\!] \Vdash \gamma(n) = 0$, hence if the second disjunct holds for $\bar{\beta}$ then it also does for β. We conclude that if we can show $\bar{\mathcal{O}}$ forces the hypothesis of WMP on $\bar{\beta}$, we will have shown the same for β.

There are two cases to consider: $\bar{\mathcal{O}}$ is disjoint from $\bigcap_n \mathcal{C}_n$, or it's not. In the former case, $\bar{\mathcal{O}}$ is covered by the disjoint clopens $\bar{\mathcal{O}} \cap \mathcal{O}_n$, each of which itself is the disjoint union of the clopens $\bar{\mathcal{O}} \cap \mathcal{O}_n \cap [\![\bar{\beta}(n) = 1]\!]$ and $\bar{\mathcal{O}} \cap \mathcal{O}_n \cap [\![\bar{\beta}(n) = 0]\!]$. The former set forces $\exists n\ \bar{\beta}(n) = 1$, and the latter $\exists n\ \gamma(n) = 1 \wedge \beta(n) = 0$, which suffices.

For the second case, we get to use the ultrafilter hypothesis. Work within $\bar{\mathcal{O}}$. (That means, for instance, reference to $\mathcal{O}_n$ implicitly means $\mathcal{O}_n \cap \bar{\mathcal{O}}$.) Let $\mathcal{N}_0$ be $\{n \mid \mathcal{O}_n \Vdash \bar{\beta}(n) = 0\}$, $\mathcal{N}_1$ be $\{n \mid \mathcal{O}_n \Vdash \bar{\beta}(n) = 1\}$, and $\mathcal{N}_2$ be the naturals in neither $\mathcal{N}_0$ nor $\mathcal{N}_1$. The $\mathcal{N}_i$'s form a partition of the natural numbers, hence one is in the ultrafilter. That means the inverse image $\mathcal{U}_i$ of some $\mathcal{N}_i \cup \{*\}$ is open. Suppose first that is the case for $i = 0$. Notice that the inverse image of $\mathcal{N}_0$ forces $\exists n\ \gamma(n) = 1 \wedge \beta(n) = 0$. Let x be any other point of $\mathcal{U}_0$, meaning x is in $\bigcap_n \mathcal{C}_n$. If $\mathcal{V}$ is an open set containing x, then $\mathcal{V} \cap \mathcal{U}_0$ must contain a point in some $\mathcal{O}_n$ with $n \in \mathcal{N}_0$, lest $\mathcal{V} \subseteq \bigcap_n \mathcal{C}_n$, whereas the latter set has empty interior. Hence $\mathcal{V} \cap \mathcal{U}_0$ forces the second disjunct (in the hypothesis of WMP). Similarly if $i = 1$ or 2. $\square$

5   BD-N and Future Directions

The principles studied above, although about sequences, are really logical principles, because they are about binary sequences. A natural extension is to include
similar analyses for analytic principles. Examples abound: whether the Cauchy
and Dedekind reals are equal [2], the Fundamental Theorem of Algebra [2,11],
the Fan Theorem [2,13], BD-N [12]. As it turns out, this is more difficult than
the current study of logical principles. Perhaps that is only to be expected, since
principles of analysis are more complicated. Be that as it may, the following is a
summary of what is known in one case, namely BD-N. The purpose of discussing
these failed attempts is to convey to the interested reader a sense of the difficulties, and to provide a springboard for future researchers. This section then
concludes with some other open questions.

By way of background, a set (of natural numbers) is **pseudo-bounded**
if every sequence (a_n) of its members is eventually bounded by the identity
sequence (i.e. for n large enough $a_n < n$). **BD-N** is the principle that every
countable pseudo-bounded set is bounded [5–7]. In [12], it was shown that the
model built over the space $\mathcal{T}$ of bounded sequences, suitably topologized, falsifies
BD-N: $\mathcal{T} \Vdash G$ is pseudo-bounded yet unbounded (where G is the generic). This
failure is strong in that there is one counter-example that works for the whole
space, and that this counter-example is not merely not forced to be bounded,
which would ultimately come down to a single point, but rather that it is posi-
tively forced to be unbounded, and that, again, by the whole space.

To get a model in which BD-N fails, it would seem as though some kind
of completeness is necessary, because if you take either the space of eventually constant sequences, or the space of bounded but never eventually constant
sequences, the generic is no longer pseudo-bounded. (The sequence that picks
out the next pair of identical entries, or the next change in the sequence, can
be leveraged to contradict pseudo-boundedness.) On the other hand, in the successful space in [12], if you remove just one point, you violate completeness, but
what's left is covered by open sets of the original space, each of which forces
¬BD-N. So the role of completeness is unclear.

It is easy to find ways to change the space so it is no longer precisely the
bounded sequences, but it may as well be, in that the bounded sequences are easily recovered from the space. For instance, take the set of always positive bounded
sequences – don't allow 0 as a value. Trivially, by shifting everything down one,
you re-create the bounded sequences. Or the space of bounded sequences in
which every entry indexed by an odd number is equal to the entry just before
(i.e. $\alpha(2n) = \alpha(2n + 1)$). By identifying each odd entry with its predecessor,
again one re-captures the bounded sequences. Clearly one could come up with
more complicated variants of these. What's not so clear is just how they would
be identified and how one could give a general procedure to extract exactly
the bounded sequences. Or, for that matter, since it's not exactly the bounded
sequences we need, how to give the general property of a space which would
make it violate BD-N.

This then leads to a general project: find a good theorem about topological spaces violating, or for that matter satisfying, BD-N; more generally, find such for other principles of analysis.

Even for logical principles, there is still more to be done. For instance, analyze some principles not studied here. Even for the ones in this paper, the theorems could be improved. For instance, the theorems proved here are implications; it would be nice to see iff's, perhaps of course calling for a tighter property.

Some logical principles, given about binary sequences, have real number correlates. For instance, assuming for instance DC, LPO is equivalent with the decidability of equality on the reals. Also, again under DC, LLPO is equivalent with the linearity of the ordering of the reals. It would be interesting to compare the requirements and restrictions on topological spaces for corresponding pairs of principles.

References

1. Diener, H., Lubarsky, R.: Separating the fan theorem and its weakenings. J. Symbolic Logic **79**(3), 792–813 (2014). https://doi.org/10.1017/jsl.2014.9
2. Fourman, M.P., Hyland, J.M.E.: Sheaf models for analysis. In: Fourman, M., Mulvey, C., Scott, D. (eds.) Applications of Sheaves. LNM, vol. 753, pp. 280–301. Springer, Heidelberg (1979). https://doi.org/10.1007/BFb0061823
3. Grayson, R.J.: Heyting-valued semantics, in Logic Colloquium '82. Stud. Logic Found. Math. **112**, 181–208 (1984)
4. Hendtlass, M., Lubarsky, R.: Separating fragments of WLEM, LPO, and MP. J. Symbolic Logic **81**(4), 1315–1343 (2016). https://doi.org/10.1017/jsl.2016.38
5. Ishihara, H.: Continuity and nondiscontinuity in constructive mathematics. J. Symbolic Logic **56**, 1349–1354 (1991)
6. Ishihara, H.: Continuity properties in constructive mathematics. J. Symbolic Logic **57**, 557–565 (1992)
7. Ishihara, H., Schuster, P.: A continuity principle, a version of Baire's theorem and a boundedness principle. J. Symbolic Logic **73**(4), 1354–1360 (2008)
8. Set Theory. Springer Monographs in Mathematics, Springer, 3rd edition (2006)
9. Krivine, J.-L.: Typed lambda-calculus in classical Zermelo-Fraenkel set theory. Arch. Math. Logic **40**(3), 189–205 (2001)
10. Krivine, J.-L.: Dependent choice, 'quote' and the clock. Theoret. Comput. Sci. **308**, 259–276 (2003)
11. Lubarsky, R.: Geometric spaces with no points. J. Logic Anal. **2**(6), 1–10 (2010). https://doi.org/10.4115/jla2010.2.6. http://logicandanalysis.org/
12. Lubarsky, R.: On the failure of BD-N and BD, and an application to the anti-Specker property. J. Symbolic Logic **78**(1), 39–56 (2013)
13. Lubarsky, R.: Separating the fan theorem and its weakenings II. J. Symbolic Logic **84**, 1484–1509 (2019). https://doi.org/10.1017/jsl.2019.1

On the Compatibility Between the Minimalist Foundation and Constructive Set Theory

Samuele Maschio$^{(\boxtimes)}$ and Pietro Sabelli

Dipartimento di Matematica "Tullio Levi-Civita", Università di Padova, Padua, Italy
maschio@math.unipd.it

Abstract. The Minimalist Foundation **MF** was ideated by M.E. Maietti and G. Sambin and then completed as a formal system by M.E. Maietti in order to provide a foundation for constructive mathematics compatible with the main classical and intuitionistic, predicative and impredicative, foundational theories. Here we show that **MF** is in fact compatible with Aczel's constructive set theory **CZF**. We prove this by extending the extensional level of **MF** with rules obtaining a system which turns out to be equivalent to **CZF**.

1 Introduction

Classical mathematics leans on a standard foundational theory, that is Zermelo-Fraenkel axiomatic set theory **ZF**. The situation in constructive mathematics is very different: there are many foundational theories in the literature and no one of them has already reached the privileged status of "standard".

Moreover, the foundational tendency in constructive mathematics changed after Bishop's work (see *A constructive Manifesto* in [4]). The modern view on constructivism is far from that of Brouwer's intuitionism or that of Russian computable mathematics. The notion of *compatibility* plays an important role nowadays: constructive mathematics is in fact understood by most mathematicians working in the field as ordinary mathematics done with intuitionistic logic and for this reason it must lay in a common core between classical mathematics, Brouwer's intuitionism and Russian computable mathematics. In particular, a foundational theory corresponding to such a notion of constructivism should be itself a common core between the main classical and intuitionistic, predicative and impredicative foundational theories available in the literature; intuitively, such a foundational theory should admit interpretations in the other ones preserving logic and the intended meaning of set-theoretical constructors. Maietti and Sambin in [9] identified properties that such a common core foundation should satisfy for meeting this requirement. Later in [8] Maietti proposed a precise foundational theory, called *Minimalist Foundation* (for short **MF**), satisfying these properties. The formal system **MF** consists of two levels formulated as dependent type theories: the intensional level **mTT** and the extensional level **emTT** connected by a setoid model of the second in the first. The intensional level should be an account of all the computational aspects of the theory, while the extensional level is the one in which ordinary mathematics should be performed. In particular, **mTT** is compatible (see [8]) with type theoretic foundations like Martin-Löf type theory [10] and Coquand's Calculus of Constructions [5], while **emTT** should be compatible with axiomatic set-theoretical foundations. In [8] an argument for the compatibility of **emTT** with Aczel's constructive Zermelo-Fraenkel set theory **CZF** in [3] is sketched. In this paper we want to make precise that statement by showing that **emTT** is compatible with **CZF** in a strong sense. We will in fact extend **emTT** with some rules, obtaining a type theory **emTT**$_{CZF}$ equivalent to **CZF**. The theory **emTT**$_{CZF}$ can be seen as an envelope of **CZF** embodying (meta)theoretical concepts of set theory like those of definable class, definable set and Δ_0-formula.

The work done here has strict connections with Aczel's interpretation of constructive set theory in type theory [1] and Aczel and Gambino's one in [2]. Indeed, in [1] the author adds a "universe of sets" type to Martin-Löf type theory in order to provide a model of **CZF** in it. This idea is similar to our, but Martin-Löf type theory is quite different from the extensional level of the minimalist foundation. In **emTT** e.g. propositions-as-types does not hold. Our framework is instead more similar to that of [2] since type theory is enriched with logic there. This distinction is present also in **emTT**, although it lacks W-types and a universe, which are used in [2] to construct an interpretation for the universe of sets. There, indeed, the models are type theoretical renderings of a cumulative universe of sets, and cannot be adapted to models of impredicative set theories like **IZF** or **ZF**. On the contrary, our construction is modular in that it works also if we remove ε-induction, or if we add other principles in order to obtain impredicative theories equivalent, for example, to **IZF** or **ZF**. Eventually, apart from differences and analogies between our approach and those adopted in [2] and [1], the aim itself of this paper is very different: our goal is not the definition of a model of set theory in **emTT**, but rather an extension of **emTT** equivalent to **CZF**.

The extensional level **emTT** of the Minimalist Foundation in [8] is formulated as a variant of Martin-Löf type theory in [7]. First, **emTT** contains four kinds of types (small propositions, propositions, sets and collections) which allow to keep a distinction between logical and mathematical entities and different degrees of complexity: **small propositions** include the falsum constant and propositional identities of terms in sets, and are closed under connectives and quantifiers with respect to sets; **propositions** include all small propositions and propositional identities, and are closed under connectives and quantifiers; **sets** include the empty set N_0, a singleton set N_1, all small propositions and are closed under constructors Σ, Π, $+$, List and under quotients of sets with respect to small propositional equivalence relations. Each set and each proposition is a collection and **collections** are closed under Σ and include power-collections of sets. In particular, every type turns out to be a collection in **emTT**. A crucial characteristic of **emTT** is the fact that elimination rules of propositional constructors act only toward propositions; for this reason the axiom of choice is not a theorem of **emTT**. Moreover, propositions are proof-irrelevant, that is every term of a proposition is equal to a canonical term true. Propositional identities reflect definitional equalities and extensionality of functions holds. Finally, in **emTT** the construction of W-types is not available and there are no universes. For sake of readability we will write $a =_A b$ instead of $\mathsf{Eq}(A, a, b)$.

2   An Alternative Presentation of CZF

Here we present Aczel's constructive set theory **CZF** (see [3]) using a language which is different from the usual one, but which is more suitable for our purposes. The language of **CZF** consists of terms and formulas, including a subclass of Δ_0-formulas, and is defined as the following grammar, where φ and ψ are metavariables for formulas, φ_0 and ψ_0 for Δ_0-formulas, a, b for terms, and x for a variable that does not appear free in a.

$$\text{terms} ::= x \mid \emptyset \mid \omega \mid \{a, b\} \mid \bigcup a \mid \{x \,\varepsilon\, a \mid \varphi_0\}$$

$$\text{formulas} ::= \bot \mid a = b \mid a \,\varepsilon\, b \mid \varphi \to \psi \mid \varphi \land \psi \mid \varphi \lor \psi \mid \forall x \varphi \mid \exists x \varphi$$

$$\Delta_0\text{-formulas} ::= \bot \mid a = b \mid a \,\varepsilon\, b \mid \varphi_0 \to \psi_0 \mid \varphi_0 \land \psi_0 \mid \varphi_0 \lor \psi_0$$
$$\mid \forall x (x \,\varepsilon\, a \to \varphi_0) \mid \exists x (x \,\varepsilon\, a \land \varphi_0)$$

Note that in a term of the form $\{x \,\varepsilon\, a \mid \varphi_0\}$ the variable x is bounded.

We use $\neg \varphi$, $\top$, $\varphi \leftrightarrow \psi$, $a \subseteq b$, $\exists! x \varphi$, $\exists x \,\varepsilon\, t \,\varphi$ and $\forall x \,\varepsilon\, t \,\varphi$ with their standard meaning. We will write 0 for $\emptyset$, 1 for $\{\emptyset\}$, $\{a\}$ for $\{a, a\}$, (a, b) for $\{\{a\}, \{a, b\}\}$, $a \cup b$ for $\bigcup\{a, b\}$, $p_1(a)$ for $\bigcup\{x \,\varepsilon\, \bigcup a \mid \forall y (y \,\varepsilon\, a \to x \,\varepsilon\, y)\}$, $p_2(a)$ for $\bigcup\{x \,\varepsilon\, \bigcup a \mid x = p_1(a) \to a = \{\{p_1(a)\}\}\}$, $\ell(a)$ for $\{x \,\varepsilon\, \omega \mid \exists y ((x, y) \,\varepsilon\, a)\}$ and $a^\frown b$ for $a \cup \{(\ell(a), b)\}$. The terms $p_1(a)$ and $p_2(a)$ represent the first and second component of a when a has the form (b, c); while, when a is a list (i.e. a function whose domain is a natural number), $\ell(a)$ represents the length of a and $a^\frown b$ represents the list obtained by appending b to a. We will use $\mathsf{Fun}(f)$ as an abbreviation for the formula which expresses the fact that f is a function:

$$\forall u (u \,\varepsilon\, f \to \exists v \exists w \, u = (v, w)) \land \forall v \forall w \forall w' ((v, w) \,\varepsilon\, f \land (v, w') \,\varepsilon\, f \to w = w')$$

When we think f as a function, we will write, $\mathsf{dom}(f)$ and $\mathsf{im}(f)$ to mean, respectively, $\{x \,\varepsilon\, \bigcup\bigcup f \mid \exists y \,\varepsilon\, \bigcup\bigcup f ((x, y) \,\varepsilon\, f)\}$ and $\{x \,\varepsilon\, \bigcup\bigcup f \mid \exists y \,\varepsilon\, \bigcup\bigcup f ((y, x) \,\varepsilon\, f)\}$, and we will write $f(a) = b$ as a shorthand for $(a, b) \,\varepsilon\, f$.

Besides the axioms and rules of intuitionistic first-order logic, the specific axioms of **CZF** are the universal closures of the following formulas:

1. $\forall z (z \,\varepsilon\, x \leftrightarrow z \,\varepsilon\, y) \to x = y$
2. $\neg (x \,\varepsilon\, \emptyset)$
3. $x \,\varepsilon\, \{y, z\} \leftrightarrow x = y \lor x = z$
4. $x \,\varepsilon\, \bigcup y \leftrightarrow \exists z (x \,\varepsilon\, z \land z \,\varepsilon\, y)$
5. $z \,\varepsilon\, \{x \,\varepsilon\, y \mid \varphi\} \leftrightarrow z \,\varepsilon\, y \land \varphi[z/x]$ for every Δ_0-formula φ

6. $0 \,\varepsilon\, \omega \wedge \forall x \,\varepsilon\, \omega(x \cup \{x\} \,\varepsilon\, \omega) \wedge \forall y(0 \,\varepsilon\, y \wedge \forall z \,\varepsilon\, y(z \cup \{z\} \,\varepsilon\, y) \to \omega \subseteq y)$

7. $(\forall x \,\varepsilon\, z \exists y \varphi) \to \exists w(\forall x \,\varepsilon\, z \exists y \,\varepsilon\, w \, \varphi \wedge \forall y \,\varepsilon\, w \exists x \,\varepsilon\, z \, \varphi)$ for every formula φ in which w is not free.

8. $\forall v \forall w \exists z \forall u(\forall x \,\varepsilon\, v \exists y \,\varepsilon\, w \, \varphi \to \exists z' \,\varepsilon\, z(\forall x \,\varepsilon\, v \exists y \,\varepsilon\, z' \, \varphi \wedge \forall y \,\varepsilon\, z' \exists x \,\varepsilon\, v \, \varphi))$ for every formula φ in which z is not free.

9. $\forall x(\forall y \,\varepsilon\, x \, \varphi[y/x] \to \varphi) \to \forall x \varphi$ for every formula φ in which y is not free.

The axiom schemas 7. and 8. above are called *strong collection* and *subset collection*, respectively. For further details on **CZF** the reader can refer to [3].

3 The Type Theory emTT$_{\mathbf{CZF}}$

We define the type theory **emTT**$_{\mathbf{CZF}}$ by adding rules to **emTT**. The idea behind this extension is that collections can be thought as definable classes of set theory, sets (of type theory) as definable classes which can be proven to be sets, while sets (of set theory) correspond to elements of a universal collection $\mathbf{V}$. Moreover, propositions of type theory will correspond to propositions of set theory, while small propositions will correspond to Δ_0-formulas. We will add the rules in four steps[1].

Step 1: Collections as definable classes

The first step consists in forcing the identification between collections and definable classes of set theory. We first introduce a universal collection $\mathbf{V}$[2]:

$$\frac{}{\mathbf{V}\,col} \qquad \frac{a \in A}{a \in \mathbf{V}}$$

We also need to norm the relation between definitional equality in an arbitrary collection and in the universal collection:

$$\frac{a = b \in A}{a = b \in \mathbf{V}} \qquad \frac{a \in A \quad b \in A \quad a = b \in \mathbf{V}}{a = b \in A} \qquad \frac{a \in A \quad b \in \mathbf{V} \quad a = b \in \mathbf{V}}{b \in A}$$

We require the definitional equality with respect to $\mathbf{V}$ to be a small proposition:

$$\frac{a \in \mathbf{V} \quad b \in \mathbf{V}}{a =_{\mathbf{V}} b \, prop_s}$$

We also need to introduce atomic small propositions representing set-theoretic membership and atomic propositions internalizing type-theoretic membership[3]:

$$\frac{a \in \mathbf{V} \quad b \in \mathbf{V}}{a \,\varepsilon\, b \, prop_s} \qquad \frac{a \in \mathbf{V} \quad A \, col}{a \,\varepsilon\, A \, prop} \qquad \frac{a \in A}{true \in a \,\varepsilon\, A} \qquad \frac{A \, col \quad true \in a \,\varepsilon\, A}{a \in A}$$

---

[1] Following the standard type-theoretic practice, we will omit the initial part of context common to all judgments in the premises and conclusion of each rule.

[2] We recall that, in each of the following rules, we never need to declare a type to be a collection, since in **emTT** any type can be proven to be a collection.

[3] Although we will use the same symbol ε for these two atomic propositions, the premises of each rule involving them will always unravel any possible ambiguity.

These constructors must be well-behaved with respect to definitional equality:

$$\frac{a = a' \in \mathbf{V} \qquad b = b' \in \mathbf{V}}{a \,\varepsilon\, b = a' \,\varepsilon\, b' \, prop_s} \qquad \frac{a = a' \in \mathbf{V} \qquad A = A' \, col}{a \,\varepsilon\, A = a' \,\varepsilon\, A' \, prop}$$

We introduce now a new constructor which allows us to form collections by comprehension, that is, to include definable classes among collections, together with a rule describing the relationship between the new constructor and propositional membership, and a rule of extensional equality for collections:

$$\frac{\varphi \, prop \, [x \in \mathbf{V}]}{\{x \mid \varphi\} \, col}$$

$$\frac{\varphi \, prop \, [x \in \mathbf{V}] \qquad a \in \mathbf{V}}{\mathsf{true} \in \varphi[a/x] \leftrightarrow a \,\varepsilon\, \{x \mid \varphi\}} \qquad \frac{\mathsf{true} \in (\forall x \in \mathbf{V})(x \,\varepsilon\, A \leftrightarrow x \,\varepsilon\, B)}{A = B \, col}$$

The previous rules will, in turn, force the desired identification between collections and definable classes. Indeed, from the last two rules, one can derive the following:

$$\frac{A \, col}{A = \{x \mid x \,\varepsilon\, A\} \, col}$$

Finally, we add the following four rules describing bounded quantifiers in terms of quantifiers over the universal collection $\mathbf{V}$.

$$\frac{\varphi \, prop \, [x \in A]}{x \,\varepsilon\, A \wedge \varphi \, prop \, [x \in \mathbf{V}]} \qquad \frac{\varphi \, prop \, [x \in A]}{\mathsf{true} \in (\exists x \in A)\varphi \leftrightarrow (\exists x \in \mathbf{V})(x \,\varepsilon\, A \wedge \varphi)}$$

$$\frac{\varphi \, prop \, [x \in A]}{x \,\varepsilon\, A \rightarrow \varphi \, prop \, [x \in \mathbf{V}]} \qquad \frac{\varphi \, prop \, [x \in A]}{\mathsf{true} \in (\forall x \in A)\varphi \leftrightarrow (\forall x \in \mathbf{V})(x \,\varepsilon\, A \rightarrow \varphi)}$$

The rules on the left side could look dangerous, since one could prove in $\mathbf{emTT_{CZF}}$ that $b \,\varepsilon\, A \rightarrow \varphi[b/x]$ is a proposition whenever $\varphi \, prop \, [x \in A]$ and $b \in \mathbf{V}$, without being able to prove $\varphi[b/x]$ to be itself a proposition. However, this is not a real problem, since one can never prove that $\varphi[b/x]$ is true applying the elimination rules of conjunction and implication without being able to prove that b is in A. In the practice of mathematics such expressions are nothing new, consider e.g. a proposition like $x \in \mathbb{N}^+ \rightarrow \frac{x}{x} = 1$, where the consequent $\frac{x}{x} = 1$ makes sense only if we already know that x is different from 0.

Step 2: Sets as definable sets

The next rules aim to identify type-theoretic sets with definable sets of $\mathbf{CZF}$.

First, a collection extensionally equal to an element of $\mathbf{V}$ is a set.

$$\frac{A \, col \qquad \mathsf{true} \in (\exists y \in \mathbf{V})(\forall x \in \mathbf{V})(x \,\varepsilon\, A \leftrightarrow x \,\varepsilon\, y)}{A \, set}$$

The converse is obtained by introducing a name in **V** for each definable set:

$$\frac{A\,set}{\lceil A\rceil \in \mathbf{V}} \qquad \frac{A\,set}{true \in (\forall x \in \mathbf{V})(x\,\varepsilon\,A \leftrightarrow x\,\varepsilon\,\lceil A\rceil)}$$

Finally, we add three rules which collapse all type definitional equalities to definitional equalities between collections.

$$\frac{A = B\,col \qquad A\,type \qquad B\,type}{A = B\,type} \qquad (\text{with } type \in \{set, prop, prop_s\})$$

Notice that, using names $\lceil A\rceil$ in **V**, it can be easily shown that if two collections are equal and one of them is a set, then the other one is a set too.

Step 3: Axiomatic set theory via the universal collection

In this step the axioms of set theory are embodied in the system via the universal collection **V**. We adopt here the usual abbreviations $\neg$ and $\leftrightarrow$.

$$\frac{a \in \mathbf{V} \qquad b \in \mathbf{V}}{true \in (\forall x \in \mathbf{V})(x\,\varepsilon\,a \leftrightarrow x\,\varepsilon\,b) \to a =_{\mathbf{V}} b}$$

$$\frac{}{\emptyset \in \mathbf{V}} \qquad \frac{a \in \mathbf{V} \qquad b \in \mathbf{V}}{\{a, b\} \in \mathbf{V}} \qquad \frac{a \in \mathbf{V}}{\bigcup a \in \mathbf{V}} \qquad \frac{a \in \mathbf{V}}{true \in \neg(a\,\varepsilon\,\emptyset)}$$

$$\frac{a \in \mathbf{V} \qquad b \in \mathbf{V} \qquad c \in \mathbf{V}}{true \in c\,\varepsilon\,\{a, b\} \leftrightarrow c =_{\mathbf{V}} a \vee c =_{\mathbf{V}} b} \qquad \frac{b \in \mathbf{V}}{true \in b\,\varepsilon\,\bigcup a \leftrightarrow (\exists x \in \mathbf{V})(b\,\varepsilon\,x \wedge x\,\varepsilon\,a)}$$

$$\frac{}{\omega \in \mathbf{V}} \qquad \frac{}{true \in \mathsf{Ind}(\omega)} \qquad \frac{a \in \mathbf{V}}{true \in a\,\varepsilon\,\omega \to (\forall y \in \mathbf{V})(\mathsf{Ind}(y) \to a\,\varepsilon\,y)}$$

where $\mathsf{Ind}(y)$ is an abbreviation for $\emptyset\,\varepsilon\,y \wedge (\forall z \in \mathbf{V})(z\,\varepsilon\,y \to \bigcup\{z, \{z, z\}\}\,\varepsilon\,y)$.

$$\frac{a \in \mathbf{V} \qquad \varphi\,prop\,[x \in \mathbf{V}]}{true \in (\forall x \in \mathbf{V})((\forall y \in \mathbf{V})(y\,\varepsilon\,x \to \varphi[y/x]) \to \varphi) \to \varphi[a/x]}$$

$$\frac{a \in \mathbf{V} \qquad \varphi\,prop_s\,[x \in \mathbf{V}]}{\{x\,\varepsilon\,a\,|\,\varphi\} \in \mathbf{V}} \qquad \frac{a \in \mathbf{V} \qquad \varphi\,prop_s\,[x \in \mathbf{V}] \qquad b \in \mathbf{V}}{true \in b\,\varepsilon\,\{x\,\varepsilon\,a\,|\,\varphi\} \leftrightarrow b\,\varepsilon\,a \wedge \varphi[b/x]}$$

$$\frac{\varphi\,prop\,[x \in \mathbf{V}, y \in \mathbf{V}, z \in \mathbf{V}]}{true \in \mathsf{SCol}(\varphi)}$$

where $\mathsf{SCol}(\varphi)$ is:

$$(\forall z \in \mathbf{V})[(\forall x \in \mathbf{V})(x\,\varepsilon\,z \to (\exists y \in \mathbf{V})\varphi) \to$$

$$(\exists w \in \mathbf{V})((\forall x \in \mathbf{V})(x\,\varepsilon\,z \to (\exists y \in \mathbf{V})(y\,\varepsilon\,w \wedge \varphi)) \wedge (\forall y \in \mathbf{V})(y\,\varepsilon\,w \to (\exists x \in \mathbf{V})(x\,\varepsilon\,z \wedge \varphi)))]$$

$$\frac{\varphi\,prop\,[x \in \mathbf{V}, y \in \mathbf{V}, z \in \mathbf{V}, v \in \mathbf{V}, w \in \mathbf{V}, u \in \mathbf{V}, z' \in \mathbf{V}]}{true \in \mathsf{SubCol}(\varphi)}$$

where $\mathsf{SubCol}(\varphi)$ is:

$$(\forall v \in \mathbf{V})(\forall w \in \mathbf{V})(\exists z \in \mathbf{V})(\forall u \in \mathbf{V})[(\forall x \in \mathbf{V})(x \,\varepsilon\, v \rightarrow (\exists y \in \mathbf{V})(y \,\varepsilon\, w \wedge \varphi)) \rightarrow$$

$$(\exists z' \in \mathbf{V})(z' \,\varepsilon\, z \wedge (\forall x \in \mathbf{V})(x \,\varepsilon\, v \rightarrow$$

$$(\exists y \in \mathbf{V})(y \,\varepsilon\, z' \wedge \varphi)) \wedge (\forall y \in \mathbf{V})(y \,\varepsilon\, z' \rightarrow (\exists x \in \mathbf{V})(x \,\varepsilon\, v \wedge \varphi)))]$$

Let us conclude this step with two remarks. First, the axiom of extensionality of set theory which we embodied in the system as the first rule above in this step guarantees that the newly defined term constructors relative to $\mathbf{V}$ (including $\lceil A \rceil$) are well-behaved with respect to definitional equality. Indeed, each of these constructors appears in the theory equipped with a rule which describes exactly its elements. Moreover, we can establish a binary correspondence (up to the respective notions of equality) between type-theoretic sets and terms of type $\mathbf{V}$ by sending A to $\lceil A \rceil$, and a to $\{x \mid x \,\varepsilon\, a\}$ in the opposite direction. Indeed we can derive the following rules:

$$\frac{A \, set}{A = \{x \mid x \,\varepsilon\, \lceil A \rceil\} \, set} \qquad \frac{a \in \mathbf{V}}{a = \lceil \{x \mid x \,\varepsilon\, a\} \rceil \in \mathbf{V}}$$

Step 4: Interpretation as rules

To recover the usual interpretation of types as classes, it suffices to specify the interpretation of the canonical elements of each type via the following rules.

$$\frac{}{\star = \emptyset \in \mathsf{N}_1} \qquad \frac{A \, col \qquad B \, col \, [x \in A] \qquad a \in A \qquad b \in B[a/x]}{\langle a, b \rangle = (a, b) \in (\Sigma x \in A)B}$$

where (t, s) means $\{\{t\}, \{t, s\}\}$ and $\{t\}$ means $\{t, t\}$.

$$\frac{A \, set \qquad B \, set \, [x \in A] \qquad b \in B \, [x \in A]}{\lambda x^A.b = \{z \,\varepsilon\, \lceil (\Sigma x \in A)B \rceil \mid (\exists x \in A)(z =_{\mathbf{V}} (x, b))\} \in (\Pi x \in A)B}$$

where z is a fresh variable.

$$\frac{A \, set \qquad B \, set \qquad a \in A}{\mathsf{inl}(a) = (\emptyset, a) \in A + B} \qquad \frac{A \, set \qquad B \, set \qquad b \in B}{\mathsf{inr}(b) = (\{\emptyset\}, b) \in A + B}$$

$$\frac{A \, set}{\epsilon = \emptyset \in \mathsf{List}(A)} \qquad \frac{A \, set \qquad a \in \mathsf{List}(A) \qquad b \in A}{\mathsf{cons}(a, b) = \bigcup\{a, \{(\ell(a), b)\}\} \in \mathsf{List}(A)}$$

where $\ell(a) := \mathsf{El}_{\mathsf{List}}(a, \emptyset, (x, y, z) \bigcup\{z, \{z\}\})$ is a term of type $\{v \mid v \,\varepsilon\, \omega\}$.

$$\frac{\begin{array}{c} A \, set \qquad R \, prop_s \, [x \in A, y \in A] \qquad a \in A \\ \mathsf{true} \in (\forall x \in A)R[x/y] \\ \mathsf{true} \in (\forall x \in A)(\forall y \in A)(R \leftrightarrow R[y/x, x/y]) \\ \mathsf{true} \in (\forall x \in A)(\forall y \in A)(\forall z \in A)(R \wedge R[y/x, z/y] \rightarrow R[z/y]) \end{array}}{[a] = \{x \,\varepsilon\, \lceil A \rceil \mid R[a/y]\} \in A/R}$$

$$\frac{\varphi \, prop_s}{[\varphi] = \{x \, \varepsilon \, \{\emptyset\} \mid x =_{\mathbf{V}} \emptyset \wedge \varphi\} \in \mathcal{P}(1)}$$

where x is a fresh variable.

$$\frac{A \, set \qquad b \in \mathcal{P}(1) \, [x \in A]}{\lambda x^A.b = \lceil \{z \mid (\exists x \in A)(z =_{\mathbf{V}} (x,b))\} \rceil \in A \to \mathcal{P}(1)}$$

where z is fresh and the rule of strong collection together with the fact that A is a set, guarantees that the right-hand side of the conclusion is well-defined.

$$\frac{\varphi \, prop \qquad \mathbf{true} \in \varphi}{\mathbf{true} = \emptyset \in \varphi}$$

Then, thanks to extensional equality for collections and the elimination and η-conversion rules of **emTT**, we can derive the following rules characterizing sets and collections as definable classes (the variable z is always assumed to be fresh).

$$\frac{}{\mathsf{N}_0 = \{z \mid \bot\} \, col} \qquad \frac{A \, col \qquad B \, col \, [x \in A]}{(\Sigma x \in A)B = \{z \mid (\exists x \in A)(\exists y \in B)(z =_{\mathbf{V}} (x,y))\} \, col}$$

$$\frac{}{\mathsf{N}_1 = \{z \mid z =_{\mathbf{V}} \emptyset\} \, col} \qquad \frac{A \, set \qquad B \, set \, [x \in A]}{(\Pi x \in A)B = \{z \mid \mathsf{Rel}(z,A,B) \wedge \mathsf{Svl}(z) \wedge \mathsf{Tot}(z,A)\} \, col}$$

where

1. $\mathsf{Rel}(z,A,B)$ is $(\forall w \in \mathbf{V})(w \, \varepsilon \, z \to (\exists x \in A)(\exists y \in B)(w =_{\mathbf{V}} (x,y)))$
2. $\mathsf{Svl}(z)$ is $(\forall x \in \mathbf{V})(\forall y \in \mathbf{V})(\forall y' \in \mathbf{V})((x,y) \, \varepsilon \, z \wedge (x,y') \, \varepsilon \, z \to y =_{\mathbf{V}} y')$
3. $\mathsf{Tot}(z,A)$ is $(\forall x \in A)(\exists y \in \mathbf{V})((x,y) \, \varepsilon \, z)$

$$\frac{A \, set \qquad B \, set}{A + B = \{z \mid (\exists y \in A)(z =_{\mathbf{V}} (\emptyset,y)) \vee (\exists y \in B)(z =_{\mathbf{V}} (\{\emptyset\},y))\} \, col}$$

$$\frac{A \, set}{\mathsf{List}(A) = \{z \mid (\exists n \in \mathbf{V})(n \, \varepsilon \, \omega \wedge \mathsf{Rel}(z,n,A) \wedge \mathsf{Svl}(z) \wedge \mathsf{Tot}(z,n))\} \, col}$$

where

1. $\mathsf{Rel}(z,n,A)$ is $(\forall w \in \mathbf{V})(w \, \varepsilon \, z \to (\exists x \in \mathbf{V})(\exists y \in A)(w =_{\mathbf{V}} (x,y) \wedge x \, \varepsilon \, n))$
2. $\mathsf{Tot}(z,n)$ is $(\forall x \in \mathbf{V})(x \, \varepsilon \, n \to (\exists y \in \mathbf{V})((x,y) \, \varepsilon \, z))$

$$\frac{\begin{array}{c} A \, set \qquad R \, prop_s \, [x \in A, y \in A] \\ \mathbf{true} \in (\forall x \in A)R[x/y] \qquad \mathbf{true} \in (\forall x \in A)(\forall y \in A)(R \leftrightarrow R[y/x, x/y]) \\ \mathbf{true} \in (\forall x \in A)(\forall y \in A)(\forall z \in A)(R \wedge R[y/x, z/y] \to R[z/y]) \end{array}}{A/R = \{z \mid (\exists x \in A)(\forall y \in \mathbf{V})(y \, \varepsilon \, z \leftrightarrow y \, \varepsilon \, A \wedge R)\} \, col}$$

$$\frac{}{\mathcal{P}(1) = \{z \mid (\forall y \in \mathbf{V})(y \, \varepsilon \, z \to y =_{\mathbf{V}} \emptyset)\} \, col}$$

$$\frac{A \; set}{A \to \mathcal{P}(1) = \{z| \; \mathsf{Rel}(z, A, \mathcal{P}(1)) \land \mathsf{Svl}(z) \land \mathsf{Tot}(z, A)\} \, col}$$

$$\frac{\varphi \, prop}{\varphi = \{z| \; z =_\mathbf{V} \emptyset \land \varphi\} \, col}$$

As a byproduct of the last rule together with the fact that propositions which are equal as collections are equal, we obtain that two propositions φ and ψ are equal if and only if they are equivalent, that is true $\in \varphi \leftrightarrow \psi$. Finally, notice that we do not need to add rules for the interpretation of the elimination terms, since the relative computation rules in **emTT** suffice to uniquely determine them.

4 Translations

In this section we introduce two translations: one from the syntax of **CZF** to the pre-syntax of **emTT**$_\mathbf{CZF}$, and the other one in the opposite direction[4].

The pre-syntax of **emTT**$_\mathbf{CZF}$ is defined as the following grammar, where A and B are metavariables for pre-collections, a, b and c for pre-terms, φ and ψ for pre-propositions, and x, y and z for variables[5].

A pre-collection ::=
$\quad \mathsf{N}_0| \, \mathsf{N}_1| \, \mathsf{List}(A)| \, A + B| \, (\Sigma x \in A)B| \, (\Pi x \in A)B|$
$\quad A/(x, y)\varphi| \, \mathcal{P}(1)| \, A \to \mathcal{P}(1)| \, \{x| \, \varphi\}| \, \varphi| \, \mathbf{V}$
a pre-term ::=
$\quad x| \, \mathsf{emp}_0(a)| \, \star| \, \mathsf{El}_{\mathsf{N}_1}(a, b)| \, \epsilon| \, \mathsf{cons}(a, b)| \, \mathsf{El}^A_{\mathsf{List}}(a, b, (x, y, z)c)|$
$\quad \mathsf{inl}(a)| \, \mathsf{inr}(a)| \, \mathsf{El}_+(a, (x)b, (y)c)| \, \langle a, b\rangle| \, \mathsf{El}_\Sigma(a, (x, y)b)| \, \lambda x^A.a| \, \mathsf{Ap}(a, b)|$
$\quad [a]_{A,(x,y)\varphi}| \, \mathsf{El}_{A/(x,y)\varphi}(a, (x)b)| \, \mathsf{true}| \, [\varphi]| \, \lceil A \rceil| \, \emptyset| \, \{a, b\}| \, \bigcup a| \, \{x \varepsilon a| \, \varphi\}| \, \omega$
φ pre-proposition ::=
$\quad \perp| \, a \, \varepsilon \, b| \, a \, \varepsilon \, A| \, a =_A b| \, \varphi \to \psi| \, \varphi \land \psi| \, \varphi \lor \psi| \, (\exists x \in A)\varphi| \, (\forall x \in A)\varphi$

Pre-contexts of **emTT**$_\mathbf{CZF}$ are finite lists of declarations of variables in pre-collection defined by the following clauses: the empty list [ ] is a pre-context; and if Γ is a pre-context, x is a variable not appearing in Γ and A is a pre-collection, then $[\Gamma, x \in A]$ is a pre-context.

The first translation is then defined as follows:

Definition 1. *Every term a of* **CZF** *is translated into a pre-term $\tilde{a}$ of* **emTT**$_\mathbf{CZF}$ *and every formula φ of* **CZF** *is translated into a pre-proposition $\tilde{\varphi}$ of* **emTT**$_\mathbf{CZF}$ *according to the following clauses:*

1. $\tilde{x} := x$, $\tilde{\emptyset} := \emptyset$ *and* $\tilde{\omega} := \omega$;
2. $\widetilde{\{a, b\}} := \{\tilde{a}, \tilde{b}\}$, $\widetilde{\bigcup a} := \bigcup \tilde{a}$ *and* $\widetilde{\{x \varepsilon a| \, \varphi\}} := \{x \, \varepsilon \, \tilde{a}| \, \tilde{\varphi}\}$;

---

[4] The techniques employed in the translation from **emTT**$_\mathbf{CZF}$ to **CZF** are reminiscent of the formulae-as-classes interpretation in [11]. However, in our case we have to deal with a broader variety of constructors.

[5] Notice that we decided to annotate some of the pre-collections and pre-terms in order to keep track of pieces of information which are crucial for an effective translation.

3. $\widehat{\bot} :\equiv \bot$, $\widehat{a = b} :\equiv \tilde{a} =_{\mathbf{V}} \tilde{b}$ and $\widehat{a\,\varepsilon\,b} :\equiv \tilde{a}\,\varepsilon\,\tilde{b}$;

4. $\widehat{\varphi\kappa\psi} :\equiv \widehat{\varphi}\,\kappa\,\widehat{\psi}$ for κ being $\wedge$, $\vee$ or $\rightarrow$;

5. $\widehat{Qx\,\varphi} :\equiv (Qx \in \mathbf{V})\widehat{\varphi}$ for Q being $\exists$ or $\forall$.

Now we define the second translation: each pre-collection of **emTT**$_{\mathbf{CZF}}$ is translated into a formula $\eta_A(u)$ depending on a fresh variable u which would determine the interpretation of A by comprehension as $\{u\,|\,\eta_A(u)\}$; each pre-term a of **emTT**$_{\mathbf{CZF}}$ is translated into a formula $\delta_a(u)$ of **CZF**, depending on a fresh variable u, providing a well-defined interpretation of a as the unique u for which $\delta_a(u)$ holds; each pre-proposition of **emTT**$_{\mathbf{CZF}}$ is translated into a formula of **CZF** having the same free variables.

Definition 2. *For every pre-collection A of* **emTT**$_{\mathbf{CZF}}$ *we define a (unary) predicate η_A in* **CZF**, *for every pre-term a of* **emTT**$_{\mathbf{CZF}}$ *we define a (unary) predicate δ_a in* **CZF** *and we translate every pre-proposition φ of* **emTT**$_{\mathbf{CZF}}$ *into a formula $\widehat{\varphi}$ of* **CZF** *according to the following clauses, where the variables $\xi, u, v, w, w', w_1, w_2, w_3$ and n are meant to be fresh:*

1. $\widehat{\bot} :\equiv \bot$ and $\widehat{a\,\varepsilon\,b} :\equiv \exists u \exists v(\delta_a(u) \wedge \delta_b(v) \wedge u\,\varepsilon\,v)$;

2. $\widehat{a\,\varepsilon\,A} :\equiv \exists u(\delta_a(u) \wedge \eta_A(u))$ and $\widehat{a =_A b} :\equiv \exists u(\delta_a(u) \wedge \delta_b(u) \wedge \eta_A(u))$;

3. $\widehat{\varphi\,\kappa\,\psi} :\equiv \widehat{\varphi}\,\kappa\,\widehat{\psi}$ for κ being $\wedge$, $\vee$ or $\rightarrow$;

4. $\widehat{(\forall x \in A)\varphi} :\equiv \forall x(\eta_A(x) \rightarrow \widehat{\varphi})$ and $\widehat{(\exists x \in A)\varphi} :\equiv \exists x(\eta_A(x) \wedge \widehat{\varphi})$;

5. $\delta_x(\xi) :\equiv \xi = x$;

6. $\eta_\varphi(\xi) :\equiv \xi = 0 \wedge \widehat{\varphi}$ and $\delta_{\mathsf{true}}(\xi) :\equiv \xi = 0$;

7. $\eta_{\mathsf{N_0}}(\xi) :\equiv \bot$ and $\delta_{\mathsf{emp_0}(a)}(\xi) :\equiv \xi = 0$;

8. $\eta_{\mathsf{N_1}}(\xi) :\equiv \xi = 0$, $\delta_\star(\xi) :\equiv \xi = 0$ and $\delta_{\mathsf{EIN_1}(a,b)}(\xi) :\equiv \delta_b(\xi)$;

9. $\eta_{(\Sigma x \in A)B}(\xi) :\equiv \exists v \exists w(\eta_A(v) \wedge \eta_B(w)[v/x] \wedge \xi = (v, w))$,
   $\delta_{\langle a,b\rangle}(\xi) :\equiv \exists v \exists w(\delta_a(v) \wedge \delta_b(w) \wedge \xi = (v, w))$ and
   $\delta_{\mathsf{EI_\Sigma}(a,(x,y)b)}(\xi) :\equiv \exists v(\delta_a(v) \wedge \delta_b(\xi)[p_1(v)/x, p_2(v)/y])$;

10. $\eta_{(\Pi x \in A)B}(\xi) :\equiv \mathsf{Fun}(\xi) \wedge \forall u(u \in \mathsf{dom}(\xi) \leftrightarrow \eta_A(u)) \wedge \forall x \forall y(\xi(x) = y \rightarrow \eta_B(y))$
    $\delta_{\lambda x^A.b}(\xi) :\equiv \forall v(v\,\varepsilon\,\xi \leftrightarrow \exists w \exists w'(\eta_A(w) \wedge \delta_b(w')[w/x] \wedge v = (w, w')))$ and
    $\delta_{\mathsf{Ap}(a,b)}(\xi) :\equiv \exists v \exists w(\delta_a(v) \wedge \delta_b(w) \wedge \xi = p_2(\bigcup\{z\,\varepsilon\,v\,|\,p_1(z) = w\}))$;

11. $\eta_{A+B}(\xi) :\equiv \exists v(\eta_A(v) \wedge \xi = (0, v)) \vee \exists w(\eta_B(w) \wedge \xi = (1, w))$,
    $\delta_{\mathsf{inl}(a)}(\xi) :\equiv \exists v(\delta_a(v) \wedge \xi = (0, v))$, $\delta_{\mathsf{inr}(a)} :\equiv \exists v(\delta_a(v) \wedge \xi = (1, v))$ and
    $\delta_{\mathsf{EI_+}(a,(x)b,(y)c)}(\xi) :\equiv$
    $\qquad \exists v(\delta_a(v) \wedge ((p_1(v) = 0 \wedge \delta_b(\xi)[p_2(v)/x]) \vee (p_1(v) = 1 \wedge \delta_c(\xi)[p_2(v)/x])))$;

12. $\eta_{\mathsf{List}(A)}(\xi) :\equiv \exists n(n\,\varepsilon\,\omega \wedge \mathsf{Fun}(\xi) \wedge \mathsf{dom}(\xi) = n \wedge \forall u(u\,\varepsilon\,\mathsf{im}(\xi) \rightarrow \eta_A(u)))$
    $\delta_\epsilon(\xi) :\equiv \xi = 0$,
    $\delta_{\mathsf{cons}(a,b)}(\xi) :\equiv \exists v \exists w(\delta_a(v) \wedge \delta_b(w) \wedge \xi = v \cup \{(\ell(v), w)\})$ and
    $\delta_{\mathsf{EI^A_{List}}(a,b,(x,y,z)c)}(\xi) :\equiv \exists f\Big(\mathsf{Fun}(f) \wedge \forall u(u\,\varepsilon\,\mathsf{dom}(f) \rightarrow \eta_{\mathsf{List}(A)}(u)) \wedge$
    $\exists v(\delta_b(v) \wedge f(0) = v) \wedge \forall w_1 \forall w_2 \forall w_3 \forall v$
    $(f(w_1) = w_3 \wedge \eta_A(w_2) \wedge \delta_c(v)[w_1/x, w_2/y, w_3/z] \rightarrow f(w_1 \frown w_2) = v) \wedge$
    $\exists w'(\delta_a(w') \wedge f(w') = \xi)\Big)$;

13. $\eta_{A/(x,y)\varphi}(\xi) :\equiv \exists w(\eta_A(w) \wedge \forall v(v\,\varepsilon\,\xi \leftrightarrow \eta_A(v) \wedge \widehat{\varphi}[w/x, v/y]))$,
    $\delta_{[a]_{A,(x,y)\varphi}}(\xi) :\equiv \exists w(\delta_a(w) \wedge \forall v(v\,\varepsilon\,\xi \leftrightarrow \eta_A(v) \wedge \widehat{\varphi}[w/x, v/y]))$ and
    $\delta_{\mathsf{EI_Q}(a,(x)b)}(\xi) :\equiv \exists v(\delta_a(v) \wedge \exists w(w\,\varepsilon\,v) \wedge \forall w(w\,\varepsilon\,v \rightarrow \delta_b(\xi)[w/x])))$;

14. $\eta_{\mathcal{P}(1)}(\xi) :\equiv \xi \subseteq \{0\}$ and $\delta_{[\varphi]}(\xi) :\equiv \forall v(v \,\varepsilon\, \xi \leftrightarrow v = 0 \wedge \widehat{\varphi})$;
15. $\eta_{A \to \mathcal{P}(1)}(\xi) :\equiv \eta_{(\Pi x \in A)\mathcal{P}(1)}(\xi)$ where x is fresh;
16. $\eta_{\mathbf{V}}(\xi) :\equiv \xi = \xi$, $\delta_{\lceil A \rceil}(\xi) :\equiv \forall v(v \,\varepsilon\, \xi \leftrightarrow \eta_A(v))$, $\delta_{\emptyset}(\xi) :\equiv \xi = \emptyset$,
    $\delta_{\{a,b\}}(\xi) :\equiv \exists v \exists w (\delta_a(v) \wedge \delta_b(w) \wedge \xi = \{v, w\})$, $\delta_{\bigcup a}(\xi) :\equiv \exists v(\delta_a(v) \wedge \xi = \bigcup v)$,
    $\delta_{\omega}(\xi) :\equiv \xi = \omega$ and $\delta_{\{x \,\varepsilon\, a | \,\varphi\}}(\xi) :\equiv \exists v(\delta_a(v) \wedge \forall x(x \,\varepsilon\, \xi \leftrightarrow x \,\varepsilon\, v \wedge \widehat{\varphi}))$;
17. $\eta_{\{x | \,\varphi\}}(\xi) :\equiv \widehat{\varphi}[\xi/x]$.

Finally, if Γ is a pre-context of $\mathbf{emTT_{CZF}}$, we define the formula $\widehat{\Gamma}$ of $\mathbf{CZF}$ as follows: $\widehat{[\,]} :\equiv \top$, while $\widehat{[\Gamma, x \in A]} :\equiv \widehat{\Gamma} \wedge \eta_A(x)$.

The composition of the two translations in one order results in an equivalence:

Proposition 1. *Let a be a term of $\mathbf{CZF}$, ψ a formula of $\mathbf{CZF}$ and u a fresh variable. Then $\mathbf{CZF} \vdash u = a \leftrightarrow \delta_{\widehat{a}}(u)$ and $\mathbf{CZF} \vdash \psi \leftrightarrow \widehat{\widetilde{\psi}}$.*

Proof. By simultaneous induction on the complexity of terms and formulas.

The next lemmas can be proven by induction on the complexity of the pre-syntax.

Lemma 1. *Let t be a pre-term of $\mathbf{emTT_{CZF}}$ and let u, v be fresh variables. Then $\mathbf{CZF} \vdash \delta_t(u) \wedge \delta_t(v) \to u = v$.*

Lemma 2 (Substitution Lemma). *Let t and a be pre-terms of $\mathbf{emTT_{CZF}}$, A a pre-collection of $\mathbf{emTT_{CZF}}$ and φ a pre-proposition of $\mathbf{emTT_{CZF}}$. Then:*

1. $\mathbf{CZF} \vdash \exists v(\delta_t(v)) \wedge \delta_{a[t/x]}(u) \leftrightarrow \exists v(\delta_t(v) \wedge \delta_a(u)[v/x])$;
2. $\mathbf{CZF} \vdash \exists v(\delta_t(v)) \wedge \eta_{A[t/x]}(u) \leftrightarrow \exists v(\delta_t(v) \wedge \eta_A(u)[v/x])$;
3. $\mathbf{CZF} \vdash \exists v(\delta_t(v)) \wedge \widehat{\varphi}[t/x] \leftrightarrow \exists v(\delta_t(v) \wedge \widehat{\varphi}[v/x])$.

where u and v are assumed to be fresh variables.

The next proposition is the counterpart of Proposition 1. It can be proven by induction on complexity of proof-trees using the previous lemmas.

Proposition 2. *Let A, a and φ be a pre-collection, a pre-term and a pre-proposition of $\mathbf{emTT_{CZF}}$, respectively. Then:*

1. *if $\mathbf{emTT_{CZF}} \vdash A \, col \, [\Gamma]$, then $\mathbf{emTT_{CZF}} \vdash A = \widetilde{\{z | \eta_A(z)\}} \, col \, [\Gamma]$;*
2. *if $\mathbf{emTT_{CZF}} \vdash a \in A \, [\Gamma]$, then $\mathbf{emTT_{CZF}} \vdash \mathsf{true} \in (\forall z \in \mathbf{V}) (\widetilde{\delta_a(z) \leftrightarrow z =_{\mathbf{V}} a}) \, [\Gamma]$ where z is a fresh variable;*
3. *if $\mathbf{emTT_{CZF}} \vdash \varphi \, prop \, [\Gamma]$, then $\mathbf{emTT_{CZF}} \vdash \mathsf{true} \in \varphi \leftrightarrow \widetilde{\widehat{\varphi}} \, [\Gamma]$.*

5   The Main Result

The first theorem says that $\mathbf{emTT_{CZF}}$ can be seen as an extension of **CZF**.

Theorem 1. *Let ψ be a formula of* **CZF** *whose free variables are among $x_1, ..., x_n$. If* $\mathbf{CZF} \vdash \psi$, *then* $\mathbf{emTT_{CZF}} \vdash \mathsf{true} \in \widetilde{\psi}\,[x_1 \in \mathbf{V}, ..., x_n \in \mathbf{V}]$.

Proof. This is essentially an immediate consequence of the rules in Step 3 in Sect. 3 and the rules for propositions in **emTT**.

The next theorem shows how the judgements of $\mathbf{emTT_{CZF}}$ are interpreted in **CZF**. However, before proceeding we need to introduce the concept of Δ_0-formula relative to a formula Γ of **CZF**. Such formulas are nothing but Δ_0-formulas in which some variables are substituted by elements which are definable in presence of Γ, but which can possibly lack a representation as terms. The class of formulas $\widetilde{\Delta_0}[\Gamma]$ is the smallest one respecting the following clauses:

1. $\bot$, $x = y$ and $x\,\varepsilon\,y$ are in $\widetilde{\Delta_0}[\Gamma]$ for every pair of variables x, y;
2. if φ and ψ are in $\widetilde{\Delta_0}[\Gamma]$, then $\varphi \wedge \psi$, $\varphi \vee \psi$ and $\varphi \to \psi$ are in $\widetilde{\Delta_0}[\Gamma]$;
3. if φ is a formula in $\widetilde{\Delta_0}[\Gamma]$, y is a variable, z is a fresh variable and δ is a formula such that $\mathbf{CZF} \vdash \Gamma \to \exists! z\,\delta$, then $\exists z(\delta \wedge \exists y\,\varepsilon\,z\,\varphi)$, $\exists z(\delta \wedge \forall y\,\varepsilon\,z\,\varphi)$ and $\exists z(\delta \wedge \varphi)$ are in $\widetilde{\Delta_0}[\Gamma]$.

Then, the class $\Delta_0[\Gamma]$ contains those formulas φ in $\widetilde{\Delta_0}[\Gamma]$ such that $\mathbf{free}(\varphi) \subseteq \mathbf{free}(\Gamma)$.

Lemma 3. *If φ is a formula in $\Delta_0[\Gamma]$, v, v' are fresh variables and x is a variable, then* $\mathbf{CZF} \vdash \Gamma \to \forall v \exists v' \forall x(x\,\varepsilon\,v' \leftrightarrow x\,\varepsilon\,v \wedge \varphi)$.

Theorem 2. *The following hold if u and v are assumed to be fresh variables:*

1. *if* $\mathbf{emTT_{CZF}} \vdash A = B\,type\,[\Gamma]$ *(for type being col, set, prop or $prop_s$), then* $\mathbf{CZF} \vdash \widehat{\Gamma} \to \forall u(\eta_A(u) \leftrightarrow \eta_B(u))$;
2. *if* $\mathbf{emTT_{CZF}} \vdash A\,set\,[\Gamma]$, *then* $\mathbf{CZF} \vdash \widehat{\Gamma} \to \exists z \forall u(u\,\varepsilon\,z \leftrightarrow \eta_A(u))$;
3. *if* $\mathbf{emTT_{CZF}} \vdash \varphi\,prop_s\,[\Gamma]$, *then there exists a formula ψ in $\Delta_0[\widehat{\Gamma}]$ such that* $\mathbf{CZF} \vdash \widehat{\Gamma} \to (\widehat{\varphi} \leftrightarrow \psi)$;
4. *if* $\mathbf{emTT_{CZF}} \vdash a \in A\,[\Gamma]$, *then* $\mathbf{CZF} \vdash \widehat{\Gamma} \to \exists u(\delta_a(u) \wedge \eta_A(u))$;
5. *if* $\mathbf{emTT_{CZF}} \vdash a = b \in A\,[\Gamma]$, *then* $\mathbf{CZF} \vdash \widehat{\Gamma} \to \exists u(\delta_a(u) \wedge \delta_b(u) \wedge \eta_A(u))$;

Proof. This is a long but straightforward proof made simultaneously by induction on complexity of proof-trees in $\mathbf{emTT_{CZF}}$. As an example, we show only one case relative to item 3, namely that of a small proposition obtained through a bounded universal quantifier with respect to a set. Assume that the judgement $(\forall x \in A)\varphi\,prop_s\,[\Gamma]$ is deduced in $\mathbf{emTT_{CZF}}$ from the judgements $A\,set\,[\Gamma]$ and $\varphi\,prop_s\,[\Gamma, x \in A]$. Then, by inductive hypothesis, we know that $\mathbf{CZF} \vdash \widehat{\Gamma} \to \exists z \forall u(\eta_A(u) \leftrightarrow u\,\varepsilon\,z)$ and that there exists a $\Delta_0[\widehat{[\Gamma, x \in A]}]$-formula ψ such that $\mathbf{CZF} \vdash \widehat{[\Gamma, x \in A]} \to (\widehat{\varphi} \leftrightarrow \psi)$. The first one is equivalent to $\mathbf{CZF} \vdash \widehat{\Gamma} \to \exists z \delta_{\lceil A \rceil}(z)$ while from the second one we obtain $\mathbf{CZF} \vdash$

S. Maschio and P. Sabelli

$\widehat{\Gamma} \to \forall x(\eta_A(x) \to (\widehat{\varphi} \leftrightarrow \psi))$. Assuming $\widehat{\Gamma}$, from these it follows in **CZF** that $\widehat{(\forall x \in A)\varphi} :\equiv \forall x(\eta_A(x) \to \widehat{\varphi})$ is equivalent to $\forall x(\eta_A(x) \to \psi)$ which is equivalent to $\exists z(\delta_{\lceil A \rceil}(z) \wedge \forall x \, \varepsilon \, z \, \psi)$. Since this is a $\Delta_0[\widehat{\Gamma}]$-formula, we can conclude.

Corollary 1. *Let φ be a pre-proposition of* $\mathbf{emTT_{CZF}}$. *If* $\mathbf{emTT_{CZF}} \vdash \mathsf{true} \in \varphi[\Gamma]$, *then* $\mathbf{CZF} \vdash \widehat{\Gamma} \to \widehat{\varphi}$.

Proof. From 4. in Theorem 1, if $\mathbf{emTT_{CZF}} \vdash \mathsf{true} \in \varphi[\Gamma]$, then $\mathbf{CZF} \vdash \widehat{\Gamma} \to \exists u(\delta_{\mathsf{true}}(u) \wedge \eta_\varphi(u))$ that is $\mathbf{CZF} \vdash \widehat{\Gamma} \to \exists u(u = 0 \wedge \widehat{\varphi})$. Thus $\mathbf{CZF} \vdash \widehat{\Gamma} \to \widehat{\varphi}$.

The theorems above show that $\mathbf{emTT_{CZF}}$ and **CZF** are equivalent. Indeed:

1. every formula of **CZF** is equivalent to one of the form $\widehat{\psi}$;
2. every proposition of $\mathbf{emTT_{CZF}}$ is equivalent to one of the form $\widetilde{\varphi}$;
3. if φ is a theorem of **CZF**, then $\widetilde{\varphi}$ is a theorem of $\mathbf{emTT_{CZF}}$;
4. if ψ is a theorem of $\mathbf{emTT_{CZF}}$, then $\widehat{\psi}$ is a theorem of **CZF**.

6 Conclusions

We have proven here that it is possible to extend the extensional level of the Minimalist Foundation to **CZF**, and thus to the main intuitionistic and classical axiomatic set theories, such as **IZF**, **ZF** and **ZFC**, by adding rules and preserving the logical meaning. This provides a very strong notion of compatibility between **emTT** and these theories, confirming the fact that the Minimalist Foundation is a suitable common ground for comparison between set-theoretical foundational theories and intuitionistic type theories.

There are at least two possible future directions of investigation. Firstly, one could exploit the modularity of the construction of $\mathbf{emTT_{CZF}}$ to study weaker subsystems and their possible set-theoretical counterparts. Secondly, one could apply similar techniques to prove a strong compatibility between **emTT** and other predicative theories like Feferman's Explicit Mathematics [6].

References

1. Aczel, P: The type theoretic interpretation of constructive set theory. In: Logic Colloquium 1977 (Proc. Conf., Wrocław, 1977), pp. 55–66. North Holland, Amsterdam (1977)
2. Aczel, P., Gambino, N.: The generalized type-theoretic interpretation of constructive set theory. J. Symbolic Logic **71**(1), 67–103 (2006)
3. Aczel, P., Rathjen, M.: Notes on Constructive Set Theory. (2010). http://www1.maths.leeds.ac.uk/~rathjen/book.pdf
4. Bishop, E., Bridges, Douglas: Constructive Analysis. GW, vol. 279. Springer, Heidelberg (1985). https://doi.org/10.1007/978-3-642-61667-9
5. Coquand, T., Huet, G.: The calculus of constructions. Inf. Comput. **76**(2–3), 95–120 (1988)

6. Feferman, S.: A language and axioms for explicit mathematics. In: Crossley, J.N. (ed.) Algebra and Logic. LNM, vol. 450, pp. 87–139. Springer, Heidelberg (1975). https://doi.org/10.1007/BFb0062852
7. Martin-Löf, P.: Intuitionistic type theory. Notes by G.Sambin of a series of lectures given in Padua. Bibliopolis, Naples (1984)
8. Maietti, M.E.: A minimalist two-level foundation for constructive mathematics. Ann. Pure Appl. Logic **160**(3), 319–354 (2009)
9. Maietti, M.E., Sambin, G.: Toward a minimalist foundation for constructive mathematics. In: From Sets and Types to Topology and Analysis: Practicable Foundations for Constructive Mathematics, pp. 91–114, Oxford Logic Guides 48, Oxford University Press (2005)
10. Nordström, B., Petersson, K., Smith, J.M.: Programming in Martin-Löf Type Theory. An Introduction. Oxford University Press, Oxford (1990)
11. Rathjen, M.: The Formulae-as-Classes Interpretation of Constructive Set Theory, Proof technology and computation, 279–322, NATO Science Series III Computer and Systems Sciences, 200. IOS, Amsterdam (2006)

Reducing Reachability in Temporal Graphs: Towards a More Realistic Model of Real-World Spreading Processes

Kitty Meeks[✉][iD]

School of Computing Science, University of Glasgow, Glasgow G12 8RZ, UK
kitty.meeks@glasgow.ac.uk

Abstract. In many settings there is a need to reduce the spread of something undesirable, such as a virus, through a network. Typically, the network in which the spreading process takes place is not fixed but is subject to discrete changes over time; a natural formalism for such networks is that of *temporal graphs*. In this paper we survey three types of modifications that have been proposed in order to reduce reachability in temporal graphs, as well as the computational complexity of identifying optimal strategies for reducing reachability using each type of modification. We then go on to discuss several limitations of the current frameworks as models for intervention against real-world spreading processes, and suggest how these might be addressed in future research.

Keywords: Reachability · Temporal graphs · Spreading processes · Computational complexity · Parameterized algorithms

1 Introduction

Reachability is a crucial concept in understanding the spread of all kinds of things – good and bad – through networks. Sometimes we would like to restrict the spread of something undesirable, be it a virus or fake news, through a network; in other cases it is desirable to maximise the reachability subject to certain constraints, for example when preparing an advertising campaign or designing a transportation schedule. Here we focus on the problem of reducing reachability in the presence of an undesirable spreading process.

Many of the networks in which we are concerned with reachability – be these networks representing physical or virtual social contact, or transport networks – are inherently temporal: trains depart at specified times, and people do not interact continuously with all of their contacts. The relative timing of connections in the network clearly has an important impact on the reachability of individual

The work described here has been supported by EPSRC grants EP/T004878/1 and EP/V032305/1, and a Royal Society of Edinburgh Personal Research Fellowship (funded by the Scottish Government).

vertices, as illustrated in Fig. 1. These observations motivate the study of reachability in temporal graphs, whose edge-sets are subject to discrete changes over time.

Formally, following the foundational work of Kempe et al. [13], we define a *temporal graph* to be a pair (G, λ) where G is a (static) graph, often called the *underlying graph*, and $\lambda : E(G) \to 2^{\mathbb{N}} \setminus \{\emptyset\}$ maps edges of G to non-empty sets of times. A pair (e, t) where $e \in E(G)$ and $t \in \lambda(e)$ is called a *time-edge* of $\mathcal{G}$. We define the *lifetime* of $\mathcal{G} = (G, \lambda)$ to be the maximum time assigned to any edge by λ; throughout, we will consider only those temporal graphs whose lifetime is finite.

Crucial to the notion of reachability in temporal graphs is the notion of a temporal path. A *temporal path* in $\mathcal{G} = (G, \lambda)$ is a sequence of time-edges $(e_1, t_1), \ldots, (e_p, t_p)$ such that the edges $e_1, \ldots, e_p$ form a path in G and, for $1 \leq i \leq p - 1$, we have $t_i \leq t_{i+1}$. If all inequalities are strict, we say this is a *strict temporal path*.

Armed with these notions, we can define the concept of reachability sets in temporal graphs. The *(strict) temporal reachability set* of the vertex v in $\mathcal{G}$ is the set of all vertices u such that there exists a (strict) temporal path from v to u in $\mathcal{G}$; by convention, we assume that each vertex v also reaches itself. For a set of vertices S, the temporal reachability set of S is the union of the temporal reachability sets of vertices in S. The *temporal reachability* of a vertex (or set of vertices) is the size of its temporal reachability set, and the *maximum* (respectively *minimum*) *temporal reachability* of a temporal graph is the maximum (respectively minimum) temporal reachability of any vertex in the graph.

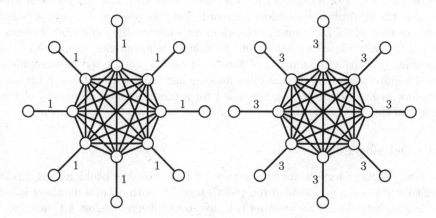

Fig. 1. Changing the relative order of edges can have an arbitrarily large impact on the maximum temporal reachability. Assuming that all edges within the clique are active only at time 2 in both examples (with times on the other edges as indicated), every vertex of the clique in the right-hand example reaches the entire graph, whereas no vertex in the left-hand example reaches any vertex outside the clique other than itself.

While there is clear motivation for studying reachability in the temporal setting, there are many associated challenges. Concepts that are well-understood or even trivial in the static setting become much more complex in the temporal world. For example, reachability is no longer symmetric: often, in the temporal setting, we will find that vertex u is reachable from vertex v even when v is not reachable from u. Classical graph theoretic results on connectivity, including Menger's Theorem, also fail to hold in the temporal setting [13] (although, in the case of Menger's Theorem, a more subtle temporal analogue has been developed [14]).

Motivated by the observation above that it is often desirable to decrease the extent to which something can spread through a network, a major recent focus for research in the temporal reachability setting has been on identifying optimal modifications to decrease the maximum or average temporal reachability of some set of nodes. Unsurprisingly, these kinds of optimisation problems typically turn out to be computationally intractable except in very specific cases.

In Sect. 2, we will introduce the three main types of modifications that have been studied in the literature to date, and summarise the key results regarding the computational complexity of using these modifications to minimise reachability. In Sect. 3 we then go on to discuss some limitations of the current models and how these might be extended to better encode real-world scenarios, before concluding in Sect. 4 with some thoughts on the main challenges for future work in this area.

2   Modifying Temporal Graphs to Reduce Reachability

Three main types of modification to reduce reachability have so far been proposed in the literature: edge deletions, reordering of edges, and delaying of edges. In recognition of the fact that modifications are likely costly, some kind of restriction is typically placed on the extent to which the graph can be modified (for example, by limiting the number of permitted modifications), but more sophisticated requirements that the modifications are not too disruptive to the network have not been investigated (see Sect. 3.4 for a more detailed discussion of this issue). In this section we discuss each of the types of modification in turn.

2.1   Deleting Edges

Enright, Meeks, Mertzios and Zamaraev [7] introduce the problem TR EDGE DELETION: given a temporal graph (G, λ), together with natural numbers k and h, the goal is to determine whether it is possible to delete at most k time-edges[1] so that the maximum temporal reachability of the resulting temporal graph is at most h. This is a direct temporal analogue of earlier work by Enright and Meeks which considered edge deletion in static graphs as a means of limiting the size of

---

[1] The work in [7] focusses on the special case in which each $|\lambda(e)| = 1$ for every edge e, so deletion of time-edges is equivalent to deletion of static edges in the underlying graph.

an epidemic in cattle trade networks [9]; "deleting" an edge in this setting might correspond to enforcing additional checks or quarantine periods when animals are moved a certain route, thereby reducing the risk of disease transmission along this route to something close to zero. This static version of the problem is already NP-complete [9], so it is unsurprising that TR EDGE DELETION remains intractable even under strong restrictions: the problem is NP-hard even when h, the maximum degree of the underlying input graph, and the lifetime of the input temporal graph are all bounded by constants. Moreover, assuming the Exponential Time Hypothesis, there is no hope achieving a running time in terms of the input size and the number k of permitted deletions that improves significantly on a brute-force approach; from the parameterised perspective, this also demonstrates that the problem is W[1]-hard with respect to the parameter k.

On the positive side, the authors obtain two polynomial-time algorithms which approximate the minimum number of deletions needed: one computes an h-approximation on arbitrary graphs, while the other computes a c-approximation whenever the underlying input graph has cutwidth at most c. While at first sight these approximation ratios seem to leave a lot of room for improvement, it is also shown that the problem is unlikely to admit a polynomial-time constant-factor approximation in general, even when restricted to temporal graphs with lifetime two. From the parameterised perspective, the problem is also shown to admit an exact FPT algorithm when parameterised simultaneously by h, the maximum degree of the underlying input graph, and the treewidth of the underlying input graph. Many of these results are also extended to a setting in which restrictions are placed on the permitted waiting time at each vertex along a temporal path.

2.2   Reordering Edges

A different method for reducing reachability in temporal graphs was proposed by Enright, Meeks and Skerman [10]: given a static underlying graph as input, the goal is to assign times to the edges so as to minimise the maximum temporal reachability of the resulting temporal graph. Formally, they introduce the problem MIN-MAX REACHABILITY TEMPORAL ORDERING, which takes as input a static graph $G = (V, E)$, a list $\mathcal{E} = \{E_1, \ldots, E_\ell\}$ of subsets of E, and a positive integer h, and asks whether there is a bijective function $t : \mathcal{E} \to [\ell]$ such that the maximum temporal reachability of the temporal graph in which every edge in E_i is active at time $t(E_i)$ is at most k. The requirement that the time-labelling function t be bijective is to rule out trivial solutions in the case of strict reachability (since, in this case, reachability can always be minimised by making all edges active at the same time); for non-strict reachability, there is always an optimal solution in which no two edge-sets are assigned the same time since, if E_1 and E_2 are initially assigned the same time, altering the assignment so that they are given consecutive times (in arbitrary order, and without changing the relative order of any other sets) will not increase the reachability of any vertex. This model was once again inspired by the spread of disease in livestock: many livestock trades are mediated through markets, with named events (e.g. "Spring

Bull Sale") taking place on specific dates; thus certain sets of trades will take place on the same day, but the relative order of this set of trades and another set (of another class of animal, but potentially involving many of the same farms) could be changed by an auction company.

The general version of this problem turns out to be extremely computationally challenging: MIN-MAX REACHABILITY TEMPORAL ORDERING is NP-complete even on trees and DAGs, and from the parameterised perspective is W[1]-hard parameterised by the vertex-cover number of the input graph, even when the input graph is required to be a tree. The only positive result in this setting is a constant-factor approximation to the optimisation problem when the input satisfies several strong structural restrictions.

In the quest for more positive results, the authors consider a special case – further removed from the motivating application – in which each edge set E_i is a singleton (so that all edges can be reordered independently). In this case the problem is still NP-complete on general graphs, but does admit a linear-time constant-factor approximation algorithm when restricted to graphs of bounded maximum degree. This restriction of the problem can also be solved exactly in polynomial time on DAGs, and on trees it admits an FPT algorithm parameterised by either the maximum permitted reachability h or the maximum degree.

2.3 Delaying Edges

A third family of modifications that could be used to reduce temporal reachability was introduced by Deligkas and Potapov [6]: they consider the operations of either *merging* a sequence of consecutive timesteps (so that all edges previously active at any timestep in the sequence are now only active at the last timestep in the sequence), or *delaying* individual edges by some number of timesteps. They propose that, in some settings, these merging and delaying operations are less disruptive to the infrastructure than the deletion or more general reordering approaches discussed above. Again, the goal[2] is to reduce the reachability of the resulting temporal graph: in addition to considering the maximum temporal reachability, they also consider the problems of minimising the average temporal reachability over all vertices and of minimising the temporal reachability of some specific set of vertices given as part of the input. Determining whether it is possible to achieve a specified bound for any of the three notions of temporal reachability using merging operations turns out to be NP-complete, even on trees of maximum degree three. In the setting of delaying operations, the authors adapt a reduction from [7] to show that, when the number of permitted delaying operations is bounded by k, all three problems are NP-complete and W[1]-hard with respect to the parameter k. On the positive side, however, they give a polynomial-time algorithm to optimise all three notions of temporal reachability when an arbitrary number of delaying operations can be applied.

---

[2] Beyond the scope of this paper, the authors in [6], and a subsequent related work [5], also consider goals related to increasing reachability using the same operations.

Molter, Renken and Szchoche [15] recently investigated the relationship between the complexity of minimising temporal reachability by respectively deleting and delaying edges. In addition to showing that the maximum temporal reachability of any vertex in some specified set of source vertices can, in both cases, be minimised in polynomial time when the underlying graph is a tree, they provide a general reduction from the delaying version to the deletion version of the problem. However, when parameterised by the permitted number of reachable vertices, this relationship is reversed: the delaying version is in FPT while the deletion version remains W[1]-hard.

3   Limitations of Current Models

While all of the work described above draws on real-world applications for motivation, there are a number of common features in all of these models which limit their practical applicability. In this section we will discuss some of these, and the ways in which future research might address the current shortcomings.

3.1   Arbitrary Waiting Times

With the exception of some results on deletion [7], the work described above allows the most flexible notion of temporal paths, whereby there is no restriction on the waiting time at a single vertex. This is not necessarily a realistic model of many spreading processes: for example, in the setting of disease spread, there will typically only be a limited time-window during which an individual is infectious and can potentially pass on infection to their contacts; similarly, when considering the spread of information it seems more likely that an individual will share gossip they have just learnt than that received a year ago. Enright, Meeks, Mertzios and Zamaraev [7] consider the edge-deletion problem in the setting of so-called (α, β)-reachability as a more realistic model for disease spread, in which the waiting time at a vertex must be at least α and at most β timesteps. However, their results implicitly assume a disease for which recovery does not confer immunity (or a network in which vertices correspond to groups of individuals, e.g. animals on a farm, and so multiple infections of different individuals within the group are possible), as (α, β)-reachability is defined in terms of temporal *walks* which satisfy this restriction, meaning that the same vertex may be visited multiple times: this is primarily for pragmatic computational reasons, since the existence or otherwise of such a walk between two vertices can be determined in polynomial time [1], whereas determining the existence or otherwise of a so-called *restless* temporal path, in which the waiting time at each vertex can be at most Δ, is known to be NP-complete [4].

It would be particularly interesting to investigate the impact of restrictions on waiting times in the two models in which times are changed: for example, a delay could either create or destroy restless temporal paths without changing the set of (traditional) temporal paths in the graph. However, this restriction has not yet been considered in either the reordering or delaying model; this seems a fruitful line for future research.

3.2 Deterministic Spreading Only

Perhaps the most obvious limitation of all the models discussed above is that they consider only deterministic worst-case spread, whereas in reality transmission along a single time-edge will be associated with some probability. There are certain applications for worst-case analysis of this kind, for example if all potential contacts of a diseased individual need to be identified and required to isolate, but in other settings we are likely to be more interested in the expected reachability of a vertex (or other measures associated with the random variable denoting the size of the reachable set).

This natural generalisation has been proposed as an extension to current work [10], but probabilistic spreading has not so far been considered within any of the models introduced above. One reason for this is that probabilistic spreading vastly changes the nature of the computation: computing the probability of transmission between a pair of vertices is equivalent to counting the number of weighted temporal paths between the two (where weights are multiplied along the path, and correspond to the transmission probabilities associated with the corresponding time-edges), and even without weights this problem is known to be intractable in many settings [8]. Thus even the problem of verifying whether a given intervention (based on deleting or changing the times on edges) is sufficient to achieve a specified goal (in terms of the expected reachability) will be intractable unless the input is highly restricted. However, it would nevertheless be worthwhile to carry out further research in this direction, even if the only realistic goal is that of obtaining approximation algorithms in restricted settings.

3.3 Only One Type of Modification Allowed

Several different kinds of modification are encapsulated in the various models discussed above, each of which may be realistic in particular settings, but each model considered allows only one type of modification to be applied to a single instance. However, it is credible that, in many scenarios, it might for example be feasible to change the timing of some edges while removing others completely. The complexity of carrying out combinations of these modifications to achieve a specific reachability goal is entirely unexplored.

To make hybrid models of this kind more realistic and flexible, it would be natural to introduce a cost function that allows different kinds of modifications to be more or less costly (for example, delaying an edge by a short time should intuitively be less costly than removing it altogether). A cost function of this kind could also be used to enforce restrictions on which kinds of modifications are permitted at each edge: for example, there might be some edges that we cannot delete but whose time we are allowed to change.

More generally, cost functions would also be a valuable extension within any of the models that allows only a single type of modification. For example, some edges may be more costly to delete than others. However, the notion of cost is even more powerful in the reordering or delaying setting: here the cost could depend not only on the edge under consideration, but also the duration and/or direction of the time modification (assuming that some initial default configuration is given in the reordering model). This would reflect the intuition that changing the time on an edge by a small amount is likely to be less disruptive than a larger change, and also the fact that in some settings either advancing or delaying will be easier; potentially in some settings, if the change to the time is large enough, it is no less disruptive to delete the edge entirely. Moreover, the relationship between time difference and cost need not be monotonic: it might for example be easier (or indeed only possible) to reschedule a connection to take place on the same day of the week as originally scheduled.

3.4   Independence of Modifications

With the exception of a few results in the reordering setting, the models described here assume that edges can be modified independently from one another; however, this is not necessarily realistic. In the deletion setting, for example, there might be some minimum connectivity requirements that must be maintained – if we were dealing with a transport network, say, we might want to ensure that every vertex is still able to reach some vertex corresponding to a location providing basic essential services. The potential dependencies between different modifications are perhaps even clearer in the delaying setting: again considering a transport network, if particular edges use the same vehicle or driver then delaying one edge may necessarily force other related edges to be delayed; on the other hand, we might not be allowed to increase the gap between two such related edges by too much without violating legal requirements on working hours for the driver.

These observations motivate the development of refined models in which the dependencies between different edges can be captured. Once again, such generalisations will only serve to increase the computational complexity of problems that are already intractable in many cases, but it would be instructive to determine whether any of the restricted settings that admit efficient algorithms in the independent versions of the models also give tractability when some level of dependency is considered. Moreover, investigations in this direction would motivate the development of parameters to capture the structure of the dependencies. This could, for example, be done by considering the structure of the graph whose vertex-set is the set of (time-)edges in the input graph, and in which there is an edge between two (time-)edges if and only if the two cannot be modified independently. The maximum size of a connected component in this auxiliary graph was implicitly considered as a parameter in the reordering model [10], but other parameters such as the maximum degree or treewidth of the auxiliary graph would also likely be of interest.

3.5   Perfect Knowledge

All of the models discussed above assume that (where appropriate) we have complete knowledge of the initial schedule and can carry out precise modifications (so that we specify exactly the new time assigned to an edge after delaying or reordering). However, in real-world scenarios, information and our control of changes is likely to be imperfect, so we may have to operate under uncertainty. For example, we might not know (or be able to specify) the precise time at which a journey will be made, but instead a window in which it will occur; if this is the case for two incident edges in the network, their relative order might not be known. Moreover, a pre-determined schedule might be subject to unplanned disruption, for example in a transport network where a certain number of unforeseen delays can be expected. It would be natural to consider both random and adversarial models of changes to the schedule, with some bound on the number and/or scale of changes.

These observations motivate the development of techniques to deal with uncertainty and identify modification strategies that are in some sense robust to small changes in the schedule, or provide a good approximation to the best strategy regardless of when connections occur during their permitted windows. Very recently, Füchsle, Molter, Niedermeier and Renken [11,12] made a first step in this direction, considering the simpler goal of determining whether there is a temporal path between two vertices that is robust against some small number of delays (as, for example, when planning a multi-leg train journey). They already encounter intractability in several settings, indicating that optimising reachability in such settings will certainly be challenging.

4   Discussion

In spite of much recent work in this area, we have only scratched the surface in understanding the complexity of determining optimal sets of modifications to minimise reachability in realistic temporal settings. There is a strong motivation for generalising the models that have been studied so far to incorporate more realistic features; however, given the extreme computational tractability that has already been encountered in the more basic variants, this will require new approaches to dealing with intractability. We have seen that restricting only the structure of the underlying graph is rarely enough to give rise to efficient algorithms, as many of the problems remain intractable even when the underlying graph is (for example) a tree. A promising research direction that has emerged recently is the development of parameters that describe aspects of the *temporal* structure of temporal graphs in combination with structural properties of the underlying graph. Recent parameters of this kind include the timed feedback-vertex number [4] and the (vertex-)interval-membership-width [2,3] of temporal graphs; vertex-interval-membership-width has already been exploited in the reachability setting to give an FPT algorithm to minimise the number of vertices reachable from a fixed source under deletion operations [3], but the values of both parameters on real-world networks of interest have yet to be investigated.

References

1. Bentert, M., Himmel, A.-S., Nichterlein, A., Niedermeier, R.: Efficient computation of optimal temporal walks under waiting-time constraints. Appl. Netw. Sci. **5**(1), 1–26 (2020). https://doi.org/10.1007/s41109-020-00311-0

2. Bumpus, B.M., Meeks, K.: Edge exploration of temporal graphs. In: Flocchini, P., Moura, L. (eds.) IWOCA 2021. LNCS, vol. 12757, pp. 107–121. Springer, Cham (2021). https://doi.org/10.1007/978-3-030-79987-8_8

3. Bumpus, B.M., Meeks, K.: Edge exploration of temporal graphs. CoRR abs/2103.05387 (2021)

4. Casteigts, A., Himmel, A.-S., Molter, H., Zschoche, P.: Finding temporal paths under waiting time constraints. Algorithmica **83**(9), 2754–2802 (2021). https://doi.org/10.1007/s00453-021-00831-w

5. Deligkas, A., Eiben, E., Skretas, G.: Minimizing reachability times on temporal graphs via shifting labels (2021). https://arxiv.org/pdf/2112.08797

6. Deligkas, A., Potapov, I.: Optimizing reachability sets in temporal graphs by delaying. In: The Thirty-Fourth AAAI Conference on Artificial Intelligence, AAAI 2020, The Thirty-Second Innovative Applications of Artificial Intelligence Conference, IAAI 2020, The Tenth AAAI Symposium on Educational Advances in Artificial Intelligence, EAAI 2020, New York, NY, USA, 7–12 February 2020, pp. 9810–9817. AAAI Press (2020)

7. Enright, J., Meeks, K., Mertzios, G.B., Zamaraev, V.: Deleting edges to restrict the size of an epidemic in temporal networks. J. Comput. Syst. Sci. **119**, 60–77 (2021). https://doi.org/10.1016/j.jcss.2021.01.007

8. Enright, J., Meeks, K., Molter, H.: Counting temporal paths (2022). https://arxiv.org/pdf/2202.12055

9. Enright, J., Meeks, K.: Deleting edges to restrict the size of an epidemic: a new application for treewidth. Algorithmica **80**(6), 1857–1889 (2017). https://doi.org/10.1007/s00453-017-0311-7

10. Enright, J.A., Meeks, K., Skerman, F.: Assigning times to minimise reachability in temporal graphs. J. Comput. Syst. Sci. **115**, 169–186 (2021). https://doi.org/10.1016/j.jcss.2020.08.001

11. Füchsle, E., Molter, H., Niedermeier, R., Renken, M.: Delay-robust routes in temporal graphs, **219**, 30:1–30:15 (2022). https://doi.org/10.4230/LIPIcs.STACS.2022.30

12. Füchsle, E., Molter, H., Niedermeier, R., Renken, M.: Temporal connectivity: coping with foreseen and unforeseen delays (2022). https://arxiv.org/pdf/2201.05011

13. Kempe, D., Kleinberg, J., Kumar, A.: Connectivity and inference problems for temporal networks. J. Comput. Syst. Sci. **64**(4), 820–842 (2002). https://doi.org/10.1006/jcss.2002.1829

14. Mertzios, G.B., Michail, O., Spirakis, P.G.: Temporal network optimization subject to connectivity constraints. Algorithmica **81**(4), 1416–1449 (2018). https://doi.org/10.1007/s00453-018-0478-6

15. Molter, H., Renken, M., Zschoche, P.: Temporal reachability minimization: delaying vs. deleting. In: Bonchi, F., Puglisi, S.J. (eds.) 46th International Symposium on Mathematical Foundations of Computer Science, MFCS 2021, 23–27 August 2021, Tallinn, Estonia. LIPIcs, vol. 202, pp. 76:1–76:15. Schloss Dagstuhl - Leibniz-Zentrum für Informatik (2021). https://doi.org/10.4230/LIPIcs.MFCS.2021.76

Hilbert's Tenth Problem for Term Algebras with a Substitution Operator

Juvenal Murwanashyaka[(✉)] [ID]

Department of Mathematics, University of Oslo, Oslo, Norway
juvenalm@math.uio.no

Abstract. We introduce a first-order theory of finite full binary trees and show that the analogue of Hilbert's Tenth Problem is undecidable by constructing a many-to-one reduction of Post's Correspondence Problem.

1 Introduction

Hilbert's Tenth Problem asks whether there exists an algorithm that given a polynomial $f \in \mathbb{Z}[x_1, x_2, \ldots, x_n]$ decides whether f has a zero in $\mathbb{Z}^n$. In 1970, Yuri Matiyasevich proved that Hilbert's Tenth Problem is undecidable by showing that the exponential function is existentially definable in terms of addition and multiplication (see for example Davis [1]). After this, a standard technique for showing that a structure has undecidable existential theory has been to show that it existentially interprets the first-order structure of arithmetic $(\mathbb{N}, 0, 1, +, \times)$ (see Sects. 5.3 and 5.4a of Hodges [2] for more details). In this paper, we introduce a first-order structure $\mathcal{T}(\mathcal{L}_{\mathsf{BT}})$ of finite full binary trees (see Sect. 2) and prove that the analogue of Hilbert's Tenth Problem for $\mathcal{T}(\mathcal{L}_{\mathsf{BT}})$ is undecidable without interpreting arithmetic, that is, without relying on the solution to Hilbert's Tenth Problem (such a proof can also be produced by modifying slightly the coding in Sect. 5 to translate multiplication).

2 Preliminaries

We consider the first-order language $\mathcal{L}_{\mathsf{BT}} = \{\bot, \langle \cdot, \cdot \rangle, \cdot[\cdot \mapsto \cdot]\}$ where $\bot$ is a constant symbol, $\langle \cdot, \cdot \rangle$ is a binary function symbol and $\cdot[\cdot \mapsto \cdot]$ is a ternary function symbol. The intended structure $\mathcal{T}(\mathcal{L}_{\mathsf{BT}})$ is a term model: The universe $\mathbf{H}$ is the set of all variable-free terms in the language $\{\bot, \langle \cdot, \cdot \rangle\}$ (equivalently, finite full binary trees). The constant symbol $\bot$ is interpreted as itself. The function symbol $\langle \cdot, \cdot \rangle$ is interpreted as the function that maps the pair (s, t) to the term $\langle s, t \rangle$. The function symbol $\cdot[\cdot \mapsto \cdot]$ is interpreted as a term substitution operator: $t[r \mapsto s]$ is the term we obtain by replacing each occurrence of r in t with s. We define $t[r \mapsto s]$ by recursion as follows: If $t = r$, then $t[r \mapsto s] = s$. If $r \neq \bot$, then $\bot[r \mapsto s] = \bot$. If $r \neq t = \langle t_1, t_2 \rangle$, then $t[r \mapsto s] = \langle t_1[r \mapsto s], t_2[r \mapsto s] \rangle$.

To improve readability, it will occasionally be more convenient to represent finite binary trees using notation that is closer to their visual form: By recursion, for $n \geq 2$, let $\langle x_1, \ldots, x_n, x_{n+1} \rangle$ be shorthand for $\langle \langle x_1, \ldots, x_n \rangle, x_{n+1} \rangle$. By recursion, let $\bot^1 = \bot$ and $\bot^{n+1} = \langle \bot^n, \bot \rangle$.

U. Berger et al. (Eds.): CiE 2022, LNCS 13359, pp. 196–207, 2022.
https://doi.org/10.1007/978-3-031-08740-0_17

We let $\mathsf{Th}^{\exists}(\mathcal{T}(\mathcal{L}_{\mathsf{BT}}))$ denote the set of all existential $\mathcal{L}_{\mathsf{BT}}$-sentences that are true in $\mathcal{T}(\mathcal{L}_{\mathsf{BT}})$. We let $\mathsf{Th}^{\mathsf{H10}}(\mathcal{T}(\mathcal{L}_{\mathsf{BT}}))$ denote the set of all $\mathcal{L}_{\mathsf{BT}}$-sentences of the form $\exists \vec{x} \, [\, s = t \,]$ that are true in $\mathcal{T}(\mathcal{L}_{\mathsf{BT}})$. In Sect. 7, we prove that $\mathsf{Th}^{\exists}(\mathcal{T}(\mathcal{L}_{\mathsf{BT}}))$ is undecidable by constructing a reduction of Post's correspondence problem. The coding techniques that form the basis of the encoding are developed in Sects. 3, 4, 5, 6. In Sect. 8, we show that undecidability of $\mathsf{Th}^{\exists}(\mathcal{T}(\mathcal{L}_{\mathsf{BT}}))$ implies undecidability of $\mathsf{Th}^{\mathsf{H10}}(\mathcal{T}(\mathcal{L}_{\mathsf{BT}}))$.

Definition 1. *Let $\{0,1\}^+$ denote the set of all nonempty binary strings. The Post Correspondence Problem (PCP) is given by*

- *Instance: a list of pairs $\langle a_1, b_1 \rangle, \ldots, \langle a_n, b_n \rangle$ where $a_i, b_i \in \{0,1\}^+$*
- *Solution: a finite nonempty sequence $i_1, \ldots, i_m$ of indexes such that we have the equality $a_{i_1} a_{i_2} \ldots a_{i_m} = b_{i_1} b_{i_2} \ldots b_{i_m}$.*

To analyze further what we can and cannot effectively decide over $\mathcal{T}(\mathcal{L}_{\mathsf{BT}})$, we introduce bounded quantifiers. We let $x \sqsubseteq t$ and $x \not\sqsubseteq t$ be shorthand for $t[\,x \mapsto \langle x,x \rangle\,] \neq t$ and $t[\,x \mapsto \langle x,x \rangle\,] = t$, respectively. Observe that $\sqsubseteq$ is the subtree relation on finite binary trees. In [5], Venkataraman shows that the existential theory of the structure we obtain by taking $\mathcal{T}(\mathcal{L}_{\mathsf{BT}})$ and replacing the substitution operator with the subtree relation is decidable and the decision problem is NP-complete. Let $\forall x \sqsubseteq t \, \phi$ be shorthand for $\forall x \, [\, x \sqsubseteq t \rightarrow \phi \,]$. Let $\Sigma_{1,0,1}^{\mathcal{T}(\mathcal{L}_{\mathsf{BT}})}$ denote the set of all $\mathcal{L}_{\mathsf{BT}}$-sentences that are true in $\mathcal{T}(\mathcal{L}_{\mathsf{BT}})$ and are of the form $\exists x \, \forall y \sqsubseteq x \, \phi$ where ϕ is quantifier-free. In Sect. 9, we show that $\Sigma_{1,0,1}^{\mathcal{T}(\mathcal{L}_{\mathsf{BT}})}$ is undecidable. We cannot prove this result by encoding Post's correspondence problem since this problem is about sequences of pairs and therefore necessitates the use of two bounded universal quantifiers. Instead, we encode the Modulo Problem of Kristiansen & Murwanashyaka [3].

Definition 2. *Let $f^0(x) = x$ and $f^{n+1}(x) = f(f^n(x))$. The Modulo Problem is given by*

- *Instance: a list of pairs $\langle A_0, B_0 \rangle, \ldots, \langle A_{M-1}, B_{M-1} \rangle$ where $M > 1$ and $A_i, B_i \in \mathbb{N}$ for $i = 0, \ldots, M-1$.*
- *Solution: a natural number N such that $f^N(3) = 2$ where $f(x) = A_j z + B_j$ if there exists $j \in \{0, 1, \ldots, M-1\}$ such that $x = Mz + j$.*

3   Numbers

To encode Post's correspondence problem, we need to associate strings over a finite alphabet with finite binary trees. As a step towards this, we show that certain classes of number-like objects are existentially definable in $\mathcal{T}(\mathcal{L}_{\mathsf{BT}})$.

Definition 3. *Let $\alpha \in \mathbf{H}$. Let $s_1, \ldots, s_n \in \mathbf{H}$ be such that α is not a subtree of s_i for all $i \leq n$ and $s_n \neq s_j$ for all $j < n$. Let*

$$\frac{1}{\alpha, \vec{s}} \equiv \langle \alpha, s_1, \ldots, s_n \rangle \quad \text{and} \quad \frac{m+1}{\alpha, \vec{s}} \equiv \frac{1}{\alpha, \vec{s}}[\alpha \mapsto \frac{m}{\alpha, \vec{s}}] \;.$$

Let $\mathbb{N}_{\vec{s}}^{\alpha} = \{\, \frac{m}{\alpha, \vec{s}} \in \mathbf{H} : \; m \in \mathbb{N} \; \wedge \; m \geq 1 \, \}$.

Lemma 1. *Let $\alpha \in \mathbf{H}$. Let $s_1, \ldots, s_n \in \mathbf{H}$ be such that α is not a subtree of s_i for all $i \leq n$ and $s_n \neq s_j$ for all $j < n$. Then, for all $T \in \mathbf{H}$*

$$T \in \mathbb{N}_{\vec{s}}^{\alpha} \Leftrightarrow T = \frac{1}{\alpha, \vec{s}} \vee \left(\frac{2}{\alpha, \vec{s}} \sqsubseteq T \wedge T = \frac{1}{\alpha, \vec{s}} \left[\alpha \mapsto T \left[\frac{2}{\alpha, \vec{s}} \mapsto \frac{1}{\alpha, \vec{s}} \right] \right] \right).$$

Proof. The left-right implication of the claim is straightforward. Let the size of a binary tree T be the number of nodes in T. We prove by induction on the size of T that

$$T = \frac{1}{\alpha, \vec{s}} \vee \left(\frac{2}{\alpha, \vec{s}} \sqsubseteq T \wedge T = \frac{1}{\alpha, \vec{s}} \left[\alpha \mapsto T \left[\frac{2}{\alpha, \vec{s}} \mapsto \frac{1}{\alpha, \vec{s}} \right] \right] \right) \qquad (*)$$

implies $T \in \mathbb{N}_{\vec{s}}^{\alpha}$.

Assume T satisfies $(*)$. We need to show that $T \in \mathbb{N}_{\vec{s}}^{\alpha}$. If $T = \frac{1}{\alpha, \vec{s}}$, then certainly $T \in \mathbb{N}_{\vec{s}}^{\alpha}$. Otherwise, by the second disjunct in $(*)$, we have $\frac{2}{\alpha, \vec{s}} \sqsubseteq T$. Let $S = T \left[\frac{2}{\alpha, \vec{s}} \mapsto \frac{1}{\alpha, \vec{s}} \right]$. Then, S is strictly smaller than T. By the second disjunct in $(*)$, we have $T = \frac{1}{\alpha, \vec{s}} [\alpha \mapsto S]$. By Definition 3, $\frac{1}{\alpha, \vec{s}} = \langle \alpha, s_1, \ldots, s_n \rangle$. Since α is not a subtree of any s_i

$$T = \frac{1}{\alpha, \vec{s}} [\alpha \mapsto S] = \langle \alpha, s_1, \ldots, s_n \rangle [\alpha \mapsto S] = \langle S, s_1, \ldots, s_n \rangle . \qquad (**)$$

We know that $\frac{2}{\alpha, \vec{s}} \sqsubseteq T$. By Definition 3, $\frac{2}{\alpha, \vec{s}} = \langle \alpha, s_1, \ldots, s_n, s_1, \ldots, s_n \rangle$. Since $s_n \neq s_j$ for all $1 \leq j < n$, it follows from $\frac{2}{\alpha, \vec{s}} \sqsubseteq T$ and $(**)$ that we have one of the following cases: (i) $S = \frac{1}{\alpha, \vec{s}}$, (ii) occurrences of $\frac{2}{\alpha, \vec{s}}$ in T can only be found in S. In case of (ii), we have

$$S = T \left[\frac{2}{\alpha, \vec{s}} \mapsto \frac{1}{\alpha, \vec{s}} \right] = \langle S, s_1, \ldots, s_n \rangle \left[\frac{2}{\alpha, \vec{s}} \mapsto \frac{1}{\alpha, \vec{s}} \right] = \langle S \left[\frac{2}{\alpha, \vec{s}} \mapsto \frac{1}{\alpha, \vec{s}} \right], s_1, \ldots, s_n \rangle$$

$$= \langle \alpha, s_1, \ldots, s_n \rangle \left[\alpha \mapsto S \left[\frac{2}{\alpha, \vec{s}} \mapsto \frac{1}{\alpha, \vec{s}} \right] \right] = \frac{1}{\alpha, \vec{s}} \left[\alpha \mapsto S \left[\frac{2}{\alpha, \vec{s}} \mapsto \frac{1}{\alpha, \vec{s}} \right] \right].$$

We see that in case of either (i) or (ii), S satisfies $(*)$. Thus, by the induction hypothesis, $S \in \mathbb{N}_{\vec{s}}^{\alpha}$. It then follows from $(**)$ that $T \in \mathbb{N}_{\vec{s}}^{\alpha}$. $\square$

4   Strings

Given a finite alphabet $A = \{a_1, \ldots, a_m\}$, let ε denote the empty string and let A^* denote the set of all finite strings over A. Let $A^+ = A^* \setminus \{\varepsilon\}$. We will now associate A^* with an existentially definable class of finite binary trees.

Definition 4. *Let $A = \{a_1, \ldots, a_m\}$ be a finite alphabet. For each natural number $i \geq 1$, let $\mathbf{g}_i \equiv \langle \perp^{3+i}, \perp^{3+i} \rangle$. Let $\alpha \in \mathbf{H}$ be incomparable with $\mathbf{g}_i$ with respect to the subtree relation for all i. We define a one-to-one map $\tau_\alpha : A^* \to \mathbf{H}$ by recursion*

$$\tau_\alpha(w) = \begin{cases} \alpha & \text{if } w = \varepsilon \\ \langle \alpha, \mathbf{g}_i \rangle & \text{if } w = a_i \\ \tau_\alpha(w_0) [\alpha \mapsto \tau_\alpha(w_1)] & \text{if } w = w_0 w_1 \text{ and } w_0 \in A . \end{cases}$$

Given $s \in A^*$, we write $\frac{s}{\alpha}$ for $\tau_\alpha(s)$. Furthermore, we write a_i for g_i.

For example, $\frac{a_1 a_1 a_3 a_1 a_2}{\alpha} = \langle \alpha, a_2, a_1, a_3, a_1, a_1 \rangle$.

Lemma 2. *Let $A = \{a_1, \ldots, a_m\}$ be a finite alphabet. Then, $\tau_\alpha(A^*)$ is existentially definable in $T(\mathcal{L}_{\mathsf{BT}})$.*

Proof. We need the following property to prove that $\tau_\alpha(A^*)$ is existentially definable

(*) $g_1, \ldots, g_m$ are incomparable with respect to the subtree relation.

Lemma 1 tells us that the classes $\mathbb{N}_{g_i}^\alpha \cup \{\alpha\}$ are existentially definable in $T(\mathcal{L}_{\mathsf{BT}})$. The idea is to show that $s \in \tau_\alpha(A^*)$ if and only if we can transform s into an element of $\mathbb{N}_{g_i}^\alpha \cup \{\alpha\}$. We show that $\tau_\alpha(A^*)$ is defined by the formula
$$\phi(x) \equiv x[g_2 \mapsto g_1] \cdots [g_m \mapsto g_1] \in \mathbb{N}_{g_1}^\alpha \cup \{\alpha\}.$$
Clearly, each element in $\tau_\alpha(A^*)$ has the property $\phi(x)$. To see that the converse holds, assume $\phi(s)$. We need to show that $s \in \tau_\alpha(A^*)$. Since $\mathbb{N}_{g_i}^\alpha \cup \{\alpha\} \subseteq \tau_\alpha(A^*)$, it suffices to show that for each $1 \leq i \leq n$ and each finite binary tree t, if $t[g_i \mapsto g_1] \in \tau_\alpha(A^*)$, then $t \in \tau_\alpha(A^*)$. We prove this by induction on the size of t.

Assume $t[g_i \mapsto g_1] \in \tau_\alpha(A^*)$. We need to show that $t \in \tau_\alpha(A^*)$. If g_i is not a subtree of t, then $t = t[g_i \mapsto g_1] \in \tau_\alpha(A^*)$. Assume now g_i is a subtree of t. Let $t = \langle t_0, t_1 \rangle$. We cannot have $t = g_i$ since $g_1 \notin \tau_\alpha(A^*)$. Hence, $t[g_i \mapsto g_1] = \langle t_0[g_i \mapsto g_1], t_1[g_i \mapsto g_1]\rangle$. By how the elements of $\tau_\alpha(A^*)$ are defined, $t_0[g_i \mapsto g_1] \in \tau_\alpha(A^*)$ and $t_1[g_i \mapsto g_1] = g_j$ for some $1 \leq j \leq n$. Since $t_0[g_i \mapsto g_1] \in \tau_\alpha(A^*)$, by the induction hypothesis, $t_0 \in \tau_\alpha(A^*)$. If g_i is not a subtree of t_1, then $t_1 = t_1[g_i \mapsto g_1] = g_j$. Assume now g_i is a subtree of t_1. Then, g_1 is a subtree of g_j since $t_1[g_i \mapsto g_1] = g_j$. By (*), $g_1 = g_j$, which implies $t_1 = g_i$. Hence, $t_0 \in \tau_\alpha(A^*)$ and $t_1 = g_l$ for some $1 \leq l \leq n$. Then, $t = \langle t_0, t_1 \rangle \in \tau_\alpha(A^*)$ by how the elements of $\tau_\alpha(A^*)$ are defined.

Thus, by induction, if $t[g_i \mapsto g_1] \in \tau_\alpha(A^*)$, then $t \in \tau_\alpha(A^*)$. $\square$

5 Sequences of Strings I

Recall that the instance $\langle a_1, b_1 \rangle, \ldots, \langle a_n, b_n \rangle$ of PCP has a solution if and only if there exist a finite nonempty sequence $i_1, \ldots, i_m$ of indexes such that we have $a_{i_1} a_{i_2} \cdots a_{i_m} = b_{i_1} b_{i_2} \cdots b_{i_m}$. So, given a finite sequence $C = \langle c_1, c_2, \ldots, c_n \rangle$ of nonempty binary strings, we need to express that a sequence $w_1, w_2, \ldots, w_k$ of binary strings satisfies the following two properties: (A) there exists $i \in \{1, \ldots, n\}$ such that $w_1 = c_i$, (B) for all $j \in \{1, \ldots, k-1\}$ there exists $i \in \{1, \ldots, n\}$ such that $w_{j+1} = w_j c_i$. In other words, we need to give an existential definition of the class $\mathbb{P}(C)$ of all sequences $w_1, w_2, \ldots, w_k$ that satisfy (A)-(B). In this section, we give a formal definition of $\mathbb{P}(C)$, as a class of finite binary trees, and show that it is existentially definable.

Since we are interested in describing sequences that satisfy (A)-(B), it is not the set $\{0, 1\}^*$ we are interested in, but rather the subset generated by

$\{c_1, c_2, \ldots, c_n\}$ under concatenation. We also need to treat the c_i's as distinct objects since we intend to replace C with one of the sequences $\langle a_1, \ldots, a_n \rangle$, $\langle b_1, \ldots, b_n \rangle$ where $\langle a_1, b_1 \rangle, \ldots, \langle a_n, b_n \rangle$ is an instance of PCP. To capture this, we associate elements of $\{c_1, c_2, \ldots, c_n\}^+$ with strings over a larger alphabet $\{0, 1, \mu_1, \mu_2, \ldots, \mu_n\}$ where μ_i represents the last letter of c_i. Assume for example $c_1 = 110$, $c_2 = 011$ and $c_3 = 1010$. Then, we associate the binary string $c_2 c_1 c_3$ with the string $01\mu_2 11\mu_1 101\mu_3$.

Definition 5. *Let* $C = \langle c_1, c_2, \ldots, c_n \rangle$ *be a sequence of nonempty binary strings. We associate* c_i *with a finite binary tree in* $\tau_\alpha(\{0, 1, \mu_1, \ldots, \mu_n\}^*)$ *as follows*

$$\frac{c_i}{C, \alpha} \equiv \frac{w_i \mu_i}{\alpha} \quad where \quad c_i = w_i d \wedge w_i \in \{0, 1\}^* \wedge d \in \{0, 1\}.$$

We let $\frac{\varepsilon}{C, \alpha} \equiv \alpha$. *We associate the string* $c_{i_1} c_{i_2} \ldots c_{i_m}$ *with a finite binary tree in* $\tau_\alpha(\{0, 1, \mu_1, \ldots, \mu_n\}^*)$ *as follows*

$$\frac{c_{i_1} c_{i_2} \ldots c_{i_m}}{C, \alpha} \equiv \frac{w_{i_1} \mu_{i_1} w_{i_2} \mu_{i_2} \ldots w_{i_m} \mu_{i_m}}{\alpha}.$$

We are finally ready to give a formal definition of the class of those finite binary trees that encode sequences that satisfy (A)-(B).

Definition 6. *Let* $C = \langle c_1, c_2, \ldots, c_n \rangle$ *be a sequence of nonempty binary strings. Let* $\alpha, \gamma \in \mathbf{H}$ *be incomparable with respect to the subtree relation. Assume* α *also satisfies the condition in Definition 4. Let* $\mathbb{P}(C, \alpha, \gamma)$ *be the smallest subset of* $\mathbf{H}$ *that satisfies*

- $\langle \gamma, \frac{c_i}{C, \alpha} \rangle \in \mathbb{P}(C, \alpha, \gamma)$ *for all* $i \in \{1, \ldots, n\}$
- *if* $T \in \mathbb{P}(C, \alpha, \gamma)$ *where* $T = \langle R, \frac{c_{i_1} c_{i_2} \ldots c_{i_m}}{C, \alpha} \rangle$, *then* $\langle T, \frac{c_{i_1} c_{i_2} \ldots c_{i_m} c_j}{C, \alpha} \rangle \in \mathbb{P}(C, \alpha, \gamma)$ *for all* $j \in \{1, \ldots, n\}$.

Lemma 3. *Let* $C = \langle c_1, c_2, \ldots, c_n \rangle$ *be a sequence of nonempty binary strings. Let* $\alpha, \gamma \in \mathbf{H}$ *be incomparable with respect to the subtree relation. Assume* α *also satisfies the condition in Definition 4. Let* $\delta = \langle \alpha, \alpha \rangle$. *Let* $F_\delta^\alpha(L) = L[\alpha \mapsto \delta]$ *for all* $L \in \mathbf{H}$. *Let* $T \in \mathbf{H}$. *Then,* $T \in \mathbb{P}(C, \alpha, \gamma)$ *if and only if*

(1) $\delta \not\sqsubseteq T$
(2) there exists $m \in \{1, \ldots, n\}$ *such that* $\langle \gamma, \frac{c_m}{C, \alpha} \rangle \sqsubseteq T$
(3) there exists $S \in \tau_\alpha(\{0, 1, \mu_1, \ldots, \mu_n\}^*)$ *such that*

$$T = \left\langle F_\delta^\alpha(T) \left[\langle \gamma, \frac{c_m}{C, \delta} \rangle \mapsto \gamma, \frac{c_1}{C, \delta} \mapsto \alpha, \ldots, \frac{c_n}{C, \delta} \mapsto \alpha \right], S \right\rangle.$$

Before we prove the lemma, we illustrate why the left-right implication holds. First, observe that (1) holds if $T \in \mathbb{P}(C, \alpha, \gamma)$. Now, assume for example $T = \left\langle \gamma, \frac{c_2}{C, \alpha}, \frac{c_2 c_3}{C, \alpha}, \frac{c_2 c_3 c_1}{C, \alpha} \right\rangle$. The tree $F_\delta^\alpha(T)$ is just the tree we obtain by replacing each one of the three occurrences of α in T with δ. Hence, $F_\delta^\alpha(T) =$

$\left\langle \gamma, \frac{c_2}{C,\delta}, \frac{c_2 c_3}{C,\delta}, \frac{c_2 c_3 c_1}{C,\delta} \right\rangle$. Since there is only one occurrence of $\left\langle \gamma, \frac{c_2}{C,\delta} \right\rangle$ in $F_\delta^\alpha(T)$, we have $R_0 := F_\delta^\alpha(T)\left[\left\langle \gamma, \frac{c_2}{C,\delta} \right\rangle \mapsto \gamma \right] = \left\langle \gamma, \frac{c_2 c_3}{C,\delta}, \frac{c_2 c_3 c_1}{C,\delta} \right\rangle$. We replace the one occurrence of $\frac{c_1}{C,\delta}$ in R_0 and obtain $R_1 := R_0\left[\frac{c_1}{C,\delta} \mapsto \alpha \right] = \left\langle \gamma, \frac{c_2 c_3}{C,\delta}, \frac{c_2 c_3}{C,\alpha} \right\rangle$. Since $\frac{c_2 c_3}{C,\alpha}$ does not contain a subtree of the form $\frac{c_i}{C,\delta}$ by the choice of δ, there is no occurrence of $\frac{c_2}{C,\delta}$ in R_1. Hence, $R_2 := R_1\left[\frac{c_2}{C,\delta} \mapsto \alpha \right] = R_1$. We replace the occurrence of $\frac{c_3}{C,\delta}$ in R_2 and obtain $R_3 := R_2\left[\frac{c_3}{C,\delta} \mapsto \alpha \right] = \left\langle \gamma, \frac{c_2}{C,\alpha}, \frac{c_2 c_3}{C,\alpha} \right\rangle$. Now, observe that R_3 is the left subtree of T.

Proof (Proof of Lemma 3).
The left-right implication is obvious. We prove right-left implication by induction on the size of T. We need the following properties:

(A) Since γ and α are incomparable with respect to the subtree relation, the binary tree $\left\langle \gamma, \frac{c_m}{C,\alpha} \right\rangle$ is not a subtree of elements of $\tau_\alpha(\{0,1,\mu_1,\ldots,\mu_n\}^*)$.
(B) Since γ and δ are incomparable with respect to the subtree relation, the binary tree $\left\langle \gamma, \frac{c_m}{C,\alpha} \right\rangle$ is not a subtree of elements of $\tau_\delta(\{0,1,\mu_1,\ldots,\mu_n\}^*)$.

Assume T satisfies (1)-(3). We need to show that $T \in \mathbb{P}(C,\alpha,\gamma)$. By assumption, we have a natural number $m \in \{1,\ldots,n\}$ and a string $s \in \{0,1,\mu_1,\ldots,\mu_n\}^*$ such that the following three properties hold: (i) $\delta \not\sqsubseteq T$, (ii) $\left\langle \gamma, \frac{c_m}{C,\alpha} \right\rangle \sqsubseteq T$, (iii) $T = \left\langle F_\delta^\alpha(T)\left[\left\langle \gamma, \frac{c_m}{C,\delta} \right\rangle \mapsto \gamma, \frac{c_1}{C,\delta} \mapsto \alpha, \ldots, \frac{c_n}{C,\delta} \mapsto \alpha \right], \frac{s}{\alpha} \right\rangle$. Let $T_0 = F_\delta^\alpha(T)\left[\left\langle \gamma, \frac{c_m}{C,\delta} \right\rangle \mapsto \gamma, \frac{c_1}{C,\delta} \mapsto \alpha, \ldots, \frac{c_n}{C,\delta} \mapsto \alpha \right]$.

Assume $T_0 = \gamma$. By (ii), $\left\langle \gamma, \frac{c_m}{C,\alpha} \right\rangle \sqsubseteq T$. By (A), $\left\langle \gamma, \frac{c_m}{C,\alpha} \right\rangle \not\sqsubseteq \frac{s}{\alpha}$. Hence, $T = \left\langle T_0, \frac{s}{\alpha} \right\rangle = \left\langle \gamma, \frac{c_m}{C,\alpha} \right\rangle \in \mathbb{P}(C,\alpha,\gamma)$.

Assume now $T_0 \neq \gamma$. Since $T_0 \sqsubseteq T$, it follows from (i) that $\delta \not\sqsubseteq T_0$. Since $\left\langle \gamma, \frac{c_m}{C,\alpha} \right\rangle \sqsubseteq T$, $T \neq \left\langle \gamma, \frac{c_m}{C,\alpha} \right\rangle$ and $\left\langle \gamma, \frac{c_m}{C,\alpha} \right\rangle \not\sqsubseteq \frac{s}{\alpha}$, we have $\left\langle \gamma, \frac{c_m}{C,\alpha} \right\rangle \sqsubseteq T_0$. Finally, we have

$$T_0 = F_\delta^\alpha(T)\left[\left\langle \gamma, \frac{c_m}{C,\delta} \right\rangle \mapsto \gamma, \frac{c_1}{C,\delta} \mapsto \alpha, \ldots, \frac{c_n}{C,\delta} \mapsto \alpha \right]$$

$$= F_\delta^\alpha(\left\langle T_0, \frac{s}{\alpha} \right\rangle)\left[\left\langle \gamma, \frac{c_m}{C,\delta} \right\rangle \mapsto \gamma, \frac{c_1}{C,\delta} \mapsto \alpha, \ldots, \frac{c_n}{C,\delta} \mapsto \alpha \right]$$

$$= \left\langle F_\delta^\alpha(T_0), \frac{s}{\delta} \right\rangle\left[\left\langle \gamma, \frac{c_m}{C,\delta} \right\rangle \mapsto \gamma, \frac{c_1}{C,\delta} \mapsto \alpha, \ldots, \frac{c_n}{C,\delta} \mapsto \alpha \right]$$

$$= \left\langle F_\delta^\alpha(T_0)\left[\left\langle \gamma, \frac{c_m}{C,\delta} \right\rangle \mapsto \gamma, \frac{c_1}{C,\delta} \mapsto \alpha, \ldots, \frac{c_n}{C,\delta} \mapsto \alpha \right], S_0 \right\rangle$$

where

$$S_0 = \frac{s}{\delta}\left[\left\langle \gamma, \frac{c_m}{C,\delta} \right\rangle \mapsto \gamma, \frac{c_1}{C,\delta} \mapsto \alpha, \ldots, \frac{c_n}{C,\delta} \mapsto \alpha \right]$$

$$= \frac{s}{\delta}\left[\frac{c_1}{C,\delta} \mapsto \alpha, \ldots, \frac{c_n}{C,\delta} \mapsto \alpha \right] \qquad \text{(by } (B) \text{)}$$

$$= \frac{s's''}{\delta}\left[\frac{c_k}{C,\delta} \mapsto \alpha \right] = \frac{s'}{\alpha} \in \tau_\alpha(\{0,1,\mu_1,\ldots,\mu_n\}^*)$$

where we have used that $s = s's''$ and $\frac{s''}{\delta} = \frac{c_k}{C,\delta}$ for some $k \in \{1, \ldots, n\}$ since we would otherwise have $\frac{s}{\delta}\left[\frac{c_1}{C,\delta} \mapsto \alpha , \ldots , \frac{c_n}{C,\delta} \mapsto \alpha\right] = \frac{s}{\delta}$ while $\delta \not\sqsubseteq T$ by (1). Since T_0 satisfies (1)-(3), $T_0 \in \mathbb{P}(C, \gamma)$ by the induction hypothesis. It then follows that $T \in \mathbb{P}(C, \gamma)$.

Thus, by induction, $T \in \mathbb{P}(C, \alpha, \gamma)$ if T satisfies (1)-(3). $\square$

6   Sequences of Strings II

Recall that the instance $\langle a_1, b_1 \rangle, \ldots, \langle a_n, b_n \rangle$ of PCP has a solution if and only if there exist a finite nonempty sequence $i_1, \ldots, i_m$ of indexes such that we have $a_{i_1} a_{i_2} \ldots a_{i_m} = b_{i_1} b_{i_2} \ldots b_{i_m}$. Let $C = \langle c_1, c_2, \ldots, c_n \rangle$ be one of the sequences $\langle a_1, \ldots, a_n \rangle$, $\langle b_1, \ldots, b_n \rangle$. Each element $T \in \mathbb{P}(C, \alpha, \gamma)$ represents a sequence of the form $w_1, w_2, \ldots, w_m$ where $w_k = c_{i_1} c_{i_2} \ldots c_{i_k}$ and $i_j \in \{1, \ldots, n\}$ for all $j \in \{1, \ldots, m\}$. We need the sequence $i_1, i_2, \ldots, i_m$ to verify the equality $a_{i_1} a_{i_2} \ldots a_{i_m} = b_{i_1} b_{i_2} \ldots b_{i_m}$. We need an existential $\mathcal{L}_{\mathsf{BT}}$-formula that extracts this information from T. To achieve this, we need to encode sequences that are more complex than those we encountered in Sect. 5.

The class $\mathbb{P}(C, \alpha, \gamma)$ consists of finite binary trees that encode sequences of the form $w_1, w_2, \ldots, w_k$ where $w_i \in \tau_\alpha(\{0, 1, \mu_1, \ldots, \mu_n\}^*)$ for all $i \in \{1, \ldots, k\}$. We need to consider the class of those binary trees that encode sequences of the form $W_1, W_2, \ldots, W_k$ where $W_i \in \mathbb{P}(C, \alpha, \gamma)$ for all $i \in \{1, \ldots, k\}$. To illustrate how this helps us identify the sequence $i_1, i_2, \ldots, i_m$, let $T = \left\langle \gamma, \frac{c_2}{C,\alpha}, \frac{c_2 c_3}{C,\alpha}, \frac{c_2 c_3 c_1}{C,\alpha} \right\rangle$ where $c_1 = 01$, $c_2 = 00$, $c_3 = 10$. We need to find an existential $\mathcal{L}_{\mathsf{BT}}$-formula $\Psi(T, X)$ that is true in $\mathcal{T}(\mathcal{L}_{\mathsf{BT}})$ if and only if X represents the string $\mu_2 \mu_3 \mu_1$. Instead of working with T, we work with the binary tree $W_1 = \Gamma_n^\alpha(T)$ in Fig. 1. It contains the information μ_2, μ_3, μ_1 and has the advantage of having a simpler structure. We give a formal definition of the operator $\Gamma_n^\alpha : \mathbf{H} \to \mathbf{H}$ that takes T and gives us $\Gamma_n^\alpha(T)$. It is really the restriction of Γ_n^α to $\mathbb{P}(C, \alpha, \gamma)$ we are interested in. It will follow from the definition that Γ_n^α is existentially definable.

Definition 7. *Let $\alpha, 0, 1, \mu_1, \ldots, \mu_n$ be as in Definition 5. Let $\mu_{n+1}, \ldots, \mu_{2n}$ be distinct fresh letters. Let $\Gamma_n^\alpha : \mathbf{H} \to \mathbf{H}$ be the function defined by $\Gamma_n^\alpha(T) = T_2$ where*

$$T_0 = T\left[\frac{\mu_1}{\alpha} \mapsto \frac{\mu_1}{\mu_{n+1}} , \ldots , \frac{\mu_n}{\alpha} \mapsto \frac{\mu_n}{\mu_{n+n}} \right]$$

$$T_1 = T_0\left[1 \mapsto 0 , \mu_1 \mapsto 0 , \mu_2 \mapsto 0 , \ldots , \mu_n \mapsto 0 \right]$$

$$T_2 = T_1\left[\mu_{n+1} \mapsto \mu_1 , \mu_{n+2} \mapsto \mu_2 , \ldots , \mu_{n+n} \mapsto \mu_n \right].$$

Recall that we are interested in specifying an existential $\mathcal{L}_{\mathsf{BT}}$-formula $\Psi(T, X)$ that is true if and only if X encodes the string $\mu_2 \mu_3 \mu_1$. As we have just seen,

$\Gamma_n^\alpha(T)$ contains also the information μ_2, μ_3, μ_1. So, we let $\Psi(T, X)$ be a formula of the form $\exists W\, \Phi(T, X, W)$ where W is a finite binary tree that encodes a sequence $W_1, W_2, \ldots, W_k$ where $W_1 = \Gamma_n^\alpha(T)$ and $W_k = X$. Before we give a formal definition of the class $\mathbb{P}_2(C, \alpha, \gamma)$ of all W with this property, we use the binary tree $T = \left\langle\, \gamma, \frac{c_2}{C,\alpha}, \frac{c_2 c_3}{C,\alpha}, \frac{c_2 c_3 c_1}{C,\alpha}\,\right\rangle$ to illustrate the form of W. Let $W_1, \ldots, W_7$ be the binary trees in Fig. 1. Then, W can for example be the binary tree $\left\langle\, \alpha, W_7, W_6, W_5, W_4, W_3, W_2, W_1\,\right\rangle$ or the binary tree $\left\langle\, \alpha, W_7, W_7, W_6, W_5, W_4, W_3, W_2, W_1\,\right\rangle$. It is not a problem that there are many choices for W. What is important is that $\Gamma_n^\alpha(T)$ is the unique right subtree of W, and W_7 encodes the information we need in a simple format and is the unique subtree X of W which is such that $\langle\alpha, X\rangle \sqsubseteq W$.

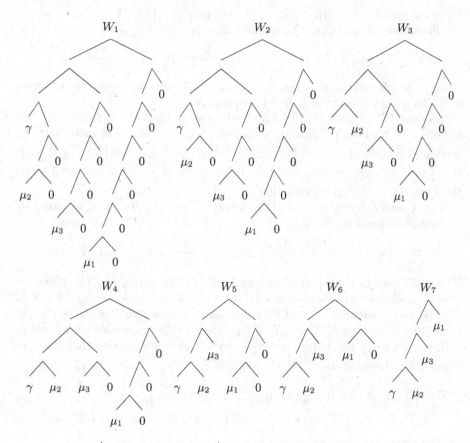

Fig. 1. Let $T = \left\langle\, \gamma, \frac{c_2}{C,\alpha}, \frac{c_2 c_3}{C,\alpha}, \frac{c_2 c_3 c_1}{C,\alpha}\,\right\rangle$. Then, $W_1 = \Gamma_n^\alpha(T)$. Binary trees of the form $W = \left\langle\, \alpha, W_7, \ldots, W_7, W_6, W_5, W_4, W_3, W_2, W_1\,\right\rangle$ are elements of $\mathbb{P}_2(C, \alpha, \gamma)$.

Definition 8. *Let $C = \langle c_1, c_2, \ldots, c_n \rangle$ be a sequence of nonempty binary strings. Let $\alpha, \gamma \in \mathbf{H}$ be incomparable with respect to the subtree relation. Assume α satisfies the condition in Definition 4. Assume γ is not a subtree of μ_i for all $i \in \{1, \ldots, n\}$. Let $W \in \mathbb{P}_2(C, \alpha, \gamma)$ if and only if there exists a sequence $W_1, W_2, \ldots, W_k \in \mathbf{H}$ such that there exists $T \in \mathbb{P}(C, \alpha, \gamma)$ such that $W_1 = \Gamma_n^\alpha(T)$, $W = \langle \, \alpha \,, W_k, W_{k-1}, \ldots, W_1 \, \rangle$, $W_k \in \tau_\gamma(\{\mu_1, \ldots, \mu_n\}^+)$ and $W_{i+1} = W_i \left[\frac{0}{\mu_1} \mapsto \mu_1 \,, \frac{0}{\mu_2} \mapsto \mu_2 \,, \ldots, \frac{0}{\mu_n} \mapsto \mu_n \right]$ for all $i \in \{1, 2, \ldots, k-1\}$.*

We prove that $\mathbb{P}_2(C, \alpha, \gamma)$ is existentially definable.

Lemma 4. *Let $C = \langle c_1, c_2, \ldots, c_n \rangle$ be a sequence of nonempty binary strings. Let $\alpha, \gamma \in \mathbf{H}$ be incomparable with respect to the subtree relation. Assume α satisfies the condition in Definition 4. Assume γ is not a subtree of μ_i for all $i \in \{1, \ldots, n\}$. Let $W \in \mathbf{H}$. Then, $W \in \mathbb{P}_2(C, \alpha, \gamma)$ if and only if*

(1) there exists $X \in \tau_\gamma(\{\mu_1, \ldots, \mu_n\}^+)$ such that $\langle \alpha, X \rangle \sqsubseteq W$
(2) there exists $T \in \mathbb{P}(C, \alpha, \gamma)$ such that $W = \langle V \,, \Gamma_n^\alpha(T) \rangle$ where

$$V = W \left[\langle \alpha, X \rangle \mapsto \alpha \,, \frac{0}{\mu_1} \mapsto \mu_1 \,, \frac{0}{\mu_2} \mapsto \mu_2 \,, \ldots, \frac{0}{\mu_n} \mapsto \mu_n \right].$$

Proof. The left-right implication is a straightforward consequence of Definition 8. We focus on proving the right-left implication.

Assume W satisfies (1)-(2). We need to show that $W \in \mathbb{P}_2(C, \alpha, \gamma)$. By Definition 8, we need to show that there exist $W_1, \ldots, W_k \in \mathbf{H}$ such that: (A) $W = \langle \, \alpha \,, W_k, W_{k-1}, \ldots, W_2, W_1 \, \rangle$, (B) $W_k \in \tau_\gamma(\{\mu_1, \ldots, \mu_n\}^+)$, (C) $W_{i+1} = W_i \left[\frac{0}{\mu_1} \mapsto \mu_1 \,, \frac{0}{\mu_2} \mapsto \mu_2 \,, \ldots, \frac{0}{\mu_n} \mapsto \mu_n \right]$ for all $i \in \{1, 2, \ldots, k-1\}$, (D) there exists $T \in \mathbb{P}(C, \alpha, \gamma)$ such that $W_1 = \Gamma_n^\alpha(T)$.

Let X and T be binary trees that satisfy clauses (1)-(2). First, we prove by (backward) induction that if $\langle \alpha, X \rangle \sqsubseteq U \sqsubseteq W$ and $U = \langle U_0, U_1 \rangle$, then

$$U_0 = U \left[\langle \alpha, X \rangle \mapsto \alpha \,, \frac{0}{\mu_1} \mapsto \mu_1 \,, \ldots, \frac{0}{\mu_n} \mapsto \mu_n \right] \text{ and } \alpha \not\sqsubseteq U_1 \,.$$

We let (*) refer to the equality, and we let (**) refer to $\alpha \not\sqsubseteq U_1$. The base case $U = W$ is Clause (2). So, assume $U = \langle V, U_1 \rangle$, $V = \langle V_0, V_1 \rangle$, $\langle \alpha, X \rangle \sqsubseteq V \sqsubseteq U \sqsubseteq W$ and U satisfies (*) and (**). We need to show that V satisfies (*) and (**). Since U satisfies (**), $\langle \alpha, X \rangle \not\sqsubseteq U_1$. Since α is incomparable with 0 and μ_i with respect to $\sqsubseteq$, the binary tree $\frac{0}{\mu_i}$ cannot equal a binary tree that has α as subtree. Furthermore, if $\alpha \sqsubseteq R$, then $\alpha \sqsubseteq R[\frac{0}{\mu_i} \mapsto \mu_i]$. Hence, by (*)

$$V = U \left[\langle \alpha, X \rangle \mapsto \alpha \,, \frac{0}{\mu_1} \mapsto \mu_1 \,, \ldots, \frac{0}{\mu_n} \mapsto \mu_n \right]$$
$$= \langle V, U_1 \rangle \left[\langle \alpha, X \rangle \mapsto \alpha \,, \frac{0}{\mu_1} \mapsto \mu_1 \,, \ldots, \frac{0}{\mu_n} \mapsto \mu_n \right] = \langle \, U', U'' \, \rangle$$

where by (**)

$$U'' = U_1 \left[\frac{0}{\mu_1} \mapsto \mu_1 \,, \ldots, \frac{0}{\mu_n} \mapsto \mu_n \right] \not\sqsupseteq \alpha$$

$$U' = V \left[\langle \alpha, X \rangle \mapsto \alpha \,, \frac{0}{\mu_1} \mapsto \mu_1 \,, \ldots, \frac{0}{\mu_n} \mapsto \mu_n \right].$$

Thus, V satisfies (*) and (**). Thus, by induction, if $\langle \alpha, X \rangle \sqsubseteq U \sqsubseteq W$ and $U = \langle U_0, U_1 \rangle$, then U satisfies (*) and (**).

Now, to prove that (A)-(D) hold, it suffices to prove by induction on the size of finite binary trees that if U is a subtree of W which is such that $\langle \alpha, X \rangle \sqsubseteq U$, then there exists a sequence $U_1, \ldots, U_m$ such that: (i) $U = \langle \alpha, U_m, U_{m-1}, \ldots, U_1 \rangle$, (ii) $U_m = X$, (iii) $U_{i+1} = U_i \left[\frac{0}{\mu_1} \mapsto \mu_1, \ldots, \frac{0}{\mu_n} \mapsto \mu_n \right]$ for all $i \in \{1, 2, \ldots, m-1\}$.

So, assume $\langle \alpha, X \rangle \sqsubseteq U \sqsubseteq W$. If $U = \langle \alpha, X \rangle$, then U satisfies (i)-(iii) trivially. Otherwise, by (**), there exist V and U_1 such that $U = \langle V, U_1 \rangle$ and $\langle \alpha, X \rangle \sqsubseteq V$. By the induction hypothesis, there exists a sequence $V_1, \ldots, V_m$ such that the following holds: (iv) $V = \langle \alpha, V_m, V_{m-1}, \ldots, V_1 \rangle$, (v) $V_m = X$, (vi) $V_{i+1} = V_i \left[\frac{0}{\mu_1} \mapsto \mu_1, \ldots, \frac{0}{\mu_n} \mapsto \mu_n \right]$ for all $i \in \{1, 2, \ldots, m-1\}$. In particular, $U = \langle V, U_1 \rangle = \langle \alpha, V_m, V_{m-1}, \ldots, V_1, U_1 \rangle$. By (v)-(vi) and (**), there can only be one occurrence of α in U. Hence $U \left[\langle \alpha, X \rangle \mapsto \alpha \right] = \langle \alpha, V_{m-1}, \ldots, V_1, U_1 \rangle$. Then, by (*) and (vi)

$$\langle \alpha, V_m, V_{m-1}, \ldots, V_1 \rangle = V =$$

$$U \left[\langle \alpha, X \rangle \mapsto \alpha, \frac{0}{\mu_1} \mapsto \mu_1, \ldots, \frac{0}{\mu_n} \mapsto \mu_n \right] =$$

$$\langle \alpha, V_{m-1}, \ldots, V_1, U_1 \rangle \left[\frac{0}{\mu_1} \mapsto \mu_1, \ldots, \frac{0}{\mu_n} \mapsto \mu_n \right] =$$

$$\langle \alpha, V_m, \ldots, V_2, U_1' \rangle$$

where $U_1' = U_1 \left[\frac{0}{\mu_1} \mapsto \mu_1, \ldots, \frac{0}{\mu_n} \mapsto \mu_n \right]$. Hence

$$U = \langle \alpha, V_m, V_{m-1}, \ldots, V_1, U_1 \rangle \text{ and } V_1 = U_1 \left[\frac{0}{\mu_1} \mapsto \mu_1, \ldots, \frac{0}{\mu_n} \mapsto \mu_n \right].$$

Thus, U satisfies (i)-(iii).

Thus, by induction, if U is a subtree of W which is such that $\langle \alpha, X \rangle \sqsubseteq U$, then U satisfies (i)-(iii).   □

7   Reduction of Post's Correspondence Problem

We are ready to specify a many-to-one reduction of Post's Correspondence Problem.

Theorem 1. *The Post Correspondence Problem is many-to-one reducible to the fragment* $\mathsf{Th}^{\exists}(\mathcal{T}(\mathcal{L}_{\mathsf{BT}}))$.

Proof. Consider an instance $\langle a_1, b_1 \rangle, \ldots, \langle a_n, b_n \rangle$ of PCP. We need to construct an existential $\mathcal{L}_{\mathsf{BT}}$-sentence ϕ that is true in $\mathcal{T}(\mathcal{L}_{\mathsf{BT}})$ if and only if $\langle a_1, b_1 \rangle, \ldots, \langle a_n, b_n \rangle$ has a solution. The instance $\langle a_1, b_1 \rangle, \ldots, \langle a_n, b_n \rangle$ has a solution if and only if there exist two sequences $u_1, u_2, \ldots, u_k$ and $v_1, v_2, \ldots, v_m$ such that

(I) there exists $f_1 \in \{1, \ldots, n\}$ such that $u_1 = a_{f_1}$ and for all $j \in \{1, \ldots, k-1\}$
     there exist $f_{j+1} \in \{1, \ldots, n\}$ such that $u_{j+1} = u_j a_{f_{j+1}}$
(II) there exists $g_1 \in \{1, \ldots, n\}$ such that $u_1 = b_{g_1}$ and for all $j \in \{1, \ldots, m-1\}$
     there exist $g_{j+1} \in \{1, \ldots, n\}$ such that $u_{j+1} = u_j b_{g_{j+1}}$
(III) $k = m$ and $f_j = g_j$ for all $j \in \{1, \ldots, k\}$
(IV) $u_k = v_m$.

Let $\alpha = \langle \perp, \perp^2 \rangle$ and $\gamma = \langle \perp, \perp^3 \rangle$. Then, α and γ satisfy the conditions in Definition 6 and Definition 8. Let $A = \langle a_1, a_2, \ldots, a_n \rangle$ and let $B = \langle b_1, b_2, \ldots, b_n \rangle$. Definition 6 tells us that the sequence $u_1, u_2, \ldots, u_k$ is encoded by a binary tree $L \in \mathbb{P}(A, \alpha, \gamma)$ and the right subtree of L, denoted U, encodes u_k. Similarly, the sequence $v_1, v_2, \ldots, v_m$ is encoded by a binary tree $R \in \mathbb{P}(B, \alpha, \gamma)$ and the right subtree of R, denoted V, encodes v_m. Lemma 3 tells us that $\mathbb{P}(A, \alpha, \gamma)$ and $\mathbb{P}(B, \alpha, \gamma)$ are existentially definable.

Definition 8 gives us binary trees X_L and $W_L \in \mathbb{P}_2(A, \alpha, \gamma)$ such that $\Gamma_n^\alpha(L)$ is the right subtree of W_L, $\langle \alpha, X_L \rangle \sqsubseteq W_L$ and X_L encodes the sequence $f_1, f_2, \ldots, f_k$. The existentially definable operator Γ_n^α is defined in Definition 7. Similarly, there exist X_R and $W_R \in \mathbb{P}_2(B, \alpha, \gamma)$ such that $\Gamma_n^\alpha(R)$ is the right subtree of W_R, $\langle \alpha, X_R \rangle \sqsubseteq W_R$ and X_R encodes the sequence $g_1, g_2, \ldots, g_m$. Lemma 4 tells us that $\mathbb{P}_2(A, \alpha, \gamma)$ and $\mathbb{P}_2(B, \alpha, \gamma)$ are existentially definable.

Now, encoding (III) corresponds to requiring that $X_L = X_R$ holds. To encode (IV), we cannot simply require that $U = V$ holds since U is the representation of u_k when viewed as an element of $\{0, 1, \mu_1, \ldots, \mu_n\}^+$ and V is the representation of v_m when viewed as an element of $\{0, 1, \mu_1, \ldots, \mu_n\}^+$. So, let $\Theta_n^A(U)$ be the binary tree we obtain by replacing μ_i with the last letter of a_i and let $\Theta_n^B(V)$ be the binary tree we obtain by replacing μ_j with the last letter of b_j. Then, encoding (IV) corresponds to requiring that $\Theta_n^A(U) = \Theta_n^B(V)$ holds.

Let $\Theta_n^A(U) = U[\, \mu_1 \mapsto d_1, \ldots, \mu_n \mapsto d_n\,]$ where d_i is the last letter of a_i. Let $\Theta_n^B(V) = V[\, \mu_1 \mapsto e_1, \ldots, \mu_n \mapsto e_n\,]$ where e_j is the last letter of b_j. Let

$$\phi \equiv \exists L \in \mathbb{P}(A, \alpha, \gamma) \; \exists U, U' \; \exists R \in \mathbb{P}(B, \alpha, \gamma) \; \exists V, V'$$

$$\exists W_L \in \mathbb{P}_2(A, \alpha, \gamma) \; \exists X_L, S_L \; \exists W_R \in \mathbb{P}_2(B, \alpha, \gamma) \; \exists X_R, S_R \; \Big[$$

$$L = \langle U', U \rangle \; \wedge \; R = \langle V', V \rangle \; \wedge \; \langle \alpha, X_L \rangle \sqsubseteq W_L \; \wedge \; W_L = \langle S_L, \Gamma_n^\alpha(L) \rangle \; \wedge$$

$$\langle \alpha, X_R \rangle \sqsubseteq W_R \; \wedge \; W_R = \langle S_R, \Gamma_n^\alpha(R) \rangle \; \wedge \; \Theta_n^A(U) = \Theta_n^B(V) \; \wedge \; X_L = X_R \Big].$$

Then, ϕ is true in $\mathcal{T}(\mathcal{L}_{\mathsf{BT}})$ if and only if $\langle a_1, b_1 \rangle, \ldots, \langle a_n, b_n \rangle$ has a solution. $\square$

8   Analogue of Hilbert's Tenth Problem

In this section, we show that the analogue of Hilbert's Tenth Problem for $\mathcal{T}(\mathcal{L}_{\mathsf{BT}})$ is undecidable.

Theorem 2. *The fragment* $\mathsf{Th}^{\mathsf{H10}}(\mathcal{T}(\mathcal{L}_{\mathsf{BT}}))$ *is undecidable.*

Proof. Since $\mathsf{Th}^{\exists}(\mathcal{T}(\mathcal{L}_{\mathsf{BT}}))$ is undecidable, it suffices to show that given an existential $\mathcal{L}_{\mathsf{BT}}$-sentence ϕ, we can compute a finite number of $\mathcal{L}_{\mathsf{BT}}$-sentences $\phi_1, \ldots, \phi_n$ of the form $\exists \vec{x}\,[\,s = t\,]$ such that $\mathcal{T}(\mathcal{L}_{\mathsf{BT}}) \models \phi \leftrightarrow \bigvee_{i=1}^{n} \phi_i$. Since $\mathcal{T}(\mathcal{L}_{\mathsf{BT}}) \models (\,s_1 = t_1 \wedge s_2 = t_2\,) \leftrightarrow \langle s_1, s_2 \rangle = \langle t_1, t_2 \rangle$, it suffices to show that given a $\mathcal{L}_{\mathsf{BT}}$-formula of the form $s \neq t$, we can compute a finite number of atomic $\mathcal{L}_{\mathsf{BT}}$-formulas $s_1 = t_1, \ldots, s_k = t_k$ such that we have $\mathcal{T}(\mathcal{L}_{\mathsf{BT}}) \models s \neq t \leftrightarrow \bigvee_{j=1}^{k} s_j = t_j$. This is the case since $s \neq t \Leftrightarrow t[s \mapsto \langle s, s \rangle] = t \vee s[t \mapsto \langle t, t \rangle] = s$. $\square$

9 Bounded Quantifiers

We end this paper by showing that $\Sigma_{1,0,1}^{\mathcal{T}(\mathcal{L}_{\mathsf{BT}})}$ is undecidable. We prove this by encoding the Modulo Problem.

Theorem 3. *The fragment $\Sigma_{1,0,1}^{\mathcal{T}(\mathcal{L}_{\mathsf{BT}})}$ is undecidable.*

Proof. We encode natural numbers as follows: $n \equiv \perp^{n+2}$. The next step is to associate linear polynomials in one variable with $\mathcal{L}_{\mathsf{BT}}$-terms. We let $L(z) \equiv z[0 \mapsto z]$. If z represents the natural number q, then $L(z)$ represents the natural number $2q$ since 0 has exactly one occurrence in z. Recall that $L^0(z) = z$ and $L^{k+1}(z) = L(L^k(z))$. Hence, if $n > 0$, then $L^{n-1}(z)$ represents the natural number nq. If $n > 0$, then the term $m[0 \mapsto L^{n-1}(z)]$ represents the natural number $nq + m$. We complete our translation of linear polynomials in one variable as follows: For any formula $\phi(x)$ where x is a free variable, $\phi(nz + m) = \phi(m)$ if $n = 0$ and $\phi(nz + m) = \phi(m[0 \mapsto L^{n-1}(z)])$ if $n > 0$.

Given an instance $\langle A_0, B_0 \rangle, \ldots, \langle A_{M-1}, B_{M-1} \rangle$, we need to compute a $\Sigma_{1,0,1}$-sentence ψ that is true in $\mathcal{T}(\mathcal{L}_{\mathsf{BT}})$ if and only if the instance has a solution. Let $x \in y$ be shorthand for $\langle x, \alpha \rangle \sqsubseteq y \wedge \alpha \not\sqsubseteq x$ where $\alpha \equiv \langle \perp, \perp^2 \rangle$. The sentence ψ needs to say that there exists a finite set T such that $3 \in T$, $2 \in T$ and if $2 \neq Mz + j \in T \wedge 0 \leq j < M$, then $A_j z + B_j \in T$. With this in mind, we let ψ be the sentence $\exists T\, \forall z \sqsubseteq T\,[\,3 \in T \wedge \psi_0\,]$ where ψ_0 is

$$\bigwedge_{j=0}^{M-1} \Big(\,(Mz + j \in T \wedge Mz + j \neq 2\,) \rightarrow A_j z + B_j \in T\,\Big).$$ $\square$

References

1. Davis, M.: Hilbert's tenth problem is unsolvable. Am. Math. Monthly **80**(3), 233–269 (1973)
2. Hodges, W.: Model Theory. Cambridge University Press, Cambridge (1993)
3. Kristiansen, L., Murwanashyaka, J.: First-order concatenation theory with bounded quantifiers. Arch. Math. Logic **60**(1–2), 77–104 (2021). https://doi.org/10.1007/s00153-020-00735-6
4. Post, E.L.: A variant of a recursively unsolvable problem. Bull. (new Ser.) Am. Math. Soc. **52**(4), 264–268 (1946)
5. Venkataraman, K.: Decidability of the purely existential fragment of the theory of term algebras. J. ACM **34**(2), 492–510 (1987)

Weak Sequential Theories of Finite Full Binary Trees

Juvenal Murwanashyaka[✉] [iD]

Department of Mathematics, University of Oslo, Oslo, Norway
juvenalm@math.uio.no

Abstract. We study a first-order theory of finite full binary trees with an axiom schema of open induction. We show that this theory is sequential by constructing a direct interpretation of Adjunctive Set Theory in a very weak finitely axiomatized subtheory. We show that weakening the latter theory by removal of an axiom which states that the subtree relation is transitive gives a theory that directly interprets Vaught's weak set theory, a non-finitely axiomatizable fragment of Adjunctive Set Theory.

1 Introduction

In this paper, we show that a very weak finitely axiomatized first-order theory of finite full binary trees is sequential. Informally, *sequential* theories are theories with a coding machinery of a certain strength. It is possible to code any finite sequence in the domain of the theory. Furthermore, it is possible to extend any sequence by adjoining an arbitrary element. The concept of sequential theories was introduced by Pudlák [7] in the study of degrees of multidimensional local interpretations. Pudlák shows that sequential theories are prime in this degree structure. An element is prime if it is not the join of two smaller elements.

As a consequence of their expressive power, sequential theories are essentially undecidable. A computably enumerable first-order theory is called *essentially undecidable* if any consistent extension, in the same language, is undecidable (there is no algorithm for deciding whether an arbitrary sentence is a theorem). A computably enumerable first-order theory is called *essentially incomplete* if any recursively axiomatizable consistent extension is incomplete. It can be proved that a theory is essentially undecidable if and only if it is essentially incomplete (see Chapter 1 of Tarski et al. [9]). Two theories that are known to be essentially undecidable are Robinson arithmetic Q and the related theory R (see Chapter 2 of [9]).

Examples of sequential theories are Adjunctive Set Theory AS (see Fig. 1 for the axioms of AS), the theory of discretely ordered commutative semirings with a least element PA⁻ (see Jeřábek [4]), Robinson Arithmetic with bounded induction IΔ₀ (see Hájek & Pudlák [3] Section V3b), Peano Arithmetic PA, Zermelo-Fraenkel Set Theory ZF. Examples of theories that are not sequential are Robinson Arithmetic Q (see Visser [11] Example 1 or Theorem 9 of [4]) and Gregorczyk's theory of concatenation TC (see Visser [12] Sect. 5).

© The Author(s), under exclusive license to Springer Nature Switzerland AG 2022
U. Berger et al. (Eds.): CiE 2022, LNCS 13359, pp. 208–219, 2022.
https://doi.org/10.1007/978-3-031-08740-0_18

The Axioms of AS

AS_1 $\exists x \, \forall y \, [\, y \notin x \,]$

AS_2 $\forall xy \, \exists z \, \forall w \, [\, w \in z \leftrightarrow (\, w \in x \, \vee \, w = y \,) \,]$

The Axioms of VS

VS_0 $\exists x \, \forall y \, [\, y \notin x \,]$

VS_n $\forall x_1 \ldots x_n \, \exists y \, \forall z \, [\, z \in y \leftrightarrow \bigvee_{i=1}^{n} z = x_i \,]$ for $0 < n < \omega$

Fig. 1. Non-logical axioms of the first-order theories AS and VS.

Formally, sequential theories are theories that directly interpret AS (see Sect. 2). A weaker notion is the concept of theories that directly interpret the weak set theory VS of Vaught [10], which is a non-finitely axiomatizable fragment of AS (see Figure 1 for the axioms of VS). Vaught introduces VS in the study of theories that are axiomatizable by a schema. A theory T is axiomatizable by a schema if there exists a formula Φ in the language of T plus a fresh relation symbol R such that the set of universal closures of formulas obtained by substituting formulas for R in Φ is an axiom set for T. Vaught shows that any computably enumerable first-order theory of finite signature that directly interprets VS is axiomatizable by a schema. For more on VS, see Sect. 3.2 of Visser [11].

In [11] and [12], Visser shows that Q and TC are not sequential by showing that they do not have pairing. A theory S has pairing if there exists a formula $\mathsf{Pair}(x,y,z)$ in the language of S such that S proves $\forall xy \, \exists z \, [\, \mathsf{Pair}(x,y,z) \,]$ and $\forall xyzuv \, [\, (\, \mathsf{Pair}(x,y,z) \, \wedge \, \mathsf{Pair}(u,v,z) \,) \rightarrow (\, x = u \, \wedge \, y = v \,) \,]$. In Kristiansen & Murwanashyaka [5], we introduce an essentially undecidable theory T with pairing (see Fig. 2 for the axioms of T). The language of T is $\mathcal{L}_\mathsf{T} = \{ \bot, \langle \cdot, \cdot \rangle, \sqsubseteq \}$ where $\bot$ is a constant symbol, $\langle \cdot, \cdot \rangle$ is a binary function symbol and $\sqsubseteq$ is a binary relation symbol. The intended model of T is a term algebra extended with the subterm relation: The universe is the set of all variable-free $\mathcal{L}_\mathsf{T}$-terms (equivalently, finite full binary trees). The constant symbol $\bot$ is interpreted as itself. The function symbol $\langle \cdot, \cdot \rangle$ is interpreted as the function that maps the pair (s,t) to the term $\langle s,t \rangle$. The relation symbol $\sqsubseteq$ is interpreted as the subterm relation (equivalently, the subtree relation): s is a subterm of t iff $s = t$ or $t = \langle t_1, t_2 \rangle$ and s is a subterm of t_1 or t_2. In [5], we show that T is essentially undecidable by showing that it interprets Q but leave open the problem of whether the converse holds. In [2], Damnjanovic shows that Q interprets T.

It is not clear to us whether T is sequential or even expressive enough to directly interpret VS. It appears as if the subtree relation does not provide a good notion of occurrence since T has models where there exist distinct elements u, v such that $u \sqsubseteq v$ and $v \sqsubseteq u$. In this paper, we consider the theory $\Sigma^\mathsf{T}_\mathrm{open}$ we obtain by extending T with an axiom schema of open induction:

$$\phi(\bot, \vec{p}) \, \wedge \, \forall xy \, [\, \phi(x, \vec{p}) \, \wedge \, \phi(y, \vec{p}) \rightarrow \phi(\langle x, y \rangle, \vec{p}) \,] \rightarrow \forall x \, \phi(x, \vec{p})$$

The Axioms of T

T_1 $\forall xy \, [\, \langle x, y \rangle \neq \perp \,]$
T_2 $\forall xyzw \, [\, \langle x, y \rangle = \langle z, w \rangle \rightarrow (\, x = z \wedge y = w \,) \,]$
T_3 $\forall x \, [\, x \sqsubseteq \perp \leftrightarrow x = \perp \,]$
T_4 $\forall xyz \, [\, x \sqsubseteq \langle y, z \rangle \leftrightarrow (\, x = \langle y, z \rangle \vee x \sqsubseteq y \vee x \sqsubseteq z \,) \,]$

Fig. 2. Non-logical axioms of the first-order theory T.

where ϕ is a quantifier-free $\mathcal{L}_T$-formula. We study two extensions of T that are subtheories of Σ_{open}^T. Let $T^{(1)}$ denote the theory we obtain by extending T with the axiom $\forall xy \, [\, \langle x, y \rangle \not\sqsubseteq x \,]$. In Sect. 4, we show that $T^{(1)}$ directly interprets VS (the proof shows that we can in fact do with $\forall xy \, [\, x \sqsubseteq x \rightarrow \langle x, y \rangle \not\sqsubseteq x \,]$). The proof we give can be easily modified to show that VS is directly interpretable in $T + \forall xy \, [\, \langle x, y \rangle \not\sqsubseteq y \,]$. Let $T^{(2)}$ denote the theory we obtain by extending T with the axioms: $\forall xyz \, [\, x \sqsubseteq y \wedge y \sqsubseteq z \rightarrow x \sqsubseteq z \,]$, $\forall xyz \, [\, x \sqsubseteq y \rightarrow \langle y, z \rangle \not\sqsubseteq x \,]$ (we could also have used $\forall xyz \, [\, x \sqsubseteq z \rightarrow \langle y, z \rangle \not\sqsubseteq x \,]$). In Sect. 5.2, we show that $T^{(2)}$ is a sequential theory by constructing a direct interpretation of AS. In Sect. 5.1, we formulate the coding technique that is the basis of this interpretation. Since Σ_{open}^T is an extension of the sequential theory $T^{(2)}$, it is also a sequential theory. One of the referees found a shorter and neat direct interpretation of AS in $T^{(2)}$. We present their proof in Sect. 5.3.

2   Sequential Theories

Hájek & Pudlák [3, p. 151] characterize sequential theories as those theories that interpret Robinson Arithmetic Q and for which there are formulas $\text{Seq}(z, u)$ (z codes a sequence of length u) and $\beta(x, v, z)$ (x is the v-th element of z) with the following two properties: (1) If z codes a sequence s of length u, then for each number v that is strictly less than u, there is a unique x that is the v-th element of z. (2) If z codes a sequence s of length u, then given y, there exists z' that codes a sequence s' of length $u + 1$ obtained by extending s with y. This definition differs slightly from the original definition of Pudlák [7]. Instead of an interpretation of Q, Pudlák requires that there exist formulas $x \leq y$, $\mathsf{N}(x)$ such that $\leq$ is a total ordering of N and each element of N has a successor in N. In this paper, we use the equivalent definition of sequentiality in terms of Adjunctive Set Theory AS (see Pudlák [7, p. 274] and Visser [11] Sect. 3.3). See Fig. 1 for the axioms of AS.

Definition 1. *Let T be a first-order theory in the language of set theory $\{\in\}$. A first-order theory S directly interprets T if there exists a formula $\phi(x, y)$ in the language of S with only x and y free such that the extension by definitions $S + \forall xy \, [\, x \in y \leftrightarrow \phi(x, y) \,]$ proves each axiom of T. A first-order theory is sequential if it directly interprets AS.*

For a more comprehensive discussion of the notion of sequentiality, we refer the reader to Visser [11]. In Mycielski et al. [6, Appendix III], it is shown that a theory of sequences can be developed in any theory that directly interprets AS. This can be used to show that AS interprets Q (see Pudlák [7] Sect. 2). See also Damnjanovic [1] for mutual interpretability of AS and Q.

3   Open Induction

In this section, we verify that $\Sigma_{\text{open}}^{\mathsf{T}}$ is an extension of $\mathsf{T}^{(1)}$ and $\mathsf{T}^{(2)}$. Thus, when we show that $\mathsf{T}^{(2)}$ is a sequential theory, it will also follow that $\Sigma_{\text{open}}^{\mathsf{T}}$ is a sequential theory.

Theorem 1. $\Sigma_{\text{open}}^{\mathsf{T}}$ *is an extension of* $\mathsf{T}^{(1)}$ *and* $\mathsf{T}^{(2)}$.

Proof. It suffices to show that $\Sigma_{\text{open}}^{\mathsf{T}}$ proves the following: (A) $\forall x\,[\,x \sqsubseteq x\,]$, (B) $\forall xyz\,[\,x \sqsubseteq y \,\wedge\, y \sqsubseteq z \to x \sqsubseteq z\,]$, (C) $\forall xyz\,[\,x \sqsubseteq y \to \langle y, z\rangle \not\sqsubseteq x\,]$.

We prove (A) by induction on x. The base case $\bot \sqsubseteq \bot$ holds by the axiom $\mathsf{T}_3 \equiv \forall x\,[\,x \sqsubseteq \bot \leftrightarrow x = \bot\,]$. The inductive case $(x \sqsubseteq x \,\wedge\, y \sqsubseteq y\,) \to \langle x, y\rangle \sqsubseteq \langle x, y\rangle$ holds by the axiom $\mathsf{T}_4 \equiv \forall xyz\,[\,x \sqsubseteq \langle y, z\rangle \leftrightarrow (\,x = \langle y, z\rangle \vee x \sqsubseteq y \vee x \sqsubseteq z\,)\,]$. Thus, by induction, $\forall x\,[\,x \sqsubseteq x\,]$ is a theorem of $\Sigma_{\text{open}}^{\mathsf{T}}$.

We prove (B) by induction on z using x and y as parameters. The base case $x \sqsubseteq y \,\wedge\, y \sqsubseteq \bot \to x \sqsubseteq \bot$ holds by T_3. We consider the inductive case $z = \langle z_0, z_1\rangle$. Assume the following formulas hold: (I) $x \sqsubseteq y \,\wedge\, y \sqsubseteq z_0 \to x \sqsubseteq z_0$, (II) $x \sqsubseteq y \,\wedge\, y \sqsubseteq z_1 \to x \sqsubseteq z_1$. We need to show that $x \sqsubseteq y \,\wedge\, y \sqsubseteq z \to x \sqsubseteq z$. So, assume $x \sqsubseteq y$ and $y \sqsubseteq z$. By T_4, we have the following cases: (1) $y = z$, (2) $y \sqsubseteq z_0$, (3) $y \sqsubseteq z_1$. Case (1) implies $x \sqsubseteq z$. We consider (2). Since $x \sqsubseteq y$ and $y \sqsubseteq z_0$, we have $x \sqsubseteq z_0$ by (I). Hence, $x \sqsubseteq \langle z_0, z_1\rangle = z$ by T_4. By similar reasoning, Case (3) also implies $x \sqsubseteq z$. Thus, $x \sqsubseteq y \,\wedge\, y \sqsubseteq z \to x \sqsubseteq z$. By induction, $\forall xyz\,[\,x \sqsubseteq y \,\wedge\, y \sqsubseteq z \to x \sqsubseteq z\,]$ is a theorem of $\Sigma_{\text{open}}^{\mathsf{T}}$.

We prove (C) by induction on x with y and z as parameters. We consider the base case $x = \bot$. By T_3 and $\mathsf{T}_1 \equiv \forall xy\,[\,\langle x, y\rangle \neq \bot\,]$, we have $\langle y, z\rangle \not\sqsubseteq \bot$. We consider the inductive case $x = \langle x_0, x_1\rangle$. Assume the following formulas hold: (IV) $x_0 \sqsubseteq y \to \langle y, z\rangle \not\sqsubseteq x_0$, (V) $x_1 \sqsubseteq y \to \langle y, z\rangle \not\sqsubseteq x_1$. We need to show that $x \sqsubseteq y \to \langle y, z\rangle \not\sqsubseteq x$. Assume for the sake of a contradiction $x \sqsubseteq y$ and $\langle y, z\rangle \sqsubseteq x$. By T_4, we have the following cases: (i) $\langle y, z\rangle = x$, (ii) $\langle y, z\rangle \sqsubseteq x_0$, (iii) $\langle y, z\rangle \sqsubseteq x_1$. We consider (i). By $\mathsf{T}_2 \equiv \forall xyzw\,[\,\langle x, y\rangle = \langle z, w\rangle \to (\,x = z \,\wedge\, y = w\,)\,]$, we have $y = x_0$. Hence, by (A), we have $x_0 \sqsubseteq y$. Since $\langle x_0, x_1\rangle \sqsubseteq y$ and $\langle x_0, x_1\rangle = \langle y, z\rangle$ and $x_0 = y$, we find $\langle y, z\rangle \sqsubseteq x_0$. But $x_0 \sqsubseteq y$ and $\langle y, z\rangle \sqsubseteq x_0$ contradicts (IV).

We consider (ii). By (A), we have $x_0 \sqsubseteq x_0$. By T_4, we have $x_0 \sqsubseteq \langle x_0, x_1\rangle$. Since $x_0 \sqsubseteq \langle x_0, x_1\rangle$ and $x \sqsubseteq y$, we have $x_0 \sqsubseteq y$ by (B). Thus, we have $x_0 \sqsubseteq y$ and $\langle y, z\rangle \sqsubseteq x_0$, which contradicts (IV). By similar reasoning, (iii) leads to a contradiction.

Thus, by induction, $\forall xyz\,[\,x \sqsubseteq y \to \langle y, z\rangle \not\sqsubseteq x\,]$ is a theorem of $\Sigma_{\text{open}}^{\mathsf{T}}$.   □

4   Direct Interpretation of VS

Recall that $T^{(1)}$ is T extended with the axiom $T_5^{(1)} \equiv \forall xy \, [\, \langle x, y \rangle \not\sqsubseteq x\,]$. In this section, we show that VS is directly interpretable in $T^{(1)}$. Since in the proof $T_5^{(1)}$ is applied to cases where x is of the form $x = \langle x_0, x_1 \rangle$, we can by T_4 do with the weaker axiom $\forall xy \, [\, x \sqsubseteq x \rightarrow \langle x, y \rangle \not\sqsubseteq x\,]$.

To improve readability, we introduce the following notation: By recursion, let $() := \bot$ and $(x_1, \ldots, x_n) := \langle (x_1, \ldots, x_{n-1}), x_n \rangle$ for $n \geq 1$. So, $(x) := \langle \bot, x \rangle$, $(x, y) := \langle \langle \bot, x \rangle, y \rangle$, and so on.

Theorem 2. VS *is directly interpretable in* $T^{(1)}$.

Proof. We translate the membership relation as follows

$$x \in y \equiv \exists uvw \, \big[\, y = \langle u, \langle w, v \rangle \rangle \ \wedge \ \langle w, x \rangle \sqsubseteq y \,\big] \ .$$

By $T_1 \equiv \forall xy \, [\, \langle x, y \rangle \neq \bot \,]$, there does not exist u, v, w such that $\bot = \langle u, \langle w, v \rangle \rangle$. Hence, $T^{(1)} \vdash \forall u \, [\, u \notin \bot \,]$. Thus, the translation of VS_0 is a theorem of $T^{(1)}$. We verify that the translation of VS_m is a theorem of $T^{(1)}$ for each $0 < m < \omega$.

We code a finite sequence $x_0, x_1, \ldots, x_n$ as $y = (\langle w, x_0 \rangle, \langle w, x_1 \rangle, \ldots, \langle w, x_n \rangle)$ where $w = (x_0, x_1, \ldots, x_n)$. By T_1 and T_4, we have $w \neq \bot$ and $w \sqsubseteq w$ by how w is defined. By $T_2 \equiv \forall xyzw \, [\, \langle x, y \rangle = \langle z, w \rangle \rightarrow (\, x = z \wedge y = w \,) \,]$, w is the unique element w' such that $y = \langle u, \langle w', v \rangle \rangle$ for some u and v. By the axiom $T_4 \equiv \forall xyz \, [\, x \sqsubseteq \langle y, z \rangle \leftrightarrow (\, x = \langle y, z \rangle \vee x \sqsubseteq y \vee x \sqsubseteq z \,) \,]$, we have $\langle w, x_i \rangle \sqsubseteq y$ for all $i \leq n$. Hence, $x_i \in y$ for all $i \leq n$. We need to show that $y = \{x_0, x_1, \ldots, x_n\}$. So, assume $z \in y$. By definition of $\in$ and uniqueness of w, this is equivalent to $\langle w, z \rangle \sqsubseteq y$. We need to show that there exists $i \leq n$ such that $z = x_i$. For $k \leq n$, let $y_0 = ()$ and $y_{k+1} = (\langle w, x_0 \rangle, \langle w, x_1 \rangle, \ldots, \langle w, x_k \rangle)$. Observe that $y_{k+1} = \langle y_k, \langle w, x_k \rangle \rangle$. By $T_3 \equiv \forall x \, [\, x \sqsubseteq \bot \leftrightarrow x = \bot \,]$ and T_1, we have $\langle w, z \rangle \not\sqsubseteq \bot = y_0$. Thus, it suffices to show that the following holds: If $\langle w, z \rangle \sqsubseteq y_{k+1}$, then $z = x_k$ or $\langle w, z \rangle \sqsubseteq y_k$.

So, assume $\langle w, z \rangle \sqsubseteq y_{k+1}$. By T_4, we have one of the following cases: (i) $\langle w, z \rangle = y_{k+1}$, (ii) $\langle w, z \rangle \sqsubseteq \langle w, x_k \rangle$, (iii) $\langle w, z \rangle \sqsubseteq y_k$. Thus, it suffices to show that (i) leads to a contradiction while (ii) implies $z = x_k$. We show that (i) leads to a contradiction. By T_2, the equality $\langle w, z \rangle = y_{k+1}$ implies $w = y_k$. If $k = 0$, then $w = y_k = \bot$ which contradicts T_1 by definition of w. If $k > 0$, then by T_4 and the definition of y_k, we have $\langle w, x_0 \rangle \sqsubseteq y_k = w$ which contradicts $T_5^{(1)}$.

We show (ii) implies $z = x_k$. By T_4, we have one of the following cases: (iia) $\langle w, z \rangle = \langle w, x_k \rangle$, (iib) $\langle w, z \rangle \sqsubseteq w$, (iic) $\langle w, z \rangle \sqsubseteq x_k$. Case (iia) implies $z = x_k$ by T_2. Case (iib) contradicts $T_5^{(1)}$. We consider (iic). We have $\langle w, z \rangle \sqsubseteq x_k$. Recall that $w = (x_0, x_1, \ldots, x_n)$. Hence, by T_4, $\langle w, z \rangle \sqsubseteq x_k$ implies $\langle w, z \rangle \sqsubseteq w$ which contradicts $T_5^{(1)}$. Thus, $z = x_k$. $\qquad\square$

It is not clear to us whether it is possible to directly interpret VS in T since it appears as if we do not have a good notion of occurrence without the axiom $\forall xy \, [\, \langle x, y \rangle \not\sqsubseteq x \,]$.

Open Problem 2. *Is* VS *directly interpretable in* T?

5   A Sequential Subtheory of $\Sigma^{\mathsf{T}}_{\text{open}}$

In this section, we show that the theory $\mathsf{T}^{(2)}$ is sequential by constructing a direct interpretation of AS. The construction is given in Sect. 5.2. In Sect. 5.1, we present the intuition behind the construction. In Sect. 5.3, we give an alternative proof that was suggested by one of the referees.

5.1   Coding Sequences

In this section, we explain how we intend to construct a formula $x \in y$ that provably in $\mathsf{T}^{(2)}$ satisfies the axioms of AS.

We reason in the standard model of T. We start by observing that there is a one-to-one correspondence between finite binary trees and finite sequences of finite binary trees. We introduce the following notation: By recursion, let $()_\alpha :=$ α and $(x_1, \ldots, x_n)_\alpha := \langle (x_1, \ldots, x_{n-1})_\alpha, x_n \rangle$ for $n \geq 1$. So, $(x)_\alpha := \langle \alpha, x \rangle$, $(x, y)_\alpha := \langle \langle \alpha, x \rangle, y \rangle$, and so on. We associate the empty sequence with $\perp$. We associate a finite sequence of finite binary trees $T_1, T_2, \ldots, T_N$ with the finite binary tree

$$T = (T_1, T_2, \ldots, T_N)_\perp . \tag{*}$$

Each non-empty finite binary tree T can be written uniquely on the form (*). Now, the idea is to let the empty tree represent the empty set and to let a finite binary tree of the form (*) represent the set $\{T_1, \ldots, T_N\}$. We observe that the finite binary tree $(T_1, T_2, \ldots, T_N, T_N)_\perp$ also represents the set $\{T_1, \ldots, T_N\}$. This is not a problem since AS does not require sets to be uniquely determined by their elements. Axiom AS_2 requires that we have an adjunction operator $\mathsf{adj}(\cdot, \cdot)$ that takes two finite binary trees T and u and gives a finite binary tree S that represents the set $T \cup \{u\}$. Clearly, $\mathsf{adj}(T, u) = \langle T, u \rangle$ does the job.

The next step is to construct an $\mathcal{L}_\mathsf{T}$-formula $x \in T$ that expresses that x is an element of T. With T as in (*), the idea is to express that there exists a finite binary tree W that encodes a sequence $V_1, V_2, \ldots, V_k$ where $V_1 = T$, for all $i \in \{1, \ldots, k-1\}$ there exists u_i such that $V_i = \langle V_{i+1}, u_i \rangle$ and there exist $j \in \{1, \ldots, k\}$ and S such that $V_j = \langle S, x \rangle$ (this is respectively what clauses (C), (D), (E) in Sect. 5.2 try to capture). We let W be of the form

$$W = (V_k, V_{k-1}, \ldots, V_2, V_1)_\alpha$$

where α is a finite binary tree whose purpose is to allow us to recognize the subtrees of W of the form $(V_k, V_{k-1}, \ldots, V_i)_\alpha$. This property is essential since the formula $x \in T$ needs to say that W is of a certain form by quantifying over subtrees of W. We require that α is not a subtree of T (this is what Clause (A) in Sect. 5.2 tries to capture). Then, the subtrees of W of the form $(V_k, V_{k-1}, \ldots, V_i)_\alpha$ are exactly those subtrees of W that have α as a subtree.

The problem with this approach is that we need to update α to find a finite binary tree W' that witnesses that x is also an element of $T' = \langle T, u \rangle$ when u is such that α is a subtree of T'. Since $x \in T'$, we need to ensure the existence of a finite binary tree of the form $W' = (V_k , V_{k-1} , V_2 , \ldots , V_1 , T')_{\alpha'}$ where α' is not a subtree of T'. Although this is not problematic when reasoning in the standard model, it appears as if we do not have in $\mathsf{T}^{(2)}$ the resources necessary to show that we can construct W' from W. Our solution is to let $x \in T$ be witnessed by infinitely many finite binary trees so that any finite binary tree that witnesses $x \in T'$ also witnesses $x \in T$. More precisely, we let $x \in T$ mean that there exists a marker α (a finite binary tree that is not a subtree of T) such that for any finite binary β that has α as a subtree, there exists a finite binary tree W_β of the form $(V_k , V_{k-1} , \ldots , V_2 , V_1)_\beta$.

The problem of markers that grow in size is similar to the problem of growing commas that is encountered when coding finite sequences of strings. In [8], W.V. Quine shows that first-order arithmetic is directly interpretable in the free semigroup with two generators by devising a way of coding arbitrary finite sequences of strings. Let a, b denote the generators of the semigroup. Let $\{a\}^*$ denote the set of all finite sequences of a's. Quine codes a finite set of strings $\{w_0, \ldots, w_n\}$ as a string of the form $w_0 b u b w_1 \ldots b u b w_n$ where $u \in \{a\}^*$ is such that if $v \in \{a\}^*$ is a substring of some w_i, then v is a proper substring of u. If u is a substring of a string w_{n+1}, we need to encode the set $\{w_0, \ldots, w_n, w_{n+1}\}$ as $w_0 b u' b w_1 \ldots b u' b w_n b u' b w_{n+1}$ where $u' \in \{a\}^*$ is longer than u. In [12], Albert Visser observes that this approach has some disadvantages in the setting of weak theories since we need to be able to update u when we wish to extend the coded sequence. The solution he provides is to represent a finite set $\{w_0, \ldots, w_n\}$ as a string of the form $b u_0 b w_0 b u_1 b w_1 \ldots b u_n b w_n$ where each u_i is in $\{a\}^*$, u_i is a substring of u_j when $i \leq j$ and if $v \in \{a\}^*$ is a substring of some w_i, then v is a proper substring of u_i. So, the commas (the u_i's) grow in length.

5.2   Direct Interpretation of AS

In this section, we construct a formula $x \in y$ that provably in $\mathsf{T}^{(2)}$ satisfies the axioms of AS. Recall that $\mathsf{T}^{(2)}$ is T extended with the following axioms $\mathsf{T}_5^{(2)} \equiv \forall xyz \, [\, (\, x \sqsubseteq y \, \wedge \, y \sqsubseteq z \,) \rightarrow x \sqsubseteq z \,]$, $\mathsf{T}_6^{(2)} \equiv \forall xyz \, [x \sqsubseteq y \rightarrow \langle y, z \rangle \not\sqsubseteq x]$.

We start by constructing a formula $W, \beta \Vdash u \in z$ which states that W is a finite binary tree using the marker β to witness that u is an element of z. Let $W, \beta \Vdash u \in z$ be shorthand for

(A) $\beta \not\sqsubseteq z$

(B) there exist z_0, z_1 such that $z = \langle z_0, z_1 \rangle$

(C) there exists W_0 such that $\beta \sqsubseteq W_0 \, \wedge \, W = \langle W_0, z \rangle$

(D) if $\langle W_1, v \rangle \sqsubseteq W \, \wedge \, \beta \sqsubseteq W_1 \, \wedge \, W_1 \neq \beta$, then there exist v_0, v_1 such that

$$v = \langle v_0, v_1 \rangle \, \wedge \, \exists W_2 \, [\beta \sqsubseteq W_2 \, \wedge \, W_1 = \langle W_2, v_0 \rangle]$$

(E) there exist W_3 and v such that $\langle W_3 , \langle v, u \rangle \rangle \sqsubseteq W \, \wedge \, \beta \sqsubseteq W_3$.

We let $W, \beta \not\Vdash u \in z$ be shorthand for $\neg (W, \beta \Vdash u \in z)$. We let $\mathsf{adj}(x,y) = \langle x, y \rangle$.

Lemma 1. $\mathsf{T} \vdash \forall W, \beta, u\, [\, W, \beta \not\Vdash u \in \bot\,]$.

Proof. By T_1, Clause (B) of $W, \beta \Vdash u \in \bot$ does not hold. □

Lemma 2. *Let* $W = \langle \beta, \mathsf{adj}(x, y) \rangle$. *Then*

$$\mathsf{T}^{(2)} \vdash (\, \beta \sqsubseteq \beta \,\wedge\, \beta \not\sqsubseteq \mathsf{adj}(x, y)\,) \rightarrow W, \beta \Vdash y \in \mathsf{adj}(x, y)\ .$$

Proof. Assume $\beta \sqsubseteq \beta \,\wedge\, \beta \not\sqsubseteq \mathsf{adj}(x, y)$ holds. We need to show that each one of the following clauses holds

(A) $\beta \not\sqsubseteq \mathsf{adj}(x, y)$
(B) there exist z_0, z_1 such that $\mathsf{adj}(x, y) = \langle z_0, z_1 \rangle$
(C) there exists W_0 such that $\beta \sqsubseteq W_0 \,\wedge\, W = \langle W_0, \mathsf{adj}(x, y) \rangle$
(D) if $\langle W_1, v \rangle \sqsubseteq W \,\wedge\, \beta \sqsubseteq W_1 \,\wedge\, W_1 \neq \beta$, then there exist v_0, v_1 such that

$$v = \langle v_0, v_1 \rangle \,\wedge\, \exists W_2\, [\, \beta \sqsubseteq W_2 \,\wedge\, W_1 = \langle W_2, v_0 \rangle\,]$$

(E) there exist W_3 and v such that $\langle W_3, \langle v, u \rangle \rangle \sqsubseteq W \,\wedge\, \beta \sqsubseteq W_3$.

Since $\beta \not\sqsubseteq \mathsf{adj}(x, y)$, (A) holds. By definition, $\mathsf{adj}(x, y) = \langle x, y \rangle$. Hence, (B) holds. It follows from $\beta \sqsubseteq \beta$ and the definition of W that (C) holds. We verify that (D) holds. Assume $\langle W_1, v \rangle \sqsubseteq W \,\wedge\, \beta \sqsubseteq W_1$. By T_4, we have

$$\langle W_1, v \rangle = \langle \beta, \mathsf{adj}(x, y) \rangle \,\vee\, \langle W_1, v \rangle \sqsubseteq \beta \,\vee\, \beta \sqsubseteq \langle W_1, v \rangle \sqsubseteq \mathsf{adj}(x, y)\ .$$

By $\mathsf{T}_5^{(2)}$, we have $\langle W_1, v \rangle = \langle \beta, \mathsf{adj}(x, y) \rangle \,\vee\, \langle W_1, v \rangle \sqsubseteq \beta \,\vee\, \beta \sqsubseteq \mathsf{adj}(x, y)$. Since $\beta \sqsubseteq W_1$, we have $\langle W_1, v \rangle \not\sqsubseteq \beta$ by $\mathsf{T}_6^{(2)}$. By assumption, $\beta \not\sqsubseteq \mathsf{adj}(x, y)$. Hence, $\langle W_1, v \rangle = \langle \beta, \mathsf{adj}(x, y) \rangle$. By T_2, we have $W_1 = \beta$. Thus, (D) holds.

Finally, we verify that (E) holds. By assumption, $\beta \sqsubseteq \beta \,\wedge\, W = \langle \beta, \mathsf{adj}(x, y) \rangle$. By T_4, $W \sqsubseteq W$. Since $\mathsf{adj}(x, y) = \langle x, y \rangle$, (E) holds. □

Lemma 3. $\mathsf{T}^{(2)}$ *proves the universal closure of*

$$(\, u \neq y \,\wedge\, \langle W, \mathsf{adj}(x, y) \rangle, \beta \Vdash u \in \mathsf{adj}(x, y)\,) \rightarrow W, \beta \Vdash u \in x\ .$$

Proof. Assume $u \neq y$ and that each one of the following clauses holds

(A) $\beta \not\sqsubseteq \mathsf{adj}(x, y)$
(B) there exist z_0, z_1 such that $\mathsf{adj}(x, y) = \langle z_0, z_1 \rangle$
(C) there exists W_0 such that $\beta \sqsubseteq W_0 \,\wedge\, \langle W, \mathsf{adj}(x, y) \rangle = \langle W_0, \mathsf{adj}(x, y) \rangle$
(D) if $\langle W_1, v \rangle \sqsubseteq \langle W, \mathsf{adj}(x, y) \rangle \,\wedge\, \beta \sqsubseteq W_1 \,\wedge\, W_1 \neq \beta$, then there exist v_0, v_1 such that

$$v = \langle v_0, v_1 \rangle \,\wedge\, \exists W_2\, [\, \beta \sqsubseteq W_2 \,\wedge\, W_1 = \langle W_2, v_0 \rangle\,]$$

(E) there exist W_3 and v such that $\langle W_3, \langle v, u \rangle \rangle \sqsubseteq \langle W, \mathsf{adj}(x, y) \rangle \,\wedge\, \beta \sqsubseteq W_3$.

Let (A'), (B'), (C'), (D'), (E') denote the corresponding clauses where we use W instead of $\langle W, \mathsf{adj}(x,y)\rangle$, and we use x instead of $\mathsf{adj}(x,y)$. We need to show that $(A')-(E')$ hold.

We show that (A') holds. By (A) , we have $\beta \not\sqsubseteq \mathsf{adj}(x,y)$. By T_4 and the definition of $\mathsf{adj}(x,y)$, $\beta \sqsubseteq x$ implies $\beta \sqsubseteq \mathsf{adj}(x,y)$. Hence, $\beta \not\sqsubseteq x$. Thus, (A') holds.

We show that (E'), (C') and (B') hold. By T_4, T_2 and (C) , we have $\beta \sqsubseteq W$ and $\langle W, \mathsf{adj}(x,y)\rangle \sqsubseteq \langle W, \mathsf{adj}(x,y)\rangle$. We show that $W \neq \beta$. By (E), there exist W_3 and v such that $\langle W_3\,, \langle v,u\rangle\rangle \sqsubseteq \langle W, \mathsf{adj}(x,y)\rangle \,\wedge\, \beta \sqsubseteq W_3$. By T_4, we have

$$\langle W_3\,, \langle v,u\rangle\rangle = \langle W, \mathsf{adj}(x,y)\rangle \vee \langle W_3\,, \langle v,u\rangle\rangle \sqsubseteq W \vee \beta \sqsubseteq \langle W_3\,, \langle v,u\rangle\rangle \sqsubseteq \mathsf{adj}(x,y)\,.$$

By T_2 and $\mathsf{T}_5^{(2)}$, we have $u = y \,\vee\, \langle W_3\,, \langle v,u\rangle\rangle \sqsubseteq W \,\vee\, \beta \sqsubseteq \mathsf{adj}(x,y)$. Since $u \neq y$ and $\beta \not\sqsubseteq \mathsf{adj}(x,y)$, we have $\langle W_3\,, \langle v,u\rangle\rangle \sqsubseteq W$. This shows that (E') holds. Since $\beta \sqsubseteq W_3$, we have $\langle W_3\,, \langle v,u\rangle\rangle \not\sqsubseteq \beta$ by $\mathsf{T}_6^{(2)}$. Hence, $W \neq \beta$. So

$$\langle W, \mathsf{adj}(x,y)\rangle \sqsubseteq \langle W, \mathsf{adj}(x,y)\rangle \,\wedge\, \beta \sqsubseteq W \,\wedge\, W \neq \beta.$$

Then, by T_2 and (D), there exists W_0 such that $\beta \sqsubseteq W_0 \,\wedge\, W = \langle W_0, x\rangle$. Thus, (C') holds. Since $\langle W_3\,, \langle v,u\rangle\rangle \sqsubseteq W = \langle W_0, x\rangle$ and $\beta \sqsubseteq W_3$, we have by T_4 and T_2

$$\langle v,u\rangle = x \vee \langle W_3\,, \langle v,u\rangle\rangle \sqsubseteq W_0 \vee \langle W_3\,, \langle v,u\rangle\rangle \sqsubseteq x\,.$$

If $\langle v,u\rangle = x$, then (B') holds. We have $\langle W_3\,, \langle v,u\rangle\rangle \not\sqsubseteq x$ since $\beta \sqsubseteq W_3$ would otherwise imply $\beta \sqsubseteq \mathsf{adj}(x,y)$ by T_4 and $\mathsf{T}_5^{(2)}$. Assume $\langle W_3\,, \langle v,u\rangle\rangle \sqsubseteq W_0$. Since $\beta \sqsubseteq W_3$, we have $W_0 \neq \beta$ by $\mathsf{T}_6^{(2)}$. Hence, by T_4, we have

$$\langle W_0, x\rangle \sqsubseteq \langle W, \mathsf{adj}(x,y)\rangle \,\wedge\, \beta \sqsubseteq W_0 \,\wedge\, W_0 \neq \beta\,.$$

Then, by (D), there exists x_0, x_1 such that $x = \langle x_0, x_1\rangle$. Thus, (B') holds.

We verify that (D') holds. Assume $\langle W_1, v\rangle \sqsubseteq W \,\wedge\, \beta \sqsubseteq W_1 \,\wedge\, W_1 \neq \beta$. By T_4, we have $\langle W_1, v\rangle \sqsubseteq \langle W, \mathsf{adj}(x,y)\rangle \,\wedge\, \beta \sqsubseteq W_1 \,\wedge\, W_1 \neq \beta$. It then follows from (D) that (D') holds. $\square$

Lemma 4. Let $W' = \langle W, \mathsf{adj}(x,y)\rangle$. Then, $\mathsf{T}^{(2)}$ proves the universal closure of

$$(\,\beta \not\sqsubseteq \mathsf{adj}(x,y) \,\wedge\, W, \beta \Vdash u \in x\,) \rightarrow W', \beta \Vdash u \in \mathsf{adj}(x,y)\,.$$

Proof. Assume $\beta \not\sqsubseteq \mathsf{adj}(x,y)$ and that each one of the following clauses holds

(A) $\beta \not\sqsubseteq x$
(B) there exist z_0, z_1 such that $x = \langle z_0, z_1\rangle$
(C) there exists W_0 such that $\beta \sqsubseteq W_0 \,\wedge\, W = \langle W_0, x\rangle$
(D) if $\langle W_1, v\rangle \sqsubseteq W \,\wedge\, \beta \sqsubseteq W_1 \,\wedge\, W_1 \neq \beta$, then there exist v_0, v_1 such that

$$v = \langle v_0, v_1\rangle \,\wedge\, \exists W_2\,[\,\beta \sqsubseteq W_2 \,\wedge\, W_1 = \langle W_2, v_0\rangle\,]$$

(E) there exist W_3 and v such that $\langle W_3\,, \langle v,u\rangle\rangle \sqsubseteq W \,\wedge\, \beta \sqsubseteq W_3$.

Let (A'), (B'), (C'), (D'), (E') denote the corresponding clauses where we use W' instead of W, and we use $\mathsf{adj}(x,y)$ instead of x. We need to show that $(A')-(E')$ hold.

By assumption, $\beta \not\sqsubseteq \mathsf{adj}(x,y)$. Thus, (A') holds. Since $\mathsf{adj}(x,y) = \langle x,y \rangle$, (B') holds. By (C), there exists W_0 such that $\beta \sqsubseteq W_0 \wedge W = \langle W_0, x \rangle$. By T_4 and the definition of W', we have $\beta \sqsubseteq W \wedge W' = \langle W, \mathsf{adj}(x,y) \rangle$. Thus, (C') holds.

We verify that (E') holds. By (E), there exist W_3 and v such that $\beta \sqsubseteq W_3$ and $\langle W_3, \langle v, u \rangle \rangle \sqsubseteq W$. By T_4 and the definition of W', we have $\beta \sqsubseteq W_3$ and $\langle W_3, \langle v, u \rangle \rangle \sqsubseteq W'$. Thus, (E') holds.

It remains to verify that (D') holds. Assume $\langle W_1, v \rangle \sqsubseteq W'$, $\beta \sqsubseteq W_1$ and $W_1 \neq \beta$. By T_4 and the definition of W', we have

$$\langle W_1, v \rangle = \langle W, \mathsf{adj}(x,y) \rangle \vee \langle W_1, v \rangle \sqsubseteq W \vee \langle W_1, v \rangle \sqsubseteq \mathsf{adj}(x,y) .$$

We cannot have $\langle W_1, v \rangle \sqsubseteq \mathsf{adj}(x,y)$ since $\beta \sqsubseteq W_1$ would otherwise by T_4 and $\mathsf{T}_5^{(2)}$ imply $\beta \sqsubseteq \mathsf{adj}(x,y)$. Hence, $\langle W_1, v \rangle = \langle W, \mathsf{adj}(x,y) \rangle \vee \langle W_1, v \rangle \sqsubseteq W$. Assume $\langle W_1, v \rangle = \langle W, \mathsf{adj}(x,y) \rangle$. By T_2 and (C), there exists W_0 such that $v = \langle x, y \rangle$, $W_1 = W = \langle W_0, x \rangle$ and $\beta \sqsubseteq W_0$. Assume now $\langle W_1, v \rangle \sqsubseteq W$. Then, by (D), there exist v_0, v_1 such that $v = \langle v_0, v_1 \rangle \wedge \exists W_2 [\beta \sqsubseteq W_2 \wedge W_1 = \langle W_2, v_0 \rangle]$. Thus, (D') holds. $\qquad\square$

We now have everything we need to show that $\mathsf{T}^{(2)}$ is sequential.

Theorem 3. AS *is directly interpretable in* $\mathsf{T}^{(2)}$.

Proof. We translate the membership relation as follows

$$u \in z \equiv \exists \alpha \left[\alpha \sqsubseteq \alpha \wedge \forall \beta \left[(\alpha \sqsubseteq \beta \wedge \beta \sqsubseteq \beta) \to \exists W [W, \beta \Vdash u \in z] \right] \right] .$$

By Lemma 1, the translation of AS_1 is a theorem of $\mathsf{T}^{(2)}$. It remains to show that the translation of AS_2 is a theorem of $\mathsf{T}^{(2)}$. It suffices to show that the sentence $\forall x y u [u \in \mathsf{adj}(x,y) \leftrightarrow (u = y \vee u \in x)]$ is a theorem of $\mathsf{T}^{(2)}$.

We show that $\mathsf{T}^{(2)} \vdash \forall x y [y \in \mathsf{adj}(x,y)]$. Let $\alpha = \langle \mathsf{adj}(x,y), \mathsf{adj}(x,y) \rangle$. By T_4, we have $\alpha \sqsubseteq \alpha$. Let β be such that $\alpha \sqsubseteq \beta$ and $\beta \sqsubseteq \beta$. We need to find W such that $W, \beta \Vdash y \in \mathsf{adj}(x,y)$. By $\mathsf{T}_5^{(2)}$, $\beta \sqsubseteq \mathsf{adj}(x,y)$ implies $\alpha \sqsubseteq \mathsf{adj}(x,y)$, which contradicts $\mathsf{T}_6^{(2)}$ since $\mathsf{adj}(x,y) \sqsubseteq \mathsf{adj}(x,y)$ by T_4. Hence, $\beta \sqsubseteq \beta$ and $\beta \not\sqsubseteq \mathsf{adj}(x,y)$. Then, by Lemma 2, we have $\langle \beta, \mathsf{adj}(x,y) \rangle, \beta \Vdash y \in \mathsf{adj}(x,y)$. Thus, $\mathsf{T}^{(2)} \vdash \forall x y [y \in \mathsf{adj}(x,y)]$.

We show that $\mathsf{T}^{(2)} \vdash \forall x y u [u \in \mathsf{adj}(x,y) \to (u = y \vee u \in x)]$. Assume $u \in \mathsf{adj}(x,y) \wedge u \neq y$. We need to show that $u \in x$. Since $u \in \mathsf{adj}(x,y)$, there exists α such that

$$\alpha \sqsubseteq \alpha \wedge \forall \beta \left[(\alpha \sqsubseteq \beta \wedge \beta \sqsubseteq \beta) \to \exists W [W, \beta \Vdash u \in \mathsf{adj}(x,y)] \right] .$$

By Clause (C) of $W, \beta \Vdash u \in \mathsf{adj}(x,y)$, we have

$$\alpha \sqsubseteq \alpha \wedge \forall \beta \left[(\alpha \sqsubseteq \beta \wedge \beta \sqsubseteq \beta) \to \exists V [\langle V, \mathsf{adj}(x,y) \rangle, \beta \Vdash u \in \mathsf{adj}(x,y)] \right] .$$

Then, by Lemma 3, we have

$$\alpha \sqsubseteq \alpha \,\wedge\, \forall \beta \left[\,(\,\alpha \sqsubseteq \beta \,\wedge\, \beta \sqsubseteq \beta \,) \to \exists V \,[\, V, \beta \Vdash u \in x \,] \,\right].$$

Thus, $\mathsf{T}^{(2)} \vdash \forall xyu \,[\, u \in \mathsf{adj}(x,y) \to (\, u = y \,\vee\, u \in x \,)\,]$.

We show that $\mathsf{T}^{(2)} \vdash \forall xyu \,[\, u \in x \to u \in \mathsf{adj}(x,y)\,]$. Assume $u \in x$ holds. Then, there exists α' such that

$$\alpha' \sqsubseteq \alpha' \,\wedge\, \forall \beta \left[\,(\,\alpha' \sqsubseteq \beta \,\wedge\, \beta \sqsubseteq \beta \,) \to \exists V \,[\, V, \beta \Vdash u \in x \,]\,\right]. \qquad (*)$$

Let $\alpha = \langle \mathsf{adj}(x,y), \alpha' \rangle$. By T_4 and $\alpha' \sqsubseteq \alpha'$, we have $\alpha \sqsubseteq \alpha \,\wedge\, \alpha' \sqsubseteq \alpha$. Hence, by $\mathsf{T}_5^{(2)}$, we have $\alpha \sqsubseteq \alpha \,\wedge\, \forall \beta \,[\alpha \sqsubseteq \beta \to \alpha' \sqsubseteq \beta]$. We have $\mathsf{adj}(x,y) \sqsubseteq \mathsf{adj}(x,y)$ by T_4. Hence, $\alpha \not\sqsubseteq \mathsf{adj}(x,y)$ by $\mathsf{T}_6^{(2)}$. Then, by $\mathsf{T}_5^{(2)}$, we have $\alpha \sqsubseteq \beta \to \beta \not\sqsubseteq \mathsf{adj}(x,y)$. It then follows from (*) and Lemma 4 that

$$\alpha \sqsubseteq \alpha \,\wedge\, \forall \beta \left[\,(\,\alpha \sqsubseteq \beta \,\wedge\, \beta \sqsubseteq \beta \,) \to \exists V \,[\, \langle V, \mathsf{adj}(x,y) \rangle, \beta \Vdash u \in \mathsf{adj}(x,y) \,] \,\right].$$

Thus, $\mathsf{T}^{(2)} \vdash \forall xyu \,[\, u \in x \to u \in \mathsf{adj}(x,y)\,]$.   □

Corollary 1. AS *is directly interpretable in* $\Sigma_{\mathsf{open}}^{\mathsf{T}}$.

Our interpretation of AS relies heavily on the transitivity of the subtree relation and it is not clear to us whether it is possible to directly interpret AS without using this property.

Open Problem 3. *Is* AS *directly interpretable in* T? *Is* AS *directly interpretable in* $\mathsf{T}^{(1)}$?

5.3   An Alternative Proof

In this final section, we present an alternative direct interpretation of AS in $\mathsf{T}^{(2)}$ that was suggested by one of the referees. Let $\mathsf{Pair}(x) \equiv \exists yz \,[\, x = \langle y, z \rangle \,]$ and $x \in' y \equiv \exists uv \,[\, y = \langle u, v \rangle \,\wedge\, \langle v, x \rangle \sqsubseteq y \,]$. Let $\mathsf{BSh}(x)$ be shorthand for: there exist u, v such that the following holds: (i) $x = \langle u, v \rangle$, (ii) $\mathsf{Pair}(v)$, (iii) $\forall v' \,[\, v \sqsubseteq v' \,\wedge\, \mathsf{Pair}(v') \to \exists u' \,\forall y \,[\, y \in' x \leftrightarrow y \in' \langle u', v' \rangle \,]\,]$. We translate the membership relation as follows: $x \in y \equiv x \in' y \,\wedge\, \mathsf{BSh}(y)$.

It is easy to verify, using T_1 and T_3, that the translation of AS_1 is a theorem of $\mathsf{T}^{(2)}$. We verify that the translation of AS_2 is a theorem of $\mathsf{T}^{(2)}$. We are given x and y and need to find z such that (1) $\forall w \,[\, w \in z \leftrightarrow (\, w \in x \,\vee\, w = y \,)\,]$. We assume first x is not an empty set according to $\in$. Then, there exist u, v such that $x = \langle u, v \rangle$, $\mathsf{Pair}(v)$ and for any $v' \sqsupseteq v$ such that $\mathsf{Pair}(v')$, there exist u' such that x and $\langle u', v' \rangle$ have the same $\in'$-elements. To construct z we pick $v' = \langle v, y \rangle$. Since $\mathsf{Pair}(v)$, we have $v \sqsubseteq v'$ by T_4. We then pick a corresponding u' and put $z = \langle \,\langle u', \langle v', y \rangle \rangle, v' \rangle$. It is easy to see that in order to verify (1) it is enough to fix arbitrary $v'' \sqsupseteq v'$ and any u'' such that $\mathsf{Pair}(v'')$ and $\forall w \,[\, w \in' \langle u', v' \rangle \leftrightarrow w \in \langle u'', v'' \rangle \,]$ and show that the $\in'$ elements of $\langle \,\langle u'', \langle v'', y \rangle \rangle, v'' \rangle$ precisely are y and all w such that $w \in' x$.

We have $w \in' \langle \langle u'', \langle v'', y \rangle \rangle, v'' \rangle$ if and only if $\langle u'', w \rangle \sqsubseteq \langle u'', \langle v'', y \rangle \rangle$. By T_4, the latter happens in exactly the following cases: (a) $\langle v'', w \rangle \sqsubseteq u''$, (b) $\langle v'', w \rangle \sqsubseteq y$, (c) $\langle v'', w \rangle \sqsubseteq v''$, (d) $\langle v'', w \rangle = \langle v'', y \rangle$, (e) $\langle v'', w \rangle = \langle u'', \langle v'', y \rangle \rangle$. By the choice of v'' and u'', (a) holds if and only if $w \in' \langle u', v' \rangle$, which in turn by the choice of v' and u' happens if and only if $w \in' x$. By T_2, Case (d) happens if and only if $w = y$. By definition, $v' = \langle v, y \rangle$. Since $\mathsf{Pair}(v)$, we have $v \sqsubseteq v' \sqsubseteq v''$ by T_4. By T_4, (b) implies $\langle u'', w \rangle \sqsubseteq \langle v, y \rangle = v' \sqsubseteq v''$. By $\mathsf{T}_5^{(2)}$, (b) implies $\langle u'', w \rangle \sqsubseteq v''$, which contradicts $\mathsf{T}_6^{(2)}$ since $v'' \sqsubseteq v''$ by T_4 as $\mathsf{Pair}(v'')$. Similarly, Case (c) contradicts $\mathsf{T}_6^{(2)}$. By T_2, Case (e) holds if and only if $v'' = u''$ and $w = \langle v'', y \rangle$. Since x is not an empty set according to $\in$, there exists w' such that $\langle v'', w' \rangle \sqsubseteq u'' = v''$ (since x and $\langle u'', v'' \rangle$ have the same $\in'$ elements) which contradicts $\mathsf{T}_6^{(2)}$. This concludes the verification of (1) when x is not an empty set according to $\in$.

If x is an empty set according to $\in$, we replace x with $\langle \bot, \langle \bot, \bot \rangle \rangle$ and proceed as above always choosing $u' = \bot$ and $u'' = \bot$. This concludes the verification of AS_2. This completes the proof.

References

1. Damnjanovic, Z.: Mutual interpretability of Robinson arithmetic and adjunctive set theory with extensionality. Bull. Symb. Logic **23**(4), 381–404 (2017)
2. Damnjanovic, Z.: Mutual interpretability of weak essentially undecidable theories. J. Symb. Logic 1–50 (2022). https://doi.org/10.1017/jsl.2022.15
3. Hájek, P., Pudlák, P.: Metamathematics of First-Order Arithmetic. Cambridge University Press, Cambridge (2017)
4. Jeřábek, E.: Sequence encoding without induction. Math. Logic Q. **58**(3), 244–248 (2012)
5. Kristiansen, L., Murwanashyaka, J.: On interpretability between some weak essentially undecidable theories. In: Anselmo, M., Della Vedova, G., Manea, F., Pauly, A. (eds.) CiE 2020. LNCS, vol. 12098, pp. 63–74. Springer, Cham (2020). https://doi.org/10.1007/978-3-030-51466-2_6
6. Mycielski, J., Pudlák, P., Stern, A.S.: A Lattice of Chapters of Mathematics (Interpretations Between Theorems), vol. 84, no. 426. Memoirs of the American Mathematical Society (1990)
7. Pudlák, P.: Some prime elements in the lattice of interpretability types. Trans. Am. Math. Soc. **280**(1), 255–275 (1983)
8. Quine, W.V.: Concatenation as a basis for arithmetic. J. Symb. Logic **11**(4), 105–114 (1946)
9. Tarski, A., Mostowski, A., Robinson, R.M.: Undecidable Theories. North-Holland, Amsterdam (1953)
10. Vaught, R.L.: Axiomatizability by a schema. J. Symb. Logic **32**(4), 473–479 (1967)
11. Visser, A.: Pairs, sets and sequences in first-order theories. Arch. Math. Logic **47**(4), 299–326 (2008). https://doi.org/10.1007/s00153-008-0087-1
12. Visser, A.: Growing commas. A study of sequentiality and concatenation. Notre Dame J. Formal Logic **50**(1), 61–85 (2009)

On Envelopes and Backward Approximations

Eike Neumann$^{(\boxtimes)}$

Swansea University, Swansea, UK
neumaef1@gmail.com

Abstract. We study the question under which assumptions the composition of a finite sequence of backwards-stable approximations of potentially discontinuous functions converges to the composition of the sequence of original functions. We give two convergence criteria with the help of continuous envelopes.

Keywords: Computable analysis · Backward stable algorithms · Continuous envelopes

1 Introduction

When working over infinite data, such as real numbers, one frequently encounters computational problems that fail to be solvable exactly (in the sense of Exact Real Computation) for continuity reasons. A common remedy is to replace such problems with approximate formulations where a slightly perturbed problem instance is solved exactly. More precisely, let $f\colon X \to Y$ be a function between computable metric spaces. Let $\mathbb{Q}_{>0}$ denote the space of strictly positive rational numbers with the discrete topology. Consider the *backward approximation*

$$^{\dagger}f\colon X \times \mathbb{Q}_{>0} \rightsquigarrow Y, \quad {}^{\dagger}f(x,\varepsilon) = \{f(\widetilde{x}) \in Y \mid \widetilde{x} \in B(x,\varepsilon)\}. \tag{1}$$

This relaxation underlies for instance the non-deterministic inequality test for real numbers, the notion of "approximate solutions" of fixed point equations [3,13], and backwards stable algorithms in numerical analysis [17, Chapter III].

Observe that the function $^{\dagger}f$ is always continuous in the sense of being computable relative to an oracle. Further, if f has a computable left inverse, then $^{\dagger}f$ is computable. The latter situation occurs frequently in practice, since discontinuous functions often arise as "inverse problems".

▨ This project has received funding from the European Union's Horizon 2020 research and innovation programme under the Marie Skłodowska-Curie grant agreement No 731143. This work has greatly benefited from discussions with Franz Brausse, Pieter Collins, Michal Konečný, Norbert Müller, Sewon Park, Florian Steinberg, and Martin Ziegler.

U. Berger et al. (Eds.): CiE 2022, LNCS 13359, pp. 220–233, 2022.
https://doi.org/10.1007/978-3-031-08740-0_19

Backward approximations can be useful for computing quantities that depend continuously on the input data. For instance, the standard algorithms for computing the eigenvalues of a matrix proceed by first diagonalising the matrix using a backwards stable algorithm, and then reading the eigenvalues off the diagonal [17, Chapter V]. This yields good approximations of the eigenvalues, despite the base change matrices not depending continuously on the input matrix.

This leads to the general question under which assumptions it is possible to make an "idealised" program that employs discontinuous functions as subroutines into a rigorous one by replacing the subroutines in question by backward approximations. We will study this question for the simplest types of programs: compositions of finite sequences of functions. We will give necessary and sufficient criteria with the help of continuous envelopes [9].

Let us first consider the following question: Given functions $f_i\colon X_i \to X_{i+1}$ between computable metric spaces $X_1,\dots,X_{n+1}$ and $x \in X_1$, when do we have convergence

$$^{\dagger}f_n(\cdot,\delta) \circ \cdots \circ {}^{\dagger}f_1(\cdot,\delta)(x) \to f_n \circ \cdots \circ f_1(x) \qquad \text{as } \delta \to 0\,? \qquad (2)$$

Here, $^{\dagger}f_i(\cdot,\delta)\colon X_i \rightsquigarrow X_{i+1}$ is the function which is obtained by binding the second parameter of $^{\dagger}f$ to δ.

A necessary condition is that the composition $f_n \circ \cdots \circ f_1$ be continuous. But this condition is not sufficient. Consider for instance the function $f\colon \mathbb{R} \to \mathbb{R}$ which sends 0 to 0 and $x \in \mathbb{R}\setminus\{0\}$ to $1/x$, and let $f_2 = f_1 = f$.

For a computable metric space Y, let $\mathcal{K}(Y)$ denote the space of compact subsets of Y endowed with the upper Vietoris topology. The space $\mathcal{K}(Y)$ carries a natural lattice structure with respect to its specialisation order, which corresponds to reverse inclusion of compact sets. Let $\mathcal{K}_{\perp}(Y)$ denote the same space with a bottom element added. Any function $f\colon X \to Y$ has a best continuous approximation $F\colon X \to \mathcal{K}_{\perp}(Y)$ in the following sense: For all $x \in X$ we have $f(x) \in F(x)$, and if a continuous map $G\colon X \to \mathcal{K}_{\perp}(Y)$ satisfies $f(x) \in G(x)$ for all $x \in X$ then $F(x) \subseteq G(x)$ for all $x \in X$. For a proof of this fact see $e.g.$ [16] or [6]. Observe that since $\mathcal{K}_{\perp}(Y)$ carries the upper Vietoris topology, continuous maps of type $X \to \mathcal{K}_{\perp}(Y)$ correspond to compact-valued upper semicontinuous maps with open domains. We obtain the following convergence criterion:

Theorem 1. Let $X_1,\dots,X_{n+1}$ be a finite sequence of computable metric spaces. Let $f_i\colon X_i \to X_{i+1}$, $i = 1,\dots,n$ be a finite sequence of functions. For $i = 1,\dots,n$, let $F_i\colon X_i \to \mathcal{K}_{\perp}(X_{i+1})$ be the best continuous approximation of f_i with values in $\mathcal{K}_{\perp}(X_{i+1})$. Assume that $F_i(x) \neq \perp$ for all $x \in X_i$. Let $\mathbb{Q}_{>0}$ denote the space of positive rational numbers with the discrete topology. Then the following are equivalent:

1. For all $x \in X_1$ and all $\varepsilon > 0$ there exists a $\delta > 0$ such that for all $y \in {}^{\dagger}f_n(\cdot,\delta) \circ \cdots \circ {}^{\dagger}f_1(\cdot,\delta)(x)$ we have $d\left(y, f_n \circ \cdots \circ f_1(x)\right) < \varepsilon$.

2. *There exists a total continuous[1] multi-valued function*

$$\Omega \colon \mathcal{K}(X_1) \times \mathbb{Q}_{>0} \rightsquigarrow \mathbb{Q}_{>0}$$

such that for all $K \in \mathcal{K}(X_1)$, all $x \in K$, all $\varepsilon > 0$, all $\delta \in \Omega(K, \varepsilon)$, and all $y \in {}^\dagger f_n(\cdot, \delta) \circ \cdots \circ {}^\dagger f_1(\cdot, \delta)(x)$ we have $d(y, f_n \circ \cdots \circ f_1(x)) < \varepsilon$.

3. *We have $F_n \circ \cdots \circ F_1(x) = \{f_n \circ \cdots \circ f_1(x)\}$ for all $x \in X_1$. Here, the composition of the F_i's is taken in the Kleisli category of the monad $\mathcal{K}_\perp$.*

When the envelopes of all functions $f_1, \ldots, f_n$ are known, checking the equality $F_n \circ \cdots \circ F_1(x) = \{f_n \circ \cdots \circ f_1(x)\}$ is arguably much simpler than proving convergence directly.

In (2) we have chosen the same δ in each f_i depending only on ε and x. The notion of convergence can be weakened by allowing a different δ_i for each ${}^\dagger f_i$ that is allowed to depend on the value of ${}^\dagger f_{i-1}(x_{i-1}, \delta_{i-1})$.

Convergence in this sense can be characterised with the help of primary co-envelopes, introduced in [10, Section 5]. The definition of this concept requires some preparation. For a represented space X, let $\mathcal{O}(X)$ denote the space of open subsets of X endowed with the Scott topology, which in this case coincides with the ω-Scott topology, cf. [15, Proposition 2.2]. A continuous map $j \colon X \to Y$ between represented spaces is called a Σ-split embedding if the induced map $j^* \colon \mathcal{O}(Y) \to \mathcal{O}(X)$ has a continuous section $s \colon \mathcal{O}(X) \to \mathcal{O}(Y)$. This means that the map s must be continuous and satisfy $j^* \circ s = \mathrm{id}_{\mathcal{O}(X)}$. A represented space X is called Σ-*split injective* if it is an injective object in the category of represented spaces relative to the class of Σ-split embeddings. More explicitly, a space X is Σ-split injective if and only if for all continuous maps $f \colon A \to X$ and all Σ-split injective maps $j \colon A \to B$ there exists a – not necessarily unique – continuous map $g \colon B \to X$ such that $f = g \circ j$. Equivalently, a represented space is Σ-split injective if and only if the natural inclusion $\eta_X \colon X \to \mathcal{O}(\mathcal{O}(X))$ which sends a point $x \in X$ to the set $\{U \in \mathcal{O}(X) \mid x \in U\}$ has a continuous left inverse $\rho_X \colon \mathcal{O}(\mathcal{O}(X)) \to X$ [9, Proposition 3.18]. Any Σ-split injective space is a complete lattice with respect to its specialisation order [9, Corollary 3.19].

For a function $f \colon X \to Y$, let $f^\circ \colon \mathcal{O}(Y) \to \mathcal{O}(X)$ denote the function which sends an open set $U \in \mathcal{O}(Y)$ to the interior of the set $f^{-1}(U)$.

A *co-envelope* of a function $f \colon X \to Y$ consists of a Σ-split injective space A together with two continuous maps $F^\star \colon A \to \mathcal{O}(X)$ and $\pi \colon A \to \mathcal{O}(Y)$ satisfying $F^\star(x) \subseteq f^\circ \circ \pi(x)$ for all $x \in A$.

To each function $f \colon X \to Y$ one can assign a unique *primary co-envelope*, consisting of a Σ-split injective space $\mathfrak{A}_f$ together with two continuous maps $\mathfrak{E}_f^\star \colon \mathfrak{A}_f \to \mathcal{O}(X)$ and $\pi_{\mathfrak{A}_f} \colon \mathfrak{A}_f \to \mathcal{O}(Y)$. Intuitively speaking, the primary co-envelope of a function f is – in a certain sense – the most efficient encoding of all continuously obtainable information on f. We will not spell out the full definition here. See [10, Section 5] for details.

---

[1] Here and throughout the rest of the paper, a multi-valued function is called *continuous* if it is computable relative to some oracle.

The map $\pi_{\mathfrak{A}_f}$ preserves arbitrary joins and hence has an upper adjoint [7, Corollary O-3.5]. This means that there exists a monotone, not necessarily continuous map $\rho\colon \mathcal{O}(Y) \to \mathfrak{A}_f$ such that for all $x \in \mathfrak{A}_f$ and all $U \in \mathcal{O}(Y)$ we have

$$\pi_{\mathfrak{A}_f}(x) \subseteq U \;\Leftrightarrow\; x \leq \rho(U).$$

In the above equation, the ordering on $\mathfrak{A}_f$ is the specialisation order. See [7, Chapter O-3] for more details on adjoints. The map ρ is continuous if and only if $\mathfrak{A}_f$ is isomorphic to $\mathcal{O}(Y)$. In this case, $\mathfrak{E}_f^{\star}$ can be identified with the greatest continuous approximation of f with values in $\mathcal{K}_{\perp}(Y)$.

We obtain the following characterisation:

Theorem 2. *Let $X_1, \ldots, X_{n+1}$ be a finite sequence of computable metric spaces. Let $f_i\colon X_i \to X_{i+1}$, $i = 1, \ldots, n$ be a finite sequence of functions. For $i = 1, \ldots, n$, let the primary co-envelope of f_i be given by the Σ-split injective space $\mathfrak{A}_{f_i}$ and the continuous maps $\pi_{\mathfrak{A}_{f_i}}\colon \mathfrak{A}_{f_i} \to \mathcal{O}(X_{i+1})$, and $\mathfrak{E}_i^{\star}\colon \mathfrak{A}_{f_i} \to \mathcal{O}(X_i)$. Let $\rho_i\colon \mathcal{O}(X_{i+1}) \to \mathfrak{A}_{f_i}$ denote the upper adjoint of the map $\pi_{\mathfrak{A}_{f_i}}\colon \mathfrak{A}_{f_i} \to \mathcal{O}(X_{i+1})$. Let $\mathbb{Q}_{>0}$ denote the space of positive rational numbers with the discrete topology. The following are equivalent:*

1. *There exist continuous multi-valued functions $\omega_i\colon X_i \times \mathbb{Q}_{>0} \rightsquigarrow \mathbb{Q}_{>0}$, with ω_1 total and*

$$(x_i, \varepsilon) \in \mathrm{dom}(\omega_i) \wedge x_{i+1} \in {}^{\dagger}f_i(x_i, \varepsilon) \;\to\; (x_{i+1}, \varepsilon) \in \mathrm{dom}(\omega_{i+1}),$$

   such that for all sequences $x_1, \ldots, x_{n+1}$, $\delta_1 > 0, \ldots, \delta_n > 0$ satisfying $\delta_i \in \omega_i(x_i, \varepsilon)$ and $x_{i+1} \in {}^{\dagger}f_i(x_i, \delta_i)$ we have $d(x_{n+1}, f_n \circ \cdots \circ f_1(x)) < \varepsilon$.
2. *We have*

$$\mathfrak{E}_1^{\star} \circ \rho_1 \circ \cdots \circ \mathfrak{E}_{n-1}^{\star} \circ \rho_{n-1} \circ \mathfrak{E}_n^{\star} \circ \rho_n(U) = (f_n \circ \cdots \circ f_1)^{-1}(U)$$

   for all $U \in \mathcal{O}(X_{n+1})$.

The notion of convergence guaranteed by Theorem 2 is much less uniform than the one guaranteed by Theorem 1. Like in Theorem 1, the function ω_1 in Theorem 2 can be extended to compact subsets of X_1, so that its dependency on its first argument can be eliminated when it is restricted to compact subsets of X_1. However, the dependency of ω_i on the first argument can in general not be eliminated for $i \geq 2$, as Example 1 below shows.

We assume familiarity with the standard terminology and notation from computable analysis. For a concise introduction see [11]. See [1, 4, 12, 18] for textbooks on the subject.

2   Proof of Theorem 1

Let us now prove Theorem 1. We will first show the implication $(3) \Rightarrow (1)$.

Observe that continuous maps of type $X \to \mathcal{K}_{\perp}(Y)$ correspond to continuous maps of type $\mathcal{K}_{\perp}(X) \to \mathcal{K}_{\perp}(Y)$ which send $\perp$ to $\perp$ and preserve compact meets.

For a map $F\colon \mathcal{K}_\perp(X) \to \mathcal{K}_\perp(Y)$ which sends $\perp$ to $\perp$ and preserves compact meets, we write

$$F^*\colon \mathcal{O}(Y) \to \mathcal{O}(X),\ F^*(U) = \{x \in X \mid F(\{x\}) \in U\}.$$

By convention, $\perp \subseteq U$ is false for all open sets $U \in \mathcal{O}(Y)$. Observe that if F sends $\perp$ to $\perp$ and preserves compact meets then

$$F(K) \subseteq U \Leftrightarrow K \subseteq F^*(U) \tag{3}$$

for all $K \in \mathcal{K}_\perp(X)$.

For a point $x \in X$ we write $B(x, \varepsilon)$ for the ball of radius $\varepsilon > 0$ about x. For a set $S \subseteq X$ we write $B(S, \varepsilon) = \cup_{x \in S} B(x, \varepsilon)$. For notational convenience, we will write x for the singleton set $\{x\}$.

Lemma 1. *Let $X_1, \ldots, X_{n+1}$ be a finite sequence of computable metric spaces. Let $F_i\colon \mathcal{K}_\perp(X_i) \to \mathcal{K}_\perp(X_{i+1})$, $i = 1, \ldots, n$ be a finite sequence of continuous maps that send $\perp$ to $\perp$ and preserve compact meets. Let $x \in X_1$. Assume that $F_n \circ \cdots \circ F_1(x) \neq \perp$. Then for all $\varepsilon > 0$ there exist $\eta_0 > 0, \ldots, \eta_{n-1} > 0, \eta_n = \varepsilon$, and $\delta > 0$, such that*

$$B\left(B\left(F_{i-1} \circ \cdots \circ F_1(x), \eta_{i-1}\right), \delta\right) \subseteq F_i^*\left(B\left(F_i \circ \cdots \circ F_1(x), \eta_i\right)\right).$$

for $i = 1, \ldots, n$ (by convention, the empty composition is the identity).

Proof. Recall that $\eta_n = \varepsilon$. We obviously have

$$F_n \circ \cdots \circ F_1(x) \subseteq B\left(F_n \circ \cdots \circ F_1(x), \eta_n\right).$$

By (3) we have

$$F_{n-1} \circ \cdots \circ F_1(x) \subseteq F_n^*\left(B\left(F_n \circ \cdots \circ F_1(x), \eta_n\right)\right).$$

Since the set $F_{n-1} \circ \cdots \circ F_1(x)$ is compact, there exists $\overline{\eta}_{n-1}$ such that

$$B\left(F_{n-1} \circ \cdots \circ F_1(x), \overline{\eta}_{n-1}\right) \subseteq F_n^*\left(B\left(F_n \circ \cdots \circ F_1(x), \eta_n\right)\right).$$

Let $\eta_{n-1} = \delta_{n-1} = \overline{\eta}_{n-1}/2$. Then

$$B\left(B\left(F_{n-1} \circ \cdots \circ F_1(x), \eta_{n-1}\right), \delta_{n-1}\right) \subseteq B\left(F_{n-1} \circ \cdots \circ F_1(x), \overline{\eta}_{n-1}\right)$$
$$\subseteq F_n^*\left(B\left(F_n \circ \cdots \circ F_1(x), \eta_n\right)\right).$$

We can apply the same argument with η_{n-1} playing the role of η_n to obtain the existence of η_{n-2} and δ_{n-2} such that

$$B\left(B\left(F_{n-2} \circ \cdots \circ F_1(x), \eta_{n-2}\right), \delta_{n-2}\right) \subseteq F_{n-1}^*\left(B\left(F_{n-1} \circ \cdots \circ F_1(x), \eta_{n-1}\right)\right).$$

By induction we obtain the existence of $\eta_0, \ldots, \eta_n$, and $\delta_0, \ldots, \delta_{n-1}$ such that

$$B\left(B\left(F_{i-1} \circ \cdots \circ F_1(x), \eta_{i-1}\right), \delta_{i-1}\right) \subseteq F_i^*\left(B\left(F_i \circ \cdots \circ F_1(x), \eta_i\right)\right)$$

for $i = 1, \ldots, n$. The claim now follows if we let $\delta = \min\{\delta_1, \ldots, \delta_{n-1}\}$.

Lemma 2. *Let $X_1, \ldots, X_{n+1}$ be a finite sequence of computable metric spaces. Let $F_i \colon \mathcal{K}_\perp(X_i) \to \mathcal{K}_\perp(X_{i+1})$, $i = 1, \ldots, n$ be a finite sequence of continuous maps that preserve compact meets. Let $f_i \colon X_i \to X_{i+1}$, $i = 1, \ldots, n$ be a finite sequence of functions satisfying $f_i(x) \subseteq F_i(\{x\})$ for all $x \in X_i$. Let $x \in X_1$. Let $\varepsilon > 0$. Assume that $F_n \circ \cdots \circ F_1(x) \subseteq B\left(f_n \circ \cdots \circ f_1(x), \varepsilon/2\right)$. For $\delta > 0$, let $P_{\delta,1} = \{x\}$ and $P_{\delta,i+1} = f_i\left(B(P_{\delta,i}, \delta)\right)$. Then there exists $\delta > 0$ such that*

$$P_{\delta,n+1} \subseteq B\left(f_n \circ \cdots \circ f_1(x), \varepsilon\right).$$

Proof. For a map $G \colon \mathcal{K}_\perp(X) \to \mathcal{K}_\perp(Y)$ that preserves compact meets and an arbitrary set $S \subseteq X$, write

$$G(S) = \begin{cases} \bigcup_{x \in S} G(x) \subseteq Y & \text{if } G(x) \neq \perp \text{ for all } x \in S, \\ \perp & \text{if } G(x) = \perp \text{ for some } x \in S. \end{cases}$$

By Lemma 1, for all $\eta_n > 0$ there exist $\eta_0 > 0, \ldots, \eta_{n-1} > 0$ and $\delta > 0$ such that

$$B\left(B\left(F_{i-1} \circ \cdots \circ F_1(x), \eta_{i-1}\right), \delta\right) \subseteq F_i^*\left(B\left(F_i \circ \cdots \circ F_1(x), \eta_i\right)\right).$$

for $i = 1, \ldots, n$. With the above notation, this implies

$$F_i\left(B\left(B\left(F_{i-1} \circ \cdots \circ F_1(x), \eta_{i-1}\right), \delta\right)\right) \subseteq B\left(F_i \circ \cdots \circ F_1(x), \eta_i\right). \tag{4}$$

Let $\eta_n = \varepsilon/2$. We claim that we have $P_{\delta,i+1} \subseteq B(F_i \circ \cdots \circ F_1(x), \eta_i)$ for $i = 1, \ldots, n$. For $i = 1$ we have by (4)

$$P_{\delta,2} = f_1\left(B(x, \delta)\right) \subseteq F_1\left(B(B(x, \eta_0), \delta)\right) \subseteq B\left(F_1(x), \eta_1\right).$$

By induction it follows that

$$\begin{aligned} P_{\delta,i+1} &= f_i\left(B\left(P_{\delta,i}, \delta\right)\right) \\ &\subseteq f_i\left(B\left(B\left(F_{i-1} \circ \cdots \circ F_1(x), \eta_{i-1}\right), \delta\right)\right) \\ &\subseteq F_i\left(B\left(B\left(F_{i-1} \circ \cdots \circ F_1(x), \eta_{i-1}\right), \delta\right)\right) \\ &\subseteq B\left(F_i \circ \cdots \circ F_1(x), \eta_i\right). \end{aligned}$$

The last inclusion follows again from (4).

We obtain, using the definition $\eta_{n-1} = \varepsilon/2$,

$$\begin{aligned} P_{\delta,n} &\subseteq B\left(F_n \circ \cdots \circ F_1(x), \varepsilon/2\right) \\ &\subseteq B\left(B\left(f_n \circ \cdots \circ f_1(x), \varepsilon/2\right), \varepsilon/2\right) \\ &\subseteq B\left(f_n \circ \cdots \circ f_1(x), \varepsilon\right). \end{aligned}$$

This proves the claim.

The implication (3) $\Rightarrow$ (1) in Theorem 1 now follows immediately.

Let us now prove the direction (1) $\Rightarrow$ (3). The proof relies on properties of uniformly $\mathcal{R}$-universal envelopes that were established in [10, Section 4].

Lemma 3. *Let $X_1, \ldots, X_{n+1}$ be a sequence of computable metric spaces. Let $f_i \colon X_i \to X_{i+1}$, $i = 1, \ldots, n$ be a sequence of functions. For $i = 1, \ldots, n$, let $F_i \colon X_i \to \mathcal{K}_\perp(X_{i+1})$ be the best continuous approximation of f_i with values in $\mathcal{K}_\perp(X_{i+1})$. Let $x \in X_1$. Assume that $F_i(x) \neq \perp$ for all $x \in X_i$. Let $x \in X_i$. Assume that for all $\varepsilon > 0$ there exists a $\delta > 0$ such that for all*

$$y \in {}^\dagger f_n(\cdot, \delta) \circ \cdots \circ {}^\dagger f_1(\cdot, \delta)(x)$$

we have $d(y, f_n \circ \cdots \circ f_1(x)) < \varepsilon$. Then $F_n \circ \cdots \circ F_1(x) = \{f_n \circ \cdots \circ f_1(x)\}$.

Proof. Since $F_i(y) \neq \perp$ for all $y \in X_i$, it follows from [10, Theorem 30] that the function f_i is uniformly $\mathcal{R}$-envelopable and F_i is an $\mathcal{R}$-universal envelope of f_i. A *robust property* of f at y is an open set $U \in \mathcal{O}(X_i)$ such that $f^{-1}(U)$ is a neighbourhood of y. See also [9, Definition 4.12]. By [10, Proposition 29] we have the following result: For all $y \in X_i$, all robust properties $U \in \mathcal{O}(X_{i+1})$ of f at y, and all $\eta > 0$ we have $F_i(y) \in B(U, \eta)$.

Let $\varepsilon > 0$. For $\delta > 0$, let $P_{1,\delta} = \{x\}$ and $P_{i+1,\delta} = f_i(B(P_{i,\delta}, \delta))$. By assumption, there exists $\delta > 0$ such that $P_{n+1,\delta} \subseteq B(f_n \circ \cdots \circ f_1(x), \varepsilon)$.

We prove by induction on $i \geq 0$ that $F_i \circ \cdots \circ F_1(x) \subseteq B(P_{i+1,\delta}, \delta)$. The claim then follows easily.

For $i = 0$ the claim is trivial.

Assume that $F_i \circ \cdots \circ F_1(x) \subseteq B(P_{i+1,\delta}, \delta)$ for $i \geq 0$. Let $y \in F_i \circ \cdots \circ F_1(x)$. Then

$$f_{i+1}(y) \in f_{i+1}(B(P_{i+1,\delta}, \delta)) = P_{i+2,\delta} \subseteq B(P_{i+2,\delta}, \delta/2).$$

We thus have $y \in B(P_{i+1,\delta}, \delta) \subseteq f_{i+1}^{-1}(B(P_{i+2,\delta}, \delta/2))$. Hence, $B(P_{i+2,\delta}, \delta/2)$ is a robust property of f_{i+1} at y. Since F_{i+1} is an $\mathcal{R}$-universal envelope of f_{i+1}, it follows that

$$F_{i+1}(y) \subseteq B(B(P_{i+2,\delta}, \delta/2), \delta/2) \subseteq B(P_{i+2,\delta}, \delta).$$

This proves the claim.

Finally, we show the equivalence of (1) and (2). Since (2) clearly implies (1) it suffices to show the implication (1) $\Rightarrow$ (2). We first show a weaker implication, where the modulus Ω ranges over points rather than compact sets:

Lemma 4. *Let $X_1, \ldots, X_{n+1}$ be a sequence of computable metric spaces. Let $f_i \colon X_i \to X_{i+1}$, $i = 1, \ldots, n$ be a sequence of functions. Assume that the sentence*

$$\forall x \in X_1. \forall \varepsilon > 0. \exists \delta > 0. \left({}^\dagger f_n(\cdot, \delta) \circ \cdots \circ {}^\dagger f_1(\cdot, \delta)(x) \subseteq B(f_n \circ \cdots \circ f_1(x), \varepsilon)\right)$$

(5)

holds true. Then there exists a total continuous multi-valued function

$$\omega \colon X_1 \times \mathbb{Q}_{>0} \rightsquigarrow \mathbb{Q}_{>0}$$

witnessing (5).

Proof. To all rational points[2] $x \in X_1$ and all rational numbers $\varepsilon > 0$ we can assign a sequence

$$0 < \delta_1(x, \varepsilon) \leq \delta_2(x, \varepsilon) \leq \ldots$$

of rational numbers such that each $\delta_i(x, \varepsilon)$ is a witness of (5). If the set of witnesses of (5) is bounded with supremum $\delta > 0$ we can further ensure that $\delta_i \to \delta$ as $i \to \infty$. If the set of witnesses of (5) is unbounded, we can ensure that the sequence $(\delta_i(x, \varepsilon))_{i \in \mathbb{N}}$ is unbounded.

Let $(x_i)_i$ be an enumeration of all rational points in X. Let $(\varepsilon_i)_i$ be an enumeration of all strictly positive rational numbers. We obtain a function $\Phi \colon \mathbb{N}^3 \to X \times \mathbb{Q}^2$ which sends (i, j, k) to $(x_i, \varepsilon_j, \delta_k(x_i, \varepsilon_j))$. The function $f_n \circ \cdots \circ f_1$ is necessarily continuous, so that it has a continuous modulus of continuity $\mu \colon X_1 \times \mathbb{Q}_{>0} \to (0, +\infty)_<$, where $(0, +\infty)_<$ is the space of positive reals with the Scott topology induced by the usual ordering. We may assume that μ is monotonically increasing in its second argument.

We now compute a suitable function ω relative to the oracles Φ and μ. Given $x \in X_1$ and $\varepsilon \in \mathbb{Q}_{>0}$, search for (i, j, k) such that $\varepsilon_j < \varepsilon$, $x \in B(x_i, \delta_k(x_i, \varepsilon_j))$, and $\delta_k(x_i, \varepsilon_j) < \mu(x, \varepsilon - \varepsilon_j)$. Output a positive rational lower bound δ on $\delta_k(x_i, \varepsilon_j) - d(x, x_i) > 0$.

We claim that δ is a witness for (5). By assumption we have

$$^\dagger f_n(\cdot, \delta_k(x_i, \varepsilon_j)) \circ \cdots \circ {}^\dagger f_1(\cdot, \delta_k(x_i, \varepsilon_j))(x_i) \subseteq B(f_n \circ \cdots \circ f_1(x_i), \varepsilon_j). \quad (6)$$

Since $\delta_k(x_i, \varepsilon_j) < \mu(x, \varepsilon - \varepsilon_j)$ and $d(x, x_i) < \delta_k(x_i, \varepsilon_j)$ we have

$$d\left(f_n \circ \cdots \circ f_1(x_i), f_n \circ \cdots \circ f_1(x)\right) < \varepsilon - \varepsilon_j$$

which implies

$$B(f_n \circ \cdots \circ f_1(x_i), \varepsilon_j) \subseteq B(f_n \circ \cdots \circ f_1(x), \varepsilon) \quad (7)$$

We prove by induction on ℓ that

$$^\dagger f_\ell(\cdot, \delta) \circ \cdots \circ {}^\dagger f_1(\cdot, \delta)(x) \subseteq {}^\dagger f_\ell(\cdot, \delta_k(x_i, \varepsilon_j)) \circ \cdots \circ {}^\dagger f_1(\cdot, \delta_k(x_i, \varepsilon_j))(x_i).$$

Combining this with (6) and (7) we obtain the claim. Consider the case $\ell = 1$. We have $B(x, \delta) \subseteq B(x_i, \delta_k(x_i, \varepsilon_j))$ by construction. This implies:

$$^\dagger f_1(\cdot, \delta)(x) = f_1(B(x, \delta)) \subseteq f_1(B(x_i, \delta_k(x_i, \varepsilon_j))) = {}^\dagger f_1(\cdot, \delta_k(x_i, \varepsilon_j))(x_i).$$

The induction step is trivial, observing that $\delta < \delta_k(x_i, \varepsilon_j)$.

We have shown that the algorithm outputs a witness for (5) whenever it halts. It remains to show that the algorithm halts on all inputs. Let $(x, \varepsilon) \in X_1 \times \mathbb{Q}_{\geq 0}$.

---

[2] Recall that a computable metric space is presented by a dense sequence $(x_n)_n$ and a map $\mathbb{N}^2 \to \mathbb{R}$ which sends (n, m) to the distance of x_n and x_m. We call the elements of the sequence $(x_n)_n$ the *rational points* of X, in analogy to the rational numbers, that play this role for the computable metric space of real numbers.

By assumption, there exists $\delta > 0$ such that

$$^\dagger f(\cdot, \delta) \circ \cdots \circ {}^\dagger f(\cdot, \delta)(x) \subseteq B(f_n \circ \cdots \circ f_1(x), \varepsilon/4).$$

There exists a rational point x_i with

$$d(x, x_i) < \min\{\delta/4, \tfrac{1}{2}\mu(x, \varepsilon/4)\}.$$

We have

$$B(x_i, 2d(x, x_i)) \subseteq B(x, \delta).$$

This implies:

$$^\dagger f_n(\cdot, 2d(x, x_i)) \circ \cdots \circ {}^\dagger f_1(\cdot, 2d((x, x_i))(x_i) \subseteq {}^\dagger f_n(\cdot, \delta) \circ \cdots \circ {}^\dagger f_1(\cdot, \delta)(x)$$
$$\subseteq B(f_n \circ \cdots \circ f_1(x), \varepsilon/4).$$

Now, since $d(x, x_i) < \mu(x, \varepsilon/4)$, we have

$$B(f_n \circ \cdots \circ f_1(x), \varepsilon/4) \subseteq B(f_n \circ \cdots \circ f_1(x_i), \varepsilon/2).$$

It follows that $2d(x, x_i)$ witnesses the existential quantifier in (5) when the variables in the universal quantifier are bound to x_i and $\varepsilon/2$ respectively. Let $\varepsilon_j \in (\varepsilon/2, 3\varepsilon/4)$ be a rational number. By construction, there exists a number $\delta_k(x_i, \varepsilon_j)$ in our sequence such that $d(x, x_i) < \delta_k(x_i, \varepsilon_j) < 2d(x, x_i)$.

By construction we have $\varepsilon_j < \varepsilon$. Again by construction, x is contained in $B(x_i, \delta_k(x_i, \varepsilon_j))$. Finally, we have $\varepsilon - \varepsilon_j > \varepsilon/4$ and thus

$$\mu(x, \varepsilon - \varepsilon_j) > \mu(x, \varepsilon/4) > 2d(x, x_i) > \delta_k(x_i, \varepsilon_j).$$

Here we have used that μ is monotonically increasing in its second argument. Thus, the search will terminate on input $(x_i, \varepsilon_j, \delta_k(x_i, \varepsilon_j))$.

Finally we extend the modulus ω to a modulus Ω as in the statement of the theorem:

Corollary 1. *Let $X_1, \ldots, X_{n+1}$ be a sequence of computable metric spaces. Let $f_i \colon X_i \to X_{i+1}$, $i = 1, \ldots, n$ be a sequence of functions. Assume that the sentence (5) holds true.*

Then there exists a total continuous multi-valued function

$$\Omega \colon \mathcal{K}(X_1) \times \mathbb{Q}_{>0} \rightsquigarrow \mathbb{Q}_{>0}$$

such that for all $K \in \mathcal{K}(X_1)$, all $x \in K$, all $\varepsilon > 0$, any $\delta \in \Omega(K, \varepsilon)$ is a witness for the existential quantifier in (5).

Proof. By Lemma 4 there exists $\omega \colon X_1 \times \mathbb{Q}_{>0} \rightsquigarrow \mathbb{Q}_{>0}$ witnessing the existential quantifier in (5).

The computable metric space X_1 admits a computably open representation, so that given $K \in \mathcal{K}(X_1)$, $\varepsilon > 0$, and $\delta > 0$ we can semi-decide the sentence

$$\forall x \in K. \exists \eta \in \omega(x, \varepsilon). (\eta > \delta) \tag{8}$$

relative to some realiser of ω. By a straightforward compactness argument, for all compact sets K there exists a uniform lower bound $\delta > 0$ such that the sentence (8) holds true. This allows us to compute Ω relative to ω by unbounded search for a suitable δ.

3   Proof of Theorem 2

For a function $f\colon X \to Y$ between represented spaces, let

$$f^\circ\colon \mathcal{O}(Y) \to \mathcal{O}(X), \; f^\circ(U) = f^{-1}(U)^\circ,$$

where for a set $S \subseteq X$, S° denotes the interior of S. The proof of the second result relies on the following observation, which follows from the proof of [10, Theorem 41]:

Lemma 5. *Let* $f\colon X \to Y$ *be a function between represented spaces. Let the primary co-envelope of* f *be given by the* Σ-*split injective space* $\mathfrak{A}_f$ *and the continuous maps* $\pi_{\mathfrak{A}_f}\colon \mathfrak{A}_f \to \mathcal{O}(Y)$ *and* $\mathfrak{C}_f^\star\colon \mathfrak{A}_f \to \mathcal{O}(X)$. *Let* $\rho\colon \mathcal{O}(Y) \to \mathfrak{A}_f$ *denote the upper adjoint of the map* $\pi_{\mathfrak{A}_f}\colon \mathfrak{A}_f \to \mathcal{O}(Y)$. *Then* $\mathfrak{C}_f^\star \circ \rho = f^\circ$.

We now turn to the proof of Theorem 2. We first prove the direction (2) $\Rightarrow$ (1). Thus, assume that we have

$$\mathfrak{C}_1^\star \circ \rho_1 \circ \cdots \circ \mathfrak{C}_{n-1}^\star \circ \rho_{n-1} \circ \mathfrak{C}_n^\star \circ \rho_n(U) = (f_n \circ \cdots \circ f_1)^{-1}(U)$$

for all $U \in \mathcal{O}(X_{n+1})$. By Lemma 5 we have $\mathfrak{C}_i^\star \circ \rho_i = f_i^\circ$ for $i = 1, \ldots, n$. Since $f_n \circ \cdots \circ f_1$ is continuous, the assumption hence says

$$f_n^\circ \circ \cdots \circ f_1^\circ = (f_n \circ \cdots \circ f_1)^\circ = (f_n \circ \cdots \circ f_1)^{-1}. \tag{9}$$

For $i = 1, \ldots, n+1$, let $(a_{i,m})_{m \in \mathbb{N}}$ be a dense sequence in X_i. Let $m \in \mathbb{N}$. Let $\varepsilon > 0$ be a positive rational number. Let $y_m = f_n \circ \cdots \circ f_1(a_{1,m})$. We have by (9):

$$(f_n \circ \cdots \circ f_1)^{-1} (B(y_m, \varepsilon/2)) = (f_n \circ \cdots \circ f_1)^\circ (B(y_m, \varepsilon/2))$$
$$= f_1^\circ \circ \cdots \circ f_n^\circ (B(y_m, \varepsilon/2)).$$

We obtain open sets $U_{i,m,\varepsilon}$ by letting $U_{n+1,m,\varepsilon} = B(y_m, \varepsilon/2)$ and $U_{i,m,\varepsilon} = f_i^\circ (U_{i+1,m,\varepsilon})$. We have

$$U_{1,m,\varepsilon} = (f_n \circ \cdots \circ f_1)^{-1} (B(y_m, \varepsilon/2)). \tag{10}$$

We can make the countable collection $U_{i,m,\varepsilon}$ where $i = 1, \ldots, n+1$, $m \in \mathbb{N}$, and $\varepsilon > 0$ is rational into an oracle, by listing for each $U_{i,m,\varepsilon}$ the set of all rational balls contained in $U_{i,m,\varepsilon}$. More precisely, there exist functions

$$\ell\colon \{1, \ldots, n+1\} \times \mathbb{Q}_{>0} \times \mathbb{N}^2 \to \mathbb{N}$$

and

$$\eta\colon \{1, \ldots, n+1\} \times \mathbb{Q}_{>0} \times \mathbb{N}^3 \to \mathbb{N}$$

such that the following holds true:

1. For all $(i, \varepsilon, m, j, k) \in \{1, \ldots, n+1\} \times \mathbb{Q}_{>0} \times \mathbb{N}^3$ the open ball

$$B(a_{i, \ell(i, \varepsilon, m, j)}, \eta(i, \varepsilon, m, j, k))$$

   is contained in $U_{i, m, \varepsilon}$.
2. Whenever $a_{i, p}$ is a rational point in X_i and $r > 0$ is a positive real number with $B(a_{i, p}, r) \subseteq U_{i, m, \varepsilon}$ for some $m \in \mathbb{N}$ and $\varepsilon > 0$, then there exists $j \in \mathbb{N}$ such that $p = \ell(i, \varepsilon, m, j)$, and for all $0 < s < r$ there exists $k \in \mathbb{N}$ with $\eta(i, \varepsilon, m, j, k) > s$.

We now compute ω_i with help of the oracles ℓ and η. Given $x_i \in X_i$ and a rational number $\varepsilon > 0$, search for $m, j, k \in \mathbb{N}$ such that

$$x_i \in B\left(a_{i, \ell(i, \varepsilon, m, j)}, \eta(i, \varepsilon, m, j, k)\right).$$

Output any rational number δ satisfying $0 < \delta < \eta(i, \varepsilon, m, j, k) - d(x_i, a_{i, \ell(i, \varepsilon, m, j)})$. Observe that this implies that if $\delta \in \omega_i(x, \varepsilon)$ then

$$B(x_i, \delta) \subseteq B\left(a_{i, \ell(i, \varepsilon, m, j)}, \eta(i, \varepsilon, m, j, k)\right) \subseteq U_{i, m, \varepsilon}. \tag{11}$$

Further observe that the search terminates on input x_i and $\varepsilon > 0$ if and only if there exists $m \in \mathbb{N}$ such that $x_i \in U_{i, m, \varepsilon}$. In other words,

$$(x_i, \varepsilon) \in \text{dom}\, \omega_i \Leftrightarrow x_i \in \bigcup_{m \in \mathbb{N}} U_{i, m, \varepsilon} \tag{12}$$

We claim that ω_1 is a total function. Let $x_1 \in X_1$ and $\varepsilon > 0$. Since $f_n \circ \cdots \circ f_1$ is continuous, there exists a rational point $a_{1, m} \in X_1$ such that $f_n \circ \cdots \circ f_1(x_1) \in B(f_n \circ \cdots \circ f_1(a_{1, m}), \varepsilon)$. By definition, this implies $x_1 \in U_{1, m, \varepsilon}$. The claim follows with (12).

Next, we show that

$$\left((x_i, \varepsilon) \in \text{dom}(\omega_i) \wedge \delta \in \omega_i(x_i, \varepsilon) \wedge x_{i+1} \in {}^\dagger f_i(x_i, \delta)\right) \rightarrow (x_{i+1}, \varepsilon) \in \text{dom}(\omega_{i+1}).$$

Assume that $(x_i, \varepsilon) \in \text{dom}(\omega_i)$. By (12) we have $x_i \in U_{i, m, \varepsilon}$ for some $m \in \mathbb{N}$. Let $\delta \in \omega_i(x_i, \varepsilon)$. Then by (11) we have $B(x_i, \delta) \subseteq U_{i, m, \varepsilon}$. Thus,

$$f_i(B(x_i, \delta)) \subseteq f_i(U_{i, m, \varepsilon}) \subseteq U_{i+1, m, \varepsilon}.$$

The last inclusion follows directly from the definition of $U_{i, m, \varepsilon}$. The claim follows.

Finally, let $x_1, \ldots, x_{n+1}, \delta_1 > 0, \ldots, \delta_n > 0$ be sequences which satisfy $\delta_i \in \omega_i(x_i, \varepsilon)$ and $x_{i+1} \in {}^\dagger f_i(x_i, \delta_i)$. By the preceding arguments, we have $x_1 \in U_{1, m, \varepsilon}$ for some $m \in \mathbb{N}$ and $f_i(B(x_i, \delta)) \subseteq U_{i+1, m, \varepsilon}$ for $i = 1, \ldots, n$. Thus,

$$x_{n+1} \in U_{n+1, m, \varepsilon} = B(f_n \circ \cdots \circ f_1(a_{1, m}), \varepsilon/2).$$

By (10) we have $f_n \circ \cdots \circ f_1(x_1) \in B(f_n \circ \cdots \circ f_1(a_{1, m}), \varepsilon/2)$. Hence,

$$d(x_{n+1}, f_n \circ \cdots \circ f_1(x_1)) < \varepsilon.$$

This establishes the direction (2) ⇒ (1). Let us now prove the converse direction. Thus, assume the existence of continuous multi-valued maps

$$\omega_i \colon X_i \times \mathbb{Q}_{>0} \rightsquigarrow \mathbb{Q}_{>0},$$

as in the statement of the theorem.

Let $U \in \mathcal{O}(X_{n+1})$ be an open set. By Lemma 5, our aim is to show that

$$(f_n \circ \cdots \circ f_1)^{-1}(U) = f_1^\circ \circ \cdots \circ f_n^\circ(U).$$

Let $x_1 \in X_1$ be such that $f_n \circ \cdots \circ f_1(x_1) \in U$. Let $\varepsilon > 0$ be such that we have $B(f_n \circ \cdots \circ f_1(x_1), \varepsilon) \subseteq U$.

Let $\delta_1 \in \omega_1(x_1, \varepsilon)$. Let $V_1 = B(x_1, \delta_1)$. For $2 \leq i \leq n-1$, let

$$V_{i+1} = \bigcup_{x_{i+1} \in f_i(V_i)} \bigcup_{\delta_{i+1} \in \omega_{i+1}(x_{i+1}, \varepsilon)} B(x_{i+1}, \delta_{i+1}).$$

Essentially by definition we have $V_{n+1} \subseteq B(f_n \circ \cdots \circ f_1(x), \varepsilon) \subseteq U$.

By definition, each V_i is an open set. A straightforward induction, using the assumption about the domains of the ω_i's, shows that $(x_{i+1}, \varepsilon) \in \operatorname{dom} \omega_{i+1}$ whenever $x_{i+1} \in f_i(V_i)$. Thus, the set V_{i+1} contains the set $f_i(V_i)$. Thus, $f_i^\circ(V_{i+1}) \supseteq V_i$. Hence,

$$f_1^\circ \circ \cdots \circ f_n^\circ(U) \supseteq f_1^\circ \circ \cdots \circ f_n^\circ(V_{n+1}) \supseteq V_1 = B(x_1, \delta_1) \ni x.$$

This proves the claim.

4 Examples

Our first example shows that the dependency of ω_i on x_i for $i > 1$ in Theorem 2 cannot be eliminated in general.

Example 1. Let

$$f \colon \mathbb{R} \to \mathbb{R}, \; f(x) = \begin{cases} -x & \text{if } x < 0, \\ 1 & \text{otherwise.} \end{cases}$$

One easily verifies that the best continuous approximation of f with values in $\mathcal{K}_\perp(\mathbb{R})$ is given by the map

$$F(x) = \begin{cases} \{-x\} & \text{if } x < 0, \\ \{0, 1\} & \text{if } x = 0, \\ \{1\} & \text{if } x > 0. \end{cases}$$

We have $f \circ f(x) = 1$ for all $x \in \mathbb{R}$, but $F \circ F(0) = \{0, 1\}$. Thus, Theorem 1 is not applicable. Indeed, let $0 < \varepsilon < 1$. For all $\delta > 0$, we have

$$^\dagger f(\cdot, \delta) \circ {}^\dagger f(0, \delta) = (0, \delta) \cup \{1\} \not\subseteq B(f \circ f(0), \varepsilon).$$

Theorem 2 does apply. Indeed, we can choose $\omega_1(x, \varepsilon) = 1$ and $\omega_2(x, \varepsilon) = |x|$. Then any $y \in {}^\dagger f(x, \omega_1(x, \varepsilon))$ is a strictly positive number. Now, $\omega_2(y, \varepsilon)$ is equal to $|y|$, so that $^\dagger f(y, \omega_2(y, \varepsilon)) = \{1\}$.

Our second example illustrates a classic scenario where Theorem 1 is applicable.

Example 2. Let
$$P_N \colon \operatorname{Sym}_n(\mathbb{R}) \to \operatorname{Sym}_n(\mathbb{R}), \ A \mapsto A^N$$
be the operator which sends a real symmetric matrix to its Nth power.

Since diagonal matrices can be raised to the Nth power very efficiently, it makes sense to diagonalise the input matrix before applying P_N. This suggests to decompose P_N into the following chain of functions:

$$\operatorname{Sym}_n \xrightarrow{\text{diag}} \operatorname{Fin}(\mathbb{R} \times \Gamma(\mathbb{R}^n)) \xrightarrow{p_N} \operatorname{Fin}(\mathbb{R} \times \Gamma(\mathbb{R}^n)) \xrightarrow{\text{mul}} \operatorname{Sym}_n,$$

where:

1. $\Gamma(\mathbb{R}^n)$ denotes the space of linear subspaces of $\mathbb{R}^n$, identified with a closed subspace of $\mathcal{F}(B^n)$, the compact subsets of the unit ball $B^n \subseteq \mathbb{R}^n$ with the Hausdorff metric.
2. $\operatorname{Fin}(X)$ is the space of finite subsets of X, identified with a subspace of $\mathbb{N} \times \mathcal{F}(X)$, where $(n, S) \in \operatorname{Fin}(X)$ if and only if the set S has exactly n elements.
3. $p_N\left(\{(\lambda_1, E_1), \ldots, (\lambda_s, E_s)\}\right) = \left\{(\lambda_1^N, E_1), \ldots, (\lambda_s^N, E_s)\right\}.$
4. For a given finite set $S = \{(\lambda_1, E_1), \ldots, (\lambda_s, E_s)\}$, if $\dim E_1 + \cdots + \dim E_s \neq n$, then $\operatorname{mul}(S) = 0$. Otherwise, $\operatorname{mul}(S) = QDQ^T$, where D is a diagonal matrix with entries $\lambda_1, \ldots, \lambda_s$, such that each λ_i occurs $\dim E_i$ often and Q is a matrix whose columns are of the form $v_{1,1}, \ldots, v_{1,m_1}, \ldots, v_{s,1}, \ldots, v_{s,m_s}$, where $v_{i,1}, \ldots, v_{i,m_i}$ is an orthonormal basis of E_i. Observe that mul is well-defined.
5. $\operatorname{diag}(A) = \{(\lambda_1, E_1), \ldots, (\lambda_s, E_s)\}$, where $\lambda_1, \ldots, \lambda_s$ are the distinct eigenvalues of A and E_i is the eigenspace of λ_i.

The maps p_N and mul are computable. Computability of mul follows for example from the results in [19]. The map diag however, is discontinuous. Let $F \colon \operatorname{Sym}_n(\mathbb{R}) \to \mathcal{K}_\perp(\operatorname{Fin}(\mathbb{R} \times \Gamma(\mathbb{R}^n)))$ denote its best continuous approximation with values in $\mathcal{K}_\perp(\operatorname{Fin}(\mathbb{R} \times \Gamma(\mathbb{R}^n)))$. It is not difficult to see that for $A \in \operatorname{Sym}_n(\mathbb{R})$, the set $F(A)$ is the compact set of all finite sets $\{(\lambda_1, E_1), \ldots, (\lambda_s, E_s)\}$ such that $\lambda_1, \ldots, \lambda_s$ are (not necessarily distinct) eigenvalues of A, E_i is an eigenspace for λ_i for all i, $E_i \perp E_j$ for $i \neq j$, and $\dim E_1 + \cdots + \dim E_s = n$. We have $\operatorname{mul} \circ p_N \circ F(\{A\}) = \{P_N(A)\}$, so that by Theorem 1,

$$^\dagger\operatorname{mul}(\cdot, \delta) \circ {}^\dagger p_N(\cdot, \delta) \circ {}^\dagger\operatorname{diag}(\cdot, \delta) \to P_N$$

as $\delta \to 0$, uniformly on compact sets.

References

1. Brattka, V., Hertling, P. (eds.): Handbook of Computability and Complexity in Analysis. THEOAPPLCOM. Springer, Cham (2021). https://doi.org/10.1007/978-3-030-59234-9

2. Brattka, V., Presser, G.: Computability on subsets of metric spaces. Theoret. Comput. Sci. **305**(1–3), 43–76 (2003)
3. Brouwer, L.: An intuitionist correction of the fixed point theorem on the sphere. Proc. Roy. Soc. Lond. Ser. A. **213**, 1–2 (1952)
4. Collins, P.: Computable analysis with applications to dynamic systems. Math. Struct. Comput. Sci. **30**(2), 173–233 (2020)
5. Escardó, M.H.: PCF extended with real numbers: a domain-theoretic approach to higher-order exact real number computation. Ph.D. thesis, Imperial College London (1996)
6. Escardó, M.H.: Properly injective spaces and function spaces. Topol. Appl. **89**(1), 75–120 (1998)
7. Gierz, G., Hofmann, K.H., Keimel, K., Lawson, J.D., Mislove, M.W., Scott, D.: Continuous Lattices and Domains. Cambridge University Press, Cambridge (2003)
8. Hofmann, K.H., Lawson, J.D.: On the order-theoretical foundation of a theory of quasicompactly generated spaces without separation axiom. J. Aust. Math. Soc. Ser. A. Pure Math. Stat. **36**(2), 194–212 (1984)
9. Neumann, E.: Universal envelopes of discontinuous functions. Ph.D. thesis, Aston University (2019)
10. Neumann, E.: Uniform envelopes. arXiv:2103.16156 (2021)
11. Pauly, A.: On the topological aspects of the theory of represented spaces. Computability **5**(2), 159–180 (2016)
12. Pour-El, M.B., Richards, J.I.: Computability in Analysis and Physics. Springer (1989)
13. Scarf, H.: The approximation of fixed points of a continuous mapping. SIAM J. Appl. Math. **15**(5), 1328–1343 (1967)
14. Schröder, M.: Admissible representations for continuous computations. Ph.D. thesis, FernUniversität Hagen (2002)
15. Schröder, M.: A Hofmann-Mislove theorem for Scott open sets. Preprint https://arxiv.org/abs/1501.06452v1 (2015)
16. Scott, D.: Continuous lattices. In: Lawvere, F.W. (ed.) Toposes, Algebraic Geometry and Logic. LNM, vol. 274, pp. 97–136. Springer, Heidelberg (1972). https://doi.org/10.1007/BFb0073967
17. Trefethen, L.N., Bau III, D.: Numerical Linear Algebra. SIAM, Philadelphia (1997)
18. Weihrauch, K.: Computable Analysis. Springer, Heidelberg (2000). https://doi.org/10.1007/978-3-642-56999-9_9
19. Ziegler, M., Brattka, V.: Computability in linear algebra. Theoret. Comput. Sci. **326**(1–3), 187–211 (2004)

On Trees Without Hyperimmune Branches

Keng Meng Ng[1], Frank Stephan[2,3]([✉]), Yue Yang[3], and Liang Yu[4]

[1] Division of Mathematical Sciences, School of Physical and Mathematical Sciences,
Nanyang Technological University, 21 Nanyang Link,
Singapore 637371, Republic of Singapore
kmng@ntu.edu.sg
[2] School of Computing, National University of Singapore, 13 Computing Drive,
Block COM1, Singapore 117417, Republic of Singapore
fstephan@comp.nus.edu.sg
[3] Department of Mathematics, National University of Singapore,
10 Lower Kent Ridge Road, Block S17, Singapore 119076, Republic of Singapore
matyangy@nus.edu.sg
[4] Mathematical Department, Nanjing University,
Nanjing 210093, Jiangsu, People's Republic of China

Abstract. The current work includes a result announced in the year 2012 which was unproven until now. The result shows that there is a co-r.e. tree with uncountably many infinite branches such that the non-isolated infinite branches of the constructed tree are all nonrecursive, generalised low, hyperimmune-free and form a perfect tree.

1 Introduction

The connections between trees and their branches are well-studied. A major result is Jockusch and Soare's Low Basis Theorem [8] which showed that every infinite binary recursive (or co-r.e.) tree has an infinite branch of low Turing degree; similarly they showed that it also has an infinite branch of hyperimmune-free Turing degree. This shows that trees (this word denotes from now on infinite binary trees) which are recursive or co-r.e. have hyperimmune-free infinite branches. Downey [3] provided a tree where all branches are hyperimmune-free and some are nonrecursive. Downey's construction left open the question whether such trees can be made to have uncountably many infinite branches.

Ng, Stephan, Yang and Yu constructed in 2011 and 2012 recursive trees with uncountably many infinite branches such that every infinite branch is of hyperimmune-free Turing degree. They furthermore studied various related results

Frank Stephan and Yang Yue have been supported in part by the Singapore Ministry of Education Tier 2 grant AcRF MOE2019-T2-2-121/R146-000-304-112 as well as by the NUS Tier 1 grants AcRF R146-000-337-114 and R252-000-C17-114. Keng Meng Ng is supported by the Singapore Ministry of Education grant RG23/19 at NTU. Liang Yu was supported by NSFC grant No. 12025103.

U. Berger et al. (Eds.): CiE 2022, LNCS 13359, pp. 234–245, 2022.
https://doi.org/10.1007/978-3-031-08740-0_20

and announced in 2012 [12, Theorem 2.4] the result that there is a recursive binary tree with uncountably many infinite branches of Cantor-Bendixson rank 1 (thus removing the isolated branches makes it perfect) such that all infinite branches are hyperimmune-free and generalised low$_1$. They gave a proof sketch and announced the full details of the proof in the journal version which never got ready due to the construction becoming more and more lengthy and remaining incomplete. The reason was that Ng, Stephan, Yang and Yu tried to follow the proof-sketch of the initial approach of their paper [12, Theorem 2.4] and intended to use the "full approximation method" which is a complicated infinite injury construction. The alternative proof in the present work uses a K-recursive guidance tree U whose infinite branches form a perfect tree of 2-generic inversions of the double jumps of sets in the cone above K'. This guidance tree brought down the complexity of the construction from infinite injury to finite injury in the translation of U to the final co-r.e. tree T.

The result is from the field of classical recursion theory and it connects two major notions of the field, namely that of hyperimmune-free Turing degrees (which are those Turing degrees where all functions computed are majorised by a recursive function) with that of recursive or co-r.e. trees having uncountably many infinite branches. Recursive functions are, in easy terms, those which can be computed by a abstract machine without any bounds on computation time and storage space; alternatively one can also say, due to a result of Matiyasevich [10], that a recursive function is one whose graph is Diophantine, that is, satisfies that there is a polynomial p with integer coefficients in variables $x, y, z_1, \ldots, z_k$ such that, for all $x, y \in \mathbb{N}$, $f(x) = y$ iff there are values for $z_1, \ldots, z_k \in \mathbb{N}$ with $p(x, y, z_1, \ldots, z_k) = 0$. This also works with partial-recursive functions and thus recursively enumerable sets. The classes of the infinite branches of such trees are also called Π_1^0 and subject to detailed studies. The authors want also refer to standard text books on recursion theory and related fields for further reading of the background [1, 9, 15, 16, 18]. The main innovation of [12] was to show that Π_1^0-classes can be both uncountable and only have members of hyperimmune-free Turing degree. The add-on properties are introduced below one by one together with definitions or characterisations explaining them.

Theorem 1. *There is a co-r.e. tree T without finite branches which has $2^{\aleph_0}$ many infinite branches such that the nonisolated infinite branches are all hyperimmune-free, generalised low$_1$, Schnorr-trivial, of minimal Turing degree, jump traceable and form a perfect tree.*

Besides the above mentioned announcement [12, Theorem 2.4], the proof was never published and is also not in the follow-up works, that is, works citing the 2012 paper [6, 7, 13, 22]. A result proven by Hirschfeldt, Jockusch and Schupp [7, Lemma 6.7] was also announced without proof [12] and states that every hyperimmune-free infinite branch A on a K-recursive tree is also on a recursive tree not containing any additional infinite branches. Here some detailed explanations on the used notions.

Co-r.e. tree: This is a downward closed infinite subset of binary strings such that the set of strings outside it is recursively enumerable. Branches are finite or infinite strings such that all finite prefixes of them are in the tree. Co-r.e. trees can be made such that all branches are infinite by enumerating for each node σ into the complement of the tree where before both $\sigma 0$ and $\sigma 1$ had been enumerated into the complement. The infinite branches of a co-r.e. tree form a Π_1^0-class and the concepts recursive tree, co-r.e. tree and Π_1^0-class are interchangeable when talking about the class of infinite branches of a tree.

Remark 2. One can prune of the finite branches of an existing recursive tree S and receives a co-r.e. tree T in which every node has either one or two successors, but which does not have any deadends. The infinite branches of both are the same. This co-r.e. tree is notationally easier to handle, due to the direct correspondence of the branching bits of its nonrecursive infinite branches in T and these are the union of all branching strings (branching bits used until some level) form a K-r.e. tree whose infinite branches correspond in a one-one way with the nonisolated infinite branches of T.

Hyperimmune-free: The easiest characterisation of a set A being hyperimmune-free is that every A-recursive function is majorised by a recursive function. Formally, it means that no set $B \leq_T A$ is hyperimmune, that is, for every infinite set $B \leq_T A$ there is a recursive array $I_0, I_1, \ldots$ of finite disjoint sets given by canonical indices with each I_k intersecting B. Hyperimmune sets were introduced by Post [20]. Dekker [2] showed that every nonrecursive r.e. Turing degree contains a hyperimmune set and Miller and Martin [11] showed that on one hand every nonrecursive Turing degree below the halting problem K contains a hyperimmune set while on the other hand there are also nonrecursive Turing degrees without hyperimmune sets, such degrees and the sets in them are called hyperimmune-free. Jockusch and Soare [8] showed that every co-r.e. tree with an infinite branch contains actually an infinite hyperimmune-free branch.

Schnorr-trivial: Franklin and Stephan [4] gave the following characterisation which serves as a definition: A set A is Schnorr-trivial if for every $f \leq_{tt} A$ there is a recursive function g such that $\forall n \, \exists m \leq 2^n \, [f(n) = g(n, m)]$.

Remark 3. Above notions have the following properties: Schnorr-trivial plus hyperimmune-free equals to a property called recursively traceable; however, the property Schnorr-trivial is easier to achieve in a construction, as one needs only to consider truth-table reductions and not to worry about Turing reductions. Furthermore, if φ_e^A is a truth-table reduction then it is assumed that there is a recursive function g such that $\varphi_e^A(x)$ needs, independently of the choice of A, at most $g(x)$ steps and queries only below $g(x)$ and outputs a value y with $y < g(x)$. Similarly, if φ_e is a Turing reduction and $\varphi_e^A(x)$ needs s steps to converge then all places queried are below s and $\varphi_e^A(x) < s$. In particular, terminating computations $\varphi_e^\sigma(x)$ query σ only at values in the domain σ. Two partial functions φ_e^σ and φ_e^τ are consistent at stage s iff for all x where both $\varphi_e^\sigma(x)$ and $\varphi_e^\tau(x)$ output values y and z within s steps, it holds that $y = z$.

Jump Traceable: A set A is jump traceable if there are a recursive function h and a partial-recursive function g such that $\forall n \, \exists m \leq h(n) \, [\varphi_n^A(n) = g(n,m)]$. Here one uses the diagonal jump function $n \mapsto \varphi_n^A(n)$ in place of its domain A' and equality "$=$" of partial function values means that either both sides are undefined or both sides are defined and equal.

Generalised Low: A set A is generalised low$_1$ if $A' \leq_T A \oplus K$. This property was introduced to generalise the notion "low" in a senseful way beyond the classes of Turing degrees below the halting problem. Note that "generalised low$_1$" and "high" are not disjoint properties and some sets have both properties, for example the 1-generic set obtained by inverting the jump of K'. Nies showed the following proposition which allows to construct jump-traceable sets when one actually wants generalised low ones.

Proposition 4 (Nies [14]). *If A is jump traceable then $A' \leq_T A \oplus K$.*

Minimal Turing Degree: A set A is of minimal Turing degree iff A is not recursive and for every $B \leq_T A$, either B is recursive or $A \leq_T B$. Spector [19] constructed a minimal Turing degree which is below the jump K' of the halting problem K and Sacks [17] constructed a minimal Turing degree below K. A sufficient criterion to show that A is minimal is to show that for every Turing reduction φ_e there is a co-r.e. tree S such that A is an infinite branch of S and a node $\sigma \preceq A$ such that one of the following three conditions holds:

1. The function φ_e^A is total and every $B \succeq \sigma$ on S satisfies that $\varphi_e^A = \varphi_e^B$ and thus φ_e^A is recursive;
2. Every $B \succeq \sigma$ on S with $B \neq A$ satisfies that there is an x with $\varphi_e^A(x) \neq \varphi_e^B(x)$ where both values are defined and thus $A \leq_T \varphi_e^A$;
3. There is an x with $\varphi_e^A(x)$ being undefined and thus φ_e^A is partial.

A tree S is e-splitting along A if it satisfies one of the three conditions and Spector [19] used this method to construct a minimal Turing degree.

Perfect Tree: A tree is perfect iff every infinite branch is the pointwise limit of other infinite branches which are different to it; in particular perfect trees have $2^{\aleph_0}$ many infinite branches and do not have isolated infinite branches. The tree T constructed in the main result will satisfy that its nonisolated branches form a perfect tree and that there is furthermore set of size $\aleph_0$ of isolated branches added to this tree; these additional recursive branches cannot be avoided as T must have low branches by the Low Basis Theorem [8] and these branches are then recursive by being both hyperimmune-free and low and thus isolated by the construction that all infinite branches on the perfect tree are nonrecursive.

Proposition 5. *If V is a K'-recursive tree, then V is contained in a K-r.e. tree U such that every infinite branch A of U is also one of V and vice versa.*

Proof. This is a folklore result which holds relative to any oracle, not only relative K. However, it is needed here only relative to K. By the limit lemma, there is a K-recursive approximation V_s such that for all $\mu \in V$, $V_s(\mu) = V(\mu)$

for almost all s. Now one enumerates a node μ into U iff there is a stage $s > |\mu|$ such that all prefixes ν of μ are in V_s. If A is an infinite branch of V then clearly all prefixes of A are enumerated into U and A is an infinite branch of U. If A is not an infinite branch of V there is a prefix μ of A which is not in V and so there is a stage t such that $V_s(\mu) = 0$ for all $s \geq t$ and then no prefix of A longer than $|\mu| + t$ will ever be enumerated into U; thus A is not an infinite branch of U. $\square$

Proposition 6 (Based on Friedberg Jump Inversion Theorem [5]**).** *There is a perfect K'-recursive tree V such that each infinite branch of it is 2-generic and that all Turing degrees above K' are double jumps of infinite branches of V.*

Proof. Given a set $B \subseteq \mathbb{N}$ and oracle K', one starts with the root $\sigma_0 = \varepsilon$ and puts it into the tree. Then one checks whether there is an extension η of σ_n in W_e^K and if so then one lets $\sigma_{n+1} = \eta B(n)$ for the first such η found else one lets $\sigma_{n+1} = \sigma_n B(n)$. This case-distinction is clearly K'-recursive. The resulting tree V is the union of this construction for all oracles B and $V[B]$ refers to the encoded infinite branch for B. For two oracles $B, \tilde{B}$ first differing at position n, the respective strings σ_{n+1} in the construction of $V[B]$ and $V[\tilde{B}]$ will differ exactly on the last bit and therefore $V[B]$ and $V[\tilde{B}]$ will be different infinite branches of V. The tree V will be uniformly K'-recursive.

The sets $V[B]$ are always 2-generic and thus $V[B]'' \equiv_T B \oplus K'$. Note that the 2-genericity is coded explicitly into the set $V[B]$ by using an extension η of σ_n in W_e^K whenever such an extension exists. Further note that $V[B] \oplus K'$ can recover B and $B \leq_T V[B] \oplus K'$. As $V[B]$ is 2-generic, $V[B]'' \equiv_T V[B] \oplus K'$ and if $B \geq_T K'$ then $V[B]'' \equiv_T B$. Thus the class of infinite branches of V has cardinality $2^{\aleph_0}$ and their double jumps cover the whole cone above K'. $\square$

Corollary 7. *There is a K-r.e. tree $U = \{u(0), u(1), u(2), \ldots\}$ such that all its infinite branches are 2-generic and that the Turing degrees of the double jumps of these branches cover the whole cone above K'.*

2   The Main Result and Its Construction

The following theorem implies Theorem 1 and uses the above constructed trees from Proposition 6 and Corollary 7.

Theorem 8. *Given U, V as in Proposition 6 and Corollary 7, there is a co-r.e. tree T with uncountably many infinite branches such that every nonisolated infinite branch of T is of hyperimmune-free Turing degree, minimal Turing degree, generalised low_1, jump traceable and Schnorr-trivial. Furthermore, for each nonisolated infinite branch A of T there is an infinite branch B of U with $A \oplus K \equiv_T B \oplus K$ and B consists of the branching bits of A in T.*

Construction. The construction works with markers c_n which are initialised as $c_{n,0} = n$ and move at stages t from $c_{n,t}$ to $c_{n,t+1}$; in parallel to the movement of markers, a co-r.e. tree will be constructed which has branching nodes only on levels on which a marker sits. This tree is called T and $T_0 = \{0,1\}^*$. Furthermore, $u_t(k)$ is the t-th approximation to $u(k)$ for the K-recursive enumeration $u(0), u(1), u(2), \ldots$ of the tree U; note that this approximation exists by the Limit Lemma and for each k and almost all t, $u_t(k) = u(k)$.

Recall that a finite tree up to a level can be described by the leave nodes in that level; furthermore, one can for each leaf describe the string of branching bits which are those bits in the path to the leaf where one has to make a choice between two possibilities in order to select the leaf to which one wants to go; those where there is only one choice are omitted from the string.

At stage t, one first considers for each n with $c_{n,t} \leq t+1$ the finite tree L_n which contains all words $\sigma \in T_t$ with $dom(\sigma) \subseteq \{0, 1, \ldots, c_{n,t} - 1\}$. The branching bits of a $\sigma \in L_n$ are the last bits a of those prefixes $\eta a \prec \sigma$ where both $\eta 0, \eta 1 \in L_n$ and the branching string is the sequence of branching bits in the given order from the root to the node σ. One considers an extension of H_n of L_n and calls it admissible when it satisfies the following conditions:

1. The leaves of H_n have the domain $\{0, 1, \ldots, t+1\}$ and $H_n \subseteq T_t$;
2. For each leaf σ of L_n there is exactly one $\tau \in H_n$ extending σ and having domain $\{0, 1, \ldots, t\}$; furthermore, for the branching bits μ of σ in L_n, if $\mu \in \{u_{t+1}(0), u_{t+1}(1), \ldots, u_{t+1}(n)\}$ then $\tau 0, \tau 1 \in H_n$ else only $\tau 0 \in H_n$;
3. There is progress from L_n to H_n in the way that certain enumeration, definability or splitting goals are obtained; more precisely there are $\sigma, \sigma' \in L_n$ with the corresponding τ, τ' such that $c_{n,t} \leq t+1$ and at least one of the following conditions is satisfied:
   (a) Some element $m \leq n$ became enumerated into K between time $c_{n,t}$ and $t+1$ or $u_{t+1}(m) \neq u_s(m)$ for some $s \in \{c_{n,t}, c_{n,t}+1, \ldots, t\}$;
   (b) There is an $e \leq n$ for which the function φ_e^σ is not defined on all of $0, 1, \ldots, n$ within $c_{n,t}$ steps while φ_e^τ is defined on all of $0, 1, \ldots, n$ within $t+1$ steps;
   (c) There is an $e \leq n$ for which $\varphi_e^\sigma(e)$ is not defined within $c_{n,t}$ steps while $\varphi_e^\tau(e)$ is defined within $t+1$ steps;
   (d) For some $e \leq n$ there is an x such that φ_e^σ and $\varphi_e^{\sigma'}$ are consistent at time $c_{n,t}$ while $\varphi_e^\tau(x), \varphi_e^{\tau'}(x)$ are defined and different for an $x < t+1$ within $t+1$ steps;
   (e) $|\sigma| = |\tau|$ and $c_{n,t} = t+1$.

For the least n where one can find L_n, H_n as above, one does the following:

1. For $m < n$, $c_{m,t+1} = c_{m,t}$ and $c_{n,t+1} = t+1$ and for $m > n$, $c_{m,t+1} = t+1+m-n$;
2. Furthermore, one lets T_{t+1} consist of all the nodes which are comparable to one of the leaves of H_n, that is, one prunes off the tree all nodes which are extending some leaf σ of L_n but which are incomparable to all leaves of H_n.

Note that such an n is always found as the n with $c_{n,t} = t+1$ can be selected when no smaller n qualifies.

Note that in the above, if H_n was defined at stage s, then the L_n at the next first stage t where $c_{n,t+1} > c_{n,s+1}$ satisfies that the leaves of that L_n at stage

t are one bit shorter than the leaves of the H_n at stage s; this is to make sure that when $U_{t+1}(m) \neq u_{s+1}(m)$ for some $m \leq n$ then the sprouting of the leaves of H_n can be undone for the new H_n and is not incorporated into the new L_n.

Notation 9. In the following, the final value of L_n and H_n refer to the trees with leaves of level $c_{n,t} - 1$ and $c_{n,t}$, respectively, where t is so large that $c_{n,t}$ does not change at t or later.

The following proposition is true first due to the fact that when the last H_m with $m < n$ has been defined then $L_n = H_{m-1}$ and from then onwards, whenever L_n and H_n change, the extension of L_n extends each leaf σ of the old L_n uniquely to a leaf τ of the new L_n and furthermore puts two successor leaves into H_n iff the branching bits μ form a string in $\{u_{t+1}(0), u_{t+1}(1), \ldots, u_{t+1}(n)\}$.

Proposition 10. *Each leaf σ of L_n has two successors in H_n iff its branching string η is in $\{u(0), u(1), \ldots, u(n)\}$ and each leaf of σa of H_n extends in a unique way to a leaf τ of L_{n+1}.*

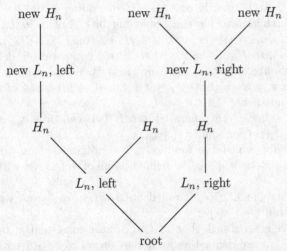

The above picture shows how a tree L_n gets updated due to changes in $\{u_s(0), u_s(1), \ldots, u_s(n)\}$ where the updates from the old s to the larger new s removes 0 from the list (branching string for left) and add 1 into the list (branching string for right). Nodes denoted with L_n and H_n denote the leaves of these trees, where the new left leaf of L_n is above the old left leaf of H_n and the old left right leaf of H_n is enumerated into the complement of T. The new leaves of H_n have the branching strings 0, 10, 11. Left successors have branching bit 0 and right successors have branching bit 1 at each branching which survives.

3   Proof of the Properties of Infinite Branches

The following fact is useful. It is just based on the fact that given a K-recursive enumeration $v(0), v(1), v(2), \ldots$ of the above tree U, one can replace it by a new enumeration $u(\langle i,j\rangle)$ which has the following approximation: If $v_j(i) = v_s(i)$ for $s = j, j+1, \ldots, j+t$ then $u_t(\langle i,j\rangle) = v_j(i)$ else $u_t(\langle i,j\rangle)$ is some fixed element of U, say the root of the tree.

Fact 11. *Every nonempty K-r.e. set has a K-recursive enumeration in which the enumerating function can be approximated such that it makes at most one mind change in the computation of each number in the enumeration.*

Proposition 12. *Every infinite branch A of T is jump traceable and, by Proposition 4, also generalised low$_1$.*

Proof. One can see by induction that L_n has always prior to step t at most 2^n leaves and that H_n (due to the branching nodes on the level of $c_{n,t+1}$ being there) can have at most 2^{n+1} leaves. Furthermore, if one enumerates the various possibilities for progress in item 3, one sees that the overall number of mind changes is bounded by $1 + (n+1) \cdot (2 + 2^n + 2^n + 4^n) \leq 8^{n+2}$. Now taking into account that activity of smaller c_m cause c_n to act again, one gets that c_n is modified at most 8^{n+2} times between any two changes of lower markers, so in total at most $8^{(n+1)(n+2)}$ times. Now one can for each leaf τ of each version of L_n enumerate at most one value of $\varphi_e^\sigma(e)$ and for each infinite branch A of T where $\varphi_e^A(e)$ is defined, $\varphi_e^A(e) = \varphi_e^\sigma(e)$ for one of the leaves of the final version of L_n after the last time that the marker $c_{n,t}$ moved, thus every infinite branch A is jump traceable with bound $2^{3n^2+10n+6}$. □

Proposition 13. *An infinite branch A of T is isolated iff there is an n such that the leaf of A restricted to final version of L_n has branching string μ with $\mu \notin U$.*

Proof. The reason for this that if μ is not in U then $\mu \notin \{u(0), u(1), \ldots, u(n)\}$ for all n and the final versions of L_n and H_n will have that the leaf $\tau a \preceq A$ in H_n is of the form $\tau 0$ and $\tau 1 \notin H_n$. The same will be true for all $m \geq n$, as in them the restriction of A to $L_m = H_{m-1}$ will have the same branching string η. Thus the corresponding τ in H_m will have the unique extension and leaf $\tau 0$ in H_m and therefore the infinite branch A is isolated and thus recursive.

Now consider the case that all branching strings of A are in U. Then, for each L_m there is a first $n \geq m$ such that the branching string μ of A in L_m is in $\{u(0), u(1), \ldots, u(n)\}$. It follows that the leaf τ of L_n extended by A will also have two extensions $\tau 0, \tau 1 \in H_n$ and so there is a branching node in T which is a leaf of L_n and a prefix of A. As this happens for infinitely many n, the infinite branch A is not isolated. □

Proposition 14. *Every infinite branch A of T is of hyperimmune-free Turing degree.*

Proof. Let A be an infinite branch of T which is not isolated and which therefore might be non-recursive; note that all isolated infinite branches are recursive. Now $A = U[B]$ for some 2-generic B, that is, the set B if viewed as an infinite sequence defines the branching bits of A in the tree T.

For a given Turing reduction φ_e, consider the following set: $W^K = \{\mu : \exists n \geq e$ [the final L_n has a leaf σ with branching string μ and $\varphi_e^\sigma(x)$ being undefined for some $x < n]\}$. This set is K-r.e. and note that when $\varphi_e^A(x)$ would be defined for some infinite branch A of T extending σ, then some progress would be possible and the L_n would not be the final one.

If an $A = T[B]$ satisfies that there are above every σ some infinite branch $\tilde{A} = T[\tilde{B}]$ of T such that $\tilde{A}$ also extends σ and $\varphi_e^{\tilde{A}}$ is not total, then there is an x with $\varphi_e^{\tilde{A}}(x)$ being undefined and any $n \geq x$ satisfies that some prefix $\tilde{\sigma}$ of $\tilde{A}$ is in L_n as a leaf and $\varphi_e^{\tilde{\sigma}}(m)$ is undefined on some $m \leq n$ and therefore its branching string ν is in W^K. Thus B has above every node some extension in W^K and so B has a prefix itself which is in W^K. This implies that φ_e^A is not total by the definition of W^K.

So one sees that there is a $\sigma \preceq A$ such that for all infinite branches $\tilde{A}$ of T which extend σ it holds that $\varphi_e^{\tilde{A}}$ is total. Thus one can, for every x, simulate the coenumeration of T and the pruning of the tree until a stage is found and a level ℓ such that for all $\tau \in \{0,1\}^\ell$ which extend σ and which are still in T it holds that $\varphi_e^\tau(x)$ converges within ℓ steps and then the maximum of these values is an upper bound for $\varphi_e^A(x)$; as this upper bound is computed by a recursive function, φ_e^A has a recursive upper bound. Thus, for each e, either φ_e^A is partial (as indicated in the preceding paragraph) or φ_e^A has a recursive upper bound and therefore every nonisolated infinite branch of T is of hyperimmune-free Turing degree. The isolated infinite branches are recursive and therefore of hyperimmune-free Turing degree as well.   □

Proposition 15. *Every infinite branch A of T is Schnorr-trivial.*

Proof. If φ_e is a truth-table reduction with bound function g for the computation time then it will happen for almost all n that $c_{n,t}$ is eventually above $g(n)$; this is due to the fact that the time to enumerate the halting time of K up to n is a dominating function with respect to n. Thus one can, for all sufficiently large n, simulate the construction until the final value of the $c_{n,t}$ is above the use and then enumerate the 2^n values which are defined by the various branches of the co-r.e. tree which survive. The finitely many smaller values can be patched. Thus A is Schnorr-trivial.   □

Proposition 16. *The double jumps A'' of the infinite branches A of T form the cone above K'.*

Proof. Assume A is a non-isolated infinite branch of T; then $A = T[B]$ for some infinite branch B of U; furthermore, the bits of B are the branching bits of A in T. Note that the double jumps of the infinite branches B of V and thus U cover all Turing degrees above K' due to the B being obtained by uniform double jump inversion; furthermore, each B is 2-generic and $B'' \equiv_T B \oplus K'$.

The halting problem K allows to reconstruct all branching nodes of T and these allow to recover the set B from $A \oplus K$. Thus $B \leq_T A \oplus K$. As B is 2-generic, $B'' \equiv_T B \oplus K' \leq_T A \oplus K'$. Furthermore, Marcus Triplett mentions in his bachelor thesis [21] that every hyperimmune free set A satisfies $A'' \equiv_T A \oplus K'$, thus the above infinite branch A satisfies $A'' \equiv_T B''$.

As the constructions of V and U included for every Turing degree above K' a two-generic infinite branch B of U such that the double jump B'' is in the given Turing degree, one has that the double jumps of the infinite branches of T cover all Turing degrees above K'.   □

Proposition 17. *Every nonrecursive infinite branch A of T has minimal Turing degree.*

Proof. Let A be a non-recursive infinite branch of T. Consider a total function φ_e^A. By Proposition 14 there is a σ such that all infinite branches $\tilde{A}$ of T above σ, $\varphi_e^{\tilde{A}}$ is total.

If now there is such an infinite branch $\tilde{A}$ extending σ which is different from A but for which φ_e^A and $\varphi_e^{\tilde{A}}$ coincide, then it follows that above the branching node σ' of A and $\tilde{A}$, all infinite branches of S produce the same function φ_e^A and so this function is recursive; otherwise $\sigma'0$ or $\sigma'1$ would be extended into a sufficiently long prefixes of $\hat{A}$ and the respective of A and $\tilde{A}$ in order to achieve that these prefixes are mapped by φ_e on some value to different images and so either A or $\tilde{A}$ would be cut off.

So one has that there is a $\sigma'' \preceq A$ such that, for all infinite branches $\tilde{A}$ of S extending σ'', either the functions $\varphi_e^{\tilde{A}}$ are all different or are all the same.

If they are all different, one can Turing reduce A to φ_e^A. Whenever there are two different extensions above some $\sigma''' \succeq \sigma''$, one coenumerates T and simulates φ_e until either an e-splitting at some x above $\sigma'''0$ and $\sigma'''1$ is found so that $\varphi_e^A(x)$ says which branch to follow or one of the two nodes $\sigma'''0$ and $\sigma'''1$ has been enumerated out of T. Thus $A \equiv_T \varphi_e^A$ by the usual e-splitting analysis.

If the infinite branches of T above σ'' are mapped by φ_e all the same image, then one can for each input x coenumerate T until a level $\ell > |\sigma''|$ and a time t are found such that all $\tau \in \{0,1\}^\ell \cap S_t$ which extend σ'' satisfy that $\varphi_{e,t}^\tau(x)$ is a unique value y and equals to $\varphi_e^A(x)$. Thus φ_e^A is recursive in this case. Thus the minimality of A is verified.   □

Proposition 18. *The nonisolated branches of T form a perfect tree.*

Proof. Recall that every infinite branch B of U is 2-generic and that the infinite branches of U form a perfect subtree V of U by Proposition 6 and Corollary 7.

There is a K-recursive operator which maps the infinite branch B of U to the infinite branch $A = T[B]$ where the "branching string" of A in T is exactly the set B. This mapping is one-one and continuous. Furthermore, if $B_0, B_1, \dots$ converge pointwise against B and all $B_k \neq B$ then the infinite branches $T[B_k]$ converge pointwise to $A = T[B]$. Hence the nonrecursive infinite branches of U are mapped in a bijection to the nonisolated infinite branches of T and this bijection preserves pointwise limits; as the class of infinite branches of U and its image in T are both closed in the sense of topology, the limits of each convergent sequence is again an infinite branch of the corresponding tree. Thus the nonisolated infinite branches of T form a perfect subtree of T which is recursive in K'.   □

4   Concluding Remarks

The presented proof shows that one can construct a co-r.e. tree such that every branch is infinite and that every infinite branch is either isolated or has all of the following properties: nonrecursive, hyperimmune-free, generalised low$_1$, minimal Turing degree, Schnorr-trivial and jump traceable. Furthermore, the nonisolated infinite branches form a perfect tree and its double jumps cover the cone above K' and each of its jumps is also the jump of a 2-generic set. The key idea was to use the guidance tree U and to transform it into the final co-r.e. tree T so that every non-isolated infinite branch A of T has the branching bits from an infinite branch B of U which guides the building of the tree. The construction could be a bit varied to get the following related results.

First, instead of taking V to be the union of all $V[\tilde{B}]$ in Proposition 6, one could take a K'-recursive tree with uncountably many K'-hyperimmune-free and 2-generic branches and then get the result that there is a tree T with uncountably many infinite branches such that every infinite branch is hyperimmune-free, hyperimmune-free relative to K', jump-traceable and jump-traceable relative to K'. It is possible to iterate this.

Second, if $B \leq_T K'$ is 2-generic then one can construct an K-r.e. tree U with B being its unique infinite branch. The resulting tree T has then exactly one nonisolated and nonrecursive branch which is $A = T[B]$. This gives a co-r.e. tree of Cantor-Bendixson rank 2 with exactly one nonisolated branch $A = T[B]$ which is nonrecursive, hyperimmune-free, generalised low$_1$ and satisfies $A \oplus K = B \oplus K$.

Third, note that a perfect co-r.e. tree T without deadends has always an infinite branch which is high, thus one cannot avoid the isolated branches in the construction of T which make the tree T to be a nonperfect enlargement of a perfect tree. If T would not have isolated infinite branches then one can by the finite extension method construct an infinite branch A such that each σ_{k+1} is the first branching node above $\sigma_k K'(k)$ where σ_0 is the least branching node in the tree. Now $A \oplus K$ allows to check which of the nodes in the infinite branch A are branching nodes and thus $K' \leq_T A \oplus K$. Thus A is high and cannot be hyperimmune-free. So the Cantor-Bendixson rank of the tree T constructed in Theorem 1 must be at least 1, as was also stated without proof by Ng, Stephan, Yang and Yu [12]. The same applies to trees with uncountably many infinite branches where the jumps of all infinite branches avoid some upper cone.

The following questions are left open. For the first, it was claimed by Ng, Stephan, Yang and Yu [12, Theorem 3.6] that a modification of the proof of the main result of this paper would give the result; however, this proof is now a new proof by other means and the authors are not aware how to incorporate the Robinson guessing into it.

Open Problem 19. *1. Are there uncountably many hyperimmune-free sets which are hyperimmune-free relative to every low recursively enumerable set?*
2. Is every jump of a nonrecursive hyperimmune-free set also the jump of a 2-generic set? The converse is [12, Theorem 4.4].
3. Is the jump of every hyperimmune-free set also the jump of a hyperimmune-free Schnorr-trivial set?

References

1. Calude, C.S.: Information and Randomness - An Algorithmic Perspective, 2nd edn. Springer, Heidelberg (2002). https://doi.org/10.1007/978-3-662-04978-5
2. Dekker, J.C.: A theorem on hypersimple sets. Proc. Am. Math. Soc. **5**, 791–796 (1954)
3. Downey, R.G.: On Π_1^0-classes and their ranked points. Notre Dame J. Formal Logic **32**(4), 499–512 (1991)
4. Franklin, J., Stephan, F.: Schnorr-trivial sets and truth-table reducibility. J. Symb. Logic **75**(2), 501–521 (2010)
5. Friedberg, R.: A criterion for completeness of degrees of unsolvability. J. Symb. Logic **22**, 159–160 (1957)
6. Hölzl, R., Porter, C.P.: Randomness for computable measures and initial segment complexity. Ann. Pure Appl. Logic **168**(4), 860–886 (2017)
7. Hirschfeldt, D.R., Jockusch Jr, C.G., Schupp, P.E.: Coarse computability, the density metric, Hausdorff distances between Turing degrees, perfect trees, and reverse mathematics. Technical report on http://arxiv.org/abs/2106.13118 (2021)
8. Jockusch, C.G., Soare, R.I.: Π_1^0 classes and degrees of theories. Trans. Am. Math. Soc. **173**, 33–56 (1972). https://doi.org/10.1007/s00153-012-0310-y
9. Li, M., Vitányi, P.: An Introduction to Kolmogorov Complexity and its Applications. Springer, New York (2019). https://doi.org/10.1007/978-0-387-49820-1
10. Matiyasevich, Y.V.: Diofantovost' perechislimykh mnozhestv. Doklady Akademii Nauk SSSR, 191, 297-282 (1970). (in Russian). English translation: Enumerable sets are Diophantine. Soviet Math. Doklady 11, 354-358 (1970)
11. Miller, W., Martin, D.: The degrees of hyperimmune sets. Z. für Math. Logik und Grundl. der Math. **14**, 159–166 (1968)
12. Ng, K.M., Stephan, F., Yang, Y., Yu, L.: The computational aspects of hyperimmunefree degrees. In: Proceedings of the Twelfth Asian Logic Conference, pp. 271–284. World Scientific (2013)
13. Ng, K.M., Yu, H.: Effective domination and the bounded jump. Notre Dame J. Formal Logic **61**(2), 203–225 (2020)
14. Nies, A.: Reals which compute little. In: Proceedings of Logic Colloquium 2002, Lecture Notes in Logic, vol. 27, pp. 261–275 (2002)
15. Nies, A.: Computability and Randomness. Oxford University Press, Oxford (2009)
16. Odifreddi, P.: Classical Recursion Theory. North-Holland, Amsterdam (1989)
17. Sacks, G.E.: On the degrees less than $0'$. Ann. Math. **77**, 211–231 (1963)
18. Soare, R.: Recursively Enumerable Sets and Degrees: A Study of Computable Functions and Computably Generated Sets. Springer, Heidelberg (1987)
19. Spector, C.: On degrees of unsolvability. Ann. Math. **64**, 581–592 (1956)
20. Post, E.L.: Recursively enumerable sets of positive integers and their decision problems. Bull. Am. Math. Soc. **50**, 284–316 (1944)
21. Triplett, M.A.: Algorithmic Complexity and Triviality. Bachelor Thesis, The University of Auckland, New Zealand (2014)
22. Yu, H.: On equivalence relations and bounded Turing degrees. Ph.D. dissertation. Nanyang Technological University, Singapore (2018)

Algebras of Complemented Subsets

Iosif Petrakis[1]([⊠]) [iD] and Daniel Wessel[2] [iD]

[1] Mathematics Institute, University of Munich, Theresienstrasse 39,
80333 Munich, Germany
petrakis@math.lmu.de
https://www.mathematik.uni-muenchen.de/~petrakis/
[2] Department of Computer Science, University of Verona, Strada le Grazie 15,
37134 Verona, Italy
daniel.wessel@univr.it
https://www.di.univr.it/?ent=persona&id=33101&lang=en

Abstract. Complemented subsets were introduced by Bishop, in order
to avoid complementation in terms of negation. In his two approaches
to measure theory Bishop used two sets of operations on complemented
subsets. Here we study these two algebras and we introduce the notion of
Bishop algebra as an abstraction of their common structure. We translate
constructively the classical bijection between subsets and boolean-valued
functions by establishing a bijection between the proper classes of complemented subsets and of strongly extensional, boolean-valued, partial
functions. Avoiding negatively defined concepts, most of our results are
within minimal logic.

Keywords: Bishop sets · complemented subsets · partial functions

1 Introduction

Bishop's "official" theory of sets (oBST)[1], presented in a condensed way in
Chap. 3 of [2,4], motivated Martin-Löf's type theory (MLTT) [14,15] and most
of the formal studies of the 70's (see [1]). In [2] Bishop introduced subsets in a
categorical manner, he treated the powerset mainly as a proper class, he defined
only the empty subset of a set, and not the empty set, and he used a fully
positive notion of an inequality, or apartness relation. However, in the practice
of Bishop-style constructive mathematics a more "naive" theory of Bishop sets
(nBST) was employed. In the work of Bridges and Richman [5,13] subsets were
defined by separation, the powerset was considered to be a set, the empty set
was used, and an almost positive notion of an inequality was studied. In [20] a

---

[1] The type-theoretic interpretation of Bishop's set theory into the theory of setoids [17,
18] is nowadays the standard way to understand Bishop sets. A categorical interpretation of Bishop sets is Palmgren's constructive adaptation [16] of Lawvere's
elementary theory of the category of sets. In [9] Coquand views Bishop sets as a
natural sub-presheaf of the universe in the cubical set model.

U. Berger et al. (Eds.): CiE 2022, LNCS 13359, pp. 246–258, 2022.
https://doi.org/10.1007/978-3-031-08740-0_21

reconstruction (BST) of oBST is given, highlighting the use of dependent assignment routines, of predicative definitions, and of set-indexed families of sets and subsets.

In [2] Bishop defined for a set X, equipped with an equality $=_X$ and an inequality $\neq_X$, a positive notion of disjoint subsets of X and through the latter the concept of a complemented subset of X. Complemented subsets are easier to handle than plain subsets, as their partial, characteristic functions are constructively defined and their complement behaves a lot like the classical complement of a subset. These two features of complemented subsets were crucial to Bishop's reconstruction of measure theory (BMT) in [2] and in Bishop-Cheng measure theory (BCMT), a constructive counterpart to the classical Daniell approach to measure theory, developed first in [3] and extended significantly in [4].

The two different measure theories of Bishop involve different operations between complemented subsets. In BMT the, so-called here, first algebra of complemented subsets is considered, while in BCMT the second. Here we study these two algebras, some of the properties of which, as we explain, depend on the underlying theory of Bishop sets. For all basic notions and results mentioned here without further explanation or proof, we refer to [20]. In a proposition we write (INT) to denote that its proof is within intuitionistic logic. Otherwise, all proofs presented here are within minimal logic. Due to lack of space, some proofs are omitted. We structure this paper as follows:

- In Sect. 2 we introduce the extensional empty subset $\not\varnothing_X$ of a set X, as a positive notion of empty subset.
- In Sect. 3 we present complemented subsets and partial functions.
- In Sect. 4 we describe the first algebra of complemented subsets and the constructive translation of the classical bijection between subsets and boolean-valued functions (Proposition 8).
- In Sect. 5 we describe the second algebra of complemented subsets and its relation to boolean-valued, partial functions.
- In Sect. 6 we introduce Bishop algebras as an abstraction of the two algebras of complemented subsets.

2   Inequalities, and a Positive Notion of Empty Subset

In oBST a *subset* of a set $(X, =_X)$ is a pair (A, i_A^X), where A is a set and $i_A^X \colon A \hookrightarrow X$ is an embedding[2] of A into X. If (A, i_A^X), (B, i_B^X) are subsets of X, then $(A, i_A^X) \subseteq (B, i_B^X)$, or simpler $A \subseteq B$, if there is (an embedding) $f \colon A \hookrightarrow B$, in symbols $f \colon A \subseteq B$, such that the following diagram commutes

---

[2] If X, Y are totalities an *assignment routine* f from X to Y is denoted by $f \colon X \rightsquigarrow Y$. If X, Y are sets, $f \colon X \rightsquigarrow Y$ is a *function*, if it respects their equalities. Their set is denoted by $\mathbb{F}(X, Y)$. A function is an embedding, if it is an injection.

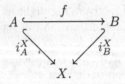

The totality of the subsets of X is the *powerset* $\mathcal{P}(X)$ of X, equipped with the equality $(A, i_A^X) =_{\mathcal{P}(X)} (B, i_B^X) :\Leftrightarrow A \subseteq B \ \& \ B \subseteq A$. Since the membership condition for $\mathcal{P}(X)$ requires quantification over the universe $\mathbb{V}_0$ of (predicative) sets, $\mathcal{P}(X)$ is a proper class. A bounded formula $P(x)$ is an *extensional property* on X, if $\forall_{x,y \in X} \big([x =_X y \ \& \ P(x)] \Rightarrow P(y)\big)$. The totality X_P, defined by $x \in X_P :\Leftrightarrow x \in X \ \& \ P(x)$ and $x =_{X_P} y :\Leftrightarrow x =_X y$, is an *extensional subset* of X, where $i_P^X \colon X_P \rightsquigarrow X$ is defined by $i_P^X(x) := x$, for every $x \in X_P$. Clearly, i_P^X is an embedding. As usual, we write $X_P := \{x \in X \mid P(x)\}$.

Bishop never defined the empty set, only the empty subset of an inhabited set! According to [2], p. 65, if $x_0 \in X$, the totality $\emptyset_X$ is defined by $z \in \emptyset_X :\Leftrightarrow x_0 \in X \ \& \ 0 =_{\mathbb{N}} 1$. If $i_\emptyset^X \colon \emptyset_X \rightsquigarrow X$ is defined by $i(z) := x_0$, for every $z \in \emptyset_X$, let $z =_{\emptyset_X} w :\Leftrightarrow i(z) =_X i(w) :\Leftrightarrow x_0 =_X x_0$. The pair $(\emptyset_X, i_\emptyset^X)$ is the *empty subset* of X. As Bishop writes in [2], p. 65,

> The definition of $\emptyset_X$ is negativistic, and we prefer to mention the void set as seldom as possible.

In contrast to the recursion rule of the empty type in MLTT, in order to define an assignment routine $f \colon \emptyset_X \rightsquigarrow A$, we need an element of A. If $A \subseteq X$ is inhabited, one needs Ex falso to show $\emptyset_X \subseteq A$. Moreover, $\emptyset_A \subseteq X$, but no connection can be established between $\emptyset_A$ and $\emptyset_X$. Alternatively, the empty subset can be defined as an extensional subset of X. Clearly, the definition $\emptyset_X := \{x \in X \mid \neg(x =_X x)\}$ is negativistic. In [4], and also in nBST, the following almost positive, due to (Ap_1), notion of inequality is considered.

Definition 1. *Let $(X, =_X)$ be a set. An inequality on X, or an apartness relation on X, is a relation $x \neq_X y$ such that the following conditions are satisfied:*

(Ap_1) $\forall_{x,y \in X} \big(x =_X y \ \& \ x \neq_X y \Rightarrow 0 =_{\mathbb{N}} 1\big)$.
(Ap_2) $\forall_{x,y \in X} \big(x \neq_X y \Rightarrow y \neq_X x\big)$.
(Ap_3) $\forall_{x,y \in X} \big(x \neq_X y \Rightarrow \forall_{z \in X}(z \neq_X x \vee z \neq_X y)\big)$.

If $\big(A, i_A^X\big) \subseteq X$, the canonical inequality on A induced by $\neq_X$ is defined by

$$a \neq_A a' :\Leftrightarrow i_A^X(a) \neq_X i_A^X(a'),$$

for every $a, a' \in A$, while its $\neq_X$-complement is the extensional subset of X

$$A^{\neq_X} := \big\{x \in X \mid \forall_{a \in A}\big(x \neq_X i_A^X(a)\big)\big\}.$$

If $(Y, =_Y, \neq_Y)$ is a set with inequality, a function $f \colon X \to Y$ is strongly extensional, if $f(x) \neq_Y f(x') \Rightarrow x \neq_X x'$, for every $x, x' \in X$.

An inequality $x \neq_X y$ is extensional on $X \times X$ i.e., if $x, y \in X$ with $x \neq_X y$, and if $x', y' \in X$ with $x' =_X x$ and $y' =_X y$, then $x' \neq_X y'$. In [2] the following completely positive notion of inequality is used.

Definition 2. *Let* $(X, =_X)$ *be a set and* F *an extensional subset of the set* $\mathbb{F}(X)$ *of real-valued functions on* X. *The inequality on* X *induced by* F *is defined by*

$$x \neq_X^F y :\Leftrightarrow \exists_{f \in F}\big(f(x) \neq_{\mathbb{R}} f(y)\big),$$

for every $x, y \in X$, *where* $a \neq_{\mathbb{R}} b :\Leftrightarrow |a - b| > 0$, *for every* $a, b \in \mathbb{R}$. *We call an inequality* $\neq_X$ *on* X *an* f-*inequality, if there is an extensional subset* F *of* $\mathbb{F}(X)$, *such that* $x \neq_X y \Leftrightarrow x \neq_X^F y$, *for every* $x, y \in X$.

An f-inequality is an inequality, but no negation of some sort is used in its definition. Moreover, the proof of its extensionality avoids negation. If F is a Bishop topology of functions (see [19,21,22,24]), then $x \neq_X^F y$ is the canonical inequality of a Bishop space. The inequality $a \neq_{\mathbb{R}} b$ is an f-inequality, as $a \neq_{\mathbb{R}} b \Leftrightarrow a \neq_{\mathbb{R}}^{\mathrm{Bic}(\mathbb{R})} b$, where Bic$(\mathbb{R})$ is the topology of Bishop-continuous functions of type $\mathbb{R} \to \mathbb{R}$ (see [19], Proposition 5.1.2.). By its extensionality, an (f$-$)inequality provides a (fully) positive definition of the *extensional empty subset*. With its help a positive definition of the property "a subset is empty", defined negatively as "it is not inhabited" in [5], p. 8, is possible. From now on, X, Y are sets with an (f$-$)inequality $\neq_X, \neq_Y$, respectively.

Definition 3. *Let* $\not{\emptyset}_X := \{x \in X \mid x \neq_X x\}$ *be the extensional, empty subset of* X. *If* $(A, i_A^X) \subseteq X$, *we call* A *empty, in symbols* empty(A), *if* $A \subseteq \not{\emptyset}_X$ *in* $\mathcal{P}(X)$.

Proposition 1. *Let* $A, B \in \mathcal{P}(X)$.

(i) $\not{\emptyset}_A \subseteq A$ *in* $\mathcal{P}(X)$, *and* $A \cap \not{\emptyset}_X \subseteq \not{\emptyset}_X$.
(ii) *If* $A \subseteq B$, *then* $\not{\emptyset}_A \subseteq \not{\emptyset}_B$ *in* $\mathcal{P}(X)$.
(iii) (INT) *If* A *is inhabited, then* $\not{\emptyset}_X \cup A =_{\mathcal{P}(X)} A$, *and hence* $\not{\emptyset}_X \subseteq A$.

Proof. We show only (ii). By the definition of $\neq_A$ on $A \subseteq X$ we get

$$\not{\emptyset}_A := \{a \in A \mid a \neq_A a\} := \{a \in A \mid i_A^X(a) \neq_X i_A^X(a)\}.$$

If $f : A \subseteq B$, its restriction (denoted by f again) to $\not{\emptyset}_A$ witnesses the required inequality; if $a \in \not{\emptyset}_A$, then by the following left commutativity we get $i_B^X(f(a)) =_X i_A^X(a) \neq_X i_A^X(a) =_X i_B^X(f(a))$ i.e., $f(a) \in \not{\emptyset}_B$

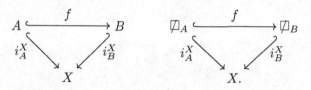

The right commutativity above follows immediately from the left one.   □

Proposition 2. *If $A \in \mathcal{P}(X)$, the following are equivalent:*

(i) $\texttt{empty}(A)$.
(ii) $A \subseteq \not\!\emptyset_A$.
(iii) $A =_{\mathcal{P}(X)} \not\!\emptyset_A$.

Proof. (i) $\Rightarrow$ (ii): Let $f : A \subseteq \not\!\emptyset_X$ i.e., $i_A^X(a) =_X f(a) \neq_X f(a)$. The identity
    proves $A \subseteq \not\!\emptyset_A$: if $a \in A$, then $i_A^X(a) =_X f(a) \neq_X f(a) =_X i_A^X(a)$.
(ii) $\Rightarrow$ (iii): It follows immediately from Proposition 1(i).
(iii) $\Rightarrow$ (i): By Proposition 1(ii) we have that $A \subseteq \not\!\emptyset_A \subseteq \not\!\emptyset_X$.

$\square$

As $\texttt{empty}(\not\!\emptyset_A)$, By Proposition 2 we get $\not\!\emptyset_A =_{\mathcal{P}(X)} \not\!\emptyset_{\not\!\emptyset_A}$.

3   Complemented Subsets and Partial Functions

An inequality induces a positive notion of disjoint subsets $(A, i_A^X), (B, i_B^X)$ of X.

Definition 4. $(A, i_A^X), (B, i_B^X)$ *are $\neq_X$-disjoint, in symbols $A]]_x B$, or $A][B$, if*

$$\forall_{a \in A} \forall_{b \in B} (i_A^X(a) \neq_X i_B^X(b)),$$

A complemented subset of X is a pair $\boldsymbol{A} := (A^1, A^0)$, where $(A^1, i_{A^1}^X), (A^0, i_{A^0}^X) \in \mathcal{P}(X)$ and $A^1][A^0$. Its characteristic function $\chi_A : A^1 \cup A^0 \to \boldsymbol{2}$ is given by

$$\chi_A(x) := \begin{cases} 1, & x \in A^1 \\ 0, & x \in A^0. \end{cases}$$

Let $\mathcal{P}^{][}(X)$ be the proper class of complemented subsets of X, $\boldsymbol{A} \subseteq \boldsymbol{B} :\Leftrightarrow A^1 \subseteq B^1$ & $B^0 \subseteq A^0$ and $\boldsymbol{A} =_{\mathcal{P}^{][}(X)} \boldsymbol{B} :\Leftrightarrow \boldsymbol{A} \subseteq \boldsymbol{B}$ & $\boldsymbol{B} \subseteq \boldsymbol{A}$. We call $\boldsymbol{A}$ total, if $Dom(\boldsymbol{A}) := A^1 \cup A^0 =_{\mathcal{P}(X)} X$, and inhabited (coinhabited), if $A^1 (A^0)$ is inhabited.

Proposition 3. *Let $\boldsymbol{A}, \boldsymbol{B} \in \mathcal{P}^{][}(X)$ and $A \in \mathcal{P}(X)$.*

(i) $(A, A^{\neq_X}), (A^{\neq_X}, A) \in \mathcal{P}^{][}(X)$, *and $A^1 \cap A^0 \subseteq \not\!\emptyset_X$.*
(ii) $\not\!\emptyset_X][A$, *and hence $(\not\!\emptyset_X, A), (A, \not\!\emptyset_X) \in \mathcal{P}^{][}(X)$.*

Definition 5. *A partial function from X to Y is a triplet (A, i_A^X, f_A^Y), where $(A, i_A^X) \subseteq X$, and $f_A^Y \in \mathbb{F}(A, Y)$. Usually, we write f_A^Y instead of (A, i_A^X, f_A^Y). We call f_A^Y total, if $A =_{\mathcal{P}(X)} X$. Let $(A, i_A^X, f_A^Y) \leq (B, i_B^X, f_B^Y)$, or $f_A^Y \leq f_B^Y$, if there is $e_{AB} : A \hookrightarrow B$ such that the following triangles commute*

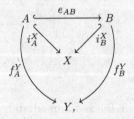

and we write $e_{AB} \colon f_A^Y \leq f_B^Y$. The partial function space $\mathfrak{F}(X,Y)$ is a proper class, equipped with the equality $f_A^Y =_{\mathfrak{F}(X,Y)} f_B^Y :\Leftrightarrow f_A^Y \leq f_B^Y$ & $f_B^Y \leq f_A^Y$. Let $\mathfrak{F}^{\mathrm{se}}(X,\mathbf{2})$ be the proper class of strongly extensional elements of $\mathfrak{F}(X,\mathbf{2})$.

If $A \in \mathcal{P}^{\mathrm{ll}}(X)$, then $(A^1 \cup A^0, i_{A^1 \cup A^0}^X, \chi_A) \in \mathfrak{F}(X,\mathbf{2})$. If $f,g \in \mathfrak{F}(X,\mathbf{2})$, let $\sim f := 1 - f$, and $f \vee g := \max\{f,g\}$, $f \cdot g := f \wedge g := \min\{f,g\}$ on $\mathrm{dom}(f) \cap \mathrm{dom}(g)$.

Proposition 4. *If $A \in \mathcal{P}^{\mathrm{ll}}(X)$, then χ_A is strongly extensional.*

Proof. Let $z,w \in A^1 \cup A^0$ with $\chi_A(z) \neq_2 \chi_A(w)$. Let $\chi_A(z) := 1$ and $\chi_A(w) := 0$. In this case $z \in A^1$, $w \in A^0$. Since $A^1][A^0$, we get $i_{A^1}^X(z) \neq_X i_{A^0}^X(w) \Leftrightarrow: z \neq_{A^1 \cup A^0} w$. If $\chi_A(z) := 0$ and $\chi_A(w) := 1$, we work similarly. $\square$

4   The First Algebra of Complemented Subsets

Definition 6. *If $A, B \in \mathcal{P}^{\mathrm{ll}}(X)$, let $A \cup B := (A^1 \cup B^1, A^0 \cap B^0)$, $A \cap B := (A^1 \cap B^1, A^0 \cup B^0)$, $-A := (A^0, A^1)$, and $A - B := A \cap (-B)$. More generally, if $\big(\lambda(i)\big)_{i \in I}$ is a family of complemented subsets of X indexed by the set[3] I i.e., $\lambda(i) := \big(\lambda^1(i), \lambda^0(i)\big) \in \mathcal{P}^{\mathrm{ll}}(X)$, for every $i \in I$, let*

$$\bigcup_{i \in I} \lambda(i) := \left(\bigcup_{i \in I} \lambda^1(i), \bigcap_{i \in I} \lambda^0(i) \right) \in \mathcal{P}^{\mathrm{ll}}(X),$$

$$\bigcap_{i \in I} \lambda(i) := \left(\bigcap_{i \in I} \lambda^1(i), \bigcup_{i \in I} \lambda^0(i) \right) \in \mathcal{P}^{\mathrm{ll}}(X),$$

Within (INT), if A is total, then $(A \cup -A) \cap B =_{\mathcal{P}^{\mathrm{ll}}(X)} B$. Clearly, $A \subseteq B \Leftrightarrow A \cap B = A$. Next diagram depicts $A \cap B$:

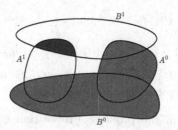

Proposition 5. *The first algebra $\mathfrak{B}_1(X) := \big(\mathcal{P}^{\mathrm{ll}}(X), \cap, \cup, -\big)$ is a distributive lattice such that $-(-A) = A$, for every $A \in \mathcal{P}^{\mathrm{ll}}(X)$. If I is a set and $\big(\lambda(i)\big)_{i \in I}$ is an I-family of complemented subsets of X, the following hold:*

(i) $-\bigcup_{i \in I} \lambda(i) =_{\mathcal{P}^{\mathrm{ll}}(X)} \bigcap_{i \in I} \big(-\lambda(i)\big)$.

---

[3] For the exact definition of this concept within BST, see [20], Sect. 4.9.

(ii) $(A \cup -A) \cap \left(A \cup \bigcap_{i \in I} \lambda(i) \right) =_{\mathcal{P}\mathrm{ll}(X)} (A \cup -A) \cap \left[\bigcap_{i \in I} (A \cup \lambda(i)) \right].$

The dual to condition (i) follows immediately. Condition (ii) is the constructive counterpart to the following distributivity property (D_I)[4]:

$$(D_I) \qquad\qquad A \cup \bigcap_{i \in I} \lambda(i) =_{\mathcal{P}\mathrm{ll}(X)} \bigcap_{i \in I} (A \cup \lambda(i)).$$

Next we show that $(D_\mathbb{N})$ cannot be accepted constructively, avoiding $\emptyset_\mathbb{R}$ (see [2], p. 67) and employing an $\mathbb{N}$-family of inhabited and coinhabited complemented subsets. According to LPO, a "taboo" of constructive mathematics, every boolean-valued sequence is constant 0, or it takes the value 1 on some $n \in \mathbb{N}$.

Proposition 6. (i) *The distributivity property $(D_\mathbb{N})$ implies LPO.*
(ii) (INT) *If $A \in \mathcal{P}\mathrm{ll}(X)$ is total, then (D_I) holds for A.*

Proof. (i) If $\alpha : \mathbb{N} \to 2$, let the $\mathbb{N}$-family of complemented subsets of $\mathbb{R}$

$$\lambda(n) := \begin{cases} (\{n\}^{\neq_\mathbb{R}}, \{n\}), & \alpha_n = 0 \\ (\{n\}, \{n\}^{\neq_\mathbb{R}}), & \alpha_n = 1. \end{cases}$$

If $A := \bigcup_{n \in \mathbb{N}} -\lambda(n) := \left(\bigcup_{n \in \mathbb{N}} \lambda^0(n), \bigcap_{n \in \mathbb{N}} \lambda^1(n) \right)$, then

$$A \cup \bigcap_{n \in \mathbb{N}} \lambda(n) = \left(\left(\bigcup_{n \in \mathbb{N}} \lambda^0(n) \right) \cup \left(\bigcap_{n \in \mathbb{N}} \lambda^1(n) \right), \left(\bigcap_{n \in \mathbb{N}} \lambda^1(n) \right) \cap \left(\bigcup_{n \in \mathbb{N}} \lambda^0(n) \right) \right),$$

$$\bigcap_{n \in \mathbb{N}} (A \cup \lambda(n)) = \left(\bigcap_{n \in \mathbb{N}} \left(\bigcup_{n \in \mathbb{N}} \lambda^0(n) \cup \lambda^1(n) \right), \bigcup_{n \in \mathbb{N}} \left(\bigcap_{n \in \mathbb{N}} \lambda^1(n) \cap \lambda^0(n) \right) \right).$$

As $\bigcup_{n \in \mathbb{N}} \lambda^0(n) \cup \lambda^1(n) \supseteq \{n\}^{\neq_\mathbb{R}}$, we get $\bigcap_{n \in \mathbb{N}} \left(\bigcup_{n \in \mathbb{N}} \lambda^0(n) \cup \lambda^1(n) \right) \supseteq \mathbb{N}^{\neq_\mathbb{R}}$. By

$(D_\mathbb{N})$ $\frac{1}{2} \in \left(\bigcup_{n \in \mathbb{N}} \lambda^0(n) \right) \cup \left(\bigcap_{n \in \mathbb{N}} \lambda^1(n) \right)$. If $\frac{1}{2} \in \bigcup_{n \in \mathbb{N}} \lambda^0(n)$, then $\frac{1}{2} \in \lambda^0(n)$ and $\alpha_n = 1$, for some n. If $\frac{1}{2} \in \bigcap_{n \in \mathbb{N}} \lambda^1(n)$, then $\alpha_n = 0$, for every $n \in \mathbb{N}$. (ii) It follows immediately by Proposition 3(iii) and Proposition 5(ii). $\qquad\square$

The final argument in the proof of Proposition 6(i) also shows that the hypothesis of the totality of A employed in that proof implies LPO.

---

[4] The dual to condition (ii), which is equivalent to it, is the equality

$$(A \cap -A) \cup \left(A \cap \bigcup_{i \in I} \lambda(i) \right) =_{\mathcal{P}\mathrm{ll}(X)} (A \cap -A) \cup \left[\bigcup_{i \in I} (A \cap \lambda(i)) \right],$$

and it is the constructive counterpart to $A \cap \bigcup_{i \in I} \lambda(i) =_{\mathcal{P}\mathrm{ll}(X)} \bigcup_{i \in I} (A \cap \lambda(i))$.

Proposition 7 (INT). *Let $A \in \mathcal{P}^{]l}(X)$.*

(i) *If A is coinhabited, then $A \subseteq (X, \not\!\varnothing_X)$.*
(ii) *If A is inhabited, then $(\not\!\varnothing_X, X) \subseteq A$.*
(iii) *If A is inhabited and coinhabited, then $(\not\!\varnothing_X, X) \subseteq A \subseteq (X, \not\!\varnothing_X)$.*

Within nBST $\mathbf{0}_X := (\varnothing, X)$ and $\mathbf{1}_X := (X, \varnothing)$ are the bottom and top elements of $\mathfrak{B}_1(X)$, respectively[5]. However, even within nBST, $\mathfrak{B}_1(X)$ is neither a Boolean algebra, as $A \cap (-A) := (A^1 \cap A^0, A^1 \cup A^0) = (\varnothing, \mathrm{Dom}(A))$, nor a Heyting algebra (if $-A = A \Rightarrow \mathbf{0}_X$, the adjunction property for any definition of the exponential $B \Rightarrow A$ fails). Next we translate constructively the classical bijection between $\mathcal{P}(X)$ and 2^X. As the only operation involved is that of complementation, Proposition 8 pertains to both algebras of complemented subsets.

Proposition 8. *Let consider the proper class-assignment routines*

$$\chi \colon \mathcal{P}^{]l}(X) \rightsquigarrow \mathfrak{F}^{se}(X, \mathbf{2}) \quad \& \quad \delta \colon \mathfrak{F}^{se}(X, \mathbf{2}) \rightsquigarrow \mathcal{P}^{]l}(X),$$

$$A \mapsto \chi(A) =: \chi_A := \left(A^1 \cup A^0, i^X_{A^1 \cup A^0}, \chi^2_{A^1 \cup A^0} \right),$$

$$f_A := (A, i^X_A, f^2_A) \mapsto \delta(f_A) := \left(\delta^1(f^2_A), \delta^0(f^2_A) \right),$$

$$\delta^1(f^2_A) := \{ a \in A \mid f^2_A(a) =_2 1 \} =: [f^2_A =_2 1],$$

$$\delta^0(f^2_A) := \{ a \in A \mid f^2_A(a) =_2 0 \} =: [f^2_A =_2 0],$$

for every $A := (A^1, i^X_{A^1}, A^0, i^X_{A^0}) \in \mathcal{P}^{]l}(X)$ and $f_A := (A, i^X_A, f^2_A) \in \mathfrak{F}^{se}(X, \mathbf{2})$.

(i) *χ is a well-defined, proper class-function.*
(ii) *δ is a well-defined, proper class-function.*
(iii) *χ and δ are inverse to each other.*
(iv) *$\delta(\sim f) =_{\mathcal{P}^{]l}(X)} -\delta(f)$ and $\chi_{-A} =_{\mathfrak{F}(X, \mathbf{2})} \sim \chi_A$, for every $f \in \mathfrak{F}^{se}(X, \mathbf{2})$ and $A \in \mathcal{P}^{]l}(X)$, respectively.*

Proof. We show only (i) and (ii). Let $A, B \in \mathcal{P}^{]l}(X)$. By Proposition 4 χ is a well-defined routine. If $(e_1, j_1) \colon A^1 =_{\mathcal{P}(X)} B^1$ and $(e_0, j_0) \colon A^0 =_{\mathcal{P}(X)} B^0$

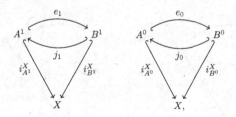

it is straightforward to show that $(e, j) \colon \chi_A =_{\mathfrak{F}^{se}(X, \mathbf{2})} \chi_B$

---

[5] These definitions are also used in [8], in order to show that the second algebra of complemented subsets is a Boolean semiring with unit.

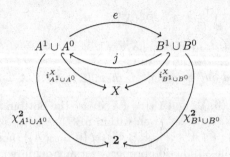

where $e\colon A^1 \cup A^0 \to B^1 \cup B^0$ and $j\colon B^1 \cup B^0 \to A^1 \cup A^0$ are defined by

$$e(z) := \begin{cases} e_1(z)\,, & z \in A^1 \\ e_0(z)\,, & z \in A^0 \end{cases}, \quad j(w) := \begin{cases} j_1(w)\,, & w \in B^1 \\ j_0(w)\,, & w \in B^0. \end{cases}$$

(ii) First we show that $\delta(f_A) \in \mathcal{P}^{]\![}(X)$. Let $a \in \delta^1(f_A^2)$ and $b \in \delta^0(f_A^2)$. As $f_A^2(a) =_2 1 \neq_2 0 =_2 f_A^2(b)$, by the strong extensionality of f_A^2, and according to the definition of the canonical inequality of the subset (A, i_A^X), we get $a \neq_A b :\Leftrightarrow i_A^X(a) \neq_X i_A^X(b)$. If $\left(A, i_A^X, f_A^2\right) =_{\mathfrak{F}^{\mathrm{se}}(X,\mathbf{2})} \left(B, i_B^X, f_B^2\right)$, then the commutativities $(\#_1)$ and $(\#_2)$ of the following outer diagrams

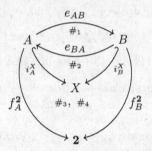

imply that $(e_{AB})_{|\delta^1(f_A^2)}\colon \delta^1(f_A^2) \to \delta^1(f_B^2)$ and $(e_{BA})_{|\delta^1(f_B^2)}\colon \delta^0(f_A^2) \to \delta^0(f_B^2)$ are well-defined, and the commutativities $(\#_3),(\#_4)$ of the above inner diagrams (A, B, X) imply the commutativity of the following diagrams

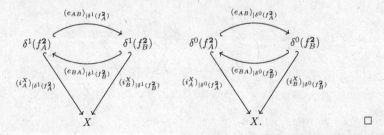

The use of $\mathfrak{F}^{\mathrm{se}}(X, \mathbf{2})$, and not of $\mathfrak{F}(X, \mathbf{2})$, is crucial to the well-definability of δ. In general the operations $\cup, \cap$ of $\mathfrak{B}_1(X)$ are not preserved by χ and δ.

Proposition 9. Let $A, B \in \mathcal{P}^{]\![}(X)$ and $f, g \in \mathfrak{F}^{\mathrm{se}}(X, \mathbf{2})$.

(i) *If $A\ (f)$ is total, then $\chi_A\ (\delta(f))$ is total.*

(ii) *If A, B are total, then $A \cup B, A \cap B$ are total, and $\chi_{A \cup B} =_{\mathfrak{F}(X,2)} \chi_A \vee \chi_B$, $\chi_{A \cap B} =_{\mathfrak{F}(X,2)} \chi_A \wedge \chi_B$.*

(iii) *If f_A, f_B are total, then $f_A \vee f_B, f_A \wedge f_B$ are total, and $\delta(f_A) \cup \delta(f_B) = \delta(f_A \vee f_B)$, $\delta(f_A) \cap \delta(f_B) = \delta(f_A \wedge f_B)$.*

5   The Second Algebra of Complemented Subsets

Definition 7. *If $A, B \in \mathcal{P}^{\parallel}(X)$, let*

$$A \vee B := ([A^1 \cap B^1] \cup [A^1 \cap B^0] \cup [A^0 \cap B^1],\ A^0 \cap B^0),$$

$$A \wedge B := (A^1 \cap B^1,\ [A^1 \cap B^0] \cup [A^0 \cap B^1] \cup [A^0 \cap B^0]),$$

and $A \ominus B := A \wedge (-B)$. More generally, if $(\lambda(i))_{i \in I}$ is a family of complemented subsets of X indexed by the set I, let

$$\bigvee_{i \in I} \lambda(i) := \left(\left[\bigcap_{i \in I} (\lambda^1(i) \cup \lambda^0(i)) \right] \cap \left[\bigcup_{i \in I} \lambda^1(i) \right],\ \bigcap_{i \in I} \lambda^0(i) \right),$$

$$\bigwedge_{i \in I} \lambda(i) := \left(\bigcap_{i \in I} \lambda^1(i),\ \left[\bigcap_{i \in I} (\lambda^1(i) \cup \lambda^0(i)) \right] \cap \left[\bigcup_{i \in I} \lambda^0(i) \right] \right).$$

In contrast to $\mathfrak{B}_1(X)$, $A \wedge B \nsubseteq A$. Next diagram depicts $A \wedge B$:

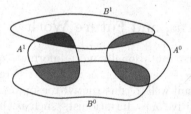

Proposition 10. *The second algebra $\mathfrak{B}_2(X) := (\mathcal{P}^{\parallel}(X), \wedge, \vee, -)$ satisfies all properties of $\mathfrak{B}_1(X)$ except the absorption equalities[6].*

Using a similar argument, the corresponding distributivity $(D_{\mathbb{N}})$ for $\mathfrak{B}_2(X)$ implies LPO. Although $\mathfrak{B}_2(X)$ is not a lattice, its crucial advantage over $\mathfrak{B}_1(X)$, and the main reason for its introduction by Bishop and Cheng, is that $\vee$ and $\wedge$ are preserved by the proper class-functions χ and δ.

Proposition 11. *Let $A, B \in \mathcal{P}^{\parallel}(X)$ and $f, g \in \mathfrak{F}^{\mathrm{se}}(X, 2)$.*

---

[6] In [4], p. 74, Bishop and Bridges mention that $\mathfrak{B}_2(X)$ satisfies "all the usual finite algebraic laws that do not involve the operation of set complementation". In [8], p. 695, Coquand and Palmgren rightly notice that $\mathfrak{B}_2(X)$ does not satisfy the absorption equalities $(A \wedge B) \vee A = A$ and $(A \vee B) \wedge A = A$.

(i) $\chi_{A \vee B} =_{\mathfrak{F}(X,2)} \chi_A \vee \chi_B$ *and* $\chi_{A \wedge B} =_{\mathfrak{F}(X,2)} \chi_A \wedge \chi_B$.

(ii) $\delta(f_A) \vee \delta(f_B) = \delta(f_A \vee f_B)$ *and* $\delta(f_A) \wedge \delta(f_B) = \delta(f_A \wedge f_B)$.

Proof. We show only $\chi_{A \wedge B} =_{\mathfrak{F}(X,2)} \chi_A \wedge \chi_B$. By definition

$$\chi_A \wedge \chi_B := \big(\mathrm{Dom}(A) \cap \mathrm{Dom}(B), i^X_{\mathrm{Dom}(A) \cap \mathrm{Dom}(B)}, (\chi_A \wedge \chi_B)^2_{\mathrm{Dom}(A) \cap \mathrm{Dom}(B)}\big),$$

$$(\chi_A \wedge \chi_B)^2_{\mathrm{Dom}(A) \cap \mathrm{Dom}(B)}(u, w) := \chi_A(u) \wedge \chi_B(w),$$

for every $(u, w) \in \mathrm{Dom}(A) \cap \mathrm{Dom}(B)$. The partial function $\chi_{A \wedge B}$ is the triplet

$$\chi_{A \wedge B} := \big(\mathrm{Dom}(A \wedge B), i^X_{\mathrm{Dom}(A \wedge B)}, (\chi_{A \wedge B})^2_{\mathrm{Dom}(A \wedge B)}\big).$$

As $\mathrm{Dom}(A \wedge B) =_{\mathcal{P}(X)} \mathrm{Dom}(A) \cap \mathrm{Dom}(B)$, if $(f, g) : \mathrm{Dom}(A \wedge B) =_{\mathcal{P}(X)} \mathrm{Dom}(A) \cap \mathrm{Dom}(B)$, the following outer diagram also commutes

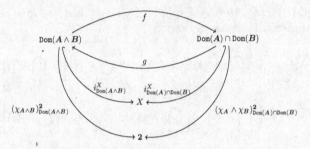

and hence the two partial functions are equal in $\mathfrak{F}(X, 2)$.   □

6 Bishop Algebras, and Future Work

Mathematics becomes computationally more informative, if, instead of classical logic, intuitionistic logic is used. Pioneers, such as Brouwer, realised early on that negation does not suit well to constructive reasoning and replaced negatively defined concepts by positive ones. Intuitionists, such as Griss [10], even suggested to avoid negation completely in mathematics. Bishop, motivated by Brouwer's inequalities, defined, the so-called here, f-inequalities in a fully positive manner. Moreover, by extending the idea of positive separation from points to subsets, Bishop introduced the notion of complemented subset.

As we saw, the complement $-A$ of A behaves a lot like the classical complement $X \setminus A$, where $A \subseteq X$. Moreover, a characteristic function χ_A is defined through A. However, χ_A is partial. The correspondence between complemented subsets and strongly extensional, boolean-valued, partial functions, described here in Propositions 8 and 11, is behind the successful reconstruction of the Daniell approach to measure theory within Bishop-style constructive mathematics BISH. Moreover, the fruitfulness of Bishop-Cheng measure theory turned complemented subsets and partial functions into "first-class citizens" in BISH.

Here, after introducing a positive definition of the empty subset, we presented the basic properties of the two algebras of complemented subsets. From the point of view of abstract lattice theory, Bishop's first algebra of complemented subsets is an instance of a widely used construction of *Kleene lattices*, commonly ascribed to Kalman [11]. Using intuitionistic logic, this is to say that $\mathfrak{B}_1(X)$ is a distributive lattice with contravariant involution – such that, $A \cap -A \subseteq B \cup -B$, for every inhabited (or coinhabited) $A, B \in \mathcal{P}^{][}(X)$.

As opposed to $\mathfrak{B}_1(X)$, Bishop's second algebra $\mathfrak{B}_2(X)$ is not a lattice by lack of the absorption identities, of which any abstract generalisation must take account. Pinning down common properties of $\mathfrak{B}_1(X)$ and $\mathfrak{B}_2(X)$, we thus define a *Bishop algebra* $\mathfrak{A}$, or better an *I-Bishop algebra* in order to avoid impredicativity, to be an algebra $\mathfrak{A} = (A, \wedge, \vee, -)$ where both reducts $(A, \wedge)$ and $(A, \vee)$ are *I*-complete semilattices such that $\wedge$ distributes over $\vee$, along with an involutive homomorphism – of semilattices such that the following *I*-distributive law holds

$$(x \vee -x) \wedge \left(x \vee \bigwedge_{i \in I} x_i\right) =_A (x \vee -x) \wedge \left[\bigwedge_{i \in I}(x \vee x_i)\right].$$

Note that – is subject to both De Morgan laws, which moreover implies that $\vee$ in turn distributes over $\wedge$. Hence, every Bishop algebra is a *distributive De Morgan bisemilattice* [12], on top of which we further require the above *I*-distributivity. Several questions naturally arise, among which those of a suitable representation theorem for Bishop algebras, as well as of categorical aspects[7]. It might be interesting to relate Bishop algebras to *overlap algebras* [6,7]. While the latter provide a constructive view of complete Boolean algebras, and thus of powerset lattices, the former should serve towards an analogous and point-free treatment of algebras of complemented subsets.

References

1. Beeson, M.J.: Foundations of Constructive Mathematics, Ergebnisse der Mathematik und ihrer Grenzgebiete. Springer, Heidelberg (1985)
2. Bishop, E.: Foundations of Constructive Analysis. McGraw-Hill, New York (1967)
3. Bishop, E., Cheng, H.: Constructive measure theory. Mem. Amer. Math. Soc. **116** (1972)
4. Bishop, E., Bridges, D.S.: Constructive Analysis. Grundlehren der Mathematischen Wissenschaften. Springer, Heidelberg (1985)
5. Bridges, D.S., Richman, F.: Varieties of Constructive Mathematics. Cambridge University Press, Cambridge (1987)
6. Ciraulo, F., Sambin, G.: The overlap algebra of regular opens. J. Pure Appl. Algebra **214**(11), 1988–1995 (2010)
7. Ciraulo, F., Contente, M.: Overlap algebras: a constructive look at complete Boolean algebras. Log. Methods Comput. Sci. **16**(1), 13:1–13:15 (2020)
8. Coquand, T., Palmgren, E.: Metric Boolean algebras and constructive measure theory. Arch. Math. Logic **41**, 687–704 (2002)
9. Coquand, T.: Universe of Bishop sets. Manuscript (2017)

---

[7] The relation of complemented subsets to Chu categories was noticed by Shulman [25], and it is also studied in [23].

10. Griss, G.F.: Negationless intuitionistic mathematics I. Indag. Math. **8**, 675–681 (1946)
11. Kalman, J.A.: Lattices with involution. Trans. Amer. Math. Soc. **87**, 485–491 (1958)
12. Ledda, A.: Stone-type representations and dualities for varieties of bisemilattices. Stud. Logica. **106**(2), 417–448 (2017). https://doi.org/10.1007/s11225-017-9745-9
13. Mines, R., Richman, F., Ruitenburg, W.: A Course in Constructive Algebra. Springer, New York (1988). https://doi.org/10.1007/978-1-4419-8640-5
14. Martin-Löf, P.: An intuitionistic theory of types: predicative part. In: Rose, H.E., Shepherdson, J.C. (eds.) Logic Colloquium 1973, Proceedings of the Logic Colloquium. Studies in Logic and the Foundations of Mathematics, vol. 80, pp. 73–118. North-Holland (1975)
15. Martin-Löf, P.: An intuitionistic theory of types. In: Sambin, G., Smith, J.M. (eds.) Twenty-Five Years of Constructive Type Theory (Venice, 1995). Oxford Logic Guides, vo. 36, pp. 127–172. Oxford University Press (1998)
16. Palmgren, E.: Constructivist and structuralist foundations: Bishop's and Lawvere's theories of sets. Ann. Pure Appl. Log. **163**, 1384–1399 (2012)
17. Palmgren, E., Wilander, O.: Constructing categories and setoids of setoids in type theory. Log. Methods Comput. Sci. **10**(3), 25 (2014)
18. Palmgren, E.: Constructions of categories of setoids from proof-irrelevant families. Arch. Math. Log. **56**, 51–66 (2017)
19. Petrakis, I.: Constructive topology of Bishop spaces. Ph.D. Thesis, LMU Munich (2015)
20. Petrakis, I.: Families of sets in Bishop set theory. Habilitationsschrift, LMU, Munich (2020). https://www.mathematik.uni-muenchen.de/~petrakis/
21. Petrakis, I.: Embeddings of Bishop spaces. J. Log. Comput. exaa015 (2020). https://doi.org/10.1093/logcom/exaa015
22. Petrakis, I.: Direct spectra of Bishop spaces and their limits. Log. Methods Comput. Sci. **17**(2), 4:1–4:50 (2021)
23. Petrakis, I.: Chu representations of categories related to constructive mathematics. arXiv:2106.01878v1 (2021)
24. Petrakis, I.: Bases of pseudocompact Bishop spaces. In: Bridges, D.S., et al. (eds.) Handbook of Constructive Mathematics. Cambridge University Press (2022)
25. Shulman, M.: Affine logic for constructive mathematics. arXiv:1805.07518v2 (2021)

On the Weihrauch Degree of the Additive Ramsey Theorem over the Rationals

Pierre Pradic[(⊠)] and Giovanni Soldà

Swansea University, Swansea, UK
p.r.a.pradic@swansea.ac.uk

Abstract. We characterize the strength, in terms of Weihrauch degrees, of certain problems related to Ramsey-like theorems concerning colourings of the rationals. The theorems we are chiefly interested in assert the existence of almost-homogeneous sets for colourings of pairs of rationals satisfying properties determined by some additional algebraic structure on the set of colours.

In the context of reverse mathematics, most of the principles we study are equivalent to Σ_2^0-induction over RCA_0. The associated problems in the Weihrauch lattice are related to $\mathsf{TC}_{\mathbb{N}}^*$, $(\mathsf{LPO}')^*$ or their product, depending on their precise formalizations.

Keywords: Weihrauch reducibility · Reverse mathematics · Additive ramsey · Σ_2^0-induction

1 Introduction

The infinite Ramsey theorem is a central object of study in the field of computability theory. It says that for any colouring c of n-uples of a given arity of an infinite set X, there exists a infinite subset $H \subseteq X$ such that the set of n-tuples $[H]^n$ of elements of H is homogeneous. This statement is non-constructive: even if the colouring c is given by a computable function, it is not the case that we can find a computable homogeneous subset of X. Various attempts have been made to quantify how non-computable this problem and some of its natural restrictions are. This is in turn linked to the axiomatic strength of the corresponding theorems, as investigated in *reverse mathematics* [12] where Ramsey's theorem is a privileged object of study [7].

This paper is devoted to a variant of Ramsey's theorem with the following restrictions: we colour pairs of rational numbers and we require some additional structure on the colouring, namely that it is *additive*. A similar statement first appeared in [11, Theorem 1.3] to give a self-contained proof of decidablity of the Monadic Second-order logic of $(\mathbb{Q}, <)$. We will also analyse a simpler statement we call the *shuffle principle*, a related tool appearing in more modern decidability proofs [4, Lemma 16]. The shuffle principle states that every $\mathbb{Q}$-indexed word

---

The second author was supported by an LMS Early Career Fellowship.

© The Author(s), under exclusive license to Springer Nature Switzerland AG 2022
U. Berger et al. (Eds.): CiE 2022, LNCS 13359, pp. 259–271, 2022.
https://doi.org/10.1007/978-3-031-08740-0_22

(with letters in a finite alphabet) contains a convex subword in which every letter appears densely or not at all. Much like the additive restriction of the Ramsey theorem for pairs over $\mathbb{N}$, studied from the point of view of reverse mathematics in [8], we obtain a neat correspondence with Σ_2^0-induction (Σ_2^0-IND).

Theorem 1. *In the weak second-order arithmetic* RCA$_0$, Σ_2^0-IND *is equivalent to both the shuffle principle and the additive Ramsey theorem for* $\mathbb{Q}$.

We take this analysis one step further in the framework of Weihrauch reducibility that allows to measure the uniform strength of general multi-valued functions (also called *problems*) over Baire space. Let Shuffle and ART$_\mathbb{Q}$ be the most obvious problems corresponding to the shuffle principle and additive Ramsey theorem over $\mathbb{Q}$ respectively. We relate them, as well as various weakenings cShuffle, cART$_\mathbb{Q}$, iShuffle and iART$_\mathbb{Q}$ that only output sets of colours or intervals, to the standard (incomparable) problems TC$_\mathbb{N}$ and LPO$'$.

Theorem 2. *We have the following equivalences*

- Shuffle $\equiv_W$ ART$_\mathbb{Q}$ $\equiv_W$ TC$_\mathbb{N}^*$ $\times$ (LPO$'$)*
- cShuffle $\equiv_W$ cART$_\mathbb{Q}$ $\equiv_W$ (LPO$'$)*
- iShuffle $\equiv_W$ iART$_\mathbb{Q}$ $\equiv_W$ TC$_\mathbb{N}^*$

2   Background

In this section, we will introduce the necessary background for the rest of the paper, and fix most of the notation that we will use, except for formal definitions related to weak subsystems of second-order arithmetic, in particular RCA$_0$ (which consists of Σ_1^0-induction and recursive comprehension) and RCA$_0$ + Σ_2^0-IND. A standard reference for that material and, more generally, systems of interest in reverse mathematics, is [12].

2.1   Generic Notations

We identify $k \in \mathbb{N}$ with the finite set $\{0, \ldots, k-1\}$. For every linear order $(X, <_X)$, we write $[X]^2$ for the set of pairs (x, y) with $x <_X y$. In this paper, by an *interval* I we always mean a pair $(u, v) \in [\mathbb{Q}]^2$, regarded as the set $]u, v[$ of rationals; we never use interval with irrational extrema.

2.2   Additive and Ordered Colourings

For the following definition, fix a linear order $(X, <_X)$. For every poset $(P, \prec_P)$, we call a colouring $c : [X]^2 \to P$ *ordered* if we have $c(x, y) \preceq_P c(x', y')$ when $x' \leq_X x <_X y \leq_X y'$. A colouring $c : [X]^2 \to S$ is called *additive* with respect to a semigroup structure $(S, \cdot)$ if we have $c(x, z) = c(x, y) \cdot c(y, z)$ whenever $x <_X y <_X z$.

A subset $A \subseteq X$ is *dense in* X if for every $x, y \in A$ with $x <_X y$ there is $z \in A$ such that $x <_X z <_X y$. Given a colouring $c : [X]^n \to k$ and some interval $Y \subseteq X$, we say that Y is *c-densely homogeneous* if there exists a finite partition of Y into dense subsets D_i such that each $[D_i]^n$ is monochromatic (that is, $|c([D_i]^n)| \leq 1$). We will call those *c-shuffles* if c happens to be a colouring of $\mathbb{Q}$ (i.e. $X = \mathbb{Q}$ and $n = 1$). Finally, given a colouring $c : \mathbb{Q} \to k$, and given an interval $I \subseteq \mathbb{Q}$, we say that a colour $i < k$ *occurs densely in* I if the set of $x \in \mathbb{Q}$ such that $c(x) = i$ is dense in I.

Definition 1. *The following are statements of second-order arithmetic:*

- $\mathrm{ORT}_{\mathbb{Q}}$: *for every finite poset* $(P, \prec_P)$ *and ordered colouring* $c : [\mathbb{Q}]^2 \to P$, *there exists a c-homogeneous interval* $]u, v[\subset \mathbb{Q}$.
- Shuffle: *for every* $k \in \mathbb{N}$ *and colouring* $c : \mathbb{Q} \to k$, *there exists an interval* $I =]x, y[$ *such that* I *is a c-shuffle*.
- $\mathrm{ART}_{\mathbb{Q}}$: *for every finite semigroup* $(S, \cdot)$ *and additive colouring* $c : [\mathbb{Q}]^2 \to S$, *there exists an interval* $I =]x, y[$ *such that* I *is c-densely homogeneous*.

As mentioned before, a result similar to $\mathrm{ART}_{\mathbb{Q}}$ was originally proved by Shelah in [11, Theorem 1.3 & Conclusion 1.4] and Shuffle is a central lemma when analysing labellings of $\mathbb{Q}$ (see e.g. [4]). We will establish that $\mathrm{ART}_{\mathbb{Q}}$ and Shuffle are equivalent to Σ_2^0-induction over RCA_0 while $\mathrm{ORT}_{\mathbb{Q}}$ is provable in RCA_0.

We introduce some more terminology that will come in handy later on. Given a colouring $c : [\mathbb{Q}]^n \to k$, a set $C \subseteq k$ and an interval $I =]u, v[$ that is a c-shuffle, we say that I is a *c-shuffle for the colours in* C, or equivalently that I is *c-homogeneous for the colours of* C, if we additionally have $c(I) = C$.

2.3   Preliminaries on Weihrauch Reducibility

We now give a brief introduction to the Weihrauch degrees of problems and the operations on them that we will use in the rest of the paper. We stress that here we are able to offer but a glimpse of this vast area of research, and we refer to [2] for more details on the topic.

We deal with partial multifunctions $f : \subseteq \mathbb{N}^{\mathbb{N}} \rightrightarrows \mathbb{N}^{\mathbb{N}}$, which we call *problems*, for short. We will most often define problems in terms of their *inputs* and of the *outputs* corresponding to those inputs.

We stress that, differently from [2], we do not define problems for arbitrary represented spaces (domains and codomains of the problems we consider admit a straightforward coding as subspaces of $\mathbb{N}^{\mathbb{N}}$).

A partial function $F : \subseteq \mathbb{N}^{\mathbb{N}} \to \mathbb{N}^{\mathbb{N}}$ is called a *realizer for* f, which we denote by $F \vdash f$, if, for every $x \in \mathrm{dom}(f)$, $F(x) \in f(x)$. Given two problems f and g, we say that g is *Weihrauch reducible* to f, and we write $g \leq_{\mathrm{W}} f$, if there are two computable functionals H and K such that $K\langle FH, \mathrm{id}\rangle$ is a realizer for g whenever F is a realizer for f. We define strong Weihrauch reducibility similarly: for every two problems f and g, we say that g *strongly Weihrauch reduces to* f, written $g \leq_{\mathrm{sW}} f$, if there are computable functionals H and K such that $KFH \vdash g$ whenever $F \vdash f$. We say that two problems f and g are (strongly) Weihrauch equivalent if both $f \leq_{\mathrm{W}} g$ and $g \leq_{\mathrm{W}} f$ (respectively $f \leq_{\mathrm{sW}} g$ and $g \leq_{\mathrm{sW}} f$). We write this $\equiv_{\mathrm{W}}$ (respectively $\equiv_{\mathrm{sW}}$).

There are a number of useful structural operations on problems, which respect the quotient to Weihrauch degrees, that we need to introduce. The first one is the *parallel product* $f \times g$, which has the power to solve an instance of f and instance of g at the same time. The *finite parallelization* of a problem f, denoted f^*, has the power to solve an arbitrary number of instances of f, provided that number is given as part of the input. Finally, the *compositional product* of two problems f and g, denoted $f * g$, corresponds basically to the most complicated problem that can be obtained as a composition of f paired with the identity, a recursive function and g paired with identity (that last bit allows us to keep track of the initial input when applying f).

Now let us list some of the most important[1] problems that we are going to use in the rest of the paper.

- $\mathsf{C_N}$: $\subseteq \mathbb{N}^{\mathbb{N}} \rightrightarrows \mathbb{N}$ (*closed choice on* $\mathbb{N}$) is the problem that takes as input an enumeration e of a (strict) subset of $\mathbb{N}$ and such that, for every $n \in \mathbb{N}$, $n \in \mathsf{C_N}(e)$ if and only if $n \notin \mathrm{ran}(e)$ (where $\mathrm{ran}(e)$ is the *range* of e).
- $\mathsf{TC_N}$: $\subseteq \mathbb{N}^{\mathbb{N}} \rightrightarrows \mathbb{N}$ (*totalization of closed choice on* $\mathbb{N}$) is the problem that takes as input an enumeration e of *any* subset of $\mathbb{N}$ (hence now we allow the possibility that $\mathrm{ran}(e) = \mathbb{N}$) and such that, for every $n \in \mathbb{N}$, $n \in \mathsf{TC_N}(e)$ if and only if $n \notin \mathrm{ran}(e)$ or $\mathrm{ran}(e) = \mathbb{N}$.
- LPO: $2^{\mathbb{N}} \rightarrow \{0,1\}$ (*limited principle of omniscience*) takes as input any infinite binary string p and outputs 0 if and only if $p = 0^{\mathbb{N}}$.
- $\mathsf{LPO'}$: $\subseteq 2^{\mathbb{N}} \rightarrow \{0,1\}$: takes as input (a code for) an infinite sequence $\langle p_0, p_1, \dots \rangle$ of binary strings such that the function $p(i) = \lim_{s \to \infty} p_i(s)$ is defined for every $i \in \mathbb{N}$, and outputs $\mathsf{LPO}(p)$.

The definition of $\mathsf{LPO'}$ could have been obtained by composing the one of LPO and the definition of jump as given in [2]: we include it for convenience. Intuitively, $\mathsf{LPO'}$ corresponds to the power of answering a single binary Σ_2^0-question. In particular, $\mathsf{LPO'}$ is easily seen to be (strongly) Weihrauch equivalent to both $\mathsf{IsFinite}$ and $\mathsf{IsCofinite}$, the problems accepting as input an infinite binary string p and outputting 1 if p contains finitely (respectively, cofinitely) many 1s, and 0 otherwise.

We will use this fact throughout the paper.

Another problem of combinatorial nature, introduced in [5], will prove to be very useful for the rest of the paper.

Definition 2. ECT *is the problem whose instances are pairs* $(n, f) \in \mathbb{N} \times \mathbb{N}^{\mathbb{N}}$ *such that* $f \colon \mathbb{N} \to n$ *is a colouring of the natural numbers with* n *colours, and such that, for every instance* (n, f) *and* $b \in \mathbb{N}$, $b \in \mathsf{ECT}(n, f)$ *if and only if*

$$\forall x > b \, \exists y > x \, (f(x) = f(y)).$$

---

[1] Whereas LPO and $\mathsf{C_N}$ have been widely studied, $\mathsf{TC_N}$ is somewhat less known (and does not appear in [2]): we refer to [9] for an account of its properties, and to [1] for a deeper study of some principles close to it.

Namely, ECT is the problems that, upon being given a function f of the integers with finite range, outputs a b such that, after that b, the palette of colours used is constant (hence its name, which stands for *eventually constant palette tail*). We will refer to suitable bs as *bounds* for the function f.

A very important result concerning ECT and that we will use throughout the paper is its equivalence with $\mathsf{TC}_\mathbb{N}^*$.

Lemma 1 ([5, Theorem 9]). $\mathsf{ECT} \equiv_\mathrm{W} \mathsf{TC}_\mathbb{N}^*$

Another interesting result concerning ECT is the following: if we see it as a statement of second-order arithmetic (ECT can be seen as the principle asserting that for every colouring of the integers with finitely many colours there is a bound), then ECT and Σ_2^0-IND are equivalent over RCA_0 (actually, over RCA_0^*).

Lemma 2 ([5, Theorem 7]). *Over* RCA_0, *ECT and* Σ_2^0-IND *are equivalent.*

Hence, thanks to the results above, it is clear why $\mathsf{TC}_\mathbb{N}^*$ appears as a natural candidate to be a "translation" of Σ_2^0-IND in the Weihrauch degrees.

We end this section with two technical results about Weihrauch degrees. The first one asserts that the two main problems that we use as benchmarks in the sequel, namely $(\mathsf{LPO}')^*$ and $\mathsf{TC}_\mathbb{N}^*$, are incomparable in the Weihrauch lattice.

Lemma 3. $(\mathsf{LPO}')^*$ *and* $\mathsf{TC}_\mathbb{N}^*$ *are Weihrauch incomparable. Hence, we have that* $(\mathsf{LPO}')^*, \mathsf{TC}_\mathbb{N}^* <_\mathrm{W} (\mathsf{LPO}')^* \times \mathsf{TC}_\mathbb{N}^*$.

The second result asserts that the sequential composition of $\mathsf{LPO}' \times \mathsf{TC}_\mathbb{N}$ after $\mathsf{C}_\mathbb{N}$ can actually be computed by the parallel product of LPO', $\mathsf{TC}_\mathbb{N}^n$ and $\mathsf{C}_\mathbb{N}$. As customary, for every problem P we write P^n to mean $\underbrace{\mathsf{P} \times \cdots \times \mathsf{P}}_{n \text{ times}}$.

Lemma 4. *For every integers* a *and* b *and every problem* $\mathsf{P} \leq_\mathrm{W} \mathsf{C}_\mathbb{N}$, *it holds that* $((\mathsf{LPO}')^a \times \mathsf{TC}_\mathbb{N}^b) * \mathsf{P} \leq_\mathrm{W} (\mathsf{LPO}')^a \times \mathsf{TC}_\mathbb{N}^b \times \mathsf{P}$.

2.4   Green Theory

Green theory is concerned with analysing the structure of ideals of finite semi-groups, be they one-sided on the left or right or even two-sided. This gives rise to a rich structure to otherwise rather inscrutable algebraic properties of finite semigroups. We will need only a few related results, all of them relying on the definition of the *Green preorders* and of idempotents (recall that an element s of a semigroup is idempotent when $ss = s$).

Definition 3. *For a semigroup* $(S, \cdot)$, *define the* Green preorders *as follows:*

- $s \leq_\mathcal{R} t$ *if and only if* $s = t$ *or* $s \in tS = \{ta : a \in S\}$ *(suffix order)*
- $s \leq_\mathcal{L} t$ *if and only if* $s = t$ *or* $s \in St = \{at : a \in S\}$ *(prefix order)*
- $s \leq_\mathcal{H} t$ *if and only if* $s \leq_\mathcal{R} t$ *and* $s \leq_\mathcal{L} t$
- $s \leq_\mathcal{J} t$ *if and only if* $s \leq_\mathcal{R} t$ *or* $s \leq_\mathcal{L} t$ *or* $s \in StS = \{atb : (a, b) \in S^2\}$

(infix order)

The associated equivalence relations are written $\mathcal{R}$, $\mathcal{L}$, $\mathcal{H}$, $\mathcal{J}$; *their equivalence classes are called respectively* $\mathcal{R}$, $\mathcal{L}$, $\mathcal{H}$, *and* $\mathcal{J}$-*classes.*

We conclude this section reporting, without proof, the two technical lemmas that will be needed in Sect. 4. Although not proved in second-order arithmetic originally, it is clear that their proofs goes through in RCA$_0$: besides straightforward algebraic manipulations, they only rely on the existence, for each finite semigroup $(S, \cdot)$, of an index $n \in \mathbb{N}$ such that s^n is idempotent for any $s \in S$.

Lemma 5 ([10, Proposition A.2.4]). *If* $(S, \cdot)$ *is a finite semigroup,* $H \subseteq S$ *an* $\mathcal{H}$-*class, and some* $a, b \in H$ *satisfy* $a \cdot b \in H$ *then for some* $e \in H$ *we know that* $(H, \cdot, e)$ *is a group.*

Lemma 6 ([10, Corollary A.2.6]). *For any pair of elements* $x, y \in S$ *of a finite semigroup, if we have* $x \leq_{\mathcal{R}} y$ *and* x, y $\mathcal{J}$-*equivalent, then* x *and* y *are also* $\mathcal{R}$-*equivalent.*

3 The Shuffle Principle and Related Problems

3.1 The Shuffle Principle in Reverse Mathematics

We start by giving a proof[2] of the shuffle principle in RCA$_0$ + Σ_2^0-IND, since, in a way, it gives a clearer picture of some properties of shuffles that we use in the rest of the paper.

Lemma 7. RCA$_0$ + Σ_2^0-IND $\vdash$ Shuffle

Proof. Let $c : \mathbb{Q} \to n$ be a colouring of the rationals with n colours. For any natural number k, consider the following Σ_2^0 formula $\varphi(k)$: "there exists a finite set $L \subseteq n$ of cardinality k and there exist $u, v \in \mathbb{Q}$ with $u < v$ such that $c(w) \in L$ for every $w \in \,]u, v[$". Since $\varphi(n)$ is true, it follows from the Σ_2^0 minimization principle that there exists a minimal k such that $\varphi(k)$ holds. Consider $u, v \in \mathbb{Q}$ and the set of colours L corresponding to this minimal k. We now only need to show that $]u, v[$ is a c-shuffle to conclude.

Let $a = c(x)$ for some $x \in \,]u, v[$. We need to prove that a occurs densely in $]u, v[$. Consider arbitrary $x, y \in \,]u, v[$ with $x < y$. We are done if we show that there exists some $w \in \,]x, y[$ with $c(w) = a$. So, suppose that there is no such w. By bounded Σ_1^0-comprehension, there exists a finite set $L' \subset n$ consisting of exactly those $b \in n$ which occur as values of $c|_{]x,y[}$. Clearly, $\varphi(|L'|)$ holds. However, $L' \subseteq L$, and by assumption $a \notin L'$, so $|L'| < k$, contradicting the choice of k as the minimal number such that $\varphi(k)$ holds. $\square$

The proof above shows an important feature of shuffles: given a certain interval $]u, v[$, any of its subintervals having the fewest colours is a shuffle.

Interestingly, the above implication reverses, so we have the following equivalence.

---

[2] From Leszek A. Kołodziejczyk, personal communication.

Theorem 3. *Over* RCA$_0$, Shuffle *is equivalent to* Σ^0_2-IND.

We do not offer a proof of the reversal here; such a proof can easily be done by taking inspiration from the argument we give for Lemma 11. With this equivalence in mind, we now introduce Weihrauch problems corresponding to Shuffle, beginning with the stronger one.

Definition 4. *We regard* Shuffle *as the problem with instances* $(k, c) \in \mathbb{N} \times \mathbb{N}^{\mathbb{N}}$ *such that* $c : \mathbb{Q} \rightarrow k$ *is a colouring of the rationals with* k *colours, and such that, for every instance* (k, c), *for every pair* $(u, v) \in [\mathbb{Q}]^2$ *and for every* $C \subseteq k$, $(u, v, C) \in$ Shuffle(k, c) *if and only if* $]u, v[$ *is a* c-*shuffle for the colours in* C.

Note that the output of Shuffle contains two components that cannot be easily computed from one another. It is thus natural to define two weakenings that we also study here.

Definition 5. iShuffle *("i" for "interval") is the same problem as* Shuffle *save for the fact that a valid output only contains the interval* $]u, v[$ *which is a* c-*shuffle. Complementarily,* cShuffle *("c" for "colour") is the problem that only outputs a possible set of colours taken by a* c-*shuffle.*

We will first start analysing the weaker problems cShuffle and iShuffle and show they are respectively equivalent to $(\mathsf{LPO}')^*$ and $\mathsf{TC}^*_{\mathbb{N}}$. This will also imply that Shuffle is stronger than $(\mathsf{LPO}')^* \times \mathsf{TC}^*_{\mathbb{N}}$, but the converse will require an entirely distinct proof.

3.2   Weihrauch Complexity of the Weaker Shuffle Problems

We first start by discussing cShuffle briefly. Showing that it is stronger than $(\mathsf{LPO}')^*$ is relatively straightforward.

Lemma 8. $(\mathsf{LPO}')^* \leq_{\mathrm{W}}$ cShuffle

Proof Idea. By noting that cShuffle$^2 \leq_{\mathrm{W}}$ cShuffle by considering pairing of distinct colourings, it suffices to show $\mathsf{LPO}' \leq_{\mathrm{W}}$ cShuffle.

The reduction is then obtained by computing, from the input of LPO', a map $f : \mathbb{Q} \rightarrow \mathbb{N}$ such that infinite sets are taken to dense sets by f^{-1}. □

The reversal is more difficult; in this case, it is helpful to be more precise, and give a better estimate of the number of instances of LPO' necessary to solve an instance (n, c) of cShuffle.

Lemma 9. *Let* cShuffle$_n$ *be the restriction of* cShuffle *to the instances of the form* (n, c). *Then,* cShuffle$_n \leq_{\mathrm{W}} (\mathsf{LPO}')^{2^n-1}$

Proof Idea. We use one instance of LPO' for each non-empty subset C of n, to decide if there is an interval in which only colours from C appear. The $\subseteq$-minimal C for which it happens are guaranteed to correspond to a c-shuffle. □

Putting the two previous results together, we have the following.

Theorem 4. $(LPO')^* \equiv_W cShuffle$

Now we move to iShuffle.

Lemma 10. *Let* $iShuffle_n$ *be the restriction of* iShuffle *to the instances of the form* (n, c). *For every* $n \in \mathbb{N}$ *with* $n \geq 2$, $iShuffle_n \leq_{sW} TC_\mathbb{N}^{n-1}$.

Proof Idea. Fix an enumeration of the intervals of $\mathbb{Q}$ and let (n, c) be an instance of $iShuffle_n$. The idea of the reduction is the following. With the first instance e_{n-1} of $TC_\mathbb{N}$, we look for an interval I on which c takes only $n-1$ colours: if no such interval exists, then this means that every colour is dense in every interval, and so every inverval would be a valid solution to c. Hence, we can suppose that such an interval is eventually found: we will then use the second instance e_{n-2} of $TC_\mathbb{N}$ to look for a subinterval of I_j where c takes only $n-2$ values. Again, we can suppose that such an interval is found. We proceed like this for $n-1$ steps, so that in the end the last instance e_1 of $TC_\mathbb{N}$ is used to find an interval I' inside an interval I on which we know that at most two colours appear. Again, we look for c-monochromatic intervals: if we do not find any, then I' is already a c-shuffle, whereas if we do find one, then that interval is a solution.

Although not apparent in the sketch given above, an important part of the proof is that the $n-1$ searches we described can be performed *in parallel*: the fact that this can be accomplished relies on the fact that any subinterval of a shuffle is a shuffle. □

Lemma 11. *Let* ECT_n *be the restriction of* ECT *to the instances of the form* (n, f). *For every* $n \in \mathbb{N}$ *with* $n \geq 2$, $ECT_n \leq_{sW} iShuffle_n$.

Proof. Let (n, f) be an instance of ECT_n. We will slightly abuse notation, in the following sense: we will define a colouring $c : \mathbb{D} \to n$ of the dyadics, instead of directly defining a colouring of the rationals. We will then exploit the fact that there is a computable order-preserving bijection between the dyadic numbers $\mathbb{D}$ and $\mathbb{Q}$, and we will apply $iShuffle_n$ to (n, c).

We define $c : \mathbb{D} \to n$ as follows: let $d = \frac{m}{2^h}$ be a dyadic number, then we let $c(d) = f(h)$. Hence, all the points of the same denominator have the same colour according to c. Let $(\frac{u}{2^k}, \frac{v}{2^\ell}) \in iShuffle_n(n, c)$. Let b be such that $\frac{1}{2^b} < \frac{v}{2^\ell} - \frac{u}{2^k}$. We claim that b is a bound for f. Suppose not, then there is a colour $i < n$ and a number $x \in \mathbb{N}$ such that $x > b$ and $f(x) = i$, but for no $y > x$ it holds that $f(y) = i$. Hence, all the dyadics of the form $\frac{w}{2^x}$ are given colour i, but i does not appear densely often in any interval of $\mathbb{D}$. But by definition of b, there is a $z \in \mathbb{N}$ such that $\frac{z}{2^x} \in \left] \frac{u}{2^k}, \frac{v}{2^\ell} \right[$, which is a contradiction. Hence b is a bound for f. □

We can then relate this to $TC_\mathbb{N}$; the next lemma follows directly by inspecting the second half of [5, Theorem 9].

Lemma 12. *For every* $n \in \mathbb{N}$ *with* $n \geq 2$, $TC_\mathbb{N}^{n-1} \leq_W ECT_n$ *(and this cannot be improved to a strong Weihrauch reduction).*

Putting things together, we finally have a characterization of iShuffle.

Theorem 5. *For every $n \geq 2$, we have the Weihrauch equivalence*

$$\mathsf{ECT}_n \equiv_W \mathsf{iShuffle}_n \equiv_W \mathsf{TC}_{\mathbb{N}}^{n-1} \qquad whence \qquad \mathsf{ECT} \equiv_W \mathsf{iShuffle} \equiv_W \mathsf{TC}_{\mathbb{N}}^*$$

3.3 The Full Shuffle Problem

The main result of this section is that $\mathsf{Shuffle} \equiv_W \mathsf{TC}_{\mathbb{N}}^* \times (\mathsf{LPO}')^*$, which will be proved in Theorem 6. In order to do that, it is convenient to observe that, similarly to cShuffle and iShuffle, Shuffle is closed under finite parallelization.

Lemma 13. $\mathsf{Shuffle} \times \mathsf{Shuffle} \leq_W \mathsf{Shuffle}$. *Therefore,* $\mathsf{Shuffle}^* \equiv_W \mathsf{Shuffle}$.

This enables one to easily prove the following lemma.

Lemma 14. $\mathsf{TC}_{\mathbb{N}}^* \times (\mathsf{LPO}')^* \leq_W \mathsf{Shuffle}$

Proof. From Theorem 4 and Theorem 5, we have that $\mathsf{TC}_{\mathbb{N}}^* \times (\mathsf{LPO}')^* \leq_W$ iShuffle $\times$ cShuffle, and since clearly iShuffle $\sqcup$ cShuffle $\leq_W$ Shuffle, by Lemma 13 we have that $\mathsf{TC}_{\mathbb{N}}^* \times (\mathsf{LPO}')^* \leq_W$ Shuffle. $\qquad\square$

For the other direction, again, we want to be precise as to the number of instances of $\mathsf{TC}_{\mathbb{N}} \times (\mathsf{LPO}')$ needed to solve an instance of Shuffle.

Lemma 15. *Let* $\mathsf{Shuffle}_n$ *be the restriction of* $\mathsf{Shuffle}$ *to the instances of the form* (n, c). *Then,* $\mathsf{Shuffle}_n \leq_W (\mathsf{TC}_{\mathbb{N}} \times \mathsf{LPO}')^{2^n - 1}$

Proof Idea. Let (n, c) be an instance of Shuffle. Essentially, the main idea for the proof of $\mathsf{Shuffle}_n \leq_W (\mathsf{TC}_{\mathbb{N}} \times \mathsf{LPO}')^{2^n - 1}$ is to combine the proofs of Lemma 10 and of Theorem 4: we want to use $\mathsf{TC}_{\mathbb{N}}$ to find a candidate interval for a certain subset C of n, and on the side we use LPO' (or equivalently, IsFinite) to check for every such set C whether a c-shuffle for the colours of C actually exists. The main difficulty with the idea described above is that the two proofs must be intertwined, in order to be able to find both a c-shuffle and the set of colours that appear on it. $\qquad\square$

Putting the previous results together, we obtain the following.

Theorem 6. $\mathsf{Shuffle} \equiv_W \mathsf{TC}_{\mathbb{N}}^* \times (\mathsf{LPO}')^*$

4 $\mathsf{ART}_{\mathbb{Q}}$ and Related Problems

We now analyse the logical strength of the principle $\mathsf{ART}_{\mathbb{Q}}$. As in the case of Shuffle, we start with a proof of $\mathsf{ART}_{\mathbb{Q}}$ in $\mathsf{RCA}_0 + \Sigma_2^0\text{-IND}$. This will give us enough insights to assess the strength of the corresponding Weihrauch problems.

4.1   Additive Ramsey over $\mathbb{Q}$ in Reverse Mathematics

As a preliminary step, we figure out the strength of $\mathsf{ORT}_\mathbb{Q}$, the ordered Ramsey theorem over $\mathbb{Q}$. It is readily provable from RCA_0 and is thus much weaker than most other principles we analyse. We can be a bit more precise by considering RCA_0^* which is basically the weakening of RCA_0 where induction is restricted to Δ_1^0 formulas (see [12, Definition X.4.1] for a nice formal definition).

Lemma 16. $\mathsf{RCA}_0^* \vdash \mathsf{RCA}_0 \Leftrightarrow \mathsf{ORT}_\mathbb{Q}$

We now show that the shuffle principle is equivalent to $\mathsf{ART}_\mathbb{Q}$. So overall, much like the Ramsey-like theorems of [8], they are equivalent to Σ_2^0-induction.

Lemma 17. $\mathsf{RCA}_0 + \mathsf{Shuffle} \vdash \mathsf{ART}_\mathbb{Q}$. Hence, $\mathsf{RCA}_0 + \Sigma_2^0\text{-}\mathsf{IND} \vdash \mathsf{ART}_\mathbb{Q}$.

Proof. Fix a finite semigroup $(S, \cdot)$ and an additive colouring $c : [\mathbb{Q}]^2 \to S$. Say a colour $s \in S$ *occurs* in $X \subseteq \mathbb{Q}$ if there exists $(x, y) \in [X]^2$ such that $c(x, y) = s$.

We proceed in two stages: first, we find an interval $]u, v[$ such that all colours occurring in $]u, v[$ are $\mathcal{J}$-equivalent to one another. Then we find a subinterval of $]u, v[$ partitioned into finitely many dense homogeneous sets. For the first step, we apply the following lemma to obtain a subinterval $I_1 =]u, v[$ of $\mathbb{Q}$ where all colours lie in a single $\mathcal{J}$-class.

Lemma 18. *For every additive colouring c, there exists $(u, v) \in [\mathbb{Q}]^2$ such that all colours of $c|_{]u,v[}$ are $\mathcal{J}$-equivalent to one another.*

Proof. If we post-compose c with a map taking a semigroup element to its $\mathcal{J}$-class, we get an ordered colouring. Applying $\mathsf{ORT}_\mathbb{Q}$ yields a suitable interval. $\square$

Moving on to stage two of the proof, we want to look for a subinterval of I_1 partitioned into finitely many dense homogeneous sets. To this end, define a colouring $\gamma : I_1 \to S^2$ by setting $\gamma(z) = (c(u, z), c(z, v))$.

By Shuffle, there exist $x, y \in I_1$ with $x < y$ such that $]x, y[$ is a γ-shuffle. For $l, r \in S$, define $H_{l,r} := \gamma^{-1}(\{(l, r)\}) \subseteq]x, y[$; note that this is a set by bounded recursive comprehension. Clearly, all $H_{l,r}$ are either empty or dense in $]x, y[$, and moreover $]x, y[= \bigcup_{l,r} H_{l,r}$. Since there are finitely many pairs (l, r), all we have to prove is that each non-empty $H_{l,r}$ is homogeneous for c.

Let $s = c(w, z)$ such that $w, z \in H_{l,r}$ with $w < z$. By additivity of c and the definition of $H_{l,r}$,

$$s \cdot r = c(w, z) \cdot c(z, v) = c(w, v) = r. \tag{1}$$

In particular $r \leq_\mathcal{R} s$. But we also have $r \, \mathcal{J} \, s$, which gives $r \, \mathcal{R} \, s$ by Lemma 6. This shows that all the colours occurring in $H_{l,r}$ are $\mathcal{R}$-equivalent to one another. A dual argument shows that they are all $\mathcal{L}$-equivalent, so they are all $\mathcal{H}$-equivalent. The assumptions of Lemma 5 are satisfied, so their $\mathcal{H}$-class is actually a group.

All that remains to be proved is that any colour s occurring in $H_{l,r}$ is actually the (necessarily unique) idempotent of this $\mathcal{H}$-class. Since $r \, \mathcal{R} \, s$, there exists a

such that $s = r \cdot a$. But then by (1), $s \cdot s = s \cdot r \cdot a = r \cdot a = s$, so s is necessarily the idempotent. Thus, all sets $H_{l,r}$ are homogeneous and we are done.   □

We conclude this section by showing that the implication proved in the Lemma above reverses., thus giving the precise strength of $\mathsf{ART}_\mathbb{Q}$ over RCA_0.

Theorem 7. $\mathsf{RCA}_0 + \mathsf{ART}_\mathbb{Q} \vdash \mathsf{Shuffle}$. *Hence,* $\mathsf{RCA}_0 \vdash \mathsf{ART}_\mathbb{Q} \leftrightarrow \Sigma_2^0\text{-IND}$.

Proof. Let $f \colon \mathbb{Q} \to n$ be a colouring of the rationals. Let $(S_n, \cdot)$ be the finite semigroup defined by $S_n = n$ and $a \cdot b = a$ for every $a, b \in S_n$. Define the colouring $c \colon [\mathbb{Q}]^2 \to S_n$ by setting $c(x, y) = f(x)$ for every $x, y \in \mathbb{Q}$. Since for every $x < y < z$, $c(x, z) = f(x) = c(x, y) \cdot c(y, z)$, c is additive. By additive Ramsey, there exists $]u, v[$ which is c-densely homogeneous and thus a f-shuffle. □

4.2 Weihrauch Complexity of Additive Ramsey

We now start the analysis of $\mathsf{ART}_\mathbb{Q}$ in the context of Weihrauch reducibility. We will mostly summarize results, relying on the intuitions we built up so far. First off, we determine the Weihrauch degree of the ordered Ramsey theorem over $\mathbb{Q}$.

Theorem 8. *Let* $\mathsf{ORT}_\mathbb{Q}$ *be the problem whose instances are ordered colourings* $c \colon [\mathbb{Q}]^2 \to P$, *for some finite poset* $(P, \prec)$, *and whose possible outputs on input* c *are intervals on which* c *is constant. We have that* $\mathsf{ORT}_\mathbb{Q} \equiv_W \mathsf{LPO}^*$.

Proof Idea. $\mathsf{LPO}^* \leq_{sW} \mathsf{ORT}_\mathbb{Q}$: given n sequences $p_0, \ldots, p_{n-1} \in 2^\mathbb{N}$, build a coloring $c \colon [\mathbb{Q}]^2 \to 2^n$ such that, for every $(x, y) \in [\mathbb{Q}]^2$ and $l \in \mathbb{N}$ such that $2^{-l-1} \leq y - x < 2^{-l}$, $i \in c(x, y)$ if and only if there is $k < l$ such that $p_i(k) = 1$. This is an ordered coloring, and the color associated to any homogeneous set gives answer to $\mathsf{LPO}(p_i)$.

$\mathsf{ORT}_\mathbb{Q} \leq_W \mathsf{LPO}^*$: without loss of generality, assume that the input is a coloring $c \colon [\mathbb{Q}]^2 \to k$ where k is ordered as usual. There is a straightforward procedure that, taking an interval I and a color $i \in k$, checks if there exists a pair of $(x, y) \in [I]^2$ such that $c(x, y) < i$, and returns that pair if it exists (and otherwise does not terminate). Now run that procedure for $i = k - 1$ and some arbitrary interval I_{k-1}, and if it returns some (x, y), run it for $i = k - 2$ and the interval $]x, y[$, and so forth (note that we cannot drop below $i = 0$ since the coloring is ordered). Calling $(x_s, y_s)_{s \in \mathbb{N}}$ the sequence of pairs that are tested, define the sequences p_i for every $i < k$ by $p_i(s) = 1 \Leftrightarrow c(x_s, y_s) < i$. The largest i such that $\mathsf{LPO}(p_i) = 0$ will be the color of some monochromatic interval that can be determined by the first s such that $p_{i+1}(s) = 1$ (or is I_{k-1} if $i = k - 1$). □

Now let us discuss Weihrauch problems corresponding to $\mathsf{ART}_\mathbb{Q}$.

Definition 6. *Regard* $\mathsf{ART}_\mathbb{Q}$ *as the following Weihrauch problem: the instances are pairs* (S, c) *where* S *is a finite semigroup and* $c \colon [\mathbb{Q}]^2 \to S$ *is an additive colouring of* $[\mathbb{Q}]^2$, *and such that, for every* $C \subseteq S$ *and every interval* I *of* $\mathbb{Q}$, $(I, C) \in \mathsf{ART}_\mathbb{Q}$ *if and only if* I *is* c-*densely homogeneous for the colours of* C.

Similarly to what we did in Definition 5, we also introduce the problems $\mathsf{cART}_\mathbb{Q}$ *and* $\mathsf{iART}_\mathbb{Q}$ *that only return the set of colours and the interval respectively.*

We start by noticing that the proof of Theorem 7 can be readily adapted to show the following.

Lemma 19. – cShuffle $\leq_{sW}$ cART$_\mathbb{Q}$, *hence* (LPO$'$)* $\leq_W$ cART$_\mathbb{Q}$.
- iShuffle $\leq_{sW}$ iART$_\mathbb{Q}$, *hence* TC$_\mathbb{N}^*$ $\leq_W$ iART$_\mathbb{Q}$.
- Shuffle $\leq_{sW}$ ART$_\mathbb{Q}$, *hence* (LPO$'$)* $\times$ TC$_\mathbb{N}^*$ $\leq_W$ ART$_\mathbb{Q}$.

The rest of the section is devoted to find upper bounds for cART$_\mathbb{Q}$, iART$_\mathbb{Q}$ and ART$_\mathbb{Q}$. The first step to take is a careful analysis of the proof of Lemma 17. For an additive colouring $c\colon [\mathbb{Q}]^2 \to S$, the proof can be summarized as follows:

- we start with an application of ORT$_\mathbb{Q}$ to find an interval $]u, v[$ such that all the colours of $c|_{]u,v[}$ are all $\mathcal{J}$-equivalent (Lemma 18).
- define the colouring $\gamma\colon \mathbb{Q} \to S^2$ and apply Shuffle to it, thus obtaining the interval $]x, y[$.
- the rest of the proof consists simply in showing that $]x, y[$ is a c-densely homogeneous interval.

Hence, from the uniform point of view, this shows that ART$_\mathbb{Q}$ can be computed via a composition of Shuffle and ORT$_\mathbb{Q}$. Whence the next theorem.

Theorem 9. – cART$_\mathbb{Q}$ $\leq_W$ (LPO$'$)* $\times$ LPO*, *therefore* cART$_\mathbb{Q}$ $\equiv_W$ (LPO$'$)*.
- iART$_\mathbb{Q}$ $\leq_W$ TC$_\mathbb{N}^*$ $\times$ LPO*, *therefore* iART$_\mathbb{Q}$ $\equiv_W$ TC$_\mathbb{N}^*$.
- ART$_\mathbb{Q}$ $\leq_W$ (LPO$'$)* $\times$ TC$_\mathbb{N}^*$ $\times$ LPO*, *therefore* ART$_\mathbb{Q}$ $\equiv_W$ (LPO$'$)* $\times$ TC$_\mathbb{N}^*$.

5   Conclusion and Future Work

We have analysed the strength of an additive Ramseyan theorem over the rationals from the point of view of reverse mathematics and found it to be equivalent to Σ_2^0-induction, and then refined that analysis to a Weihrauch equivalence with TC$_\mathbb{N}^*$ $\times$ (LPO$'$)*. We have also shown that the problem decomposes nicely: we get the distinct complexities (LPO$'$)* or TC$_\mathbb{N}^*$ if we only require either the set of colours or the location of the homogeneous set respectively. The same holds true for another equally and arguably more fundamental shuffle principle.

For further work, we believe it should be straightforward to carry out a similar analysis for Ramsey theorem over $\mathbb{N}$ (known to be equivalent to Σ_2^0-induction in the context of reverse mathematics [8]). Related to $\mathbb{Q}$, there are also weaker combinatorial principles of interest to look at like $(\eta)_{<\infty}^1$ from [6]. More generally, it would be interesting to study standard mathematical theorems that are known to be equivalent to Σ_2^0-IND in reverse mathematics: this can be considered to contribute to the larger endevour of studying principles already analyzed in reverse mathematics in the framework of the Weihrauch degrees. In the particular case of Σ_2^0-IND, it can be interesting to see which degrees are necessary for such an analysis. We refer to [3] for more on this topic, and for a more comprehensive study of Ramsey's theorem in the Weihrauch degrees.

Acknowledgements. We are very grateful to Arno Pauly for many inspiring discussions that led to this work and many technical contributions that cannot be neatly decoupled from the main results. The first author also warmly thanks Leszek Kołodziejczyk for the proof of Lemma 7 as well as Henryk Michalewski and Michał Skrzypczak for numerous discussions on a related project.

References

1. Brattka, V., Gherardi, G.: Completion of choice. Ann. Pure Appl. Logic **172**(3), 102914 (2021). https://doi.org/10.1016/j.apal.2020.102914
2. Brattka, V., Gherardi, G., Pauly, A.: Weihrauch complexity in computable analysis. In: Brattka, V., Hertling, P. (eds.) Handbook of Computability and Complexity in Analysis. TAC, pp. 367–417. Springer, Cham (2021). https://doi.org/10.1007/978-3-030-59234-9_11
3. Brattka, V., Rakotoniaina, T.: On the uniform computational content of Ramsey's theorem. J. Symbolic Logic **82** (2015). https://doi.org/10.1017/jsl.2017.43
4. Carton, O., Colcombet, T., Puppis, G.: Regular languages of words over countable linear orderings. In: Aceto, L., Henzinger, M., Sgall, J. (eds.) ICALP 2011, Part II. LNCS, vol. 6756, pp. 125–136. Springer, Heidelberg (2011). https://doi.org/10.1007/978-3-642-22012-8_9
5. Davis, C., Hirschfeldt, D.R., Hirst, J.L., Pardo, J., Pauly, A., Yokoyama, K.: Combinatorial principles equivalent to weak induction. Computability **9**(3–4), 219–229 (2020). https://doi.org/10.3233/COM-180244
6. Frittaion, E., Patey, L.: Coloring the rationals in reverse mathematics. Computability **6**(4), 319–331 (2017). https://doi.org/10.3233/COM-160067
7. Hirschfeldt, D.R.: Slicing the Truth. World Scientific (2014). https://doi.org/10.1142/9208
8. Kolodziejczyk, L.A., Michalewski, H., Pradic, P., Skrzypczak, M.: The logical strength of Büchi's decidability theorem. Log. Methods Comput. Sci. **15**(2) (2019). https://doi.org/10.23638/LMCS-15(2:16)2019
9. Neumann, E., Pauly, A.: A topological view on algebraic computation models. J. Complex. **44**, 1–22 (2018). https://doi.org/10.1016/j.jco.2017.08.003
10. Perrin, D., Pin, J.E.: Infinite Words: Automata, Semigroups, Logic and Games. Pure and Applied Mathematics (2004)
11. Shelah, S.: The monadic theory of order. Ann. Math. **102**(3), 379–419 (1975)
12. Simpson, S.G.: Subsystems of Second Order Arithmetic. Perspectives in Mathematical Logic (1999). https://doi.org/10.1007/978-3-642-59971-2

Reverse Mathematics
of the Uncountability of ℝ

Sam Sanders[✉]

Department of Philosophy II, RUB Bochum, Bochum, Germany
sasander@me.com
https://sasander.wixsite.com/academic

Abstract. In his first set theory paper (1874), Cantor establishes the uncountability of ℝ. We study the latter in Kohlenbach's *higher-order* Reverse Mathematics, motivated by the observation that one cannot study concepts like 'arbitrary mappings from ℝ to ℕ' in second-order Reverse Mathematics. Now, it was recently shown that the statement

NIN : *there is no injection from* $[0, 1]$ *to* ℕ

is *hard to prove* in terms of conventional comprehension. In this paper, we show that NIN is *robust* by establishing equivalences between NIN and NIN restricted to mainstream function classes, like: bounded variation, semi-continuity, and Borel. Thus, the aforementioned hardness of NIN is **not** due to the quantification over *arbitrary* ℝ → ℕ-functions in NIN. Finally, we also study NBI, the restriction of NIN to *bijections*, and the connection to Cousin's lemma and Jordan's decomposition theorem.

1 Introduction and Preliminaries

1.1 Aim and Motivation

In a nutshell, we study the *the uncountability of* ℝ from the point of view of *Reverse Mathematics*. We now explain the aforementioned italicised notions.

First of all, Reverse Mathematics (RM hereafter) is a program in the foundations of mathematics initiated by Friedman [11,12] and developed extensively by Simpson and others [34,35]; an introduction to RM for the 'mathematician in the street' is in [36]. In a nutshell, RM seeks to identify the minimum axioms needed to prove theorems of ordinary, i.e. non-set theoretic, mathematics. We assume basic familiarity with RM, including Kohlenbach's *higher-order* RM introduced in [18], with more recent results -including our own- in [26–29,31,32].

Now, the biggest difference between 'classical' RM and higher-order RM is that the former makes use of L_2, the language of *second-order* arithmetic, while

This research was supported by the *Deutsche Forschungsgemeinschaft* (DFG) via the grant *Reverse Mathematics beyond the Gödel hierarchy* (SA3418/1-1). I thank Ulrich Kohlenbach and Dag Normann for all helpful advise regarding Sect. 2.1. I also thank the anonymous referees for their many helpful suggestions.

U. Berger et al. (Eds.): CiE 2022, LNCS 13359, pp. 272–286, 2022.
https://doi.org/10.1007/978-3-031-08740-0_23

the latter uses L_ω, the language of *higher-order* arithmetic. Thus, higher-order objects are only indirectly available via so-called codes or representations in classical RM. In particular, L_2 cannot talk about 'arbitrary mappings from $\mathbb{R}$ to $\mathbb{N}$'. Thus, Simpson (only) proves that the real numbers $\mathbb{R}$ cannot be enumerated as a sequence in classical RM (see [35, II.4.9]). Hence, the higher-order RM of the *uncountability of* $\mathbb{R}$, discussed next, is a natural (wide-open) topic of study.

Secondly, the uncountability of $\mathbb{R}$ was established in 1874 by Cantor in his *first* set theory paper [6], which even has its own Wikipedia page, namely [39]. We will study the uncountability of $\mathbb{R}$ in the guise of the following principles:

– NIN: *there is no injection from* $[0, 1]$ *to* $\mathbb{N}$,
– NBI: *there is no bijection from* $[0, 1]$ *to* $\mathbb{N}$.

It was established in [29] that NIN and NBI are *hard* to prove in terms of (conventional) comprehension, as explained in detail in Remark 1. One obvious way of downplaying these results is to simply attribute the hardness of NIN to the fact that one quantifies over *arbitrary* third-order objects, namely $\mathbb{R} \to \mathbb{N}$-functions.

In this paper, we establish RM-equivalences involving NIN and NBI, where some are straightforward (Sect. 2.1) and others advanced or surprising (Sect. 2.2). We also study the connection between NIN and *Cousin's lemma* and *Jordan's decomposition theorem* (Sect. 2.3). In particular, we show that NIN is equivalent to the statement that there is no injection from $[0, 1]$ to $\mathbb{Q}$ that enjoys 'nice' mainstream properties like *bounded variation*, *semi-continuity*, and related notions. Hence, the aforementioned hardness of NIN and NBI is not due to the latter quantifying over arbitrary third-order functions as *exactly* the same hardness is observed for *mathematically natural* subclasses. A recent FOM-discussion initiated by Friedman via [13], brought about this insight, while our results establish that NIN is *robust* in the sense of Montalbán, as follows.

> [...] gaining a greater understanding of [the big five] phenomenon is currently one of the driving questions behind reverse mathematics. To study the big five phenomenon, one distinction that I think is worth making is the one between robust systems and non-robust systems. A system is *robust* if it is equivalent to small perturbations of itself. This is not a precise notion yet, but we can still recognize some robust systems. All the big five systems are very robust. [...] Apart from those systems, weak weak König's Lemma (WWKL$_0$) is also robust, and we know no more than one or two other systems that may be robust. ([23, p. 432])

Thirdly, as to the structure of this paper, we introduce some essential axioms and definitions in Sect. 1.2 while our main results may be found in Sect. 2. We note that some of our results are proved using IND$_0$, a non-trivial fragment of the induction axiom from Sect. 1.2.1. It is a natural RM-question, posed previously by Hirschfeldt (see [23, §6.1]), whether these extra axioms are needed for the reversal. Neeman provides an example of the necessary use of extra induction in a reversal in [24]. We finish this introductory section with a conceptual remark.

Remark 1 (Conventional comprehension). First of all, the goal of RM is to find the minimal axioms that prove a given theorem. In second-order RM, these minimal axioms are fragments of the comprehension axiom (and related notions), i.e. the statement that the set $\{n \in \mathbb{N} : \varphi(n)\}$ exists for a certain class of L_2-formulas. Higher-order RM similarly makes use of 'comprehension functionals', i.e. *third-order* objects that decide formulas in a certain sub-class of L_2. Examples include Kleene's quantifier $\exists^2$ and the Suslin functional S^2, to be found in Sect. 1.2.1. We are dealing with *conventional* comprehension here, i.e. only first- and second-order objects are allowed as parameters.

Secondly, second-order arithmetic Z_2 has two natural higher-order formulations Z_2^ω and Z_2^Ω based on comprehension functionals, both to be found in Sect. 1.2.1. The systems Z_2, Z_2^ω, and Z_2^Ω prove the same second-order sentences by [15, Cor. 2.6]. Nonetheless, the system Z_2^ω **cannot** prove NIN or NBI, while Z_2^Ω proves both. Here, Z_2^ω and NIN can be formulated in the language of third-order arithmetic, i.e. there is no 'type mismatch'. The previous negative result is why we (feel obliged/warranted to) say that *the principle* NIN *is hard to prove in terms of conventional comprehension*. Finally, NIN and NBI seem to be the weakest natural third-order principles with this hardness property.

1.2 Preliminaries

We introduce axioms and definitions from RM needed below. We refer to [18, §2] or [26, §2] for Kohlenbach's base theory RCA_0^ω, and basic definitions like the real numbers $\mathbb{R}$ in RCA_0^ω. As in second-order RM (see [35, II.4.4]), real numbers are represented by fast-converging Cauchy sequences. To avoid the details of coding real numbers and sets, we often assume the axiom $(\exists^2)$ from Sect. 1.2.1, which can however sometimes be avoided, as discussed in Remark 10.

1.2.1 Some Axioms of Higher-Order Arithmetic

First of all, the functional φ in $(\exists^2)$ is clearly discontinuous at $f = 11\dots$; in fact, $(\exists^2)$ is equivalent to the existence of $F : \mathbb{R} \to \mathbb{R}$ such that $F(x) = 1$ if $x >_{\mathbb{R}} 0$, and 0 otherwise ([18, §3]).

$$(\exists\varphi^2 \leq_2 1)(\forall f^1)\big[(\exists n)(f(n) = 0) \leftrightarrow \varphi(f) = 0\big]. \qquad (\exists^2)$$

Related to $(\exists^2)$, the functional μ^2 in (μ^2) is also called *Feferman's* μ ([18]).

$$(\exists\mu^2)(\forall f^1)\big[((\exists n)(f(n) = 0) \to [f(\mu(f)) = 0 \wedge (\forall i < \mu(f))(f(i) \neq 0)]) \qquad (\mu^2)$$
$$\wedge\, [(\forall n)(f(n) \neq 0) \to \mu(f) = 0]\big].$$

Intuitively, μ^2 is the least-number-operator, i.e. $\mu(f)$ provides the least $n \in \mathbb{N}$ such that $f(n) = 0$, if such number exists. We have $(\exists^2) \leftrightarrow (\mu^2)$ over RCA_0^ω and $\mathsf{ACA}_0^\omega \equiv \mathsf{RCA}_0^\omega + (\exists^2)$ proves the same L_2-sentences as ACA_0 by [15, Theorem 2.5]. Working in ACA_0^ω, one readily defines a functional $\eta : [0,1] \to 2^{\mathbb{N}}$ that converts real numbers to their[1] binary representation.

---

[1] In case there are two binary representations, we choose the one with a tail of zeros.

Secondly, we sometimes need more induction than is available in RCA_0^ω. The connection between 'finite comprehension' and induction is well-known from second-order RM (see [35, X.4.4]).

Principle 2 (IND_0). *Let Y^2 satisfy $(\forall n \in \mathbb{N})(\exists$ at most one $f \in 2^\mathbb{N})(Y(f,n) = 0)$. For $k \in \mathbb{N}$, there is w^{1^*} such that for any $m \le k$, we have*

$$(\exists i < |w|)((w(i) \in 2^\mathbb{N} \wedge Y(w(i), m) = 0)) \leftrightarrow (\exists f \in 2^\mathbb{N})(Y(f,m) = 0).$$

Thirdly, *the Suslin functional* S^2 is defined in [18] as follows:

$$(\exists \mathsf{S}^2 \le_2 1)(\forall f^1)\big[(\exists g^1)(\forall n^0)(f(\bar{g}n) = 0) \leftrightarrow \mathsf{S}(f) = 0\big]. \tag{S^2}$$

The system $\Pi_1^1\text{-}\mathsf{CA}_0^\omega \equiv \mathsf{RCA}_0^\omega + (\mathsf{S}^2)$ proves the same Π_3^1-sentences as $\Pi_1^1\text{-}\mathsf{CA}_0$ by [32, Theorem 2.2]. By definition, the Suslin functional S^2 can decide whether a Σ_1^1-formula as in the left-hand side of (S^2) is true or false. We similarly define the functional S_k^2 which decides the truth or falsity of Σ_k^1-formulas from L_2; we also define the system $\Pi_k^1\text{-}\mathsf{CA}_0^\omega$ as $\mathsf{RCA}_0^\omega + (\mathsf{S}_k^2)$, where (S_k^2) expresses that S_k^2 exists. We note that the operators ν_n from [5, p. 129] are essentially S_n^2 strengthened to return a witness (if existant) to the Σ_n^1-formula at hand.

Finally, second-order arithmetic Z_2 readily follows from $\cup_k \Pi_k^1\text{-}\mathsf{CA}_0^\omega$, or from:

$$(\exists E^3 \le_3 1)(\forall Y^2)\big[(\exists f^1)(Y(f) = 0) \leftrightarrow E(Y) = 0\big], \tag{$\exists^3$}$$

and we therefore define $\mathsf{Z}_2^\Omega \equiv \mathsf{RCA}_0^\omega + (\exists^3)$ and $\mathsf{Z}_2^\omega \equiv \cup_k \Pi_k^1\text{-}\mathsf{CA}_0^\omega$, which are conservative over Z_2 by [15, Cor. 2.6]. Despite this close connection, Z_2^ω and Z_2^Ω can behave quite differently, as discussed in Remark 1. The functional from $(\exists^3)$ is also called '$\exists^3$', and we use the same convention for other functionals.

1.2.2 Some Basic Definitions

We introduce the higher-order definitions of 'set' and 'countable', as can be found in e.g. [27,29,31].

First of all, open sets are represented in second-order RM as countable unions of basic open sets ([35, II.5.6]), and we refer to such sets as 'RM-open'. By [35, II.7.1], one can effectively convert between RM-open sets and (RM-codes for) continuous characteristic functions. Thus, a natural extension of the notion of 'open set' is to allow *arbitrary* (possibly discontinuous) characteristic functions, as is done in e.g. [27,31]. To make sure (basic) RM-open sets have characteristic functions, we shall always assume ACA_0^ω when necessary.

Definition 3 [Subsets of $\mathbb{R}$]. We let $Y : \mathbb{R} \to \{0,1\}$ represent subsets of $\mathbb{R}$ as follows: we write '$x \in Y$' for '$Y(x) = 1$'.

The notion of 'subset of $2^\mathbb{N}$ or $\mathbb{N}^\mathbb{N}$' now has an obvious definition. Having introduced our notion of set, we now turn to countable sets.

Definition 4 [Enumerable sets of reals]. A set $A \subset \mathbb{R}$ is *enumerable* if there exists a sequence $(x_n)_{n \in \mathbb{N}}$ such that $(\forall x \in \mathbb{R})(x \in A \leftrightarrow (\exists n \in \mathbb{N})(x =_\mathbb{R} x_n))$.

This definition reflects the RM-notion of 'countable set' from [35, V.4.2]. Note that given Feferman's μ^2, we can remove all elements from a sequence of reals $(x_n)_{n \in \mathbb{N}}$ that are not in a given set $A \subset \mathbb{R}$.

The definition of 'countable set of reals' is now as follows in RCA_0^ω, while the associated definitions for Baire space are obvious.

Definition 5 [Countable subset of $\mathbb{R}$]. A set $A \subset \mathbb{R}$ is *countable* if there exists $Y : \mathbb{R} \to \mathbb{N}$ such that $(\forall x, y \in A)(Y(x) =_0 Y(y) \to x =_{\mathbb{R}} y)$. The functional Y is called *injective* on A or *an injection* on A. If $Y : \mathbb{R} \to \mathbb{N}$ is also *surjective*, i.e. $(\forall n \in \mathbb{N})(\exists x \in A)(Y(x) = n)$, we call A *strongly countable*. The functional Y is then called *bijective* on A or *a bijection* on A.

The first part of Definition 5 is from Kunen's set theory textbook ([20, p. 63]) and the second part is taken from Hrbacek-Jech's set theory textbook [14] (where the term 'countable' is used instead of 'strongly countable'). According to Veldman ([38, p. 292]), Brouwer studied set theory based on injections. Hereafter, 'strongly countable' and 'countable' shall exclusively refer to Definition 5.

Finally, note that the principles NIN and NBI from Sect. 1 have now been defined. We have previously studied the RM of cocode_i for $i = 0, 1$ in [29,31], where the index $i = 0$ expresses that a countable set in the unit interval can be enumerated (for $i = 1$, we restrict to strongly countable sets).

2   Main Results

We establish the results sketched in Sect. 1.1. We generally assume $(\exists^2)$ from Sect. 1.2.1 to avoid the technical details involved in the representation of sets and real numbers. Given that NIN cannot be proved in Z_2^ω by Remark 1, this seems like a weak assumption.

2.1   Basic Robustness Results

In this section, we show that NIN, NBI, and related principles are relatively robust when it comes to the domain of the mappings therein.

First of all, let $\mathsf{NIN}^{\mathsf{X}}$ express that there is no injection $Y : \mathsf{X} \to \mathbb{N}$, for X equal to either the reals $\mathbb{R}$, Cantor space $2^{\mathbb{N}}$ (also denoted as C), or Baire space $\mathbb{N}^{\mathbb{N}}$.

Theorem 6. *The system* ACA_0^ω *proves* $\mathsf{NIN} \leftrightarrow \mathsf{NIN}^C \leftrightarrow \mathsf{NIN}^{\mathbb{N}^{\mathbb{N}}} \leftrightarrow \mathsf{NIN}^{\mathbb{R}}$.

Proof. First of all, $\mathsf{NIN} \to \mathsf{NIN}^{\mathbb{R}}$ and $\mathsf{NIN}^C \to \mathsf{NIN}^{\mathbb{N}^{\mathbb{N}}}$ are trivial, while $\mathsf{NIN}^{\mathbb{R}} \to \mathsf{NIN}$ follows by considering the injection $\frac{1}{2}(1 + \frac{x}{1+|x|})$ from $\mathbb{R}$ to $(0, 1)$.

Secondly, assume NIN and use the usual interval-halving technique (using $\exists^2$) to obtain $\eta : [0, 1] \to 2^{\mathbb{N}}$ such that $\eta(x)$ is the binary representation of $x \in [0, 1]$, choosing a tail of zeros in the non-unique case. Fix $Y : 2^{\mathbb{N}} \to \mathbb{N}$ and define $Z : [0, 1] \to \mathbb{N}$ as $Z(x) := Y(\eta(x))$, which satisfies the axiom of extensionality[2]

---

[2] Functions $F : \mathbb{R} \to \mathbb{R}$ are represented by $\Phi : \mathbb{N}^{\mathbb{N}} \to \mathbb{N}^{\mathbb{N}}$ mapping equal reals to equal reals, i.e. extensionality as in $(\forall x, y \in \mathbb{R})(x =_{\mathbb{R}} y \to \Phi(x) =_{\mathbb{R}} \Phi(y))$ (see [18, p. 289]).

on $\mathbb{R}$ by definition. By NIN, there are $x, y \in [0,1]$ with $x \neq_\mathbb{R} y$ and $Z(x) = Z(y)$. Clearly, $\eta(x) \neq_1 \eta(y)$ and $Y(\eta(x)) = Y(\eta(y))$, and NIN^C follows.

Thirdly, assume NIN^C, fix $Z : [0,1] \to \mathbb{N}$ and let $(q_n)_{n\in\mathbb{N}}$ be a list of all rational numbers with non-unique binary representation. Define $Y : 2^\mathbb{N} \to \mathbb{N}$ as follows: $Y(f) := 3Z(\mathfrak{r}(f))$ in case $\mathfrak{r}(f) := \sum_{n=0}^\infty \frac{f(n)}{2^{n+1}}$ has a unique binary representation, $Y(f) := 3n+1$ in case $\mathfrak{r}(f) = q_n$ and f has a tail of zeros, and $Y(f) = 3n+2$ in case $\mathfrak{r}(f) = q_n$ and f has a tail of ones. By NIN^C, there are $f, g \in 2^\mathbb{N}$ such that $f \neq_1 g$ and $Y(f) = Y(g)$. Clearly, this is only possible in the first case of the definition of Z, i.e. we have $Y(f) = 3Z(\mathfrak{r}(f)) = 3Z(\mathfrak{r}(g)) = Y(g)$. Since also $\mathfrak{r}(f) \neq_\mathbb{R} \mathfrak{r}(g)$, NIN follows and we obtain $\mathsf{NIN} \leftrightarrow \mathsf{NIN}^C$.

Finally, let $Y : 2^\mathbb{N} \to \mathbb{N}$ be an injection. For $f \in \mathbb{N}^\mathbb{N}$, define its graph $X_f := \{(n, f(n)) : n \in \mathbb{N}\}$ in $\mathbb{N}^2$ and code the latter as a binary sequence $\tilde{X}_f$. Note that $f(n) := (\mu m)[(n,m) \in X_f]$ recovers the function f from its graph X_f. Modulo this coding, define $Z : \mathbb{N}^\mathbb{N} \to \mathbb{N}$ as $Z(f) := Y(\tilde{X}_f)$. By the assumption on Y, $Z(f) =_0 Z(g)$ for $f, g \in \mathbb{N}^\mathbb{N}$ implies $\tilde{X}_f =_1 \tilde{X}_g$, which implies $f =_1 g$, by the definition of X_f. Hence, $\neg\mathsf{NIN}^C \to \neg\mathsf{NIN}^{\mathbb{N}^\mathbb{N}}$, and we are done. $\square$

Similarly, cocode_0^X is the statement that any countable subset of X can be enumerated, while cocode_1^X is the restriction to strongly countable sets.

Theorem 7 (ACA_0^ω). *For $i = 0, 1$, we have* $\mathsf{cocode}_i \leftrightarrow \mathsf{cocode}_i^\mathbb{R} \leftrightarrow \mathsf{cocode}_i^C$.

Proof. The implication $\mathsf{cocode}_i^\mathbb{R} \to \mathsf{cocode}_i$ is trivial while the (rescaled) arctangent function is a bijection from $\mathbb{R}$ to $(0,1)$, which readily yields the reversal.

Now assume cocode_0^C and let $Z : [0,1] \to \mathbb{N}$ be injective on $A \subset [0,1]$. The functional $Y : 2^\mathbb{N} \to \mathbb{N}$ defined by $Y(f) := Z(\mathfrak{r}(f))$ is clearly injective on $B := \{\eta(x) : x \in A\}$ where η is as in the proof of Theorem 6. Let $(f_n)_{n\in\mathbb{N}}$ be a list of all elements in B and note that $(\mathfrak{r}(f_n))_{n\in\mathbb{N}}$ is a list of all elements in A, i.e. cocode_0 follows. Note that if Z is bijective on A, then Y is bijective on B by definition, i.e. $\mathsf{cocode}_1^C \to \mathsf{cocode}_1$.

Next, assume cocode_0, let $Y : 2^\mathbb{N} \to \mathbb{N}$ be injective on $A \subset 2^\mathbb{N}$, and define $Z(x) := Y(\eta(x))$. Then $Z : [0,1] \to \mathbb{N}$ witnesses that $B = \{\mathfrak{r}(f) : f \in A\}$ is countable, and let $(x_n)_{n\in\mathbb{N}}$ be an enumeration of B. This list is readily converted to a list of all elements in A via η and by noting that μ^2 can list all $f \in A$ such that $\mathfrak{r}(f)$ has a non-unique binary representation; we thus have cocode_0^C.

We now prove $\mathsf{cocode}_1^\mathbb{R} \to \mathsf{cocode}_1^C$. Let $Y : 2^\mathbb{N} \to \mathbb{N}$ be bijective on $A \subset 2^\mathbb{N}$ and let $(f_n)_{n\in\mathbb{N}}$ be the list of all $f \in A$ such that $\mathfrak{r}(f)$ has a non-unique binary representation. Now define $D \subset \mathbb{R}$ as: $x \in D$ if either of the following holds:

- $x \in [0,1]$, x has a unique binary representation, and $\eta(x) \in A$,
- there is $n \in \mathbb{N}$ with $x \in (n, +1, n+2]$ and $x - (n+1) =_\mathbb{R} \mathfrak{r}(f_n)$.

Define $W : \mathbb{R} \to \mathbb{N}$ as $W(x) := Y(\eta(x))$ if $x \in [0,1]$ and $W(x) := Y(f_n)$ in case $|x| \in (n+1, n+2]$ as in the second case of the definition of D. Then W is a bijection on D since Y is a bijection on A. The list provided by $\mathsf{cocode}_1^\mathbb{R}$ for D now readily yields the list required for A as in cocode_1^C. $\square$

Finally, NBI^X is the statement that there is no bijection from X to $\mathbb{N}$, where X is e.g. $\mathbb{R}$ or $\mathbb{N}^{\mathbb{N}}$. We have the following theorem.

Theorem 8. *The system* ACA_0^ω *proves* $\mathsf{NBI} \leftrightarrow \mathsf{NBI}^{\mathbb{R}}$ *and* $\mathsf{NBI} \to \mathsf{NBI}^{\mathbb{N}^{\mathbb{N}}}$.

Proof. The implication $\mathsf{NBI} \to \mathsf{NBI}^{\mathbb{R}}$ is immediate as the (rescaled) tangent function provides a bijection from $(0,1)$ to $\mathbb{R}$. The inverse of tangent, called *arctangent*, yields a bijection in the other direction (also with rescaling), i.e. the first equivalence is immediate, as well as $\mathsf{NBI} \leftrightarrow \mathsf{NBI}^{\mathbb{R}_{\geq 0}}$. We now define a (continuous) bijection from $\mathbb{N}^{\mathbb{N}}$ to $\mathbb{R}_{\geq 0}$ based on *continued fractions*. Intuitively, a sequence $(a_n)_{n \in \mathbb{N}}$ of natural numbers is mapped to the real $x \in \mathbb{R}_{\geq 0}$ via the following (generalised) continued fraction:

$$x = a_0 + \cfrac{1}{1 + \cfrac{1}{a_1 + \cfrac{1}{1 + \cfrac{1}{a_2 + \ddots}}}} \tag{CF}$$

The real $x \in \mathbb{R}_{\geq 0}$ in (CF) exists in ACA_0^ω in the sense that there is an explicit function $F : (\mathbb{N}^{\mathbb{N}} \times n) \to \mathbb{Q}$ such that $x =_{\mathbb{R}} \lim_{n \to \infty} F(f)(n)$, where $F(f)(n) \in \mathbb{Q}$ is essentially the continued fraction in (CF) 'broken off' after encountering a_n. The definition of F can be be found in e.g. [22, Ch.1, p. 7-9]. One readily shows that the mapping defined by (CF) is a bijection from $\mathbb{N}^{\mathbb{N}}$ to $\mathbb{R}_{\geq 0}$ in ACA_0^ω. $\square$

We could prove similar results for *a countable set in the unit interval has measure*[3] *zero*, which is intermediate between cocode_0 and NIN, which is shown in [31] as an illustration how weak NIN is. Nonetheless, we have the following result.

Theorem 9 (ACA_0^ω). *A countable set* $A \subset [0,1]$ *has* weak[4] *measure zero.*

Proof. Fix $A \subset [0,1]$ and $Y : [0,1] \to \mathbb{N}$ injective on A. For $\varepsilon > 0$, define $\varepsilon_n := \frac{\varepsilon}{2^{n+1}}$, $B := \{(a,b) \in \mathbb{R}^2 : \frac{a+b}{2} \in A \wedge |b-a| = 2^{-Y(\frac{a+b}{2})}\}$, and $Z((a,b)) := Y(\frac{a+b}{2})$. Clearly, this shows that A has weak measure zero, as required. $\square$

We say that a property holds *weakly almost everywhere* (wae) in case it holds outside a set of weak measure zero as in Footnote 4.

We finish this section with a conceptual remark regarding our base theory.

---

[3] For $A \subset \mathbb{R}$, let 'A has measure zero' mean that for any $\varepsilon > 0$, there is a sequence of closed intervals $(I_n)_{n \in \mathbb{N}}$ covering A and such that $\varepsilon > \sum_{n=0}^{\infty} |J_n|$ for $J_0 := I_0$ and $J_{i+1} := I_{i+1} \setminus \cup_{j \leq i} I_j$. This follows from the usual definition as used in mathematics.

[4] For $A \subset \mathbb{R}$, let 'A has weak measure zero' mean that for any $\varepsilon > 0$, there is a sequence $(\varepsilon_n)_{n \in \mathbb{N}}$, a set B of closed intervals, and $Z : \mathbb{R}^2 \to \mathbb{N}$ injective on B, such that $(\forall a \in A)(\exists (b,c) \in B)(a \in (b,c))$ and $(\forall (b,c) \in B, \forall n \in \mathbb{N})(Z((b,c)) = n \to |b-c| \leq \varepsilon_n)$ and $\varepsilon \geq \sum_{n=0}^{\infty} \varepsilon_n$. Given cocode_0, this is the same as 'measure zero'.

Remark 10. We have used ACA_0^ω as the base theory for the above results, since our notion of 'set-as-characteristic function' as in Definition 3 is poorly behaved in the absence of $(\exists^2)$. One *can* obtain equivalences over RCA_0^ω, and let us establish $\mathsf{NIN}^{\mathbb{N}^\mathbb{N}} \to \mathsf{NIN}^C$ over RCA_0^ω as an example via the following steps.

- Fix any $Y : 2^\mathbb{N} \to \mathbb{N}$, which may or may not be continuous.
- In case Y is *continuous*, it is immediate that $Y(00\dots) = Y(00\dots00 * 11\dots)$ for enough instances of 0 on the right.
- In case Y is *discontinuous*, use the results in [18, §3] to derive $(\exists^2)$ over RCA_0^ω. We can now use the proof of Theorem 6 in ACA_0^ω.

The above proof of course heavily relies on the law of excluded middle.

2.2   Advanced Robustness Results

In this section, we show that NIN is equivalent to various restrictions involving notions from mainstream mathematics, like semi-continuity and bounded variation; we first introduce the latter.

First of all, an important weak continuity notion is *semi-continuity*, introduced by Baire in [2] around 1899. By [2, §84, pp. 94–95], the notion of quasi-continuity goes back to Volterra; any cliquish function is the sum of two quasi-continuous functions. Moreover, while the limits in the following definition may not exist in RCA_0^ω, the associated inequalities always make sense.

Definition 11. [Weak continuity]

- $f : \mathbb{R} \to \mathbb{R}$ is *upper semi-continuous* if for all $x_0 \in \mathbb{R}$, $f(x_0) \geq_\mathbb{R} \limsup_{x \to x_0} f(x)$.
- $f : \mathbb{R} \to \mathbb{R}$ is *lower semi-continuous* if for all $x_0 \in \mathbb{R}$, $f(x_0) \leq_\mathbb{R} \liminf_{x \to x_0} f(x)$.
- $f : X \to \mathbb{R}$ is *quasi-continuous* (resp. *cliquish*) at $x \in X$ if for any $\epsilon > 0$ and any open neighbourhood U of x, there is a non-empty open ball $G \subset U$ with $(\forall y \in G)(|f(x) - f(y)| < \varepsilon)$ (resp. $(\forall y, z \in G)(|f(z) - f(y)| < \varepsilon)$).

Secondly, Jordan introduces the notion of *bounded variation* in [16] around 1881, also studied in second-order RM [19,25]. Moreover, Jordan proves in [17, §105] that functions of bounded variation are exactly those for which the notion of 'length of the graph' makes sense; the latter boast[5] an even 'earlier' history. What is more, Lakatos in [21, p. 148] claims that Jordan did not invent or introduce the notion of bounded variation in [16], but rather discovered it in Dirichlet's 1829 paper [8].

---

[5] The notion of arc length was studied for discontinuous regulated functions in 1884 ([33, §1–2]), where it is also claimed to be essentially equivalent to Duhamel's 1866 approach from [10, Ch. VI]. Around 1833, Dirksen, the PhD supervisor of Jacobi and Heine, provides a definition of arc length that is (very) similar to the modern one (see [9, §2, p. 128]), but with some conceptual problems as discussed in [7, §3].

Definition 12 [Bounded variation]. Any $f : [a, b] \to \mathbb{R}$ *has bounded variation* on $[a, b]$ if there is $k_0 \in \mathbb{N}$ such that $k_0 \geq \sum_{i=0}^{n} |f(x_i) - f(x_{i+1})|$ for any partition $x_0 = a < x_1 < \cdots < x_{n-1} < x_n = b$.

Functions of bounded variation have only got countably many points of discontinuity (see e.g. [1, Ch. 1]); Dag Normann and the author study this property in higher-order computability theory in [30]. In the latter, we also study regulated functions (called 'regular' in [1]), defined as follows (say in ACA_0^ω).

Definition 13 [Regulated function]. A function $f : [0, 1] \to \mathbb{R}$ is *regulated* if for every $x_0 \in [0, 1]$, the 'left' and 'right' limit $f(x_0-) = \lim_{x \to x_0-} f(x)$ and $f(x_0+) = \lim_{x \to x_0+} f(x)$ exist.

Thirdly, Borel functions are defined in Definition 14; the usual definition of Borel set makes sense in ACA_0^ω, where $(\exists^2)$ is used to define countable unions.

Definition 14 [Borel function]. Any $f : [0, 1] \to \mathbb{R}$ is a Borel function in case $f^{-1}((a, +\infty)) := \{x \in [0, 1] : f(x) > a\}$ is a Borel set for any $a \in \mathbb{R}$.

Fourth, recall the induction axiom IND_0 from Sect. 1.2.2. Let Y be any property such that '$f : [0, 1] \to \mathbb{R}$ satisfies Y' follows from 'f has bounded variation on $[0, 1]$' and where this implication can be established over (say) ACA_0^ω.

Theorem 15 ($\mathsf{ACA}_0^\omega + \mathsf{IND}_0$). *The following are equivalent to* NIN:

- $\mathsf{NIN}_{\mathsf{bv}}$: *there is no injection from* $[0, 1]$ *to* $\mathbb{Q}$ *that has bounded variation,*
- $\mathsf{NIN}_{\mathsf{Y}}$: *there is no injection from* $[0, 1]$ *to* $\mathbb{Q}$ *that has property* Y,
- $\mathsf{NIN}_{\mathsf{Riemann}}$: *there is no injection from* $[0, 1]$ *to* $\mathbb{Q}$ *that is Riemann integrable,*
- $\mathsf{NIN}_{\mathsf{Borel}}$: *there is no Borel function that is an injection from* $[0, 1]$ *to* $\mathbb{Q}$,
- $\mathsf{NIN}_{\mathsf{reg}}$: *there is no injection from* $[0, 1]$ *to* $\mathbb{Q}$ *that is regulated,*
- $\mathsf{NIN}_{\mathsf{cliq}}$: *there is no injection from* $[0, 1]$ *to* $\mathbb{Q}$ *that is cliquish,*
- $\mathsf{NIN}_{\mathsf{semi}}$: *there is no upper semi-continuous injection from* $[0, 1]$ *to* $\mathbb{Q}$,
- $\mathsf{NIN}'_{\mathsf{semi}}$: *there is no lower semi-continuous injection from* $[0, 1]$ *to* $\mathbb{Q}$.

Only the implications involving the final five items require the use of IND_0.

Proof. As there is an injection from $\mathbb{Q}$ to $\mathbb{N}$ in RCA_0, we only need to prove that $\mathsf{NIN}_{\mathsf{bv}} \to \mathsf{NIN}$ over ACA_0^ω for the first equivalence. To this end, let $Y : [0, 1] \to \mathbb{N}$ be an injection and define $W : [0, 1] \to \mathbb{Q}$ by $W(x) := \frac{1}{2^{Y(x)+1}}$. Then W has bounded variation with upper bound 2. Indeed, since Y is an injection on $[0, 1]$, any sum $\sum_{i=0}^{n} |W(x_n) - W(x_{n+1})|$ is at most $\sum_{i=0}^{n} \frac{1}{2^{i+1}}$. By $\mathsf{NIN}_{\mathsf{bv}}$, there are $x, y \in [0, 1]$ with $x \neq_\mathbb{R} y$ and $W(x) =_\mathbb{Q} W(y)$. This implies the contradiction $Y(x) =_0 Y(y)$, and $\mathsf{NIN} \leftrightarrow \mathsf{NIN}_{\mathsf{bv}}$ follows. For $\mathsf{NIN}_{\mathsf{Riemann}} \to \mathsf{NIN}$, the function W is Riemann integrable following the ε-δ-definition. Indeed, fix $\varepsilon_0 > 0$ and find $k_0 \in \mathbb{N}$ such that $\frac{1}{2^{k_0}} < \varepsilon_0$. Since Y is an injection, if P is a partition of $[0, 1]$ consisting of $|P|$-many points and with mesh $\|P\| \leq \frac{1}{2^{k_0}}$, it is immediate that the Riemann sum $S(W, P)$ is smaller than $\frac{1}{2^{k_0}} \sum_{n=0}^{|P|} \frac{1}{2^{i+1}}$, which is at most $\frac{1}{2^{k_0}}$.

For the implication $\mathsf{NIN}_{\mathsf{semi}} \to \mathsf{NIN}$, consider the same $W : [0, 1] \to \mathbb{R}$ and note that $[\limsup_{x \to x_0} W(x)] =_\mathbb{R} 0 <_\mathbb{R} W(x_0)$ for any $x_0 \in [0, 1]$ in case $Y :$

$[0,1] \to \mathbb{N}$ is an injection. Hence, $W(x)$ is upper semi-continuous and $Z(x) := 1 - W(x)$ is similarly *lower* semi-continuous, since $[\liminf_{x \to x_0} Z(x)] =_{\mathbb{R}} 1 >_{\mathbb{R}} Z(x_0)$ for any $x_0 \in [0,1]$. The finite sequences provided by IND_0 seem essential to establish these semi-continuity claims. One proves $\mathsf{NIN}_{\mathsf{cliq}} \to \mathsf{NIN}$ in the same way, namely using IND_0 to exclude the finitely many 'too large' function values. For the implication $\mathsf{NIN}_{\mathsf{Borel}} \to \mathsf{NIN}$, note that for an injection $Y : [0,1] \to \mathbb{N}$ the above function $W(x)$ is Borel as $W^{-1}((a, +\infty))$ for any $a \in \mathbb{R}$ is either finite or $[0,1]$, and that these are Borel sets is immediate in $\mathsf{ACA}_0^\omega + \mathsf{IND}_0$. For the implication $\mathsf{NIN}_{\mathsf{reg}} \to \mathsf{NIN}$, consider the same $W : [0,1] \to \mathbb{R}$ and note that $W(0+) = W(1-) = W(x+) = W(x-) = 0$ for $x \in (0,1)$ in the same way as for the semi-continuity of W. Thus, W is regulated and we are done.   □

As noted above, a function has bounded variation iff it has finite arc length. The proof of this equivalence ([1, Prop. 3.28]) goes through in RCA_0^ω, i.e. we may replace 'bounded variation' by 'finite arc length' in the previous theorem.

Fifth, we say that a function has *total variation equal to* $a \in \mathbb{R}$ in case the supremum over all partitions of $\sum_{i=0}^n |f(x_i) - f(x_{i+1})|$ in Definition 12 equals a.

Corollary 16 ($\mathsf{ACA}_0^\omega + \mathsf{IND}_0$). *The following are equivalent to* NBI:

- $\mathsf{NBI}_{\mathsf{Riemann}}$: *there is no bijection from* $[0,1]$ *to* $\mathbb{Q}$ *that is Riemann integrable,*
- $\mathsf{NBI}_{\mathsf{bv}}$: *there is no injection from* $[0,1]$ *to* $\mathbb{Q}$ *that has total variation* 1,
- $\mathsf{NBI}_{\mathsf{Borel}}$: *there is no Borel function that is a bijection from* $[0,1]$ *to* $\mathbb{Q}$,
- $\mathsf{NBI}_{\mathsf{cliq}}$: *there is no bijection from* $[0,1]$ *to* $\mathbb{Q}$ *that is cliquish,*
- $\mathsf{NBI}_{\mathsf{semi}}$: *there is no upper semi-continuous bijection from* $[0,1]$ *to* $\mathbb{Q}$,
- $\mathsf{NBI}'_{\mathsf{semi}}$: *there is no lower semi-continuous bijection from* $[0,1]$ *to* $\mathbb{Q}$.

Only the implications involving the final four items require the use of IND_0.

Proof. For the first equivalence, $W : [0,1] \to \mathbb{R}$ from the proof has total variation *exactly* 1 in case Y is also surjective. The other equivalences are now immediate by the proof of the theorem.   □

As an intermediate conclusion, one readily proves that there are no *continuous* injections from $\mathbb{R}$ to $\mathbb{Q}$ (say over ACA_0^ω). However, Theorem 15 and Corollary 16 show that admitting countably many points of discontinuity, one obtains principles that are extremely hard to prove following Remark 1.

Finally, one can greatly generalise Theorem 15 based on Remark 17. Indeed, there are many spaces intermediate between bounded variation and regulated, each of which yields a natural and equivalent restriction of NIN.

Remark 17 (Intermediate spaces). The following spaces are intermediate between bounded variation and regulated; all details may be found in [1]. Wiener spaces from mathematical physics are based on *p-variation*, which amounts to replacing '$|f(x_i) - f(x_{i+1})|$' by '$|f(x_i) - f(x_{i+1})|^p$' in the definition of variation. Young generalises this to ϕ-*variation* which instead involves $\phi(|f(x_i) - f(x_{i+1})|)$ for so-called Young functions ϕ, yielding the Wiener-Young spaces. Perhaps a simpler construct is the Waterman variation, which involves $\lambda_i |f(x_i) - f(x_{i+1})|$

and where $(\lambda_n)_{n\in\mathbb{N}}$ is a sequence of reals with nice properties; in contrast to bounded variation, any continuous function is included in the Waterman space ([1, Prop. 2.23]). Combining ideas from the above, the *Schramm variation* involves $\phi_i(|f(x_i) - f(x_{i+1})|)$ for a sequence $(\phi_n)_{n\in\mathbb{N}}$ of well-behaved 'gauge' functions. As to generality, the union (resp. intersection) of all Schramm spaces yields the space of regulated (resp. bounded variation) functions, while all other aforementioned spaces are Schramm spaces ([1, Prop. 2.43 and 2.46]). In contrast to bounded variation and the Jordan decomposition theorem, these generalised notions of variation have no known 'nice' decomposition theorem. The notion of *Korenblum variation* does have such a theorem (see [1, Prop. 2.68]) and involves a distortion function acting on the *partition*, not on the function values.

2.3   Connections to Mainstream Mathematics

We establish the connection between NIN and two theorems from mainstream mathematics, namely *Cousin's lemma* and *Jordan's decomposition theorem*.

First of all, our results have significant implications for the RM of Cousin's lemma. Indeed, as shown in [26], Z_2^ω cannot prove Cousin's lemma as follows:

$$(\forall \Psi : \mathbb{R} \to \mathbb{R}^+)(\exists y_0, \ldots, y_k \in [0,1])([0,1] \subset \cup_{i\le k} B(y_i, \Psi(y_i))), \qquad \text{(HBU)}$$

which expresses that the *canonical covering* $\cup_{x\in[0,1]} B(x, \Psi(x))$ has a finite sub-covering, namely given by $y_0, \ldots, y_k \in [0,1]$. In [4], it is shown that HBU formulated using *second-order codes* for Borel functions is provable in ATR_0 plus some induction. We now show that this result from [4] is entirely due to the presence of second-order codes. Indeed, by Theorem 18, the restriction of HBU to Borel functions still implies NIN, which is not provable in Z_2^ω by Remark 1. To this end, let HBU_{semi} (resp. $\text{HBU}_{\text{Borel}}$) be HBU restricted to $\Psi : [0,1] \to \mathbb{R}^+$ that are upper semi-continuous (resp. Borel) as in Definition 11 (resp. Definition 14).

Theorem 18 ($ACA_0^\omega + IND_0$). NIN *follows from* HBU_{semi} *and from* $\text{HBU}_{\text{Borel}}$; *extra induction is only needed in the first case.*

Proof. Let $Y : [0,1] \to \mathbb{N}$ be an injection and consider $\Psi(x) := \frac{1}{2^{Y(x)+3}}$, which is upper semi-continuous and Borel by the proof of Theorem 15. Now consider the uncountable covering $\cup_{x\in[0,1]} B(x, \frac{1}{2^{Y(x)+3}})$ of $[0,1]$. Since Y is an injection, we have $\sum_{i\le k} |B(x_i, \frac{1}{2^{Y(x_i)+3}})| \le \sum_{i\le k} \frac{1}{2^{i+2}} \le \frac{1}{2}$ for any finite sequence $x_0, \ldots, x_k$ of distinct reals in $[0,1]$. In this light, HBU_{semi} and $\text{HBU}_{\text{Borel}}$ are false. We note that the required basic measure theory (for finite sequences of intervals) can be developed in RCA_0 ([35, X.1]). $\qquad\square$

We now show that we can replace 'Borel' by 'Baire class 2' in Theorem 18, assuming the right (equivalent) definition. Now, *Baire classes* go back to Baire's 1899 dissertation ([2]) and a function is 'Baire class 0' if it is continuous and 'Baire class $n + 1$' if it is the pointwise limit of Baire class n functions. Baire's *characterisation theorem* ([3, p. 127]) expresses that a function is Baire class 1 iff there is a point of continuity of the induced function on each perfect set.

Now let B2 be the class of all $g : [0,1] \to \mathbb{R}$ such that $g = \lim_{n\to\infty} g_n$ on $[0,1]$ and where for all $n \in \mathbb{N}$ and perfect $P \subset [0,1]$, the restriction $g_{n\restriction P}$ has a point of continuity on P. We have the following corollary.

Corollary 19 ($\mathsf{ACA}_0^\omega + \mathsf{IND}_0$). *We have* $\mathsf{HBU}_{\mathsf{B2}} \to \mathsf{NIN}$ *where the former is the restriction of* HBU *to* $\Psi : [0,1] \to \mathbb{R}^+$ *in* B2.

Proof. Fix $A \subset [0,1]$ and $Y : [0,1] \to \mathbb{N}$ with Y is injective on A. Define $\Psi :$ $[0,1] \to \mathbb{R}^+$ as follows: $\Psi(x)$ is $\frac{1}{2^{Y(x)+5}}$ in case $x \in A$, and $1/8$ otherwise. Define Ψ_n as Ψ with the condition '$Y(x) \leq n+5$' in the first case. Clearly $\Psi = \lim_{n\to\infty} \Psi$ and $\Psi \in$ B2, as Ψ_n only has at most $n + 5$ points of discontinuity (the set of which is not perfect in $\mathsf{ACA}_0^\omega + \mathsf{IND}_0$). For a finite sub-covering $x_0, \ldots, x_k \in [0,1]$ of $\cup_{x\in[0,1]} B(x, \Psi(x))$, there must be $j \leq k$, with $x_j \notin A$. Indeed, the measure of $\cup_{i\leq k} B(x_i, \Psi(x_i))$ is otherwise below $\sum_{n=0}^k \frac{1}{2^{i+5}} < 1$, a contradiction as the required basic measure theory can be developed in RCA_0 ([35, X.1]). $\square$

Secondly, Jordan proves the following fundamental theorem about functions of bounded variation around 1881 in [16].

Theorem 20 (Jordan decomposition theorem). *Any* $f : [0,1] \to \mathbb{R}$ *of bounded variation is the difference of two non-decreasing functions* $g, h : [0,1] \to \mathbb{R}$.

Formulated using second-order codes, Theorem 20 is provable in ACA_0 (see [19, 25]); we now show that the third-order version is *hard to prove* as in Remark 1.

Theorem 21 (ACA_0^ω). *Each item implies the one below it.*

- *The Jordan decomposition theorem for the unit interval.*
- $\mathsf{HBU}_{\mathsf{bv}}$, *i.e.* HBU *restricted to* $\Psi : [0,1] \to \mathbb{R}^+$ *of bounded variation.*
- NIN: *there is no injection from* $[0,1]$ *to* $\mathbb{N}$.

Assuming IND_0, *we may replace the principle* $\mathsf{HBU}_{\mathsf{bv}}$ *by the following one:*

- *For* $f : [0,1] \to \mathbb{R}$ *of bounded variation, there is* $x \in [0,1]$ *such that* f *is continuous (or: quasi-continuous) at* x.

Proof. The points of discontinuity of a non-decreasing function can be enumerated in ACA_0^ω by [30, Lemma 3.3]. Now assume the Jordan decomposition theorem and fix some $\Psi : [0,1] \to \mathbb{R}^+$ of bounded variation. If $(x_n)_{n\in\mathbb{N}}$ enumerates all the points of discontinuity of Ψ, then the following also covers $[0,1]$.

$$\cup_{q\in\mathbb{Q}\cap[0,1]} B(q, \Psi(q)) \bigcup \cup_{n\in\mathbb{N}} B(x_n, \Psi(x_n)).$$

The second-order Heine-Borel theorem (provable in WKL_0 by [35, IV.1]) now yields a finite sub-covering, and $\mathsf{HBU}_{\mathsf{bv}}$ follows. Now assume the latter and suppose $Y : [0,1] \to \mathbb{N}$ is an injection. Define $\Psi : [0,1] \to \mathbb{N}$ as $\Psi(x) := \frac{1}{2^{Y(x)+3}}$. As in the proof of Corollary 19, any finite sub-covering of $\cup_{x\in[0,1]} B(x, \Psi(x))$ must have measure at most $1/2$, a contradiction; NIN follows and the first part is done.

For the second part of the theorem, we use the first part of the proof, namely that for $f : [0,1] \to \mathbb{R}$ of bounded variation, the points of discontinuity can be enumerated, say by $(x_n)_{n \in \mathbb{N}}$. By [35, II.4.9], the unit interval cannot be enumerated, i.e. there is $y \in [0,1]$ such that $(\forall n \in \mathbb{N})(x_n \neq y)$. By definition, f is continuous at y. For the final implication, consider $\Psi : [0,1] \to \mathbb{R}^+$ from the first part of the proof. The function Ψ is everywhere discontinuous in case Y is an injection; one seems to need IND_0 to prove this. Similarly, Ψ is not quasi-continuous at any $x \in [0,1]$, and we are done.   □

In conclusion, basic third-order theorems like Cousin's lemma and Jordan's decomposition theorem are 'hard to prove' in terms of conventional comprehension following Remark 1. Rather than measuring logical strength in terms of the one-dimensional scale provided by conventional comprehension, we propose an alternative *two-dimensional* scale, where the first dimension is based on conventional comprehension and the second dimension is based on the *neighbourhood function principle* NFP (see e.g. [37]). Thus, higher-order RM should seek out the minimal axioms needed to prove a given theorem of third-order arithmetic **and** these minimal axioms are in general a pair, namely a fragment of conventional comprehension and a fragment of NFP. This two-dimensional picture already exists in set theory where one studies which fragment of ZF and which fragments of AC are needed for proving a given theorem of ZFC. Note that ZF proves NFP as the choice functions in the latter are *continuous*.

References

1. Appell, J., Banaś, J., Merentes, N.: Bounded Variation and Around, vol. 17. De Gruyter, Berlin (2014)
2. Baire, R.: Sur les fonctions de variables réelles. Ann. Mat. **3**, 1–123 (1899)
3. Baire, R.: Leçons sur les fonctions discontinues. Les Grands Classiques Gauthier-Villars. Éditions Jacques Gabay. Reprint of the 1905 original (1995)
4. Barrett, J., Downey, R., Greenberg, N.: Cousin's lemma in second-order arithmetic. Preprint, arxiv: https://arxiv.org/abs/2105.02975 (2021)
5. Buchholz, W., Feferman, S., Pohlers, W., Sieg, W.: Iterated inductive definitions and subsystems of analysis. LNM, vol. 897. Springer, Heidelberg (1981)
6. Cantor, G.: Ueber eine eigenschaft des inbegriffs aller reellen algebraischen zahlen. J. Reine Angew. Math. **77**, 258–262 (1874)
7. Coolidge, J.L.: The lengths of curves. Amer. Math. Monthly **60**, 89–93 (1953)
8. Dirichlet, L.P.G.: Über die Darstellung ganz willkürlicher Funktionen durch Sinus- und Cosinusreihen. Repertorium der physik, bd. 1 (1837)
9. Dirksen, E.: Ueber die anwendung der analysis auf die rectification der curven. Akademie der Wissenschaften zu Berlin, pp. 123–168 (1833)
10. Dunham, J.M.C.: Application des méthodes générales à la science des nombres et à la science de l'étendue, vol II. Gauthier-Villars (1886)
11. Friedman, H.: Some systems of second order arithmetic and their use, pp. 235–242 (1975)
12. Friedman, H.: Systems of second order arithmetic with restricted induction, I & II (abstracts). J. Symb. Log. **41**, 557–559 (1976)

13. Friedman, H.: Remarks on reverse mathematics/1. FOM mailing list, 21 September 2021. https://cs.nyu.edu/pipermail/fom/2021-September/022875.html
14. Hrbacek, K., Jech, T.: Introduction to Set Theory. Monographs and Textbooks in Pure and Applied Mathematics, 3 edn., vol. 220. Marcel Dekker (1999)
15. Hunter, J.: Higher-order reverse topology. ProQuest LLC, Ann Arbor, MI. Thesis Ph.D. the University of Wisconsin - Madison (2008)
16. Jordan, C.: Sur la série de fourier. Compt. Rendus l'Acad. Sci. Paris Gauthier-Villars 92, 228–230 (1881)
17. Jordan, C.: Cours d'analyse de l'École polytechnique. Tome I. Les Grands Classiques Gauthier-Villars. Éditions Jacques Gabay. Reprint of the third (1909) edition (1991). First edition: 1883
18. Kohlenbach, U.: Higher order reverse mathematics, pp. 281–295 (2005)
19. Kreuzer, A.P.: Bounded variation and the strength of Helly's selection theorem. Log. Methods Comput. Sci. 10(4), 16, 15 (2014)
20. Kunen, K.: Set Theory. Studies in Logic, vol. 34. College Publications (2011)
21. Lakatos, I.: (2015)
22. Lorentzen, L., Waadeland, H.: Continued Fractions with Applications. Studies in Computational Mathematics, vol. 3. North-Holland (1992)
23. Montalbán, A.: Open questions in reverse mathematics. Bull. Sym. Log. 17(3), 431–454 (2011)
24. Neeman, I.: Necessary use of Σ_1^1 induction in a reversal. J. Symb. Log. 76(2), 561–574 (2011)
25. Nies, A., Triplett, M.A., Yokoyama, K.: The reverse mathematics of theorems of Jordan and Lebesgue. J. Symb. Log. 86, 1–18 (2021)
26. Normann, D., Sanders, S.: On the mathematical and foundational significance of the uncountable. J. Math. Log. 19, 1950001 (2019)
27. Normann, D., Sanders, S.: Open sets in reverse mathematics and computability theory. J. Log. Comput. 30(8), 40 (2020)
28. Normann, D., Sanders, S.: Pincherle's theorem in reverse mathematics and computability theory. Ann. Pure Appl. Log. 171(5), 102788, 41 (2020)
29. Normann, D., Sanders, S.: On robust theorems due to Bolzano, Weierstrass, and Cantor in reverse mathematics. https://arxiv.org/abs/2102.04787, p. 30 (2021, submitted)
30. Normann, D., Sanders, S.: Betwixt turing and kleene. In: Artemov, S., Nerode, A. (eds.) LFCS 2022. LNCS, vol. 13137, pp. 236–252. Springer, Cham (2022). https://doi.org/10.1007/978-3-030-93100-1_15
31. Normann, D., Sanders, S.: On the uncountability of ℝ. J. Symb. Log. 40 (2022, to appear). https://arxiv.org/abs/2007.07560
32. Sakamoto, N., Yamazaki, T.: Uniform versions of some axioms of second order arithmetic. MLQ Math. Log. Q. 50(6), 587–593 (2004)
33. Scheeffer, L.: Allgemeine untersuchungen über rectification der curven. Acta Math. 5(1), 49–82 (1884)
34. Simpson, S.G. (ed.): Reverse Mathematics 2001. Lecture Notes in Logic, vol. 21. ASL, La Jolla (2005)
35. Simpson, S.G.: Subsystems of Second Order Arithmetic. Perspectives in Logic, 2nd edn. Cambridge University Press, Cambridge (2009)
36. Stillwell, J.: Reverse Mathematics, Proofs from the Inside Out. Princeton University Press, Princeton (2018)
37. Troelstra, A.S., van Dalen, D.: Constructivism in Mathematics I. Studies in Logic and the Foundations of Mathematics, vol. 121. North-Holland (1988)

38. Veldman, W.: Understanding and using Brouwer's continuity principle. In: Schuster, P., Berger, U., Osswald, H. (eds.) Reuniting the Antipodes - Constructive and Nonstandard Views of the Continuum. Synthese Library, vol. 306, pp. 285–302. Springer, Dordrecht (2001). https://doi.org/10.1007/978-94-015-9757-9_24

39. Wikipedia, The Free Encyclopedia. Cantor's first set theory article (2022). https://en.wikipedia.org/wiki/Cantor%27s_first_set_theory_article

Boole vs Wadge: Comparing Two Basic Tools of Descriptive Set Theory

Victor Selivanov[✉] [iD]

A.P. Ershov Institute of Informatics Systems, and S.L. Sobolev Institute
of Mathematics, Novosibirsk, Russia
vseliv@iis.nsk.su

Abstract. We systematically compare ω-Boolean classes and Wadge classes, e.g. we complement the result of W. Wadge that the collection of non-self-dual levels of his hierarchy coincides with the collection of classes generated by Borel ω-ary Boolean operations from the open sets in the Baire space. Namely, we characterize the operations, which generate any given level in this way, in terms of the Wadge hierarchy in the Scott domain. As a corollary we deduce the non-collapse of the latter hierarchy. Also, the effective version of this topic is developed.

Keywords: ω-ary Boolean operation · Wadge hierarchy · quasi-Polish space · Baire space · Cantor space · Scott domain

1 Introduction

Set operations were central tools of classical descriptive set theory from its very beginning at the end of 19th century (E. Borel, H. Lebesgue, N.N. Luzin, M.Y. Suslin, A.N. Kolmogorov, F. Hausdorff, L.V. Kantorovich, E.M. Livenson, and many others). The set operations, now better known as ω-ary Boolean operations, gave rise to many important hierarchies in Polish and then quasi-Polish (QP-) spaces, including the Borel, Luzin, and Hausdorff hierarchies [1,3].

Only in the 1970s new basic tools of DST, namely the Wadge reducibility and Gale-Stewart games, were introduced giving rise to the Wadge hierarchy (WH) of Borel sets [21] in the Baire space. Under suitable set-theoretic assumptions, the WH was extended to arbitrary subsets of the Baire space [19] which subsumes the mentioned classical hierarchies, as well as many others. This approach to WH maybe developed without using the ω-ary Boolean operations at all.

Nevertheless, both approaches are closely related, as was demonstrated in [21] by showing that the collection of non-self-dual levels of the Borel WH coincides with the collection of classes (called ω-Boolean classes in the sequel), obtained by applying Borel ω-ary Boolean operations to the class of open sets in the

This work was supported by Mathematical Center in Akademgorodok under agreement No. 075-15-2022-281 from 05.04.2022 with the Ministry of Science and Higher Education of the Russian Federation.

Baire space; below we refer to this fact as the Wadge theorem. Again, this may be extended to arbitrary subsets of the Baire space under suitable set-theoretic assumptions [19]. For simplicity, we avoid foundational discussions and use the standard ZFC axioms, so some of our results are proved only for the Borel sets.

Outside zero-dimensional spaces, the relation between ω-Boolean classes and WH (which was recently extended to all QP-spaces [15]) is quite intricate, and some principal questions remained open even for the Baire space (e.g., the problem of characterizing the ω-ary Boolean operations which yield a given level of the WH as explained in the previous paragraph); below we sometimes refer to this question as the main problem of this paper. A systematic study of such questions was initiated in [9] and continued in [11,12] where some particular cases of the main problem were established.

In this paper we continue this investigation, in particular give a complete solution of the main problem. The corresponding characterization is based on the relation of this problem to the WH in Scott domain discovered in [11] when this WH was not yet defined. Thus, the complete answer would not be possible without the extension of the WH in [15]. Modulo this extension, our proofs here are easy. We also establish some basic facts on the WH in the Scott domain and some other quasi-Polish spaces (including the fundamental non-collapse property). This is interesting on its own because the WH in non-zero-dimensional spaces was not seriously studied before [15] where the corresponding questions were raised.

After recalling some basic notions and facts (including some new observations) in the next section, we provide relevant information about the ω-Boolean classes in Sect. 3. In Sect. 4 we prove our main results. In the last two sections we shortly outline the extension of this topic from sets to k-partitions and its effective version relevant to the fast evolving effective descriptive set theory; more detailed exposition should appear in the journal version of this paper.

2   Preliminaries

We use standard set-theoretic notation and terminology, in particular X^Y denotes the set of functions from Y to X. We often identify (using the characteristic functions) $P(X) = \{Y \mid Y \subseteq X\}$ with 2^X where $2 = \{0,1\}$.

We recall the definition of ω-ary Boolean operations introduced in [4]. Associate with any $A \subseteq 2^\omega$ an infinitary Boolean term d_A (in the signature $\{\cup, \cap, \overline{}\}$) with variables $v_0, v_1, \ldots$ as follows:

$$d_A = d_A(v_0, v_1, \ldots) = \bigcup_{a \in A} c_a(v_0, v_1, \ldots)$$

where

$$c_a(v_0, v_1, \ldots) = \left(\bigcap_{a(i)=1} v_i \right) \cap \left(\bigcap_{a(i)=0} \overline{v}_i \right).$$

Note that c_a is an infinitary analog of "elementary conjunctions" and d_A—of "disjunctive normal forms" in propositional logic.

The term d_A induces in the obvious way an ω-ary Boolean operation $d_A :$ $P(X)^\omega \to P(X)$ on $P(X)$ for every set X (actually on every complete Boolean algebra). Namely, for any $X_i \subseteq X$, let $d_A(X_0, \ldots)$ is the value of d_A under substitution $v_i = X_i$. We call two infinitary Boolean terms *equivalent* if they define the same infinitary operation in any complete Boolean algebra.

Let us formulate some known properties of the introduced notions. Let $\langle \cdot, \cdot \rangle$ be the standard computable bijection between $\omega \times \omega$ and ω.

Lemma 1. 1. The sets $c_a(X_0, \ldots) = \{x \in X \mid \forall i (x \in X_i \leftrightarrow i \in a)\}$, $a \subseteq \omega$, are pairwise disjoint.

2. $d_A(X_0, \ldots) = g^{-1}(A)$ where the function $g = g_{(X_0, \ldots)} : X \to P(\omega)$ is defined by $g(x) = \{i \in \omega \mid x \in X_i\}$.

3. $A \mapsto d_A(X_0, \ldots)$ is a homomorphism between complete Boolean algebras $(P(P(\omega)); \cup, \cap, \bar{}, \varnothing, P(\omega))$ and $(P(X); \cup, \cap, \bar{}, \varnothing, X)$.

4. $d_{\uparrow a}(X_0, \ldots) = \bigcap_{i \in a} X_i$, where $\uparrow a = \{b \subseteq \omega \mid a \subseteq b\}$ for every $a \subseteq \omega$.

5. $f^{-1}(d_A(X_0, \ldots)) = d_A(f^{-1}(X_0), f^{-1}(X_1), \ldots)$ for every $f : Y \to X$.

6. Any countable Boolean term is equivalent to the term d_A for some Borel set $A \subseteq 2^\omega$, and vice versa.

7. For any subsets $A, B_0, B_1, \ldots$ of 2^ω there is a unique $C \subseteq 2^\omega$ such that

$$d_C(X_0, \ldots) = d_A(d_{B_0}(X_{\langle 0,0 \rangle}, X_{\langle 0,1 \rangle}, \ldots), d_{B_1}(X_{\langle 1,0 \rangle}, X_{\langle 1,1 \rangle}, \ldots), \ldots)$$

uniformly on $X, X_0, \ldots$.

Proof Hints. Items (1–5) are well known and straightforward. Item (6) was observed in Theorem 6.4 of [9] where countable Boolean terms are also called ω_1-Boolean terms. For item (7) see e.g. Section 1.4 of [7].   □

In this paper we apply Boolean operations only to subsets of (topological) spaces, so we assume acquaintance with basic notions of topology. By a cb$_0$-space we mean a countably based T_0-space. Most often, we work with QP-spaces introduced in [1] which include Polish spaces, ω-continuous domains, and countably based spectral spaces.

A basic example of a QP-space is the Baire space $\mathcal{N} = \omega^\omega$. There are two natural topologies on $P(\omega) = 2^\omega$: the Cantor topology on 2^ω which gives rise to the Cantor space $\mathcal{C}$, and the Scott topology on $P(\omega)$ which gives rise to the Scott domain $P\omega$. Recall that a basis of the Cantor topology is given by the cones $[\sigma] = \sigma \cdot \mathcal{C}$, $\sigma \in 2^{<\omega}$, which are clopen sets in $\mathcal{C}$. A subbasis of the Scott topology is given by the sets $\uparrow i = \uparrow \{i\} = \{A \subseteq \omega \mid i \in A\}$. The precise relation between Cantor and Scott topologies are described in Theorem 5.3 of [11]; in particular, the Borel sets in both topologies are the same. Both spaces $\mathcal{C}, P\omega$ are QP.

The next lemma relates some properties of the operation $d_A : P(X^\omega) \to P(X)$ to topological properties of A w.r.t. the Cantor and Scott topologies.

Lemma 2. 1. For any open sets $X_0, X_1, \ldots$ in X, the function $g_{(X_0, \ldots)} : X \to P\omega$ is continuous.

2. For any $X_i \subseteq X$ and $\sigma \in 2^{<\omega}$ we have $g_{(X_0, \ldots)}^{-1}([\sigma]) = c_\sigma(X_0, \ldots, X_{|\sigma|-1})$, where $c_\sigma(v_0, \ldots, v_{|\sigma|-1}) = (\bigcap_{\sigma(i)=1} v_i) \cap (\bigcap_{\sigma(i)=0} \bar{v}_i)$ is the finitary version of the term c_a in Sect. 2.

3. Let $X = P(\omega)$. Then $g^{-1}_{(\uparrow 0, \uparrow 1, \ldots)}$ is the identity function on $P(\omega)$, and $A = d_A(\uparrow 0, \uparrow 1, \ldots)$.

4. For any Borel subsets $A, B_0, B_1, \ldots$ of $\mathcal{C}$, the set $C \subseteq 2^\omega$ from Lemma 1(7) is also Borel.

Proof. (1) It suffices to show that $g^{-1}_{(X_0, \ldots)}(\uparrow i)$ is open in X for every $i \in \omega$. This holds because $g^{-1}_{(X_0, \ldots)}(\uparrow i) = X_i$ by Lemma 1(4).

(2) Straightforward by the definitions.

(3) The first assertion holds by Lemma 1(2), and it immediately implies the second one.

(4) Follows from Theorem 6.4 of [9].   □

Next we recall the technical notion of a family of pointclasses from [13]. A *pointclass* $\Gamma(X)$ in a space X is a subset of $P(X)$. A *family of pointclasses* is a family $\Gamma = \{\Gamma(X)\}$ parametrized by arbitrary spaces (or by spaces in a natural class, say by the QP-spaces) such that $\Gamma(X) \subseteq P(X)$ for any space X, and $f^{-1}(A) \in \Gamma(X)$ for any $A \in \Gamma(Y)$ and any continuous function $f : X \to Y$. In particular, any pointclass $\Gamma X)$ in such a family is downward closed under the Wadge reducibility in X. Recall that $B \subseteq X$ is *Wadge reducible* to $A \subseteq X$ (in symbols $B \leq^X_W A$) if $B = f^{-1}(A)$ for some continuous function f on X. A basic example of a family of pointclasses is $\mathbf{O} = \{\mathbf{O}(X)\}$ where $\mathbf{O}(X)$ is the class of open sets in X. Another example is the family $\mathbf{B}$ of Borel pointclasses.

Let $A \subseteq 2^\omega$. With any pointclass $\Gamma(X)$ we associate the pointclass $\Gamma(X)_A = \{d_A(X_0, \ldots) \mid X_0, \ldots \in \Gamma(X)\}$. We also associate with A the operator $\Gamma \mapsto \Gamma_A$ on families of pointclasses defined by $\Gamma_A(X) = \Gamma(X)_A$.

Such operators $\Gamma \mapsto \Gamma_A$ subsume many useful concrete operators including the operator $\Gamma \mapsto \Gamma_\sigma$ where $\Gamma_\sigma(X)$ is the set of all countable unions of sets in $\Gamma(X)$, the operator $\Gamma \mapsto \Gamma_c$ where $\Gamma_c(X)$ is the set of all complements of sets in $\Gamma(X)$, the operator $\Gamma \mapsto \Gamma_d$ where $\Gamma_d(X)$ is the set of all differences of sets in $\Gamma(X)$, and the operator $\Gamma \mapsto \Gamma_p$ defined by $\Gamma_p(X) = \{pr_X(B) \mid B \in \Gamma(\mathcal{N} \times X)\}$ where $pr_X(B)$ is the projection to the second coordinate.

Iterating the operators from the previous paragraph in a familiar way (see e.g. [13] for details), we obtain the classical Borel $\{\boldsymbol{\Sigma}^0_\alpha\}_{\alpha < \omega_1}$, Luzin $\{\boldsymbol{\Sigma}^1_\alpha\}_{\alpha < \omega_1}$, and Hausdorff $\{\boldsymbol{\Sigma}^{-1}_\alpha\}_{\alpha < \omega_1}$ hierarchies treated as families of pointclasses. We use the standard $\boldsymbol{\Sigma}, \boldsymbol{\Pi}, \boldsymbol{\Delta}$-notation for the related levels of these and other hierarchies. We will freely use nice properties of these hierarchies in Polish spaces [3] which were extended to the QP-spaces in [1].

Many natural properties of families of pointclasses are preserved by the operators $\Gamma \mapsto \Gamma_A$. E.g., a family of pointclasses Γ is *reasonable* if for any numbering $\nu : \omega \to \Gamma(X)$ its universal set $U_\nu = \{(n, x) \mid x \in \nu(n)\}$ is in $\Gamma(\omega \times X)$; note that the family $\mathbf{O}$ is reasonable. Similarly, a representation $\nu : \mathcal{N} \to \Gamma(X)$ is a Γ-*total representation (TR)* if $U_\nu = \{(a, x) \mid x \in \nu(a)\}$ is in $\Gamma(\mathcal{N} \times X)$, and ν is a *principal* Γ-*TR* if it is a Γ-TR and any Γ-TR is reducible to ν.

Lemma 3. *1. If Γ is a family of pointclasses then so is also Γ_A.*

2. If Γ is reasonable then so is also Γ_A.

3. If X be a cb_0-space and $\Gamma(X)$ has a principal Γ-TR then so does $\Gamma_A(X)$.
4. Let X be a countably based space and let $\Gamma(X)$ be an arbitrary non-self-dual level of the above-mentioned classical hierarchies. Then $\Gamma(X)$ has a principal Γ-TR.
5. There is a binary operation $*$ on $P(2^\omega)$ such that $\Gamma(X)_{A*B} = (\Gamma(X)_A)_B$ for every pointclass $\Gamma(X)$. The class $\mathbf{B}(\mathcal{C})$ is closed under $*$.

Proof Hints. Item (1) follows from Lemma 1(5). Proofs of (2–4) may be found in [13]. Item (5) follows from Lemma 1(7) and Lemma 2(4) where $B_i = B$ for $i < \omega$, see Sect. 1.7 of [7] for details. □

We conclude this section with recalling some notation and facts about the WH. The quotient-poset of the preorder $(P(\mathcal{N}); \leq_W)$ under the induced equivalence relation $\equiv_W$ is called *the structure of Wadge degrees* in $\mathcal{N}$. W. Wadge [21] has characterised the structure of Wadge degrees of Borel sets (i.e., the quotient-poset of $(\mathbf{B}(\mathcal{N}); \leq_W)$) up to isomorphism. Namely, it is well founded and for every Borel sets A, B we have $A \leq_W B$ or $\mathcal{N} \setminus B \leq_W A$; in particular it has no 3 pairwise incomparable elements. He has also computed the rank v of this structure and has shown that if a Borel set A is self-dual, i.e. $A \leq_W \overline{A}$, (resp. non-self-dual) then any Borel set of the next Wadge rank is non-self-dual (resp. self-dual), any Borel set of Wadge rank of countable cofinality is self-dual, and any Borel set of Wadge rank of uncountable cofinality is non-self-dual.

In [18] the following separation theorem was established: For any non-self-dual Borel set A exactly one of the principal ideals $\{X \mid X \leq_W A\}$, $\{X \mid X \leq_W \overline{A}\}$ has the separation property. The mentioned results give rise to the WH which is, by definition, the sequence $\{\Sigma_\alpha(\mathcal{N})\}_{\alpha < v}$ of all non-self-dual principal ideals of $(\mathbf{B}(\mathcal{N}); \leq_W)$ that do not have the separation property and satisfy for all $\alpha < \beta < v$ the strict inclusion $\Sigma_\alpha(\mathcal{N}) \subset \Delta_\beta(\mathcal{N})$ where, as usual, $\Delta_\alpha(\mathcal{N}) = \Sigma_\alpha(\mathcal{N}) \cap \Pi_\alpha(\mathcal{N})$. The Σ, Π, and Δ-levels of WH are known as *Wadge classes*. The collection of Wadge classes is semi-well-ordered (SWO) by inclusion, i.e., it is well founded and for any Wadge classes $\mathcal{A}, \mathcal{B}$ we have: $\mathcal{A} \subseteq \mathcal{B}$ or $\mathcal{B}_c \subseteq \mathcal{A}$.

The WH was originally defined only for the Baire space, though the SWO-property is easily extended to all zero-dimensional Polish spaces. Since for many natural non-zero-dimensional spaces the structure of Wadge degrees was shown to be far from being SWO (this is e.g. the case for $P\omega$, see below), the extension of the WH to such spaces (say, to Polish or QP-spaces) is not obvious. To obtain an extension of WH to the QP-spaces that preserves the SWO-property, one can use the characterization of non-empty QP-spaces as precisely the cb_0-spaces X such that there is a continuous open surjection ξ from $\mathcal{N}$ onto X [1].

As suggested independently in [8,14], one can define the WH $\{\Sigma_\alpha(X)\}_{\alpha < v}$ in X by $\Sigma_\alpha(X) = \{A \subseteq X \mid \xi^{-1}(A) \in \Sigma_\alpha(\mathcal{N})\}$. One easily checks that the definition of $\Sigma_\alpha(X)$ does not depend on the choice of ξ, $\bigcup_{\alpha < v} \Sigma_\alpha(X) = \mathbf{B}(X)$, $\Sigma_\alpha(X) \subseteq \Delta_\beta(X)$ for all $\alpha < \beta < v$, and any $\Sigma_\alpha(X)$ is downward closed under the Wadge reducibility in X. Using modified versions of set operations in [21], relatively simple set-theoretic descriptions of levels of the WH in X was suggested in [15]. The description was used to prove some basic properties of the WH in X; it will also be used to deduce main results of this paper.

3 ω-Boolean Classes Under Inclusion

By ω-*Boolean classes* we mean classes of the form $\mathbf{\Gamma}(X)_A$, for some pointclass $\mathbf{\Gamma}(X)$ in a space X and $A \subseteq \mathcal{C}$. Let $\mathbf{\Gamma}(X)^+ = \{\mathbf{\Gamma}(X)_A \mid A \in \mathbf{B}(\mathcal{C})\}$ (resp. $\mathbf{\Gamma}(X)^* = \{\mathbf{\Gamma}(X)_A \mid A \subseteq \mathcal{C}\}$) be the collections of ω-Boolean classes generated from $\mathbf{\Gamma}(X)$ by the Borel (resp. by arbitrary) ω-ary Boolean operations. Since the aim of this paper is to compare such collections with the corresponding collections of Wadge classes in X, it is natural to ask when the collections of ω-Boolean classes are SWO by inclusion.

As mentioned in the introduction, most often the collections of ω-Boolean classes were considered over the family $\mathbf{\Gamma} = \mathbf{\Sigma}_1^0$ which is of course very natural. This case is also principal for our paper but other cases (e.g., other levels of the Borel hierarchy) are also natural. The next result, attributed in [20] to A. Miller, solves the analogue of the main problem of this paper for $\mathbf{\Delta}_1^0(\mathcal{C})$ as generating class.

Proposition 1. *For any $A \subseteq \mathcal{C}$ we have $d_A(\mathbf{\Delta}_1^0(\mathcal{C})) = \{B \mid B \leq_W^{\mathcal{C}} A\}$, hence $\mathbf{\Delta}_1^0(\mathcal{C})^*$ coincides with the collection of all Wadge classes in $\mathcal{C}$.*

Corollary 1. *The map $A \mapsto d_A(\mathbf{\Delta}_1^0(\mathcal{C}))$ induces an isomorphism between the structure of all Wadge degrees in $\mathcal{C}$ and the poset $(\mathbf{\Delta}_1^0(\mathcal{C})^*; \subseteq)$. Therefore, the poset $(\mathbf{\Delta}_1^0(\mathcal{C})^+; \subseteq)$ is SWO.*

The next broad extension of one direction of this corollary was obtained in Theorem 6.5 of [9] (we adjust the notation of [9] to this paper). It applies e.g. to all $\mathbf{\Delta}$-levels of Borel hierarchies as generator sets.

Proposition 2. *[9] Let $\mathbf{\Gamma}(X)$ be a subalgebra of the Boolean algebra $P(X)$. Then $A \leq_W^{\mathcal{C}} B$ implies $\mathbf{\Gamma}(X)_A \subseteq \mathbf{\Gamma}(X)_B$. Therefore, $(\mathbf{\Gamma}(X)^+; \subseteq)$ is SWO.*

This proposition implies that $(\mathbf{\Gamma}(X)^+; \subseteq)$ is SWO for many natural families of pointclasses $\mathbf{\Gamma}$.

Corollary 2. *1. Let X be an arbitrary space and $\mathbf{\Gamma} = \mathbf{\Delta}_{1+\alpha}^0$ for some $\alpha < \omega_1$. Then $(\mathbf{\Gamma}(X)^+; \subseteq)$ is SWO.*
2. Let X be a cb_0-space and $\mathbf{\Gamma} = \mathbf{\Sigma}_{2+\alpha}^0$ for some $\alpha < \omega_1$, or X be a zero-dimensional cb_0-space and $\mathbf{\Gamma} = \mathbf{\Sigma}_1^0$. Then $(\mathbf{\Gamma}(X)^+; \subseteq)$ is SWO.

Proof. Item (1) is immediate by Proposition 2, so consider item (2). Let $A = P(\omega) \setminus \{\varnothing\}$, then $\mathbf{E}_A = \mathbf{E}_\sigma$ for every family of pointclasses $\mathbf{E}$. Then $\mathbf{\Gamma}(X) = \mathbf{\Delta}(X)_A$, where $\mathbf{\Delta} = \mathbf{\Gamma} \cap \mathbf{\Gamma}_c$. For every set $B \in \mathbf{B}(\mathcal{C})$ we then have $\mathbf{\Gamma}(X)_B = \mathbf{\Delta}(X)_{A*B}$ and $A * B \in \mathbf{B}(\mathcal{C})$ by Lemma 3(5), so $\mathbf{\Gamma}(X)^+ \subseteq \mathbf{\Delta}(X)^+$. Since $(\mathbf{\Delta}(X)^+; \subseteq)$ is SWO by Proposition 2, so is also $(\mathbf{\Gamma}(X)^+; \subseteq)$.   □

Next we discuss the collection of ω-Boolean classes generated by the open sets in $P\omega$. The next result, which is a slight improvement of Theorem 6.3 in [10], is similar to Proposition 1 where Cantor space is replaced by Scott domain and clopen sets by open sets.

Proposition 3. *For any $A \subseteq P\omega$, $d_A(\mathbf{\Sigma}_1^0(P\omega)) = \{B \mid B \leq_W^{P\omega} A\}$.*

Proof. By Lemma 2(3), $A = d_A(\uparrow 0, \uparrow 1, \ldots) \in d_A(\Sigma^0_1(P\omega))$. Let now $B \leq^{P\omega}_W A$, so $B = f^{-1}(A)$ for some continuous function f on $P\omega$. By Lemma 1(5), $B = d_A(f^{-1}(\uparrow 0), f^{-1}(\uparrow 1), \ldots)$, hence $B \in d_A(\Sigma^0_1(P\omega))$. This proves the inclusion from right to left.

For the converse inclusion, let $B \in d_A(\Sigma^0_1(P\omega))$. Then, by Lemma 1(2), $B = g^{-1}_{(X_0,\ldots)}(A)$ for some open set X_i in $P\omega$. Since $g_{(X_0,\ldots)}$ is a continuous function on $P\omega$ by Lemma 2(1), $B \leq^{P\omega}_W A$. $\square$

Corollary 3. *The map $A \mapsto d_A(\Sigma^0_1(P\omega))$ induces an isomorphism between the structure of all Wadge degrees in $P\omega$ and $(\Sigma^0_1(P\omega)^*; \subseteq)$.*

In contrast with Corollary 1, the structure $(\Sigma^0_1(P\omega)^+; \subseteq)$ is far from being SWO, as it follows from the results in [2,10] about the structure of Wadge degrees in $P\omega$. In fact, as shown in [2], this structure (and even its small substructure of $\Delta^0_2(P\omega)$-degrees) has infinite antichains and infinite descending chains. Since the Borel Wadge classes in every QP-space is SWO, there is no hope to obtain a wide extension of the Wadge theorem beyond zero-dimensional spaces.

4 ω-Boolean Classes vs Wadge Classes

In this section we establish our main results, in particular we characterize the Borel ω-ary Boolean operations which generate any given non-self-dual level of the WH from the open sets in $\mathcal{N}$. This characterization is closely related to the WH in $P\omega$, as discovered in [11]; our main result is a broad extension of some partial results of that paper. The extension became possible after extending the WH to arbitrary spaces and establishing its useful properties in QP-spaces [15]. We also establish some new properties of these hierarchies which are interesting on their own. In particular, we prove the non-collapse of the WH in $P\omega$.

We start with a general fact about the WH in QP-spaces. The proof does not immediately follow from the definition of WH in QP-spaces at the end of Sect. 2. Instead, we use the equivalent set-theoretic definition of level $\Sigma_\alpha(X)$ of the WH in X and its properties described in [15]. Since these are rather technical, we give only a proof sketch. We think that reading the sketch with the paper [15] at hand should suffice for verification of the proof. We very briefly recall the corresponding terminology.

The definition is in terms of iterated $\{0,1\}$-labeled well founded trees T. In non-trivial cases (which hold in the proof) T is a well founded tree in $2^{<\omega}$ labeled by similar iterated trees $T(\tau) = \{\sigma \in 2^{<\omega} \mid \tau\sigma \in T\}$, $\tau \in T$ of lesser rank. With any such tree T we associate iterated T-families F of sets over $\mathcal{L} = \{\Sigma_{1+\gamma}(X)\}_{\gamma < \omega_1}$. Such a family F has the form $(\{U_\tau\}, \{F_\tau\}$ where $\{U_\tau\}_{\tau \in T}$ is a T-family of open sets and, for each $\tau \in T$, F_τ is an iterated $T(\tau)$-family of sets over $\mathcal{L} = \{\Sigma_{2+\gamma}(X)\}_{\gamma < \omega_1}$ of lesser rank. Intuitively, F represents a complex mind-change procedure (uniformly on the levels $\Sigma_{1+\gamma}(X)$) that defines a subset of X.

Let $\mathcal{L}(X,T)$ be the pointclass of sets defined by the T-families over $\mathcal{L}$. Then we can associate with any $\alpha < \upsilon$ an iterated $\{0,1\}$-labeled tree T_α in such a way that $\Sigma_\alpha(X) = \mathcal{L}(X, T)$. By the results in [15], the collection of all such $\mathcal{L}(\mathcal{N}, T)$ coincides with the collection of non-self-dual Borel Wadge classes in $\mathcal{N}$.

Recall that any T_0-space X has a partial order $\leq_X$ (the specialization order) defined as follows: $x \leq_X y$, if $x \in U$ implies $y \in U$, for any open set U.

Theorem 1. *Let X be a quasi-Polish space which has a smallest element $\perp$ w.r.t. the specialization order. Then the Wadge hierarchy in X is discrete, i.e., $\Delta_\alpha(X) = \bigcup_{\beta<\alpha}(\Sigma_\beta(X) \cup \Pi_\beta(X))$ for every $\alpha < \upsilon$.*

Proof Sketch. We argue by cases. The case $\alpha = 0$ is trivial since $\Delta_0 = \varnothing$. Let now α be a limit ordinal of uncountable cofinality. By the properties of WH in $\mathcal{N}$, we have $\Delta_\alpha(\mathcal{N}) = \bigcup_{\beta<\alpha} \Sigma_\beta(\mathcal{N})$. By the preservation property of the WH in X (see Theorem 4.6 in [15]), we obtain $\Delta_\alpha(X) = \bigcup_{\beta<\alpha} \Sigma_\beta(X)$. Note that the existence of the smallest element is not in fact needed in this case.

Let now α be a limit ordinal of countable cofinality (note that in this case the equality $\Delta_\alpha(\mathcal{N}) = \bigcup_{\beta<\alpha}(\Sigma_\beta(\mathcal{N}) \cup \Pi_\beta(\mathcal{N}))$ fails, hence the argument of the previous paragraph does not work). By the inclusions of levels of the WH X, it suffices to show the inclusion $\Delta_\alpha(X) \subseteq \bigcup_{\beta<\alpha}(\Sigma_\beta(X) \cup \Pi_\beta(X))$. Let $S \in \Delta_\alpha(X)$, then both $S, \overline{S}$ are in $\Sigma_\alpha(X)$, hence S (resp. $\overline{S}$) is defined by a T_α-family $F = (\{U_\tau\}, \{F_\tau\}$ (resp. $G = (\{V_\tau\}, \{G_\tau\})$.

From Definition 3.1 in [15], the countable cofinality of α, and the structure of WH [21] it is not hard to deduce that the root label of T_α is 0 and, since $S \cup \overline{S} = X$, $X = (U_0 \cup U_1 \cup \cdots) \cup (V_0 \cup V_1 \cup \cdots)$. Therefore, $\perp$ is in one of these sets U_i, V_i, let e.g. $\perp \in U_i$. Since U_i is open and $\perp$ is smallest w.r.t. $\leq_X$, we get $X = U_i$. By Lemma 3.34(3) in [15] we get $S \in \mathcal{L}(X, T_\alpha(i))$, hence $\xi^{-1}(S) \in \mathcal{L}(\mathcal{N}, T_\alpha(i))$ where $\xi : \mathcal{N} \to X$ is a continuous open surjectiion. But $T_\alpha(i) \lhd T_\alpha$, hence $\xi^{-1}(S)$ is in $\Sigma_\beta(\mathcal{N}) \cup \Pi_\beta(\mathcal{N})$ for some $\beta < \alpha$. By the preservation property, $S \in \Sigma_\beta(X) \cup \Pi_\beta(X)$.

Finally, let $\alpha = \beta + 1$ be a successor ordinal, then we have to prove that $\Delta_\alpha(X) = \Sigma_\beta(X) \cup \Pi_\beta(X)$ (note that the equality $\Delta_\alpha(\mathcal{N}) = \Sigma_\beta(\mathcal{N}) \cup \Pi_\beta(\mathcal{N})$ fails, hence again the result again does not follow directly from the preservation property). The argument used for ordinals of countable cofinality, also works in this case, and shows that $\Delta_\alpha(X) \subseteq \Sigma_\beta(X) \cup \Pi_\beta(X)$. $\square$

By Wadge theorem, $\{d_A(\Sigma_1^0(\mathcal{N}) \mid A \in \mathbf{B}(P\omega)\} = \{\Sigma_\alpha(\mathcal{N}), \Pi_\alpha(\mathcal{N}) \mid \alpha < \upsilon\}$. A natural question is to characterize, for any given $\alpha < \upsilon$, the Borel sets $A \subseteq P\omega$ for which $d_A(\Sigma_1^0(\mathcal{N})) = \Sigma_\alpha(\mathcal{N})$. The answer is given in the next theorem that extends several particular cases obtained in [11, 12].

Theorem 2. *Let $A \in \mathbf{B}(P\omega)$ and $\alpha < \upsilon$. Then $d_A(\Sigma_1^0(\mathcal{N})) = \Sigma_\alpha(\mathcal{N})$ iff $A \in \Sigma_\alpha(P\omega) \setminus \Pi_\alpha(P\omega)$.*

Proof. Let first $A \in \Sigma_\alpha(P\omega) \setminus \Pi_\alpha(P\omega)$. By Lemma 2(1), the function $g_{(X_0,\dots)} : \mathcal{N} \to P\omega$ is continuous for all $X_i \in \Sigma_1^0(\mathcal{N})$. As $A \in \Sigma_\alpha(P\omega)$, by Proposition 4.2 in [15] we obtain $g_{(X_0,\dots)}^{-1}(A) \in \Sigma_\alpha(\mathcal{N})$, for all $X_i \in \Sigma_1^0(\mathcal{N})$. Therefore, $d_A(\Sigma_1^0(\mathcal{N})) \subseteq \Sigma_\alpha(\mathcal{N})$ by Lemma 1(2).

For the converse inclusion, consider the open continuous surjection $\rho : \mathcal{N} \to P\omega$ where $\rho(x) = \{n \mid \exists i(x(i) = n + 1)\}$. Then $\rho^{-1}(A) \in \boldsymbol{\Sigma}_\alpha(\mathcal{N}) \setminus \boldsymbol{\Pi}_\alpha(\mathcal{N})$ by the preservation property, hence $\rho^{-1}(A)$ is Wadge complete in $\boldsymbol{\Sigma}_\alpha(\mathcal{N})$. As $d_A(\boldsymbol{\Sigma}_1^0(\mathcal{N}))$ is downward closed under $\leq_W^{\mathcal{N}}$ by Lemma 3(1), it suffices to show that $\rho^{-1}(A) \in d_A(\boldsymbol{\Sigma}_1^0(\mathcal{N}))$. But $A = d_A(\uparrow 0, \uparrow 1, \ldots)$ by Lemma 2(3), hence $\rho^{-1}(A) = d_A(\rho^{-1}(\uparrow 0), \rho^{-1}(\uparrow 1), \ldots)$ by Lemma 1(5), and $\rho^{-1}(\uparrow 0), \rho^{-1}(\uparrow 1), \ldots$ are open in $\mathcal{N}$.

For the opposite implication, let $d_A(\boldsymbol{\Sigma}_1^0(\mathcal{N})) = \boldsymbol{\Sigma}_\alpha(\mathcal{N})$. Let β be the least ordinal such that $A \in \boldsymbol{\Sigma}_\beta \cup \boldsymbol{\Pi}_\beta$. Since $P\omega$ is a QP-space and $\varnothing$ is the smallest element w.r.t. $\leq_{P\omega}$, by Theorem 1 we get that either $A \in \boldsymbol{\Sigma}_\beta \setminus \boldsymbol{\Pi}_\beta$ or $A \in \boldsymbol{\Pi}_\beta \setminus \boldsymbol{\Sigma}_\beta$. By the proof above, either $d_A(\boldsymbol{\Sigma}_1^0(\mathcal{N})) = \boldsymbol{\Sigma}_\beta(\mathcal{N})$ or $d_A(\boldsymbol{\Sigma}_1^0(\mathcal{N})) = \boldsymbol{\Pi}_\beta(\mathcal{N})$. By the properties of WH in $\mathcal{N}$, the first alternative holds and $\beta = \alpha$. $\qquad\square$

We conclude this section with some corollaries of the above results concerning the non-collapse property of the WH in some natural QP-spaces. We say that the WH in X does not collapse, if $\boldsymbol{\Sigma}_\alpha(X) \nsubseteq \boldsymbol{\Pi}_\alpha(X)$ for all $\alpha < \upsilon$. The non-collapse property was investigated in [17] where its close relation to the preorder $\leq_{co}$ on spaces was established, where $X \leq_{co} Y$ iff there is a continuous open surjection from Y onto X.

Theorem 3. *Let X be a quasi-Polish space such that $P\omega \leq_{co} X$. Then the WH in X does not collapse, and Theorem 2 holds for X in place of $P\omega$.*

Proof. As noticed in the proof of Theorem 2, the WH in $P\omega$ is discrete. We show that it also does not collapse, i.e., $\boldsymbol{\Sigma}_\alpha(P\omega) \nsubseteq \boldsymbol{\Pi}_\alpha(P\omega)$ for every $\alpha < \upsilon$. By the Wadge theorem, $d_A(\boldsymbol{\Sigma}_1^0(\mathcal{N})) = \boldsymbol{\Sigma}_\alpha(\mathcal{N})$ for some Borel $A \subseteq P\omega$. By Theorem 2, $A \in \boldsymbol{\Sigma}_\alpha(P\omega) \setminus \boldsymbol{\Pi}_\alpha(P\omega)$, so the WH in $P\omega$ does not collapse. Since $P\omega \leq_{co} X$, the FH in X does not collapse as well by Proposition 3(1) in [17]. Let $f : X \to P\omega$ be a continuous open surjection. Repeating the proof of Theorem 2 with X in place of $\mathcal{N}$ and f in place of ρ, we get the proof of the remaining statement. $\square$

The above theorems apply to several natural spaces. We illustrate this by only one example. Let $\omega_\perp^\omega$ be the Kleene domain considered in [10,11], i.e., the set of partial functions on ω with the Scott topology. It is well known and easy to see that $\omega_\perp^\omega$ is an ω-algebraic domain.

Corollary 4. *The Wadge hierarchy in $\omega_\perp^\omega$ is discrete, and Theorem 3 holds for $X = \omega_\perp^\omega$.*

Proof. Since $\omega_\perp^\omega$ is an ω-algebraic domain, it is also a QP-space [1]. Since the empty function $\perp$ is the smallest element w.r.t. the specialization order $\sqsubseteq$ in $\omega_\perp^\omega$, the WH in $\omega_\perp^\omega$ is discrete by Theorem 1. Since $rng : \omega_\perp^\omega \to P\omega$ is a continuous open surjection, the remaining assertion follows by Theorem 3. $\qquad\square$

5   Extension to k-partitions

The Wadge theory has an interesting extension from sets to k-partitions, and even to Q-partitions, for any better quasiorder (BQO) Q [5,15]. Here we very briefly and informally discuss the extension of above results to this context, focusing on k-partitions.

Instead of the sets $A \subseteq 2^\omega$ used to define the ω-ary Boolean operations, we now use k-partitions $A : 2^\omega \to \bar{k}$, where $2 \leq k < \omega$ and $\bar{k} = \{0, \ldots, k-1\}$ is an antichain with k elements; sets correspond to 2-partitions. The operation $d_A : P(X)^\omega \to P(X)$ from Sect. 2 now becomes the operation $d_A : P(X)^\omega \to \bar{k}^X$ defined by $d_A(X_0, \ldots) = A \circ g_{(X_0, \ldots)}$. It is easy to check that all items in Lemmas 1 and 2 which make sense under this extension, remain true.

The extension of results about pointclasses requires a straightforward extension of the notion of a family of pointclasses to that of a family of partition-classes described in [13]; in particular, the Wadge reducibility $\leq_W^X$ is extended to k-partitions as follows: for $A, B \in \bar{k}^X$, $A \leq_W^X B$ iff $A = B \circ f$ for some continuous function f on X. With this at hand, we associate with any $A \subseteq 2^\omega$ the operator $\mathbf{\Gamma} \mapsto \mathbf{\Gamma}_A$ sending families of pointclasses to families of partitionclasses by $\mathbf{\Gamma}_A(X) = \mathbf{\Gamma}(X)_A$ where $\mathbf{\Gamma}(X)_A = \{A \circ g_{(X_0, \ldots)} \mid X_i \in \mathbf{\Gamma}(X)\}$. The analogue of Lemma 3 is now straightforward. As already mentioned, the extension of WH in $\mathcal{N}$ to k-partition was made in [5], and to all spaces in [15]. Note that the collections of levels of these hierarchies are BQOs under inclusion.

The versions of the collections $\mathbf{\Gamma}(X)^+ = \{\mathbf{\Gamma}(X)_A \mid A \in \mathbf{B}(\mathcal{C})\}$ and $\mathbf{\Gamma}(X)^* = \{\mathbf{\Gamma}(X)_A \mid A \subseteq \mathcal{C}\}$ from Sect. 3 are defined in the same way, only now A range over the Borel k-partitions of $\mathcal{C}$ in the first case and over all k-partitions of $\mathcal{C}$ in the second case. With these modifications, analogues of the results in Sect. 3 hold with almost the same proofs, only in the formulations which mention the SWO-property it should be replaced by the BQO-property.

The main results in the previous section also extend to k-partitions but the proof of the extension of Theorem 2 requires some additional efforts because it essentially depends on the Wadge theorem. Its extension to k-partitions may be proven with a heavy use on notions and techniques from [15]; full details cannot be included in this conference paper.

6   Effectivization

The effective version of descriptive set theory was first developed in computability theory for concrete popular zero-dimensional spaces. More recently, it was extended to broader classes of effective spaces interesting to computer science. Here we briefly and informally discuss effective aspects of the topic developed in this paper.

Instead of abstract spaces, we now have to deal with effective spaces, and several classes of such spaces (say, the effective cb_0-spaces) are now commonly known. In such spaces one always has a numbering of a base which induces effective versions of basic topological notions, including those of effectively open sets, computable functions, effectively open functions, and so on. A more recent notion is that of a computable QP-space; this is an effective cb_0-space X such that there exists a computable effectively open surjection $\xi : \mathcal{N} \to X$ onto X (see e.g. [16] for details). A lot of important spaces are computable QP. Also, the classical hierarchies are readily effectivized; levels of the effective versions are denoted in the same manner as levels of the corresponding classical ones, but using the lightface letters Σ, Π, Δ instead of the boldface $\boldsymbol{\Sigma}, \boldsymbol{\Pi}, \boldsymbol{\Delta}$ used for the classical hierarchies.

An *effective family of pointclasses* is a family $\Gamma = \{\Gamma(X)\}$ parametrized by effective cb_0-spaces (or, say the computable QP-spaces such that $\Gamma(X) \subseteq P(X)$ and $f^{-1}(A) \in \Gamma(X)$ for any $A \in \Gamma(Y)$ and any computable function $f : X \to Y$. In particular, any effective pointclass $\Gamma(X)$ is downward closed under the effective Wadge reducibility $\leq_{eW}^{X}$ in X, where $B \leq_{eW}^{X} A$ iff $B = f^{-1}(A)$ for some computable function f on X. Natural examples are the family $O = \{O(X)\}$ where $O(X)$ is the class of effectively open sets in X, the family $B = \{B(X)\}$ of the effectively Borel pointclasses, and any level of the effective versions of the classical hierarchies. An effective family Γ is *numbered* if there are numberings $\gamma_X : \omega \to \Gamma(X)$ such that $U_{\gamma_X} \in \Gamma(\omega \times X)$ for all X; all mentioned examples of effective families are numbered. As above, we associate with any $A \subseteq 2^{\omega}$ and any numbered effective family Γ the family Γ_A by $\Gamma_A(X) = \Gamma(X)_A$, where $\Gamma(X)_A = \{g_{(X_0,...)}^{-1}(A) \mid \{X_i\}$ is computable w.r.t. $\gamma_X\}$. With these notions at hand, many effective analogues of facts in Sect. 2 hold. In particular, $\Gamma \mapsto \Gamma_A$ is an operator on the effective families of pointclasses.

The effective versions

$$\Gamma(X)^{+} = \{\Gamma(X)_A \mid A \in B(\mathcal{C})\}, \ \Gamma(X)^{*} = \{\Gamma(X)_A \mid A \subseteq \mathcal{C}\}$$

of the collections

$$\boldsymbol{\Gamma}(X)^{+} = \{\boldsymbol{\Gamma}(X)_A \mid A \in \mathbf{B}(\mathcal{C})\}, \ \boldsymbol{\Gamma}(X)^{*} = \{\boldsymbol{\Gamma}(X)_A \mid A \subseteq \mathcal{C}\}$$

from Sect. 3 are defined in the same way, only now A range over the effectively Borel subsets of $\mathcal{C}$ in the first case. With these modifications at hand, analogues of the results in Sect. 3 hold with almost the same proofs, with only important difference that now the SWO- and BQO-properties fail because the effective Wadge reducibility induces very rich structures (e.g., in the space ω this reducibility is just the many-one reducibility).

There are at least two natural ways to obtain modifications leading to results resembling the results in the previous sections, also with the SWO- and BQO-properties. The first one is to restrict considerations to finite-ary Boolean operations instead of the ω-ary ones. This approach was explored already in [9] and led to a nice theory for the case of sets; this approach may also be straightforwardly extended to the case of k-partitions if we apply the finitary effective WH developed in [16].

Another approach is to develop the effective infinitary version of the WH from [6]. We guess that the effective version WH in QP-spaces from [15] based on the ideas and results of [6] will lead to a satisfactory effective analogues of the main results, including Theorem 2. We hope to do this in the journal version of this paper.

References

1. de Brecht, M.: Quasi-Polish spaces. Ann. Pure Appl. Logic **164**, 356–381 (2013)
2. Duparc, J., Vuilleumier, L.: The Wadge order on the Scott domain is not a well-quasi-order. J. Symb. Log. **85**(1), 300–324 (2020)
3. Kechris, A.S.: Classical Descriptive Set Theory. Graduate Texts in Mathematics, vol. 156. Springer, New York (1995). https://doi.org/10.1007/978-1-4612-4190-4
4. Kantorovich, L.V., Livenson, E.M.: Memoir on the analytical operations and projective sets I. Fund. Math. **18**, 214–271 (1932)
5. Kihara, T., Montalbán, A.: On the structure of the Wadge degrees of bqo-valued Borel functions. Trans. Amer. Math. Soc. **371**(11), 7885–7923 (2019)
6. Louveau, A.: Some results in the Wadge hierarchy of Borel sets. In: Kechris, A.S., Martin, D.A., Moschovakis, Y.N. (eds.) Cabal Seminar 79–81. Lecture Notes in Mathematics, vol. 1019, pp. 28–55. Springer, Heidelberg (1983). https://doi.org/10.1007/BFb0071692
7. Ochan, Y.S.: Theory of operations over sets. Uspekchy Mat. Nauk **10**(3), 71–128 (1955). (in Russian)
8. Pequignot, Y.: A Wadge hierarchy for second countable spaces. Arch. Math. Log. **54**, 659–683 (2015). https://doi.org/10.1007/s00153-015-0434-y
9. Selivanov, V.L.: Fine hierarchies and Boolean terms. J. Symb. Logic **60**(1), 289–317 (1995)
10. Selivanov, V.L.: Variations on the Wadge reducibility. Sib. Adv. Math. **15**(3), 44–80 (2005)
11. Selivanov, V.L.: Hierarchies in φ-spaces and applications. Math. Logic Q. **51**(1), 45–61 (2005)
12. Selivanov, V.L.: Classifying countable Boolean terms. Algebra Logic **44**(2), 95–108 (2005)
13. Selivanov, V.L.: Total representations. Log. Methods Comput. Sci. **9**(2), 1–30 (2013)
14. Selivanov, V.L.: Towards a descriptive theory of cb$_0$-spaces. Math. Struct. Comput. Sci. **28**(8), 1553–1580 (2017). Earlier version in arXiv: 1406.3942v1 [Math.GN] 16 June 2014
15. Selivanov, V.: A Q-Wadge hierarchy in quasi-Polish spaces. J. Symb. Log. (2019). https://doi.org/10.1017/jsl.2020.52
16. Selivanov, V.L.: Effective Wadge hierarchy in computable quasi-Polish spaces. Sib. Electron. Math. Rep. **18**(1), 121–135 (2021) https://doi.org/10.33048/semi.2021.18.010. arXiv:1910.13220v2
17. Selivanov, V.: Non-collapse of the effective wadge hierarchy. In: De Mol, L., Weiermann, A., Manea, F., Fernández-Duque, D. (eds.) CiE 2021. LNCS, vol. 12813, pp. 407–416. Springer, Cham (2021). https://doi.org/10.1007/978-3-030-80049-9_40
18. Steel, J.: Determinateness and the separation property. J. Symbol. Logic **45**, 143–146 (1980)
19. Wesep, R.: Wadge degrees and descriptive set theory. In: Kechris, A.S., Moschovakis, Y.N. (eds.) Cabal Seminar 76–77. LNM, vol. 689, pp. 151–170. Springer, Heidelberg (1978). https://doi.org/10.1007/BFb0069298
20. Van Wesep, R.: Subsystems of second-order arithmetic, and descriptive set theory under the axiom of determinateness. Ph.D. thesis, University of California, Berkeley (1977)
21. Wadge, W.: Reducibility and Determinateness in the Baire Space. Ph.D. thesis, University of California, Berkely (1984)

Computational Complexity of Classical Solutions of Partial Differential Equations

Svetlana Selivanova[✉]

KAIST, School of Computing, Daejeon, Republic of Korea
sweseliv@gmail.com

Abstract. This paper provides a brief survey of recent achievements in characterizing computational complexity of partial differential equations (PDEs), as well as computing solutions with guaranteed precision within the exact real computation approach. The emphasis is on classical solutions and linear PDE systems, since these are the cases where most of the progress has been achieved so far. Complexity, as it turns out, heavily depends on the smoothness of the initial data, which has similarities with the situation for ordinary differential equations (ODEs).

1 Introduction

Differential equations model various processes in physics, engineering and many other areas, which requires solving them exactly or approximately. Especially for safety critical and small scale applications it is important to compute the solutions with arbitrary guaranteed prescribed precision. While explicit solutions formulas can be derived for some particular cases, most problems are solved numerically which often leads to computational instabilities.

The computable analysis paradigm [2,25,34] provides a rigorous framework for computation over continuous structures, which gives rise to the exact real computation approach, see [22] and references therein. This approach is different from symbolic computation in computer algebra, as well as being different from traditional reliable numerical methods. In particular, real numbers are treated as exact entities (as opposed to intervals, see, e.g., [23]), and the solutions to various continuous problems are computed by approximation up to guaranteed absolute error $1/2^n$, where n is the desirable number of the output digits (as opposed to intermediate precision propagation).

In order to assess the efficiency of such computations, it is important to characterize the bit-cost of the considered algorithms, and also potentially find the

Supported by the National Research Foundation of Korea (grant 2017R1E1A1 A03071032) and by the International Research & Development Program of the Korean Ministry of Science and ICT (grant 2016K1A3A7A03950702) and by the NRF Brain Pool program (grant 2019H1D3A2A02102240) and by the RFBR-JSPS Grant 20-51-50001. The author is thankful to Victor Selivanov, Holger Thies and Martin Ziegler for valuable discussions.

U. Berger et al. (Eds.): CiE 2022, LNCS 13359, pp. 299–312, 2022.
https://doi.org/10.1007/978-3-031-08740-0_25

optimal complexity class corresponding to the original problem, as well as the optimal algorithm. In [3,8,14,15,35] the real bit-complexity approach is developed (see also the survey [13] and references therein); bit-cost is measured w.r.t. the output precision parameter n. In particular, the real-valued counterparts of the classical "discrete" complexity classes can be defined:

$$NC \subseteq P_1 \subseteq P \subseteq NP \subseteq \#P_1 \subseteq \#P \subseteq PSPACE = PAR \subseteq EXP. \qquad (1)$$

For simplicity of notation, we identify decision and functional complexity classes, e.g., write P instead of FP.

There has been significant progress in relating broad classes of ordinary differential equations (ODEs) to these complexity classes: [1,7,9,10,12,24], see also the recent survey [6] and references therein. The survey [6] extensively covers the current achievements in computability of ODEs and of partial differential equations (PDEs); as mentioned therein, most computability results are for particular cases of practically important PDEs, some of them nonlinear, e.g. Korteweg de Vries [5] and Navier-Stokes [33] equations.

However, there is hope to relate broad classes of PDEs to the complexity classes (1) in a similar way as being pursued for ODEs, as well as for other problems on continuous structures. This is a natural program of investigations that should be highly rewarding for both classical analysis/numerical methods and computability/complexity theories.

One of the main goals of the present survey is to highlight the current progress and possible directions of future research in computational complexity and exact real computation of PDEs systematically, in order to potentially achieve as clear and full picture as there is for ODEs. See a brief summary of ODE/PDE complexity results in Table 1 below and detailed formulations for PDEs in Sects. 2, 3. For ODEs (2) (below), it has been proved that computing the solution $\vec{u} = \vec{u}(t)$ is in general PSPACE-complete [7,9], and there is a polynomial time algorithm, if the right-hand side function is analytic and polynomial time computable (see [10] for a uniform result, and [24] for the case of unbounded domains). For PDEs, which also involve spatial derivatives of the unknown function $\vec{u} = \vec{u}(t, x_1, \ldots, x_d)$, there are more possibilities to consider:

- Linear (w.r.t. the derivatives of $\vec{u}$; the coefficients may nonlinearly depend on $\vec{x}$), quasilinear (the coefficients may also depend on $\vec{u}$) and nonlinear;
- With coefficients, initial and/or boundary conditions belonging to different functional classes, such as analytic, finitely continuously differentiable or Sobolev spaces;
- Hyperbolic, parabolic or elliptic types in the 2-dimensional case; in the general case there is no full classification, but there are other important subclasses, e.g., subelliptic, subparabolic, etc.

Currently only the classical (analytic and finitely continuously differentiable) solutions of PDEs have been considered from the real complexity viewpoint, since the real complexity approach is based on evaluating the function, while integrable/Sobolev functions cannot be evaluated at a given point. Therefore the definitions of bit-complexity of such generalized functions still need to be fully worked out; such work is started in [19, 32]. Most of the progress has been by now achieved for linear (systems of) PDEs, and the complexity classification for them is close to clear, while for quasilinear systems there are only upper bounds such as 2-EXP.

Table 1. Brief summary of ODE/PDE complexity results; see the cited papers for detailed assumptions.

ODEs	Evolutionary PDEs (including Hyperbolic and Parabolic)	Other Types of PDEs (including Elliptic)
$$\begin{cases} \frac{d}{dt}\vec{u} = f(t,\vec{u}), \\ \vec{u}(0) = \vec{v} \end{cases} \quad (2)$$	$$\begin{cases} \vec{u}_t = \sum_{\lvert \vec{j} \rvert} \mathbf{B}_{\vec{j}}(\vec{x}) \cdot \partial^{\vec{j}}\vec{u}, \\ \vec{u}(0,\vec{x}) = \varphi(\vec{x}) \end{cases}$$	$$\begin{cases} \sum_{j=1}^{d} \frac{\partial^2}{\partial x_j^2} u = f \text{ in } B^d \\ u\mid_{\partial B^d} = g(\vec{x}) \end{cases}$$
▷ $f \in$ P analytic $\Longrightarrow \vec{u} \in$ P ([10] uniform parametrized complexity result; [24] for unbounded domains and polynomial f) ▷ $f \in$ P linear $\Longrightarrow \vec{u} \in$ Log²-SPACE [18] ▷ $f \in$ P Lipschitz or $C^1 \Longrightarrow \vec{u}$ PSPACE-"complete" [7, 9]	▷ $\varphi, B_j \in$ P analytic $\Longrightarrow \vec{u} \in$ P ([18]; [29] uniform version; [27, 30] analysis of dependence on constant matrix coefficients $B_j = B_j^*$ over various real closed fields) ▷ $\varphi, B_j \in$ P: $C^k, k \geq 1$ (well posed) $\Longrightarrow$ [16,17] • $\vec{u} \in$ PSPACE-"complete" (general case) • $\vec{u} \in \#$P (constant periodic case) • $\vec{u}\#$P$_1$-"hard" (heat equation) • $\vec{u} \in$ P for constant mutually commuting matrices ▷ for the quasilinear case $B_j = B_j(\vec{x},\vec{u})$ upper bound 2-EXP [18].	▷ $f, g \in$ P $\Longrightarrow u \in \#$P; $\#$P$_1$-"hard" [11]

Thus far it has been productive to study bit-complexity of classical numerical and analytic approaches adapted to the computable analysis framework, and try to optimize them; as well as prove hardness results, demonstrating the best potentially possible lower bound. Most of the results are currently obtained for linear systems of PDEs; some of the methods can be extended to nonlinear PDEs as well (by now with "bad" upper bounds only). The evolutionary PDEs (4), discussed below, include such practically important examples as the heat, wave and Schroedinger equations, as well as acoustics, elasticity and Maxwell systems. Similarly to the ODE case, analytic initial data yield polynomial time computable solutions in many important cases, while finitely continuously differentiable ones yield PSPACE or $\#$P.

Section 2 is essentially based on the papers [11, 16, 18] and overviews the recent results on characterizing complexity of computing the solution from the fixed polynomial time computable initial data. Section 3 is based on [27,29,30] and focuses on complexity of solution operators. Section 4 contains concluding remarks and possible future research directions.

2   Complexity of the Solutions with Fixed Initial Data

The real complexity classes are defined in [15]; the equivalent formulations below are from [13,16,17]; see also the more subtle definitions of #P and #P_1 therein.

Definition 1. *For a partial real function $f \subseteq \mathbb{R}^d \to \mathbb{R}^{d'}$, computing f means converting, for every $x \in dom(f)$, any sequence $(\vec{a}_m) \subseteq \mathbb{Z}^d$ with $||\vec{x} - \frac{\vec{a}_m}{2^m}|| \leq 1/2^m$ into some sequence $(\vec{b}_n) \subseteq \mathbb{Z}^{d'}$ with $||f(\vec{x}) - \frac{\vec{b}_n}{2^n}|| \leq 1/2^n$.*

Such a computation is said to run in polynomial (exponential) time if $\vec{b}_n$ appears within a number of steps at most polynomial (exponential) in n; similarly for polynomial space. The (real counterparts of the) complexity classes P, EXP, PSPACE *are defined accordingly.*

The papers [11,16] analyze bit-complexity of linear PDEs with finitely continuously differentiable initial data. In [11], the Dirichlet problem for the (elliptic) Poisson's equation on an open Euclidean unit ball $B^d = \{\vec{x} \in \mathbb{R}^d : |\vec{x}| < 1\}$ is studied:

$$\sum_{j=1}^d \frac{\partial^2}{\partial x_j^2} u = f \text{ in } B^d, \qquad u\mid_{\partial B^d} = g(\vec{x}). \tag{3}$$

Theorem 1. *[11, Theorem 2.1]*

a) *If* P = #P, *then for every choice of polynomial time computable functions $f : B^d \to \mathbb{R}$ and $g : \partial B^d \to \mathbb{R}$, the solution $u : B^d \to \mathbb{R}$ to (3) is again computable in polynomial time.*
b) *There exist polynomial time computable functions f, g such that the solution u is not polynomial time computable unless* P_1 = #P_1.

Theorem 1a can be strengthened to "u is computable in #P"; see also a comment in [16, Conclusion] regarding Theorem 1b and the inaccuracy ("P = #P" instead of "P_1 = #P_1") in the original formulation in [11]. Note that P, #P, P_1, #P_1 in Theorem 1 are the corresponding "discrete" complexity classes.

In [16,18] the main focus is on the linear evolutionary systems of PDEs with initial conditions

$$\begin{cases} \vec{u}_t = \sum_{|\vec{j}|} \mathbf{B}_{\vec{j}}(\vec{x}) \cdot \partial^{\vec{j}} \vec{u}, & 0 \leq t \leq 1, \quad \vec{x} \in \Omega, \\ \vec{u}\mid_{t=0} = \varphi(\vec{x}), & \vec{x} \in \Omega, \end{cases} \tag{4}$$

and, possibly, boundary conditions

$$\mathcal{L}\vec{u}(t,\vec{x})\,|_{\partial\Omega} = 0, \quad (t,\vec{x}) \in [0,1] \times \partial\Omega, \tag{5}$$

where $\Omega = [0,1]^d$ is the unit cube (for technical simplicity); $\partial\Omega$ is its boundary; the solution $\vec{u} = (u_1, \ldots, u_{d'}) = \vec{u}(t,\vec{x})$ is an unknown function on Ω with values in $\mathbb{R}^d$; $\mathcal{L}$ in the boundary condition is a linear differential operator of order strictly less than the order of the differential operator $\sum_{|\vec{j}|} \mathbf{B}_{\vec{j}}(\vec{x}) \cdot \partial^{\vec{j}}$. The coefficients are $d' \times d'$ matrices $\mathbf{B}_{\vec{j}}$ that may depend on $\vec{x}$, but not on t (autonomous case); $\vec{j} = (j_1, \ldots, j_d)$ denotes a multi-index of order $|\vec{j}| = j_1 + j_2 + \ldots + j_d$, $\partial^{\vec{j}} = \partial_1^{j_1} \cdots \partial_d^{j_d}$ denotes the corresponding differential operator, where $\partial_k^{j_k} = \frac{\partial^{j_k}}{\partial x_k^{j_k}}$; and $\varphi(\vec{x})$ is the initial condition. Note that the equations (4) are linear in the derivatives, but the matrix coefficients $\mathbf{B}_{\vec{j}}$ can depend on $\vec{x}$ non-linearly.

The following results (Theorem 3 below) study the bit-cost of the difference scheme approach adapted to the computable analysis/exact real computation paradigms. Recall that for a linear differential operator $\mathcal{A}$, the matrix $\mathbf{A}_{(h)}$ (constructed using a uniform grid on Ω with the grid step $h = h(n)$) defines the corresponding *difference scheme*

$$u^{(h,(l+1)\tau)} = \mathbf{A_h}u^{(h,l\tau)}, \quad u^{(h,0)} = \varphi^{(h)}. \tag{6}$$

Its entries are denoted $(\mathbf{A}_{(h)})_{I,J}$, $1 \leq I, J \leq K$. Here $K \sim 2^{\mathcal{O}(n)}$ is the dimension of the vectors $\vec{u}^{(h,m\tau)}$ approximating the solution $\vec{u}(m\tau, \vec{x},)$ at time $m\tau \leq 1$, i.e., for $1 \leq m \leq M := 1/\tau \sim 2^n$. $\tau, h \sim 1/2^n$ denote the temporal and spatial grid widths, respectively.

Items (i), (ii) of the following hypotheses, necessary for the bit-complexity results, are very natural and easy to check. Item (iii) assumes the difference scheme converging to the solution w.r.t. the maximum norm, which is not always considered in numerical analysis, but such schemes can be constructed in particular cases, usually under stronger smoothness assumptions (see Example 1 below). The L_2-norm convergence is more standard; however, as mentioned in the introduction, the current bit-complexity notions are based on the evaluation of the function and the sup-norm while an L_2 function cannot be evaluated pointwise; development of coding theory for integrable functions is in progress.

Hypotheses 2. *(i) The problem (4), (5) is well-posed (Hadamard) in that the classical solution $\vec{u}(t,\vec{x})$ to (4) exists, is unique and depends continuously on the initial data in the following sense:*

$$\varphi(\vec{x}) \in \mathcal{C}^l(\bar{\Omega}), \quad \mathbf{u}(t,\vec{x}) \in \mathcal{C}^2([0,1] \times \bar{\Omega}), \quad \|\mathbf{u}\|_{C^2([0,1]\times\bar{\Omega})} \leq C_0 \|\varphi\|_{C^l(\Omega)}, \tag{7}$$

for some fixed C_0, $l \geq 2$.
(ii) The initial functions $\varphi(\vec{x})$ and matrix coefficients $\mathbf{B_j}(\vec{x})$ as well as their partial derivatives up to order l are polynomial time computable.
(iii) The system (4) admits a difference scheme $\mathbf{A}_{h(n)}$ (see (6) above) which is polynomial time computable, and its solution $u^{(n)}$ converges to the solution

$\vec{u}$ of (4) *w.r.t. the maximum norm on the uniform grid* $G_{h(n)}$ *with the step* $h = h(n)$:

$$\max_{x \in G_{h(n)}} \left| \vec{u} |_{G_{h(n)}} - u^{(n)} \right| < C \cdot h(n), \quad C \text{ does not depend on } n.$$

Note that technically a difference scheme is a family $\mathbf{A}_{h(n)}$ of matrices of dimension growing exponentially in $n \to \infty$ such as to approximate the operator $\mathcal{A} = \sum_{|\vec{j}|} \mathbf{B}_{\vec{j}}(\vec{x}) \cdot \partial^{\vec{j}}$ with increasing precision; the approximating solution $u^{(n)}$ is a sequence of vectors of dimension growing exponentially in n. See [16, Definition 5] for adjustment of the complexity classes to this case.

Theorem 3. *[16, Theorem 2a,b]*

a) *The solution* $\vec{u}$ *of (4) under Hypotheses 2 is computable in* PSPACE.
b) *If additionally the difference scheme* $\mathbf{A}_h$ *from (iii) is a sum of tensor products of circulant block matrices of constant bandwidth, then evaluating the solution* $(t, \vec{x}) \mapsto \vec{u}(t, \vec{x})$ *of (4) is computable in* #P.

Remark 1. (i) Difference scheme matrices of Theorem 3b correspond to the case of constant matrix coefficients $\mathbf{B}_{\vec{j}}$ in (4) and periodic boundary conditions, see (10) below.
(ii) An important tool for proving Theorem 3 is recursive matrix powering (instead of step-by-step iterations (6)), and its reduction to multinomial powering for Theorem 3b.
(iii) In [17], Theorem 3a is strengthened to proving PSPACE, in general, optimal for the class (4), via a reduction to (characteristic) ODE systems, solutions of which are proved PSPACE-hard in [7].

An important and rich class of PDEs of the form (4) are the first-order systems

$$\vec{u}_t = \sum_{j=1}^{d} \mathbf{B}_j(\vec{x}) \cdot \partial_{x_j} \vec{u}, \quad \vec{u}(0, \vec{x}) = \varphi(\vec{x}). \tag{8}$$

The discrete solutions of (8) are proved to be in polynomial parallel time in [21] by means of multigrids.

Example 1. [16, Example 2] Many linear evolutionary PDEs admit difference schemes that satisfy the Hypotheses 2 and thus can be computed in PSPACE or #P according to Theorem 3, including:

a) The heat equation

$$u_t = a^2 \sum_{j=1}^{d} \partial^2_{x_j} u, \quad \vec{u}(0, \vec{x}) = \varphi(\vec{x}) \tag{9}$$

with periodic boundary conditions

$$u(t, x_1, \ldots, x_{j-1}, 0, x_{j+1}, \ldots, x_d) = u(t, x_1, \ldots, x_{j-1}, 1, x_{j+1}, \ldots, x_d) \tag{10}$$

(same equalities hold also for u_x, u_y), and a polynomial time computable initial function, provided that $u(t, \vec{x}) \in C^{(1,4)}([0, T] \times \bar{\Omega})$.

b) The Wave Equation

$$u_{tt} = a^2 \sum_{j=1}^{d} \partial_{x_j}^2 u$$

with periodic boundary conditions and polynomial time computable initial functions, provided that $u(t, x, y) \in C^{(4,5)}([0, T] \times \bar{\Omega})$.

c) The two-dimensional acoustics system

$$\begin{cases} \rho_0 \dfrac{\partial u}{\partial t} + \dfrac{\partial p}{\partial x} = 0, \\ \rho_0 \dfrac{\partial v}{\partial t} + \dfrac{\partial p}{\partial y} = 0, \\ \dfrac{\partial p}{\partial t} + \rho_0 c_0^2 \left(\dfrac{\partial u}{\partial x} + \dfrac{\partial v}{\partial y} \right) = 0 \end{cases}$$

can be equivalently reduced to the two-dimensional wave equation; as well as some other symmetric hyperbolic systems ((8) with constant coefficients $\mathbf{B}_j = \mathbf{B}_j^*$), which are equivalent to higher-order wave equations.

For the heat equation, the hardness result is similar to Theorem 1b for the Poisson equation:

Theorem 4. *[16, Theorem 2d] For the heat equation (9), (10) there exists a polynomial time computable initial condition φ such that the solution u is classical but cannot be computed in polynomial time unless* $\mathsf{P}_1 = \#\mathsf{P}_1$.

For a particular case (basically reducible to a 1-dimensional system) polynomial time complexity is established via the characteristics method:

Theorem 5. *[16, Theorem 2c] Evaluating the solution $\vec{u}$ of (8) is polynomial time computable if the matrices $\mathbf{B}_j$ are constant and mutually commute for $j = 1, \ldots d$.*

Evaluating the solution $\vec{u}$ of (8) is also polynomial time computable for the case of *analytic* variable coefficients and initial functions, i.e., the Cauchy-Kovalevskaya case: see [18, Theorem 3] and the uniform version in Theorem 10 in Subsect. 3.2 below. Note that for quasilinear equations, when $\mathbf{B}_j = \mathbf{B}_j(\vec{x}, \vec{u})$ the situation is more complicated, and, even in the analytic Cauchy-Kovalevskaya setting, the best known upper bound is by now 2-EXP.

To summarize, for fixed polynomial time computable initial and matrix coefficient functions, there is a pretty clear picture for complexity of linear PDEs. Computing solutions of linear evolutionary PDE systems with variable coefficients (4) (which include hyperbolic and parabolic systems) is, in general, PSPACE-complete (Theorem 3a and Remark 1(iii)), which is similar to the general ODE case. For the case of constant coefficients and periodic boundary conditions, the complexity bound can be improved to #P (Theorem 3a and Remark 1(i)), which is same as for the (elliptic) Poisson equation (Theorem 1a); both Poisson and heat equations are $\#\mathsf{P}_1$-hard (Theorem 1b, Theorem 4). For the analytic case, solutions of both ODEs and linear evolutionary PDEs are polynomial time computable, which makes them feasible to compute in exact real computation packages (see further comments at end of Subsect. 3.2).

3   Complexity of Solution Operators

This section summarizes results on complexity of solution *operators* of several important subclasses of PDEs (4).

3.1   Restricting to Computable Real Closed Fields

In [27,30,31], computability and complexity of solution operators of symmetric hyperbolic systems (a particular and practically important subclass of the systems (8))

$$A\vec{u}_t + \sum_{j=1}^d B_j \cdot \partial_{x_j}\vec{u} = f(t,\vec{x}), \quad \vec{u}(0,\vec{x}) = \varphi(\vec{x}), \tag{11}$$

where $A = A^* > 0, B_j = B_j^*$ are constant matrices, were investigated based on the difference scheme approach.

It is important to emphasize that the situation here is rather subtle, since the schemes behave well only if spectral decompositions of the involved matrices and matrix pencils are known. But the spectral decomposition even for a symmetric 2×2-matrix is known to be non-computable [36]. As observed in [26], the problem becomes computable (even for $d' \times d'$-matrices uniformly on d') if matrix coefficients range over any fixed computable ordered field of reals. This observation led to some new facts on computable, primitive recursive (PR), and polynomial time computable real closed fields of reals and their applications to the computability and complexity issues for solution operators in [27,30], shortly discussed below. For basics of computable structure theory see e.g. [4].

The domain H of existence and uniqueness of the Cauchy problem is the intersection of semi-spaces $t \geq 0$, $x_i - \mu_{\max}^{(i)}t \geq 0$, $x_i - 1 - \mu_{\min}^{(i)}t \leq 0$, ($i = 1,\ldots,d$) of $\mathbb{R}^{d+1}$ where $\mu_{\min}^{(i)}, \mu_{\max}^{(i)}$ are respectively the minimum and maximum of the eigenvalues of the matrix $A^{-1}B_i$. Therefore, the computation of H reduces to the computation of the eigenvalues of the matrices $A^{-1}B_i$, and can be done in polynomial time [30, Theorem 4].

By computing the solution $\vec{u} \in C^2(\Omega)$ of (11), in the paper [30] we mean to output the following: (codes of) a rational $T > 0$ with $H \subseteq [0,T] \times Q$, a spatial rational grid step h dividing 1, a time grid step τ dividing T and a rational h, τ-grid function $v : G_N^\tau \to \mathbb{Q}$ such that

$$||\vec{u} - \widetilde{v\,|_H}||_{sL_2} < \frac{1}{a}. \tag{12}$$

Denote

$$\mathbf{M}_1(A, B, f) = \max_i\left\{||B_i||_2, ||(A^{-1}B_i)^2||_2, \max_k\{|\mu_k| : \det(\mu_k A - B_i) = 0\}, \sup_{t,x}||\frac{\partial^2 f}{\partial x_i \partial t}(t,\vec{x})||_2\right\},$$

$$\mathbf{M}_2(A, B, f, \varphi) = \max_{i,j}\left\{||A^{-1}B_iA^{-1}B_j - A^{-1}B_jA^{-1}B_i||_2, \sup_{t,x}||\frac{\partial^2 f}{\partial x_i \partial x_j}(t,\vec{x})||_2, \sup_x||\frac{\partial^2 \varphi}{\partial x_i \partial x_j}(\vec{x})||_2\right\}.$$

Theorem 6. *[30, Theorem 5] Let the dimension d be fixed; $A, B_1, \ldots, B_d \in M_{d'}(\mathbb{R}_{alg})$ where $\mathbb{R}_{alg}$ is the field of algebraic real numbers, $\varphi_1 \ldots, \varphi_{d'} \in \mathbb{Q}[x_1 \ldots, x_d]$ and $f_1 \ldots, f_{d'} \in \mathbb{Q}[t, x_1 \ldots, x_d]$. Then*

a) The solution u is computable from $A, B_1, \ldots, B_d, f, \varphi, a, d'$ in EXP.
b) If additionally d', a and M are fixed and such that

$$\max\{|M_1(A, B, f)|, |M_2(A, B, f, \varphi)|\} \leq M,$$

then u is computable from $A, B_1, \ldots, B_d, f, \varphi$ in polynomial time.

The proof of this theorem is based on the following difference scheme approach modification, which can be used for guaranteed precision computations:

1. Computation of steps (for technical simplicity, for the 2-dimensional case):

$$h \leq \frac{1}{2a\mathcal{P}(A, B_1, B_2, \varphi)}, \text{ where } \mathcal{P}(A, B_1, B_2, \varphi) = \frac{\lambda_{max}(A)}{\lambda_{min}(A)} \cdot \max\{\|\frac{\partial^2 \varphi}{\partial x_i \partial x_j}\|_s\}.$$

$$\cdot \max\{\|A\|_2, \|B_1\|_2, \|B_2\|_2, \|(A^{-1}B_1)^2\|_2, \|(A^{-1}B_2)^2\|_2,$$
$$\|A^{-1}B_1 A^{-1}B_2 - A^{-1}B_2 A^{-1}B_1\|_2\};$$

$$\tau \leq h \cdot \left(\frac{1}{\max_i\{|\mu_i| : \det(\mu_i A - B_1) = 0\}} + \frac{1}{\max_i\{|\mu_i| : \det(\mu_i A - B_2) = 0\}}\right)^{-1}.$$

Both h and τ can be computed in polynomial time, since all the expressions in $\mathcal{P}(A, B_1, B_2, \varphi)$ (eigenvalues, matrix multiplication, taking an inverse matrix, differentiating rational polynomials) are polynomial time computable.
2. Applying the difference scheme based on standard algorithms.

The modification consists in (i) explicitly computing the grid steps and domain of existence and uniqueness, via polynomial time algorithms; and (ii) computing the arising on Step 2 eigenvectors of the matrix pencils $(\mu A - B_j)$ via symbolic computations; see [30] for all details and encodings, as well as comments in the beginning of this subsection.

In [27] primitive recursive (PR) computability of the solution operator for (11) is proved (the natural precise notion of PR-computability in PR-metric spaces may be found in the arXiv version [28] of [27]). By a PRAS-field we mean a PR-presentable ordered subfield $\mathbb{A}$ of the reals such that given $b \in \mathbb{A}$, one can primitive recursively find $k \in \mathbb{N}$ with $b < k$, and given a polynomial in $\mathbb{A}[x]$, one can primitive recursively find its factorization to irreducible polynomials; $\hat{\mathbb{A}}$ denotes the real closure of $\mathbb{A}$.

Theorem 7. *[27, Theorem 14] Let $M, p \geq 2$ be integers. Then the operator $(A, B_1, \ldots, B_d, \varphi) \mapsto \mathbf{u}$ for (11) is a PR-computable function from the space $S_+ \times S^d \times C_s^{p+1}(Q, \mathbb{R}^{d'})$ to $C_{sL_2}^p(H, \mathbb{R}^{d'})$ where S and S^+ are respectively the sets of all symmetric and symmetric positively definite matrices from $M_{d'}(\hat{\mathbb{A}})$, $\|\frac{\partial \varphi}{\partial x_i}\|_s \leq M$ and $\|\frac{\partial^2 \varphi}{\partial x_i \partial x_j}\|_s \leq M$ for $i, j = 1, 2, \ldots, d$.*

Theorem 8. *[27, Theorem 15] Let $M, p \geq 2$ be integers and $A, B_1, \ldots, B_d \in M_{d'}(\mathbb{R}_p)$ be fixed matrices, where $\mathbb{R}_p$ is the field of PR real numbers. Then the solution operator $\varphi \mapsto \mathbf{u}$ for (11) is a PR-computable function (uniformly on d, d') from $C_s^{p+1}(Q, \mathbb{R}^{d'})$ to $C_{sL_2}^p(H, \mathbb{R}^{d'})$, $\|\frac{\partial \varphi}{\partial x_i}\|_s \leq M$ and $\|\frac{\partial^2 \varphi}{\partial x_i \partial x_j}\|_s \leq M$ for $i, j = 1, 2, \ldots, d$.*

We conclude with the following PR-version of results of [30] (Theorem 6 above). The formulation of Theorem 9 is broader than of Theorem 6, because now the algorithm is uniform on d, d', a and works not only with algebraic numbers; all computations are precise and performed within the real closure $\widehat{\mathbb{A}}$ of any PRAS-field $\mathbb{A}$.

Theorem 9. *[27, Theorem 16] Given integers $d, d', a \geq 1$, matrices $A, B_1 \ldots, B_d \in M_{d'}(\widehat{\mathbb{A}})$, and rational functions $\varphi_1 \ldots, \varphi_{d'} \in \widehat{\mathbb{A}}(x_1 \ldots, x_d)$, $f_1 \ldots, f_{d'} \in \widehat{\mathbb{A}}(t, x_1 \ldots, x_d)$ as in (11), one can primitive-recursively compute a rational $T > 0$ with $H \subseteq [0, T] \times Q$, a spatial rational grid step h dividing 1, a time grid step τ dividing T and an h, τ-grid function $v : G_N^\tau \to \widehat{\mathbb{A}}$ such that $\|\vec{u} - \widetilde{v\,|_H}\|_{sL_2} < a^{-1}$.*

In this way, informally speaking, the class of PR functions is closed under solution operators of (11), while the class of polynomial-time computable functions is not. In Theorem 6b, stating polynomial-time computability of the solution, the output precision parameter is fixed (in all other results it is not).

3.2   Uniform Complexity for Analytic Inputs

In [29] we prove a uniform polynomial time computable version of the Cauchy-Kovalevskaya theorem (first formulated nonuniformly in [18]), as well as uniform polynomial time computability of the heat and Schroedinger equations for the case of analytic initial data. The following definition introduces coefficient bounds used in Theorems 10, 11 below.

Definition 2. *[29, Definition 2] Fix $d \in \mathbb{N}$.*

a) *Consider a multi-index $\boldsymbol{\alpha} \in \mathbb{N}^d$ and $\vec{x} \in \mathbb{R}^d$. Abbreviate $\vec{x}^{\boldsymbol{\alpha}} := x_1^{\alpha_1} \cdots x_d^{\alpha_d}$ and $\partial^{\boldsymbol{\alpha}} := \partial_1^{\alpha_1} \cdots \partial_d^{\alpha_d}$ and $\boldsymbol{\alpha}! = \alpha_1! \cdots \alpha_d!$ and $|\boldsymbol{\alpha}| = \alpha_1 + \cdots + \alpha_d$.*
b) *Consider a complex multi-sequence $(a_{\boldsymbol{\alpha}}) : \mathbb{N}^d \to \mathbb{C}$. A pair (M, L) with $M, L \in \mathbb{N}$ is called a coefficient bound for $(a_{\boldsymbol{\alpha}})$ if it satisfies*

$$|a_{\boldsymbol{\alpha}}| \leq M \cdot L^{|\boldsymbol{\alpha}|} \quad \text{for all} \quad \boldsymbol{\alpha} \in \mathbb{N}^d. \tag{13}$$

c) *Consider a complex function f analytic in some neighborhood of $[-1; 1]^d$. A pair (M, L) with $M, L \in \mathbb{N}$ is called a coefficient bound for f if it is a coefficient bound for the multi-sequence $\partial^{\boldsymbol{\alpha}} f(\vec{x})/\boldsymbol{\alpha}!$ for every $\vec{x} \in [-1; 1]^d$. Same for a complex function f analytic on the hyper-torus*

$$\Omega = \big([0; 1) \bmod 1\big)^d.$$

The latter means that, for some L and for every $\vec{x} \in \Omega$,

$$\left(-1/L, +1/L\right)^d \ni \vec{y} \mapsto f(\vec{x} + \vec{y} \bmod \vec{1}) = \sum_\alpha f_\alpha \vec{y}^\alpha$$

is a converging power series, with complex Taylor coefficient sequence (f_α) depending on $\vec{x}$. Here $1/L$ is a radius of convergence of f.

Theorem 10. *[29, Theorem 3] Fix $d \in \mathbb{N}$ and consider the solution operator that maps any analytic right-hand sides $B_1, \ldots, B_d : [-1; 1]^d \to \mathbb{C}^{d' \times d'}$ and initial condition $\varphi : [-1; 1]^d \to \mathbb{C}^{d'}$ and 'small' enough $t \in \mathbb{C}$ to the solution $u = u(t, \cdot)$ of (8).*

This operator is computable in parameterized time polynomial in $n + L + \log M$, where $\varphi, B_1, \ldots, B_d$ are given via their (componentwise) Taylor expansions around $\vec{0}$ as well as integers (M, L) as coefficient bounds to $\varphi, B_1, \ldots, B_d$ componentwise.

The heat and Schrödinger's equations are not covered by the Cauchy-Kovalevskaya Theorem.

Theorem 11. *[29, Theorem 4] Fix $d \in \mathbb{N}$ and consider the following linear partial differential equations on the d-dimensional hypercube with periodic boundary conditions $\Omega = \left([0; 1) \bmod 1\right)^d$, that is, analytic initial data $\varphi : [0; 1]^d \to \mathbb{C}$ satisfying*

$$\partial^\alpha \varphi(x_1, \ldots, x_{j-1}, 0, x_{j+1}, \ldots, x_d) = \partial^\alpha \varphi(x_1, \ldots, x_{j-1}, 1, x_{j+1}, \ldots, x_d) \quad (14)$$

for all $\alpha \in \mathbb{N}^d$, all $j = 1, 2 \ldots, d$ and all $\vec{x} \in \Omega$; similarly for the solution $u(t, \cdot) : [0; 1]^d \to \mathbb{C}$ for all $t > 0$. Recall that $\Delta = \partial_1^2 + \partial_2^2 + \cdots + \partial_d^2$ denotes the Laplace operator.

a) Consider the heat equation

$$u_t = \Delta u, \qquad u(0, \cdot) = v. \quad (15)$$

b) Consider the Schrödinger equation of a free particle

$$u_t = i\Delta u, \qquad u(0, \cdot) = v. \quad (16)$$

For any $t > 0$ and for any initial data φ given by coefficient bounds (M, L) and φ's power series expansion at each $\vec{x} = (2\vec{\ell} + \vec{1})/(2L) \in \Omega$, $\ell \in \{0, 1, \ldots, L - 1\}^d$, the unique analytic solution $u(t, \cdot) : \Omega \to \mathbb{C}$ to each of the above PDEs is computable in parameterized time polynomial in $n + \log t + L + \log M$.

The uniform complexity notions for the case of analytic functions, extending Definition 1, as well as details of the exact real computation approach applied to the considered setting, are collected in [29, Section 2]. The algorithms developed in proofs of Theorems 10, 11 have been used to create exact real computation solvers (implemented in iRRAM [20]) for the corresponding classes of analytic PDEs [29].

4   Conclusion

The existing rich theories of PDEs, as well as of analytic and numerical methods of their solutions do not directly yield a bit-complexity classification of PDEs. Apart from being a natural general program of study, such a classification would be very helpful in developing reliable and efficient algorithms within the exact real computation approach based on the computable analysis framework.

This survey shows the current status and outlines possible future directions of obtaining such a classification, in particular emphasizing the impact of:

▷ Adding or removing input parameters: it can increase or decrease bit-cost, as well as allow obtaining uniform results;
▷ Smoothness of the solutions: similarly to the ODE case, linear analytic systems of PDEs allow polynomial time algorithms, while computation of finitely and infinitely continuously differentiable solutions is possible only in PSPACE or #P (and proved $\#P_1$-hard for the Poisson and heat equations);
▷ Type of PDEs under consideration: linear systems have predictably better computational properties compared to the quasilinear ones; while hyperbolic, parabolic and elliptic types (within the linear type) show similar behaviour in terms of computational complexity.

The following are natural directions of future investigations:

▷ Finalizing the complexity classification for the case of linear systems of PDEs and extending it to quasilinear and general nonlinear PDEs;
▷ Developing a sound complexity theory for generalized solutions and extending the classification to this case;
▷ Extending the currently existing exact real computation PDE solvers from linear analytic to more general PDE systems.

In this way, bridging classical differential equations and numerical methods theories with computability and complexity theories, via computable analysis and exact real computation, gives hope to achieve deep insight into algorithmic complexity of PDEs (and ODEs), as well as provide optimal and reliable methods of computing their solutions with guaranteed arbitrary precision.

References

1. Bournez, O., Graça, D.S., Pouly, A.: Solving analytic differential equations in polynomial time over unbounded domains. In: Murlak, F., Sankowski, P. (eds.) MFCS 2011. LNCS, vol. 6907, pp. 170–181. Springer, Heidelberg (2011). https://doi.org/10.1007/978-3-642-22993-0_18
2. Brattka, V., Hertling, P., Weihrauch, K.: A tutorial on computable analysis. In: Cooper, S.B., Löwe, B., Sorbi, A. (eds.) New Computational Paradigms: Changing Conceptions of What Is Computable, pp. 425–491. Springer, New York (2008). https://doi.org/10.1007/978-0-387-68546-5_18
3. Braverman, M., Cook, S.A.: Computing over the reals: foundations for scientific computing. Notices AMS **53**(3), 318–329 (2006)

4. Ershov, Y., Goncharov, S.: Constructive Models. Novosibirsk, Scientific Book (in Russian, there is an English Translation) (1999)
5. Gay, W., Zhang, B.Y., Zhong, N.: Computability of solutions of the Korteweg-de Vries equation. Math. Log. Q. **47**(1), 93–110 (2001)
6. Graça, D., Zhong, N.: Computability of differential equations. In: Handbook of Computability and Complexity in Analysis (Editors: Vasco Brattka and Peter Hertling), pp. 71–99. Theory and Applications of Computability (2021)
7. Kawamura, A.: Lipschitz continuous ordinary differential equations are polynomial-space complete. Comput. Complex. **19**(2), 305–332 (2010). https://doi.org/10.1007/s00037-010-0286-0
8. Kawamura, A., Cook, S.: Complexity theory for operators in analysis. In: Proceedings of the 42nd ACM Symposium on Theory of Computing, STOC 2010, pp. 495–502. ACM, New York (2010). https://doi.org/10.1145/1806689.1806758
9. Kawamura, A., Ota, H., Rösnick, C., Ziegler, M.: Computational complexity of smooth differential equations. Log. Methods Comput. Sci. **10**(1:6), 15 (2014). https://doi.org/10.2168/LMCS-10(1:6)2014
10. Kawamura, A., Steinberg, F., Thies, H.: Parameterized complexity for uniform operators on multidimensional analytic functions and ODE solving. In: Proc 25th International Workshop on Logic, Language, Information, and Computation (WOLLIC), pp. 223–236 (2018). https://doi.org/10.1007/978-3-662-57669-4_13
11. Kawamura, A., Steinberg, F., Ziegler, M.: On the computational complexity of the Dirichlet problem for Poisson's equation. Math. Struct. Comput. Sci. **27**(8), 1437–1465 (2017). https://doi.org/10.1017/S096012951600013X
12. Kawamura, A., Thies, H., Ziegler, M.: Average-case polynomial-time computability of hamiltonian dynamics. In: Potapov, I., Spirakis, P.G., Worrell, J. (eds.) 43rd International Symposium on Mathematical Foundations of Computer Science, MFCS 2018, 27–31 August 2018, Liverpool, UK. LIPIcs, vol. 117, pp. 30:1–30:17. Schloss Dagstuhl - Leibniz-Zentrum für Informatik (2018)
13. Kawamura, A., Ziegler, M.: Invitation to real complexity theory: algorithmic foundations to reliable numerics with bit-costs (2018). https://arxiv.org/abs/1801.07108
14. Ko, K., Friedman, H.: Computational complexity of real functions. Theoret. Comput. Sci. **20**(3), 323–352 (1982). https://doi.org/10.1016/S0304-3975(82)80003-0
15. Ko, K.I.: Complexity Theory of Real Functions. Progress in Theoretical Computer Science, Birkhäuser, Boston (1991)
16. Koswara, I., Pogudin, G., Selivanova, S., Ziegler, M.: Bit-complexity of solving systems of linear evolutionary partial differential equations. In: Santhanam, R., Musatov, D. (eds.) CSR 2021. LNCS, vol. 12730, pp. 223–241. Springer, Cham (2021). https://doi.org/10.1007/978-3-030-79416-3_13
17. Koswara, I., Pogudin, G., Selivanova, S., Ziegler, M.: Bit-complexity of classical solutions of linear evolutionary systems of partial differential equations. J. Complex. (2022, submitted)
18. Koswara, I., Selivanova, S., Ziegler, M.: Computational complexity of real powering and improved solving linear differential equations. In: van Bevern, R., Kucherov, G. (eds.) CSR 2019. LNCS, vol. 11532, pp. 215–227. Springer, Cham (2019). https://doi.org/10.1007/978-3-030-19955-5_19
19. Lim, D., Selivanova, S., Ziegler, M.: Complexity and coding theory of hilbert spaces: what is a polynomial-time computable l_2 function? In: Proceedings of Computability and Complexity in Analysis (CCA 2020), pp. 41–42 (2020)

20. Müller, N.T.: The iRRAM: exact arithmetic in C++. In: Blanck, J., Brattka, V., Hertling, P. (eds.) CCA 2000. LNCS, vol. 2064, pp. 222–252. Springer, Heidelberg (2001). https://doi.org/10.1007/3-540-45335-0_14

21. Pan, V., Reif, J.: The bit-complexity of discrete solutions of partial differential equations: compact multigrid. Comput. Math. Appl. **20**, 9–16 (1990)

22. Park, S., et al.: Foundation of computer (algebra) analysis systems: semantics, logic, programming, verification (2020). https://arxiv.org/abs/1608.05787

23. Plum, M.: Computer-assisted proofs for semilinear elliptic boundary value problems. Japan J. Indust. Appl. Math. **26**(2–3), 419–442 (2009)

24. Pouly, A., Graça, D.S.: Computational complexity of solving polynomial differential equations over unbounded domains. Theoret. Comput. Sci. **626**, 67–82 (2016). https://doi.org/10.1016/j.tcs.2016.02.002

25. Pour-El, M., Richards, J.: Computability in Analysis and Physics. Cambridge University Press, Cambridge (2017)

26. Selivanova, S., Selivanov, V.: Computing solution operators of boundary-value problems for some linear hyperbolic systems of PDEs. Log. Methods Comput. Sci. **13**(4:13), 1–31 (2017)

27. Selivanov, V., Selivanova, S.: Primitive recursive ordered fields and some applications. In: Boulier, F., England, M., Sadykov, T.M., Vorozhtsov, E.V. (eds.) CASC 2021. LNCS, vol. 12865, pp. 353–369. Springer, Cham (2021). https://doi.org/10.1007/978-3-030-85165-1_20

28. Selivanova, S., Selivanov, V.: Primitive recursive ordered fields and some applications (2021). arXiv:2010.10189

29. Selivanova, S., Steinberg, F., Thies, H., Ziegler, M.: Exact real computation of solution operators for linear analytic systems of partial differential equations. In: Boulier, F., England, M., Sadykov, T.M., Vorozhtsov, E.V. (eds.) CASC 2021. LNCS, vol. 12865, pp. 370–390. Springer, Cham (2021). https://doi.org/10.1007/978-3-030-85165-1_21

30. Selivanova, S., Selivanov, V.: Bit complexity of computing solutions for symmetric hyperbolic systems of PDEs with guaranteed precision. Computability **10**(2), 123–140 (2021). https://doi.org/10.3233/COM-180215

31. Selivanova, S., Selivanov, V.L.: Computing solution operators of boundary-value problems for some linear hyperbolic systems of PDEs. Log. Methods Comput. Sci. **13**(4) (2017). https://doi.org/10.23638/LMCS-13(4:13)2017

32. Steinberg, F.: Complexity theory for spaces of integrable functions. Log. Methods Comput. Sci. **13**(3), Paper No. 21, 39 (2017). https://doi.org/10.23638/LMCS-13(3:21)2017

33. Sun, S.-M., Zhong, N., Ziegler, M.: Computability of the solutions to navier-stokes equations via effective approximation. In: Du, D.-Z., Wang, J. (eds.) Complexity and Approximation. LNCS, vol. 12000, pp. 80–112. Springer, Cham (2020). https://doi.org/10.1007/978-3-030-41672-0_7

34. Weihrauch, K.: Computable Analysis. Springer, Berlin (2000). https://doi.org/10.1007/978-3-642-56999-9

35. Weihrauch, K.: Computational complexity on computable metric spaces. Math. Log. Q. **49**(1), 3–21 (2003)

36. Ziegler, M., Brattka, V.: Computability in linear algebra. Theoret. Comput. Sci. **326**(1–3), 187–211 (2004)

Barendregt's Problem #26
and Combinatory Strong Reduction

William Stirton[✉] [iD]

Edinburgh Leisure Ltd., 139 London Road, Edinburgh EH7 6AE, UK
William_Stirton@yahoo.co.uk

Abstract. The goal of the paper is to make a start on the following problem: to define a function f taking simply typed combinator terms to natural numbers and prove that, when b is such a term formed by contracting a strong redex within another term a, then $f(b) < f(a)$. An exact definition of strong reduction, in the axiomatic style introduced by J. R. Hindley, is presented in Sect. 2 to make the paper self-contained. A function f is then defined which has the property that $f(b) < f(a)$ when b is formed from a by contracting either a weak redex or a strong redex of the shape $[x].\mathbf{S}abc$, where the variable x occurs in all three terms a, b, c. Reasons are given for thinking that the most challenging part of the problem as a whole will be the treatment of redexes of the shape $[x_1, x_2, \ldots, x_m].\mathbf{S}abc$. In view of the connection between strong reduction and $\lambda\eta$-reduction, a comprehensive solution to the problem described here will bring with it the solution to a long-standing open problem concerning the simply typed λ-calculus.

Keywords: Simply typed combinatory logic · Strong normalization · Gödel's Koan

1 Introduction

Let $\Lambda_\rightarrow$ be the set of simply typed λ-terms and $CL_\rightarrow$ the set of simply typed combinator terms. Let R be a reduction relation defined over either of these sets and let a function f which takes $\Lambda_\rightarrow$ or $CL_\rightarrow$ into the natural numbers be called *R-reducing* iff, whenever a single R-reduction step takes X to Y, we have $f(Y) < f(X)$.

Let WR be combinatory weak reduction (defined by Definition 1 below) and let SR be combinatory strong reduction (defined in Sect. 2 below). For each well-known reduction relation R, a proof that some function f is R-reducing will be all the more interesting if f is computationally undemanding enough to be acceptable as a proof-theoretic ordinal assignment. What this requirement amounts to is not easy to state exactly, but a minimal requirement is that f should be feasible. Study of examples like [3] suggests that calculating the ordinal number assigned to a finitary proof or term should take not much more work than writing down the proof or term itself.

© The Author(s), under exclusive license to Springer Nature Switzerland AG 2022
U. Berger et al. (Eds.): CiE 2022, LNCS 13359, pp. 313–326, 2022.
https://doi.org/10.1007/978-3-031-08740-0_26

An exhibition of an SR-reducing function, which meets the standards required by ordinal-theoretic proof theory, would be of the greatest interest, not least because it would bring with it the solution to a long-standing problem (see [1]) concerning $\lambda\beta$-reduction over $\Lambda_\rightarrow$. It is not being claimed that this is the best way to tackle the problem posed in [1]. Strictly speaking, there are infinitely many shapes of strong redex [4] but even disregarding the number of variables abstracted, which can be equal to any finite number, the number of shapes a strong redex can have is still quite large and a proof that a function is SR-reducing may well require a great many case-distinctions.

On the other hand, investigating a subrelation of SR that is comparatively weak (but still stronger than WR) can be heuristically illuminating. Work is currently in progress on an attempt to prove that a certain function from $\Lambda_\rightarrow$ into the natural numbers is $\lambda\beta$-reducing. If the attempt succeeds, the treatment of SR and the treatment of $\lambda\beta$-reduction will each throw some light upon the other. In general, the definitions come out simpler when working on $CL_\rightarrow$, but when working on $\Lambda_\rightarrow$ far fewer case-distinctions are needed in the proofs.

The goal of the present paper is to exhibit (in Definition 7) a function from $CL_\rightarrow$ into the natural numbers and prove that it is SR^0-reducing, where SR^0 is a relatively simple subrelation of SR, which includes WR. It is hoped that the proof presented here will illustrate both the difficulties that arise when one advances from weak to strong reduction and the sort of tricks that are needed to overcome them.

2   Definitions of Weak and Strong Reduction

The set $CL_\rightarrow$ is defined as in [5] (p. 115f.). That is, the following are taken as atomic terms: typed versions of **S**, **K**, **I** and typed variables. Throughout this paper, "term" will mean a *term of $CL_\rightarrow$*.

Weak reduction (WR) is the relation on $CL_\rightarrow$ defined by:

Definition 1. *1. For any a, b, c such that* $\boldsymbol{S}_{ABC}abc$ *is a term of $CL_\rightarrow$, the pair* $\langle \boldsymbol{S}_{ABC}abc, ac(bc)\rangle$ *is in WR;*

2. For any a, b such that $\boldsymbol{K}_{AB}ab$ *is a term of $CL_\rightarrow$,* $\langle \boldsymbol{K}_{AB}ab, a\rangle$ *is in WR;*

3. For any a of type A $\langle \boldsymbol{I}_{A}a, a\rangle$ *is in WR;*

4. If $\langle b, c\rangle \in WR$ *and ab, bd are terms of $CL_\rightarrow$, then* $\langle ab, ac\rangle$ *and* $\langle bd, cd\rangle$ *are in WR;*

5. If $\langle a, b\rangle$ *and* $\langle b, c\rangle$ *are in WR, so is* $\langle a, c\rangle$.

This definition is standard: see, for example, [5] (p. 24). If $\langle a, b\rangle \in WR$ in virtue of clause (i), (ii) or (iii), then a is a *weak redex* and b its *contractum*.

The notion of *abstracting a variable* from a term of $CL_\rightarrow$ has been defined in various ways; but the authors of [2] (p. 88) have argued that, for the purpose of considering strong reduction, only the following definition will work.

Definition 2. *For any term a of type C and any variable x^A, there is a term $[x^A]a$ of type $A\rightarrow C$, defined by:*

1. If x^A is not in a, $[x^A]a$ is $\boldsymbol{K}_{CA}a$;
2. If x^A is a, $[x^A]a$ is $\boldsymbol{I}_A$;
3. If A is $a_0 x^A$ for some a_0 in which x^A does not occur, $[x^A]a$ is a_0;
5. If the antecedents of the foregoing clauses are all false and a is $a_0 a_1$ for some a_0 of type $B{\to}C$, then $[x^A]a$ is $\boldsymbol{S}_{ABC}[x^A]a_0[x^A]a_1$.

If other combinators like the typed instances of $\boldsymbol{B}$ had been included among the primitive terms of $CL_{\to}$, it would have been possible to incorporate other clauses into Definition 2 and this would make $[x^A]a$ simpler in some cases. Specifically:

4. If a is $a_0 a_1$ for some a_0 of type $B{\to}C$ in which x^A does not occur and some a_1 of which x^A is a proper subterm, then $[x^A]a$ is $\boldsymbol{B}_{ABC}\, a_0\, [x^A]a_1$.

When (as in the present paper) the combinators $\boldsymbol{B}_{ABC}$ are not taken as primitive, clause 4 is derivable provided $\boldsymbol{B}_{ABC}\, a_0$ be identified with $\boldsymbol{S}_{ABC}(\boldsymbol{K}_{(B{\to}C)A}a_0)$. The authors of [2] (p. 40) have introduced the notation $\boldsymbol{B}_{ABC}: a_0$ with the stipulation that $\boldsymbol{B}_{ABC}: a_0$ is $\boldsymbol{B}_{ABC}\, a_0$ in a system in which $\boldsymbol{B}_{ABC}$ is taken as primitive and is $\boldsymbol{S}_{ABC}(\boldsymbol{K}_{(B{\to}C)A}a_0)$ when $\boldsymbol{B}_{ABC}$ is not taken as primitive but typed instances of $\boldsymbol{S}$ and $\boldsymbol{K}$ are. This notation will be used in Sect. 4 below.

Just as the relation WR can be defined by first defining a set of redex-contractum pairs, as is done in clauses $1-3$ of Definition 1, and then closing this set under the operations mentioned in clauses 4 and 5, so SR can be defined[1] by first defining a set of (strong) redex-contractum pairs RC and then closing RC under the operations mentioned in clauses 4 and 5 of Definition 1.

Definition 3. 1. If a is a weak redex and b its contractum, then $\langle a, b \rangle \in RC$;
2. For any a of type $A{\to}C$, $\langle \boldsymbol{S}_{AAC}(\boldsymbol{K}_{(A{\to}C)A}a)\boldsymbol{I}_A, a \rangle \in RC$;
3. For any a of type $B{\to}C$ and b of type B, $\langle \boldsymbol{S}_{ABC}(\boldsymbol{K}_{(B{\to}C)A}a)(\boldsymbol{K}_{BA}b)$, $\boldsymbol{K}_{CA}(ab) \rangle \in RC$;
4. For any A, $\langle \boldsymbol{S}_{(A{\to}A)(A{\to}A)(A{\to}A)}(\boldsymbol{K}_{((A{\to}A){\to}A{\to}A)(A{\to}A)}\boldsymbol{I}_{A{\to}A}), \boldsymbol{I}_{A{\to}A} \rangle \in RC$;
5. If $\langle a, b \rangle$ is in RC, so is $\langle [x^D]a, [x^D]b \rangle$ for every variable x^D.[2]

This paper will not prove anything about SR as a whole but only its subrelation SR^0, defined by:

Definition 4. 1. If $\langle d, e \rangle$ is either a weak redex-contractum pair or $\langle [x^D]\boldsymbol{S}_{ABC}abc, [x^D]ac(bc) \rangle$ for some terms a, b, c, each of which contains x^D, then $\langle d, e \rangle$ is in SR^0;
2. SR^0 is closed under the operations mentioned in clauses 4 and 5 of Definition 1.

---

[1] That it can be so defined was a discovery of Hindley [4]. The original definition was different. See [2] (Sect. 11E).

[2] That RC can be defined in this way is the content of theorem 11(ii) on p. 118 of [2]. An alternative possibility is to define RC as the set of pairs that can be formed by making substitutions for variables in certain schemata. See [2] (p. 117) or [4] (p. 233).

3   A Mapping of $CL_\rightarrow$ into the Natural Numbers

Proposition 1. *Every term is $Xa_1a_2...a_n$ for some atom X and some (possibly empty) sequence $a_1, ..., a_n$ of terms.*

Definition 5. *1. The* rank *of a type is the number of arrows in it.*
2. The rank of a term is the rank of its type.
3. For any type A or term a, the rank of A resp. a shall be $\rho(A)$ resp. $\rho(a)$.

Definition 6. *The* multiset *of* associated terms *of $Xa_1a_2...a_n$ of rank i (henceforth: $\mathcal{A}(Xa_1a_2...a_n, i)$) is defined by:*

1. For any $j \in [1, n]$, if $\rho(a_j) = i$, a_j is in $\mathcal{A}(Xa_1a_2...a_n, i)$.
2. For any $j \in [1, n]$, if $i < \rho(a_j)$ and b is in $\mathcal{A}(a_j, i)$, b is in $\mathcal{A}(Xa_1a_2...a_n, i)$.
3. No other terms are in $\mathcal{A}(Xa_1a_2...a_n, i)$.

The next definition defines the *measure of $Xa_1a_2...a_n$ at rank $i-$* in symbols, $[Xa_1a_2...a_n]_i-$ by course-of-values recursion on lengths of terms not larger than $Xa_1a_2...a_n$ and, within that, on $\rho(X)-i$. For any $i < \rho(X)$, let the terms of $\mathcal{A}(Xa_1a_2...a_n, i)$ be $f_1^i, f_2^i, ..., f_{\ell(i)}^i$ and let the sum $[f_1^i]_i + [f_2^i]_i + \cdots + [f_{\ell(i)}^i]_i$ be abbreviated to $[\boldsymbol{f}^i]_i$.

Definition 7. *1. $[Xa_1a_2...a_n]_i = 0$ if $\rho(X) < i$.*
2. $[Xa_1a_2...a_n]_{\rho(X)} = 0$ if X is a variable and $= 1$ if X is a combinator.
3. $[Xa_1a_2...a_n]_i$ for $i < \rho(X)$ is $2^{[Xa_1a_2...a_n]_{i+1}} \cdot (max\{1, [\boldsymbol{f}^i]_i\})$.

Stipulation: to avoid notational clutter, simply $2^{[Xa_1a_2...a_n]_{i+1}} \cdot [\boldsymbol{f}^i]_i$ will be written in place of $2^{[Xa_1a_2...a_n]_{i+1}} \cdot (max\{1, [\boldsymbol{f}^i]_i\})$.

Proposition 2. *If $\rho(a_{n+1}) < i$, then $[Xa_1a_2...a_na_{n+1}]_i = [Xa_1a_2...a_n]_i$*

Theorem 1. *The function $a \mapsto [a]_0$ is WR-reducing.*

Proof. See the Appendix at the end of this paper.

Discussion: let the *level* of a type be defined in the usual way, that is, the level of an atomic type is 0 and the level of $A \rightarrow B$ is the largest number in the set {level of A plus 1, level of B}. For any term a, the level of a (henceforth: $\delta(a)$) shall be the level of the type of a. Then $a \mapsto [a]_0$ would be WR-reducing even if the variable "i" in Definition 7 ranged over levels rather than ranks and, indeed, most normalizability proofs make reference to level but not rank.

Schütte ([6], p. 106f.) defined a function $a, i \mapsto |a|_i$ by a definition equivalent to:

1. $|Xa_1a_2...a_n|_i = 0$ if $\delta(X) < i$.
2. For every $i \leq \delta(X)$, $|X|_i = 0$ if X is a variable and $= 1$ if X is a combinator.
3. $|Xa_1a_2...a_n|_i = |Xa_1a_2...a_{n-1}|_i$ if $\delta(a_n) < i \leq \delta(X)$.
4. Otherwise $|Xa_1a_2...a_n|_i = 2^{|Xa_1a_2...a_n|_{i+1}} \cdot (|Xa_1a_2...a_{n-1}|_i + |a_n|_i)$.

and proved that $a \mapsto |a|_0$ is WR-reducing ([6], pp. 107–112).

The proof of Theorem 1 has been relegated to an appendix because it will be easy enough to reconstruct for anyone who is familiar with Schütte's proof or who has mastered the proof of Theorem 2 below. The main point to be stressed here is that, if we were concerned with weak reduction only, it might be natural to let "i" in Definition 7 range over levels, but in order to tackle strong reduction it has to range over ranks.

It would be possible to modify Schütte's definition by replacing δ with ρ. Whether the function so defined would have any useful applications which $a, i \mapsto [a]_i$ does not have, or conversely, is not yet known.

4   Strong Reduction

As the weak redexes that present the greatest difficulty when proving Theorem 1 are of the shape $\mathbf{S}_{ABC}abc$, it seems reasonable to conjecture that the most difficult class of strong redexes will be those of the shape $[x_1, x_2, \ldots, x_m]\mathbf{S}_{ABC}abc$ and that, if the case $m = 1$ can be treated, the general case probably can. This paper will concentrate on the class of strong redexes that are formed by abstracting a single variable x^D from a weak redex $\mathbf{S}_{ABC}abc$. Unfortunately there are nine different shapes such a redex can have, depending on exactly where the variable x^D occurs within a, b, c. I will assume x^D occurs in all three subterms.

Let the terms $[x^D]a, [x^D]b, [x^D]c$ be called a', b', c' for short.

When Definition 2 together with the colon notation is used to write $[x^D]\mathbf{S}_{ABC}abc$ without square brackets, the result is:

$$\mathbf{S}_{DAC}\,(\mathbf{S}_{D(A\to B)(A\to C)}(\mathbf{B}_{D(A\to B\to C)((A\to B)\to A\to C)} : \mathbf{S}_{ABC}\,a')b')c' \qquad (1)$$

and when the same is done to its contractum $[x^D]ac(bc)$ the result is:

$$\mathbf{S}_{DBC}(\mathbf{S}_{DA(B\to C)}a'c')(\mathbf{S}_{DAB}b'c') \qquad (2)$$

To save space, $\mathbf{B}_{D(A\to B\to C)((A\to B)\to A\to C)}$ will be written without its subscript.

Proposition 3. $[\mathbf{S}_{DA(B\to C)}a']_i \quad < \quad [\mathbf{B} \quad : \quad \mathbf{S}_{ABC}\,a']_i \quad$ for all $i \le \rho(\mathbf{S}_{D(A\to B\to C)((A\to B)\to A\to C)}).$

Proof. The term mentioned on the right side of the inequality, written without the colon, is $\mathbf{S}_{D(A\to B\to C)((A\to B)\to A\to C)}(\mathbf{K}_{((A\to B\to C)\to(A\to B)\to A\to C)D}\mathbf{S}_{ABC})\,a'$. The head combinator of this term has a higher rank[3] than $\mathbf{S}_{DA(B\to C)}$ on the left. From this the proposition follows using Definition 7.

Proposition 4. $[\mathbf{S}_{DAB}b']_i < [\mathbf{S}_{D(A\to B)(A\to C)}v^{D\to(A\to B)\to A\to C}b']_i$ for every $i \le \rho(\mathbf{S}_{D(A\to B)(A\to C)}).$

---

[3] Readers who are curious as to why the variable "i" in Definition 7 ranges over ranks, not levels, should note that if "i" ranged over levels the measure of $\mathbf{S}_{DA(B\to C)}a'$ at levels above the level of $\mathbf{K}_{((A\to B\to C)\to(A\to B)\to A\to C)D}\mathbf{S}_{ABC}$ could be the same as the measure of $\mathbf{B} : \mathbf{S}_{ABC}\,a'$.

Proof. This follows from the fact[4] that $\rho(\mathbf{S}_{DAB}) < \rho(\mathbf{S}_{D(A\to B)(A\to C)})$.

Definition 8. $\phi(b, i)$ *shall be* 1 *if* $\rho(b) = i$ *and* 0 *otherwise.*

In the following proofs, the variable $v^{D\to(A\to B)\to A\to C}$ will be written without its superscript. A sequence comprising the terms belonging to $\mathcal{A}(a', i)$ resp. $\mathcal{A}(b', i)$ resp. $\mathcal{A}(c', i)$ shall be called $\boldsymbol{f}^i, \boldsymbol{g}^i, \boldsymbol{h}^i$ for short. If the terms of $\boldsymbol{f}^i$ be $f_1^i, f_2^i, \ldots, f_{\ell(i)}^i$, then the sum $[f_1^i]_i + [f_2^i]_i + \cdots + [f_{\ell(i)}^i]_i$ shall be called $[\boldsymbol{f}^i]_i$ for short. Likewise for $\boldsymbol{g}^i$ and $\boldsymbol{h}^i$.

Proposition 5. *If* $\rho(b') \le i < \rho(a')$ *then*

$$[\mathbf{S}_{DA(B\to C)}a']_i + [\mathbf{S}_{DAB}b']_i + [\mathbf{S}_{D(A\to B)(A\to C)}]_i < [\mathbf{S}_{D(A\to B)(A\to C)}(\boldsymbol{B}:\mathbf{S}_{ABC}\,a')b']_i$$

Proof. If $\rho(b') \le i < \rho(a')$, the following equalities and inequalities hold:

$$[\mathbf{S}_{DA(B\to C)}a']_i + [\mathbf{S}_{DAB}b']_i + [\mathbf{S}_{D(A\to B)(A\to C)}]_i$$

$$< \quad [\mathbf{B}:\mathbf{S}_{ABC}\,a']_i + [\mathbf{S}_{D(A\to B)(A\to C)}vb']_i + [\mathbf{S}_{D(A\to B)(A\to C)}]_i$$

by Propositions 3 and 4, as $i < \rho(a') < \rho(\mathbf{S}_{D(A\to B)(A\to C)}) < \rho(\mathbf{S}_{D(A\to B\to C)((A\to B)\to A\to C)})$

$$= \quad [\mathbf{B}:\mathbf{S}_{ABC}\,a']_i + 2^{[\mathbf{S}_{D(A\to B)(A\to C)}]_{i+1}} \cdot ([b']_i \cdot \phi(b', i)) + [\mathbf{S}_{D(A\to B)(A\to C)}]_i$$

$$< \quad 2^{[\mathbf{S}_{D(A\to B)(A\to C)}]_{i+1}} \cdot ([\mathbf{B}:\mathbf{S}_{ABC}\,a']_i + [b']_i \cdot \phi(b', i))$$

because $[\mathbf{S}_{D(A\to B)(A\to C)}]_i < [\mathbf{B}:\mathbf{S}_{ABC}\,a']_i$

$$< \quad 2^{[\mathbf{S}_{D(A\to B)(A\to C)}]_{i+1}} \cdot (2^{[\mathbf{B}:\mathbf{S}_{ABC}a']_{i+1}} \cdot ([\mathbf{S}_{ABC}]_i \cdot \phi(\mathbf{S}_{ABC}, i) + [\boldsymbol{f}^i]_i) + [b']_i \cdot \phi(b', i))$$

$$\le \quad 2^{[\mathbf{S}_{D(A\to B)(A\to C)}]_{i+1} + [\mathbf{B}:\mathbf{S}_{ABC}a']_{i+1}} \cdot ([\mathbf{S}_{ABC}]_i \cdot \phi(\mathbf{S}_{ABC}, i) + [\boldsymbol{f}^i]_i + [b']_i \cdot \phi(b', i))$$

$$< \quad 2^{[\mathbf{S}_{D(A\to B)(A\to C)}(\mathbf{B}:\mathbf{S}_{ABC}\,a')]_{i+1}} \cdot ([\mathbf{S}_{ABC}]_i \cdot \phi(\mathbf{S}_{ABC}, i) + [\boldsymbol{f}^i]_i + [b']_i \cdot \phi(b', i))$$

because $i+1 \le \rho(a') < \rho(\mathbf{B}:\mathbf{S}_{ABC}\,a')$

$$= \quad [\mathbf{S}_{D(A\to B)(A\to C)}(\mathbf{B}:\mathbf{S}_{ABC}\,a')b']_i$$

In comparing the measures of respective redexes and contractums, a critical part is played by the type of $[x^D]c$, which is $D\to A$. Let the rank of this type be j and let $\rho(D\to B\to C)$ be l.

Proposition 6. *If* $j < i < \rho(b')$ *then*

$$[\mathbf{S}_{DA(B\to C)}a']_i + [\mathbf{S}_{DAB}b']_i + [\mathbf{S}_{D(A\to B)(A\to C)}]_i < [\mathbf{S}_{D(A\to B)(A\to C)}(\boldsymbol{B}:\mathbf{S}_{ABC}\,a')b']_i$$

---

[4] See footnote 3.

Hint of proof: very similar to Proposition 5, except that in place of $[b]_i$ the sum $[g^i]_i$ is used.

Proposition 7. *If* $i \leq j$ *and if* $2 < [S_{DAC}]_i$, *then*

$$[S_{DA(B\to C)}a'c']_i + [S_{DAB}b'c']_i + [S_{DAC}]_i < [S_{DAC}(S_{D(A\to B)(A\to C)}(B : S_{ABC}a')b')c']_i$$

Proof. By induction on $j-i$. When $i = j$, we have:

$$[S_{DA(B\to C)}a'c']_j + [S_{DAB}b'c']_j + [S_{DAC}]_j$$

$$= \quad 2^{[S_{DA(B\to C)}a']_{j+1}} \cdot ([f^j]_j + [c']_j) + 2^{[S_{DAB}b']_{j+1}} \cdot ([g^j]_j + [c']_j) + [S_{DAC}]_j$$

$$\leq \quad 2^{[S_{DA(B\to C)}a']_{j+1}+[S_{DAB}b']_{j+1}+1} \cdot ([f^j]_j + [g^j]_j + [c']_j) + [S_{DAC}]_j$$

$$< \quad 2^{[S_{D(A\to B)(A\to C)}(B:S_{ABC}a')b']_{j+1}} \cdot ([f^j]_j + [g^j]_j + [c']_j) + [S_{DAC}]_j$$

by Proposition 6[5], as $1 < [S_{D(A\to B)(A\to C)}]_{j+1}$

$$< \quad 2^{[S_{D(A\to B)(A\to C)}(B:S_{ABC}a')b']_{j+1}+[S_{DAC}]_{j+1}} \cdot ([f^j]_j + [g^j]_j + [c']_j)$$

$$< \quad 2^{[S_{DAC}(S_{D(A\to B)(A\to C)}(B:S_{ABC}a')b')]_{j+1}} \cdot ([f^j]_j + [g^j]_j + [c']_j)$$

because $j{+}1 \leq \rho(S_{D(A\to B)(A\to C)}(B : S_{ABC}a')b')$

$$= \quad [S_{DAC}(S_{D(A\to B)(A\to C)}(B : S_{ABC}a')b')c']_j$$

The proof of the induction step is similar but uses $[h^i]_i$ in place of $[c']_i$ and the I.H. in place of Proposition 6.

Proposition 8. *When* $\rho(D\to B) < i \leq l \leq j$, *then*

$$[S_{DBC}(S_{DA(B\to C)}a'c')(S_{DAB}b'c')]_i + [S_{DAB}b'c']_i + 2$$
$$< \quad [S_{DAC}(S_{D(A\to B)(A\to C)}(B : S_{ABC}a')b')c']_i$$

Proof. By induction on $l-i$. Let $q(i)$ be $[c']_i$ if $i = j$ and $[h^i]_i$ if $i < j$. When $i = l$, we have:

$$[S_{DBC}(S_{DA(B\to C)}a'c')(S_{DAB}b'c')]_l + [S_{DAB}b'c']_l + 2$$

$$= \quad 2^{[S_{DBC}]_{l+1}} \cdot [S_{DA(B\to C)}a'c']_l + [S_{DAB}b'c']_l + 2$$

---

[5] This is another place where it is crucial that we are working with ranks rather than levels. If "i" in Definition 7 ranged over levels, it would be possible that $[S_{DA(B\to C)}a']_{j+1} + [S_{DAB}b']_{j+1}+1$ should be equal to 3 while $[S_{D(A\to B)(A\to C)}(B : S_{ABC}a')b']_{j+1}$ would be equal to 1, and the last inequality would be false.

because $\rho(\mathbf{S}_{DAB}b'c') = \rho(D{\rightarrow}B) < l$

$$= \quad 2^{[\mathbf{S}_{DBC}]_{l+1}+[\mathbf{S}_{DA(B\rightarrow C)}a'c']_{l+1}} \cdot ([\boldsymbol{f}^l]_l + q(l)) + 2^{[\mathbf{S}_{DAB}b'c']_{l+1}} \cdot ([\boldsymbol{g}^l]_l + q(l)) + 2$$

$$\leq \quad 2^{[\mathbf{S}_{DBC}]_{l+1}+[\mathbf{S}_{DA(B\rightarrow C)}a'c']_{l+1}+[\mathbf{S}_{DAB}b'c']_{l+1}+2} \cdot ([\boldsymbol{f}^l]_l + [\boldsymbol{g}^l]_l + q(l))$$

$$< \quad 2^{[\mathbf{S}_{DAC}\,(\mathbf{S}_{D(A\rightarrow B)(A\rightarrow C)}(\boldsymbol{B}:\mathbf{S}_{ABC}\,a')b')c']_{l+1}} \cdot ([\boldsymbol{f}^l]_l + [\boldsymbol{g}^l]_l + q(l))$$

by Proposition 7[6], using the fact that $[\mathbf{S}_{DBC}]_{l+1} + 2 \leq [\mathbf{S}_{DAC}]_{l+1}$ when $l \leq j$

$$= \quad [\mathbf{S}_{DAC}\,(\mathbf{S}_{D(A\rightarrow B)(A\rightarrow C)}(\boldsymbol{B}:\mathbf{S}_{ABC}\,a')b')c']_l$$

The proof of the induction step is again fairly similar.

Proposition 9. *If* $l \leq j$ *and* $\rho(D{\rightarrow}B) = m$, *then*

$$[\mathbf{S}_{DBC}(\mathbf{S}_{DA(B\rightarrow C)}a'c')(\mathbf{S}_{DAB}b'c')]_m < [\mathbf{S}_{DAC}\,(\mathbf{S}_{D(A\rightarrow B)(A\rightarrow C)}(\boldsymbol{B}:\mathbf{S}_{ABC}\,a')b')c']_m$$

Proof.

$$[\mathbf{S}_{DBC}(\mathbf{S}_{DA(B\rightarrow C)}a'c')(\mathbf{S}_{DAB}b'c')]_m$$

$$= \quad 2^{[\mathbf{S}_{DBC}(\mathbf{S}_{DA(B\rightarrow C)}a'c')]_{m+1}} \cdot ([\boldsymbol{f}^m]_m + [\boldsymbol{h}^m]_m + [\mathbf{S}_{DAB}b'c']_m)$$

$$= \quad 2^{[\mathbf{S}_{DBC}(\mathbf{S}_{DA(B\rightarrow C)}a'c')]_{m+1}} \cdot ([\boldsymbol{f}^m]_m + [\boldsymbol{h}^m]_m + 2^{[\mathbf{S}_{DAB}b'c']_{m+1}} \cdot ([\boldsymbol{g}^m]_m + [\boldsymbol{h}^m]_m))$$

$$\leq \quad 2^{[\mathbf{S}_{DBC}(\mathbf{S}_{DA(B\rightarrow C)}a'c')]_{m+1}+[\mathbf{S}_{DAB}b'c']_{m+1}+1} \cdot ([\boldsymbol{f}^m]_m + [\boldsymbol{g}^m]_m + [\boldsymbol{h}^m]_m)$$

$$< \quad 2^{[\mathbf{S}_{DAC}\,(\mathbf{S}_{D(A\rightarrow B)(A\rightarrow C)}(\boldsymbol{B}:\mathbf{S}_{ABC}\,a')b')c']_{m+1}} \cdot ([\boldsymbol{f}^m]_m + [\boldsymbol{g}^m]_m + [\boldsymbol{h}^m]_m)$$

by Proposition 8

$$= \quad [\mathbf{S}_{DAC}\,(\mathbf{S}_{D(A\rightarrow B)(A\rightarrow C)}(\boldsymbol{B}:\mathbf{S}_{ABC}\,a')b')c']_m$$

Propositions 8 and 9 rested on the assumption $l \leq j$. It is time now to investigate what happens when $j < l$.

Definition 9. *For any* b *and* l, $\psi(b,l) =_{df.} 1$ *if* $l < \rho(b)$ *and* $=_{df.} 0$ *otherwise.*

Proposition 10. *If* $\max\{m,j\} < i \leq l$, *then*

$$[\mathbf{S}_{DBC}(\mathbf{S}_{DA(B\rightarrow C)}ac')]_i + [\mathbf{S}_{DAB}b'c']_i + 2 < [\mathbf{S}_{D(A\rightarrow B)(A\rightarrow C)}(\boldsymbol{B}:\mathbf{S}_{ABC}\,a')b']_i$$

---

[6] A similar remark to that made in footnote 5 applies here. If "i" in Definition 7 ranged over levels, the exponent of the l.h.s. of the last inequality could have the numerical value 5 while the exponent of the r.h.s. had the numerical value 1.

Proof. By induction on $l-i$. If $i = l$, then

$$[S_{DBC}(S_{DA(B \to C)}ac')]_l + [S_{DAB}b'c']_l + 2$$

$$= \quad 2^{[S_{DBC}]_{l+1}} \cdot [S_{DA(B \to C)}a']_l + [S_{DAB}b']_l + 2$$

because by hypothesis, $\rho(c') = j < l$

$$< \quad 2^{[S_{DBC}]_{l+1} + [S_{DA(B \to C)}a']_{l+1} + [S_{DAB}b']_{l+1} + 1} \cdot ([f^l]_l + [b']_l \cdot \phi(b', l) + [g^l]_l \cdot \psi(b', l))$$

$$< \quad 2^{[S_{D(A \to B)(A \to C)}(B:S_{ABC}a')b']_{l+1} + 1} \cdot ([f^l]_l + [b']_l \cdot \phi(b', l) + [g^l]_l \cdot \psi(b', l))$$

by Proposition 6, seeing as $[S_{DBC}]_{l+1} + 1 < [S_{D(A \to B)(A \to C)}]_{l+1}$

$$= \quad [S_{D(A \to B)(A \to C)}(B : S_{ABC}a')b']_l$$

The induction step can be proven by a fairly similar argument, using the I.H. in place of Proposition 6.

Proposition 11. *If $j < i \le m$, then*

$$[S_{DBC}(S_{DA(B \to C)}ac')(S_{DAB}b'c')]_i + 2 < [S_{D(A \to B)(A \to C)}(B : S_{ABC}a')b']_i$$

Proof. By induction on $m-i$. If $i = m$, then

$$[S_{DBC}(S_{DA(B \to C)}ac')(S_{DAB}b'c')]_m + 2$$

$$= \quad 2^{[S_{DBC}(S_{DA(B \to C)}ac')]_{m+1}} \cdot ([f^m]_m + [S_{DAB}b']_m) + 2$$

$$= \quad 2^{[S_{DBC}(S_{DA(B \to C)}ac')]_{m+1}} \cdot ([f^m]_m + 2^{[S_{DAB}b']_{m+1}} \cdot [g^m]_m) + 2$$

$$\le \quad 2^{[S_{DBC}(S_{DA(B \to C)}ac')]_{m+1} + [S_{DAB}b']_{m+1} + 1} \cdot ([f^m]_m + [g^m]_m)$$

$$< \quad 2^{[S_{D(A \to B)(A \to C)}(B:S_{ABC}a')b']_{m+1}} \cdot ([f^m]_m + [g^m]_m)$$

by Proposition 10

$$= \quad [S_{D(A \to B)(A \to C)}(B : S_{ABC}a')b']_m$$

Again, the induction step is straightforward and fairly similar.

For the remainder of this paper, let h be $\rho(D \to A \to C)$.

Proposition 12. *If $j < i \le h$ and $j < l$, then*

$$[S_{DBC}(S_{DA(B \to C)}a'c')(S_{DAB}b'c')]_i + 2 < [S_{DAC}(S_{D(A \to B)(A \to C)}(B : S_{ABC}a')b')c']_i$$

Proof. By induction on $h-i$. If $l < h$, the basis of the induction follows by Definition 7, from

$$[\mathbf{S}_{DBC}]_h + 2 < [\mathbf{S}_{DAC}(\mathbf{S}_{D(A\to B)(A\to C)}(\mathbf{B}:\mathbf{S}_{ABC}\,a')b')c']_h$$

which is obvious given Definition 7. If $h \leq l$, then, as $j < h$, the inequality

$$[\mathbf{S}_{DBC}(\mathbf{S}_{DA(B\to C)}a'c')(\mathbf{S}_{DAB}b'c')]_h < [\mathbf{S}_{D(A\to B)(A\to C)}(\mathbf{B}:\mathbf{S}_{ABC}\,a')b']_h \quad (3)$$

holds by Propositions 10 and 11. From (3), the inequality

$$[\mathbf{S}_{DBC}(\mathbf{S}_{DA(B\to C)}a'c')(\mathbf{S}_{DAB}b'c')]_h + 2 < [\mathbf{S}_{DAC}(\mathbf{S}_{D(A\to B)(A\to C)}(\mathbf{B}:\mathbf{S}_{ABC}\,a')b')c']_h \quad (4)$$

can be proven using the fact that the term on the r.h.s. of (3) is a rank h associated term of the term on the r.h.s. of (4). The induction step is straightforward.

Proposition 13. *If $j < l$, then*

$$[\mathbf{S}_{DBC}(\mathbf{S}_{DA(B\to C)}a'c')(\mathbf{S}_{DAB}b'c')]_j + 2 < [\mathbf{S}_{DAC}(\mathbf{S}_{D(A\to B)(A\to C)}(\mathbf{B}:\mathbf{S}_{ABC}\,a')b')c']_j$$

Proof. Either $m \leq j$ or $j < m$. If $m \leq j$, then

$$[\mathbf{S}_{DBC}(\mathbf{S}_{DA(B\to C)}a'c')(\mathbf{S}_{DAB}b'c')]_j + 2$$

$$= \quad 2^{[\mathbf{S}_{DBC}(\mathbf{S}_{DA(B\to C)}a'c')]_{j+1}} \cdot ([f^j]_j + [c']_j + [\mathbf{S}_{DAB}b'c']_j \cdot \phi(\mathbf{S}_{DAB}b'c',j)) + 2$$

$$\leq \quad 2^{[\mathbf{S}_{DBC}(\mathbf{S}_{DA(B\to C)}a'c')]_{j+1} + [\mathbf{S}_{DAB}b']_{j+1} + 2} \cdot ([f^j]_j + [g^j]_j + [c']_j)$$

$$< \quad 2^{[\mathbf{S}_{D(A\to B)(A\to C)}(\mathbf{B}:\mathbf{S}_{ABC}\,a')b']_{j+1}} \cdot ([f^j]_j + [g^j]_j + [c']_j)$$

by Proposition 10

$$< \quad 2^{[\mathbf{S}_{DAC}(\mathbf{S}_{D(A\to B)(A\to C)}(\mathbf{B}:\mathbf{S}_{ABC}\,a')b')]_{j+1}} \cdot ([f^j]_j + [g^j]_j + [c']_j)$$

because $j+1 < \rho(\mathbf{S}_{D(A\to B)(A\to C)}(\mathbf{B}:\mathbf{S}_{ABC}\,a')b')$

$$= \quad [\mathbf{S}_{DAC}(\mathbf{S}_{D(A\to B)(A\to C)}(\mathbf{B}:\mathbf{S}_{ABC}\,a')b')c']_j$$

If, on the other hand, $j < m$, then

$$[\mathbf{S}_{DBC}(\mathbf{S}_{DA(B\to C)}a'c')(\mathbf{S}_{DAB}b'c')]_j + 2$$

$$\leq \quad 2^{[\mathbf{S}_{DBC}(\mathbf{S}_{DA(B\to C)}a'c')(\mathbf{S}_{DAB}b')]_{j+1} + 2} \cdot ([f^j]_j + [g^j]_j + [c']_j)$$

from which the conclusion follows by Proposition 12.

Proposition 14. *If $i \leq \rho(D\to C)$, then*

$$[\mathbf{S}_{DBC}(\mathbf{S}_{DA(B\to C)}a'c')(\mathbf{S}_{DAB}b'c')]_i + 2 < [\mathbf{S}_{DAC}(\mathbf{S}_{D(A\to B)(A\to C)}(\mathbf{B}:\mathbf{S}_{ABC}\,a')b')c']_i$$

Proof. When $l \leq j$, an inequality of the form shown has been established for $i \in [m, j]$ by Propositions 8 and 9, so all that is necessary is to prove it for $i \in [0, m)$ by induction on $m-i$, which is straightforward. Moreover, when $l \leq j$ we also have $\rho(D \rightarrow C) < j$, so the inequality holds *a fortiori* for $i \leq \rho(D \rightarrow C)$.

When $j < l$, an inequality of the form shown has been proven for $i \in [j, h]$ by Propositions 12 and 13. By induction on $j-i$, a similar inequality can be easily proven for $i < j$. Moreover, $\rho(D \rightarrow C) < h$, so the needed inequality holds *a fortiori* for $i \leq \rho(D \rightarrow C)$. This completes the proof of Proposition 14.

The main goal of this paper was to prove that the reduction relation SR^0, which was defined by Definition 4, has the following property:

Theorem 2. *The function* $a \mapsto [a]_0$ *is* SR^0-*reducing.*

Proof. Let d reduce to e by a single SR^0-reduction step. The case where the redex contracted is weak is covered by Theorem 1. The case where d is $[x^D].\mathbf{S}_{ABC}abc$ and the variable x^D occurs in all the terms a, b, c is covered by Proposition 14, given that d then is (1) and e is (2). The only other possibility is that the redex contracted has that shape and is a proper subterm of d. The crucial fact for the treatment of this last case is that the rank $\rho(D \rightarrow C)$, at which the inequality shown in Proposition 14 holds, is precisely the rank of $[x^D].\mathbf{S}_{ABC}abc$ and its contractum. That this suffices is a consequence of Definition 7 (see Proposition 22 below for more detail).

Acknowledgement. The author wishes to express his thanks to Andreas Weiermann for drawing his attention to Barendregt's problem #26 in the first place and to three anonymous reviewers whose comments on an earlier version have, he hopes, enabled him to improve it considerably.

Appendix: Proof of Theorem 1

Throughout this appendix, let a, b, c, t be such that $\mathbf{S}_{ABC}abct \in CL_{\rightarrow}$. Likewise for $\mathbf{K}_{AB}abt$ and $\mathbf{I}_A at$. Let the sequences of terms belonging to $\mathcal{A}(a, i)$, $\mathcal{A}(b, i)$, $\mathcal{A}(c, i)$ be $\boldsymbol{f}^i, \boldsymbol{g}^i, \boldsymbol{h}^i$ respectively. Let the sequence $\boldsymbol{t}^i$ comprise both those of the t that have rank i and the rank i associated terms of those of the t that have ranks $> i$.

Proposition 15. *For any* i *such that* $\rho(b) < i \leq \rho(a)$,

$$[ac(bc)t]_i + 1 \quad < \quad [\mathbf{S}_{ABC}abct]_i$$

Proof. By induction on $\rho(a)-i$. If $i = \rho(a)$, then $[ac(bc)t]_i + 1 = [a]_i + 1 < [\mathbf{S}_{ABC}a]_i$. The induction step is straightforward.

Proposition 16. *For any* i *such that* $max\{\rho(c), \rho(bc)\} < i \leq \rho(b)$,

$$[ac(bc)t]_i + [b]_i + 2 \quad < \quad [\mathbf{S}_{ABC}abct]_i$$

Proof. By induction on $\rho(b)-i$. If $i = \rho(b)$, then

$$[ac(bc)t]_i + [b]_i + 2 \quad \leq \quad 2^{[ac(bc)t]_{i+1}} \cdot ([\boldsymbol{f}^i]_i + [\boldsymbol{t}^i]_i) + [b]_i + 2$$

by Definition 7, as $max\{\rho(c), \rho(bc)\} < \rho(b)$

$$\leq \quad 2^{[ac(bc)t]_{i+1}+1} \cdot ([\boldsymbol{f}^i]_i + [b]_i + [\boldsymbol{t}^i]_i) + 1$$

by the stipulation following Definition 7, which entails that the measure $2^{[ac(bc)t]_{i+1}} \cdot ([\boldsymbol{f}^i]_i + [b]_i + [\boldsymbol{t}^i]_i)$ is not less than 1

$$< \quad 2^{[\mathbf{S}_{ABC}a]_{i+1}} \cdot ([\boldsymbol{f}^i]_i + [b]_i + [\boldsymbol{t}^i]_i)$$

by Proposition 15

$$= \quad [\mathbf{S}_{ABC}abct]_i$$

as $\rho(c) < i$. The induction step is again straightforward.

Proposition 17. *If $\rho(c) \leq \rho(bc)$, then for any i such that $i \leq \rho(bc)$,*

$$[ac(bc)t]_i + [bc]_i + 2 \quad < \quad [\mathbf{S}_{ABC}abct]_i$$

Proof. By induction on $\rho(bc)-i$. If $i = \rho(bc)$, then

$$[ac(bc)t]_i + [bc]_i + 2 = 2^{[ac(bc)t]_{i+1}} \cdot ([\boldsymbol{f}^i]_i + [bc]_i + [c]_i \cdot \phi(c,i) + [\boldsymbol{t}^i]_i) + [bc]_i + 2$$

$$\leq \quad 2^{[ac(bc)t]_{i+1}+1} \cdot ([\boldsymbol{f}^i]_i + [bc]_i + [c]_i \cdot \phi(c,i) + [\boldsymbol{t}^i]_i) + 2$$

$$\leq \quad 2^{[ac(bc)t]_{i+1}+[b]_{i+1}+2} \cdot ([\boldsymbol{f}^i]_i + [\boldsymbol{g}^i]_i + [c]_i \cdot \phi(c,i) + [\boldsymbol{t}^i]_i) + 2$$

$$< \quad 2^{[\mathbf{S}_{ABC}abct]_{i+1}} \cdot ([\boldsymbol{f}^i]_i + [\boldsymbol{g}^i]_i + [c]_i \cdot \phi(c,i) + [\boldsymbol{t}^i]_i)$$

because $2 \leq [ac(bc)t]_{i+1} + [b]_{i+1} + 2 < [\mathbf{S}_{ABC}abct]_{i+1}$ by Proposition 16

$$= \quad [\mathbf{S}_{ABC}abct]_i$$

The induction step is again straightforward.

Proposition 18. *If $\rho(bc) < i \leq \rho(c)$, then*

$$[ac(bc)t]_i + [bc]_i + 2 \quad < \quad [\mathbf{S}_{ABC}abct]_i$$

Proof. By induction on $\rho(c)-i$. If $i = \rho(c)$, then

$$[ac(bc)t]_i + [bc]_i + 2 \quad = \quad 2^{[ac(bc)t]_{i+1}} \cdot ([\boldsymbol{f}^i]_i + [c]_i + [\boldsymbol{t}^i]_i) + [bc]_i + 2$$

$$\leq \quad 2^{[ac(bc)t]_{i+1}} \cdot ([\boldsymbol{f}^i]_i + [bc]_i + [c]_i + [\boldsymbol{t}^i]_i) + 2$$

$$\leq \quad 2^{[ac(bc)t]_{i+1}+[b]_{i+1}+1} \cdot ([\boldsymbol{f}^i]_i + [\boldsymbol{g}^i]_i + [c]_i + [\boldsymbol{t}^i]_i) + 2$$

$$< \quad 2^{[\mathbf{S}_{ABC}abct]_{i+1}} \cdot ([\boldsymbol{f}^i]_i + [\boldsymbol{g}^i]_i + [c]_i + [\boldsymbol{t}^i]_i)$$

because $2 \leq [ac(bc)t]_{i+1} + [b]_{i+1} + 2 < [\mathbf{S}_{ABC}abct]_{i+1}$ by Proposition 16

$$= \quad [\mathbf{S}_{ABC}abct]_i$$

The induction step is again straightforward.

Proposition 19. *If $\rho(bc) < \rho(c)$, then for any i such that $i \leq \rho(bc)$,*

$$[ac(bc)t]_i + [bc]_i + 2 \quad < \quad [\mathbf{S}_{ABC}abct]_i$$

Proof. By induction on $\rho(c)-i$. The proof is like the proof of Proposition 17, but uses Proposition 18 in place of Proposition 16.

Proposition 20. *If $i \leq \rho(a)$, then*

$$[at]_i < [\mathbf{K}_{AB}abt]_i \quad \text{and} \quad [at]_i < [\mathbf{I}_A at]_i$$

Definition 10. *An a-chain is a sequence of terms so constituted that each term other than the first is an associated term of the preceding one.*

Proposition 21. *For every redex R in a, one of the following possibilities holds:*

(i) R is at the head of a; or
(ii) R is at the head of one of the associated terms of a; or
(iii) R is at the head of a term which is the last term of an a-chain starting with a and of length > 2.

Proof. By induction on the length of a. Let a be $Xa_1a_2...a_n$. If a redex R in a is not at the head of a, it must be inside one of $a_1, a_2, \ldots, a_n$. Taking the three possibilities, of which by the I.H. one must hold, in turn:

1. If R is at the head of one of $a_1, a_2, \ldots, a_n$, it is at the head of an associated term of a.
2. If R is at the head of an associated term b of a_j $(1 \leq j \leq n)$ then if $\rho(b) < \rho(a_j)$, b is an associated term of a by Definition 6. Otherwise, R is connected to a by an a-chain of length 3.
3. If R is merely at the head of a term d to which a_j is connected by an a-chain, R is also connected to a by an a-chain.

Proposition 22. *If the following condition holds:*

For every term b which has a weak redex S in head position, contraction of S yields a term b' such that $[b']_i < [b]_i$ for every $i \leq \rho(S)$

then, for any c, c' such that c' is the result of contracting an arbitrary weak redex R within c, $[c']_i < [c]_i$ for every i not exceeding $\rho(R)$ (if R is at the head of c) or (otherwise) the rank of the second term of the unique a-chain connecting c to a term which has R at its head.

Proof. The three possibilities concerning R are distinguished by Proposition 21. When (1) holds, the succedent of the proposition is identical to its antecedent. When (2) holds, the succedent follows from the antecedent by Definition 7. When (3) holds, the proposition is proven by induction on the length of the (unique) a-chain connecting c to some term with R at its head.

Theorem 1 can now be seen to hold in virtue of the fact that the condition mentioned in Proposition 22 holds by Propositions 15–20.

References

1. Barendregt, H.P.: Problem #26 in a list of open problems maintained by the università di torino. http://tlca.di.unito.it/opltlca/opltlcasu33.html. Accessed 20 Apr 2022
2. Curry, H.B., Hindley, J.R., Seldin, J.P.: Combinatory Logic, vol. 2. North-Holland, Amsterdam (1972)
3. Gentzen, G.: Neue Fassung des Widerspruchsfreiheitsbeweises für die reine Zahlentheorie. Hirzel, Leipzig (1938)
4. Hindley, J.R.: Axioms for strong reduction in combinatory logic. J. Symb. Log. **32**(2), 224–236 (1967)
5. Hindley, J.R., Seldin, J.P.: Lambda Calculus and Combinators: An Introduction. Cambridge University Press, Cambridge (2008)
6. Schütte, K.: Proof Theory. Springer, Heidelberg (1977)

Author Index

Printed in the United States
by Baker & Taylor Publisher Services